THE OXFORD HANDBOOK OF

CHILDREN'S MUSICAL CULTURES

THE OXFORD HANDBOOK OF

CHILDREN'S MUSICAL CULTURES

Edited by

PATRICIA SHEHAN CAMPBELL

and

TREVOR WIGGINS

OXFORD
UNIVERSITY PRESS

OXFORD
UNIVERSITY PRESS

Oxford University Press is a department of the University of Oxford.
It furthers the University's objective of excellence in research, scholarship,
and education by publishing worldwide.

Oxford   New York
Auckland   Cape Town   Dar es Salaam   Hong Kong   Karachi
Kuala Lumpur   Madrid   Melbourne   Mexico City   Nairobi
New Delhi   Shanghai   Taipei   Toronto

With offices in
Argentina   Austria   Brazil   Chile   Czech Republic   France   Greece
Guatemala   Hungary   Italy   Japan   Poland   Portugal   Singapore
South Korea   Switzerland   Thailand   Turkey   Ukraine   Vietnam

Oxford is a registered trademark of Oxford University Press
in the UK and certain other countries.

Published in the United States of America by
Oxford University Press
198 Madison Avenue, New York, NY 10016

© Oxford University Press 2013

First issued as an Oxford University Press paperback, 2014.

Library of Congress Cataloging-in-Publication Data
The Oxford handbook of children's musical cultures / edited by Patricia Shehan Campbell
and Trevor Wiggins.
p. cm.
Includes bibliographical references and index.
ISBN 978-0-19-973763-5 (hardcover : alk. paper); 978-0-19-020641-3 (paperback : alk. paper)
1. Music—Juvenile—History and criticism.
2. World music—History and criticism.   3. Ethnomusicology.
I. Campbell, Patricia Shehan.   II. Wiggins, Trevor, 1953–
ML83.O94 2013
780.83—dc23
2012006708

Contents

PART 1. ENGAGEMENTS WITH CULTURE: SOCIALIZATION AND IDENTITY

PART 1A. (RE)MAKING CULTURES FOR/ BY CHILDREN/UPDATING TRADITION

PART 1B. CULTURAL IDENTITIES WITH MULTIPLE MEANINGS

PART 2. PERSONAL JOURNEYS IN/ THROUGH CULTURE

PART 3. MUSIC IN EDUCATION AND DEVELOPMENT

Editorial Acknowledgments

We wish to thank mentors, colleagues, and students who have inspired us in our studies of musical children, including contributors to this volume. Many thanks to our life partners, too: Charlie Campbell, who occasionally comes up for air from his science projects to hear the stories and songs of children and to offer his logical comments, and Vivienne Wells, who demands I take breaks to walk dogs and regain my perspective as well as editing me. We remember and acknowledge Rita Klinger, whose incisive remarks, based on her rich history of teaching music to children in Israel and the United States, helped to inform the shape of this project.

About the Companion Website
WWW.OUP.COM/US/OHCMC

....

OXFORD has created a password-protected website to accompany *The Oxford Handbook of Children's Musical Cultures*, and the reader is encouraged to take full advantage of it. The authors of the chapters have many additional examples to support and illustrate their writing and the locations they describe and research. There are additional images (in color, of course), as well as audio and video extracts. These additional visual and sonic elements support the reader in a more rounded understanding of the world of children in different locations as they play and interact with each other and their environment. Here are brass bands from India, circle games from the Gambia and India, and songs from Japan, Ghana, Brazil, and many other places. The musical cultures of children are constrained only by their imagination and resources, and this website opens more doors on to their world to complement the book. Additional materials available online are found throughout the text as "web figures" and are signaled with the following symbols:

- 🔊 Audio recordings
- ▶ Video recordings
- 📷 Photos or diagrams
- 🔗 Links, sheet music, and other supplementary documents

You can access the companion website by using the username Music5 and the password Book1745.

About the Contributors

Carlos R. Abril is associate professor and director of music teacher education at the University of Miami, FL, USA. He is coeditor of the book, *Musical Experience in Our Lives* (Rowman & Littlefield, 2009) and has published book chapters and articles focusing on the sociocultural nature of music education.

Mayumi Adachi is professor of music psychology at Hokkaido University and the editor/translator of *Enso o Sasaeru Kokoro to Kagaku 2011 Seishin Shobo* (Japanese translation of *The Science and Psychology of Music Performance*, 2002, Oxford University Press).

Sarah J. Bartolome is assistant professor of music education at Louisiana State University. She has published several chapters and journal articles on issues related to children's musical culture, ethnomusicology and music education, and music teaching and learning.

Marisol Berríos-Miranda is an ethnomusicologist who specializes in Caribbean and Latin American music. She has published extensively on salsa music and Latino identity, music and social change, and community music. She is curator of the Smithsonian traveling exhibit "American Sabor: Latinos in US Popular Music," a senior Ford fellow, and a Jubilation Foundation fellow.

Tyler Bickford received his PhD in ethnomusicology in 2011 from Columbia University, where he teaches as a lecturer in the core curriculum. He studies US schoolchildren's media consumption and expressive culture and is writing a book about the tween music industry.

Sally Bodkin-Allen is the academic leader for the bachelor of contemporary music at the Southern Institute of Technology in Invercargill, New Zealand. She is a mother of five budding musicians, has a keen interest in music education, and has composed four musicals, including two for schoolchildren.

Gregory D. Booth is associate professor of ethnomusicology in the department of anthropology at the University of Auckland. He is the author of *Brass Baja: Stories from the World of Indian Wedding Bands* (Oxford University Press, 2005) and *Behind the Curtain: Making Music in Mumbai's Film Studios* (Oxford University Press, 2008).

Patricia Shehan Campbell is Donald E. Peterson Professor of Music at the University of Washington. Her published works include *Songs in Their Heads: Music and Its*

Meaning in Children's Lives ([1998], 2010), *Teaching Music Globally* (2004), *Musician and Teacher* (2008), and *Music in Childhood* (fourth edition, 2013). She serves on the board of Smithsonian Folkways and is president of The College Music Society.

Lily Chen-Hafteck is associate professor of music education at Kean University, New Jersey, USA. She has published numerous journal articles and book chapters on early childhood music, the relationship between children's singing and languages, and cultural issues in music education.

Judah M. Cohen is the Lou and Sybil Mervis Professor of Jewish Culture and associate professor of folklore and ethnomusicology at Indiana University. In addition to numerous essays, he has authored three monographs, including *The Making of a Reform Jewish Cantor: Musical Authority, Cultural Investment* (Indiana University Press, 2009), and coedited *The Culture of AIDS in Africa: Hope and Healing in Music and the Arts* (Oxford University Press, 2011).

Eugene Dairianathan is head of the Visual and Performing Arts academic group at the National Institute of Education, Nanyang Technological University, Singapore. His publications focus on interdisciplinary perspectives on music.

Sonja Lynn Downing is assistant professor of ethnomusicology at Lawrence University in Appleton, Wisconsin. Her article "Agency, Leadership, and Gender Negotiation in Balinese Girls' Gamelans" was published in *Ethnomusicology* (2010).

Andrea Emberly is an ethnomusicologist who specializes in research on children's musical cultures in South Africa and Australia. She completed her PhD at the University of Washington in 2009 and conducted postdoctoral research at the University of Western Australia from 2009 to 2011 before becoming assistant professor of Children's Studies at York University in Toronto, Canada.

Kristin Harris Walsh holds a PhD in folklore from Memorial University of Newfoundland and an MA in dance from York University. Her research focuses on vernacular dance practices, children's culture, and dance education. She is currently adjunct professor and project coordinator at the MMaP Research Centre at Memorial University's School of Music.

Anna Hoefnagels is associate professor at Carleton University in Ottawa, Canada. Her teaching and research specializes in first peoples' musics in Canada, music and gender, folk and traditional music in Canada, and ethnomusicology. Her publications have focused primarily on intertribal music genres and issues of gender, performance, and tradition in Central Canadian aboriginal communities.

Beatriz Ilari is assistant professor of music education at the University of Southern California in Los Angeles. She has conducted research on children's musical engagement throughout Brazil and in Japan and by different groups—from urban school children to the Amazonian riverine.

Alan M. Kent is lecturer for the Open University, United Kingdom and visiting lecturer in Celtic Studies at the University of La Coruña, Galicia. His publications include *The Literature of Cornwall: Continuity, Identity, Difference* (Redcliffe Press, 2000) and *The Theatre of Cornwall: Space, Place, Performance* (Redcliffe Press, 2010). He has also written on the enthnomusicology of Cornwall for numerous journals.

Alexandra Kertz-Welzel, PhD, is professor and chair of the department of music education at Ludwig Maximilian University in Munich, Germany and, in addition to numerous articles in leading journals, author of the book *Every Child for Music: Musikpädagogik und Musikunterricht in den USA* (Blaue Eule, 2006).

Young-Youn Kim holds a PhD in music education from the University of Washington, USA. She is a professor at Silla University (Korea) and the chief editor of the *Korean Journal of Music Education*. Her main research area is early childhood music education.

Magali Kleber teaches at Londrina State University (UEL) in Brazil. She coordinates a research group for music education and social movements at the National Research Council in Brazil and is the president of the Brazilian Association for Music Education. She also chairs the Community Music Activity Commission and is leader of the research group Music Education and Social Movements for the International Society for Music Education.

Lisa Huisman Koops, PhD, is assistant professor of music education at Case Western Reserve University. Her research focuses on the vital role of the family in optimizing early music development and education.

Chee-Hoo Lum is assistant professor in music education at the National Institute of Education, Nanyang Technological University, Singapore. He is also director for UNESCO-NIE Centre for Arts Research in Education, part of a regional network of observatories stemming from the UNESCO Asia-Pacific Action Plan. His publications focus on children's musical cultures, creativity and improvisation in children's music, elementary music methods, and world musics in education.

Elizabeth Mackinlay is associate professor in the School of Education at the University of Queensland. Liz is involved in a number of different research projects including drumming circles for primary students, Indigenous Australian studies and education, music and mothering, and feminism in higher education. She is currently the editor of the *Music Education Research and Innovation* (MERI) and co-editor of the *Australian Journal of Indigenous Education* (AJIE).

Noriko Manabe is assistant professor of music at Princeton University, an ethnomusicologist and music theorist, and an affiliate in East Asian and Latin American Studies. She has published articles on Japanese rap and DJs, Cuban music, and music and mobile media in *Ethnomusicology*, the *Latin American Music Review*, *Asian Music*, and the volume *Internationalizing Internet Studies*.

Kedmon Mapana is an assistant lecturer at the University of Dar es Salaam, Tanzania, Department of Fine and Performing Arts, and is completing doctoral studies at Seattle Pacific University. His publications are included in the *African Cultural Studies Journal* and the *British Journal of Music Education.* He is the recipient of a recent award from AIRS (Advancing Interdisciplinary Research on Singing, Canada) for his work on Wagogo children's music and was named a Jubilation Foundation fellow in 2009.

Kathryn Marsh is associate professor and former chair of music education at the Sydney Conservatorium of Music, University of Sydney and is the author of *The Musical Playground: Global Tradition and Change in Children's Songs and Games* (Oxford University Press, 2008).

Terry E. Miller, primarily known for his research in mainland Southeast Asia, has also researched folk religious music traditions of the United States, Scotland, and the English-speaking West Indies. He, along with Dr. Sara Stone Miller, has researched the Church of God and Saints of Christ since 1982 in the USA, Jamaica, and South Africa. Miller coedited and wrote part of *The Garland Encyclopedia of World Music (Southeast Asia)* and co-authored *World Music: A Global Journey.*

Sara Stone Miller is an ethnomusicologist and music educator and was on the faculty at Kent State University for nineteen years. Her major area of study is the Church of God and Saints of Christ, with additional ethnomusicological research in East and Southeast Asia, the Caribbean, the United Kingdom, South Africa, and the USA with her husband, Terry E. Miller.

Amanda Minks is assistant professor of anthropology in the Honors College of the University of Oklahoma. She is author of the forthcoming book *Voices of Play: Miskitu Children's Speech and Song on the Atlantic Coast of Nicaragua* (University of Arizona Press, 2013).

Marvelene C. Moore, professor of music education and James A. Cox endowed chair at the University of Tennessee, Knoxville, is editor of *Critical Essays in Music Education* (Ashgate, 2012) and *Kaleidoscope of Cultures* (R&L Education, 2010) and movement author for the Pearson Education textbook series, *Making Music, K–8* (2005).

Sylvia Nannyonga-Tamusuza is associate professor of music at Makerere University (Uganda) and has written on popular music, music, and social identity. Her recent book is titled *Baakisimba: Gender in Music and Dance of the Baganda People of Uganda* (Routledge, 2005).

Robert Pitzer taught instrumental music in the public schools of Washington State for twenty-three years and now teaches music education courses at Western Washington University in Bellingham, Washington. His research interests include jazz education and multicultural music in schools.

Christopher Roberts received his Ph.D. from the University of Washington. His scholarly and instructional interests include children's songs and singing style, world music pedagogy, and music teacher education.

Natalie Sarrazin, PhD, is associate professor at The College at Brockport, State University of New York and an ethnomusicologist and music educator. Her recently published book is titled *Indian Music for the Classroom* (MENC and Rowman Littlefield Press, 2008).

Hope Munro Smith is assistant professor in the department of music at California State University, Chico. She is an ethnomusicologist who specializes in the music of the Caribbean.

Jusamara Souza is professor of music education in the Institute of Arts at the Universidade Federal do Rio Grande do Sul. Her research interests include formal and informal music education, mass media, and music education.

Janet Sturman is professor of music and ethnomusicology at the University of Arizona in Tucson and author of *Zarzuela: Spanish Operetta, American Stage* (University of Illinois Press, 2000).

Polo Vallejo holds a PhD in ethnomusicology and is associate professor at the Universidad Complutense de Madrid, collaborator at the Association Polyphonies Vivants (Paris), and a member of MCAM (University of Montreal) and the Carl Orff Foundation. He is the author of *Mbudi Mbudi na Mhanga* (Musical Universe of Wagogo Children, Tanzania), published in 2004.

Peter Whiteman is deputy head of the Institute of Early Childhood, Macquarie University, Australia. His research focuses on early childhood music education, with particular interests in reconstructed childhoods and children's voices in research.

Trevor Wiggins was director of music at Dartington College of Arts, UK and is now a research associate at SOAS, University of London, and a freelance musician-scholar. His publications include books, CDs, and articles covering ethnomusicology and music education, with a particular focus on West Africa.

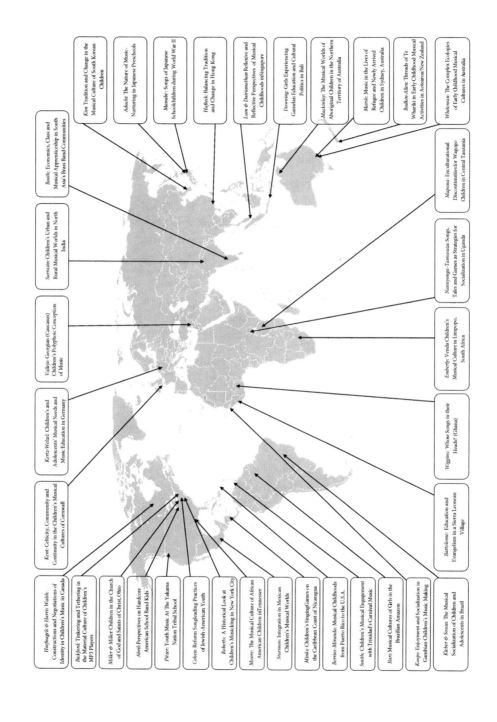

Kim: Tradition and Change in the Musical Culture of South Korean Children

Adachi: The Nature of Music-Nurturing in Japanese Preschools

Manabe: Songs of Japanese Schoolchildren during World War II

Hufbeck: Balancing Tradition and Change in Hong Kong

Lum & Dairianathan Reflective and Reflexive Perspectives of Musical Childhoods inSingapore

Downing: Girls Experiencing Gamelan Education and Cultural Politics in Bali

Mackinlay: The Musical Worlds of Aboriginal Children in the Northern Territory of Australia

Marsh: Music in the Lives of Refugee and Newly Arrived Children in Sydney, Australia

Bodkin-Allen: Threads of Te Whariki in Early Childhood Musical Activities in Aotearoa/New Zealand

Whiteman: The Complex Ecologies of Early Childhood Musical Cultures in Australia

Booth: Economics, Class and Musical Apprenticeship in South Asia's Brass Band Communities

Sarrazin: Children's Urban and Rural Musical Worlds in North India

Vallejo: Georgian (Caucasus) Children's Polyphoic Conception of Music

Kertz-Welzel: Children's and Adolescents' Musical Needs and Music Education in Germany

Kent: Celticity, Community and Continuity in the Children's Musical Cultures of Cornwall

Mapoma: Enculturational Discontinuities or Wagogo Children in Central Tanzania

Nannyonga-Tamusuza: Songs, Tales and Games as Strategies for Socialization in Uganda

Emberly: Venda Children's Musical Cultures in Limpopo, South Africa

Wiggins: Whose Songs in their Heads? (Ghana)

Bartolome: Education and Evangelism in a Sierra Leonean Village

Kléber & Souza: The Musical Socialization of Children and Adolescents in Brazil

Hoefnagels & Harris Walsh: Constructions and Negotiations of Identity in Children's Music in Canada

Bickford: Tinkering and Tethering in the Material Culture of Children's MP3 Players

Miller & Miller: Children in the Church of God and Saints of Christ, Ohio

Abril: Perspectives on Hardcore American School Band Kids

Pitzer: Youth Music At The Yakama Nation Tribal School

Cohen: Reform Songleading Practices of Jewish-American Youth

Roberts: A Historical Look at Children's Musicking in New York City

Moore: The Musical Culture of African American Children inTennessee

Sturman: Integration in Mexican Children's Musical Worlds

Minks: Children's SingingGames on the Caribbean Coast of Nicaragua

Berrios-Miranda: Musical Childhoods from Puerto Rico to the U.S.A.

Smith: Children's Musical Engagement with Trinidad's Carnival Music

Ilari: Musical Cultures of Girls in the Brazilian Amazon

Knapp: Enjoyment and Socialization in Gambian Children's Music Making

THE OXFORD HANDBOOK OF

CHILDREN'S MUSICAL CULTURES

GIVING VOICE TO CHILDREN

PATRICIA SHEHAN CAMPBELL AND TREVOR WIGGINS

CHILDREN's engagement with music is universal. They are awash with music, and the rhythms and melodies they exude from an early age are evidence of ways in which the music of their culture lives within them. From infancy, across their childhood years, and onward into their adolescence, they sing, dance, and play music because they must. They consume it as they also create it. As avid listeners, they escape to it and find safe haven in it. Their natural propensity for musical engagement is fostered and facilitated by families, communities, schools, and the media. Music defines them as children even as it distances them from those who do not share the same interests. They evolve a pastiche repertoire that grows from their living in cultures in which music is valued, and they find their way into music somehow—even if societal odds are against it. Children develop their musical sensibilities as their surroundings allow it, and from their innate instinct to be musical they grow more musical through cultural interaction and education. Yet they are not passive recipients of the music they value but active agents in choosing the music they will take time to listen and respond to, to make, and to choose to preserve, reinvent, or discard.

This volume represents an interdisciplinary inquiry into children and their musical worlds—their songs, chants, rhythmic speech, movement and dance routines, listening interests, sociomusical interactions, and creative expressions, alone and together, and on instruments and a diversity of everyday objects. Scholars from ethnomusicology and education, as well as those with expertise in folklore and developmental psychology, have contributed to this collection on the content and context of children's music making and the function and meaning of these musical expressions to them. They provide circumstantial evidence and critical commentary for why children engage musically; how music is differentiated by age, gender, race and ethnicity, and socioeconomic circumstances; and whether the music children make is associated with the adult music of their experience or linked cross-culturally to the expressive practices of childhood that happen everywhere.

The thirty-five essay-chapters offer perspectives on children's musical cultures from a broad geographic base of mostly musical ethnographies from around the globe. They provide descriptions and assessments of the musical world of children in specific settings, their enculturation and possibilities for their musical education and training, the sources of knowledge and materials, and the range of music available to them, taught, expressed, invented, and preserved by them. Some chapters survey the extent of local music in children's use, or in particular contexts in which children gather (e.g., schools, homes, and playgrounds), and others offer an understanding of music from a "child's eye" perspective, investigating children's musical world and allowing their voices to be heard. The volume involves looking both at the nature, structures, and styles of the music preferred and used by children—with a broad definition of "childhood" encompassing early childhood well on into adolescence—and the meanings and messages that this music acquires and conveys both for the children and for those who are providing the music to them. It considers the ways in which particular musical styles or even specific pieces known and valued by children may represent different views of the world or of cultural heritage. An underlying weave in the writing is the premise that there are processes common to children's development regardless of where in the world they may live, and yet there are cultural factors—local, national, and global—that influence their thoughts and ways of being.

A RETROSPECT OF STUDIES OF MUSICAL CHILDREN

The study of children has long challenged scholars working across a number of disciplines. Such a challenge has necessitated the development of manuals and reflective words that advise methodological approaches and issues (Bluebond-Langner 2007; Graue and Walsh 1998; Holmes 1998; Montgomery 2009). Anthropologists have historically refrained from examining the life worlds of children, viewing them as imperfect and unimportant because they are only in the gradual process of becoming culturally competent adults (James and James 2008; Lancy 2008). Yet this view has been contested, such that anthropology is based on the premise that "culture is learned, not inherited" and children's capacity to learn culture is remarkably strong to have merited so little interest in the annals of contemporary anthropology. Hirschfeld observes that, although there have been a number of individual studies of children since the 1930s, "this work has not coalesced into a sustained tradition of child-focused research" (2002: 611). Only since the advent of the twenty-first century has there been a substantial increase of interest in the study of children within the discipline of anthropology, leading to the setting up of a special interest group for Children and Childhood within the American Anthropological Association in 2007 (American Anthropological Association 2011).

Ethnomusicology had also paid little attention to children, and reviews of the field have turned up a surprisingly small body of literature and research (Minks 2002). John Blacking's historic study of the Venda children of South Africa (1967) broke a new pathway, although his impetus was the study of adult musical culture to which the children belong. Even earlier, Richard Waterman's study of the Yirkalla, an Australian indigenous group, examined musical enculturation in the life cycle of boys and girls, who were socialized into their cultural values and traditions through song (1956). The bimusical environment in which young Australian Aboriginal children were raised (this time, the Pitjanjara) was noted in Margaret Kartomi's study of their experience with traditional songs as well as Western popular music and missionary hymns (1980). More recently, the oral-kinetic texts in double-dutch competitions of African American girls was studied ethnomusicologically by Kyra Gaunt (2006), bringing attention to the communally valued rhythmic, timbral, and melodic effects of vernacular speech in their performance practice. Yet despite a few scattered studies of children here and there, ethnomusicologists are just now making strides in their views of children as autonomous and separated from the adults of their culture. Like their colleagues in anthropology, they are emerging from a history of observational reports of their own making, into an understanding that children are capable of expressing themselves (James 2007: 261). Further, in ethnomusicology as in anthropology, the emphasis given to diversity over commonality has prevented the examination of patterns of children's practices (Minks 2006: 217) when in fact childhood may be best viewed for its global as well as cultural-specific entities.

From the end of the nineteenth century to the last years of the twentieth century, children's song appeared to be of great interest to scholars who collected, dissected, and discussed their composite parts. Children's song was seen by folklorists as a fixed cultural artifact that, like all folk song, could be examined for text, melody, and rhythm. Collections amassed, such as William Wells Newell's *Games and Songs of American Children* (1884) and Lady Alice Gomme's two-volume *Traditional Games* (1894–1898). Folklorists were particularly keen to study the texts of songs, chants, and rhymes as well as riddles, teases, and taunts. Beginning in the 1950s, the works of folklorists Iona and Peer Opie paid heed to children's songs and singing games for their lore and language and for the steady state of some characteristics as well as the variations across renderings of the song, in various regions and contexts. Their classic work, *The Singing Game* (1985), was intended to document the "final flowering" period of children's song, for fear that it would soon disappear (although it continues to this day).

A number of significant features of the music of childhood have become evident in the analysis by music scholars of collections of songs, chants, rhythms, and musical utterances, particularly of children in North America, Australia, and northern and western Europe (Campbell 2007; Marsh and Young 2006; Nettl 2005).

Children's invented and reinvented songs and singing games are seen as featuring small vocal ranges of less than an octave, typically a sixth, and sometimes only a fourth. Three-tone, four-tone, and pentatonic melodies are frequent, and major and minor seconds and minor thirds are prominent. Duple-metered songs are common, although the complexities of cross-rhythms come into play when children sing in duple and move (as in clapping hands) in rhythms felt in triple meter. Syncopations abound in the melodies of children's songs, although straightforward binary rhythms are also evident. Children's songs, especially in English-speaking communities, tend to fall into repetitive and cyclical forms, particularly strophic form, although there is a sizable number of through composed songs in their invented song repertoire, too. The rhymed chants of children may be rhythmic but not pitched, or they may feature just two alternating pitches of a second or a third. Of their spontaneous singing, children engage in musical utterances, short melodic segments that include sustained pitches of a few notes to a wide diatonic spread of pitches, adding words and nontranslatable sounds that flow freely and expressively (Campbell [1998]2010). The music of children reflects their environmental influences, such that the idiomatic nuances of popular song and other adult-made music surface in their melodies and rhythms. Elsewhere in the world, in parts of Africa and Asia, children's music exhibits similar features in the way of their uses of music and its social meanings as well as some of its sonic properties (Blacking 1995; Dzansi 2002; Lew 2005).

Educationists have traditionally approached children as recipients of knowledge transmitted to them by adults with training in subject matter and developmentally appropriate delivery techniques and systems. Researchers have viewed children as blank slates and have represented children as primitive, as copycats, as personality trainees, as monkeys, and as critics (Holmes 1998: 109–111). Only since the early 1990s have specialists in music education sought to expand their views of children, utilizing ethnographic fieldwork techniques to query their musical engagement outside the realm of formal schooling. One early project was Campbell's, *Songs in Their Heads,* published in 1998 and updated in 2010 (Campbell [1998] 2010). Campbell sought to construct a multidisciplinary study of children's musical interests and actions that allowed children to speak for themselves, with conversations set alongside standard descriptions and interpretations inherent in fieldwork. Of this same ilk are the works of music educators who have examined the processes by which children create and recreate songs, preserve them intact and vary them, and transmit and learn them through processes that fuse watching, listening, and imitating (Corso 2003; Harwood 1998; Lum, 2007; Marsh 2008; Riddell 1990). Recent years have also seen the publication of three volumes of children and their music, many of the essays written by those attuned to the musical education of children: McPherson's edited volume *The Child as Musician* (2006) is a thorough review of the musical development of children and the ways in which they engage with music, *Musical Childhoods and the Cultures of Youth* (edited by Boynton and Kok 2006) is a collection of essays by musicologists and ethnomusicologists that addresses the manner in which children are socialized into the musical life of their communities, both in past and contemporary circumstances, and *Musical Childhoods of Asia and the*

Pacific (Lum and Whiteman 2012) offers views of children in their musical worlds through methodological lenses prominent in education research.

The historic and continuing efforts of specialists across several disciplines and fields contribute to an understanding of children and the music they make, know, and value. Yet musical childhood is largely overlooked and underresearched, particularly with attention to a child-centered approach that gives voice to the children who create their culture, in which music plays a significant role. The intent of this volume is to advance a perspective of the world of music as children know it, in their own words, and as articulated by adults who can foreground children and their social realities, however ensnarled and entwined that process may be. The great leap forward from what has come before has resulted in further discovery of the complexities of the roles and meanings of music in the lives of children.

DEFINING CHILDHOOD

The struggle to define childhood is long and varied. From the Middle Ages, when children were depicted as miniature adults (with heads and bodies out of their child-like proportions), the emphasis has been on who children would become rather than who they really are (Ariès 1962). They were described as less developed, compared to adults, and defined more by what was missing than by the essence of this rich period of their early years. Even now, children are defined by age but not fully recognized for their agency and are assigned roles rather than allowed to experience and discover what is meaningful for themselves. Childhood is not so easily defined, and the simple and straightforward descriptions of the past may be tidy but also off the mark.

Children are in a unique liminal position, one that continues from birth clear through to their achievement of independence from the family in later adolescence, as subjects and objects of enculturation, education, training, induction, consumerism, peer pressure, and exploitation. They are variously accommodated, amused, or educated, often through the media, in a community—a *reservation* of sorts—that is made for them and by them in schools, after-school programs, sports activities, and social and service clubs especially designed for their needs. Even as the construct of childhood is defined by maturational, social, and cultural factors, so also are children, and they are fashioned by adults to fit into cubbyholed conceptualizations of who they are and are not, with little attention to their own sense of themselves. Children define themselves differently than adults define them (Valentine 2000), and we might predict that there is also variance in children's self-definitions as children from one place in the world to the next as they respond and interact with specific contexts.

Within the English language, there is a wealth of literature that has established some of the attributes of children in ways that emphasize aspects of the adult view of childhood. In the Bible, for example, St. Paul advised the Corinthians, "When I was a child, I spoke like a child, thought like a child, and reasoned like a child. When I became a man, I gave up my childish ways" (1 Corinthians 13, International Standard Version). This view attends to the progression of children toward adulthood, and proposes that the giving up of "childish" ways is the indicator of progression to the state of "man" through personal autonomy rather than the control of society. William Shakespeare (1623) also offered a vision of childhood in *As You Like It*, when Jacques observed:

> At first the infant,
> Mewling and puking in the nurse's arms;
> And then the whining school-boy, with his satchel
> And shining morning face, creeping like snail
> Unwillingly to school. (act 2, sc. 7)

For Shakespeare, representing views of his time, the early stages of life are bounded by the body; the physical inabilities that inhibit action and communication by the intellect. In the twentieth century, we now know that those early weeks and months of "childishness" are the site of the most rapid learning, growth, and experimentation of the entire human existence. Children experiment with their new bodies, trying out their voices as they acquire language but also exploring a far wider range of vocalizations. It says much for some societies that this enthusiasm can be reduced to "creeping to school" within a few short years.

Outside the English-speaking world, however, there are points of pause on recognition of the challenges of the universal child (or childhood), when the meaning of words like "children" or "children's musical culture," and even "music," take on different meanings as they translate problematically between languages. In some locations, children are expected to be responsible for contributing to the economic necessities of an adult world, and there is little time for childhood wonder, exploration and experimentation, and play. Children grow up quickly in these climes, if ever they were permitted to behave like children. They may know brief childhoods, too, with little recognition of the vast spaces between childhood and adulthood when, in their adolescence, they teeter between dependence and independence. Children are at one level and in some settings highly sophisticated in their interactions with others, learning very quickly to draw meaning from a large range of cultural and social indicators and behaviors, while they are at the same time naïve about the possible intentions and manipulations practiced on them. They can articulate their feelings, emotions, and preferences straight from the heart, spontaneously and in emotionally unrestricted ways, even as they are also capable of thoughtful and deliberate choices and (at a certain age) explanations and reflections on the experiences of their childhood.

THE PRINCIPAL THEMES OF THIS VOLUME

Principal themes and supporting strands of inquiry and intrigue emerge in the varied contexts of this volume. These function to create a framework for an examination of children, their musical lives, and their identities in music. Local cultures in which children are living, learning, and developing are described, with attention to their homes and families, their neighborhoods, schools, community centers, and social groups, as well as national and cultural imperatives that press upon the young lives of children within school and on the far outside. On numerous occasions, historical streams of influence within local, regional, and national realms are traced as they function to shape children's lives, their learning, and their interests and values, and attention is paid to traditional and imported cultural strands that influence children's perceptions of music, the arts, and culture. The chapters collect around three broad topics:

- Engagements with Culture: Socialization and Identity, within which there are determinate subthemes of (re)making cultures by and for children, including updating tradition, cultural identities with multiple meanings, and personal journeys in and through culture
- Music in Education and Development
- Technologies: Impacts, Uses, and Responses (particularly as they influence their musical engagement and interests)

This framework for the study of children's musical culture is an assemblage of front-end questions that launched the volume and is furthered by emergent themes from the chapters within. They are not discrete themes but overlap and deepen understandings of the nexus of children, music, and culture. Although these themes and strands have been used to order the chapters, the contributors are not constrained by them, so that authors' views of the factors affecting their specific contexts may appropriately range across a wider range of inquiry than the specific section title. Some of the threads will be teased out later in this introduction.

ENGAGEMENTS WITH CULTURE: SOCIALIZATION AND IDENTITY

(Re)Making Cultures for/by Children/Updating Tradition

Ethnomusicologists have always acknowledged "traditional" music as an area of primary interest, while recognizing that musical traditions by men and women have to be created, invented, and constantly refreshed if they are not to enter a state of preservation (or made static through the process of museumization). Concern for the preservation of traditional music, also often termed "folk" music, has been evident in the United Kingdom for at least three centuries since it began to be "collected" (Harker 1985). During the past half century, publications and professional organizations dealing with "tradition" in some way are almost too numerous to mention and include, for example, The International Council for Traditional Music, the now classic *Folk and Traditional Musics of the Western Continents* (Nettl 1965), *Music & Tradition* (Widdess and Wolpert 1981), and *Cahiers de Musiques Traditionnelles*, from volume 1 of 1998 to the latest, volume 23 of 2010 (Ateliers d'ethnomusicologie). These all tend to focus on the nature of the adult-made music and the circumstances of its transmission as well as the meaning and place of the music within its culture. There are few mentions of children in relation to tradition, save the occasional reference to a specific genre of children's music or a group of children learning traditional music as part of an initiation into adulthood. Expert adult musicians and cultural elders assume the role of culture bearers, responsible for remembering and performing cultural tradition, overseeing its performances by adult members of the community, and ensuring that it is passed on at an appropriate time and fully understood by the following generation. This is, of course, a partial view, since children also frequently play a part of musical traditions, both contributing to them and absorbing their heritage. But within the realities of formal education across the majority of the world, children are typically removed from the adult world and located in a special enclave called "school" for much of their time, where they are taught adult-valued knowledge and offered adult-structured experiences. Curricular content for children is typically that knowledge believed by adults to have universal application, for communication or for a community's economic development via technology, manufacturing, or farming. If the arts are ever included in a school curriculum, they are more likely to be offered from a national or international canonic standard rather than local perspective, and they may be taught more as knowledge rather than through direct experience, which then alters the nature of learning as well as precisely what is learned. In the end, these societal decisions for children's education may offer little recognition of, and support for, their own valued traditions and their own culture-bearing qualities.

Children's lives, their learning, and their interests and values are the outcomes of historical streams of influence that have existed for generations, or even centuries, within local, regional, and national realms. Time-honored cultural traditions in music and the arts may be untraceable to the circumstances of their origin and evolution, and yet they may have always been there—innate, inherited, indigenous. Some of the strongest traditions are as likely to have been imported as they are indigenous, and their presence may be wrapped into colonial histories in which some nations once exerted undue pressure and influence upon other nations. The music of a culture, including the music that children make, preserve, and pass on, may be embedded in a colonial heritage. The music children learn at school, or perform at churches, may well be vestiges of that earlier history: English-language songs in Hong Kong preschools (see the chapter by Chen-Hafteck—subsequent references to chapters in this volume will give just the author name) and in English-language classes in the Gambia (Koops); the study of Western classical instruments (and the examinations of the Associated Board of the Royal Schools of Music) in the schools of Hong Kong and Singapore (Chen-Hafteck; Lum and Dairianathan); the use of Wesleyan hymnals in the children's choir of a village church in Sierra Leone (Bartolome).

The continuation of traditions within indigenous societies is complicated by their locations within the priorities of a second nation, as in the case of the Aboriginal Australians (Mackinlay) and the Yakama of the western United States (Pitzer). In fact, children of these societies live in two worlds, code switching in and out of two cultural systems, their values, and their languages. They know the music of their first nation from birth and in all of the customary rituals and practices that thread through the seasons of their childhoods, even as they learn the music of their second nation through its mediated sources as well as the government-sponsored standards of the school curriculum. Their cultural histories are complicated and continuing, and they struggle with their multiple identities at large and in music.

The element of a familial history emerges, too, in considerations of children's musical lives, one that is linked in a linear way to living generations ahead of them, including parents and grandparents as well as aunts and uncles, who surround children and contribute to their musical sensibilities. Such is the account of three generations in a family that traces its musical heritage to Puerto Rico (Berríos-Miranda), where a first generation remembered the live music of *carnaval* and the *bomba* and *plena* music on the Motorola radio, a second generation was raised on salsa's rhythms and instrumental improvisations, and a third generation now responds to reggaeton's electronic mix of hip-hop and reggae. The pathways of young musicians are rooted as well in a family history of professional musicians, in which fathers and grandfathers, steeped in musical knowledge of the brass band world, were the influential models for a third generation (Booth). As mentioned earlier, a colonial heritage or context is a significant historical element in many places. While there is not space in this volume to reexamine the extensive research from the perspective of children's musical heritage, the chapters by Lum and Dairianathan, Chen-Hafteck, Wiggins, Koops, Bartolome, Mapana, Nannyonga-Tamusuza, Smith, Mackinlay, Berríos-Miranda, Moore, Pitzer, Sturman, and Vallejo all offer some comment on and insight into colonial legacies.

In her chapter, Downing specifically explores issues of young girls as tradition bearers in creating a new gamelan ensemble in Bali, a dichotomy that both subverts tradition by innovating a girls' gamelan and propagates gamelan tradition more widely, as the girls' gamelan is a popular tourist attraction. Cultural continuity is mostly a concern of adults who want to ensure that a succeeding generation is inculcated with appropriate attitudes and mores, often carried and indicated by the performance of songs in which the musical qualities render the words more memorable. This use of songs is explored in two religious contexts in the United States (Cohen; Miller and Miller), as part of the creation of Japanese identity in the first part of the twentieth century (Manabe), and in traditional gender roles and expectations in Uganda (Nannyonga-Tamusuza). A unique choral repertoire, supported by an equally unique written script to communicate the language, is the subject of Vallejo's research in Georgia. This area has become known for its adult choral tradition, and Vallejo begins the process of inquiry into the ways in which children learn in this context. Singing, as well as learning an instrument, is also the medium through which children learn in the Mexican context explored by Sturman. The development of orchestral playing by children in Latin America has achieved wide notice, often referred to as "*El Sistema*," but Sturman's inquiry also encompasses the ways in which children are the medium for the creation of a culture that sets out to bring together traditional music and language with adopted skills. Other fascinating insights come from Pitzer, who provides evidence that the Yakama traditions are becoming reenergized and owned by a new generation, and from Moore, who delves into the traditions of African American children that have survived as the culture of and for children for multiple generations.

A view of children as passive recipients of adult culture is also partial and does not recognize the capacities of children to change adult culture (rather than only imitating it), aligning it more with their interests. In some cultures, there are genres of children's music, passed between generations of children, who are then also culture bearers. Children often live in a plural context that is the nexus of local and national issues, dealing with different identities as well as a variety of inheritances from immigrant communities. Several chapters explore the relationship between local identities and a sense of nationality, mostly located in Africa (Bartolome; Emberly; Koops; Mapana; Wiggins) where postcolonial national boundaries include more than one indigenous ethnicity as well as a colonial legacy. Bodkin-Allen has a different view of parallel issues in New Zealand/Aotearoa as children "play" with their identities, and Kent both traces a historical tradition and maps the contemporary situation for an underrepresented Cornish culture within the United Kingdom. Mackinlay observes the issues in Australia for culture bearers located within a dominant culture whose policies are not always supportive of Aboriginal traditions, while Marsh examines the cultural heritage and materials of newly arrived immigrant children. National cultural imperatives for the transmission of appropriate materials also appear as issues in Hong Kong (Chen-Hafteck), Singapore (Lum and Dairianathan), and Korea (Kim), where Western classical music is the state-sponsored music of choice over indigenous forms.

Discussions about culture and interactions with it tend to assume a model of an individual who interacts directly with that culture as an autonomous person: an adult. For children, the situation is more complex and there is a series of modalities affecting their interaction with cultural materials, with their domestic setting providing a major context within which they are first exposed to cultural materials. Children are gradually allowed autonomy in their choice of their active engagement within the culture, subject to social and economic constraints. With the increasing availability of music through the media, the home is less the site of active family music making than was formerly the case, but perhaps most mothers still sing to their children—at least in private. Whiteman explores the ways in which young children construct their world at micro- and macrolevels in relation to their family and local community, considering locations in Australia and Hawaii.

The tendency in many households to leave the radio or television (or perhaps both) playing and to use big-screen entertainment as placeholders for absent parents and caregivers, means that children may hear more music in their childhood than they would previously have heard in a lifetime. This may contribute to the phenomenon of "continuous partial attention" in which an individual monitors several diverse sources, trying to avoid missing anything (Stone 2010) but also pays less specific attention to any source and is more easily distracted by something else because it might be significant. Parents may leave their choice of media playing but are also likely introduce a child to radio or TV programs made specifically for them at an early age. There is little quality control, such that programs made for children range from educational, through edutainment, to programs whose sole aim seems to be to sell merchandise. Hoefnagels and Harris Walsh explore some of these issues in Canada, looking at the repertoire and intentions of the performers. The extent to which this is a local culture is complex; some aspects of the repertoire present a global village where the world comes to a given locality, but this is also culture at the national level, inducting children into a North American context. By contrast, the family and locality of the culture that Miller and Miller observe in an American church is highly focused. It rejects many aspects of the surrounding general culture but is linked to other churches internationally by shared beliefs. Parental control of what is heard and done by the children continues for longer in the church setting so that the children are better prepared to pass on this aural-oral culture. Nannyonga-Tamusuza also reports on a local culture in Uganda, where music and songs support and inculcate family roles and there is a designated person, a paternal aunt, who is responsible for the transmission of knowledge and culture.

The Amazonian riverine culture that Ilari explores is very local, mostly due to geographic location, and there is a sense that this is a liminal community from a wider Brazilian perspective. Very local family and community cultures may find themselves under pressure from media access in the future, as such access enables children to identify the individuality of their cultural behavior and to question it; music is often a powerful tool to ensure that the traditional behaviors and roles are embedded within children's consciousness at an early stage. The Aboriginal culture in Australia that Mackinlay reports on is already under pressure from a dominant national culture. Thus, the indigenous culture, based on the extended family, is struggling for meaningful survival and exploring how they will respond to the influences of this dominant culture. In contrast, Kleber and Souza report on community projects in Brazil, where cultural activities, particularly music that extends across both traditional and more international styles, are offering a medium through which socioeconomic hardship, antisocial behavior, and low self-esteem are being addressed. Of course, because children are not simply recipients of local culture, they create their own culture within peer groups, negotiating an environment drawing on the cultural inheritance from their families and their own experience. The detailed observation of a group of children in Nicaragua by Minks shows how the rules and behaviors for games work within this cultural web.

Cultural Identities with Multiple Meanings

An important element in the journey through childhood and adolescence is the development of a conscious identity. This personal identity is shaped and defined by language, ethnicity, and religious beliefs and is often publicly expressed (and personally determined from tween-age, or even earlier) through dress, music, and dance. Derived from a sense of belonging to a particular group, identity is frequently oversimplified, summarized by a single word or reference. Saïd observed,

> No one today is purely *one* thing. Labels like Indian, or woman, or Muslim or American are no more than starting points.... Yet just as human beings make their own history, they also make their cultures and ethnic identities. (1994: 407–408)

As young as they are, children make their own identities, and these are not purely *one* thing. They are familiar with and sensitive to labels, and they learn early on their power to include, exclude, and cause hurt. Yet childhood is marked by a growing awareness of the meaning of multiple symbols of cultural and social location. Young children use music because they find it appealing, and it is only as they mature that they recognize the symbolic meanings attached to music's place in the construction of their personal identity. The widespread availability of global materials through locally available media such as radio, TV, films, and the internet has led to a "glocal" situation for many children, so their identity is shaped by elements and influences in local, national, and global spheres. The question of how local identities are recognized at the national level, the materials that support local identity, and the presence and attraction of national and international media, is in play for children in New Zealand (Bodkin-Allen), Sierra Leone (Bartolome), South Africa (Emberly), Brazil (Ilari), the United Kingdom (Kent), the Gambia (Koops), Australia (Marsh), the United States (Pitzer), India (Sarrazin), and Trinidad (Smith). In contrast, Hoefnagels and Harris Walsh examine the glocal world specifically created for children by adult performers in Canada. Language usage is another interesting aspect often associated with songs. Although linguistic code switching is not always indicative of identity (Depperman 2007: 35), Minks explores the linguistic codes in operation around a children's game in Nicaragua.

Personal Journeys in/through Culture

It would be surprising if reflections on the role and function of music within the spheres of culture, socialization, and identity did not result in the reexamination by some authors of their own childhood development and experience. This might have resulted in the reinvention of history with 20/20 hindsight, such that what would come forward would be either a glowing reminiscence of a childhood in which it was always a golden summer or a damning indictment of past practices that did not measure up to our present advanced state of knowledge. In fact, a balanced and reasoned set of personal journeys emerged instead through autoethnography, a mode of writing that has become established relatively recently as an accepted form of academic inquiry (see, e.g., Holman-Jones 2005 and the 2009 music-focused collection by Bartleet and Ellis). Four contributors to this volume examine issues for a community specifically through their own experience, often studying children who are now at a similar stage as a comparator and reference point. Lum and Dairianathan explore the acculturative issues raised by the strong presence of Western instruments and examinations in Singapore, with its continuation of Chinese (and Malay and Indian) cultural traditions and values. Mackinlay interrogates the childhood experiences for Aboriginal children in northern Australia, where there are many unresolved cultural differences between a traditional upbringing and the values expressed by state-controlled educational practice. Moore reflects on both the delights and challenges of an African American upbringing in the southern United States, while Berríos-Miranda considers the continuities and changes for her mother, herself, and her children in Santurce, Puerto Rico and Seattle, United States, over the course of these three generations. In parallel with Lum and Dairianathan, and with Mackinlay, Mapana considers music education in Tanzania, focusing on his experience in the Wagogo cultural region and probing how music experiences in and out of school can be local and national, while Chen-Hafteck explores the ongoing dialogue around identity for herself and children today in Hong Kong.

Music in Education and Development

The place of the arts, and specifically music, in formal education has always been a matter of debate and justification, particularly after the early years when "play" is valued. Reasons put forward for music's maintenance in educational institutions, communities, and individual families include its inherent artistic qualities, its impact on children's cognitive development, its contribution to children's emotional well-being, its communication (in song texts) of social values and required behaviors, its long-standing presence in a traditional school curriculum, its prospects for the economic livelihoods of adults who have amassed skills from their school years onward, and even its social status. National and cultural imperatives press upon the presence of music in schools for children's greater good, even as there are local communities that stand in support of its place in their state-sponsored system of education. In the case of governments that recognize the arts as an economic product, there are attempts to maximize their income from it, in which case they may sponsor the training of highly productive young musicians while providing little musical education for all others. In various societal circumstances, children learn music more or less well as a result of the education and training that is offered to them in schools, preschools, free or family-afforded special music schools, after-school programs, or private tuition (as in the case of piano lessons). Children's musical education may function to develop their musicianship, their creative thinking processes, and their knowledge of history and culture. For very few, music may become their livelihood and professional work (e.g., Booth; Lum and Dairianathan), while for most children, their musical education will lead to later leisure activity and an outlet for their personal expression alone and in groups.

In the schools, musical study by children frequently leads to the acquisition of skill sets and repertoires by children through their participation in instrumental and vocal music ensembles as well as through listening lessons and guided experiences in creative musical invention. Such aims fall short when students' musical needs and music education actualities are ill matched, as has happened in those German schools where lessons are more tailored to passive listening than to engaging children in the process of making music (Kertz-Welzel). Likewise, the government-mandated content of Euro-American art music within the schools of Singapore (Lum and Dairianathan), Tanzania (Mapana) and other nations with European colonial histories does little to develop a connection of students to their own living local musical cultures. In Brazilian programs, where there is an honoring of children's social realities, the results of musical training and education are positive and meaningful (Kleber and Souza). Membership in musically demanding school programs in Hong Kong, Mexico, the United States, and elsewhere fire up children and youth, who forge their personal, social, and cultural identities alongside the development of their musical skills (Abril; Sturman). Government, religious, and private sponsors of schools are well aware that the musical content of the curriculum may be chockfull of societal values and mores, too, and that songs are vessels of language learning (Chen-Hafteck; Koops) and cultural understandings that are deemed important for children to acquire (Manabe).

The rise of attention in many of the world's nations to the early education of young children, especially infants, toddlers, and prekindergarten children, has prompted specialist-teachers to seek out playful and multisensory experiences that enhance children's cognitive and socioemotional growth. Increasingly, music is a compulsory subject of study in the certification training of early childhood educators. Preschool children are commonly engaged in singing, listening, moving, and playing rhythm instruments (Adachi; Kim; Whiteman), and for some there are the additional after-school experiences through the global network of trademarked music education providers such as Kindermusik and Gymboree (Chen-Hafteck). While the musical education of young children figures importantly in a wide array of national and regional policy papers, it is valued within local cultural communities as well, where musical threads are woven through kindergartens, childcare centers, and immersion centers as a means of teaching language and cultural values (Bodkin-Allen).

Children learn music formally in after-school programs, in nongovernment organization–sponsored projects (Kleber and Souza), and in specially designated music schools (Vallejo), where they may go once their academic studies at school are finished for the day. They may know "an education through music," arranged by their parents who immerse them in private lessons and daily practice routines and even a carefully selected list of required Euro-American musical works for listening and learning (Lum and Dairianathan). The regulated study of piano, violin, flute, trumpet, guitar, and a host of instruments is its own industry and encompasses adult performers who teach, specially trained music pedagogues, an industry of instrument makers, books, recordings, tuners and repair services, and the supply of supplemental materials such as metronomes, strings, and reeds. The music(al) education of children is at once a humanistic endeavor, a social system, and a business enterprise.

The shifting spheres of children's interests and engagements in music are associated with their age and development. The gamut of childhood, from infancy through the teen years, offers them a grand variety of musical encounters in which they may become increasingly involved (and at more sophisticated levels of involvement). As children grow physically, intellectually, socially, and emotionally, their capacities to listen, respond to, and actively make music undergo considerable change. Children's potential for skill development continues across their childhood years, as does their understanding of music, its structures, and its meanings. The way children use music in their lives also evolves, often in response to changes to their emotional needs and social circumstances.

Developmental psychologists have long been interested in children's growth, and a rich literature has amassed on children's ability to perceive and make cognitive sense of music (Trainor 2005), to sing in tune and in time (Welch 1998), to move in rhythmically responsive ways to music (Metz 1989), and to developing the motor skills and aural acuity to play instruments (McPherson 2005). Attention to infants and toddlers is considerable, and musicologists and biologists alike are finding fascination in mother-baby chatter for the qualities of a communicative musicality (Malloch and Trevarthen 2009) that arise within the first months of life. This interest has now begun to map skills of language and music that develop before birth, with a recent report stating, "Human fetuses are able to memorize auditory stimuli from the external world by the last trimester of pregnancy, with a particular sensitivity to melody contour in both music and language" (Mampe et al. 2009: 1994). Neuromusical researchers intent on finding keys to incipient language and its development are finding parallels in the ways in which the sustained pitch vocalizations of song are emerging simultaneously with the building blocks of language—phonemes, words, short phrases—that are sounded by infants and toddlers (Patel 2008). Motivational studies are also considerable, too, in discerning from a sociopsychological perspective how musically impassioned children continue their musical studies into adolescence while others slow their interest or drop out altogether (McPherson and Davidson 2006). Music educationists have contributed to the literature on children's musical growth, especially on questions that pertain to establishing a schedule of instruction that is resonant with children's readiness to learn within formal school programs (Campbell and Scott-Kassner 2010).

Across the cases of children's musical cultures that comprise this volume, children of various ages are documented and described. Whiteman observed that even very young children of indigenous Hawaiian and various Australian families are active agents in determining which of the songs and rhythms from home, church, and preschool they will value and share. Preschools are the sites of examination by Bodkin-Allen, where music is threaded through the day's activities in New Zealand childcare centers and kindergartens to deliver to young children a sense of their nation's bicultural identity and multicultural society. Chen-Hafteck, and Kim turn their lenses, albeit briefly, to preschools in Hong Kong and Korea as the portal of formal education in music, where children's songs are sung, rhythm patterns are chanted and played, and learning through play is held as an ideal that merits continuous reminding in order to be achieved. They observe children's socialization through a repertoire of songs and listening experiences and ways in which early learning is consciously linked to some of the national imperatives to preserve and transmit culture to young children. Adachi's review of preschools in Japan suggests that children engage regularly in teacher-directed activities of singing familiar and new songs, listening to music, and movement to music. The early education of young children appears replete with musical experiences, perhaps in acknowledgement of the natural appeal that music has had for them in their early years of development.

School-age children, especially between the ages of five and twelve years, are in the midst of a time of singing, dancing, and playing music "for fun," with increasing proficiency as a result of their maturation, experience, and learning opportunities. They sing in school the songs they are taught by teachers (Ilari; Kent; Manabe; Nannyonga-Tamusuza), with some of the repertoire embedded with political meaning or cultural values they may not yet fully grasp. Beginning with their entrance to school, children may engage in individual and group lessons for honing skills and repertoire on instruments such as piano—as in Singapore (Lum and Dairianathan), Hong Kong (Chen-Hafteck), and Mexico (Sturman). In institutionalized settings outside school, they play in ensembles especially meant for them, including junior-sized gamelans in Bali (Downing) and steel pan ensembles in Trinidad (Smith). They sing in community choirs in the former Soviet republic of Georgia (Vallejo), in regional cultural pageants and festivals (Kent), and in church choirs in Sierra Leone (Bartolome) and in African American communities (Miller and Miller). In specially funded after-school social programs in Brazil, they start as children and continue into adolescence the development of necessary skills to play music in a range of instrumental ensemble styles that include Brazilian *chorinho*, *pagode*, samba, and hip-hop (Kleber and Souza).

Music happens among children on the far outside of school in peer and mixed age groups, especially between the ages of five and twelve years, whether they are singing together and playing singing games (Emberly; Koops; Marsh; Minks; Moore; Roberts; Sarrazin), dancing to music in the family home (Berríos-Miranda), or listening to the songs supplied by the music industry at home or in family-oriented concerts of children's singer-songwriters (Hoefnagels and Harris Walsh). The songs children invent, appropriate from mediated sources (Emberly; Marsh), or transmit intact (or with variation from earlier generations of it), are playful, sometimes teasing, reflective of their valuing of friends and family (Moore), present and future relationships—both real and imagined (Koops; Minks; Sarrazin)—and cultural customs passed to them that they do not yet understand (Nannyonga-Tamusuza). Occasionally, these songs are intended by children to have shock value as they role-play situations through the songs that are within their experience (Roberts). Children collect and share these songs in same-age (and same-grade) groups, with peak interest by children ages five to eight years, and older children may also model these songs for younger children coming into the fold of singing games. As they progress into their middle childhood years, children are increasingly prone to share music via the available technology (Bickford; Chen-Hafteck; Mackinlay; Marsh; Sarrazin), and this activity continues through their adolescent years (Kertz-Welzel; Kim; Wiggins).

In their search for identity as adolescents, music becomes them. It sweeps over them, fascinates them, and subsumes them. Children generally graduate from "childhood" at about age eleven into what is referred sometimes referred to as "youth," when the growing pains are as much socioemotional as they are physical. The search for identity intensifies through the teen years, especially ages thirteen to eighteen as they make their ways through junior and senior secondary schools and as they gradually figure out who they are personally and collectively and to which groups they belong. Some continue the musical involvement that they knew as children, whether in perpetuating children's songs (Emberly), participating in ensembles (Downing; Smith; Vallejo), or playing on solo instruments (Lum and Dairianathan; Sturman). A coming to grips with who speaks for them, sometimes through the mediated songs they listen to, is very much within the midst of the adolescent angst that they negotiate (Ilari; Kertz-Welzel; Sarrazin). As well, adolescents are exploring their identity through the songs they invent (Pitzer) and in the roles they fill within the school ensembles that they join (Abril). Some adolescents are making their way to the work they will do in the world, and the music that they have played from childhood onward occasionally develops into their economic mainstay (Kleber and Souza; Booth).

Technologies: Impacts, Uses, and Responses

An important feature of this volume is children's engagement with the glocal elements in their lives, now made so apparent through the rapid inclusion, almost as toys, of social networking, cell phones, and DVD and MP3 players in children's lives. This is, in some ways, an inversion of the concept of "glocal," usually defined as "think globally, act locally." Children may act globally by virtue of their developmental passage but think locally. Even where socioeconomic circumstances or remote location mean that some children may have less direct access to these technological "toys," children are aware of them via friends or people passing through. New technologies are also starting to make a significant impact on the documentation of many cultures, occasionally by the children themselves. In earlier times, anthropologists and ethnomusicologists arrived at a location, pointed their lens and microphone at those things they considered important, and later considered ceding some control to local people as researchers became more aware both of the effect of their work and the implications for their relationship with the people being observed. Emberly offers a telling anecdote of tables turned on her by a child, who pointed the video camera at her and asked direct questions; she willingly gave the floor to the child as she had yearned for such an opportunity to learn since the inception of her work. Culture-bearing adults, and now children, are becoming more aware of the value of documenting their lives, both to demonstrate what they have achieved and for the status this demonstrates. Audio and video recorders, and even cell phones, have been used and become progressively cheaper and more readily available in most parts of the world, with economic circumstances as the only barrier to children as researchers.

Technology and the media are increasingly evident in children's lives, and their impact has not gone unnoticed by parents and teachers. Current generations of children are growing up in a "digital-ready" world, and they accept as standard practice the ability to communicate easily with others, build their social network of friends from near and far, and access information immediately. If given the opportunity, children are rapid learners in how to access the menu-driven methods of commanding, organizing, and accessing most digital devices. Booth observes the presence of the digital age in India as a young man (and gender seems to be a part of the complex equation) organizes the family technology and learns how to operate and program a keyboard, in spite of not understanding the manual. In the United States, Bickford documents the use by children in an American school of these new technologies in remarkable ways: splitting earbuds to share mediated music with a friend and tapping out text messages in lieu of passing notes or whispering. Kim mentions the gamut of electronics in use by Korean schoolchildren, from MP3 players and cellular phones, to gaming activity on computers and via the internet; she notes also the strong influence of media stars on the preferred songs that Korean children listen to and learn.

The pervasive presence of television, radio, film, DVDs, CDs, and the internet in homes, and sometimes at school and in community settings, offers images that have a marked influence on children's real and fantasy worlds. Chandler's review of research suggested that children's perception of reality changes substantially over the course of their development between the ages of four and twelve (Chandler 1997). He reported that although young children from the age of three realized they could not influence events on television, they invariably assumed that it was all "real" in a number of ways. From the age of around seven or eight, children tend to discriminate on the basis of their knowledge that "things like that do happen" as one of the factors. This is a significant backdrop for understanding the world that Hoefnagels and Harris Walsh observe, in which children are inducted into the "global village" created for them by adults, so that they know songs from many places around the world—all of it presented to them in a context and arrangement that is familiar, with the world represented as happy and carefree. This contrasts strongly with India, where Sarrazin charts the impact of the video CD and the sound systems of passing buses on children. These media experiences offer an "other" world in many respects and enable many children to access the Bollywood film music, a marker of their membership in Indian society.

In some societies, the range of music available through technology and the media is of concern for the sustainability of traditional music. Music broadcasts by even the most local radio or TV stations are often dominated by the availability of prerecorded and imported media, and the ability of stations to represent the diversity of local culture is very limited—as is the case for localities in Ghana (Wiggins) and South Africa (Emberly). In comparison, Lum and Dairianathan observe music in Singapore, a highly technologized society, where the media availability of Western classical music supports the genre's preeminent position in society, which is substantially funded by the government.

As was mentioned earlier, the threads of interest and inquiry in this volume are not bounded by the headings under which the chapters have been grouped. In this following section, we enumerate and explore other strands that have emerged from our collected writings.

A Children's World?

For a majority of adults, and parents in particular, the creation and maintenance of a world for children where they are not exposed to the worst of the adult world is a high priority. Adults recognize that children understand in ways appropriate to their maturity and create music that they believe will appeal to children (Hoefnagels and Harris Walsh). They intentionally provide songs for children's contemporary enjoyment that carry encoded messages for future socially appropriate behaviors and values (Nannyonga-Tamusuza). There is, of course, potentially a darker side to this adult-sponsored music for children, with notions of induction typically summarized by the phrase, "Give me the child until he is seven, and I will show you the man" (Singer 2000). Music may be used as an element of control, as children are recipients of the embedded morality of songs that were intentionally selected by parents, teachers, and caregivers to distance them from matters they perceive to be harmful to their ethical development. Some elements of this can be seen in Manabe's writing about children in Japan during World War II, and some of these darker issues also emerge in Roberts's analysis of historical recordings from New York. Children may also themselves use the power of song to make negative comments on others more immediate and memorable (see, e.g., Bjørkvold 1992: 71; Campbell 2010: 44–45). Given the extent of hardship and conflict around the world, fascinating work lies ahead as to the role of music for children in challenging situations of work as child soldiers and of their struggles in families suffering the effects of failing economies. Such research would be difficult to arrange, and it should be no surprise that there is very little extant literature about the darker side of music by and for children that could be included in this volume.

Subversive Behaviors by Children

Children have a great facility for imitation. This appears in the form of mimicry, which serves a key role in the identification and cohesion of a social group. Children intentionally use and adapt words, graffiti, labels, and clothing for personal and group ends. Moore reports children's imitation at play of adults talking to them ("Oh-oo-oo child, I'm so tired, I've got to go home"). Bickford observes many aspects of imitation as well as invention in children's use of MP3 players. As they listen to adult-made mediated music, children decorate their players in individual ways, sometimes showing disregard for the economic value over the social function of technology in ways that adults find subversive, such as breaking a pair of head-phones in order to share them. This subversion also extends to the musical realm of fidelity and quality. MP3 players, although using a compressed format, are capable of delivering high-quality music, usually downloaded via a computer. This is of lit-tle importance to the children who swap tracks among themselves using the head-phones and built-in microphones, which greatly reduces the quality of the sound and introduces additional environmental sounds to the track. That fidelity is less important than social function is clearly illustrated when a child refuses an offered download because he has already recorded that track via the microphone in a car. Cohen illustrates the ways in which American adolescents create and maintain their own subculture through subverting the words of songs, with the knowledge and collusion of the "adult" world, all of whom have passed through this same process of induction and inclusion and have now graduated or been excluded from this world by the function they now assume. Similar processes in a different setting are also described by Roberts who examined historical recordings of children in New York City in the mid-twentieth century, where children take and remake music from the adult world that surrounds them.

Children, Music, and Gender

The extent of musical engagement of children does not tilt in the direction of one gender over the other, and boys as well as girls are enmeshed in music as children, though somewhat differently. Gendered codes are in active play in some cultures, which then elicit expectations for gender-specific roles. In Bali, for example, it is traditionally expected that boys are noisy and boisterous while girls are silent and demure, such that government-funded cultural projects are now underway to engage women and children in artistic practices once reserved for men alone. Downing reports on the establishment of a girls-only gamelan in which players feel a sense of pride in preserving Balinese culture even as they simply enjoy being together as friends, as they would in any girls' club, sharing stories, laughing, and joking. Gender roles have been inculcated through song texts, too, as the Japanese military marches (*gunka*) of World War II memorialized male soldiers for their loyalty and bravery on the battlefield (Manabe); gunka texts declared the primary activity of boys and men in wartime while also conveying the implicit message that supporting roles be played by girls and women.

Particularly in infancy, in toddlerhood, and until entrance to school, most boys and girls enjoy making music, listening to it, and responding to it through move-ment and dance—and they do so together, with little notable differences between genders (Opie 1985: 27–28). Societal notions begin to affect the course of musical activity by school age, however, and girls more than boys embrace the singing games of playground practice (Marsh; Minks; Moore). The content of songs sung mostly by girls encompasses subjects that include boy-girl flirtation, romantic relationships, and even forecasts of marriage (Sarrazin), which girls particularly enjoy playfully mentioning to partners or around the circle. Girls may use singing games to construct and contest forms of gender and sexuality, as information on eventual sex roles emerges in songs (Nannyonga-Tamusuza), and sexual innuendo surfaces even when the meaning may not be understood (Nannyonga-Tamusuza; Roberts).

In the dances in which Puerto Rican children engage, girls learn to develop a sense of personal security, understanding how to negotiate the physical advances of male partners—a behavior that is socially significant far beyond the dance floor (Berríos-Miranda). Some of the myths that thread through songs sung by riverine girls of the Brazilian Amazon feature supernatural creatures (*encantados*) who warn young girls of the dangers of city life, handsome young men, and becoming pregnant too soon (Ilari). Likewise, junior calypsonians in Trinidad create songs that warn against crime, HIV/AIDS, and the consequences of sexual relationships before marriage (Smith).

Boys of school age are frequently less active than girls in informally organized singing groups and in choirs, although membership in choirs in the former Soviet republic of Georgia (Vallejo) and a village choir in Sierra Leone (Bartolome) appears to maintain a gender balance. In one denomination of an African American church choir, there are particular tasks that belong only to boys, including the Shepherd Boy with his staff leading the procession of children, and the bugler, who signals the beginning of a service, and thus boys remain active musical participants (Miller and Miller). Where rural children in India continue to fill traditional gender roles, the extent of their musical play reflects these roles; boys who attend school regularly devote their time to study over play, including musical play (Sarrazin).

In many cultures, there are tendencies among adolescents toward male or female behaviors in accordance with traditions that are strictly monitored by the youth themselves. In North America, traditional gender stereotypes are continued in the selection of instruments to play in the school band, where flutes are almost exclusively "girl instruments" and lower and larger brass instruments remain within the realm of boys and, once selected, are played clear through secondary school (Abril). Song leader positions at the Reform Jewish summer camps are open to adolescent girls and boys who play guitar and sing with a strong voice, although boys appear to rise more frequently than girls to these leadership opportunities (Cohen). Until recently, only boys of the Yakama Nation Tribal School played drums, while girls were permitted to dance to and sing some (but not all) songs; Pitzer observes that this gender barrier has been lifted. In India's Muslim communities in which men work to earn money while women stay home to raise children and keep house, Booth documents how boys raised in musical families acquire skills fit for working their way into lives as professional musicians. In many venues worldwide, cultural expectations have it that girls often continue in musical activities they began in childhood, be it group singing and singing competitions, piano lessons, various instrumental ensembles, dancing, or informal listening.

Conclusion

This volume will expand and deepen understandings of children for their expressive practices in music. Varied circumstances of children are depicted, dissected, and then drawn together for their shared and distinctive features of music for its sonic and sociocultural qualities and for its meanings and values to children who listen to it and make and remake it to their personal taste. The chapters are ordered by some central themes but can be interrogated through many other links, as we have set out to show. A map of the world illustrates the geographical distribution—for every fascinating location, another is omitted and awaits future research. Each chapter offers its own explicit lens and, like children, is not only *one* thing or approach (nor is it located solely under one heading) but consists of multiple themes that overlap and intersect. Together, the collected chapters comprise a rich weave of understandings of children's musical cultures.

References

American Anthropological Association. 2011. "American Anthropological Association Children and Childhood Interest Group." Accessed July 18, 2011. http://aaacig.usu. edu.

Ariès, Philippe. 1962. *Centuries of Childhood*, translated by Robert Baldick. London: Jonathan Cape.

Bartleet, Brydie-Leigh, and Carolyn Ellis, eds. 2009. *Music Autoethnographies.* Brisbane, Australia: Australian Academic Press.

Bjørkvold, Jon Roar. 1992. *The Muse within: Creativity and Communication, Song and Play from Childhood through Maturity.* New York: Harper Collins.

Blacking, John. 1967. *Venda Children's Songs: A Study in Ethnomusicological Analysis.* Johannesburg: Witwatersrand University Press.

Bluebond-Lagner, Myra. 2007. *Children, Childhoods, and Childhood Studies.* Berkeley: University of California Press.

Campbell, Patricia Shehan. [1998] 2010. *Songs in Their Heads: Music and Its Meaning in Children's Lives.* New York: Oxford University Press.

Campbell, Patricia Shehan. 2007. "Musical Meaning in Children's Cultures." In *Handbook on Research in Arts Education*, edited by Liora Bresler, 881–894. Dordrecht, The Netherlands: Springer.

Campbell, Patricia Shehan, and Carol Scott-Kassner. 2010. *Music in Childhood.* 3rd ed. Boston: Cengage.

Chandler, Daniel. 1997. "Children's Understanding of What Is 'Real' on Television: A Review of the Literature." *Journal of Educational Media* 23 (1): 67–82.

Corso, Dawn T. 2003. "'Smooth as Butter': Practices of Music Learning amongst African American Children." PhD diss., University of Illinois at Urbana-Champaign.

Deppermann, Arnulf. 2007. "Playing with the Voice of the Other: Stylized Kanaksprak Conversations among German Adolescents." In *Style and Social Identities: Alternative Approaches to Linguistic Heterogeneity,* edited by P. Auer, 325–360. Berlin: Mouton de Gruyter.

Dzansi, Mary P. 2002. "Some Manifestations of Ghanaian Indigenous Culture in Children's Singing Games." *International Journal of Education and the Arts* 3 (7). Accessed July 18, 2011. www.ijea.org/v3n7/index.html.

Gaunt, Kyra D. 2006. *The Games Black Girls Play: Learning the Ropes from Double-Dutch to Hip-Hop.* New York: New York University Press.

Gomme, Lady Alice B. (1894–1898) 1994. *The Traditional Games of England, Scotland, and Ireland with Tunes, Singing-Rhythms, and Methods of Playing according to Variants Extant and Recording in Different Parts of the Kingdom.* 2 vols. London: David Nutt. Reprint, London: Thames and Hudson.

Graue, M. E., and D. J. Walsh. 1998. *Studying Children in Context.* Thousand Oaks, CA: Sage.

Harker, David. 1985. *Fakesong: The Manufacture of British "Folksong" 1700 to the Present Day.* Milton Keynes, UK: Open University Press.

Harwood, Eve. 1998. "'Go on Girl' Improvisation in African-American Girls' Singing Games." In *In the Course of Performance: Studies in the World of Musical Improvisation,* edited by B. Nettl and M. Russell, 113–125. Chicago: University of Chicago Press.

Hirschfeld, Lawrence A. 2002. "Why Don't Anthropologist Like Children?" *American Anthropologist* 104 (2): 611–627.

Holman-Jones, S. 2005. "Autoethnography: Making the Personal Political." In *The Sage Handbook of Qualitative Research.* 3rd ed., edited by N. K. Denzin and Y. S. Lincoln, 763–792. Thousand Oaks: Sage.

Holmes, Robyn M. 1998. *Fieldwork with Children.* Thousand Oaks, CA: Sage.

James, Alison, and Adrian James. 2008. *Key Concepts in Childhood Studies.* Los Angeles: Sage.

James, Allison. 2007. "Giving Voice to Children's Voices: Practices and Problems, Pitfalls and Potentials." *American Anthropologist* 109 (2): 261–272.

Kartomi, Margaret. 1980. "Childlikeness in Play Songs: A Case Study among the Pitjantjara at Yalata, South Australia." *Miscellanea Musicologica* 11: 172–214.

Lancy, David F. 2008. *The Anthropology of Childhood: Cherbus, Chattel, Changelings.* Cambridge: Cambridge University Press.

Lew, Jackie Chooi-Theng. 2005. "The Musical Lives of Young Malaysian Children: In School and at Home." PhD diss., University of Washington.

Lum, Chee-Hoo. 2007. "Musical Networks of Children: An Ethnography of Elementary School Children in Singapore." PhD diss., University of Washington.

Lum, Chee-Hoo, and Peter Whiteman, eds. 2012. *Musical Childhoods of Asia and the Pacific.* New York: Information Age Publishing.

Malloch, Stephen, and Colwyn Trevarthen. 2009. *Communicative Musicality: Exploring the Basis of Human Companionship.* Oxford: Oxford University Press.

Mampe, Birgit, Angela D. Friederici, Anne Christophe, and Kathleen Wermke. 2009. "Newborns' Cry Melody Is Shaped by Their Native Language." *Current Biology* 19 (23): 1994–1997.

Marsh, Kathryn, and Susan Young. 2006. "Musical Play." In *The Child as Musician*, edited by Gary E. McPherson, 289–310. New York: Oxford University Press.

McPherson, Gary E. 2005. "From Child to Musician: Skill Development during the Beginning Stages of Learning an Instrument." *Psychology of Music* 33: 5–35.

McPherson, Gary E., and Jane Davidson. 2006. "Playing an Instrument." In *The Child as Musician*, edited by Gary E. McPherson, 331–352. Oxford: Oxford University Press.

McPherson, Gary E., ed. 2006. *The Child as Musician.* Oxford: Oxford University Press.

Metz, Elayne. 1989. "Movement as a Musical Response among Preschool Children." *Journal of Research in Music Education* 37 (1): 48–60.

Minks, Amanda. 2002. "From Children's Song to Expressive Practices: Old and New Directions in the Ethnomusicological Study of Children." *Ethnomusicology* 46 (3): 379–408.

Minks, Amanda. 2006. "Afterword." In *Musical Childhoods and the Cultures of Youth*, edited by Susan Boyton and Roe-Min Kok, 209–218. Middletown: Wesleyan University Press.

Montgomery, Heather. 2009. *An Introduction to Childhood: Anthropological Perspectives on Children's Lives.* Malden, MA: Wiley-Blackwell.

Nettl, Bruno. 1965. *Folk and Traditional Music of the Western Continents.* Englewood Cliffs, NJ: Prentice-Hall.

Nettl, Bruno. 2005. *The Study of Ethnomusicology: Thirty-One Issues and Concepts.* Urbana-Champaign: University of Illinois Press.

Newell, William Wells. 1884. *Games and Songs of American Children.* New York: Dover.

Opie, Peter, and Iona Opie. 1985. *The Singing Game.* Oxford: Oxford University Press.

Riddell, Cecilia. 1990. "Traditional Singing Games of Elementary School Children in Los Angeles." PhD diss., University of California, Los Angeles.

Saïd, Edward W. 1994. *Culture and Imperialism.* London: Vintage.

Shakespeare, William. (1623) 1951. *As You Like It.* In *Complete Works of Shakespeare*, edited by P. Alexander. London, Collins.

Singer, Bennett, ed. 2000. *42 Up: Give Me the Child until He Is Seven, and I Will Show You the Man: A Book Based on Michael Apted's Award-Winning Documentary.* New York: The New Press.

Stone, Linda. 2010. "Continuous Partial Attention." Accessed September 27, 2010. http://lindastone.net/qa/continuous-partial-attention.

Trainor, Laura J. 2005. "Are There Critical Periods for Musical Development?" *Developmental Psychobiology* 46: 262–278.

Valentine, Gill. 2000. "Exploring Children and Young People's Narratives of Identity." *Geoforum* 31 (2): 257–267.

Waterman, Richard. 1956. "Music in Australia Aboriginal Culture—Some Sociological and Psychological implications." In *Music Therapy 1955: Fifth Book of Proceedings of the National Association for Music Therapy: Papers from the Sixth Annual Conference, Detroit, Michigan*, edited by E. Thayer Gaston, Marcus E. Hahn, Robert F. Unkefer, and National Association for Music Therapy, 40–49. Lawrence, KS: National Association for Music Therapy.

Welch, Graham. 1998. "Early Childhood Musical Development." *Research Studies in Music Education* 11: 27–41.

Widdess, D. R., and R. F. Wolpert. 1981. *Music & Tradition.* Cambridge: Cambridge University Press.

PART 1

ENGAGEMENTS WITH CULTURE: SOCIALIZATION AND IDENTITY

(RE)MAKING CULTURES FOR/ BY CHILDREN/ UPDATING TRADITION

1

GIRLS EXPERIENCING GAMELAN EDUCATION AND CULTURAL POLITICS IN BALI

SONJA LYNN DOWNING

On the evening of July 31, 2006, an ensemble of young female gamelan (Indonesian percussion ensemble) musicians entered a temporary stage that had been set up in the soccer field in Ubud, Bali for a music festival. Placing themselves at their instruments, they sat with upright posture, confident and prepared, and were seemingly unfazed by the throngs of locals and tourists watching them from below. At the sharp cue from the lead drummer, the girls proceeded to perform their prepared repertoire of *gong kebyar* standards and new compositions, which variously included intricate interlocking parts, well-rehearsed dynamic and tempo variations, choreography, and singing (see Web Figure 1.1 ⦿). This performance was notable for three reasons: first, young girls were performing gamelan music as a highly polished, skilled, and experienced ensemble—something that would not have been likely a few decades earlier and that many Balinese still regard as novel; second, they were playing across the stage from an adult women's gamelan making this perhaps the first mock gamelan competition involving a girls' group; and third, it served as a prelude to a speech given by the Indonesian minister of culture and tourism. The minister's speech called on children to participate in Indonesian cultural arts as an act of patriotism, describing the performers as an example of both what Indonesian children should strive for and, conflictingly, what to avoid. In so doing, he discursively placed national and regional pride, the burden of upholding nationalist gender ideals, and promotion of the tourist economy on the shoulders of ten- to sixteen-year-old girls. The event illustrated the way that children's gamelan ensembles are located at the nexus of a complex web of competing forces, from nationalist educational and cultural projects to regional assertions of local or religious (Balinese-Hindu) identities. Tensions between ideologies of citizenship, gender roles, and the preservation of Balinese culture are played out in the promotion and support, or lack thereof, of children's gamelan ensembles and the *sanggar*, or private performing arts studios, that run them.

Historically, gamelan performance was the sole domain of men. Young boys and adult women have had opportunities to play for the past few decades, but only very recently and only in a few locations have girls been allowed and encouraged to perform gamelan music (Downing 2010). Despite being rooted in the community, these ensembles are subject to national and cultural imperatives of representation, preservation, and capitalism as well as both Indonesian and foreign historical influences on discourses of cultural arts. Girls' performances are used by community leaders and national politicians to promote a campaign of strengthening local cultural practices in response to perceived threats of globalization and increasing Islamic fundamentalism as well as to represent the nation internationally as an artistic and cultural paradise. They are also offered as both attractions for and antidotes to increasing tourism. In this chapter, I explore how children's gamelans bear the weight of supporting potentially conflicting ideologies of gender and childhood and how their members are negotiating alternative ways in which to move beyond those ideologies.

Three community-based performing arts organizations are featured here. The first is Sanggar Çudamani in Pengosekan village, just south of Ubud. Directed by I Dewa Putu Berata and his American wife Emiko Saraswati Susilo, this *sanggar* includes an internationally touring adult men's gamelan, one of the only continuously active girls' gamelans in Bali, dance classes for children, and an intensive study program for foreigners. The girls' gamelan was started in 2001, largely through Susilo's impetus, and is taught by Berata and other members of Çudamani's men's gamelan. The second organization is Sanggar Maha Bajra Sandhi, directed by Professor Ida Wayan Oka Granoka, in Batukandik, outside Bali's provincial capital of Denpasar. Since the late 1990s, this *sanggar* has involved boys and girls of a wide range of ages in gamelan music, dance, and traditional Balinese vocal styles. The third is Sanggar Pulo Candani Wiswakarma in Batubulan, which has been active since about 2002. This *sanggar* is directed by I Ketut Pradnya, who hires music teachers from across Bali to teach their specialties to the mixed-gender children's gamelan ensemble.

POLITICS AND THE PERFORMING ARTS IN BALI

For far too long, anthropologists and other scholars have reinforced the perceived separation between cultural arts and politics in which Bali has become a "cultural paradise" and even acts of violence are understood not in political or economic terms but as particular to Balinese culture (Robinson 1995: 274–280; Vickers 1989: 36). The early anthropologists in Bali—Margaret Mead, Jane Belo, Gregory Bateson, and composer Colin McPhee—have been heavily critiqued for their blindness to, and silence on, political issues. Mead and Bateson were fascinated by children and childhood in Bali, hoping that the study of children would uncover the key to understanding what they saw as Balinese personality traits (Bateson and Mead 1942). Belo's work on Balinese kinship and child development (1955, 1970) mirrors Mead and Bateson's work on village life and cultural transmission through families. McPhee (1955, 1966) concentrated on court and sacred music, though he was also involved with children's music making. Finally, Bateson's steady-state model of Balinese society in no way accounts for the social and political upheavals due to tensions between kingdoms up to the nineteenth century, much less those due to Dutch presence and colonization from the seventeenth century to WWII (Bateson 1970). Australian scholar Adrian Vickers discusses the legacy left by Mead and Bateson with their focus on domestic and religious arts, writing that they "ensured that culture and art would become the only topics in talking about Bali. History, economics, politics and other less savory topics were dropped or relegated to the margins of Bali's image" (Vickers 1989: 124). Despite these glaring gaps in the scholarship, all of these scholars have been immensely influential on anthropologists in general and scholars of Bali alike. Recently, scholars such as Vickers, David Harnish (2005), Andrew McGraw (2009), and Michael Tenzer (2000) have begun to account for the interconnections between politics and the performing arts, though no one has yet examined the roles of children within these interconnections.

In the early 1970s, Clifford Geertz described the prevalence of competing ideologies in Indonesia as an "ideological pandemonium" (Geertz [1973] 2000: 229), and this observation still seems true in early twenty-first-century Bali. The ideology of gender complementarity, contrasting constructions of childhood, tensions between regional and national patriotism, the discourses from the Indonesian women's movement, and the movement to strengthen Balinese customs, religion, and identity overlap and often contradict each other. As recent sociomusical formations, girls' and mixed-gender gamelan members and teachers find themselves pulled in multiple directions by these competing ideologies.

Gender categories in Bali are an overlay of national ideals of family structure and Balinese ideals of gender complementarity. The Indonesian New Order ideology of women's roles and family structure that was current from 1965 to 1998 appears to hold strong in many areas. This ideology defined women not as individuals in their own right but in relation to their husbands first, their children second, and finally to the state, implicitly through the first two relationships (Suryakusuma 2004: 169–170). This hierarchy in some ways contradicts Balinese gender ideals, in which men and women each have complementary roles to fulfill in society. New Order ideologies of women serving their husbands and their country by educating their children in national principles hold strong among older generations; however, girls in Bali are starting to overtake their male counterparts in academic success in school, implying possible future change in how these ideas are adopted and enacted.

Indonesian conceptions of childhood have also changed over time. Japanese scholar Saya Shiraishi (1997) and Dutch scholar Frances Gouda (1995) remind us that the current concept of childhood in Indonesia was imposed by the Dutch and then adopted through a Western-modeled education system. Shiraishi writes that the notion of childhood "was profoundly political from its birth, for the natives were equated with children who needed to be educated and guided, and this notion of the 'natives' as 'children' served twentieth century Dutch colonialism" (Shiraishi 1997: 13). Still, these conceptions of childhood overlap with, rather than displace, indigenous beliefs and practices, including the belief that children are closer to the spiritual realm than adults in the cycle of reincarnation (Mead 1955: 40), even while they are given adult-type responsibilities from an early age.

A few music teachers I spoke with mentioned children's brilliance and purity, drawing on the idea of children's closeness to the gods. Granoka (2005), director of Sanggar Maha Bajra Sandhi, described children as "funny, holy, sacred, and pure." Composer I Dewa Ketut Alit from Pengosekan spoke of a growing conception of children as being less capable than adults. He noted that some music teachers see performing silly, watered-down music and dance as appropriate to children's youthful characters, though he does not agree with this notion. Instead, he challenges young musicians to achieve higher goals and to strive to deeply understand what they are practicing and performing. He told me, "I believe children can do more than we think. They are terrific. They are brilliant, and have strong energy" (Dewa Ketut Alit, personal interview, Pengosekan, Bali, July 31, 2006).

Regarding children's responsibilities, a look at language is helpful. The Balinese words for girl and boy are literal: *istri alit* or *istri cenik* (small woman) and *lanang alit* or *lanang cenik* (small man). Children, especially girls, have many adult-type responsibilities at home (Parker 1997: 507). In my observations, girls often take care of their younger siblings and around puberty start to join their female relatives in making and setting out religious offerings for the house and preparing offerings to bring to temples. Simultaneously, a more Western sense of childhood as a time for play, school, and little responsibility is prevalent, being spread through the media as well as through the education system (Parker 1997: 502–503).

Many people in Bali are accustomed to weaving their daily lives through and between these varying conceptions of gender and childhood. However, the conflict between national and regional identity has recently come to the forefront as regionalism has been on the rise across Indonesia (*The Jakarta Post* 2007). Balinese regionalism, in particular, has grown due to a fear of the loss of culture due to tourism and globalization and has increased dramatically in reaction to the two terrorist bombings in 2002 and 2005 and the resulting suspicion of Muslims and non-Balinese Indonesians. It has coalesced within the *Ajeg Bali* campaign, defined by Elizabeth Rhoads as "a discourse on strengthening Balinese identity through promoting and protecting Balinese Hinduism, language and *adat* (custom and customary law)" (Rhoads 2007). The root word *ajeg* means to uphold, preserve, and safeguard, so *Ajeg Bali* means to preserve

Balinese culture and identity as distinct from other ethnic groups in Indonesia and beyond.

Ajeg Bali as a slogan has been supported publicly by local officials (McGraw 2004: 15, 2009: 313). The campaign promotes a strengthening and standardization of Balinese customs though the deliberate propagation of lessons on everything from offering making and Balinese dress to Hindu religion via print and broadcast media. Among other results, the *Ajeg Bali* movement dehistoricizes and commodifies Balinese cultural and religious practices. The *Ajeg Bali* campaign also serves to depoliticize and undermine local and individual control over education and cultural practices, including the performing arts. This aids the perpetuation of the myth that Bali is a cultural paradise, and its combination with the subsequent depoliticization and disempowerment of *sanggar* and women's organizations alike bodes badly for women, children, artists, and educators working outside the state education system. However, Balinese cultural aims conflict directly with the national education system, as girls find themselves with not enough hours in the day to complete all of their religious and domestic tasks and their homework and other activities for school. Because the stated goals of each side in this conflict are seen as positive and because they are done in the name of strengthening Indonesian and Balinese identity and pride, children and their families have little room to resist either side.

COMMUNITY-BASED MUSIC EDUCATION

Children's gamelans and the *sanggar* that provide the umbrella for them create a space outside school and family, although most *sanggar* are located in a family compound. All children are considered potentially musical, though access to musical training is limited by financial resources and is concentrated in southern Bali, where local economies are generally stronger than in other regions of the island. Participation depends largely on the interest and motivation of the children themselves; especially in the Ubud area, many come from families in which other members are also performing or visual artists. Children's gamelan rehearsals exist in spaces beyond rigidly structured schools, more analogous to what Shiraishi calls the neighborhood community, or the space where the majority of people in Indonesia conduct their everyday lives (Shiraishi 1997: 126). During a children's gamelan rehearsal, anyone can drop by to watch, including parents, siblings, neighbors, and potentially tourists. It is a place to catch up with friends and to see how the children are improving (see Figure 1.2).

Sanggar rehearsals are contexts in which children receive positive and constructive discipline from trusted role models, as opposed to strict authoritarian discipline at school. Çudamani member and teacher I Dewa Ketut Alit Adnyana told me that he valued the encouragement and structure given by Berata when Adnyana

Figure 1.2: The Çudamani Girls' Gamelan rehearsing in the *bale banjar* (community hall) in Pengosekan, Bali. I Dewa Ketut Alit Adnyana (far left) leads the rehearsal (2002).

was first playing and learning gamelan. Adnyana now aims to provide the same supportive discipline to the younger members of the *sanggar*. Even though Berata and Susilo are the directors of Sanggar Çudamani, rehearsals of the girls' gamelan are largely managed by the young men and teenage members of the *sanggar*, who are, in many cases, the girls' cousins and older brothers. They are less than a full generation older than the girls and so do not fall into the *bapak-anak* (father-child) power dynamic present in school and other governmental institutions (Shiraishi 1997). The girls take full advantage of this when they can, requesting to rehearse certain pieces or pushing their teachers to have a longer or shorter rehearsal. Sanggar Maha Bajra Sandhi presents another alternative structure. Granoka is the director but often leaves the logistics of running rehearsals as well as the composition and choreography of new productions to his daughters (see Figure 1.3), who have the closest day-to-day interaction with the members.

Girls' and mixed-gender gamelans undermine the national ideology of women's ideal roles by contradicting the notion that adolescent girls must be quiet, if not altogether silent. Australian anthropologist Lynette Parker has observed, "The muteness of girls and the noise of boys is part of a gendered code" (Parker 1997: 508) that is present in Indonesia and implemented through both schools and societal pressures. The dichotomy of girls as silent and boys as noisy must be extended to include the fact that Balinese women sing devotional poetry in ritual settings, sometimes quite loudly. While women have found gamelan to be another outlet for noise making in the past few decades—albeit generally not as loudly as male groups—gamelan is still a relatively new location for girls and young women to appropriately "make noise." They must continually negotiate their way through this context, finding a dynamic

Figure 1.3: Ida Ayu Arya Satyani (center left) teaching members of
Sanggar Maha Bajra Sandhi (2006).

balance between their teachers' expectations of how loud or fast they should play
(or sing) and their own (also changing) levels of comfort with how bold to be in
practice and in performance.

Despite being located beyond national institutions, children's gamelans are
still subject to some ideologies, the most prevalent and explicit of which is that of
cultural preservation, itself tightly intertwined with ideas about preparing future
generations of citizens. Sanggar Pulo Candani Wiswakarma provides one way of
addressing cultural preservation (see Web Figure 1.4 🔾). Pradnya explained to
me the goals of having children learn performing arts at his *sanggar*, which are
for them to become fuller human beings and to have a better understanding of
Balinese values. He wants the members of Pulo Candani Wiswakarma to have
a balanced education. He sees what they learn in school as primarily related to
science, math, and other rational kinds of knowledge he associates with Western
influences. In order for the children to be balanced human beings, they need
to learn Balinese arts, he says, because the arts are "the root of our culture, our
identity, our principles" (I Ketut Pradnya, personal interview, Batubulan, Bali,
September 8, 2006).

Sanggar Maha Bajra Sandhi contrasts with Sanggar Pulo Candani Wiswakarma
in addressing the issue of cultural preservation. Granoka is keen to encourage
children's participation in all aspects of the *sanggar*'s activities, including playing
gamelan, dancing, practicing yoga, singing, and developing new repertoires and
rituals. He is motivated not so much to preserve Balinese culture as to create it anew,
building on forms and concepts from older performance styles. He is, in a sense,
revitalizing older forms and styles, though his emphasis is on high-quality creation,

rather than preservation. He places children at the center of this process, not only to benefit them and to prepare future generations of performing artists but also to make use of what he sees as their spiritual purity and brilliance. With participating children as the source of such purity, the rituals they create have more spiritual power. In this way, children not only are learning and rehearsing in preparation for their future but are already active members in cultural and spiritual development and practice.

One of Sanggar Çudamani's main activities is to revitalize older pieces and genres that are rarely performed anymore. Another is to run children's programs to teach both boys and girls Balinese dance and gamelan music. Çudamani's directors aim to balance their work to preserve pieces and genres by providing opportunities for their members to create new musical, vocal, and dance compositions, and they often engage in local and international collaborations. The "Çudamani" link on their 2007 tour web page states, "Çudamani's members see themselves as a community of leaders who, through their music and dance, positively contribute to the artistic, cultural and political life of their village" (Çudamani 2009b). Among other creative and boundary-pushing activities, Çudamani and other *sanggar* are doing radical work in encouraging girls to study and play gamelan. By strategically crafting their activities within the language of *Ajeg Bali* preservationism, they are able to break down past limitations of girls' musical participation in an already socially accepted context.

Case Study: Learning and Performing "Suluh" (Reflection)

On the level of individual participation, the goal of cultural preservation is partially a motivating factor. When I asked the members of the Çudamani Girls' Gamelan what they like about playing gamelan, not one of them stated anything about being one of the first continuous girls' gamelans in Bali or advancing women's rights or roles. Instead, their answers ranged from enjoying being together, laughing and joking, to being glad they are able to perform Balinese cultural arts. One answer that was given with surprising regularity, as an answer to why they joined in the first place, what they like about playing gamelan, or what is important to them about having a girls' gamelan, was a close variant of "*Supaya bisa melestarikan budaya Bali*," or "So that [I/we] can preserve Balinese culture." Most of the time I spent with them in 2005 and 2006, however, they were most immediately concerned with playing well and playing together, balancing their individual schedules, and working out their musical parts.

As these girls grew older and busier, their afternoon rehearsal schedule stopped being feasible, and they switched to rehearsing twice a week starting at 6:00 pm. On the evening of August 21, 2006, the girls started rehearsing Berata's new composition for them called "Suluh." They rehearsed in one of the *sanggar* pavilions for almost two hours straight with total patience and attention (see Web Figure 1.5 ⬤). The piece so far seemed refined with many subtle tempo changes. At one point, Adnyana tried to get them to play louder and faster. The girls responded, playing as strongly, loudly, and quickly as they could. At first the result was jumbled and messy, but by the end of the rehearsal and after many repetitions, they had cleaned up the interlocking passages. Adnyana seemed pleased, as did the girls. The *kendang* (drum) player, Dewa Ayu Eka Putri (Ayu Eka), picked up her part quickly, enjoying the challenge of new material and playing enthusiastically and even with some individual physical style. The *reyong* (row of gong chimes) players had some of the most complex parts and needed the most attention from the teachers and the most repetition; at one point I caught the eye of one reyong player, Ni Wayan Febri Lestari, and she silently mouthed, "*Kewah!*" (Difficult!). Eventually one of the teachers called an end to the rehearsal. The girls' focus finally broken, the *gangsa* (metallophone) player Ni Luh Putu Wiwik Krisnayanti suddenly gasped and asked, "What time is it?" On hearing the answer ("eight o'clock"), she clapped her hand to her forehead, crying, "Oh no, I still have so much homework!" and several other girls groaned in commiseration. They hastily threw the covers over the instruments and quickly dispersed, heading home to the rest of their long evening's tasks.

This piece, "Suluh," exemplifies the interconnection between the girls' individual lives and identities and the societal goals placed on them by others. A significant motivation for people to teach gamelan is the desire to enrich the lives of children through participation in cultural arts. The goal of children improving themselves and their moral character through musical practice and performance is expressed through the lyrics that Berata wrote for the piece, which he composed specifically for the Çudamani Girls' Gamelan. Here, the goal of improving oneself is not part of a national ideology project, as can be seen in schools in Bali, but is conveyed through distinctly Balinese modes of expression. The sung lyrics are in polite and formal Balinese language. The music is written for the *slendro* mode on Çudamani's seven-tone gamelan instruments. The piece includes choreography for the musicians taken from basic positions (*agem*) and movements from female Balinese dance forms. All of these aspects of "Suluh" contribute to its Balinese identity.

These lyrics describe how performing music and singing serve as a guide for the players to become better people and to improve their moral characters, particularly the first eight lines of the *pengawak* (middle section). The first line and fifth of the *pengecet* (last section) continues the theme of bettering oneself. The goals of becoming a better person and of participating in the preservation of the arts are symbiotic. By learning Balinese values through the arts, one can improve one's moral fiber and knowledge; in turn, one is better equipped to work at continuing, preserving, and strengthening Balinese cultural arts. The preservation of Balinese culture is mentioned in "Suluh," in lines 9 and 10 of the *pengawak* and again in the last line of the *pengecet*.

Lyrics for "Suluh" (Reflection)
Composed by I Dewa Putu Berata (2006)

Balinese	English
Pembuka	*Opening section*
Om Swastiastu	[formal Balinese greeting]
Pamur waning atur titiang ring sang rauh	We thank those who have come
Dimogi sami rahayu	May everyone receive health
Yulati manguh kasu kertan kayun.	May everyone be happy in their hearts.
Pengawak	*Middle section*
Praya katur sesidan titiange sadulur	Whatever I can give
Antuk manah liang	With a very happy heart
Megambelan magendang gending	Playing music, drumming, and singing
Anggen masesuluh	This is used as a guide
Benjang pungkur sida becik.	So that tomorrow I may become better.
Titiang sami melajah nyalanin gending	We all are studying how to engage in singing a song
Kadasarin antuk unteng kayun	Based on a heart that is good and pure
Ngainekelin angga.	As a resource within ourselves.
Mangda ye lestari	So that we can preserve
Budaya lan seni Bali.	Balinese culture and arts.
Ledangan titiang menabuh.	Allow me to play [gamelan].
Pengecet	*Last section*
Nunas sasuluh manyuluhin angga	I ask for a mirror/reflection so that I can improve myself
Kawimur dan titiang	I am still small
Melajah nabuh, magendang gending	Just beginning to learn to play, drum, and sing
Dasarin antuk mamonyah.	To develop my courage.
Nunas sasuluh manyuluhin angga	I ask for a mirror/reflection so that I can improve myself
Kawimur dan titiang	I am still small
Melajah nabuh, magendang gending	Just beginning to learn to play, drum, and sing
Dasarin antuk mamonyah.	To develop my courage.
Ida dane sami ngiring sareng ngajegan Bali.	All together we are taking care of Bali.
Penutup	*Closing*
Pamuput atur titiang mangkin mogi sida ngulangunin pikayun.	I hope my words have made people's hearts happy.

By writing these lyrics for the girls to learn and perform, Berata is effectively teaching the girls to do what they are singing. By singing about the very act in which they are participating, Berata has his musicians engaging in a performative metadiscourse, or since it is through singing, Katherine Meizel suggests the term "metacantrics," creating a clever pun on Alan Lomax's much contested system of cantometrics (Lomax 1976).[1] However, rather than referencing Lomax's assumption of a lack of awareness on the part of the singers he studied, I want to make the distinction that Berata is deliberately creating a context through which the girls immediately embody the ideals of upholding and preserving Balinese cultural identity.

Though the lyrics both teach and express a desire to preserve traditional values, the form is very modern in its execution: the performers are young girls, rather than adult men or boys or even adult women, and "Suluh" is performed on a gamelan *semarandana*, an innovative seven-tone gamelan genre developed by I Wayan Beratha in 1987 that has increased in popularity since then (McGraw 1999–2000: 63). The piece also includes choreography for the musicians, something that has become popular in new compositions especially since about 2003 (I Nyoman Windha, personal interview, Denpasar, Bali, October 8, 2006). In this way, the passing down of cultural values and Balinese identity is made up-to-date and relevant to the present day.

Notably, in their conversations, the girls focused on the musical complexities of the piece, commenting that they enjoy it because of its well-written melodies and because they are glad to have learned a new mode. Ayu Eka explained, "The piece is difficult, but I like it. It is difficult because it uses *slendro* and because it is slow. It looks easier because of this, but actually it's more difficult" (Dewa Ayu Eka Putri, personal interview, Pengosekan, Bali, August 22, 2006). In this way, Ayu Eka was not repeating stock phrases about cultural preservation or even about self-improvement but was getting straight to the heart of artistic participation and innovation.

Even though girl musicians relish learning and performing gamelan for artistic and cultural satisfaction, their performances may be supported by government officials to foster ulterior motives. State and cultural projects are often motivating factors in creating new performance venues and events to encourage artistic activity in certain regions or for certain demographic categories, in this case, women or children. As Sharon Stephens writes, "The creation of a modern state and national culture is integrally related to the creation of new sorts of gendered and age-graded subjects and spaces and the establishment of institutions variously engaged in spreading these constructions throughout society" (Stephens 1995: 15). Children's gamelan performances at festivals are often used by festival organizers or other officials as "crucial sources of 'authentic' national culture" (Minks 2006: 210) to promote national patriotism and Balinese pride. Children's placement by the national government at the crux of objectified notions of culture and tradition keeping the nation together and healthy is exemplified by the speech given by Jero Wacik, the Indonesian minister of culture and tourism (*Menteri Kebudayaan dan Parawisata*), referred to at the beginning of this chapter. His speech coincided with the night the Çudamani Girls' Gamelan performed at the month-long Ubud Festival in a *maba-rung* (competition) style performance across the stage from the women's gamelan Chandra Wati from Ubud.

The performance was the first mock competition[2] in which the Çudamani girls had participated and may even have been the first including an all-girls gamelan on the island. Noting the social importance of gamelan competitions, McGraw writes,

> The development of a truly competent generation of female Balinese musicians able to compete and perform on an equal footing with men depends on more serious and radical changes to Balinese music culture, not to mention the wider social context. Such a development would require the creation of, and competition between, girls' ensembles. (2004: 15)

This event at the Ubud Festival was not a real competition for a jury or to win place-ment or prizes, nor was it between similarly experienced or aged groups. However, it was an initial step in showing that such healthy competition is possible if there were enough girls' groups. The event was also special because Çudamani members Ayu Eka and her younger sister Dewa Ayu Swandewi, a *gangsa* player, played across the stage from their mother Desak Made Berati, who plays *kendang* for Chandra Wati (see Web Figure 1.6 ⏺). Three weeks after the performance, Ayu Eka told me, "When I performed in Ubud with my Mom, I felt very proud that I could continue [gamelan performance] from my mother's generation to my own" (Dewa Ayu Eka Putri, personal interview, Pengosekan, Bali, August 22, 2006), indicating pride as a culture bearer, despite the newness of girls playing gamelan.

The girls' and women's performances and Minister Wacik's speech exemplify many of the conflicting identities and roles of female musicians in Bali as objects of desire, as icons of Balinese regionalism, and as paradigms of Indonesian cultural pride. Wacik stated that although Indonesia is still very weak technologically and economically compared to other countries, at least it has art and culture to be proud of internationally. He said that therefore these practices should be cared for well and that if children are involved, they will be able to work toward preserving them as adults. Echoing the notion that cultural arts, supported by the family, will improve people as human beings, he said, "If they do not [participate in the cultural arts], children will dry up. And fathers and mothers from now on, I ask of you, push them to study the arts because the arts will make them complete human beings" (Jero Wacik, public speech, Ubud Festival, Ubud, Bali, July 31, 2006).

The minister held up the Çudamani's girls' performance that night as an exam-ple, though not necessarily one to be followed entirely. He referred to the girls' gamelan as merely appearing beautiful, as if they had not seriously studied what they were doing. He said, "I ask these children, who played gamelan just now so prettily and all dressed up, to also be smart and skilled. Do not only be pretty play-ing gamelan without being skilled." It seems that the girls' unusual technical abili-ties and professionalism for their age were lost on the minister, as he fell into the trap Balinese scholar Cok Sawitri identifies of only looking at female musicians as objects, without noticing or considering their musicality (Sawitri 2001).

TOURISM, CONSUMERISM, AND CHILDREN'S GAMELANS

Although the *Ajeg Bali* campaign became popular in part in resistance to the negative effects of tourism, such as increased commercialism and a fear of the loss of traditional practices, it often ends up in conjunction with goals of developing and maintaining a cultural tourism industry. *Ajeg Bali* aims to strengthen cultural practices and identity, which are then used by both Balinese and Indonesian governmental officials to promote tourism. A substantial percentage of artists in Bali actively participate in the tourist industry. Selling paintings, woven baskets, or sculptures allows them to provide for their families and afford the rising costs of fuel and sending their children to school, and in this way, tourism's presence in Bali can be a blessing (Sanger 1988; see also Harnish 2005; Picard 1996; and Vickers 1989 for more in-depth discussions of tourism in Bali). However, the benefits and effects of tourism are complex, and many artists and scholars are highly critical of the changes it has wrought on the arts and how it has disempowered Balinese artists, including young musicians.

Sanggar Çudamani was founded in part in opposition to potential detrimental effects from involvement in the tourist industry. This opposition can be seen in the language used in the "About Us" section on Çudamani's website:

> Çudamani maintains that the vitality of Balinese arts relies on the connection of performance to the religious and social life of the village. . . . Based on a traditional village model, i.e., not for financial profit or individual gain, the group sets the highest artistic standards in the service of the temple and the community. (Çudamani 2009a)

I was surprised, then, to learn that the girls' gamelan was to perform at a major hotel in Ubud for a group of tourists in August 2006. Adnyana explained to me that while they do not play for regular tourist shows, which they feel is detrimental to the spirit of their performances, when something special comes up they consider it and that the directors are always keen to increase the performance experience of and awareness about the girls' gamelan. Alit also pointed out the potential benefits of using "the opportunity of tourism to improve" their work (Dewa Ketut Alit, personal interview, Pengosekan, Bali, July 31, 2006).

Unfortunately, the hotel staff did not treat the Çudamani members and leaders with as much respect as the musicians expected. The hotel staff made the arrangements at the last minute, confirming the performance only two days before, and then the morning of the show requested an additional piece to be performed that night. It was a testament to the girls' skills, however, that they were able to pull off a clean performance with only a single review rehearsal of one piece, and the additional piece without a dress rehearsal at all. Still, the girls were disappointed and frustrated that such an upscale and successful hotel as this failed to provide the customary rice meal afterward. Already the girls could see the discrepancies between a new system governed by profits rather than longer term and community-based reciprocation.

Especially since the late 1990s, the Indonesian government has encouraged both trade and tourism, and the forces of globalization have been felt acutely in Bali. One of the negative effects of globalization and the increase in capitalization in Bali has been children turning into consumers, obsessed with buying and showing off the latest gadgets or spending countless hours with television or computer games. According to children's gamelan members, participation and membership in a gamelan offers alternatives to such potentially mind-numbing pastimes and builds a stronger self-confidence and sense of identity.

The context of children's gamelan rehearsals, outside the structure of the school and beyond the family, providing a space for creative, collaborative learning, bears some similarities to thinking about the concept of "play." Stephens's statement "Play is the ground of a notion of culture as living resource, rather than objectified product" (1995: 34) may be applied to the space of children's gamelans. Her assertion that "play also requires a certain open-endedness and a possibility of surprise—qualities that one might argue are in short supply in the solitary, efficient electronic play of some materially privileged children" (1995: 34) shows children's gamelan as a structured type of play that serves as an excellent alternative to electronic play. Ayu Eka gave an account that strongly supports this. She told me that most of her friends are supportive that she plays *kendang* in a girls' gamelan. Sometimes, however, people try to insult her for it and call playing in a gamelan *kuno*, a term that literally means ancient, though Ayu Eka explained that in this context it is used as a derogatory term analogous to the Indonesian word *jelek*, meaning bad or ugly. She uses the term herself to reclaim the balance of the interactions and, in so doing, presents a case for gamelan as an alternative to paying money for empty entertainment playing with cell phones, which have become a status symbol in Bali:

> There are people who say, "Playing gamelan is *kuno*." I tell them, "Using cell phones is what is bad (*kuno*). Tomorrow your cell phone will be out of date (*kuno*), and then you will buy another one and use up all your money. If you play gamelan and dance, you will definitely improve yourself. It is always new and there is nothing boring about it. You do not have to pay anything, and you can even make a little money at it." But sometimes I ask them in return, "Why should we be embarrassed to play gamelan? Tourists from abroad are not embarrassed to pay tens of millions of *rupiah* [thousands of dollars] to play gamelan here, while all your money is used up buying cell phones. It is better to play gamelan! Gamelan can make your mind excellent," I tell them. (Dewa Ayu Eka Putri, personal interview, Pengosekan, Bali, May 1, 2006)

Ayu Eka identifies playing gamelan as more worthwhile, gratifying, and better for the mind than playing with cell phones. She also draws on the international appeal of gamelan. Her replies are strong responses to the threats of global consumerism and the resulting detriment to local cultural practices. Perhaps her statement that gamelan improves one's mind shows how she has indeed taken up Berata's teachings through the lyrics of "Suluh."

Conclusion

Children's musical activities are located at the center of current debates about what Balinese identity is and how to best enact, embody, present, and represent it. Teaching gamelan to children is done with the motivation of cultural preservation to support local identity and establish difference from the national majority. Children's gamelans are often supported with the goal of cultural promotion for both local and national purposes to increase tourism through their performances at festivals, competitions, and tourist shows. The activities of these organizations and the experiences of their members exemplify how children, especially girls, must negotiate competing influences of national educational policy and regional cultural policy, national and regional identity, and increasing global capitalism. Despite the constraints and obstacles facing children's gamelans, community-based gamelan music education offers children a supportive learning environment, alternatives to the nationalist ideologies of family and school, and alternative activities to help combat the negative effects of consumerism. Many musicians' identities and self-confidence strengthen because of their involvement with children's gamelans, be it teachers like Alit and Adnyana, who find teaching children a highly rewarding occupation, or children and young women, like Ayu Eka, who find pride and solidarity in their musical experiences with other young female musicians.

Acknowledgment

I am grateful to the children, their families, and their music teachers and the leaders of the *sanggars* mentioned here for sharing their musical lives with me.

Notes

1 Lomax (1976) created his cantometrics project to determine correlations between vocal timbre and style with aspects of cultural and social life of particular populations.
2 Tenzer (2000: 86–88, 102–105) discusses the history of these battle-of-the-bands style contests between gamelan ensembles.

References

Bateson, Gregory, and Margaret Mead. 1942. *Balinese Character: A Photographic Analysis*. New York: New York Academy of Sciences.
Bateson, Gregory. 1970. "Bali: The Value System of a Steady State." In *Traditional Balinese Culture*, edited by Jane Belo, 384–402. New York: Columbia University Press.

Belo, Jane. 1955. "Balinese Children's Drawing." In *Childhood in Contemporary Cultures*, edited by Margaret Mead and Martha Wolfenstein, 52–69. Chicago: University of Chicago Press.

Çudamani. 2009a. "About Us." Accessed December 12, 2009. http://www.cudamani. org/about/index.html.

Çudamani. 2009b. "Odalan Bali." Accessed December 12, 2009. http://www.cudamani. org/tour/index.html.

Downing, Sonja Lynn. 2010. "Agency, Leadership, and Gender Negotiation in Balinese Girls' Gamelans." *Ethnomusicology* 54 (1): 54–80.

Geertz, Clifford. [1973] 2000. *The Interpretation of Cultures*. New York: Basic Books.

Geertz, Clifford, and Hildred Geertz. 1975. *Kinship in Bali*. Chicago: University of Chicago Press.

Gouda, Frances. 1995. "Teaching Indonesian Girls in Java and Bali, 1900–1942: Dutch Progressives, the Infatuation with 'Oriental' Refinement, and 'Western' Ideas about Proper Womanhood." *Women's History Review* 4 (1): 25–62.

Granoka, Ida Wayan Oka. 2005. "Yuganada: Maha Bajra Sandhi's Yoga Music Breaks Through the Cakra of the World." Unpublished flyer.

Harnish, David. 2005. "Teletubbies in Paradise: Tourism, Indonesianisation and Modernisation in Balinese Music." *Yearbook for Traditional Music* 37: 103–123.

Lomax, Alan. 1976. *Cantometrics: An Approach to the Anthropology of Music*. Berkeley: University of California Press.

McGraw, Andrew Clay. 1999–2000. "The Development of the 'Gamelan Semara Dana' and the Expansion of the Modal System in Bali, Indonesia." *Asian Music* 31 (1): 63–93.

McGraw, Andrew Clay. 2004. "'Playing Like Men': The Cultural Politics of Women's Gamelan." *Latitudes* 47: 12–17.

McGraw, Andrew Clay. 2009. "The Political Economy of the Performing Arts in Contemporary Bali." *Indonesia and the Malay World* 37 (109): 299–325.

McPhee, Colin. 1948. *A Club of Small Men*. New York: J. Day.

McPhee, Colin. 1955. "Children and Music in Bali." In *Childhood in Contemporary Cultures*, edited by Margaret Mead and Martha Wolfenstein, 70–98. Chicago: University of Chicago Press.

McPhee, Colin. 1966. *Music in Bali: A Study in Form and Instrumental Organization in Balinese Orchestral Music*. New Haven: Yale University Press.

Mead, Margaret. [1949] 2001. *Male and Female*. New York: HarperCollins.

Mead, Margaret. 1955. "Children and Ritual in Bali." In *Childhood in Contemporary Cultures*, edited by Margaret Mead and Martha Wolfenstein, 40–51. Chicago: University of Chicago Press.

Minks, Amanda. 2006. "Afterword." In *Musical Childhoods & the Cultures of Youth*, edited by Susan Boynton and Roe-Min Kok, 209–218. Middleton: Wesleyan University Press.

Parker, Lynette. 1997. "Engendering School Children in Bali." *The Journal of the Royal Anthropological Institute* 3 (3): 497–516.

Picard, Michel. 1996. *Bali: Cultural Tourism and Touristic Culture*, translated by Diana Darling. Singapore: Archipelago Press.

Rhoads, Elizabeth. 2007. "Bali Standing Strong." *Inside Indonesia* 89 (January–March). Accessed January 9, 2010. http://www.insideindonesia.org/edition-89/ bali-standing-strong.

Robinson, Geoffrey. 1995. *The Dark Side of Paradise: Political Violence in Bali*. Ithaca: Cornell University Press.

Sanger, Annette. 1988. "Blessing or Blight? The Effects of Touristic Dance-Drama on Village Life in Singapadu, Bali." In *Come Mek Me Hol' Yu Han': The Impact of Tourism on Traditional Music,* edited by Adrienne Kaeppler and Olive Lewin, 89–104. Kingston: Jamaica Memory Bank.

Sawitri, Cok. 2001. "Women versus Men: A Strife in the Field of the Performing Arts." In *Bali—Living in Two Worlds: A Critical Self-Portrait*, edited by Urs Ramseyer and I Gusti Raka Panji Tisna, 129–138. Basel: Verlag Schwabe.

Shiraishi, Saya S. 1997. *Young Heroes: The Indonesian Family in Politics*. Ithaca: Cornell Southeast Asia Program Publications.

Stephens, Sharon, ed. 1995. *Children and the Politics of Culture*. Princeton: Princeton University Press.

Suryakusuma, Julia I. 2004. *Sex, Power and Nation: An Anthology of Writings, 1979–2003*. Jakarta: Metafor Publishing.

Susilo, Emiko Saraswati. 2003. "Gamelan Wanita: A Study of Women's Gamelan in Bali." Southeast Asia Paper No. 43. Honolulu: Center for Southeast Asian Studies, University of Hawaii, Manoa.

Tenzer, Michael. 2000. *Gamelan Gong Kebyar: The Art of Twentieth-Century Balinese Music*. Chicago: University of Chicago Press.

The Jakarta Post. 2007. "Survey Sees Rising Tide of Regionalism." March 22. Accessed September 1, 2007. http://www.thejakartapost.com.

Vickers, Adrian. 1989. *Bali: A Paradise Created*. Singapore: Periplus Editions.

2

YOUTH MUSIC AT THE YAKAMA NATION TRIBAL SCHOOL

ROBERT PITZER

INTRODUCTION

If you travel southwest on the superhighway that swoops through the Columbia River Basin past wineries, orchards, and cattle ranches and exit at a lonely off-ramp that seems at first to lead nowhere, you'll come to a little town that calls itself "The City of Murals." The town prides itself on the historical murals of cattle drives, Conestoga wagons, and other scenes from the American Old West that are painted on nearly every building in the central business district. Turning on to the main highway on the south side of town you pass the supermarket, a fast food franchise, and a little aluminum trailer in a dusty vacant lot where you can buy what some locals say are the best tacos in town. Next to the taco vendor there is a man selling blankets out of the back of an old, battered pickup truck. Even though the murals say, "American Old West" and the signs on the storefronts and at the vendors' stands indicate a strong Mexican American influence, this town, and all the land around it for miles, is actually on the Yakama Indian Reservation in central Washington State.

If you continue straight on the highway you'll soon pass the museum and cultural center and the big casino, then accelerate westward toward the Cascade Mountains and majestic Mount Adams, which holds an important spiritual significance for the Yakama people (Daugherty 1973). Instead, turn right and follow the narrow paved road that passes a big overgrown field behind the cyclone fencing that leads to the Yakama Nation Tribal School (YNTS). Walk through the little concrete courtyard and enter the school. You're in a medium-sized room with an acoustic tiled ceiling and a linoleum floor. Next to the vending machines on the far wall are photographs of former students and tribal members who have served in the US military. Go through the double doors at the end of the room and you've entered the gymnasium, where final preparations are being made for an all-school assembly this afternoon. Three boys sit on the little recessed stage across the basketball court from the wooden seats and practice their electric guitars as the student body begins to file in. The students chide one another good-naturedly but are generally quieter than one might expect in a typical American high school during passing time.

Today's assembly is about music. Earlier in the afternoon, students from a state university who have come to do an exchange met with YNTS students enrolled in the native flute and drumming programs offered here. The university students play jazz, classical, and folk music in small groups for those gathered for the assembly. After they're finished, Elliot comes to the microphone to speak. He is the basketball coach at the school, but he is also a member of the Grammy-nominated Black Lodge singers, who have produced more than twenty CDs of Native American music. People on the small staff at this school often serve in a number of roles. Elliot[1] speaks briefly about the importance of music in his life and then introduces Joe, a nineteen-year-old student, who comes down from the bleachers and sings a "northern-style" song with vocables while accompanying himself on a frame drum. At the end of his performance he is greeted with great applause and cheering by both the YNTS students and the university music students, who exchange wide-eyed glances as if to say, "Wow!"

Next, Lawrence steps to the microphone. Lawrence is a volunteer who comes to the school, when the schedule at his job allows, and works with students wishing to learn native flute techniques. He introduces a young girl who has not performed before a large group before. She is reluctant and has to be convinced by her mentor to play. "Come on girl!" someone shouts from the crowd. Finally she agrees to play and fills the room with a beautiful melody of her own composition. At its conclusion, the crowd erupts into wild applause. The girl smiles sheepishly and hurries out of view.

The assembly concludes with all present being invited to participate in a "round dance." You step into the large circle of people gathering on the basketball court and lightly grasp the hands of the people on your left and right. Half a dozen boys with frame drums have gathered in the middle of the floor with Elliot, the basketball coach. They begin to play a steady beat on their drums, and then sing, first in vocables, and then a verse in English. As the music begins, you step left with your left foot and then drag your right to meet it as the entire circle moves in a clockwise direction. As you move you can see that everyone in the room is participating, tribal school students, teachers, university students, visitors, even the school cook and custodian have joined in. The round dance is a welcoming dance and allows all participants to see and accept the diversity of those around them. At the conclusion of the dance, the bell is ringing and the school day is over. The university students begin to pack their instruments, some YNTS students hurry to meet their bus, and the three guitarists return to the stage to play some more. You have seen a school music program that looks very different from the typical one found in American high schools, but one that reflects the values, culture, and tradition of the community in which it is located and that seeks to provide the adolescent students of the Yakama Nation with opportunities to learn about, play, and sing the music of their ancestors.

THE YAKAMA PEOPLE

Native Americans in the United States number about 2.5 million, about two-thirds of whom live outside the federally designated reservations, mostly in cities and urban areas (Banks 2009: 138). Regardless of where they call home today, Native Americans have engaged in a centuries-long struggle with European colonizers to maintain their cultural identity. As with any culture, the traditional music of these peoples has been a central factor in defining their identity and articulating their values. In addition, music in Native American culture has historically served as a primary medium for informing new generations about their heritage. Consequently, "traditional song and dance was one of the clearly identified eradication targets" of efforts by the government, and others, to "deculturalize" indigenous people from the time of first contact until the mid-twentieth century. "At the same time, [traditional song and dance] remained one of the prime cultural factors of resistance to acculturation" (Theisz 2005: 92). During the past forty years, there has been a concerted effort on the part of some Native American leaders to revitalize their traditional culture and to educate native youth about their history and heritage. This chapter provides a context for one Native American nation's history and a glimpse into the musical lives of four youth involved in the traditional music program offered by the nation's tribal school.

The Yakama people have lived on the Columbia Plateau region of what is now the state of Washington in the United States for centuries. The oldest archaeological evidence of human habitation in the area can be traced back about 14,000 years to a period when the last glaciers of the Pleistocene Ice Age began to recede and nomadic bands, "possessing a well-developed technology for the manufacture of stone and bone tools" roamed the region, "hunting small game, fishing for salmon, collecting river mussels, and gathering wild plant foods" (Daugherty 1973: 3). Over the centuries a traditional economy based on fishing, hunting, gathering, and trading with the other tribal peoples that inhabited the plateau in areas that are now Washington, Oregon, and Idaho developed. As the seasons changed, the Yakama traveled to various parts of the plateau. In winter they lived along the interior rivers in tule-mat lodges that typically housed three to five families and subsisted on dried foods gathered the previous year. In the early spring they moved to the root grounds and camped with those from neighboring tribes. In June, the fish began to run, and the Yakama moved on to the lower Columbia to catch and preserve salmon for the coming winter. In the autumn, they went to the Cascade Mountains to pick berries and hunt. Even today, in the "culture class" taught at the YNTS, youth learn the progression of the annual food gathering seasons. The Yakama, like all Native American peoples, have always felt a close kinship with nature and give thanks for their foods through spiritual ceremonies that include traditional music and dance. Much of this interconnectedness with the environment is reflected in their music (Diamond 2008; Neaman 1999; Theisz 2005).

The Yakama's first contact with Euro-American culture occurred when they encountered members of the Lewis and Clark Expedition near the confluence of the Columbia and Yakima rivers in 1805. Soon many White trappers, miners, loggers, and homesteaders would follow. By 1855 the influx of Whites, with their insatiable appetite for land and resources, led to governmental mediation and the signing of the Yakama Treaty, which was negotiated between the native population and the Indian agent and territorial governor Isaac Stevens. This treaty gave the name Yakama to the fourteen Native American bands that constitute the Yakama Nation: the Yakama, Palouse, Pisquose, Wenatchapam, Klickitat, Klinquit, Kow was sayee, Li aywas, Sk'in pah, Wis ham, Shyiks, Oche Chotes, Kah-miltpah, and See-ap-cat. Each of these tribes and bands spoke their own Sahaptin dialect (Yakama Nation Museum and Cultural Center 2009). The treaty reduced the territory of these peoples from 10.8 million acres to about 1.4 million acres, created the Yakama Indian Reservation, and gave the Indians two years to relocate to the new reservation lands. However, only two weeks after the signing of the treaty, Stevens opened the lands up to White settlers. Yakama chief Kamiakin called on his people to oppose this declaration and they, along with other tribes, fought the US Army for three years in what became known as the Yakama War. The Indians were finally defeated in the Battle of Four Lakes near Spokane in the eastern part Washington State in September of 1858. Kamiakin escaped to Canada, but other leaders were captured and executed. Most of the Indians then retreated to the reservation, where despicable living conditions led to high rates of alcoholism, disease, and infant mortality.

In 1933 the Yakama organized as the Confederated Tribes of the Yakama Nation, and since that time they have focused on self-government, self-sufficiency, and economic independence. Access to local fish runs not only has traditional and spiritual meaning to the Yakama but also is important in terms of subsistence and accounts for a significant portion of the local economy. The treaty of 1855 recognized the right of the Yakama to fish in their traditional areas, but that right was not truly realized until the historic Boldt Decision of 1974, which gave treaty tribes the right to 50 percent of the fish. Although the treaty had ensured the right to fish at their "usual and accustomed grounds and stations," tribal fishing had been severely limited because of the encroachment of White fishers into those "accustomed grounds and stations." Additionally, many of the locations where Native Americans traditionally fished were flooded with the construction of hydroelectric dams during the twentieth century. The most notable of these locations, perhaps, was the picturesque Celilo Falls on the Columbia River (or Nchiwana, as it is known in the Sahaptin dialect), which was flooded in 1957 by the construction of the Dalles Dam (Yakama Nation Museum and Cultural Center 2009). Since the Boldt Decision, and its subsequent affirmation by the Ninth Circuit Court of Appeals and the US Supreme Court, the native tribes have comanaged the fishery resources with the state of Washington (Crowley and Wilma 2003).

Today nearly 9,000 people are enrolled as members of the Yakama Confederation of Tribes and Bands, and almost 14,000 people live on or near the reservation in south-central Washington State. All tribal members over the age of eighteen are voting members of the general council, which is the basic governmental unit of the tribe. The tribe has about 600 full-time employees and another 200 seasonal employees. There is still a good deal of economic hardship among the people of the Yakama Nation, but "today's Yakama Agency [works] daily to upgrade resource management, education, health and social welfare for [their] people" (Yakama Nation Museum and Cultural Center 2009). Students at YNTS are schooled in the history of the Yakama, their struggles, and their proud tradition, and they understand that the native music they learn makes them an important link in that tradition.

The Tribal School

The YNTS, founded in 1980, is funded by the Yakama Nation and the federal Bureau of Indian Affairs (BIA). Native youth can attend at no charge. The school, located in Toppenish, Washington, is one of more than 180 BIA-sponsored schools in the United States. YNTS currently serves about 100 students in grades seven through twelve (students attending range in age roughly from thirteen through nineteen). The school has emphasized teaching and preserving Yakama culture, and, as a part of this focus, a program teaching native drumming and flute has taken root in the past several years.

THE ROLE OF MUSIC IN NATIVE AMERICAN CULTURE

It is important to note that from the time of first contact through at least the first half of the twentieth century, the policy of the US government was to promote Native American assimilation into the dominant White culture (Banks 2009: 133). This process included attempts to extinguish native language and culture, including music. Neaman notes that the "cruel justification" for this process was the claim of White settlers that the Native Americans were "uncivilized" if they did not choose to participate in the newly dominant culture. He also points out,

To our people, [being civilized] means to be in harmony with nature, to live a life close to the earth [and] to be able to communicate with a spirit greater than ourselves. This spirit exists in song; and to an Indian person, being in touch with the spirit within song means being in touch with the spirit within one's self....I sing a song sometimes to remember who I am and what makes me unique. (1999: 79)

Elliot, the basketball coach and drumming instructor, says that the adults at YNTS feel that offering a native music experience at the school is an important component of both acquainting Yakama youth with their heritage and perpetuating their culture.

Linton and Hallowell have noted,

All societies seek to perpetuate their own cultures, but they usually do this unconsciously and as a part of the normal process of individual training and socialization. Conscious efforts to perpetuate a culture can arise only when a society becomes conscious that there are cultures other than its own, and that the existence of its own culture is threatened. Such consciousness, in turn, is a by-product of close and continuous contact with other societies. (1943: 230)

Wallace has written about the nature and development of "nativistic" movements, or movements by marginalized peoples to preserve their identity within the context of a larger dominant culture. He identified five overlapping stages of nativistic movements. These stages are (1) a period of steady state before contact with other cultures, (2) a period of individual stress, (3) a period of cultural distortion, and a (4) revitalization that eventually leads to (5) a new period of steady state (Wallace 1956: 268). Herndon points out that "all nativistic movements have in common the process of selection of [the] culture elements [to be preserved] and [a] conscious, deliberate effort to perpetuate such elements. Certain current or remembered elements of culture are selected and emphasized" (1980: 131).

Christopher Small has written that making music "has always functioned...powerfully as a means of social definition and self-definition" (Small 1998: 133). Folkestad has noted that music "provides the means of defining oneself as an individual belonging to and allied with a certain group" and that "the development of a musical identity is not only a matter of age, gender, musical taste and other preferences, but is also a result of the cultural, ethnic, religious and national contexts in which people live" (2002: 151). Thomas Vennum Jr. wrote in his introduction to *American Musical Traditions: Native American Music* that, despite the effort by the European colonizers of the continent, much of the Native American musical tradition has survived and today comprises the "oldest body of music in North America." He further writes, "The pervasiveness of...song and dance in nearly every Indian community testifies to the continuing central role of music in what these people recognize as their 'traditional' culture" and "Indian people have managed to maintain a tie, however tenuous, to their ancient past through their music" (Vennum 2002: 1). Only within the past forty years or so has there been a widespread effort to recognize, celebrate, and preserve traditional cultures in the United States (Dorothy 2010).

Dolly Linseberger, a Salish elder from coastal Washington State, has said that she wants the young people to understand that their involvement with native music "is important not only because it is enjoyable, but because it helps them have pride in who they are. You should not forget your own culture, your own tradition. The young people will have to carry this on. It will make the elders that we have left feel better if they know the young people will carry on" (Arlee 1998: 77). A similar sentiment is echoed by Dorothy, the "culture teacher" at the YNTS. She recalls a period in the late twentieth century when "many of the adults on our reservation were uninterested in the culture of our ancestors" (personal communication, February 5, 2010). Dorothy feels that the young people she works with today at the tribal school show a great deal more interest in learning about their heritage and culture than did the youth of their parent's generation.

Native American Powwow Music

Youth in the drumming program at YNTS learn about music played at native powwows held annually all over North America. Elliot explains that throughout the United States and Canada there are two primary types of Native American singing that are heard widely today: the southern style and the northern style. Northern-style powwow music is most widely sung by men, although women are heard on occasion, accompanied by either frame drums or a single horizontal drum beat in unison. The singing is in a brilliant high falsetto voice. Northern-style music is derived from the tribes of the northern plains of the United States and Canada, such as the Lakota, Northern Cheyenne, Crow, Blackfeet, and Cree. Southern-style powwow music generally features men sitting around a horizontal hide drum that they beat in unison. Women stand behind the men and sing. Southern-style singing is generally slower in tempo and lower pitched than northern style and is somewhat more reserved. Southern style derives from the southern plains tribes such as the Ponca and Kiowa. At one time, geographical region defined who sang in each style, but in contemporary times that is less the case (Spotted Eagle 1997: 15). Yakama youth are schooled primarily in northern-style singing and drumming.

Native American Drum Music

Drums are the most important and most widely used instruments in Native American music (Bierhorst 1979: 24). Many types of drums are used in Native American music today: frame drums, round drums, water drums, box drums, and drums from trap sets, to name just a few. The two most widely used in powwow music today are the hand drum or frame drum, and the large, horizontal round drum. The larger round drum is often made from a standard twenty-eight–inch diameter bass drum frame with the metal hardware removed and horse-, elk-, or cowhide stretched tight for the head. Most round drums are covered both top and bottom and are usually suspended between four posts, and they are played by between four and sixteen men

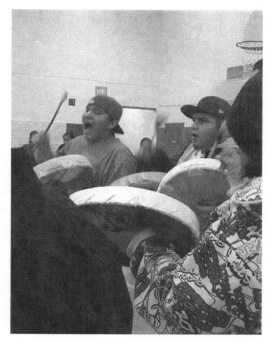

Figure 2.1: Playing the frame drum.

seated around the drum and using round headed sticks of similar length and weight (Spotted Eagle 1997: 18–19). Several frame drums may be used by a group of singers, if not by all. Frame drums are made by stretching dried animal hide over a narrow wooden frame that has bent into a circle. The drummer holds the drum in one hand and strikes the head using a mallet with his other hand (Figure 2.1). The drummer's index and middle fingers touch the underside of the head on alternate beats to create a buzzing sound (Wright-McLeod 2005: 304). Yakama youth at YNTS construct their own frame drums and use them at their performances.

Native American Flute Music

In the past several years, a flute program was added to the native music curriculum at YNTS. The only traditional melodic instruments in Native American culture are the flute and the flageolet (Nettl 195: 7). The use of these instruments can be traced back at least 2,500 years through oral traditions and ancient pictographs, and flutes can be constructed from a variety of materials, including animal antlers and bones, clay, cane, and, most commonly, wood. The end-blown block flute, the most common in use today, traces its history back to the tribes of the Great Plains and northeastern woodland areas of the continent. Such a flute is constructed by hollowing out two blocks of wood and leaving a small block of wood beneath the tone hole

Figure 2.2: Playing the flute.

that will force air through a carved depression called the "roost." After that, the two halves are glued together. Often, a carved bird is placed over the air hole (known as the nest) and then adjusted to alter the tone (Wright-McLeod 2005: 261–262). The typical end-blown block flute has three to six finger holes to create pitches and, while similar in construction, differs from the European recorder in that it does not have a thumbhole on the back (Figure 2.2). While YNTS drummers construct their own instruments, the flutes are purchased by the school from native artisans. Flute students can "earn" the right to keep their flute upon graduation by participating in a certain number of group and solo performances.

    Perhaps because it was never as pervasive in native culture as drumming during the period of systematic US governmental repression of native culture, much of the flute music tradition was lost. "Reliable historical documentation, culturally specific teachings, and knowledge about the traditions of flute-making, performance, and philosophy were largely non-existent. Colonization, government suppression, and overt cultural change forced many tribes to abandon significant portions of their oral traditions, both sacred and social" (Nakai and Demars 1996: 2). Historically, the instrument was rarely heard in the decades after European colonization of the North American continent. Native flute playing was kept alive by just a few artists during most of the twentieth century but experienced a resurgence of popularity in the 1970s. Wright-McLeod notes, though, "Sadly, this revival would also open the door to years of commercial exploitation and misinterpretation resulting from a proliferation of recordings by nonnative and New Age opportunists" (2005: 262).

Yakama Music

While located in the Pacific Northwest and bearing some similarities to the music of the coastal Salish, the music of the Yakama in many ways bears much more resemblance to that of the people of the Great Plains, or the "northern style." Brycene Neaman, a Yakama drummer, singer, storyteller, and author, has written about Yakama musical traditions in a book called *Spirit of the First People: Native American Music Traditions of Washington State*. In it, he notes important aspects of Yakama music: first, the traditional music in the Yakama culture is never written down but is transmitted through oral tradition; second, the central meaning of the music comes from the experience of the performer. Solo pieces are often improvised extemporaneously. Neaman also makes a point of music as an expression of oneness with nature (Neaman 1999). Beverley Diamond has written about the interconnectedness of the music of Native Americans and their environment. She notes that all indigenous knowledge is "bound to the knowledge of place and environment" and that Native American music reflects a "keen attention to the sonic environment" rhythmically and in timbre, as well as in text (Diamond 2008: 26).

Music at the Tribal School

Music classes at the YNTS are open to any student, but until recently, only boys were permitted to be drummers, while either boys or girls could play the flute. Within the past year, all gender barriers with regard to instrument choice have been lifted. Students learn about the traditions of music within their culture and are taught basic concepts and techniques on their instruments. Most of the flute music performed is songs that the performer has created him or herself, often extemporaneously; however students have recently begun to read familiar tunes from music books and play them on their flutes. These include Christmas carols and patriotic songs. The drum music is often based on traditional beats or chants, but there is room within the musical form for individuals to compose their own lyrics, as well. The facilitators in this program are often not regular school faculty members but tribal members that have volunteered to assist in the program. Students have regular opportunities to perform for the school and the larger tribal community and have within the past two years traveled to Seattle to perform at an international music education conference and to Hawaii for an exchange with a school for native Hawaiians.

Voices of the Yakama

Joe is a nineteen-year-old student at the tribal school and has been involved in the drumming program there since its inception. He has been interested in Native American music though his family "for as long as I can remember." Joe's family has been playing and singing Native American music for "seven generations on my dad's side, and three or four generations on my mom's." He carries on the family tradition and travels the powwow circuit throughout the plateau region, in the plains area, and into southern Canada each summer. "I guess there was never really any question that I'd be doing the music. I have been singing since I was one year old. I always remember hearing the music." He adds that "What I do at school is just a natural thing, I guess. I was playing and singing long before I came [to the school]." Joe, who can speak in great detail about the varieties and stylistic components of Native American music, thinks of his involvement with the traditional music of his people more in terms of a family tradition, than as a tribal tradition, or even as a school activity. "I am sure I'd be doing this even if it wasn't something I could do at school" says Joe. He enjoys the travel, the performances, and the camaraderie and interaction with other musicians (both of his generation and older) from throughout North America, along with participation in the musical contests that take place at many powwows. In his free time Joe does not spend much time listening to the music he performs. "I guess I listen to it some, but mostly [native music is] something I do—participate in." When asked what he does listen to for enjoyment, he says he listens to "hip-hop and rock mainly" (personal communication, February 5, 2010).

Darlene is a seventeen-year-old girl who began playing the native flute when it was first offered at YNTS three years ago. She also plays clarinet and is seriously considering attending college with an eye toward becoming a music teacher. Darlene has an appreciation of all genres of music and listens to a wide variety in her spare time. "There's a little bit of everything on my iPod," she says, "Everything from classical to hip-hop to rock. I don't really listen to Indian music on my own." Although her participation in music is "just because I love it," she does have an understanding of the greater cultural implications of playing the Native American flute and feels it connects her with her heritage. Darlene has attended summer retreats run by Denny Hurtado of the Skokomish nation, the director of Indian education for Washington State's Office of the Superintendent of Public Instruction. Hurtado's work emphasizes an understanding of Native American sovereignty through a historical view of the relationship between Indian tribes and the US government. In addition to his summer courses, Hurtado has developed a curriculum for public schools throughout Washington State that promotes a partnership between local tribes and the public schools in their area (Edmo 2008). In addition to her musical activities at the tribal school, Darlene is very involved with the activities of the "culture class," participating in autumn trips to the mountains to dig roots and gather berries as her ancestors would have done. "We pick huckleberries and choke berries out near Mount Adams. It's fun to go out and pick berries, like our grandparents did" (personal communication, February 5, 2010). Mount Adams, a 12,000-foot peak in the Cascade Mountains to the southwest of the tribal school, is a sacred peak to the Yakama people. In 1972, 21,000 acres of land near Mount Adams were returned to the Yakama Nation by the federal government, and access to that land is restricted by the tribal council (Daugherty 1973: 94). The huckleberry holds great spiritual significance for the Yakama people. It is said that "in the days of preparation for the coming of the people, it was the huckleberry who promised to sacrifice itself to fill the veins of the people: the blood. The huckleberry kept its promise in extra measure, for from its leaves comes medicine for the sick" (Yakama Nation Museum and Cultural Center 2009).

Ryan is an eleventh grader and participates in both the drumming and flute programs. When asked to describe why he participates in the native music classes at the tribal school, he describes how the music has promoted a more healthy and positive lifestyle for him: "Before I came here and started doing music, I would do lots of bad stuff in my free time. Now, instead of that other stuff, I sit in my room and make up songs on the flute and it makes me feel better, you know? Like more peaceful. Sometimes I play the guitar, too, which I am learning." Numerous studies have identified the value of school music programs in helping "at-risk" students find a place in their school community, as well as providing them with positive activities. O'Neill has stated that "every young person has the potential and capacity for engagement in musical activities" (2006: 461) and further that young people become fully engaged in these activities "in a context that provides opportunities for self-expression and self-direction" (2006: 463). Surely, the music program at the tribal school provides such opportunities with its emphasis, not only on learning traditional music that represents the students and the school in a positive light when shared with the tribal community and in performances for non-Indian audiences, but also on individual creativity and self-expression. Ryan finds both these aspects of his participation in the music program to be positive and enjoyable and of significance in his own personal growth. Since the program has now been in existence for four years, older students are encouraged to mentor newcomers. Ryan enjoys tutoring the younger students: "Yeah, it's fun showing them how to do stuff" (personal communication, February 5, 2010). With his awareness of the value the music has in his own life, Ryan mentors with an eye toward not only helping students develop musical skills, but also toward helping them see the music's transformative and self-affirming possibilities.

Jennifer, a quiet fifteen year old, transferred to the tribal school from a public high school about twenty miles away just five months ago. She has been involved with music for about ten years. "At my old school I played flute and trumpet in the band, but I switched to baritone because they needed one. I also sang in the chorus. We sang classical as well as some gospel kinds of things." She views her participation as a drummer and singer as a way to continue developing her musical skills and as a social activity—a way to integrate herself with her new classmates and contribute to the school culture. "I kind of miss playing in a regular band, but this is new and fun, and I learn a lot from the other kids. They have welcomed me and helped me a lot." When asked if she was the only girl that was playing drums, she said, "Usually" (personal communication, February 5, 2010). Dorothy, the culture class teacher explained that the previous drumming teacher had come from a family that considered it inappropriate for women to play or even touch the drums but that the new teacher's family did not have that tradition. Dorothy indicated that such traditions are not dictated by tribal norms but by the leaders of individual families within the tribe.

Lawrence volunteers as the flute teacher at the tribal school. Though born on the Yakama Reservation, he did not attend YNTS as a student but was educated at a boarding school in California. After graduation, he enlisted in the military. Lawrence tells of one night when, as a young soldier, he attended a performance of native flute music and was so inspired that he went backstage to meet the performer. The two ended up spending several hours talking. The flautist was impressed with Lawrence's enthusiasm and interest and presented him with one of his flutes as a gift. Lawrence would practice in the barracks, trying to figure out how to play songs he was familiar with by ear and making up his own songs. Once, when asked to play for a gathering of soldiers, Lawrence's performance was so beautiful that it brought his commanding officer to tears. After that, he was often asked to perform for his colleagues at his unit's military functions.

After his tour of duty had ended, Lawrence returned to his family on the reservation, where he had spent very little time since being sent to boarding school years before. While talking with a friend, who worked at the tribal school, Lawrence heard about the new program of native drumming being instituted there. Lawrence volunteered to teach interested tribal school students to play the native flute, and the school readily accepted his offer. He has now been teaching native flute at the tribal school for three years. Lawrence volunteers at the tribal school because he feels it "allows the students a chance to feel more in touch with their heritage, and at the same time gives them a chance to express their individuality." He adds, "I think it's good for the kids to play the flute and drums here. It helps them build character and it promotes personal growth" (personal communication, February 5, 2010).

Dorothy teaches the culture class at YNTS and also teaches courses for adults at a nearby college. When asked what she remembers about native music and growing up on this reservation in the 1960s, she recalls that the "pace was different. I remember spending hours swimming in the summer, and sometimes you would see some of the elders on horseback. Twelve or twenty of them riding together." When asked if this was in the 1960s, she responded, "Yes! But you don't see that anymore. I also remember that as children we did a lot of running. I mean a long way. Sometimes my brother and I would be given an empty bag that you could carry on your back and told what things to go get at the store, and we would run to the store and run home. We ran all the way, and it might be three or four miles or more." When asked what she remembered about music when she was a child on the reservation, Dorothy said she remembered how "the voices of the singers carried and flowed like the wind. The music was never performed when there was bad feeling in the heart. The music goes out and touches our people." Dorothy spoke of a man she has seen since she was a child. "He has carried his drum with him everywhere since the 1950s. Everyone is always glad to see him. He carries the history of the drum with him wherever he goes" (personal communication, February 5, 2010).

The students involved in the native music program at YNTS will be the ones "carrying the history" of their people into the future. Despite hundreds of years during which the dominant culture tried to extinguish the culture and music of the native peoples of North America, there were those, like "the man with the drum," who endeavored to preserve it. Today, YNTS teachers like Elliot, Dorothy, and Lawrence provide Yakama youth with an opportunity to reconnect with the music and culture that has been theirs for centuries. Joe has been traveling to pow-wows and playing and singing native music through his family most of his life, but Jennifer has only recently become involved. For Joe, singing and drumming allow him to continue not only a cultural tradition but a family tradition, as well. Jennifer has found that native music has given her a way to become part of the culture at her new school along with providing an opportunity to continue performing music. Ryan found that the music has helped him become more at peace with himself and enjoys perpetuating the music by tutoring younger students. Darlene loves all music and finds that native music is a natural way to express her love of Yakama culture. The native music program at YNTS has given each of these youths a slightly differ-ent experience, but all are conscious of the role music has played in the history of their people—and the part they play in that history.

Conclusion

It's lunchtime at the tribal school, and you're sitting in Dorothy's classroom where the culture classes are held. Out of the window behind her desk you can see some of the students trudging down the narrow blacktop to the highway to get some food off cam-pus. The sun is shining brightly, but it's a brisk day with just a hint of wind. Through the door come one, then two, and finally four boys and one girl to fetch the frame drums that are stored on the counter in the back of the classroom. They exit as quickly and quietly as they entered, with perhaps a little smile or a quick, "hello," to acknowl-edge you. They don't have much time, as the lunch period is quite short. Soon, from the cement courtyard between the portable classrooms, you hear the sound of the drums, pulsing together like a heartbeat, and then singing. You step outside to see and hear better. Joe is leading the song, and after he has identified the song with his opening vocal pattern, the others join in. The drummers stand in a circle facing one another. Ryan is there, and so is Jennifer, and two other drummers you recognize but don't know by name. Darlene stands outside the circle and sings, and several other students have come to stand and sing with her, surrounding the drummers. Some laugh and dance. This is not class time, and there are no impending performances, yet these youth have chosen to meet and play and sing on their own time during a break in the school day. The songs they sing may not be very old, but the way they sing them is the way such songs have been sung by the Yakama people for centuries.

Note

1 Pseudonyms have been used throughout for the names of students and informants at the YNTS. Interviews were conducted by the author in 2010.

REFERENCES

Arlee, Johnny. 1998. *Over a Century of Moving to the Drum: Salish Indian Celebrations on the Flathead Indian Reservation.* Helena, MT: Montana Historical Society Press.

Banks, James A. 2009. *Teaching Strategies for Ethnic Studies.* Boston: Pearson Education.

Bierhorst, John. 1979. *A Cry from the Earth: Music of the North American Indians.* New York: Scholastic Magazines.

Crowley, Walt, and David Wilma. 2003. "Federal Judge George Boldt Issues Historic Ruling Affirming Native American Treaty Fishing Rights on February 12, 1974." February 23, 2003. Accessed April 10, 2010. http://www.historylink.org/index.cfm?displaypage=output.cfm&file_id=5282.

Daugherty, Richard D. 1973. *The Yakima People.* Phoenix, AZ: Indian Tribal Series.

Diamond, Beverley. 2008. *Native American Music in Eastern North America.* New York: Oxford University Press.

Edmo, Se-ah-dom. 2008. "Building a Sovereignty Curriculum: A Conversation with Denny Hurtado." *Democracy and Education* 17 (2): 44–47.

Folkestad, Goran. 2002. "National Identity and Music." In *Musical Identities,* edited by Raymond R. MacDonald, David Hargreaves, and Dorothy Miell, 151–162. New York: Oxford University Press.

Herndon, Marcia. 1980. *Native American Music.* Norwood, PA: Norwood Editions.

Linton, R., and A. I. Hallowell. 1943. "Nativistic Movements." *American Anthropologist* 45 (2): 230–240.

Nakai, R. Carlos, and James Demars. 1996. *The Art of the Native American Flute.* Phoenix, AZ: Canyon Records Publishing.

Neaman, Brycene A. 1999. *Song Traditions of the Yakama.* Edited by Willie Smyth and Esme' Ryan. Seattle: University of Washington Press.

Nettl, Bruno. 1954. *North American Indian Musical Styles.* Philadelphia: American Folklore Society.

O'Neill, Susan A. 2006. "Positive Youth Musical Engagement." In *The Child as Musician,* edited by Gary E. McPherson, 461–474. New York: Oxford University Press.

Small, C. (1998). *Musicking.* Middletown, CT: Wesleyan University Press.

Spotted Eagle, Douglas. 1997. *Voices of Native America.* Liberty, UT: Eagle's View Publishing.

Theisz, R. D. 2005. *Putting Things and Order: The Discourse of Tradition.* Edited by Clyde Ellis, Luke Eric Lassiter, and Gary H. Dunham. Lincoln: University of Nebraska Press.

Vennum, Thomas Jr. 2002. "Introduction." In *American Musical Traditions: Native American Music,* edited by Jeff Todd Titon and Bob Carlin, 1–7. Vol. 1. 5 vols. New York: Schirmer Reference.

Wallace, Anthony F. C. 1956. "Revitalization Movements." *American Anthropologist* 58 (2): 264–281.

Wright-McLeod, Brian. 2005. *The Encyclopedia of Native Music.* Tucson, AZ: University of Arizona Press.

Yakama Nation Museum and Cultural Center. 2009. *Yakama Nation Museum.* Toppenish, WA: Yakama Nation Museum and Cultural Center.

3

REFORM JEWISH SONGLEADING AND THE FLEXIBLE PRACTICES OF JEWISH-AMERICAN YOUTH

JUDAH M. COHEN

INTRODUCTION: TWO SNAPSHOTS

On August 4, 2000, right before starting their Friday barbeque lunch, the high school–aged program participants attending the Kutz Camp Institute, a youth leadership camp of the Union for Reform Judaism located in Warwick, New York, seated themselves on a grassy incline. In front of them, on the basketball court below, a day camp run concurrently on the Kutz campus called Camp Shalom gave its end of session presentation. Children aged three through ten stood in two lines, with college-aged staff arranged behind them. After an introduction by Kutz Camp's assistant director, Camp Shalom's songleader, a recent college graduate, crouched in front of the children with guitar in hand and led them through a series of familiar Hebrew songs. The high school audience, including about a dozen songleaders-in-training, responded enthusiastically: singing, clapping, and mirroring the children's hand movements. After three songs the Camp

Shalom songleader stepped aside, and two college-aged counselors-in-training led the children in an Israeli folk dance. For their semiconfident efforts, the young campers received energetic cheers and applause. They then followed their counselors off the court to complete their final day of the session, while the Kutz Camp Institute's director led the high schoolers in singing the Hebrew blessing before the meal.

Eight days later, on Saturday evening, August 12, well-dressed high school–aged program participants filed into the Kutz Camp dining hall to begin the highly anticipated "banquet"—the final dinner of their camp session. Tie-dyed Woodstock-themed decorations; a large spread of fruit, vegetables, and fresh breads and pastries; and a dining hall staff in white shirts and bow ties greeted them. Participants entered, sang the blessing before the meal, ate, and then began to move the tables out of the way, preparing for the summer's most elaborate and raucous song session. Two hired post-college songleaders, who had led the main camp's communal singing over the previous three weeks, quietly went over their set list in the front of the room. Musically inclined college- and postcollege-aged staffers (including Camp Shalom's songleader) arranged themselves to the left of a central raised platform. Guitars in hand, they prepared to take turns helping the hired songleaders with the session. The campers sat, restless, as the camp leadership gave a few final thanks and announcements. With excitement building, the assemblage together sang the Hebrew grace after meals (*Birkat HaMazon*). The staff receded to the margins of the room, quietly maintaining control over the scene as the hired songleaders ascended to the central platform dressed in psychedelic t-shirts, braids, and bandannas. Long strips of paper with the order of the evening's songs dangled from the tuning pegs of their guitars. For the next hour, the songleaders facilitated a musical space in which program participants expressed themselves; hugged each other; danced in groups, in pairs, and separately; yelled out communal responses; and sang the session's twenty-nine song active repertoire at the top of their lungs. One of these songs, "Shiru Shir Chadash" ("Sing a New Song"), had also been sung at the Camp Shalom presentation earlier. Participants used the same motions as their younger counterparts, but in a much more polished form.

After leaving camp the next day, many of the high schoolers would take leadership positions within their local and national Reform Jewish youth organizations; several of the songleaders-in-training would assume jobs as youth, synagogue, and camp songleaders. Of Kutz Camp and Camp Shalom's three hired songleaders, meanwhile, two would later go on for cantorial training and one for rabbinical training at Hebrew Union College, the Union for Reform Judaism's seminary, in large part on the strength of their songleading credentials.

THE BORDERS OF CHILDREN'S MUSICAL CULTURES

These two snapshots highlight some of the challenges involved in exploring the structure of children's musical cultures. Rather than presenting a clear delineation of childhood's start and end, they show childhood to be an ambiguously multitiered phenomenon, full of dynamic shifts and manufactured stages. As James (2007) and Montgomery (2009) note, childhood is itself a constructed category, reliant on numerous social, cultural, geographical, and economic factors (among adults *and* children) for its existence. Yet research on those transitional moments between childhood and adulthood, constructed or otherwise, has been remarkably scant. Scholars seem to know childhood when they see it, describing it in demographic, aesthetic, or generational terms; but the empirical nature of childhood and its music as a time- and repertoire-based entity rarely goes challenged.[1] Instead, scholars have placed childhood music making within its own insulated category, partly as a response to earlier scholarship that framed children's music as subservient to or continuous with adult musical traditions (Blacking [1967] 1995; Gaunt 2006) and partly to establish childhood as its own legitimate topic of study (Boynton and Kok 2006; Campbell 1998; Minks 2002). With a substantial body of research and theory on childhood musical cultures now emerging, however, reexamining the musical borders between childhood and adulthood gains a new imperative as a central part of the project. How do music scholars distinguish between childhood and adult musical cultures? Can we really talk of "children's music" and "adult music"? What happens when adults practice musical cultures that are widely associated with children, or vice versa? Investigating these questions through the current lens of childhood musical studies offers the exciting potential to align the vast literature on adult music making with the emergent literature on children's musical cultures—thereby highlighting the complex interaction between two seemingly opposing constructions. Approaching children's musical culture as a function of discourse rather than age, in other words, can profoundly reconfigure the way we understand childhood—and by extension the entire musical lifecycle.

I aim here to explore the breadth of children's musical cultures via an interpretation of James's call for "revisiting a key theoretical tension within the field of childhood studies. . . . the relationship between 'childhood' as a social space, 'children' as a generational category, and 'the child' as an individual representative of that category and inhabitant of that space" (2007: 270). This call presents an opportunity to bring the multidimensional category of childhood under scrutiny and to examine how childhood and musical practices actually map onto each other. Music's ability to span social categories while taking on multiple valences can help illuminate the literal question of what it means to represent the "voice" of the child. Bringing music to James's approach thus reinforces the angle of childhood as an entity that does not define itself by age—an issue often neglected within the current literature. Remarks such as "You're acting like a child" commonly invoke behavioral definitions of childhood for disciplinary purposes; and other invocations of youth indicate naïveté, stunted intellectual growth or helplessness. Adults, moreover, regularly take on the behaviors and perspectives of children in order to create children's entertainment. Thus, invocations of childhood can serve as an important means for understanding how childhood functions throughout the cultural landscape. By recognizing that the child's voice routinely resonates beyond "children's" spaces to create its own meaning across the life spectrum, it becomes possible to engage James's call as fully as possible.

The practice of songleading at American Reform Jewish youth summer camps offers a rich opportunity to address these issues. What little has been written on music and summer camping has explored how the summer camp creates culturally sanctioned spaces where youth can fully manifest themselves while under supportive "adult" supervision (Joselit and Mittelman 1993; Posen 1974; Seeger and Seeger 2006; Tillery 1992).[2] At the same time, those who run and staff summer camps have been grouped, both anecdotally and in popular culture, with the children they oversee; while maintaining positions of responsibility, these adults and older peers encourage and participate in children's activities (as with the songleaders described earlier). Just as ethnographers aim to earn respect among the populations they study, successful summer camp staffers tend to be viewed as both mentors and "marginal youth" among the young populations they supervise. Thus youth summer camps tend to operate simultaneously as strictly hierarchical societies in which adults mediate the actions of young people, and as spaces for adults and youth to create a continuous, child-centered culture.

Since the late 1940s, songleading has manifested this simultaneity in the Reform Jewish summer camp setting. To young people it has been an indicator of creativity as well as spiritual and emotional maturity, while to adults it has represented the sonic backdrop for the Jewish summer camp experience. I have noted elsewhere that Reform Jewish songleading paralleled the rise of other American (largely Christian) pastoral music styles, maturing (so to speak) during the countercultural movements of the 1960s and 1970s (Cohen 2006a, 2006b). Yet in the years since its genesis, songleading has also become a contested representation of Reform Judaism. Young practitioners first embraced the form as a part of their developing spiritual identities. Those who had not been brought up on summer camp singing (typically campers' parents, professional synagogue musicians, and cantors) often derided it as a product of inexperienced and immature youth. As the first campers grew into adulthood, however, they increasingly brought songleading with them into Reform Jewish synagogues. The style's status as youth music consequently became confounded, even as it discursively retained its youth-based valences. Those who continued to oppose its use within formal worship services intensified their disapproval of songleading by implying that adults who favored song-led services were stuck in an arrested form of spiritual and creative development. Their invocations of camp (and "camp music") became symptomatic of more general dissipation in American Judaism, and they lamented the loss of what they described as a much older and more venerable Jewish music "tradition." While in some circles songleading had transformed over time into an adult musical practice, then, other circles saw it as an insidious musical form that made people act like overgrown children.

Songleading in American Reform Jewish summer camps, as a result, became a kind of generational borderland music: mutually practiced and mediated by children, adults, and adolescents (who in this case served as a distinct transitional demographic) but acknowledged as emerging from a space intended to focus on the youngest of these groups. Consequently, Reform Jewish youth camps developed reputations as key preserves of songleading repertoire and practice, responsible for inspiring young people to assume the franchise of religious musical activity and for giving visiting adults the opportunity to reconnect with the tradition's roots. The musical styles cultivated in these camps (and related Reform Jewish youth settings) ultimately generated a sense of authenticity among children's voices in the movement. Examining this tradition as it appeared at the cusp of the twenty-first century, then, allows us to explore how songleading has grown to represent a flexibly defined sense of childhood. Considered more expansively, the practices of Reform Jewish songleading have much to say about how the borders of "children's music" are constructed and what significance such issues have for discussions of children's musical culture, musical transmission, and the formation of communal and ethnic identity.

FINDING A VOICE: THE EMERGENCE OF REFORM JEWISH CHILDREN'S MUSIC

Before songleading gained its status as the voice of Reform Jewish childhood, children's music in the movement had been created and mediated almost entirely by adults and intended for use by ambiguously defined nonadults. Successive editions of the Reform Jewish movement's hymnal (1897, 1914, 1932) provided school-aged children with increasingly rigid scripts for effective religious behavior—from hymns, to responses, to complete service texts (Central Conference of American Rabbis [CCAR] 1897: 148–168; CCAR 1914: 272–308; CCAR 1932: 432–567). These scripts, intended as junior versions of adult rituals, allowed young voices to perform the liturgy but not to create it.

The start of the Reform movement's youth group (the National Federation of Temple Youth, or NFTY) in 1939 and the founding of its first permanent summer camp in 1952 created new, institutionally sanctioned spaces for young people to explore their own ideas of religious expression.[3] In these environments, young people sang songs of the folk revival and pioneer songs from Israel at prescribed points throughout the camp day. Yet even as Jewish leadership promoted youth initiatives as ways to reinvigorate the movement, adults remained in charge musically. Supervising faculty penned new songs to complement the social justice songs that campers sang after meals and around campfires. With a monophonic, sing-along sound, these compositions still presented a "simplified" variation on conventions of adult Reform Jewish worship hymns. The 1960 publication of the *Union Songster: Songs and Prayers for Jewish Youth* (CCAR 1960) illustrates this point well: although the book openly emphasized the significance young people had attained within the movement, the actual presence of young people's voices as composers or authors in its nearly 450 pages was negligible. These new youth settings were intended to assist young people in performing and framing Reform Jewish life; yet ultimately they continued to model youth in the image of adults.

By the early 1970s, with spaces for youth activity proliferating more generally in the United States and the gulf between adult and nonadult pursuits expanding, youth themselves began to assume the onus of creating spiritual experiences within Reform Jewish settings. College-aged students (overseen by adult camp administrators) increasingly took positions of responsibility as camps created programs for younger and younger children; by 1960, for example, the youngest unit at the movement's first summer camp in Oconomowoc, Wisconsin catered to nine- through eleven-year-olds, and the camp instituted a program for students entering third grade (age seven to eight) a few years later. Commensurately, songleading staff shifted from rabbis and rabbinical students during the 1950s, to college students in the 1960s, and to late high school students by the 1980s and 1990s. Such changes in the age-based leadership schema gave young people greater access to positions of musical (and general) authority; and eventually they began taking ownership of the songleading style and making their own additions to the repertoire. By the turn of the twenty-first century, even campers themselves had begun to lead elective courses in songwriting and composition on occasion. Kutz Camp, the movement's national leadership camp established in the late 1960s, further institutionalized the tradition by hiring college-aged songleaders to train the next high school–aged generation. Those songleaders, in turn, encouraged others to voice themselves freely during services and song sessions.

The development and spread of songleading within Reform Judaism illustrates how flexible and wide-ranging discourses on children's music can emerge over time through intergenerational dialogue. Reform Jewish leaders, in their efforts to maintain a religious tradition, prescribed for children a distinctive set of spiritual and aesthetic values. Yet the movement's leadership also needed to motivate its young people to engage with those values. Increasingly they opened spaces where children and adolescents could creatively explore Reform Judaism under less parochial guidance. Whereas children had started off in the late nineteenth century expressing themselves in a manner that adults had envisioned, they had transitioned by the twenty-first century to fashioning themselves as partners with older peers in the propagation of a youth-generated repertoire. By this time, moreover, many adults who had grown up in Reform Jewish camp settings saw songleading as key to their own spiritual maturation. Yet while youth movements and summer camps had caused the topography of Reform Jewish children's music to change, the movement's questions about the nature of children's music intensified: How did the practice of songleading actually function in relation to children's cultures? How did children and childhood factor into contemporary songleading practices? And how did the parameters for creating and disseminating children's music within the summer camp setting frame the child/youth/adult schema of progressive maturity within the Reform Jewish lifecycle?

Summer camps, in their ability to focus an entire leadership hierarchy around youth experiences, remained a significant area for understanding how musical culture created by/for children might hold broader implications about childhood. Three key types of events in particular—religious services, postmeal song sessions, and moments of instruction between older and younger campers—created a rich nexus for multigenerational conversation about the nature of childhood and the sound of Reform Judaism. During these times, young people participated in their own unique chains of spiritual and musical authority, which allowed them to shape their own musical cultures while anticipating how those cultures would factor into adolescence and adulthood. These experiences would subsequently surface in various forms during the rest of the year, including at happenings in local youth group chapters and at regional and national conferences.

To Camp: Olin-Sang-Ruby Union Institute and the Kutz Camp Institute

I observed these interactions while conducting fieldwork at two Reform Jewish youth camps (among the thirteen then operating) during summer 2000. Both camps held important roles within the Reform Jewish youth network. Olin-Sang-Ruby Union Institute (OSRUI), founded in 1952 in Oconomowoc, Wisconsin, was the first permanent summer camp sponsored by the Reform movement (Cohen 2006a). OSRUI catered to Chicago area campers between the ages of seven and seventeen by the mid-1960s and had additional staff-based training programs for young people of college age and beyond. By its very structure, the camp promoted a sense of multigenerational continuity: many of the campers "grew up" in the camp, attending year after year, transitioning into staff positions, and in many cases later sending their own children. Since 1991, OSRUI has also served as the site for the movement's national songleading retreat *Hava Nashira* (Come, let us sing), which attracted about 150 adult songleaders in 2000 and has grown ever since.

The Kutz Camp Institute in Warwick, New York, in contrast, was established in the late 1960s as a center for training the movement's high school-aged youth leadership. Since its early years, Kutz Camp's residential camping programs included a special track for participants wishing to become songleaders (Cohen 2006b). Kutz also catered to the young children of faculty and clergy-in-residence and eventually established a Jewish-themed day camp for elementary school children from the area. These younger camps remained generally separate from, but visible to, the teen programs. As with OSRUI, the Kutz "program participants" (as the teens were called during my fieldwork) maintained active yet highly regulated connections with elders. In addition to employing adult staff and clergy, the camp welcomed alumni and movement VIPs to attend Sabbath song sessions and weekend services. Parents, however, could only come to the camp during prescribed visitation hours and emergencies. These conventions maximized attendees' exposure to the camp's traditions and provided a variety of living models for attendees to extend them into adulthood and professional life.

Religious Services

At both camps, regular religious services marked the progression of spiritual time and highlighted a paradigm of fluid interaction between children and adults. Enacted at least once daily, the ritual gave campers the chance to participate in a longstanding act of Jewish identity (see Lightstone and Bird 1995), while encouraging them to cohere into a religious peer community. Services at both camps incorporated the same prayer books used widely in Reform Jewish "adult" circles, thereby linking the spiritual topography of the Jewish liturgy to the youth-based setting. Yet campers engaged with the liturgy in a different manner. Typically, a subset of campers in each unit prepared a particular day's (or week's) service(s) in consultation with a visiting rabbinic faculty member and a songleader. While many different models for service construction existed, all generally relied on this multigenerational schema. Campers thereby experimented in negotiating liturgical choices as full participants in a spiritual dialogue with the adult and college-aged authorities in charge.

The musical aspect of the service played an important underlying role in the conversation. More often than not, rabbinic faculty had themselves grown up with the songleading repertoire. The Kutz Camp staff rabbi during my fieldwork, for example, had been one of the movement's most prominent songleaders during his college and postcollege years. While negotiating the service's music (to be led by the songleader) these rabbis consequently served as secondary songleaders of sorts, addressing musical choices from both personal experience and spiritual authority. Songleaders, in turn, frequently had aspirations to the clergy, or at least to roles of movement leadership. They typically deferred to the rabbi's final decisions on music and liturgical ideas, yet they held their own authority with the campers, sometimes appearing on a par with the clergy due to their musical presence.[4] The campers themselves, in turn added their voices within the spaces allotted for them by publicly taking responsibility among their peers for their liturgical choices. Seen from outside the negotiations, the opportunities for creative input by the campers may have appeared restrictive, amounting to limited music setting options and a few select spaces for creative readings. Yet they tended to be empowering among the campers and treated as chances to shape their unit's musical and spiritual landscape.

Friday night services at the Kutz Camp Institute illustrated this dynamic. Program participants appeared, on the surface, to have limited opportunities to exercise their own voices. The rabbinic faculty member overseeing the service controlled the pace of the ritual, announced each prayer, provided many commentaries, and usually presented a parable-like sermon. Musically, the songleaders began the ritual by leading a song intended to bring the congregants into a prayerful mood and then moved to the side to await predetermined cues for leading liturgical songs with their guitars (or, in some cases, chanting without guitars). The campers in turn appeared to follow the process and choreography of the service, standing and sitting as indicated. During the service, their personal engagement with the liturgy might include peer-selected readings and songs, but more often manifested themselves through subtle responses or nonverbal cues: choosing to participate or not participate in the songs and readings, linking arms and swaying during songs with moderate tempi, "shokling" (religiously swaying) forward and back in silent prayer to communicate a personal level of religious devotion, and quietly addressing their personal social relations through whispers and side comments. Moments of planned intergenerational engagement arose within this space, including responsive readings, interactive discussions, and especially at the end of the session a student presentation or two, but as a whole the progression of the service was initiated by the camp staff. Planned by the rabbinical leadership to empower young people as the self-identified "builders" of society, the whole ritual established a layer of forced artifice in which, it was hoped, a sense of community could take root.

Although the camp religious service initially provided a structural role in encouraging a children's musical culture, the framing of these services by adults ultimately established youth-centered spaces. Campers heard their voices as full members of the congregation for perhaps the first time. Their responses and behaviors, repeated and developed over the course of weeks, gave them tools for religious self-expression considered desirable within Reform Jewish society. The structures and sounds they practiced within the service, meanwhile, became part of the broader sonic landscape of the camp experience. The rabbinical leadership and songleaders encouraged this kind of interaction, often seeing in these practices a reflection of the youth camp experiences that had been so formative to their own careers. Religious services consequently modeled a collective voice for young people and fostered a supportive environment that allowed children to link their own voices to those of their peers and mentors.

After-Meal Song Sessions

In the 1950s and 1960s, before songleading became a central part of the religious service at Reform Jewish summer camps, campers were led in singing mainly at hootenanny sessions after meals and during campfires. The practice of these gatherings, known as song sessions, continued into the twenty-first century, with all Union for Reform Judaism summer camps holding at least one after-meal song session per day in addition to a long, celebratory song session each Friday night (see Cohen 2009). Although young people tend to see themselves as having more freedom during these times, camp staff still quietly fashion the space in which campers sing and interact, fixing it within the camp's schedule, maintaining ground rules and order, and emphasizing it as an important part of the camp experience. Songleaders, too, control much of the action as the focal point of attention during song sessions: they choose the songs, regulate the campers' responses, discipline misbehaving campers, and encourage effective singing practices. Within that adult-set frame, however, youth have the opportunity to develop their own senses of empowerment and community. Since clergy are largely peripheral to song sessions, songleaders serve as a generational go-between: as both stewards of the music and advocates of the children's musical reality. Campers, in turn, interact with the songleader's leadership to solidify their own musical cultures.

Analyses of evening songleading sessions, June 14, 2000 Friday night at OSRUI, and the banquet song session at Kutz Camp on August 12, 2000 offer insight into the ways young people create their own musical cultures in collaboration with circles of older peers. The repertoire itself, originally written mostly by high school– and college-aged NFTY members and alumni, came to represent the existing tradition. Campers built upon this repertoire by inserting sung and spoken phrases, hand motions, and group movement, several of which had also been handed down over generations of campers (Cohen 2006b: 197–199). In doing so, the campers merged the original sentiments behind the songs with their own categories of belonging.

Attempts by the camp leadership to impose behavioral norms believed to be socially and spiritually compatible with the song session received a dialogic response from campers, encouraging ritualized intergenerational discourse. The camp director for OSRUI initiated this conversation at each Friday evening song session:

> I want to remind everybody in the room that tonight is Shabbat [the Sabbath] and it's time for singing songs together. It's not a time for creating cheers out of songs and it's not a time for changing the words. We want to welcome all of our guests [largely camp alumni] who are here with us tonight. We're delighted that they were able to be with us for Shabbat, and we hope that they can enjoy tonight. We'd like to remind everybody to please remain seated during *Shabbat Shirah* [the Friday night song session]. Campers, *Madrikhim* [counselors], faculty, guests, will everyone please remain seated during *Shabbat Shirah*. I also want to remind you that we need everybody to sing with the songleaders. We need you to be part of what's going on, and we need you not to be talking right now, but to be ready to join them in *Shirah* [singing], and I want to remind you all that during *Shirah* that there is no…
>
> [Campers respond:] Flash photography!

Campers eagerly awaited this moment, cameras in hand, and set off a torrent of camera flashes with their response. Repeated weekly, this familiar scene illustrated how young people creatively held their ground within a world of adult strictures. Their actions also facilitated a dynamic partnership between campers and authority figures that characterized the song session to come.

For the next forty-five minutes, songleaders walked around the middle of a circle (at OSRUI) or stood at the front of the dining hall (at Kutz), encouraging the campers to sing loudly and energetically. Campers displayed their enthusiasm and their intimate knowledge of the songs by glossing the steadily expanding repertoire (Will Boxt and Weiner 2000) with their own ideas and opinions. The high school–aged program participants at Kutz often shouted out references to popular culture as part of the singing: during a classic Zionist song that set lyrics by Theodore Herzl and Naftali Imber ("Im Tirtzu"; Debbie Friedman, 1976), they interpolated lyrics from the Disney song "When You Wish Upon a Star" (Leigh Harline and Ned Worthington, 1940); and they interpolated the entire chorus of Bill

Withers's 1972 song "Lean on Me" into a more recent popular song about Middle East peace (Sheva's 1999 "Shalom/Salaam"). The younger campers at OSRUI, in contrast, rarely went further than adding clapping patterns and repeating specific words in their singing, partly because more noticeable actions would result in disciplinary measures and partly because campers recognized the leadership's desires to maintain long-established aesthetic norms. In both cases, young people found the song session a place for limited yet self-sustaining personal expression: even in those moments when campers did not sing, the song session became a form of communal cover for side conversations, flirtations, attempts at social organization, and quiet acts of defiance.

While choosing and presenting a specific slate of songs to the campers, the songleaders maintained their own intimate relationship to the repertoire, built up over years of exposure and practice. At OSRUI in particular, where most of the songleaders had spent their childhood summers, even the song titles became a basis for creating longstanding community and insider discourse. Each week, the camp's head songleader would distribute a chit to the other songleaders with the evening's songs, keys, and guitar capo positions. On one level the list enabled the songleaders to coordinate a cohesive song session. Yet the list also included several title transformations that hinted at a more complex understanding of the musical material (see Figure 3.1). Some song titles were modified to indicate identification with a particular songleader or author. "Jeremy's Nigun," for example, indicated that one songleader had become identified with a popular Hasidic-inspired wordless tune at the camp. Likewise, "Oseh Wein B." referred to a locally written setting for the liturgical text "Oseh Shalom" (Make Peace, from the Jewish liturgy) through oblique mention of the setting's composer, Rob Weinberg.[5] In other cases, a somewhat less reverent form of a song's title lightened the mood for the songleaders (who had sung the song many times) and reinforced the songleaders' implicit collective experience as friends, colleagues, and camp alumni. Thus the song "Od Yishama" (Jeremiah 30:10–11, set by Shlomo Carlebach) became "Od Yish Your Mama" on the set list—one of two "your mama"-themed title modifications. These title transformations illustrated how the songleading repertoire acquired additional layers of meaning to those who had spent their childhood immersed in the culture and who then presented that culture to their younger peers. As songleaders led campers in a core repertoire that had changed only moderately from the previous generation, they continued to comment upon it in ways that restructured their own relationship to the music: as former campers, but not necessarily as former youth.

Campers, songleaders, and camp leadership thus used the song sessions' imposed frame of activity to experiment with more flexible perceptions of music, spirituality, and social interaction. To each group, the song session's culturally sanctioned times, places, and practices presented an opportunity for them to take ownership of a common repertoire through its repeated communal enactment.

Song	Chord	Capo
Nigun 420	Am	3
Jeremy's Nigun	Em	3
Bim Bam	Am	3
Ya Ba Beer Bong	Am	3
Snap - Crackle - Pop	Am	3
Hallelu Ivdu Avde	Am	3
Or Zarua - Lost His *&^%	Em	-
Lo Alecha	G	-
Od Yish Your Mama	Am	-
King David Melech	Em	3
Oz V'Darth Vader	Em	3
Pitchu (X2) Li	Em	3
Yisme Jew	E	-
Hallelu - I'm A Jew	Am	5
Va'anudnik Halle-Pu	G	
Oseh Wein B.	Am7	2
Matov With U?	Am	3
Hava Na Saver	G	
Hodu L'Ado Deez Nutz	G	
Kol Ha Your Mama	D	5

Figure 3.1: Reproduction of the OSRUI Friday night song session set list, July 14, 2000. Content © Jeremy Seaver, used with permission.

From Younger to Youngest

The chain of transmission from adults to counselors to campers ensured a wide distribution of a repertoire largely attributed to youth. In a number of cases, however, campers themselves were actively involved in transmitting the repertoire to still younger campers. Particularly at the Kutz Camp Institute, with its own songleading training course for high schoolers and its younger day camp, teens learning the art of songleading practiced their skills by transmitting the tradition to preschool and elementary school–aged children. On August 1, 2000, for example, several songleaders-in-training tested their technique by leading a planned communal song session with Camp Shalom. Assembled in the downstairs program room of the campus's main building, the children, aged three through ten, sat in a semicircle. Behind and between them, the young campers' college-aged counselors supervised and encouraged participation; and behind the counselors, the members of the songleading class supported their colleagues by participating in full. Furthest back, one of the postcollege-aged songleading instructors served as a point of authority, modeling appropriate behavior for the teenagers while sending occasional silent messages to the student doing the teaching. As one songleading student came to the front of the room, the transmission process began:

> DAVID [songleading student (pseudonym)]: Hello. How're you guys doin' today?
> CHILDREN: Good!
> D: Do you guys like the weather? Yes? No?

Children respond with calls of "No!" and "Yes!" One says, "I'm tired."
D: You're tired?
  Energetic calls of "Yes!" One child describes how he had been up for several hours in the middle of the night.
D [Breaking into the increasingly fragmented conversation]: All right. Everybody stand up; everybody stand up. Stretch to the sky! Get all the tiredness out of you! [The children and counselors stand and stretch their arms in the air, as the children continue to talk.] All right, everybody down! [Everyone sits back down.]
D: Okay. [Strums his guitar.] My name's David.
CHILDREN: Hi, David! *Boker tov* [Hebrew: Good morning], David! Hi, David.
D: And I'm going to sing a little song. Um, some of you may know it, so if you do, feel free to sing along. It's a very simple song, just repeat after me. It's the Hebrew alphabet, called Aleph-Bet.
  David begins, but sings in a different key from the one in which he is playing. He quickly notices and corrects himself midphrase and continues to teach the song one phrase at a time; the campers sing each phrase in response. He repeats the final phrase.
D: That was pretty good. I think you guys can do better though. Wait, who knows it? Who knows it? [Several campers raise their hands.] All right. What's your name? [Child: Maya. (pseudonym)] Maya, come up here. And who else knows it? You know it? What's your name? [Another female camper gives her name.] Come on up. [The two female campers come up and stand on either side of David.] Okay. [To the rest of the children:] You guys stand up. [To the two girls on either side of him:] And you're going to lead it, you'll help me lead it. [To the children:] And you guys are ready to help them [points to the two girls]? All right. Ready.
  David leads the song again, looking at a different girl with each phrase to help lead the song. They mostly defer, forcing David to sing quietly in encouragement. The rest of the children, however, sing along loudly.
D: Good job, guys! [Applause, mostly from the counselors and songleading students, but some from the children. David leaves the area, and the next student comes up to lead her song.]

This exchange accomplished multiple goals simultaneously: David gained songleading experience and established his musical authority with the children. The children, many of whom had known the song already (as with most of the songs in the set that morning), used the repetition to cohere further as a group and had the chance to internalize the song in their own way in a space provided by the songleader. The songleading class instructor, meanwhile, used the "teach" as a way to continue transmitting a seminal camp-associated musical tradition to the next generation of songleaders. While each demographic had to operate within a series of tight structures, together their interaction created enough spaces for each group to express itself appropriately and test the ever-stretchy parameters of its own approach to Reform Jewish musical culture. The song session also challenged more conventional scholarly understandings of children's musical activity; for even while maintaining different points of reference, all these groups engaged intimately with a broadly defined children's musical culture.

Music over the Thresholds

The three examples discussed here—two from the camps' daily schedule and one occasioned by the proximity of younger and older campers—regularly affect other aspects of camp life: from the establishment of social hierarchies, to the music the campers sing and hum to themselves throughout the day, to the nature of the campers' social interactions beyond the camp experience. At the same time, these musical activities show that children's musical spaces remain strongly circumscribed and regulated, relying more on the inheritance and interpretation of existing materials than on the creation of new music. Even the "youth" repertoires themselves were overwhelmingly created by people of college age and older. How, then, does mastering this repertoire and adopting it as a personal form of sonic expression constitute a children's musical culture?

The answer may lie more in what songleading represents culturally than in its actual content. Songleading and its associated musical knowledge appear to allow individuals both to show mastery of childhood and to transition away from it to positions of increasing authority. As mentioned earlier, many of the songleaders described here went on to take on positions of communal leadership in Reform Judaism, including several who trained to become ordained clergy. Interestingly, however, the transition to mastery did not always translate as a transition away from childhood and into adulthood. Rather, the practice of songleading adapted to maintain a dual relationship with both youth experiences and the spiritual practices of ever-older peer groups. Even as the repertoire expanded into the adult world, in other words, both OSRUI and Kutz Camp remained key sites of origin. Songleaders of all ages continually returned to these and other camps for alumni weekends, songleading conventions, and religious and communal inspiration. In doing so, the repertoire and practices of songleading became the center of intergenerational conversation, whether through moral critique, technical discussion, or debates over aesthetic parameters. The border between children's musical culture and adult culture, as a result, frequently faded into obscurity depending upon the nature and location of the interaction.

CONCLUSION

Without a significant event, such as the fabled "loss of innocence," where does (musical) childhood end? This discussion of youth songleading at Reform Jewish summer camps reveals the complicated and fraught nature of children's musical cultures. Subjected to multiple interpretations, over time songleading became a circumscribed set of discourses among young people, a transitional art practiced by songleaders straddling childhood and adulthood, and a widely practiced (and controversial) phenomenon among adults. Engaging in songleading consequently meant engaging in widespread debates over the meaning of child-hood itself. Seen through such a lens, this case study might help us to rethink the nature of children's musical cultures, not as a topic desirable for its isolation from other demographic groups but as a foundation for ever-deepening layers that illuminate both children's perceptions of life and a society's perceptions of the child's world.

NOTES

1   I exclude here the voluminous literature on rites of passage, pioneered by van Gennep 1960 and discussed by Montgomery 2009: 212–232, which is almost universally written from an adult-centered perspective.

2   The organizations that support summer camping have also commissioned numerous studies, both scholarly and anecdotal (see, e.g., Sales and Saxe 2003, 2008). I exclude most of these studies in the current discussion, however, because they often emphasize specific self-interested agendas.

3   In its earliest years, NFTY concentrated mainly on older "young" people (aged approximately eighteen through twenty-five). As time progressed, organizers opened the group to younger and younger members. By 2000, NFTY catered almost exclusively to high school students.

4   The campers' equation of songleaders with clergy was reinforced for me in June 2000 after I had filled in for a missing songleader during a morning service. Later in the day, a camper from that unit recognized me and called out, "Hi rabbi—I mean, songleader!" (field notes).

5   Significantly, two of the songwriter's nephews had also taken songleading responsibilities at OSRUI that summer, broadening the reference in the set list to include family provenance.

REFERENCES

Blacking, John. [1967] 1995. *Venda Children's Songs*. 2nd ed. Chicago: University of Chicago Press.

Boynton, Susan, and Roe-Min Kok, eds. 2006. *Musical Childhoods and the Cultures of Youth*. Middletown, CT: Wesleyan University Press.

Campbell, Patricia Shehan. 1998. *Songs in Their Heads: Music and Its Meaning in Children's Lives*. New York: Oxford University Press.

Central Conference of American Rabbis. 1897. *Union Hymnal*. New York: Wm. C. Popper and Son.

Central Conference of American Rabbis. 1914. *Union Hymnal for Jewish Worship*. 2nd ed. n.p.: Central Conference of American Rabbis.

Central Conference of American Rabbis. 1932. *Union Hymnal: Songs and Prayers for Jewish Worship*. 3rd ed. n.p.: Central Conference of American Rabbis.

Central Conference of American Rabbis. 1960. *Union Songster: Songs and Prayers for Jewish Youth*. New York: Central Conference of American Rabbis.

Cohen, Judah M. 2006a. "Singing Out for Judaism: A History of Songleaders and Songleading at Olin-Sang-Ruby Union Institute." In *A Place of Our Own: The Beginnings of Reform Jewish Camping in America*, edited by Gary Zola and Michael Lorge, 173–208. Tuscaloosa: University of Alabama Press.

Cohen, Judah M. 2006b. "'And the Youth Shall See Visions...': Summer Camps, Songleading and Musical Identity among American Reform Jewish Teenagers." In *Musical Childhoods and the Cultures of Youth*, edited by Susan Boynton and Roe-Min Kok, 187–207. Middletown, CT: Wesleyan University Press.

Cohen, Judah M. 2009. "Musical Tradition and the Crisis of Place: Reform Jewish Songleading, Shabbat Shirah, and the New Dining Hall." *Western Folklore* 67 (4): 321–349.

Gaunt, Kyra. 2006. *The Games Black Girls Play: Learning the Ropes from Double-Dutch to Hip-Hop.* New York: New York University Press.

James, Allison. 2007. "Giving Voice to Children's Voices: Practices and Problems, Pitfalls and Potentials." *The American Anthropologist* 109 (2): 261–272.

Joselit, Jenna Weissman, and Karen S. Mittelman, eds. 1993. *A Worthy Use of Summer: Jewish Camping in America.* Philadelphia: National Museum of American Jewish History.

Lightstone, Jack N., and Frederick B. Bird. 1995. *Ritual and Ethnic Identity: A Comparative Study of the Social Meaning of Liturgical Ritual in Synagogues.* Waterloo, Ontario: Wilfred Laurier University Press.

Minks, Amanda. 2002. "From Children's Song to Expressive Practices: Old and New Directions in the Ethnomusicological Study of Children." *Ethnomusicology* 46: 379–408.

Montgomery, Heather. 2009. *An Introduction to Childhood: Anthropological Perspectives on Children's Lives.* Malden, MA: Wiley-Blackwell.

Posen, I. Sheldon. 1974. "Song and Singing Traditions at Children's Summer Camps." Masters thesis, Memorial University of Newfoundland.

Sales, Amy, and Leonard Saxe. 2003. *"How Goodly Are Thy Tents": Summer Camps as Jewish Socializing Experiences.* Waltham, MA: Brandeis University Press.

Sales, Amy, and Leonard Saxe. 2008. "Summer Camps as Jewish Socializing Experiences." In *What We NOW Know about Jewish Education*, edited by Linda Dale Bloomberg, Paul Flexner, and Roberta L. Goodman, 407–416. Los Angeles: Torah Aura Productions.

Seeger, Anthony, and Kate Seeger. 2006. "Beyond the Embers of the Campfire: The Ways of Music at a Residential Children's Summer Camp." *The World of Music* 48 (1): 33–65.

Tillery, Randall. 1992. "Touring Arcadia: Elements of Discursive Simulations and Cultural Struggle at a Children's Summer Camp." *Cultural Anthropology* 7 (3): 374–388.

Van Gennep, Arnold. 1960. *The Rites of Passage.* Chicago: University of Chicago Press.

Will Boxt, Rosalie, and Robbie Weiner, eds. 2000. *Shireinu: Our Songs.* Chordster. New York: Union of American Hebrew Congregations.

4

VENDA CHILDREN'S MUSICAL CULTURE IN LIMPOPO, SOUTH AFRICA

ANDREA EMBERLY

"WHAT is your name?" "How old are you?" "What kinds of music do you like?" "Can you sing me a song?" From behind the safe lens of the video camera, these are the questions I first asked children while doing field research on children's music in Limpopo province, South Africa. One afternoon, after several of these informed "performances," one of the children with whom I worked asked me if she could use the video camera. After I gave her a few simple instructions and let her take control, she immediately turned to me, pointed the video camera close to my face and asked, "What is your name? How old are you? Can you sing me a song?" I was taken aback as my constant questions came back at me. What that particular moment revealed is what I had lost in my research to that point—the voice, the perspective, the innermost musical worlds of Venda children.

From that day, my research on children's musical identities in Limpopo changed significantly. I began to reflect on what it meant to truly represent children's musical voices without objectifying them or capitalizing on them. In the world of anthropology and ethnomusicology, representing children's experiences from the perspective of children themselves is a recent approach. My particular research seeks to integrate children's perspectives into the representations of their musical cultures. This chapter explores this idea of perspective—examining the elements needed in the creation of a relationship between the reader and the musical culture of Venda children that is representative of the viewpoint of children. I will explore the idea of perspective from three primary points: a historical vantage point—that of ethnomusicologist John Blacking; the current perspective of myself as researcher; and, most significantly, the perspective of Venda children themselves, as creators and propagators of their own distinct and collective musical cultures. Many of the musical examples discussed in this chapter are available for viewing on the EVIA (Ethnomusicological Video for Instruction and Analysis) Archives website: www.eviada.org.

There is a growing development of a "new research orthodoxy" that recognizes "children as competent social actors" (James 2007: 261). But this new recognition, which enables children to express their voices, is "not simply or only about letting children speak: it is about exploring the unique contribution to our understanding of and theorizing about the social world that children's perspectives can provide" (ibid: 262). Understanding and representing the voice of children, therefore, requires a "political enterprise" that views children as "active in the structuring of their lives and their relationships" (Mayall 2002: 138) and also recognizes the duality between adult and children's cultures. Children's voices are "standpoints, places from which any analysis sets out, rather than definitive descriptions of empirical phenomena embodied in the words children speak" (James 2007: 269).

In addition, the idea that children represent a "minority social status" recognizes the inequalities that are present when representing childhood because they are placed in a subordinate position in academic discourse (Mayall 2002; Nettl 1983). Children's agency, unlike that of other marginalized groups, can never be fully realized because unlike other groups, their dependency is somewhat biologically determined. Therefore, a discourse that acknowledges children's social and cultural agency while recognizing their dynamic relationship with adult culture allows a more inclusive understanding of the nature of children's cultures.

CHILDREN AND SOUTH AFRICA

Children in South Africa, and specifically in rural areas, are faced with maintaining their distinct traditional cultures within the legacy of apartheid that has birthed a burgeoning new "rainbow" nationhood of South Africa. The ideology of the rainbow nation, now a common term that denotes nationalistic pride, suggests that a new history of South Africa began from the time that apartheid ended (officially in 1994 with the election of Nelson Mandela) and that a new South Africa is peaceful, accepting, and moving forward. However, the ideals of the rainbow nation are not without criticism, as many argue that these ideals mask "complex configurations by foregrounding an over-simplified discourse of rainbow nationalism" (Nuttall and Michael 2000: 1).

Within the legacy of apartheid, the rainbow nationhood, and the global cultural economy, this research examines how children's musical identities are informed and shaped. Venda children's musical culture provides insight into the ways in which contemporary South African children situate and understand their identities within local, national, and global contexts and environments. These contexts build on Appadurai's notions of "scapes," in which multiple sites are "constituted by the historically situated imaginations of persons and groups from around the globe" (Appadurai 1996: 33). This approach enables us to identify the shifts between Blacking's research and contemporary, postapartheid Venda children's musical cultures and changes in research methodology to approach and situate children's perspectives within academia.

Although children no longer live under the oppressive regime of apartheid in South Africa, its history and legacy continue to affect the consciousness of children throughout the country. Apartheid was by far the most significant ideological and political social structure in South African history and was "powerful in differentially structuring racial and political consciousness in the young" (Dawes and Finchilescu 2002: 148). While acknowledging that the "economic structure of South African society has not altered radically since 1994...state ideology now stresses national unity and tolerance rather than division" (2002: 151). Therefore, "the process of tolerance building through challenging destructive ideologies, beliefs and practices has to begin if future generations of South Africans are to celebrate their diversity and commonality" (2002: 162). Children in South Africa are now faced with both the idealization of diversity and a state ideology of recognizing and accepting a communal South African identity—the "rainbow nation." Children live within this multiplicity with the social, political, and cultural history of South Africa contributing to the social construction of children's culture in Limpopo.

VENDA MUSIC AND CULTURE

Ṅwawa wa mbevha ha hangwi mukwita
The child of the mouse will never forget the mother's path (Venda proverb)

The Venda people live primarily in the Limpopo province, the most northern of the South African provinces. Within Limpopo there are five districts, with the Venda population dominating the Vhembe district, which roughly encompasses the area formally known as Vendaland, once considered an independent homeland under the apartheid government. In a groundbreaking study that drew focus to the study of children's music in ethnomusicology, John Blacking first explored the world of Venda children's music in the 1950s. Blacking's work brought musical prominence to the Venda, and he consequently dedicated the majority of his life's work to exploring the role of music in Venda culture (see Blacking 1962, 1965, 1967, 1969, 1970, 1973, 1980). In addition to Blacking, the work of Jaco Kruger explores different types of music in Venda culture (see Kruger 1989, 1996, 1999, 2004, 2006, 2007). My own research, 2005–2007 and 2009, explores children's music in Limpopo and the construction of childhood in South Africa (Emberly 2009).

In 1967, John Blacking introduced the world to the musical lives of the Venda children of South Africa with his book *Venda Children's Songs: A Study in Ethnomusicological Analysis*, which outlined the functional structure of children's songs in their community, postulating that children's music and culture was not superimposed upon them by the dominant adult culture. Blacking viewed Venda children's music as a separate musical culture that was created *by* and *for* Venda children themselves (Blacking 1967: 5). Applying structuralist/linguistic theories, he maintained that Venda children's songs were not simplified versions of adult songs but unique compositions that functioned within the culture of Venda childhood. He claimed that the surface structures of children's music were unique but that their deep musicological structures were connected to the overarching Venda musical system. The functional and cultural analysis of Venda children's songs produced a landmark exploration of children's music that continues to influence the study of children's musical cultures. Although Blacking never concluded that children's culture was self-inscribed, through his application of Alan Merriam's (1964) theory that music is human action in culture, he challenged the notion that children were mere copycats, incapable of self-creativity.

Venda children's music served as a model for Blacking's evolving analysis as he continually applied new theories to the material he collected in the 1950s. As Suzel Ana Reily notes, "Blacking used his Venda ethnography to substantiate practically every academic argument he made" and because of this "the Venda have been heralded as a group that exemplifies the power of music to generate a healthy society" (2006: 6). Through his work in South Africa and beyond, Blacking asserted that human musicality was the fabric of culture and that musical skills develop over the lifespan. It was his lifelong argument that all humans are essentially musical, a stance that continues to challenge Western views on the nature of musicality. Within Venda communities, and Venda children in particular, Blacking viewed music as the integrated product of society and culture. In so doing, Blacking opened our eyes to the need for the study of childhood in ethnomusicology.

Like Blacking, I learned about Venda children's music both from children and from adults in the community who had a vested interest in teaching children about their cultural histories (Emberly 2009). When it came to the music that was spontaneously shared outside of the category of traditional music, the games, songs, and music that children create within the community of childhood, children themselves were the primary musical directors, the knowledge bearers of their own traditions. Between these musical systems, and further supported by music education in school and mediated musical worlds, children construct their musical selves on both individual and communal levels. As active agents they are encouraged and constrained by contextual elements that significantly shape the musical sounds they receive, repeat, and create. Venda children's musical cultures are also representative of nonmusical factors that contribute to the identity of each child, from culture to social and political influences, from the media to the physical landscape. Within the local, national, and global strata, children engage with these nonmusical factors, which lead to individuality within the overarching musical culture of childhood.

Musical Identities and Matrixes of Influence

Venda children in Limpopo are united in musical languages that are uniquely personal and simultaneously communal. Therefore, it is relevant to briefly explore some of the current dynamics in identity building that children engage with: a legacy of apartheid; shifting local, national, and global identities; an education system in flux; and local and global media forces. Musical examples can illustrate this framework and highlight the significant role that music plays in identity building and the agency that children control in their own musical communities through participation and creativity.

In addition to the musical content that these confluences afford, Venda children make conscious decisions about the quality and format of their musical communities. As social agents, they make decisions about what belongs to their own musical communities and, as such, stage musical performances based on their audience. For instance, when I first arrived in several of the villages and asked the children what kind of music they wanted to perform, they inevitably began with what they identified as "traditional" music of their respective cultures. As I was typically speaking to children in the presence of Venda adults, the children often chose to perform what they believed the adults wished them to. Although this may sometimes not have been the children's first choice, these musical performances represent an important aspect of children's musical communities. The music that adults deem important in maintaining the viability of their traditions in a rapidly changing world enriches the cultural education of children and significantly contributes to their individual and local identities. Once I was able to communicate that I was interested in all aspects of children's musical cultures, from those that they were taught, to those that they encountered through the media, to those that they created spontaneously, I was presented with a rich display of musical creativity and agency.

VENDA CHILDREN'S MUSIC

> Most Venda children are competent musicians: they can
> sing and dance to traditional melodies, and many can play
> at least one musical instrument. And yet they have no
> formal musical training. (Blacking 1967: 29)

Venda children have a vast collection of music belonging solely to the category of children's songs. According to Mudzunga Davhula, an arts and culture teacher and curriculum advisor, it is possible to approach "any child in the village and they will know these songs, they have been taught these songs as a part of their cultural education" (personal communication, Tshakhuma Village, 2009). Blacking found this during his research, and its legacy remains true—Venda children are well versed in Venda children's songs. Although Venda children are expert in their knowledge of traditional music, the means by which they learn music has changed significantly since Blacking's time. Musical education, in the broad sense, has moved from the *kraal*, or chief's land, to the classroom, where the arts and culture curriculum sets guidelines for teaching music in the classroom (Emberly and Davidson 2011). Because of this significant shift, and because of changes in cultural and social structures, music maintains the agency of both tradition and of change.

On a local level, Venda children's music represents how and what it means to *be* Venda. Children learning traditional Venda songs and dance in the classroom repeatedly emphasized to me that it was important to learn this music because it would retain Venda culture and show the rest of the country that they were proud Venda people. From several local schools near Tshakhuma, children voiced that

> Learning traditional music and dance, it makes me proud for who I am, it makes me proud for what I think, it makes me proud of what God gave me.
>
> (girl, age seventeen)

> We learn these dances at our school... we just dance for enjoying our lives.
>
> (girl, age eleven)

> Being a Venda person, our language, it means a lot of things for us, because we are teaching other people to respect our language, we have to show the other languages that we respect our language and our culture.
>
> (girl, age fifteen)

And teachers in these schools voiced similar sentiments:

> Learning *tshigombela* helps them [children] learn about Venda culture.
>
> (Mrs. Munyai, grade 1 teacher, Tshirunzanani Primary School)

> It is important because at our homes and at our villages we are encouraging elders to pass their knowledge to the young ones as part of bringing back the generations.
>
> (Khosi (Chief) Ligege, principal, Ratshitanga Primary School)

The Adapting Role of Traditional Music in Venda Children's Lives

Although at one time many Venda children's songs may have provided a different context and were likely performed at specific times and events, they now represent the role of children in maintaining Venda culture under the pressure of growing up in postapartheid South Africa. This new identity that children are continually shaping includes dimensions of both Venda and South African identity. This duality is not necessarily syncretic, as the identities sometimes compete against one another.

Venda children are participants in a structured musical community that values children's songs as a legitimate and vibrant part of the overarching musical fabric of Venda culture. This role, as musical participants and ambassadors of Venda culture, is clearly defined and valued. Children know, and can perform, a significant body of songs that are considered in their communities to be Venda children's music. Children spend many hours practicing and learning songs and teaching younger children the lyrics and accompanying movements. Meeting at least once a week with a community leader or teacher, groups of children come together for the specific goal of learning these traditional songs, which they perform at cultural events and in musical competitions. On some evenings the children might stop by to practice and sing songs with one another. Sometimes older children teach younger children the patterns on the drums or specific dance patterns (see Figure 4.1).

Even though children learn the fundamental parts of the music from community leaders, teachers, and other adults, there is also a layer of child-to-child teaching that involves older children sharing advanced knowledge with younger children. The children are enthusiastic about learning the music, and even when it is not a practice day they come together to sing and dance—often trying to outdo one another on the drums or by dancing. By building skills together, children create a culture of childhood that centers on Venda music—thereby contributing to their cultural identities. Music, as an identifiable and integral part of Venda culture informs Venda children's identities and provides them with the tangible means to identify with their localized culture.

Children's roles in music making in Venda communities now reflect a more common theme that can be found throughout children's cultures: the idea that children are the ambassadors of a culture that is threatened by globalized forces

Figure 4.1: Children practicing after school.

that detract from the traditional contextual meaning of these children's songs. Adults have a vested interest in maintaining the unique culture of children's music because they want to foster children's interest in their own culture when there are external factors that may dissuade them from participating in the maintenance and perpetuation of Venda culture. These influences, as named by adult members of the community, are often attributed to television, the educational system, and the general lack of interest in Venda culture. As children grow up in rural areas and are often forced to leave for larger urban centers, there is a hope that Venda culture can be propagated through a promotion of children's music; investing in the early musical education of Venda children is an investment in the overarching community of Venda culture. Venda children learn musically about Venda culture. Inasmuch as they are learning the melodies and rhythmic patterns of children's songs that have historical relevance, they simultaneously learn about the history of Venda culture. During Blacking's research, children's participation in music making provided the foundation for many aspects of Venda culture (e.g., teaching life skills; learning life roles, puberty rites, and transitions). This cultural foundation, taught through integrated forms of music, singing, and dancing, is still present within children's musical lives. In addition, songs that belong to the *domba* or initiation schools, though less likely to be performed in context (these schools still exist, but their contexts have changed drastically; see Ramabulana 1988), represent the fundamental role of children in Venda culture. What is profoundly different, however, is the way in which children learn traditional music and the way in which they marry those traditions with emerging musical influences. Although some of the skills that particular songs used to teach Venda children may not be needed today (e.g., herding cattle, work-related skills), the songs provide cultural skills and knowledge in that children embody the essence of what it means to be Venda through music.

Venda children's musical cultures represent how music, song, and dance function in a different way in children's lives: that it now functions to educate Venda children *about* Venda children's music. The children themselves explained that this music was *their* music; when I asked them what Venda children's traditional music was, they would perform any number of historical songs or stories that they knew. Children were engaged with this genre of music; when the drums came out any number of children would take a turn playing the rhythms while others sang and danced. They were as capable of performing a traditional dance as they were in singing the latest pop song that they inevitably all knew. The musical multiplicity of children's lives is nowhere more evident than in the lives of Venda children. Participation in traditional Venda music making constitutes a new movement of cultural pride that both contributes to the "rainbow nation" and asserts the ways in which Venda culture stands out within this multiculturalism. Venda children's identities are built on local and national levels, participating simultaneously as members of Venda culture and as members of the burgeoning South African culture that is reinforced by current politics and the desire for solidarity on a national level.

THE GLOBAL: EXPLORING
THE MUSICAL WORLD

Radio, television, internet, and print media all present children with access to information on both local and global levels that contribute to their dynamic identity formation while simultaneously locating them within the global culture of childhood. But with these opportunities come competing global influences that affect local culture (see Gigli 2004). Therefore, adults teach children about their musical heritages as a way in which to protect and perpetuate local cultural identities amid a global market that is vying for children's attention. In addition, children in South Africa contribute to the global imagination, as musical influences are not unidirectional (Erlmann 1999). As active social agents, children locate themselves in the midst of local, national, and global contexts, contributing to the creation of musical cultures that are both individualistic and communal. Just as Appadurai argues that "different regions now have elaborate interests and capabilities in constructing world pictures whose very interaction affects global process" (2000: 13), children contribute to the glocalization of their own culture, which focuses on the nuances of the local within a global context.

Children's local musical communities are informed through a diversity of avenues—family, friends, and community—that further disseminate into the nation and, sometimes, eventually the world. The musical voices of children in Limpopo are unified through songs that connect them in a culture of childhood in a national sense. Songs they learn from the radio, the media, television programs, and each other all contribute to uniting children in a national culture of South Africa. Moving outward from local and national layers of identity and building up to an understanding of their identities in a global world, children are actively engaged in the intricately woven web of consumption and production. Children, as agents in the social and cultural world of South Africa and as bearers and propagators of local traditional culture, create music that engages with the national social world and participate in a global culture, illustrating how they these layers interplay within musical cultures of childhood.

During my field research I began to explore the ways in which children could be active participants in research, not as objects for study but as engaged individuals with investment in teaching others about their musical lives and identities. One way I accomplished this was by enabling children to take photographs, draw pictures, and record video. These techniques provided the opportunity to understand on a deeper level children's own perspectives on their musical identities (Thomson 2008). In one such endeavor I gave a young teenage boy my video camera because he wanted to record a rap video (see Figure 4.2). He had long been interested in a musical career and since the beginning of my research was instrumental in assisting me in many ways. On this particular afternoon in 2009 (he was fourteen years old at this time) he left for an extended period of time with the camera, and when he came back he was excited for me to burn him a copy of his first rap video. On many occasions we

Figure 4.2: Lollipop rapping.

discussed his interest in the genre because I was intrigued by his interest in the stereotypical notions of rappers, money, girls, and "homeboys." I asked him where he learned about rap music, since it was not a genre of music that all of the other young boys expressed such a dedicated interest in, and he told me he purchased CDs to learn the lyrics and sing along. He had also begun to write all of his own raps under his moniker "Lollipop," which he practiced often. In addition to writing the songs, he drew covers for all of his albums. He told me he wanted to grow up and become a rapper so he could be famous and rich. The way in which he meshes his musical lives is quite extraordinary. He is a talented musician and dancer in almost every genre and comes from a very musical family who are also very involved in the community. He is as adept at dancing a traditional dance as he is at performing a rap for anyone who will listen. Here is an abridged version of some of the lyrics from his rap:

> Yo Lollipop, c'mon
> Let's do it for the rappers
> Well tell me somethin' else
> Everyone come out and say I love you
> Well tell me somethin' else, tell me somethin' else
> Tellin' me something ridiculous
> Everything you say is a lot of rubbish
> But I am alone with my money
> Yo, yo, yo, yo....
> Everybody want to see me go right to the club
> Everybody want to sing Lol-li-pop
> Everyone is decked up in the club
> No one wants to leave me alone
> Money, money, money, money
> Because I am also paid when I think of a song
> Everybody wants to be a rapper

Everybody wants some
Ev-'ry thing
Ev-'ry thing including your mind
Everybody wants to go to the club
Where's everybody at?
Yo, there, there they are
Yeah, I see them
But I don't know what I am doing for them
Yeah, yeah....
Everybody wants to go right to the club
Yo, hey

The musical identity that he is aspiring to in this rap is a common one for many young men in South Africa. While it is not the main focus of this chapter, it does leave open avenues for exploring the role of global and local (South African rap and hip-hop, kwaito) music in the musical lives of young children in rural areas. And while Lollipop's aspirations might not be unique, it is his musical multiplicity that sets him apart from many of his contemporaries. In many ways he embodies the musical nature of childhood at its present state in Venda communities: he engages with traditional music and has the skill base and understanding to perform musically in any community context and, in addition, he is an active member of a globalized, glocalized, and mediaized youth that connects him to worlds beyond his own. Hence he embodies what it means to be Venda.

The Musical Classroom

Musical training in South African schools was once based solely on the Western European system and offered only in privileged schools. However, the revised South African arts and culture curriculum "takes South African's multicultural and multilingual diversity into account as the study of non-Western musics has been incorporated into it. It celebrates the plurality of South Africa's cultural heritage and creates awareness of other world musics" (Kwami et al. 2003: 269). At present, although the education systems is attempting a more holistic approach, learning outcomes still vary greatly between schools, and the legacy of the Bantu education system still affects the development of a unified curriculum. What Kwami et al. refer to as an "over-dependence on the Western classical music paradigm" affects the musical "diet" children are fed (2003: 270). Kwami and Lebaka see the music education system as one that "attempts to teach indigenous black African music ... using Western concepts, models and principles" (2004: 126) because African systems of music education are not often constructed in a written format. For this reason, Nzewi believes that African music education needs to be completely redefined as "the contemporary African needs to have a true and practical understanding of indigenous knowledge theory and principles" (Nzewi 2005: vii).

In the current classroom in a typical primary or secondary school in a Venda community, children are beginning to learn more about Venda traditional music alongside the diversity of musical cultures in South Africa and beyond. Whereas Blacking would have observed these musical traditions performed only in a community context, today these musical traditions are being taught in the classroom, and for many Venda children this is their primary location for learning traditional Venda music. Although children are exposed to the musical culture, language, and soundscape of Venda music from birth, formalized teaching and training, as well as competition, is now situated firmly within the formalized educational system. In many ways this has embedded the traditional Venda musical culture into the lives of young children who are now engaged directly with musical influences from South Africa and the global music economy.

LEARNING TRADITIONAL MUSIC

During my research in Limpopo, I found that children learn traditional Venda music and dance in the classroom, in their homes, and, some, in small performance groups that typically meet on the weekends. In these settings, children sing and dance, both traditional and newly composed songs, all of which are referred to as traditional Venda music. Venda children's music incorporates a wide range of songs, those that may have been sung by Venda children since the migration of the Venda from the Congo in the sixteenth century, and those that may have been composed within the past seventy years or even within the past few minutes. What constitutes tradition or what represents Venda children's culture is constantly shifting and adapting to the contexts and cultures of children's lives today therefore contributing to the overarching Venda community. For example, the following children's song, still sung today, can be traced to some of the earliest writings on Venda children's songs:

Maṱhora
Hee! Iwe Maṱhora;
Oh! Hey you Mathora (boys name)
Fhefhee!
Sound of a blown reed pipe
Wo bva wo ḽa'ni?
What was your meal this morning?
Fhefhee!
Ndo ḽa tshikhuthela;
Porridge made of maize husks
Fhefhee!
Wa sevha nga mini?
What shall you use as a relish?

Fhefhee!
Nda sevha nga ṇama;
I used meat as my relish
Fhefhee!
Ṇama tshikhuthela;
Meat that is left outside and started to smell a bit bad
Fhefhee!
Seli a hu welwi;
Don't cross the river because
Fhefhee!
Hu na ngweṇa mbili;
There are two crocodiles
Fhefhee!
Dze' kapa seli;
Their torsos are on the other riverbank
Fhefhee!

This song is regarded as a Venda children's song or *nyimbo dza vhana*—literally songs of children, *nyimbo* (songs), *vhana* (children). This song can also be found in the earliest book on Venda children's songs (Ngwana 1958: 13) and in both Blacking (1967: 64) and Kruger (2004: 22). In addition it is a song that children were still taught and sang during my own field research (2005–2007, 2009).

Blacking listed this song as one of mockery sung only by boys. Kruger (2004: 24), meanwhile, says the song is about appropriate social behavior, instructing children through a "culinary metaphor." The lyrics of the version I recorded differ from Blacking's and slightly from Kruger's (his version mentions the "meat of an Eagle," while mine has no reference to the bird) and are very close to the lyrics in the Ngwana book. Both my recorded version and Kruger's have a chorus of "fhefhee," which is the sound of a reed pipe being blown, whereas Blacking's has no chorus listed. Blacking's version is said to be sung by young boys out herding, even though he did not specifically say he learned it from boys who were herding or if he learned the song and then assumed traditional context, noting that the song traditionally had been sung while herding. Neither the version I recorded nor Kruger's mention anything about herding. Blacking also states that the song uses rude words for boys to mock one another. In the version of the song I recorded and Kruger's there is no reference to mocking.

When I asked community members in Limpopo about the contexts to which Blacking referred, they noted that many children's songs that used to be a part of children's labor (such as herding) were no longer sung in context now that children were required to attend school and could no longer be a part of the labor force. Many suggested that this probably began around the late 1960s, when formal education became more codified and the government began controlling people's farms and livestock. At this time child labor was discouraged and there were fewer and fewer herds for the boys to tend. Therefore, the context of the song has changed drastically, from only being sung by boys while herding to being sung by all children as a social lesson in behavior. The song also provides a practical warning to children about being careful at the river, where there are large crocodiles that could harm them. Indeed, there are several children's songs that refer to the crocodiles at the river, because they are an imminent threat to children's safety in the area.

Adapting Traditional Music

In another example of a children's song, children are taught about traditional healers and their significant role in Venda culture. This song has multiple layers of meaning and is significant both for its roots in tradition and its adaptation.

> *Lila lila lila ṅwana-nga (x2)*
> Cry, cry, cry, my child (x2)
> *Phumula maṱozi—Vhulwadze vhu vhavha*
> Wipe your tears—illness is painful
> *Kha ri yeni, ri ye phafula (x2)*
> Let us go, go to phafula[1]
> *Ri vhone Mungome, Mungome u a vumba*
> We shall see a healer, a healer can divine
> *Bvumba bvumba bvumba, Mungome (x2)*
> Divine, divine, divine, you diviner
> *Ṅwana u a lwala—dzi vho fara Makhadzi*
> The child is ill—*dolos*[2] are now pointing to the aunt
> *Vha na phele—phele ya gegulu (x2)*
> She has a hyena—a very old female hyena
> *Avha vho Makhulu vha na vhuloi havho*
> This granny has her own witchcraft

This song tells the story of a young child who is sick and must be taken to the traditional healer to find the source of her illness. As it turns out, the source is her aunt, who is practicing witchcraft. In Venda culture, witchcraft was historically feared and people who were deemed to be witches were killed (see Payze et al. 1992.). The song's cultural content teaches children about the role of traditional healers in Venda culture, and although many of the children would not know exactly where *phafula* was, they would know that it was a place where there would be traditional healers. When I was translating the song with the help of two young children, they knew all of the translations of the words and that the song was about traditional healers in general. The song is part of the *zwidade* tradition or folk song tradition; it teaches children about traditional healers and to be wary of those who might cast a spell on you to make you ill. The role of traditional healers throughout South Africa has been politicized and often demonized, and only now is the government recognizing the importance of traditional healers in healthcare and community development.

Figure 4.3: Children singing "Lila Lila" while passing rocks in a
circle to the beat of the song.

When I first watched this song performed by children, it was done in a circle
and the children would sing the song and pass a rock between them as they sang
(see Figure 4.3). Long before I knew the meaning of the song, I had assumed it was
a game song or counting song because it was always done in a circle passing the
rocks. When I learned the lyrics and the translation, I was confused as to the meaning of the actions that accompanied the song. In a later discussion with Mudzunga
Davhula, she revealed that she borrowed the game from the Tsonga culture and
added the Venda song to teach the children how to keep a steady beat while singing
the song. The meaning of the song to an outsider completely shifted once I learned
its context, history, and content, as the actions are a technique for learning rhythm.
It engages the notion of what makes a song traditional, because as children continue
to pair this song with the action it becomes enveloped in the genre of children's
music and accepted as a part of the song tradition even though the actions were
a recent and borrowed addition. Although cultural sharing is not a new concept
(Appadurai 2000), the song is an example of the dynamism of traditional music in
a Venda context and the notion that tradition itself is not static.

Creating Traditional Music

Another example of a song and dance performed by girls is a style known as
matangwa. In the late twentieth century, *matangwa* changed from a male-only
dance accompanied by the music of the Venda reed pipes to a dance performed

Figure 4.4: Girls dancing *matangwa*.

by women. Rather than being accompanied by the reeds, women began to sing the melodies and attach words to them, calling the genre *matangwa a mulomo* (*matangwa* of the mouth). Today, young girls readily perform this genre of group dance that marries traditional forms of music with newly composed lyrics that address current issues affecting children in the area (see Figure 4.4). This song is representational of the constantly shifting aspects of traditional music in that newly composed songs are considered traditional because they evoke the style and forms of music that have continued to dominate the musical landscape of Venda culture. Through newly composed songs and music, children shed light on issues and concerns such as education and health alongside songs that tell stories and lighthearted fables.

> *Ri hanya nga u humbela*
> We survive through asking (begging) others for something
> *Ri humbela pfunzo, tshifhato, bungu*
> We beg for education, buildings, books
> *Ri hanya nga u humbela*
> We survive through begging others for something
> *Ahe Vho Mugivhi, Ramzwa, Rammela*
> Beware Mrs. Mugivhi, Mrs. Ramzwa, Mrs. Rammela
> *Ahe ri a vha humbela*
> Beware as we beg you
> *Ri hanya nga u humbela*
> We survive through begging others for something

CONCLUSION

Children have their own vision of what their musical cultures sound like and what they *should* sound like, even if sometimes these ideals cannot be met. This agency is reflected, for instance, in children's handclapping games, popular music, and traditional musical performances. Exploring the contextualization, the experiences with which children are presented gives a metaphorical voice to children's culture and to the diversity that exists within the culture of childhood on local, national, and global levels. In the specific case of Venda children, this context locates them in musical environments from which they build their individual musical and sociocultural worlds. Although this context might be considerably distinctive from that which John Blacking found, Venda children continue to embody Venda culture through their musical worlds. As Venda children struggle to come to new understandings of what it means to be Venda, to be South African, and to locate oneself in a global culture, music remains steadfast as a founding aspect of the myriad of these identities. As so many children expressed to me through music, words, photographs, videos, and drawings, it is important to understand what it means to be Venda—and to be Venda means to understand musically your history and your future.

ACKNOWLEDGMENTS

Thanks to all the children in Limpopo for sharing your worlds with me.

NOTES

1 Phafula is a traditional place where one goes to find a traditional healer, now called a Traditional Health Practitioner (sometimes historically referred to as a witch doctor).
2 *Dolos* are a type of dice or bones that healers throw to read the illness of a person; usually they throw four *dolos*.

REFERENCES

Appadurai, A. 1996. *Modernity at Large: Cultural Dimensions of Globalization.* Minneapolis: University of Minnesota Press.

Appadurai, A. 2000. "Grassroots Globalization and the Research Imagination." *Public Culture* 12 (1): 1–19.

Blacking, J. 1962. "Musical Expeditions of the Venda." *African Music* 3 (1): 54–72.

Blacking, J. 1964. *Black Background: The Childhood of a South African Girl.* London: Abelard Schuman.

Blacking, J. 1965. "The Role of Music in the Culture of the Venda of the Northern Transvaal." In *Studies in Ethnomusicology*, edited by M. Kolinski, 2:20–52. New York: Oak Publications.

Blacking, J. 1967. *Venda Children's Songs: A Study in Ethnomusicological Analysis.* Johannesburg: Witwatersrand University Press.

Blacking, J. 1969. "Songs, Dance, Mimes and Symbolism of Venda Girl's Initiation Schools." Parts 1–4. *African Studies* 28: 28–35, 69–118, 149–199, 215–266.

Blacking, J. 1970. "Tonal Organization in the Music of Two Venda Initiation Schools." *Ethnomusicology* 14 (1): 1–54.

Blacking, J. 1973. *How Musical Is Man?* Seattle: University of Washington Press.

Blacking, J. [1980] 2001. *Domba: 1956–1958.* Bloomington, IN: Society for Ethnomusicology. Film.

Dawes, A., and G. Finchilescu. 2002. "What's Changed? The Racial Orientations of South African Adolescents during Rapid Political Change." *Childhood* 9 (2): 147–165.

Emberly, A. 2009. "'Mandela Went to China . . . and India Too': Musical Cultures of Childhood in South Africa." PhD diss., University of Washington.

Emberly, A., and J. Davidson. 2011. "From the *Kraal* to the Classroom: Shifting Musical Arts Practices from the Community to the School with Special Reference to Learning *Tshigombela* in Limpopo, South Africa." *International Journal of Music Education* 29 (3): 1–17.

Erlmann, V. 1999. *Music, Modernity, and the Global Imagination.* New York: Oxford University Press.

Gigli, S. 2004. "Children, Youth and Media around the World: An Overview of Trends and Issues." Report prepared for UNICEF 4th World Summit on Media for Children and Adolescents, Rio de Janeiro, Brazil, April 2004.

Kruger, J. 1989. "Rediscovering the Venda Ground-Bow. *Ethnomusicology* 33 (3): 391–404.

Kruger, J. 1996. "Wada: A Sacred Venda Drum." *SAMUS* 16: 49–58.

Kruger, J. 1999. "Singing Psalms with Owls: A Venda 20th Century Musical History." *African Music* 7 (4): 122–146.

Kruger, J. 2004. *Venda Lashu: Tshivenda Songs, Musical Games and Song Stories.* Potchefstroom, South Africa: School of Music, North-West University.

Kruger, J. 2006. "Tracks of the Mouse: Tonal Reinterpretation in Venda Guitar Songs." In *The Musical Human: Rethinking John Blacking's Ethnomusicology in the Twenty-First Century*, edited by S. Reily, 37–70. Burlington, VT: Ashgate.

Kruger, J., and I. le Roux. 2007. *The Flamboyant Rooster and Other Tshivenda Song Stories.* Potchefstroom, South Africa: School of Music, North-West University.

Kwami, R., and E. Lebaka. 2004. "Horses for Courses?: Indigenous African Music in Three Relocated Contexts." *Council for Research in Music Education* 161/162: 125–134.

Kwami, R. M., E. A. Akrofi, and S. Adams. 2003. "Integrating Musical Arts Cultures." In *Musical Arts in Africa*, edited by A. Herbst, M. Nzewi, and K. Agawu, 261–278. Pretoria: Unisa Press.

Mayall, B. 2002. *Towards a Sociology for Childhood: Thinking from Children's Lives.* Buckingham: Open University Press.

Merriam, A. P. 1964. *The Anthropology of Music.* Evanston, IL: Northwestern University Press.

Nettl, B. 1983. *The Study of Ethnomusicology: Twenty-Nine Issues and Concepts.* Urbana: University of Illinois Press.

Ngwana, P. 1958. *Muratho Venda-Leesreeks: Venda Readers.* Johannesburg: Voortrekkerpers.

Nuttall, S., and C. Michael. 2000. "Introduction: Imagining the Present." In *Senses of Culture: South African Culture Studies*, edited by S. Nuttall and C. Michael, 1–23. Oxford: Oxford University Press.

Nzewi, M. 2005. *Learning the Musical Arts in Contemporary Africa: Informed by Indigenous Knowledge Systems*. Pretoria, South Africa: Centre for Indigenous Instrumental African Music and Dance.

Payze, C., A. de V Minnaar, and D. Offringa. 1992. *All Women Are the Same and All Women Are Witches: Gender Violence and Its Relation to Witchcraft*. Pretoria: Human Sciences Research Council; South African Sociological Association.

Ramabulana, V. 1988. "Domba Yesterday and Today." Master's research project submitted to the Department of Anthropology, University of Venda, South Africa.

Reily, S. 2006. *The Musical Human: Rethinking John Blacking's Ethnomusicology in the Twenty-First Century*. Burlington, VT: Ashgate.

Thomson, P., ed. 2008. *Doing Visual Research with Children and Young People*. New York: Routledge.

5

SONGS OF JAPANESE SCHOOLCHILDREN DURING WORLD WAR II

NORIKO MANABE

It may seem like North Korea to you now. But at the time, we were just kids. We wanted to have fun. We sang these songs for fun.

(Chieko, World War II survivor, now in her late seventies)

AMONG the vast repertoire of Japanese school songs, perhaps the most thought provoking—and least well known—are those songs taught during World War II. Soaked with propagandistic messages, they assert the superiority of Japan over other nations, the glory of dying for one's country, the romantic imagery of conquered territories, and the joys of toiling in weapons factories, among other things. When I asked informants who had attended Japanese elementary school during World War II about these songs, they instantly and instinctively sang them, even though these songs had been banned after the war, some sixty-five years ago. Furthermore, they remembered the *gunka* (military marches) that they sang at send-off parades for soldiers and other official ceremonies; when shown Kindaichi Haruhiko's collection of *gunka* (Kindaichi and Anzai 1982), one informant sang almost all of the thirty-five songs from the period 1938–1945 with zest.

Clearly, songs were an important part of the wartime propaganda machine. For children, what values were these songs reinforcing? What behaviors were being encouraged? What legacy did they leave in the minds of the children who sang them after the war had ended? This chapter explores these issues through a discussion of the songs that were taught in schools, sung in official ceremonies and rituals, and heard over the radio from 1937 to 1945, as analyzed from their texts, the directives found in instructors' manuals, and personal testimonies.

Most of the personal stories come from interviews with informants—identified by pseudonyms in this chapter. They include two sisters, Chieko and Naoko, who were in sixth and fifth grades, respectively, in an elementary school in Kyoto at the end of the war; Naoko's husband, Akira, who attended elementary school in Osaka during the war; and Shinichi, who was a third-grade boy when he was evacuated to Tottori prefecture from Yokohama to avoid air raids. In addition, I refer to personal testimonies in published collections of diaries (e.g., Yamashita 2005).

MUSIC IN JAPANESE SCHOOLS, 1877–1933

At the beginning of the Meiji Period (1868–1912), the newly restored imperial government—well aware that two hundred years of isolation had left Japan vulnerable, technologically, economically, and militarily—initiated reforms to Westernize and modernize, including the creation of a national educational system. The government advocated *shōka* (school songs) as a way to cultivate moral character in children.[1] The first such collection, the *hoiku shōka* (nursery songs), began to be compiled in 1877. The music was composed by Imperial Court musicians in *gagaku* (court music) modes; the lyrics, by female instructors of the Tokyo Women's Normal School, drew inspiration from Japanese classical poetry. The collection was not disseminated widely and was quickly supplanted by songbooks in Western musical style by Isawa Shūji (1851–1917) and the Ministry of Education. While a student in Boston, Isawa had been tutored by Luther Whiting Mason (1818–1896), who compiled the *National Music Course*, a graded series of songbooks in extensive use in the late nineteenth century. Isawa proposed the establishment of a similar course in the Japanese educational system, arguing that music was conducive to the formation of moral character. He also argued that traditional Japanese music was unsuitable in education, as music such as *gagaku* was "too refined," while popular music, such as *shamisen*-based music for geisha, was "too vulgar"; he deemed a newly created "national" music for all classes to be more suitable (Eppstein 1994: 30–36). To implement the program, Mason was brought over to Japan.

The songbooks of the 1880s consisted almost entirely of preexisting Western songs with Japanese texts; of the thirty-three songs in the first volume (1881), only two were newly composed, neither of which was truly in a Japanese mode.[2] Texts addressed nature, famous places in Japan, and historical topics as well as the Confucian values of loyalty to the emperor, filial piety, and advancement through study. One such song was "Kazoe uta" (Counting Song, from the 1887 collection).

Adapted from a *warabeuta* (traditional Japanese children's song), the first verse of Isawa's version reminded children to be grateful to their parents. Disseminated widely by the Ministry of Education, these songbooks contributed to Japanese familiarity with Western music—and established a pattern of inculcation through music.

By the time the Ministry of Education released its next set of songbooks, Japan had emerged as a world power, having defeated imperial China in the first Sino-Japanese War (1894–1895) and czarist Russia in the Russo-Japanese War (1904–1905). Accordingly, the songbooks of 1910–1915 included texts of a more militaristic tone than the 1880s songbooks. In "Suishiei no kaiken" (Meeting at Shuishiying), an account of Russian Major-General Stoessel's surrender to Japanese General Nogi at Port Arthur (1905), Nogi says that his two sons were honored to die in battle; "Tachibana Chūsa" (Lt. Colonel Tachibana) and "Hirose Chūsa" (Commander Hirose) recount the deaths in battle of two heroes of the Russo-Japanese War. Meanwhile, the rewritten verses to "Counting Song" taught children that loyalty to the emperor and the country was their first priority. All the music in the Ministry of Education songbooks of the 1910s (except "Counting Song") was composed anew by Japanese musicians in Western scales, featuring the regular phrase structure, use of motives, and hierarchical cadences of German songwriting. Practically all schoolchildren from first to sixth grades between 1911 and 1941 sang these songs, which were also heard outside the classroom in homes, concerts, playgrounds, and on radio broadcasts.

In 1932–1933, the Ministry of Education issued small revisions to these collections. These years were volatile ones: Japan's invasion of Manchuria (1931) and the Shanghai Incident (1932) marked the beginning of protracted hostilities in China that some historians call the Fifteen-Year War. Right-wing naval officers assassinated Prime Minister Inukai (1932), which helped to precipitate a breakdown in party politics and increased military influence in government. The addition of the song "Heitai-san" (Soldiers), which taught second graders to admire soldiers, was a harbinger of dramatic changes to come.

THE WARTIME PROPAGANDA MACHINE

As the conflict in China that had begun in Manchuria erupted into the second Sino-Japanese War in 1937, the Japanese military government took control over the media. The Ministries of Foreign Affairs and Communications established the *Dōmei Tsūshin* newswire service in 1936, which controlled news distribution to newspapers and radio stations. By 1937, newspaper articles on military actions or diplomacy needed prior approval, and the government shut down smaller papers. Censored by the Defense Bureau, popular magazines valorized overseas expansion, told tales of battlefield heroics, and upheld the belief in Japan's unique national polity. The government also set up movie theaters to show propaganda films, while curtailing the distribution of foreign movies. The Ministry of Communications oversaw the content of radio programs, which was filled with *gunka* military marches. Koyama Eizō (1899–1983), the propaganda mastermind in the Cabinet Planning Agency, noted that music could be an effective means of propaganda (Kushner 2006: 33).

Gunka: The Predominant Music

Gunka (military marches) had been played since military brass bands were formed in the mid-1800s. The popularity of *gunka* rose with the Sino-Japanese War and the Russo-Japanese War. By the second Sino-Japanese War in 1937, *gunka* proliferated the Japanese soundscape, due to not only government control of communications but also growth in the diffusion of radios and phonographs. Many *gunka* were hit records, selling hundreds of thousands—and sometimes millions—of copies. As shortages in materials became more severe after 1941, record production was sharply curtailed, leaving *gunka* over the radio as one of few entertainment choices available.

Some *gunka* were effective in co-opting the people because they were perceived to have come from their own ranks. To produce new *gunka*, contests were held, inviting residents throughout the Japanese empire to submit lyrics and music. In October 1937, the Cabinet Information Office advertised such a contest to write the lyrics to a march that, "the people will love to sing for eternity." Lyrics by a young printing worker in Tottori prefecture were chosen out of 57,578 entries. Another contest was held for the music; the *gunka* composer Setoguchi Tokichi won out of 9,555 entries (Kindaichi 1979: 232). With six record companies releasing different versions, "Aikoku kōshin kyoku" (March of Patriotism, 1937) sold more than one million copies. The lyrics stirred pride in Japan, described the emperor's mission as the establishment of a "just" peace (an "ideal blooming like a fragrant flower"), called "*hakkō ichiyu*"—a slogan, translated as "universal brotherhood," which referred to the Greater East Co-Prosperity Sphere, where Japan would lead an Asian bloc independent from Western powers.

Songs such as these were sung at send-off ceremonies when soldiers were going to the front. Schoolchildren were summoned to participate in these send-offs. My informants Chieko and Naoko remembered parades at which all the schoolchildren and neighbors lined the streets, singing *gunka* and waving Japanese flags (see Web Figure 5.1 ⊙). The diary of Nakane Mihoko, a rural schoolgirl, describes an involved send-off for her teacher: he was first treated to a celebratory meal and a prayer service at the shrine, then sent off at the train station, while schoolchildren and villagers sang *gunka* and shouted "Banzai!" (Long live the emperor!) until the train disappeared (Yamashita 2005: 298–299). Similarly, Saito Keiichi, then a boy in rural Kyoto prefecture, describes saying long prayers at the shrine before sending soldiers off at the train station, singing "Roei no uta" (Song of the Camp, 1937; Saito 2008).

Another ceremony in which students were required to participate was the homecoming of deceased soldiers, called "*mugon no gaisen*" (literally, "silent, triumphant return"). A procession was led by a white banner decorated with *sakaki* (a sacred tree in Shintoism); then came the military men holding an unvarnished box, wrapped in white cloth, which contained the ashes of the deceased, followed by their families. Students, teachers, and neighbors bowed their heads silently as the procession passed by, sometimes playing sad music ("Furusato to sensō" 2007; Oba 1995: 99–101; Saitō 2008).

While both Naoko and Akira said that *gunka* were not sung during academic class time, these songs played a part in school-related activities. Whenever children went on a school outing, they sang *gunka* as they marched. *Gunka* were also sung during assemblies and in the gym during physical training, which often involved military-style drills. As more men were called to war, causing a labor shortage, schoolchildren were made to work at planting tea, potatoes, soybeans, and other foodstuffs; they sang *gunka* or *shōka* as they worked. On an informal basis, these children sang these songs frequently among themselves. Akira said that he usually sang *gunka* on the way to school and on the way home. From third grade onward, he spent time after school with fifth and sixth graders, and these boys sang *gunka* whenever they engaged in group activities or military drill games. Their favorite songs included "Chichi yo, anata wa tsuyokatta" (Father, You Were Strong, 1939), "Getsu getsu ka sui moku kin kin" (Throughout the Week, without Weekends, 1940), "Sora no shinhei" (Paratroopers, 1942), and the Kato Falcon Fighting Corps Song (1943). Chieko and Naoko also sang *gunka* at home, particularly when the lights-out policy at night (to prevent air raids from targeting populated areas) left them with little else to do. With their constant play on the radio and singing by citizens, *gunka* were ubiquitous.

Gunka Texts

Gunka typically address a small number of recurring themes. Most mention the glory of the emperor, the need to follow his will, and pride in Japan, alluding to its divine origins and beauty. Some *gunka*, such as "Getsu getsu ka sui moku kin kin," paint an idealized portrait of male camaraderie in the navy. Most, however, glamorize fighting to the death and are replete with images of death: in "Roei no uta," for example, a fellow soldier dies, smiling as he bids banzai. In "Dōki no sakura" (Cherry Blossoms of the Same Class, 1944), a pilot mourns a classmate who has preceded him in death and looks forward to meeting him again as "cherry blossoms on the same branch in Yasukuni Shrine," where falling cherry blossoms are a metaphor for young soldiers dying in battle[3]; and the Katō Falcon Fighting Song describes Colonel Katō Tateo's death in battle over the Bay of Bengal in 1942.

One *gunka* that became particularly familiar was "Umi yukaba" (Across the Seas, 1937, Web Figures 5.2 ⬤ and 5.3 ◈). Based on a poem by Ōtomo no Yakamochi from the eighth-century poetry collection *Manyōshū*, the best-known version was composed by Nobutoki Kiyoshi to stir fighting spirit, so that soldiers would not fear death to further the emperor's goals. The song was sung at send-off parades and in the announcement of victory at Pearl Harbor. It was officially designated as the second national anthem in 1943. The song came to be strongly associated with honorable deaths, as it was always played at the start of official radio announcements with such news.🔘

> Across the seas, there are corpses in the water.
> Across the mountains, there are corpses in the grass.
> We shall die at the side of our emperor.
> We shall not turn back.

The sources of the recordings and their Japanese texts can be found in Web Figure 5.2 🔘. Recordings of several of the songs discussed can be found on the linked website: "Umi yukaba" (Web Figure 5.3 🔊), "Nippon" (Web Figure 5.4 🔊), "Heitai gokko" (Web Figure 5.5 🔊), "Hotaru koi" (Web Figures 5.6 and 5.7 🔊), "Hikōki" (Web Figure 5.8 🔊).

Music Education in Wartime

While Japanese education had taught children to revere the emperor and admire the war dead since the Meiji Period, the tone of textbooks became increasingly chauvinistic starting in the 1930s. In 1937, the Ministry of Education published *Kokutai no hongi* (Cardinal Principles of National Essence), an official statement of the theory of the Japanese state. The document emphasized the divine origins of the imperial line, the emperor's place as a living deity, and his love for his subjects. Citizens were obliged to cast aside their own wishes and follow the emperor; individualism was explicitly discouraged. The mission of the armed forces was to serve the emperor. The document also addressed the uniqueness of Japanese culture and its superiority to other cultures (Ministry of Education 1937). Widely distributed, it became the basis for educational philosophy during wartime, instilling nationalism with the goal of unifying the population in the military cause (Iritani 1991: 161–167).

In March 1941, the military government issued ordinances to reorganize schools to "conform to the goals of the empire." Schools were to educate students on "the unique aspects of our national culture in relation to conditions in Asia and the world, build awareness of the emperor's position, and cultivate knowledge on the nature of our country" (Cabinet Office 1941). Music was to be taught to inspire nationalism, develop an aesthetic sensibility, teach correct pronunciation, and enhance mental acuity by developing the ability to recall sounds. Lyrics and music were to be "national" (*kokuminteki*) in nature.

The Ministry of Education issued a new set of six songbooks between March 1941 and April 1943 titled *Uta no hon* (Songbook) and *Shotōka ongaku* (Elementary

Music Course). The committee included well-known composers and lyricists of *dōyō* (commercial children's songs with artistic aspirations) and *gunka*, including Komatsu Kōsuke (1884–1966), Hashimoto Kunihiko (1904–1949), Hayashi Ryūha (1892–1974), and Shimofusa Kan'ichi (1898–1962). Several had studied in Europe, including Shimofusa, who had studied with Paul Hindemith in Berlin.

The 1941–1943 songbooks were a substantial rewrite of earlier songbooks, retaining only 17 percent of the songs from these collections. While commercially produced textbooks had been allowed in previous years (as long as the Ministry of Education approved them), all schools in Japan were now obliged to use only these new textbooks. Out of the twenty songs included for each grade, eight were explicitly marked as mandatory. These inflexible requirements made school songs an even more effective means of government propaganda than previously. The instructors' booklets were similarly explicit regarding how and why music was to be taught. First, the purpose of education was to instruct children in the "way of the emperor." The booklets told instructors to "follow the guidelines" and warned against "allowing children to follow their own course"; education was to "form children who will cooperate and work together"—not individuals. In teaching school songs, the goal was "not so much to teach musical capabilities as to inculcate them in national sentiment; that is the real purpose of music education." The primary purpose of song texts was "to ensure the absolute purity of national sentiment and train the people of the Japanese empire" (Ministry of Education 1942a: 15).

TEXTS OF THE 1941 SONGBOOKS

Instilling the National Spirit

The instructor's booklets spelled out the reasons for teaching each song. The most common purpose for a song was to cultivate the "national sentiment." This purpose was met by invoking national symbols (e.g., "Hi no maru," the national flag; "Fuji no yama," Mt. Fuji), old fables ("Momotarō," Peach Boy), and traditional holidays and their customs ("Oshōgatsu," New Year's Day; "Mochitsuki," Pounding Rice Cakes; "Mura matsuri," Village Festival). Several songs whose stated purpose was to "instill the national spirit" were adapted from *warabeuta* (traditional Japanese children's song) or were newly composed, modeled after *warabeuta*. Unlike in previous Ministry of Education songbooks, which tended to take a few stock phrases from *warabeuta*, augment them with more poetic text, and set them to Westernized music, the 1941–1943 collection preserved the original *warabeuta* texts and folk phrases of traditional games. In "Temari uta" (Song of the Handball Game), the opening lyrics, "Ten, ten, ten, Tenjin-sama" (Tenmangū shrine) are common to various regional *warabeuta*, as are the words "Pettan, pettan" (onomatopoeic for pounding rice to make rice cakes), which open "Mochitsuki" (Pounding Rice Cakes). Similarly, the lyrics to "Kakurenbo" (Hide-and-Seek) include the familiar call to potential players, "Kakurenbo suru mono, yottoide" (Those who want to play hide-and-seek, come here) and the repeated call-and-response, "Mō ii kai" (Can I come out now?) and "Mada da yō" (Not yet), all commonly heard among children playing this game. This preservation of the common, folksy language of the *warabeuta* reflected a change in educational policy away from elitism toward a homogenous, everyman orientation; these songs, which may have been considered too lowly for inclusion in previous collections, were being embraced as national expression.

The song texts also addressed the significance of the emperor (e.g., "Mitami ware"), Japan's divine origins ("Kuni hiki," Forming the Country), and the goodness and strength of the country. These sentiments are most clearly expressed in "Nippon" (Japan), a song for second graders. The first verse alludes to the Shinto myth in which the gods created the Japanese archipelago, while the second addresses its superiority to other nations. Instructors were directed to "raise nationalistic spirit and foster patriotic ardor by making the children sing about the national polity of our Japan, for which there is no comparison in the world."

> "Nippon" (Japan, 1941; Web Figures 5.2 ● and 5.4 ●)
> Japan is a good country, a noble country.
> It is the only country in the world that is the country of god.
> Japan is a good country, a strong country.
> It is an admirable country that outshines others in the world. (Ministry of Education 1941b: 129–130)

The Expanding Empire

A corollary of the assumption of Japan's superiority was its right to rule the rest of Asia in the Greater East Co-Prosperity Sphere, which is referenced in the final verse of the "Counting Song." In the first verse of this refitted version, the child is counseled to get up early, wash up, and sweep the yard by him or herself—at a time when most fathers were off to war and/or mothers were needed at munitions factories. In the tenth and final verse, the change in the political environment since 1932 is revealed:

> "Kazoe uta" (1942), Verse 10 (Web Figure 5.9 ●)
> Those who bear the burden
> of protecting Greater East Asia
> are the children of righteous Japan;
> they are we. (Ministry of Education 1942b: 142–143)

In the fifth- and sixth-grade songbooks, songs address the beauties of the acquired territories (e.g., "Dai Tōa," Greater East Asia; "Yōsukō," Yangtze River; "Manshū no hirono," Manchurian Field) and the expanses of Dai Tōa in relation to "god's country" ("Ōyashima"; Ministry of Education 1943a, 1943b).

Related to this purpose of arousing children's interest in the empire are the songs that encourage adventurousness. Some songs address historical incursions and activities in Asia by Japanese ("Momoyama," a period in the late sixteenth century; "Yamada Nagamasa," a seventeenth-century adventurer in Thailand) or contemporary military advances ("Sekidō koete," Crossing the Equator). Subtler are the songs that simply encourage children to look outward. For example, the first grader's song "Umi" (Sea, Web Figure 5.10 ◐) starts by remarking on how big the ocean is and how large the waves are. The last verse is "I want to put a boat in the sea and go to another country." According to the instructor's book, this verse was intended to "express the spirit of the people of Japan as a seafaring country," and the song was to "stimulate interest in maritime affairs" and promote a "cheerful curiosity toward far-away places"—the easier to make subjects go off to conquer new territories (Ministry of Education 1941a: 85–88).

Glorifying the Military

The 1941–1943 songbooks contain a marked increase in the number of songs extolling the military. For all six grades, about thirty-five songs, or 29 percent of the total, explicitly refer to the military; for the fifth and sixth grades, this percentage is 50 percent. This increase is particularly noticeable in the lower grades, in which songs for first and second graders teach them to admire soldiers ("Heitai-san," Soldiers) and take interest in the objects of war ("Gunkan," Battleship; "Hikōki," Airplane). Children were prodded to play war games, pretending to kill devils as "Momotarō," playing with model warships and planes, and participating in mock cavalry battles (Iritani 1991: 178–179); school songs encouraged them to play soldiers in battle in the songs "Heitai gokko" (Role-Playing as Soldiers) and "Omocha no sensha" (Toy Tanks). The lyrics to these songs feature onomatopoeia for the sound of gunfire, as illustrated in "Heitai gokko" (Figure 5.11, Web Figures 5.2 ◐; and 5.5 ◑); as the instructor's book explains in its matter-of-fact way, "'Gata gata' is the sound of machine guns. 'Ban pon' is the sound of firearms" (Ministry of Education 1941a: 131). Words (and their particles or auxiliary verbs) are separated by a "/," while clauses are separated by "//."

From the third grade on up, children sang songs that depicted battles or lauded the role of skilled military men. Several songs also recount heroic deaths in battle: the third-grade song "San yūshi" (Three Brave Soldiers) glorifies three suicide bombers who attacked the camp of the Chinese National Army during the Shanghai Incident of 1932, praising them for their willingness to die for the emperor and their country. Indeed, children were taught that fighting to the death and dying bravely were desired outcomes. The fourth-grade song "Yasukuni Jinja" (Yasukuni Shrine) states, "Even if you die in battle, your loyal, honorable, brave soul will find rest at Yasukuni Shrine," using the metaphor "*hana to chirite*" (sakura leaves blown away). The books contain many songs that glorify the roles that ordinary citizens play in the war, as seen in "Nyū ei" (Joining the Army) and "Shōnen

Figure 5.11: "Heitai gokko" (1941), Shimofusa Kan'ichi.

sensha hei" (Young Soldier of the Tank Unit). Women were expected to contribute to the war effort as well, as seen in "Hakui no tsutome" (The Duty of Nurses). Their primary role, however, was to produce and raise future soldiers, as shown in the fifth-grade song "Haha no uta" (A Song about Mothers; Web Figure 5.12 ⊙):

> Mothers are the strength of the country.
> With a brave heart, she sends her children
> to the battlefield far away.
> Doesn't the mother look brave? (Ministry of Education 1943a: 154–155)

In addition to instilling adoration of the military and heroic acts, the songs aim to cultivate behavior desirable in soldiers. According to descriptions in the instructor's books, about a fifth of all school songs were included to engender feelings of intense loyalty to the country, its emperor, and its rulers. As a third grader, my informant Chieko acted in a play and sang a song about Tajimamori, the legendary court official who sailed to distant lands for ten years in search of the fruit of immortality for Emperor Suinin, only to discover upon his return that the emperor had already died. In addition, about a quarter of the songs were meant to inspire children to be brave, while another quarter was to instill a "cheerful spirit." Since the war effort had led to a shortage of able-bodied men on the home front, children and older students were made to work; the songbooks aimed not only to raise children's spirits about doing various tasks but also to love doing them. The second-grade song "Takigi hiroi" (Collecting Firewood) describes this chore as a cheerful game; in the third-grade song "Kodomo no yaoya" (Children's Greengrocer), three young siblings, whose father has gone off to war, work together to push a heavy cart to the market, in order to purchase stock for their family store.

It is evident that the texts of these 1941–1943 songbooks sought to teach children the belief system desired for waging war effectively: the superiority of Japan, loyalty to the country and its rulers, respect for the military and its heroes, the denial of individual wants to achieve a common goal, and the glorification of heroic deaths. This military-centric vision was instilled from an early age, encouraging children to role-play as soldiers and young teenagers to work in munitions factories, while death in military service was shown as honorable—and probable.

Musical Nationalism in the 1941–1943 Songbooks

Not only the texts but also the music of the 1941–1943 songbooks was nationalistic. This characteristic in part reflected worldwide interest in musical nationalism and exoticism, which had also been extant in Japan since at least the 1920s; some *dōyō* of the 1920s and early 1930s, such as "Tōryanse" (Checkpoint, Motoori Nagayo, 1921), incorporated *warabeuta* in a Westernized harmonic setting. Foreign artists sponsored composers in this syncretic style: the Russian composer and pianist Alexander Tcherepnin (1899–1977) and the Austrian conductor Felix Weingartner (1863–1942) each sponsored competitions for Japanese composers; winners included Ifukube Akira's (1914–2006) *Nihon Kyōshikyoku* (Japanese Rhapsody, 1935) for the former and Hayasaka Fumio's (1914–1955) *Kodai no bukyoku* (Ancient Dances, 1937) for the latter (Galliano 2002: 80–83, 116).

In addition, Japanese government directives served as a powerful incentive to favor a nationalistic musical blend. In 1936, Matsumoto Manabu, the head of the Section for Supreme Control of the Ministry for the Interior, gave a speech favoring music written in Japanese style and stressing the importance of following government guidelines. The government supported musical compositions that expressed nationalist sentiments, often by using Japanese melodies within Western musical forms, and sponsored the recording, publication, and broadcast of such works. After 1938, national broadcaster NHK required commissioned works to express nationalistic sentiments (Galliano 2002: 92, 115–116). At least one composer for the 1941–1943 songbooks, Shimofusa, participated in this trend of musical nationalism, composing works such as *Shamisen kyōsōkyoku* (Shamisen Concerto, 1938) and *Koto dokusō no tame no sonata* (Sonata for Solo Koto, 1941). By 1941, musicians were obliged to apply for special licenses to continue working as musicians and hence comply with government directives. Musicians who were critical of the government were repressed through censorship, raids, and arrests (Galliano 2002: 120). Given government coercion and European approval of this style, it is not surprising that the 1941–1943 songbooks show a high level of musical nationalism.

Comments in the instructors' books for the 1941–1943 songbooks confirm the political intent of musical nationalism. For most of the songs discussed below, the instructor's books explain that by "singing Japanese songs from time immemorial, children will absorb the national spirit."

Traditional Songs

These wartime songbooks are noteworthy for their preservation of *warabeuta*, which had been considered lowly in earlier eras. Unlike the Ministry of Education songbooks of the 1880s and 1910s, which include only the "Counting Song" from the vast repertory of *warabeuta*, the 1941–1943 songbooks include several *warabeuta* and other traditional songs. In previous songbooks by the Ministry of Education, there were several instances in which some lyrics from a *warabeuta* had been taken and refitted

Figure 5.14: "Hotaru koi" (Come, Firefly, 1941), arrangement by Shimofusa, score.

with music in Western European scales. For example, the lyrics to "Chōchō" (Butterfly, 1874) were set to the melody of "Hanschen Klein"/"Lightly Row," while "Yuki" (Snow, 1911) was newly composed with Western harmonies. In contrast, the songs in the 1941–1943 songbooks retained both the texts and melodic outlines of the original *warabeuta*. One such example is "Hotaru koi" (Come, Firefly), an ancient *warabeuta* with many different regional versions that share its characteristic opening. A version from the Yokohama area (Web Figures 5.2 ⦿, 5.6 ◗, and 5.13 ⦿) has a melody that departs to the [B-D] interval in the second phrase (Obara 1994: vol. 1, 153).

In a version from Tottori prefecture, the lyric begins,

> *Ho, ho, hotaru koi.*   Firefly, come here.
> *Chiisana chōchin sagete koi.*   Come here with a small paper lantern.

Shimofusa's arrangement of "Hotaru koi" for the 1941 Ministry of Education song-book (Figure 5.14, Web Figures 5.2 ◗; and 5.7 ⦿) contains the familiar beginning, the melodic contour of the second phrase in the Yokohama version, and the text of the Tottori version (Ministry of Education 1941a: 82–85).

Newly Composed Songs on Japanese Scales

As previously mentioned, several newly composed songs—"Nawatobi" (Jump Rope), "Mochitsuki" (Pounding Rice Cakes), and "Temari uta" (Handball Song)—were inspired by *warabeuta*, with lyrics similar to the songs and chants surrounding these games. These songs were written in traditional scales that approach the sound of *warabeuta*, using traditional Japanese scales—the first time since the 1880s that newly composed songs from the Ministry of Education did not use Western scales. Furthermore, their melodies tended to outline perfect fourths, which is characteristic of traditional Japanese melodies.

Eleven other newly composed songs use Japanese scales, so Japanese scales form the musical basis for twenty-two songs—about a fifth of the collection, a significantly higher percentage than in the more Western-influenced previous collections. Recognizing that most Japanese music teachers had been trained in Western music but not Japanese music, the instructors' books contained explanations of Japanese scales (Ministry of Education 1941a: 15–16).

Harmonization of Traditional Scales

In addition, the accompaniment for most of these songs harmonizes them in a way that does not attempt to force a Western V–I cadence. As shown in "Hotaru koi" (Figure 5.14), some songs are harmonized using only the pitch sets in the traditional modes of their melodies, often beginning and ending with unisons or open fifths. Several songs in yō mode [C–D–F–G–B♭] are harmonized as if they were in Dorian; as for songs in miyako-bushi [E–F–A–B–C], "Sakura" is set as if in A minor, while "Usagi" and "Temari uta" are set in Phrygian mode. With the use of Japanese scales in such a large group of songs and accompaniments that do not impose the Western tonal paradigms, the songs retain their modal qualities while remaining within the Western practice of harmony-oriented ensembles. Hence, these songs express nationalism in a musical manner not evident in previous collections.

Songs in Western Pentatonic Scales

About 40 percent of the songs in the 1941–1943 collections are in Western pentatonic scales (i.e., [C–D–E–G–A] or [C–D–E♭–G–A♭]). However, unlike earlier collections, in which pentatonic melodies strongly imply a Western tonality through melodic patterns (such as the melodic descent 3-2-1 to the tonic or arpeggiated triads), many songs in the 1941–1943 songbooks emphasize outlines of the perfect fourth characteristic in Japanese melodies. About half of the songs in a Western pentatonic scale exhibit this pattern.

An example of a song with a Western pentatonic scale and a melody constructed around perfect fourths is "Hikōki" (Airplane, Figure 5.15, Web Figures 5.8 ◐; and 5.2 ◎), a first graders' song intended to "awaken and develop interest in airplanes and flying" (Ministry of Education 1941a: 136). The melody is entirely constructed out of a series of perfect-fourth spans, as shown in brackets. While ostensibly in C major, the song has no 3-2-1 descent; instead, the tonic is approached from scale degree 5 (G) or 6 (A) below, as in many of the gagaku-based hoiku shōka.

Between their use of revised traditional songs, traditional scales, and pentatonic melodies outlining the perfect fourth, about 40 percent of the songs in the

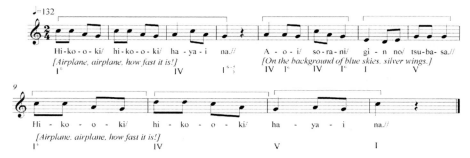

Figure 5.15: "Hikōki" (Airplanes, 1941), score.

1941–1943 songbooks have a melody reminiscent of a traditional Japanese one—a much higher percentage than in earlier collections, which are more Western in nature. In particular, close to 60 percent of the songs for the first through third grades in the 1941–1943 songbooks have melodies of a Japanese quality. They contributed to notions of "Japanese-sounding" music—which, as in postwar *enka*, is more syncretic than traditional Japanese music.

Children's Experiences with Singing in School

The instructors' guidelines recommended that children be taught music for four hours a week in first grade, five hours for second grade, and two hours a week in subsequent grades; Naoko remembered the music classes taking up about three hours each week. The teachers—a singer and a pianist—taught the children to sing by ear, first performing the songs and then having children imitate them. Children were expected to memorize these songs and sing them from memory in later classes. In some schools, songs were sung at assemblies or school concerts, but these performances appear to have become rarer as the war progressed; Naoko was picked to sing at a regional choral contest, but it was cancelled as wartime conditions worsened.

Nearly sixty years later, Naoko still recalled many school songs that were subsequently banned: the militaristic songs, such as "Dai Tōa," "Nippon," "Gunken Tone" (Tone, the Army Dog), "Shōnen sensha hei," and "Gunkan"; the older songs about war heroes, such as "Suishihei no kaikan" and "Hirose Chūsa"; and the lament-like "Mugon no gaisen" and "Hakui no tsutome." As she explained, "Having learned everything by ear and sung them repeatedly, we remembered these songs easily. We didn't feel that we were being forced to learn them" (Naoko, interview by the author, Yokohama, January 2010).

Naoko said that the music teachers simply wrote the lyrics on the board without explaining their meaning. "We just sang them lightheartedly. It wasn't the same seriousness with which we had to memorize the emperor's words." Thus, she claimed the songs did not have much impact on her thinking later in life (Naoko 2010). However, in several cases, the song texts were taken straight off the pages of the mandatory reading textbooks and hence required little additional explanation.

Therefore, these songs were reinforcing lessons already taught elsewhere in the curriculum—Japan's superiority, duty to the emperor, glorification of the military and the war dead—through the recreational act of singing.

POSTWAR DEVELOPMENTS AND
THE WARTIME LEGACY

Japan's defeat in World War II and the ensuing allied occupation (1945–1951) brought about a profound change in its ideological landscape. With the emperor forced to reject the State Shinto claim that he was an incarnate divinity, seventy of its cities reduced to rubble through American firebombing campaigns, and a quarter of its wealth destroyed, the people were suddenly told to accept defeat and occupation by the former enemy, so that the nation could rebuild itself. The hands of censorship and propaganda shifted from the Japanese military government to the supreme command for the allied powers, who employed many of the same propagandists as the wartime government, including Koyama Eizō. These men used the same mechanisms that galvanized the Japanese to fight to the death, to unify them for the purposes of rebuilding the country (Kushner 2006: 180).

The musical landscape changed too: the Far East Network Radio, operated by the US Armed Forces, invaded the airwaves, and American and British popular music, which had been banned during the war, was heard again on the radio and in bars and dance halls catering to occupation soldiers. Meanwhile, the *gunka* that had played a key role in the propaganda machine was no longer heard, and children were severely punished for singing *gunka* or the more ideological school songs (Akira, interview by the author, Yokohama, January 2010). This turn was also seen in the educational realm, where, as Chieko remarked, "Our teachers told us that everything they'd taught us was wrong, but there was nothing to replace the vacuum" (Chieko, interview by the author, Philadelphia, November 2009). Students were instructed to strike out, in black ink, those texts and songs that occupation officials regarded as militaristic or overly nationalistic or that referred to Shintoism.

In 1947, the *Kyōiku kihon hō* (Fundamental Law of Education) decreed that schools were to be remodeled according to the American system, with the purpose of shaping children into citizens of a peaceful, democratic nation. That same year, the Ministry of Education issued its last set of national music textbooks. Many songs from previous collections were excluded because their texts were perceived as nationalistic. Lyrics to other songs were changed; for example, in "Hi no maru" (Japanese Flag), a song for first graders, the description of the flag was changed from "heroic" (*isamashii*) in the 1941 version to "beautiful" (*utsukushii*) in the 1947 version. Militaristic texts were replaced with texts that emphasize cheerfulness, cooperation, and getting along with others; frequently occurring words in these songs include *nakayoku* (get along), *niko niko* (smiling), *tanoshii* (enjoyable), *ureshii* (happy), and *iiko* (good boy/girl). These changes are apparent in the 1947 version of "Counting Song" (Web Figure 5.16 🔊), in which the second verse, which regards physical fitness, has been changed to eliminate the patriotic imperative:

> "Kazoe uta," 1942, second verse, last two lines
> Become a person, a national subject,
> who is useful to the nation. (Ministry of Education 1942b: 142–143)

> "Kazoe uta," 1947, second verse, last two lines
> Always smile;
> be cheerful and energetic. (Ministry of Education 1947: 46–47)

The final verse, which had been about Japan's right to rule in East Asia in 1942, was changed to a message of "study hard, and let your learning accumulate with time."

The 1947 songbooks also signaled a reversal of the trend toward a musical Japanese identity that had taken place since the early 1900s. While the 1911, 1932, and 1941 collections of the Ministry of Education had consisted completely of songs composed by Japanese, about half of the songs in the 1947 collection were translations of Western songs with mostly Western scales, just as they had dominated Isawa's textbooks in the 1880s. Such a reversal—a rejection of things Japanese—seemed natural in the early postwar years, when poverty, displacement, and malnutrition were still rampant. Many among the disillusioned population wanted to turn away from "Japanese" culture: "I didn't like Japan. Rather, I wanted to learn about Western styles and culture" (Chieko 2009). Indeed, 1947 also saw the beginning of the postwar boom in Japanese popular songs based on the American boogie-woogie rhythm, beginning with Hattori Ryōichi's "Tokyo Boogie-Woogie."

Even with such sentiments, however, an egg cannot be unscrambled; given how pervasive wartime propaganda was in the schools and media, and how impressionable most children would have been, it would seem likely that these childhood teachings somehow affected the way these children thought as adults. The propaganda machine may have been reinvented to promote cooperation with Americans, but the apparatus they used—radio, print media, popular culture, music, the education system—were the same as in wartime. To achieve their goals of unifying the people for reconstruction, the propagandists played on the same social ideologies that they had employed during the war and that had been familiar lessons in Japanese schools since the Meiji Period: the uniqueness (and superiority) of Japanese culture, loyalty to a superior, and the need to work for the common good or the Japanese nation. These ideologies fit well with the project of reconstruction and fed seamlessly into the rapid economic growth of the 1950s–1980s, powered by employees who sacrificed personal lives to work long hours for a single company.

Hence, the children that grew up during the war internalized these values and acted upon them as adults; they also passed it on to their own children. As an adult, Chieko, along with her husband and two elementary school daughters, moved from Japan to the United States, where they were the only Japanese family in their school. She impressed upon her daughters that the family "represented Japan" to their American neighbors, requiring them to uphold the highest standards of behavior and achievement—lest the Americans consider them, and Japan more generally, to be backward. And her daughters—in collecting the high grades, school prizes, and recognition for community works that she encouraged them to obtain—demonstrated those values of discipline and hard work that Chieko had been taught in those school songs and that she passed on to the next generation.

ACKNOWLEDGMENT

Research for this chapter was funded by a fellowship from SSRC/JSPS. I thank Professor Hosokawa Shūhei and the staff at the Nichibunken and National Diet Libraries for their help in collecting materials. This chapter was originally written as part of my doctoral dissertation; I thank my committee—Professors Peter Manuel, William Rothstein, Mark Spicer, and Jane Sugarman—for their comments. I thank my CUNY colleagues Becky O'Donoghue and Andrew Pau for recording these songs. I thank my mother, uncles, and late aunt for their insights and encouragement.

NOTES

1 Manabe (2009) provides a description of the texts and music of school songs from 1877 to 1947.
2 Recordings of all school songs published by the Ministry of Education between 1881 and 1947 are available on Yamato (2000). The collection also includes a book with a short historical explanation and facsimiles of the songbooks.
3 The pilot is expecting an honorable death for himself, so that both classmates, as war dead, would be enshrined in Yasukuni Shrine. The song was a favorite of kamikaze pilots (Yamashita 2005: 232).

REFERENCES

"Furusato to sensō" [Our Hometown during Wartime]. 2007. *Furusato Isa fūdo shi* [Natural and Spiritual Features of Our Hometown, Isa, Kyoto Prefecture]. Accessed June 1, 2010. http://www15.ocn.ne.jp/~f-isa/kijio8.htm.
Cabinet Office. 1941. "Kokumin gakkō rei" [Ordinance Regarding National Schools, Edict No. 148]. Main building-3A-032-05, Monbu 02397100–051, National Archives of Japan.

Eppstein, Ury. 1994. *The Beginnings of Western Music in Meiji Era Japan*. Studies in the History and Interpretation of Music. Vol. 44. Lewiston, NY: E. Mellen Press.

Galliano, Luciana. 2002. *Yōgaku: Japanese Music in the Twentieth Century*. Lanham, MD: Scarecrow Press.

Iritani, Toshio. 1991. *Group Psychology of the Japanese in Wartime*. New York: Kegan Paul International.

Kindaichi, Haruhiko, and Anzai Aiko, eds. 1977. *Nihon no shōka: meiji hen* [Japanese School Songs: Meiji Period]. Tokyo: Kōdansha.

Kindaichi, Haruhiko, and Anzai Aiko, eds. 1979. *Nihon no shōka chū: taishō shōwa hen* [Japanese School Songs: Taisho and Showa Periods]. Tokyo: Kōdansha.

Kindaichi, Haruhiko, and Anzai Aiko, eds. 1982. *Nihon no shōka: Gakuseika, gunka, shūkyōka hen* [Japanese School Songs: Alma Maters, War Songs, and Hymns]. Tokyo: Kōdansha.

Kushner, Barak. 2006. *The Thought War: Japanese Imperial Propaganda*. Honolulu: University of Hawaii Press.

Manabe, Noriko. 2009. "Western Music in Japan: The Evolution of Styles in Children's Songs, Hip-Hop, and Other Genres." PhD diss., City University of New York.

Ministry of Education. 1937. *Kokutai no hongi* [The National Polity]. Tokyo: Ministry of Education. Accessed June 2, 2010. http://www.j-texts.com/showa/kokutaiah.html.

Ministry of Education. 1941a. *Uta no hon, kyōshiyō, jō* [First Grade Instructor's Book]. Tokyo: Ministry of Education.

Ministry of Education. 1941b. *Uta no hon, kyōshiyō, ge* [Second Grade Instructor's Book]. Tokyo: Ministry of Education.

Ministry of Education. 1942a. *Shotōka ongaku, kyōshiyō*. Vol. 1 [Third Grade Instructor's Book]. Tokyo: Ministry of Education.

Ministry of Education. 1942b. *Shotōka ongaku, kyōshiyō*. Vol. 2 [Fourth Grade Instructor's Book]. Tokyo: Ministry of Education.

Ministry of Education. 1943a. *Shotōka ongaku, kyōshiyō*. Vol. 3 [Fifth Grade Instructor's Book]. Tokyo: Ministry of Education.

Ministry of Education. 1943b. *Shotōka ongaku, kyōshiyō*. Vol. 4 [Sixth Grade Instructor's Book]. Tokyo: Ministry of Education.

Ministry of Education. 1947. *Yonensei no ongaku* [Fourth Grade Songs]. Tokyo: Ministry of Education.

National Archives of Japan. 1941. "Kokumin gakkō rei ga seitei sareru" [The National Schools Ordinance Is Established]. Accessed July 24, 2009. http://www.archives.go.jp/ayumi/kobetsu/s16_1941_01.html.

Oba, Junko. 1995. "From *Miya-san, Miya-san* to *Subaru*: The Transformation of Japanese War Songs from 1868 to Today." Masters thesis, Wesleyan University.

Obara, Akio, ed. 1994. *Nihon no warabeuta*. Kyoto: Yanagihara Shoten.

Saito, Kiichi. 2008. "Tango no densetsu" [Stories of Tango, Northern Kyoto Prefecture]. Accessed June 1, 2010. http://www.geocities.jp/k_saito_site/bunkn33.html.

Yamashita, Samuel Hideo. 2005. *Leaves from an Autumn of Emergencies: Selections from the Wartime Diaries of Ordinary Japanese*. Honolulu: University of Hawaii Press.

Yamato, Junji, ed. 2000. *Monbusho shōka shūsei: sono hensen o otte* [Collection of Songs from the Ministry of Education: Regarding Their Changes]. Tokyo: Nippon Columbia.

6

GIRLHOOD SONGS, MUSICAL TALES, AND MUSICAL GAMES AS STRATEGIES FOR SOCIALIZATION INTO WOMANHOOD AMONG THE BAGANDA OF UGANDA

SYLVIA NANNYONGA-TAMUSUZA

It was Saturday, and so the girls did not go to school. They had done all the day's gardening and had just returned from the well to fetch water, which was one of their routine daily chores. Watching and listening from a distance, I could see and hear Namuyanja, a ten-year-old girl excitedly giving instructions for the *Kibugga* musical game to her young sister and girlfriends from the neighborhood. "We should make two lines facing each other," she instructed. As I approached them, silence covered the whole place. "Which line should I join?" I asked. Amid loud laughter, an eight-year-old girl responded, "This is for children, not for big people." I was reminded that while children may participate in some musical activities with adults, there are musical activities that children claim to be theirs alone.

As it is with many cultures in Africa, music and play are part and parcel of children's life among the Baganda, the people of Buganda, formerly a powerful and dominant kingdom in central Uganda.[1] In fact, children's songs and musical tales and games[2] contribute to children's socialization[3] into adulthood, including an understanding of gender roles, which are determined the day one is born and are nurtured throughout one's life. For instance, a girl is enculturated into the ways of a woman—her expected adult gender-influenced role—through the games she plays, the tales she tells (and is told), and the songs she sings (see Blacking 1967; Gaunt 2006). Although socialization into the gender role begins at birth, the ages between seven and twelve—a period of girlhood (*obuwala*) that occurs just before the onset of menstruation—are crucial in initiating girls into their future as submissive wives and mothers. The Baganda consider menstruation one of the rituals for graduating a girl into womanhood from the age when she develops the potential to give birth.

In this chapter, I examine how the processes of creating, learning, and performing, as well as the embodied meanings of girlhood songs and musical tales and games, contribute to the socialization of rural Baganda girls into womanhood. Since these songs, tales, and games are not created and performed in isolation from social and cultural processes that create girlhood, there is a need to examine the cultural and social structures that inform the socialization process of girls in rural Buganda to contextualize this discussion. Change is happening in rural Buganda, although more slowly than in towns, so "rural" does not refer to sites of traditional, unchanging cultural practices. The majority of the Baganda live in a rural environment, but through technology, the gap between rural and urban in the Buganda region is narrowing. Since the liberation of the media in 1990s, most of rural Buganda has had access to radio and television as well as telephone networks, which enables people to access mass media information—including that which pertains to gender roles. A difficulty is that the supply of electric power is limited in rural Buganda, undermining open access to the media, so most families have to be selective about what they listen to and watch because of the cost of batteries.

GIRLHOOD SOCIALIZATION
INTO WOMANHOOD

As gender is a social behavior, it is learned (Havighurst and Davis 1943), and society uses all means (including songs, tales, and games) to ensure that its people learn acceptable gender behavior. Historically, Baganda children were socialized through the imitation of their peers as well as adults. To some extent, interactions between children have also played a role in their socialization process. According to gender constructionist theorists, socialization is not "solely private internalization of adult skills and knowledge" (Corsaro and Eder 1990: 199). While the Baganda adults consider it their responsibility to socialize girls and produce adult women who are submissive wives and mothers (see Thorne 2008: 3), some girls may contest this ascribed gendering, but discussion of this is beyond the scope of this chapter.

Of course, boys are also socialized into their adult gender role. Gender socialization is a relational experience in which the socialization of boys, for instance, reinforces the socialization of girls and vice versa. This participation is also evident in many girlhood songs and musical tales and games. Similarly, as Michael A. Messner has noted, "sometimes, children engage in 'relaxed, cross sex play'; other times—for instance, on the playground during boys' ritual invasions of girls' spaces and games" (2000: 765).

In Buganda, as in most cultures of Africa, cultural socialization into womanhood and manhood is an ongoing process, beginning when a child is born. Indeed, the Baganda have a proverb: "If you try to straighten a grown plant, which did not germinate properly, it breaks." This is understood as meaning that what you want the child to be in the future, you must train it to be when it is still young.

The socialization of a baby girl is centered on her growth into a submissive wife and mother. The identity titles and names she is given, the songs sung to her and those that she sings, the roles she is assigned, and the proverbs and sayings used in reference to her (see Walser 1982), as well as the training she receives from her parents, all support this socialization. A baby girl is generically called *ggannemeredde* meaning "I have failed and produced a failure." This title denotes weakness, powerlessness, and total failure. A baby girl is socialized into a sense of weakness, lacking power, and in need of support from men. In order to reinforce this girl socialization, a baby boy is titled *naatuukirira* (perfect child). The Baganda consider the boy more important because, in this patriarchal society, he is the one assigned to continue the family line. Moreover, most of the girls' names begin with *nna,* a feminine prefix, while boys' names usually begin with *sse,* a masculine prefix, and one can immediately tell that a person is a female or a male by the name. The syllable *nna* refers to *bugonvu* (softness), while *sse* means *busukkulumu* (powerfulness). The boys are socialized not to be emotional, as it is considered "womanish," while the expected and desirable behavior for girls is to cry. In fact, if a bride does not cry during the final blessings of her parents before she is taken to the groom, she will often be told frightening things or even pricked so that she will cry.

From seven to twelve years, before menstruation, a baby girl graduates into girlhood, *obuwala*; reference to a girl at this age is *omuwala* (*abawala,* pl.), from the verb *okuwala* (to clear, to remove, to cleanse). It also relates to *nakawala,* the tutelary deity that is believed to have the power to clear all problems in a home and guide the girl into submissiveness (Nannyonga-Tamusuza 2005: 116–117). This socialization stage is crucial, as it is the time when the girl's submissiveness must be entrenched.

Among the rural Baganda, child socialization is still mostly communal since all members of the community know and depend on each other. As such, the child belongs to the community, although the family, as the smallest unit of the community, is the major player in introducing the child to the adult world. Socialization in the family involves parents, siblings, and extended family members, especially the grandmother (*jjajja*) and paternal aunt (*ssenga*). Mothers train their girls mostly in home chores. Grandmothers are usually less strict and rarely punish their grandchildren so are often closer to them than their parents, so that parents consider grandmothers as the "spoilers of children." Because of this closeness, grandmothers are usually the teachers of songs and folktales, and yet children do not simply imitate the grandmothers but use their own creativity in developing them further.

The *ssenga* is charged with the role of socializing her nieces "in the art of becoming 'good' and subservient wives" (Tamale 2005: 16), who must satisfy the sexual desires of their husbands; if a wife does not satisfy the sexual desires of her husband, the *ssenga* is always to blame. As Sylvia Tamale has noted, "A husband who was dissatisfied with his bride's behavior, particularly her 'bedroom etiquette', would blame it on the laxity of her *Ssenga*, even returning the bride to the *Ssenga* for 'proper' training" (2005: 17). Although sexual matters are core to the training of a girl into the gendered role of wife and mother, public and direct talk about sex is considered immoral and generally not acceptable among the Baganda. The *ssenga* is exempt from this taboo; she is offered "cultural immunity" (Nannyonga-Tamusuza 2005: 136). Her advice on sexual matters is masked in metaphors, symbols, and idiomatic language (Tamale 2005). The *ssenga* also instructs the girl in *okukyalira ensiko* (visiting the bush) where a ritual takes place, "which involve[s] a procedure of stretching or elongating her inner labia [minora]" (Tamale 2005: 16–17) before she begins menstruation. Between nine and twelve years, a girl is thought to be ready to prepare her genitals for a successful sexual life, a requirement for one to become a "proper woman." In addition, the herbs (e.g., *kibugga mukasa, entengotengo, and luwoko*) used in this ritual are gathered from the bush. A Muganda woman who does not perform this ritual is "traditionally despised and regarded as having a 'pit'" (Sengendo and Sekatawa, quoted in Tamale 2005: 26). She is regarded as having "no door" to keep her "warm" and one who serves "cold" food (food being a metaphor for sex). Besides preparing the girl for her adult sexual role, the girl is trained for motherhood, as it is believed that childbirth is a result of a successful sexual life. Usually, a mother expects her daughter to play with dolls from age seven and even reinforces this by crafting dolls from banana fibers. She also teaches the girl lullabies to sing to her baby doll. It is also at this stage that a girl child begins to care for her siblings.

While the family and the immediate neighborhood community make up the major socialization context for the majority of rural girls, school education—introduced in the early twentieth century—challenges the community socialization to some extent. Until the early 1980s, it was considered sufficient for a girl to have only primary education, as parents were concerned that their girls married at the "right time." Since the mid-1980s, more girls began to acquire secondary education, and in

1992, Makerere University—the only university at the time—introduced a scheme to increase the number of female students admitted to the university. As a result, the number of women with a university education has increased, and during the sixtieth graduation of 2010, women constituted 52 percent of the graduates at Makerere University. As Deborah Kasente has reported, the introduction of Universal Primary Education (UPE) in 1996 "increased enrolment of both boys and girls aged between 6 and 12 years even among the very poor" (quoted in Kendrick and Jones 2008: 378). Through this the girls are exposed to intercultural school socialization, which brings into question some of the *ssenga's* training, especially the woman's submissiveness and the man's dominance. Girls spend more time at school than at home, and some attend school even during holidays. Attending school has also resulted in girls marrying later, with a majority of girls marrying at age eighteen or later, compared to the common practice of young marriages at fourteen years before the introduction of school education. However, the girls' school attendance, especially in rural areas, is still lagging behind that of boys, with a high dropout rate due to pregnancies and parents forcing their children into marriage before completing school.

As elsewhere in the world, the media has become an influential agent for socializing children. Consequently, Baganda girls are no longer simply imitating and reproducing Kiganda womanhood; rather they are gradually becoming "part of adult culture and contribute to its reproduction through their negotiations with adults and their creative production of a series of peer cultures with other children" (Corsaro 1990: 201). While the school and media have informed the Baganda's gendered ideologies in the twenty-first century, the community socialization of girls still takes an upper hand since a girl is still considered an adult only when she is married and has children. The *ssenga* can still check on the girls by phone when she is not able to make frequent visits.

KIGANDA CHILDREN'S MUSICAL CULTURE

The Baganda have a rich "children's musical culture," to use John Blacking's term (1967: 196). As Patricia Shehan Campbell has noted, "For children, music is a natural inclination, and it often appears to be as essential to their well-being as it is for them to be warm, fed, and well rested" (2002: 57). Among the Baganda, singing, dancing, costuming, storytelling, and acting are never separated in children's musical culture; children's games and tales are sung, acted, and costumed, while songs are acted out, danced, and sung.

While there is no strict categorization of songs and folktales that girls and boys perform, girls tend to perform particular songs and folktales to a greater extent than boys (see Minks 2002: 385–390); for example, it is common for girls to know and perform more lullabies than boys. Of course, this is not to suggest that boys do not know lullabies. In fact, boys sing lullabies to tease girls when they fail to soothe a baby (rather than singing a lullaby themselves to a crying baby). Boys laughed when I asked them to sing a lullaby and one said, "It is women who sing to babies, you cannot ask us to sing those songs!" There is a tendency for parents to restrict girls' participation in games; so a girl is usually not allowed to play ball or ride a bicycle. These kinds of games are believed to interfere with the virginity of the girls, who must keep it for their future husbands (Tamale 2005). In addition, the folktales told to girls—which of course become part of the repertoire of tales they will also tell other children—emphasize their socialization into "proper" and "true" women.

Composing is often integrated with performance, so children create new songs as well as recreating those originally composed by adults. In most cases, children learn songs and folktales from their grandmothers (Ssekamwa 1995: viii). However, Blacking reminds us that children are not mere copycats of adult musical culture, unable to create their own tales, games, and songs (1967; see also Kartomi 1980: 209). Instead, as Campbell has also noted, when performing these songs, children

> "tamper" with what they have witnessed but also adhere to its essence, ascertaining that it remains substantially the same as they had first perceived it....Children are prone to playing with the components of music in order to make them fit their expressive needs, yet they are also anchored to the values and practices of the adults who raise them. (2002: 58; see also Lew and Campbell 2005: 57–58)

As such, while the general essence of the song, game, and storyline of the folktales are kept, there are as many renditions of these songs, games, and tales as there are children performing them.

Children's creativity often transcends cultural boundaries, and a number of children's songs, games, and folktales are acculturations from both within and outside Uganda. Baganda children borrow mainly from Banyankole, Batooro, Banyoro (all from western Uganda), and Basoga (from eastern Uganda). The languages from these ethnic groups are components of the Bantu language family, as is Luganda, the language of the Baganda. "Kaleeba," a song from a folktale, combines the languages of the Banyoro, Batooro, and Banyankole in its text.

We know that "children actively create their own culture as well as affecting the adult cultures around them. Children's culture participates in, but is not entirely composed of, the material adults create for children's consumption" (Woodson 2007: 923). While Blacking (1967) argued that children have a musical culture of their own, to some extent they are certainly influenced by adult music (Lew and Campbell 2005: 57–58; Minks 2002: 391). Although the music of Baganda children may be simpler, their songs are based on the same call-and-response forms as adults, and only lullabies do not follow this pattern. The major difference between children's music and that of the adults is in the vocal style, namely *ggono* (a vocal style characterized by a blend of nasal and throaty singing with vibrato), which is adopted by adults. Children's music is also more limited metrically and usually felt in either duple or quadruple time.

Since the 1960s, children have been seen more as performers in adult musical spaces, especially when music and dance from the different cultures of Uganda were introduced into the school curriculum. Music and dance, including those of

the Baganda, became part of the school curriculum as one of the postcolonial projects for the renaissance of indigenous cultures that followed the independence of
Uganda from the British in 1962 (Hanna and Hanna 1968). Children (especially age
ten and up), perform adult music in school music and dance competitions, including
ritual music and dances of weddings, funerals, twin initiations, and ancestral worship ceremonies. However, as creativity is permitted, competitions become contexts
for redefining the performance the practice of adult music (Nannyonga-Tamusuza
2003). For example, when an adult Muganda sings a song in *baakisimba* style[4], she
or he will adapt the *ggono* style of singing, whereas a twelve-year-old is still too
young to accomplish this style.

There has been an assumption that children's musical culture is about mere
fun and entertainment and that children's expressed culture plays no "serious"
role. However, as J. C. Ssekamwa reminds us, children's folktales (and songs and
games) hold hidden philosophies (*amagezi ameekusifu*) of the Baganda (1995: vii).
Children's songs, folktales, and games can be serious education and a medium for
the communication of cultural values for a particular group of people, whether they
be children or adults (see Mans 2002: 72; Senkoro 2005: 1). As Minette Mans has
also noted, "Through play, young children are educated not only in relationships
of their societies with all their ambiguities and inconsistencies. Music and play can
be described as aspects of education for socialization" (2002: 72). Songs may be
a greater socialization force than normal language because "thoughts, ideas, feelings and comments which cannot be stated in normal language situations are more
readily expressed, thus offering kinds of information that are not otherwise easily
accessible" (Egblewogbe, quoted in Silver 2001: 53). Further, songs, games, and stories enhance socialization because they are friendlier ways of transmitting rules of
moral behavior (McQuown 1982, quoted in Silver 2001: 54).

As Campbell contends, "Music functions in children's lives as a means of linking
them to their cultural heritage and reflecting the values of their ethnic culture" (1998:
177). Accepted cultural behavior is communicated through the characters in the songs,
the meaning of the text, the contexts of song performance, and performance roles (see
Wallace 1994). However, meaning is not fixed in children's tales, songs, and games;
instead, it is assigned by both the creators of the songs and by their audiences. Music
as sound does not in itself inherit meaning. As such, meaning in children's songs, tales,
and games is fluid depending on who is constructing it and the intended purpose.

As mentioned, the Baganda are very careful not to speak vulgar language in
public and especially before children; they use symbolic, metaphoric, and idiomatic language ("dress-up words") when referring to sexual matters. Words used for
agricultural tools and activities related to growing, preparing, and eating food are
used as metaphors and symbols in communicating gendered content in children's
folktales, games, and songs. As Tamale has observed, "Such coded communications about sexuality are decipherable by women and other adults, but hidden from
children and outsiders" (2005: 20–21). As such, these songs are multivocal, communicating meaning at multiple levels, and in most cases the children do not comprehend the messages relating to sex. At this age, children are what Jeanne Klein has

called "'concrete' (literal) processors, who focus on seeing the explicit visual images and hearing the explicit verbal dialogue presented to them" (2005: 46).

Then the question is how do these games, songs, and folktales socialize girls into women when the language used is supposed to be inaccessible to them? The Baganda believe that a repeated performance enhances memory and supports behavioral change. While children may not understand the meaning of these songs, games, and tales during their childhood, when they are of age and in need of this metaphorically dressed information, they will remember it. In fact, the Baganda have a saying: "*Addingana amawolu y'agajamu omukkuto*" (One who revisits leftover food is eventually satisfied). Similarly, music has been found to significantly improve the recall of that information, explaining why teachers use nursery rhymes in early learning.

LULLABIES, SONGS, MUSICAL TALES, AND MUSICAL GAMES IN THE CONSTRUCTION OF WOMANHOOD

While school is an important space where children learn and perform music (and most studies on children's music have focused on school music education), the community constitutes the most important site for rural Baganda children to be socialized into womanhood and manhood. Songs performed in the community, as opposed to those in schools, are the focus of this discussion. Typically, there are as many renditions of these tales, games, and lullabies as there are children performing them, so I will examine just one example. The musical transcriptions come with all the usual caveats, and I aim only to give a visual representation of the sung melodies.

From as early as seven years old, Namusisi took care of Buyungo, her five-month-old brother. Namusisi told me that her mother always left her with the baby whenever she went to the gardens or to fetch water from the well. Namusisi recalled that "sometimes the baby cries so much that I also begin to cry [she laughs at herself]. However, many times, I sing some of the songs that I hear my mother sing and he stops crying." Namusisi sang to me a lullaby titled "Mwana wa Nnyabo Weesirikire" (My Mother's Baby, Do Not Cry).

Mwana wa nnyabo weesirikire	My mother's baby, do not cry
Kyenaalyako naakuterekera	Whatever I will eat, I will share with you
Baa, akaliga kanywa taba	Baa, the lamb has smoked tobacco

As girls like Namusisi perform lullabies to the babies, they too are being enculturated into their futures as mothers. From girlhood, they grow up knowing that the responsibility of providing food to children, as well as to the entire family, rests on the mother. In the lullaby, the girl is repeating her future role as the mother and food provider.

Figure 6.1: "Omwana Akaaba" (The Child Is Crying).

Indeed, Sylvia Tamale has noted, "Traditional folklore, lullabies and children's songs also provide useful metaphorical models to mediate sexuality messages among Baganda women" (2005: 22). While the apparent role of lullabies is to soothe a crying baby, some lullabies are occasions for mothers to release their marriage stresses or joys. Girls preparing for marriage are always told by their mothers and *ssenga* not to speak out on "things of the home" and that "a man is never to be answered back." Since the mother is with the child most of the time, the child becomes her audience, even when it is very young, silent, and perhaps not able to comprehend the words. F. E. M. K. Senkoro has also noted that a lullaby can be "a way of talking to oneself, where mothers would like to have silent sympathies of their children regarding their adult grievances" (2005: 2). However, as Senkoro also noted, these lullabies "do not mean to have the attention of their children regarding the actual contents of the lullabies.... [The music is] meant for one audience (children) and contents for another audience (husbands/ayahs)" (2005: 2).

An example of such lullabies is "Omwana Akaaba" (The Child Is Crying), as shown in Figure 6.1.

Omwana akaaba	The child is crying
Akaabira ki?	What is it crying for?
Akaabira ebbeere	It is crying for the breast
Bamuwe ku bbeere	Let it be given the breast
Ebbeere ddwadde	The breast is sick
Bamufumbire ka chai	They should prepare it some tea
Ebbinika mbotofu	The kettle has a hole [so it is leaking]

While this lullaby has all the musical characteristics of a lullaby, including short texts and repetitive short melodies that attract the child's attention and soothe him or her, it also contains other deeper meanings for an adult audience. One adult Muganda woman explained to me that the "crying child" is a metaphor for the man desiring to have sex and the breast is a metaphor for the sex. The leaking kettle refers to the wife who is in menstruation and therefore cannot satisfy the man's sexual desires.

Children's Musical Tales of Girlhood

In a culture in which writing was only imported in the late nineteenth century, folktales in Buganda were passed on from one generation to the other. While these tales do not offer precise factual chronologies of Buganda, they offer some explanation and legitimization of the present. The popular folktale of Kintu, told to a girl child, and its connection to the genealogy of Buganda has always been used to justify the submissive position of women in Buganda (Nannyonga-Tamusuza 2009). According to the tale, Kintu, the first man on the earth, married Nambi, who brought death to the earth because she disobeyed the rules of the land (Kaggwa 1951: 1).

Like other children's folklore, folktales do not exist in isolation but are integrated with arts that include dancing, acting, singing, and costuming. Songs are performed at the end of a folktale or may be interludes (or even preludes). Most children agree that singing makes the tales more interesting and enables them to be remembered. Storytelling in Buganda involves active participation, and children are not passive receptors of information. Instead, they react to folktales, recreate them, and adapt them to their needs.

Usually, human personalities are presented metaphorically in folktales. Animals, birds, trees, or even agricultural tools may be made to act or speak like humans. Generally, most folktales that feature real human beings as characters may begin thus, "Once upon a time, there was a man who married his wife and they gave birth to their children." Such an opening is a reminder that only heterosexual relationships are acceptable and expected when a child becomes an adult. As Senkoro has observed, through folktales, the socialization process can be presented through metaphors that manipulate various symbols to represent the society's acceptable behavior for one "to graduate into adulthood in his or her community" (2005: 1). In one such storytelling session, a twelve-year-old girl named Nakitto narrated the tale of Njabala to her siblings and neighborhood children.

Nakitto opened the tale with the phrase, "Once upon a time." The other children responded in chorus, "Our friend, go ahead." Nakitto continued with various gestures that helped to enact the story:

> There was a man who married his wife and they gave birth to a very beautiful girl called Njabala. However, Njabala's mother spoiled her; she did not teach her how to cook, dig, wash dishes, and take care of the home. Then it so happened that Njabala's mother died. After the mother died, Njabala got married. Njabala's husband was a farmer. Since Njabala did not know how to do any housework, she was always in trouble with her husband. Whenever Njabala's husband returned from the garden, he found no food, no water, and all the dishes were not done. Moreover, whenever Njabala went to the gardens, she would simply sit down. The husband got fed up and threatened to chase Njabala away. My dear, Njabala became very unhappy and one day, when she went to the gardens, Njabala began crying out to her dead mother.
>
> One day, the mother's ghost came and taught her how to dig through a song. Nakitto then commenced to sing the song "Njabala Njabala" as in Figure 6.2.

Figure 6.2: "Njabala Njabala."

Njabala Njabala Njabala	Njabala, Njabala, Njabala
Toli nsanza omuko	You should never make me meet my son in-law
Abakazi balima bati	Women dig like this
Nebatema nebawala	They chop and clear [with a hoe]
Olusuku balusalira	They trim and prune the banana plantation
N'ebinyeebwa babisekula	They also pound the groundnuts

Nakitto repeated the song, and the children then joined her, singing the chorus, "*Njabala Toli nsanza muko.*" At the end of the repetition, Nakitto interrupted and continued the tale.

> By the end of the song, the ghost of Njabala's mother had cleared the weed and pruned the banana plantation. When Njabala's husband came to the plantation, he was impressed by his wife. One day, a malicious person told Njabala's husband that he always saw a ghost singing and digging while Njabala was looking on. One day, Njabala's husband hid behind a big tree and saw Njabala's ghost mother digging while singing. Njabala's husband was very furious. I left when he had chased away Njabala and I came here to tell you this story.

All the children understood the literal meaning of this tale. One girl explained how "it teaches us to learn how to cook, to dig, to wash plates and [do] all [the] chores of the house." Indeed, this corresponds to the observation that "from her earliest years the girl is taught the correct way to hoe, to prune, to weed, to rotate the crops, to peel, and to prepare the food" (Ann 1940: 26). One young boy interpreted the Njabala tale this way: "Girls must be clean. Even if the man is dirty, the woman [wife] must be clean. She must clean the man and the home." Another girl affirmed his interpretation: "Yes, we the women must make sure that the men are clean." Still another girl added, "If you do not take care of the home, the man can throw you out of his house. Therefore, we should not allow our mothers to spoil us."

This tale has other deeper metaphorical meanings, too. For instance, the "trimming and pruning of the banana plantation" refers to the cleaning and shaving around the female genitals. To "dig" is a metaphor for having sex and to "chop," relates to movement during sex. To "pound" the groundnuts is another metaphor for having sex. Sylvia Tamale has noted, "The sexual symbolism of mortar and pestle is universal, with the...(pestle) signifying an erect phallus and...(pounding) referring to the rhythmic movements of sexual intercourse" (2005: 22). While the children may not understand the symbolism at an early age, the message becomes clear when a young woman marries.

SOCIALIZING THE GIRL THROUGH MUSICAL GAMES

The kinds of games that girls participate in are restricted and must conform to their ascribed roles as mothers and food providers. As noted earlier, when girls come of age, they "visit the bush." In reminding those who are due for the ritual and as a way of sharing experiences of those who have successfully completed the ritual, girls perform a musical game called *Kibugga* (which is also the name of one of the herbs used to elongate the labia minora). Often girls are very shy when adult women are watching them play *Kibugga*. When I asked why they did not want me to participate in the musical game, the girls remarked that the game was not meant for adults. When popular musician Halima Namakula adapted the *Kibugga* for her Afro-beat song, many adult Baganda protested at its being broadcast on television. They claimed that it was not appropriate for public performance. While the children may not know precisely why *Kibugga* should not be performed in public, they heed the advice of adults to keep the game private among themselves.

Kibugga is performed in two parallel lines that face each other, the girls kneeling and bending forward, bracing themselves with their arms on the floor. Looking at each other, they push their backs in and out. The best performer is the one who makes this movement vigorously while singing the *Kibugga* song.

Kibugga tombutulabutula   *Kibugga* do not bring me a rash
Kibugga ombutula bulungi *Kibugga* bring me a good rash
Kibugga tonkutulakutula   *Kibugga* do not tear me [badly]
Kibugga onkutula bulungi   *Kibugga* tear me well

Although the girls seemed to have enjoyed the game, none of them could speak of its meaning, which I then sought from adults. *Kibugga* is a "person" with whom girls could interact in learning the use of the herb in order to fulfill the ritual. The movement of the back in and out imitates the sexual act, whose performance is only acceptable after successfully completing this ritual. The Baganda believe that a girl who has performed this ritual successfully is bound to be successful in her marriage because she will satisfy her husband sexually.

While most times girls play games together, there are a number of games they play together with the boys. One such game is *Kyekunkuna*, the name of the main male character. In this game, there are three characters: women (wives), man (husband), and the *kabaka* (king). The game revolves around a man who is complaining to the *kabaka* about his wife, who neglects her roles. She prepares half-cooked and burnt food and sometimes serves him raw food, so he requests another wife.

There are different versions of the choreography of *Kyekunkuna*. One version begins with a big circle, depending on the number of children participating in the game, and the "king" squats in the center. A "husband" is chosen by consensus, usually one with a loud voice. The husband leads the song, pointing to a girl he accuses of being his "bad wife." His singing is dramatized as he moves to articulate his predicament and to look for a new "wife." The "bad" wife is quiet and only uses hand gestures to reject the accusations (see Figure 6.3).

Kyekunkuna	Kyekunkuna
Balijja	They will come
Ng'ekiriga	like a sheep
Ekiriga ekito	a lamb
Ekyokuttale	one that lives at the grazing hill
Ssebo Kabaka	Dear Sir, the King
Omukazi gwewampa	The woman you gave me
Tanfumbira	She does not cook for me
Afumba ewunye	She cooks burnt food
Afumba mbisi	She cooks raw food
Afumba ekonye	She prepares half-cooked food
Neefumbira	I cook for myself
Neewaatira	I peel for myself
Tolaba enjala	Don't you see my nails?
Tolaba engalo	Don't you see her fingers?
Mpa omulala	Give me another one

Then, the king offers the husband another "wife," while the rejected wife is ridiculed. In order to prolong the game, the husband rejects a number of wives, awaiting "the right wife." As a celebration, the king is lifted high in thanks for his wisdom, as shown in Figure 6.4.

Children have many interpretations of this game, and some are offered here. One boy remarked, "That game teaches girls to cook. Although boys should learn

Figure 6.3: Children playing the *Kyekunkuna* game.

how to cook, cooking is a job for girls. Indeed, it is mothers that cook at home." A girl interrupted, "Yes, our daddies do not know how to cook. They only boil water for tea." Three other boys explained, "My father has to wait for my mother to come back. In fact, when our mother is not at home, we have no cooked food." "The game teaches boys how to choose the right wives, those who know how to cook and take care of us." "Yes, it teaches us to look for girls that can do the work because it is [up to] the men to look for money and women should care for the home."

From interviews with the girls, it was clear that this game aims to create fear in girls, that if they serve burnt and half-cooked food, they will be returned to their parents. Through this game, the girls are told that cooking is their role and they have to serve well-cooked food for the security of their position in a marriage.

Figure 6.4: The king lifted high at the end of the game.

On another level, a "lamb" symbolizes a newly married man who is less experienced in sexual matters (a man who is impotent is referred to as *endiga,* a sheep). To "cook raw food" refers to a woman who does not prepare her husband well before sex (foreplay). Tamale writes that a woman who "burns the cooking pot" is one "who is not adequately lubricated" (2005: 21).

CONCLUSION

It is evident that children's folklore among the Baganda is not mere entertainment or fun. There are deep-seated meanings in their lore, which serves to socialize the children—and in this case, socialize girls into their roles as adult women. Of course, this is not to suggest that there are no other players in this socialization process. Metaphoric, symbolic, and idiomatic language; girlhood lullabies; and musical tales and games are sites where gendered information, which would not otherwise be communicated in public, is "dressed up" to communicate a discourse that is otherwise only acceptable in private. Although the girls may not understand the gendered private discourse, repeated performance of girlhood songs, tales, and games enhances memorization and storage of this information to be used at a later stage, when the girls get married. Indeed, children's music is important in the socialization of girls into womanhood and the life of a Baganda wife and mother.

NOTES

1 Muganda is singular for Baganda, and Kiganda denotes that which belongs to the Baganda.
2 Musical tales and games are those enhanced by singing or/and dancing.
3 In this discussion, socialization will refer to the ongoing process through which an individual learns the cultures, values, and norms of his or her society (see also Havighurst and Davis 1943: 29).
4 *Baakisimba* is a music and dance genre, as well as a name of a drum and a drum set, and its music is characterized by compound duple time.

REFERENCES

Ann, Mother M. O. S. F. 1940. "Notes on the Preparation of Food in Buganda." *Primitive Man* 13 (1): 26–28.
Blacking, John. 1967. *Venda Children's Songs: A Study in Ethnomusicological Analysis.* Johannesburg: Witwatersrand University Press.
Campbell, Patricia Shehan. 1998. *Songs in Their Heads: Music and Its Meanings in Children's Lives.* New York: Oxford University Press.

Campbell, Patricia Shehan. 2002. "The Musical Cultures of Children." In *The Arts in Children's Lives,* edited by L. Bresler and C. M. Thompson, 57–69. Netherlands: Kluwer Academic.

Corsaro, William A., and Donna Eder. 1990. "Children's Peer Culture." *Annual Review of Sociology* 16: 197–220.

Gaunt, Kyra D. 2006. *The Games Black Girls Play: Learning the Ropes from Double-Dutch to Hip-Hop.* New York: New York University Press.

Hanna, Lynne Judith, and William John Hanna. 1968. "Heart Beat of Africa." *African Art* 1 (3): 42–45, 85.

Havighurst, Robert J., and Allison Davis. 1943. "Child Socialization and the School." *Review of Educational Research* 13 (1): 29–37.

Kaggwa, Apolo. [1902] 1951. *Engero Za Baganda.* [The Stories of the Baganda]. London: Sheldon Press.

Kartomi, Margaret. 1980. "Childlikeness in Play Songs: A Case Study among the Pitjantjara at Yalata, South Australia." *Miscellanea Musicologica* (11): 172–214.

Kendrick, Maureen, and Shelley Jones. 2008. "Girls' Visual Representations of Literacy in A Rural Ugandan Community." *Canadian Journal of Education* 31 (2): 371–404.

Klein, Jeanne. 2005. "From Children's Perspectives: A Model of Aesthetic Processing in Theatre." *Journal of Aesthetic Education* 39 (4): 40–57.

Lew, Jackie Chooi-Theng, and, Patricia Shehan Campbell. 2005. "Children's Natural and Necessary Musical Play: Global Contexts, Local Applications." *Music Educators Journal* 91 (5): 57–62.

Mans, Minette. 2002. "Playing the Music: Comparing Performance of Children's Song and Dance in Traditional and Contemporary Namibian Education." In *The Arts in Children's Lives,* edited by L. Bresler and C. M. Thompson, 71–86. Netherlands: Kluwer Academic.

Messner, Michael A. 2000. "Barbie Girls versus Sea Monsters: Children Constructing Gender." *Gender and Society* 14 (6): 765–784.

Minks, Amanda. 2002. "From Children's Song to Expressive Practices: Old and New Directions in the Ethnomusicological Study of Children." *Ethnomusicology* 46 (3): 379–408.

Nannyonga-Tamusuza, Sylvia. 2003. "Competitions in School Festivals: A Process of: Re-Inventing Baakisimba Music and Dance of the Baganda (Uganda)." *World Music* 45 (1): 97–118.

Nannyonga-Tamusuza, Sylvia. 2005. *Baakisimba: Gender in Music and Dance of the Baganda People of Uganda.* London: Routledge.

Nannyonga-Tamusuza, Sylvia. 2009. "Female-Men, Male-Women and Others: Constructing and Negotiating Gender among the Baganda of Uganda." *Journal of Eastern African Studies* 3 (2): 367–380.

Senkoro, F. E. M. K. 2005. "Understanding Gender through Genre: Oral Literature as a Vehicle for Gender Studies in East Africa." In *Gender, Literature and Religion in Africa,* edited by Elizabeth Le Roux, Mildred A. J. Ndeda, and George Nyamndi, 5–24. Gender Series, vol. 4. Dakar: Codesria.

Silver, David. 2001. "Songs and Storytelling: Bringing Health Messages to Life in Uganda." *Education For Health* 14 (1): 51–60.

Ssekamwa, J. C. 1995. *Ebisoko n'Engero Ez'Amakulu Amakusike* [Idioms and Folktales with Their Metaphoric Meanings]. Kampala: Fountain Publishers.

Tamale, Sylvia. 2005. "Eroticism, Sensuality and 'Women's Secrets' among the
Baganda: A Critical Analysis." In "Sexual Cultures," edited by Amina Mama,
Charmaine Pereira, and Takyiwaa Manuh, special issue, *Feminist Africa* 5: 9–36.

Thorne, Barrie. 2008. *Gender Play: Girls and Boys in Schools.* New Brunswick, NJ:
Rutgers University Press.

Wallace, W. T. 1994. "Memory for Music: Effect of Melody on Recall of Text." *Journal
of Experimental Psychology: Learning, Memory, and Cognition* 20 (6): 1471–1485.

Woodson, Stephani Etheridge. 2007. "Children's Culture and Mimesis:
Representations, Rubrics, and Research." In *International Handbook of Research
in Arts Education,* edited by Liora Bresler, Dordrecht, the Netherlands: Springer,
923–938.

7

MUSICAL CULTURES OF GIRLS IN THE BRAZILIAN AMAZON

BEATRIZ ILARI

Sou o que não foi, o que vai ficar calado. Sei que agora é tarde, e temo abreviar com a vida, nos rasos do mundo. Mas, então, ao menos, que, no artigo da morte, peguem em mim, e me depositem também numa canoinha de nada, nessa água que não pára, de longas beiras: e, eu, rio abaixo, rio a fora, rio a dentro—o rio.

I am what never was—the unspeakable. I know it is too late for salvation now, but I am afraid to cut life short in the shallows of the world. At least, when death comes to my body, let them take me and put me in a wretched little canoe, and on the water that flows forever past its unending banks, let me go—down the river, away from the river, into the river—the river. (João Guimarães Rosa 1968: 36)

WITH these words, João Guimarães Rosa ends his short story "The Third Bank of the River" in which the narrator tells the story of his father, who, at a certain point in time, leaves the family to lead a solitary life on the banks of a river. Although fictitious, this story is well known in Brazil, not only for Guimarães Rosa's poetic command of Brazilian Portuguese but also for his unique perspective on the lives of people who have been nearly forgotten, due to isolation, poverty, or particular lifestyles. Guimarães Rosa knew too well the importance of the flowing waters of a river for the populations that live on its banks and immortalized it in many of his literary texts. Apart from fiction, in everyday life rivers have equally marked the lives of human beings across time and culture. For populations living in the Amazonian floodplains, rivers have been a source of imagination, seduction, and fear. They are the equivalent of a street for urban people—a sort of mirror that reflects their collective identity (Fraxe 2004).

In the Amazon, countless musical practices that both influence and characterize the lives of its inhabitants in unique ways are camouflaged by the flowing waters of its rivers. Geographical isolation and difficult access to its communities may explain why this happens. As Anthony Seeger (2008) contended, the music of the tropical forest region of South America is possibly one of the least known in the world. Although Seeger was primarily referring to the music of Amerindian societies, this seems to hold true also in the case of *populações riberinhas,* or riverine populations, living in the Amazon region. It is important to note that the term "riverine" has been used by Brazilian scholars and journalists as both a noun and an adjective to describe those populations of various races and ethnicities that live on the banks of its rivers and tributaries as well as their lifestyles and culture (Fraxe 2004).

This chapter presents the musical world of a riverine girl living on the banks of the Quianduba River in the Lower Tocantins territory, state of Pará, in the Brazilian Amazon. I adopted an ethnographic posture (Wolcott 1992), as there was not enough time for a full ethnographic account. Methods and tools from ethnography such as participant observation, field notes, and recordings of unstructured interviews and musical practices were used to document and capture meanings associated with the musical practices of children and adults. Learning about and documenting the lived experiences of riverine girls brought an awareness of the invisibility of children's musical cultures in the country. It also challenged some assumptions, including the widespread stereotypical perception that many Brazilians hold of riverine populations.

Riverine Identities

The Brazilian Amazon has been represented in diverse ways (Slater 2001). Urban, non-Amazonians often describe it in terms of the exuberance of its natural ecosystems, rich biodiversity, and traditional populations that still survive in the area (Lobo et al. 2009). Yet many are surprised by the fact that about 70 percent of Amazonians reside in urban centers (IBGE 2000). Populations living in the forest or in floodplains are a minority, and their lives continue to go rather undocumented (Lobo et al. 2009). Riverine populations living in the Amazon are an example of what Dimenstein (2005) called "nearly invisible Brazilians," or humans whose lives are ignored or forgotten by the governing authorities who have virtually no say in most important political and socioeconomic decisions. There are many reasons that might explain their invisibility, and these stem from legal, economic, and geographical to cultural factors.

The lives of riverine populations in the Amazon continue to be represented by many myths and misconceptions (Lima 1999). The small number of studies conducted to date does not alleviate this situation, although there are some exceptions, such as Gillingham's (2001) study of sustainable development in an Amazonian riverine community. Important as they are, study themes are also to blame. For example, the continuous focus on infectious diseases (Silva 2009), disadvantaged child growth in relationship to urban children (Silva and Crew 2006), and mercury contamination and/or tropical diseases (e.g., Crompton et al. 2002) continue to portray this group as both homogeneous and stereotyped. Fortunately, recent studies are helping to paint a more updated picture to challenge these stereotypes, as they confirm that riverine populations in the Brazilian Amazon continue to lead their lives in an environment of subsistence extraction and lack of electricity and basic sanitation, with limited access to education and health services (Mendes et al. 2008). Fishing and harvesting the açaí berry continue to be the main activities that fill both their economical and their nutritional needs (Siqueira 2009), as well as pottery and brickworks in specific communities (Monteiro and Ribeiro 2004).

As in many other traditional societies, riverine children take part in many activities in preparation for adulthood (Lancy 2008). Children typically help their parents early in life, and the types of chores they do are linked to their age and gender (Siqueira 2009). As they mature, many riverine youth experience a lack of opportunities, a problem that is common across the national territory. Novaes (2007) has argued that, in general, the lives of underprivileged youth in Brazil are marked by an "exclusion by address" and fears of dying young and being left out and disconnected in a connected world. In a country where childhood and youth are polysemic terms (Del Priore 2002), the combination of inequities and discrimination gives origin to different degrees of vulnerability (Novaes 2007). In the specific case of riverine youth, rural exodus is a main concern, especially in the case of girls and young women (Siqueira 2009). A recent study also suggests that riverine communities are at risk for alcohol and drug abuse and teenage pregnancy (Ford Foundation 2009). These are some contextual issues that affect the lives of riverine populations, who are often called *caboclos* (Fraxe 2004).

The *Caboclo*

Growing up in Brazil, many middle-class school-aged children learn, for example, that the mixture of white Europeans and Amerindians gave origin to the *caboclo*. Schoolbooks commonly portray rural populations in the Amazon as *caboclos*, stressing that many of them live on riverbanks (Silva and Crews 2003). Yet, the definition of *caboclo* is far more complex. As Lima (1999) suggests, the term *caboclo* refers not only to an oversimplistic classification in a traditional racial system but also to a particular lifestyle that has been looked down upon since colonial times.

It also refers to a social categorization system that is seldom used by *caboclos* themselves, as it is an etic construction but not an emic consideration.

According to Nugent (2009), *caboclos* have been negatively depicted in the anthropological literature due to their subsistence lifestyle. There is a myth that the Amazon is supposedly rich and abundant in resources that are easily accessible and that *caboclos* do not take advantage of this because they are supposedly "lazy by nature" (Nugent 2009). Likewise, the richness of Amazonian mythology has helped to create a stereotypical view of the *caboclo* as an "exotic creature" (see Fraxe 2004). Furthermore, different social groups living in the Amazon (i.e., *caboclos*, Amerindians, settlers) have been defined accordingly to ecological systems. While *caboclos* are described as the ones who live in floodplains, Amerindians and settlers are typically said to be located in uplands (Castro 2009). Yet, as Castro suggests, to define a *caboclo* one needs to balance both social and ecological categories, as these give origin to many variations. *Caboclo* is a sociopolitically loaded term, so, in this chapter, the more generic term "riverine" is employed. The focus here is turned to the influences of the river on the lives of individuals and not on a social categorization system.

LIFE ON THE SHORES OF THE QUIANDUBA RIVER

The riverine girls and women that informed the present chapter lived in the state of Pará, which is the second largest Brazilian state. It covers nearly 1,250,000 km², with a population approaching 7.5 million (IBGE 2009). In 2003 poverty levels reached approximately 45 percent of the total state population (IBGE 2003). Six main rivers (Amazonas, Pará, Tapajós, Tocantins, Xingu, and Jari) run through the state of Pará. Abaetetuba is a port city located in the lower Tocantins territory, with an estimated 139,819 inhabitants (IBGE 2009). There are seventy-five islands surrounding the city. From Abaetetuba, a motorboat ride of approximately one hour and a half leads to the Quianduba River. Although no official estimates concerning demography on the shores of the Quianduba River were found, Monteiro and Ribeiro (2004) estimated that 400 families (or approximately 2,800 people) were living in the area in 2004.

Life on the shores of the Quianduba River is demanding for children and adults alike. Everyday activities consist of a combination of school and domestic chores (Ford Foundation 2008). Swimming and rowing are considered essential for survival, and children usually learn to row during toddlerhood. Some boys are already working on the harvest of the açaí berry by the age of five, at first accompanied by an adult and later unaccompanied. Others begin to work at an early age in brickyards, as the region of Abaetetuba is well known for its bricks (Monteiro and Ribeiro 2005; Rodrigues et al. 2010). Girls tend to devote more time to domestic chores.

Time to play is scarce for both boys and girls and, according to a recent study (Ford Foundation 2008), play is but a dream for many working children. Yet, in their moments of leisure, children and adolescents play soccer and attend dance parties or festivities centered on specific Catholic saints, organized by members of their community (Ford Foundation 2008).

As in other Amazonian riverine communities (Mendes et al. 2008; Siqueira 2009), access to formal schooling is challenging for many children and adolescents of the Quianduba River. When I visited the region, the closest school was a public, multiseries (mixed class) elementary school. At the time, there was no secondary school in the community. Children and parents pointed out many problems associated with the school, including a lack of well-trained teachers, materials, and work conditions, as reported in previous studies (Ford Foundation 2008, 2009). Another problem for many children was the large distance between the school and the home. Although there were both public and private means of water transport, not all children had access to it. Furthermore, adolescents wishing to continue on with their studies had to find ways to attend secondary schools in Abaetetuba, and many could not afford it. School dropouts caused by economic exigencies were said to be common in many families (see Siqueira 2009).

Such problems, however, have not prevented riverine children and adolescents from wishing for facilities like a health center in the community, treated water, electricity, access to computers and technology, a library, a better equipped school, a university, transportation to school, safety, love, and peace for all (Ford Foundation 2009). In many of my conversations with girls like Teresa Cristina, I heard descriptions of the desire to visit places and "see the world"; indeed, she led me into an exploration of her musical world.

It is important to note that in spite of being an outsider to the visited community, my local Brazilian perspective and knowledge certainly brought many advantages to the data collection, such as the ability to communicate with children and adults in Brazilian Portuguese as well as my knowledge of Amazonian mythologies and lifestyle. This was helpful when attempting to grasp inherent meanings implicit in metaphors found in song lyrics, field observations, and interview data. However, I am fully aware of the limitations of my participation and understand that the text presented here represents the perspectives of a southeastern, urban, middle-class, nonriverine music educator (see Stock 2004). That is, I take full responsibility for the descriptions presented as well as their subsequent interpretations.

My Music, My World: A Conversation with Teresa Cristina

Teresa Cristina, or Cris as she is known in the community, is singing this song[1] (Figure 7.1) as she watches her friends swim in the river. Her light colored eyes contrast with her overtanned skin. While she sings, motorboats pass by as well as little canoes with children in charge (see Figure 7.2). Other children are diving and splashing in their clothes in the not-so-shallow waters of the Quianduba River. As

Es - se rio   é mi - nha   ru - a   mi - nha.e tu - a Mu - ru - ré.

— Pi-so no pei-to__ da lu - a   dei-to no chão da__ ma - ré.___

Figure 7.1: Notation: excerpt from "This River Is My Street."

my mind wanders across the scenery, I suddenly notice that Cris is not the only one being watched. She is also watching me:

"They dry up quickly," she says, interrupting her singing.

I laugh, embarrassed to see that she notices my surprise at the presence of fully dressed bathers. I ask her about the song that she was singing, and Cris explains that it was written by Ruy Barata, a Paraense composer. This is an "adult song" that she loves because it talks about her homeland along the river and the lifestyles of those who live there. Born in Abaetetuba, Cris spent almost her entire life on the shores of the Quianduba River. She tells me about her life and dreams. As we speak, we sometimes hear music coming from local boats, and the sounds quickly distort as they rise up in the air. Cris explains that (battery-operated) radios are the most common music-playing devices found in the area. Although there is no TV in her house (or in the neighboring wooden houses), Cris talks a lot about her love for Banda Calypso, a pop group that mixes northern and northeastern Brazilian genres with Caribbean rhythms. She talks at length about the band, the leading singer, the outfits, the CDs, and the performances. The conversation changes its focus to her favorite songs, first by Banda Calypso, then by other genres and styles. Then,

Figure 7.2: Girls rowing in the Quianduba River.

we proceed into a conversation about the music she is learning from Monica and Norberto, two university students who teach local musical traditions to children from the Quianduba River community.

> C: We learn lots of songs. We play them in the recorder first and then we go to the other instruments. And she [Monica] says that we should not make fun of those who cannot do it, that we should go slowly. Each one learns a little bit at a time. I like to learn music because sometime soon we will go places to perform.
> B: And what kind of music do you learn with Monica?
> C: *Asa Branca, A canoa virou*. Many songs.
> B: So would you sing me one of these songs?

I expect to hear a song learned in the cultural group. Instead, Cris sings a religious song (Web Figure 7.3 ⭕) in the rhythm of a Portuguese *vira*.[2]

> B: Where do you sing this song?
> C: I sing it in school and in church.
> B: And where did you learn it?
> C: From my mom. We sing it on Saturdays when we go to Catechism.
> B: Do you like to sing?
> C: Yes, I think it is a beautiful thing. When we sing, we go to many places. My dream is to become a great singer, to have my own band.
> B: And what will you sing with your band?
> C: All types of music.
> B: From the Cordão da Saracura as well?
> C: Yup.
> B: And what does Cordão da Saracura mean?
> C: It is a bird [a crane]. There are some here. It is like a hen. There are the trees, the Indians. There is Iara [a sort of siren that seduces men with her chant to later drown them], the *Curupira* [a dwarf with feet that are turned backward, who protects the forest], the *cobra grande* [big snake or anaconda]. There is the shaman and the *penico furado*.
> B: *Penico furado*? I don't know this one.
> C: Let me see how I can explain this to you. It is ... the shaman's assistant.
> B: And what about the *cobra grande*? It is a legend, right?
> C: Yes. There were three children [rowing] in quiet waters. When they looked there were some waves, very big like this [gestures]. So when they looked, they saw the big monster. The children rowed and rowed, screamed, asked for help, but no one heard them. And the big snake swallowed them. It [the *cobra grande*] exists 'til this day. She does. She lives in Abaetetuba. You have to be careful when you go there.
> C: There is also the Boto [river dolphin]. He is an animal. He lives in the deep waters of the ocean. He likes blond ladies. When there is a party, he dresses in white and puts on a hat because people say that he has a hole on his head—they say. Then he puts on his white hat and when he arrives at the party and sees a blond lady, he enchants her, he takes her to the bottom of the ocean.
> B: Are there Botos around here?
> C: Yup.
> B: Have you ever seen one?
> [João, Cris's younger brother, who is now out of the water, jumps in the conversation.]
> J: Yeah, remember that day when we were watching the game? He came here.

Figure 7.4: Notation for the Boto preto song.

B: Came here? And you were not scared? I guess not, since you are not a blond girl, right?

[Everybody laughs.]

B: Wow. So many different stories. And are there songs about them?

C: Yes, there is the song of the Boto, the *cobra grande*, the *Curupira*, Iara.
   Cris sings the Boto song.[3] (Figure 7.4)

B: What a beautiful song.

C: And there is another one, about Tia Fuloca. She gets pregnant with twenty-two children plus one. There is Tia Fuloca and her husband. And she wishes to eat the *Saracura* [the crane], so her husband fetches one for her.

Cris interrupts the story and sings the song (Web Figure 7.5 **O**),[4] praising the river and the local culture.

C: And, of course, there is the song about the *Saracura* (Figure 7.6).[5]

Figure 7.6: Notation for the Saracura song.

As she sings, the boys watch us from a distance. Cris's body is moving sideways in a choreographic motion accompanied by some impressive facial expressions. Suddenly, our names are called out. It is lunchtime and we rush inside the house. Huge amounts of açaí berries, cured meat, and manioc flour are offered, as if in a feast. Once we are done eating, Cris asks her father to tell us a story. We all head out to the dock and gather around him. Soon there are about twelve children, sitting or lying on the warm silt and listening attentively to the storyteller. The stories are about enchanted creatures that live in the forest: the Boto, Matinta Perê [a sort of Amazonian witch that whistles], the *Curupira*. At one point, the storyteller asks all children to hush and points in the distance. I am puzzled. Cris whispers in my ear, "Do you hear that whistle? It is Iara..."

LEARNING MUSIC, EXPRESSING ONESELF, AND PERPETUATING TRADITIONS

My conversation with Cris attests to the idea that music can serve as a response to very particular, complex environments. Through music she not only expresses her lifestyle but also shows a sense of pride about it—something that Monica, her teacher and mentor, is very keen to encourage. I later learn that all but the Pentecostal song[6] were learned in the context of the Cordão da Saracura, a cultural group led by Monica and Norberto Rios, our local guides, who aim to keep alive and transmit to others the traditional legends, stories, and musical practices of the region. The term "Cordão da Saracura" has two meanings here: it depicts the name of the cultural group led by Monica and Nelson, and it relates to the more general Cordão de Pássaros, a unique burlesque dramatic-musical genre that was very common in Belém and its surroundings in the late nineteenth century (Braga 2004). In both cases, the association with music and song is a central one. Interestingly, the transmission of songs in this context followed a feminine lineage. Monica learned the original *Saracura* song from Dona Nina Abreu, a respected artisan, composer, and musical leader from Abaetetuba. Later on, she taught it to Cris and other girls in the group. Yet some modifications were made to Dona Nina's original song, including changes in tonality and lyrics. In the last two verses, where Cris sang, "But nowadays TV imposes on us...." Dona Nina[7] sang "The animals singing with their loved ones, from far ahead we could hear the *quiricó* [onomatopoeic sounds, like cuckoo]." So the song became intentionally more political when it was handed down from one generation to another. There was an implicit circle of knowledge that was transmitted between women and girls in the Quianduba River, which helped to characterize girls as holders of a tradition that is undergoing transformations. Figure 7.7 shows a full performance of the *Saracura* song by Monica's students held at the local school.

Figure 7.7: Girls performing the Saracura song in a special performance organized by Monica and Norberto and held at the local school.

Interestingly, when I asked Cris to explain what the Cordão da Saracura was, she only mentioned the characters of the plot. The same happened in interviews with other girls. But in her interview, Dona Nina provided a much different picture:

> The plot of the Cordão de Pássaros is always the same. There is a farmer and her daughter, who has a birthday. [For example] in the [*cordão de*] *arara* [macaw] that I organized, the colonel's daughter was Miss Guanabara. The Indian invites the *caboclos* to go on a hunt and offers a macaw. She was the interpreter who sang "Happy Birthday" and offered it, by putting it in the hand of a clown so that he could take care of the orchard. But the clown is careless and the macaw is stolen. The party is over as she [the birthday girl] becomes sad because of the bird. Then, a *macumbeira* [type of voodoo witch] appears and does some things, and the bird reappears. When the bird appears there are festivities, with dancing, peasants, flower girls, and a huge party. In the end, the group asks permission to leave, as it is already late. And we would leave.

I kept wondering why Cris and the other girls appeared to know so little about the traditional plot of the Cordão de Pássaros. Was it just a coincidence that none of them spoke about it in their interviews? Or was their instruction more focused on the music than on its dramatic aspect? I suspect it was mostly the second, given Monica's academic training in music. If, on the one hand, having an academic training encouraged her to value and, in her own words, to "reconfigure" the musical practices of her own culture, on the other hand, she appeared to base her teaching on some traditional techniques of collective music education that are still used in conservatories, music schools, and universities across Brazil. The use of the recorder in music teaching was particularly telling in this sense. To date, many Brazilian music educators support the idea that the recorder is the best instrument for initiating groups of children in so-called formal instruction, for its price, access, and "easiness" (e.g., Teixeira 2007). In such cases, the recorder is used as a precursor to singing, moving, or performing "more difficult" instruments. Thus, the influence of an academic music education appeared to be present in music teaching and learning in the remote Quainduba river community. Here, it was combined with Monica's political agenda. Interestingly, this political dimension of music teaching and learning appears frequently in the discourses of underprivileged children and adults who take part in many sociomusical projects across Brazil (e.g., Ilari 2005, 2007, 2009; Kleber 2009), while it is unsurprisingly far less prominent in contexts where Western classical music is taught.

RIVERS AS SPACES OF TRANSGRESSION

A closer look into the lyrics of the songs offered by Cris suggests that she was not only singing about mythical creatures. She was also reinforcing the idea of rivers as spaces of transgression. As noted, rivers have always been a source of imaginary and "real" life events that mark the structures of daily life. In the Amazon, the latter is often constructed around myths and legends concerning the *encantados*, or enchanted supernatural creatures that reside under the waters or in the forests (Slater 2001). The *encantados* are entities that protect people and their communities (Fraxe 2004) in a common space (i.e., the river). For riverine Amazonians, the *encantados* are beings that did not die but became enchanted for some reason. They also hold magical powers and express themselves through particular chants, whistles, and other characteristic sounds. Omnipresent and often invisible to the human eye, under special circumstances the *encantados* may appear as particular animals or in human form, like the Boto, which has been studied at length (e.g., Slater 1994). The *encantados* were obviously a natural part of Cris's everyday life.

This comes as no surprise, as in the Amazon the *encantados* are somehow equivalent to the authorities who rule the streets, which are urban spaces of multiple transgressions (DaMatta 2001). Yet transgressions here were much more in a sense of contrasting "real" and imaginary lifeworlds (Fraxe 2004) than of the authority figures found in urban life (DaMatta 2001). For instance, the strong belief in the seductive powers of the Boto is sometimes explained as parents' ways of instilling fear in their young and chaste daughters (Slater 1994). The myth may serve the purpose of preserving young girls from the dangers of, for example, becoming pregnant too soon (Hoefle 2009) or moving to the city, where some of these dangers are close, as in Cris's rendition of the story of the *cobra grande*. Interestingly, the inverse also happens: as the "powers" of the *encantados* are deeply ingrained in the modus operandus of the riverine, a good-looking young man or young woman with a beautiful voice may also be perceived as a threat. Cris mentioned, more than once, the story of Janaína, her sixteen-year-old "idol" and the girl who was recognized as the most talented singer in the community. As with many riverine girls, Janaína already had a husband, but he was not happy about her constant singing and performing with the Cordão da Saracura and continually encouraged Janaína to abandon music and the group altogether. Interestingly, this seems to be the case for many women musicians in the region, who often abandon a more active musical life as composers or performing artists only to return to it later in life when they either abandon their husbands or their husbands die. The paradox here is that the musical lives of young riverine girls are at the same time enriched and threatened by the *encantados* and the Amazonian imagination. In some ways, participation in music is for them a form of transgression.

Concluding Thoughts

In 1542 in the upper Amazon, deep inside the Peruvian jungle, the Spanish conquistador, Francisco de Orellana, faced a group of women warriors and concluded that they were related to the fearful Greek Amazons—this is how the river got its name. Although not in the sense described by Orellana, the women that I met on the shores of the Quianduba River revealed a strong sense of fight as they dealt with isolation and the hostile environment in which they lived. This strong, warrior-like personality seemed to be present early in life in the practices, discourses, and dreams of young riverine girls.

Engagement in music was one of the means for many riverine girls to be heard and seen. Through music, they became more visible and had opportunities to "escape" their harsh realities, even if for a short while. Cris was confident that by making music she would one day be able to perform in other places outside her community. Similar experiences were found in other parts of Brazil, in studies conducted with other "invisible" children and youth (Ilari 2005, 2007, 2009; Kleber 2009). Likewise, music learning presented itself as an opportunity for girls to be enfranchised—something much valued in a country with few opportunities for underprivileged youth (Novaes 2007). By learning from older women and participating in groups like the Cordão da Saracura, riverine girls also challenged the patriarchal rule in a way that empowered them. As Cris and the other girls sang of the river, its surroundings and enchanted beings, its dangers and forbidden pleasures, not with fear but with conviction (and at times sensuality), they were also questioning the status quo.

In spite of its geographical isolation, the community in the Quianduba River was obviously affected to some extent by the media, new technologies, and Brazilian pop music. This was clear in the lyrics and musical features of the songs. For example, the many descending intervals and minor mode "feel" of the Boto song suggest some influence of pop music (e.g., *brega*), as these are not common characteristics of traditional Brazilian music. Cris's passion for the Calypso band also illustrates the pervading nature of pop music in children's lives worldwide (see Campbell [1998] 2010). Not surprisingly, such preferences also appeared in my conversations with girls the same age as Cris from the Movimento dos Trabalhadores Rurais Sem Terra in Southern Brazil and in the city of Rio de Janeiro (Ilari 2005), so, apart from her riverine lifestyle, Cris had musical preferences and dreams that were typical of other eight-year-olds across Brazil.

As noted, there was an implicit influence of a more "academic" knowledge in the music learning processes of Cris and other children who took part in the Cordão da Saracura. On the one hand, the group was recreated out of Monica's desire to "reconfigure" or keep alive some traditions of the past and have children learn and value their own culture. On the other hand, this "reconfiguration" possibly (and inevitably) altered some of the traditional ways through which music was usually transmitted and made in the community. The incorporation of the recorder as a song-teaching tool and the use of electronic instruments and microphones are some examples of these changes. However, Amazonian myths and themes (Hoefle 2007; Slater 2001) were maintained. Another interesting issue was the fact that Monica and Norberto proudly defined themselves as *caboclos* and talked at length about the *caboclo* lifestyle. None of the girls that I interviewed defined themselves in this way, so I wonder if this will happen in the future if they continue participating in the Cordão da Saracura or in similar groups. Such collective and politically engaged music learning experiences, which are likely to promote social flexibility and cohesiveness in the community (see Bowman 2009; Cross 2005), will probably bring many changes to the lives of riverine girls in the coming years.

For the character in Guimarães Rosa's story, the river offered an opportunity to escape from a life of oppression or a path to disappearance. For the Amazonian riverine girls living on the shores of the Quianduba, it is quite the opposite, as the river is a source of power, communication, and visibility. These young women are holders of a musical tradition and messengers of an age-old lifestyle. For them, music is not only a form of thought (Nettl 1995) but also a reinforcement of traditions and beliefs as well as a response to inevitable changes in their complex environment.

ACKNOWLEDGMENT

I am grateful to the Rios family, Dona Nina Abreu, and all the children and adults in the Quianduba River community who shared their lives with us. My gratitude is extended to Michelle Wibbelsman for her insightful comments on a previous version of this chapter.

NOTES

1 Lyrics in English: This river is my street, / Mine and yours *mururé* [an Amazonian plant], / I step on the moon's chest, / I lie on the grounds of the tide.
2 Lyrics in English: Zum zum zum zum / The little bee told me a little secret / That there is honey hidden in each flower, / Who made such a beautiful thing?, / Look at those who believe, / It was the hands of the creator, / I will stomp my feet, I will clap my hands, / I will clap to our Lord, the creator.
3 Lyrics in English: Black dolphin, Anaconda, Curupira, Iara of the forest, / with Matinta's [a type of witch] whistle, I invoke the powers of the waters, / Disenchant, disenchant, / Come girl, Come soon, Appear before my eyes, / To enchant these people with your chant.
4 Lyrics in English: Tia Fuloca prepare the açaí, / And also bring me some *miriti* [a local palm tree that is edible], / A taste that satisfies us, / A good thing is our local culture, / Abaetetuba, pearl of the Tocantins River, / Here the taste is açaí, / *Miriti* with cured meat and fish, La la la... / Down the river, up the river, I row in my canoe, / Bringing the joys of our children / The hopes of our people.
5 Lyrics in English: Saracura is singing, On the *igapó* tree branch, / Oh sing Saracura sing, / *Quiricó, quiricó, quiricó,* / In the past, the *cordão* was lively, / And played in the terreiros until dawn, / But nowadays, TV imposes things on us...
6 A mixture of songs from different religious beliefs was commonly found in many northern Brazilian communities that I visited, including here in the Quianduba River.
7 I interviewed Dona Nina Abreu (age seventy-three at the time) in Abaetetuba and recorded the full, original version of the Saracura song, as she conceived it.

REFERENCES

Bowman, Wayne. 2009. "The Community in Music." *International Journal of Community Music* 2 (2–3): 109–128.

Braga, Sergio Ivan Gil. 2004. "Festas religiosas e populares na Amazônia" [Popular and Religious Celebrations in the Amazon]. Paper presented at the Luso-Afro-Brazilian Social Sciences Conference, September 16–18, University of Coimbra, Coimbra, Portugal.

Campbell, Patricia Shehan. [1998] 2010. *Songs in Their Heads.* New York: Oxford University Press.

Castro, Fabio. 2009. "Patterns of Resource Use by Caboclo Communities in the Middle-Lower Amazon." In *Amazonian Peasant Societies: Modernity and Invisibility,* edited by C. Adams, W. Neves, R. Murrieta, and M. Harris, 157–177. Dordrecht, the Netherlands: Springer.

Crompton, Peter, Ana Maria Ventura, Jose Maria Sousa, Elisabeth Santos, Thomas Strickland, and Ellen Silbergeld. 2002. "Assessment of Mercury Exposure and Malaria in a Brazilian Amazon Riverine Community." *Environmental Research* 90 (2): 69–75.

Cross, Ian. 2005. "Music and Meaning, Ambiguity, and Evolution." In *Musical Communication,* edited by D. Miell, R. Macdonald, and D. J. Hargreaves, 27–44. Oxford: Oxford University Press.

DaMatta, Roberto. 2001. *O que faz o Brasil Brasil?* [What Makes Brazil, Brazil?]. Rio de Janeiro: Record.

Del Priore, Mary, ed. 2002. *História das crianças no Brasil* [History of Children in Brazil]. São Paulo: Contexto.

Dimenstein, Gilberto. 2005. *O mistério das bolas de gude: histórias de humanos quase invisíveis* [The Mystery behind Marbles: Stories of Nearly Invisible Humans]. Campinas: Papirus.

Ford Foundation, Projeto Nova Cartografia Social da Amazônia. 2008. *Crianças e adolescentes ribeirinhos e quilombolas de Abaetetuba* [Project New Social Cartography of the Amazon, Riverine and Quilombola Children and Adolescents in Abaetetuba]. Manaus: Fundação Ford.

Ford Foundation, Projeto Nova Cartografia Social da Amazônia. 2009. *Jovens de comunidades tradicionais do Baixo-Tocantins* [Project New Social Cartography of the Amazon, Youth from Traditional Communities in the Lower Tocantins]. Manaus: Fundação Ford.

Fraxe, Teresinha. 2004. *Cultura cabocla-ribeirinha* [Riverine-Cabocla Culture]. São Paulo: Annablume.

Gillingham, Sarah. 2001. "Social Organization and Participatory Resource Management in Brazilian Ribeirinho Communities: A Case Study of the Mamirauá Sustainable Development Reserve, Amazonas." *Society & Natural Resources* 14 (9): 803–814.

Guimarães Rosa, João. 1968. *The Third Bank of the River and Other Stories*. Translated by Barbara Shelby. New York: Knopf.

Hoefle, Scott William. 2009. "Enchanted (and Disenchanted) Amazonia: Environmental Ethics and Cultural Identity in Northern Brazil." *Ethics, Place & Environment* 12 (1): 107–130.

Ilari, Beatriz. 2005. "Musical Development of Brazilian Children: Regionalisms, Style and Identity." *Actes du Colloque Brésil Musical—Observatoire musical française* 31 (1): 65–81.

Ilari, Beatriz. 2007. "Música, identidade e relações humanas em um país mestiço: Implicações para a educação musical na América Latina" [Music, Identity and Human Relations in a Mixed-Race Country: Implications for Music Education in Latin America]. *Revista da ABEM* 18: 35–44.

Ilari, Beatriz. 2009. "Music Learning and the Invisible: Cultural Appropriation, Equity and Identity of Underprivileged Brazilian Children and Adolescents." In *Exploring Social Justice: How Music Education Might Matter,* edited by E. Gould, C. Morton, J. Countryman, and L. Stewart Rose, 121–139. Waterloo, Ontario: CMEA.

Kleber, Magali. 2009. "Educação musical e ONGS: Dois estudos de caso no contexto urbano brasileiro" [Music Education and NGOs: Two Case Studies in the Brazilian Urban Context]. *Em Pauta* 17 (29): 113–138.

Lancy, David. 2008. *The Anthropology of Childhood*. Cambridge: Cambridge University Press.

Lima, Deborah de Magalhães. 1999. "A construção histórica do termo *caboclo*" [Historical Construction of the Term *Caboclo*]. *Novos Cadernos NAE* 2 (2): 5–32.

Lobo, Marco Aurélio, Antonio José Lamarão Correa, and Paulo de Castro Ribeiro. 2009. "Análise comparativa de estruturas intra-urbanas Amazônicas: os casos de Abaetetuba, Castanhal, Paragominas e Santarém (PA)" [Comparative Analysis of Intraurban Structures in the Amazon: The Cases of Abaetetuba, Castanhal, Paragominas, and Santarém]. Paper presented at the 28th International Congress of the Latin American Studies Association, June 11–14, Rio de Janeiro, Brazil.

Mendes, Leila Said Assef, Fernando Augusto Ramos Pontes, Simone Souza da Costa Silva, Julia S. N. F. Bucher Maluschke, Daniela S. dos Reis, and Sarah Danielle Baia da Silva. 2008. "Inserção Ecológica no Contexto de uma Comunidade Ribeirinha Amazônica" [Ecological Engagement in the Context of an Amazon River Village]. *Interamerican Journal of Psychology* 42: 1–10.

Monteiro, Walbert, and Paula Ribeiro. 2004. "No rio Quianduba uma competição diferente" [In the Quianduba River, a Different Competition]. *Ver o Pará* 26: 18–26.

Nettl, Bruno. 1995. "Ideas about Music and Musical Thought: Ethnomusicological Perspectives." *Journal of Aesthetic Education* 30: 173–187.

Novaes, Regina. 2007. "Juventude e sociedade: jogos de espelhos" [Youth and Society: Mirror Games]. *Revista da Comunidade Virtual de Antropologia* 38. Accessed June 4, 2012. http://antropologia.com.br/arti/colab/a38-rnovaes.pdf.

Nugent, Stephen. 2009. "Utopias and Dystopias in the Amazonian Social Landscape." In *Amazon Peasant Societies in a Changing Environment*, edited by Cristina Adams, Rui Murrieta, Walter Neves, and Mark Harris, 21–32. New York: Springer.

Rodrigues, Marinês, Elisângela Castilho, and Ivo Vieira. 2010. "História do rio Quianduba: a memória viva dos seus moradores" [History of the Quianduba River: Memories of Its Inhabitants]. I Encontro Internacional de Educação do Campo. http://www.encontroobservatorio.unb.br/arquivos/artigos/123.

Seeger, Anthony. 2008. "The Tropical Forest Region." In *The Garland Handbook of Latin American Music*, edited by Dale Olson, 201–215. New York: Taylor & Francis.

Silva, Hilton. 2009. "Socio-Ecology of Health and Disease: The Effects of Invisibility on the *Caboclo* Populations of the Amazon." In *Amazon Peasant Societies in a Changing Environment*, edited by Cristina Adams, Rui Murrieta, Walter Neves, and Mark Harris, 307–333. New York: Springer.

Silva, Hilton, and Douglas Crews. 2006. "Ecology of Children's Growth: An Example from Traditional Populations of the Brazilian Amazon." *International Journal of Anthropology* 21 (2): 97–109.

Siqueira, Andrea. 2009. "Women, Gender Relations and Decision Making in *Caboclo* Households in the Amazon Estuary." In *Amazon Peasant Societies in a Changing Environment*, edited by Cristina Adams, Rui Murrieta, Walter Neves, and Mark Harris, 241–257. New York: Springer.

Slater, Candace. 1994. *Dance of the Dolphin: Transformation and Disenchantment in the Amazonian Imagination*. Chicago: University of Chicago Press.

Slater, Candace. 2001. *Entangled Edens: Visions of the Amazon*. Berkeley: University of California Press.

Stock, Jonathan. 2004. "Documenting the Musical Event: Observation, Participation, Representation." In *Empirical Musicology: Aims, Methods, Prospects*, edited by Eric Clarke and Nicholas Cook, 15–34. Oxford: Oxford University Press.

Teixeira, Walmir Marcelino. 2007. "Caderno de musicalização: canto e flauta doce" [Music Education Notebook: Singing and Recorder]. MA thesis, Universidade Federal do Paraná, Curitiba, Brazil.

Wolcott, Harry. 1992. "Posturing in Qualitative Inquiry." In *The Handbook of Qualitative Research in Education*, edited by Margaret LeCompte, Wendy Millroy, and Judith Preissle, 3–52. San Diego: Academic Press.

8

THE MUSICAL SOCIALIZATION OF CHILDREN AND ADOLESCENTS IN BRAZIL IN THEIR EVERYDAY LIVES

MAGALI KLEBER
AND JUSAMARA SOUZA

In Brazil, several studies have highlighted the importance of music in the construction of the sociocultural identity of children and adolescents who have suffered from a lack of care and social protection. The purpose of this chapter is to discuss musical socialization through family and communities and how it is developed in school and in social projects. The children and adolescents were observed and interviewed in their specific locus, such as in the nongovernmental organization (NGOs) Projeto Villa Lobinhos and Meninos do Morumbi (Kleber 2006a, 2006b) and at Escola de Porto Alegre (Müller 2000; Souza and Dias 2009), a school that assists homeless children and adolescents.

The belief is that in order to understand the musical cultures of children and adolescents, it is necessary to get to know their family experiences and their network of musical sociability. The research presented and discussed in this chapter deals with the experiences of children and teenagers living in the suburbs of major

Brazilian cities such as São Paulo and Rio de Janeiro, located in the southeast of the country, and Porto Alegre, to the south. These experiences are seen through the analytical perspective of theories that discuss everyday life. Our interest is in the values and beliefs about music education in the different cultural communities.

Music pedagogy is seen as both a process that shows the relationship between people and music and the process of music appropriation and transmission, as proposed by Kraemer (1995: 146): "Music education is concerned with relations between human beings and music under the aspects of ownership and transmission. All the music-educational practice is included in this field of study, together with what happens in and out of the institutions, as well as all the musical processes of appropriation."

As in all countries, Brazil has a variety of cultural groups sometimes classed as subcultures. One can see not only the regional differences—people who grew up in São Paulo are not like those in Rio Grande do Sul—but also differences within the same city. In Rio de Janeiro, for example, there are people who live in the slums, in contrast to those who live in penthouses in Copacabana, not far from each other. These subcultures are different in many aspects, such as social class, income, occupation, access to education, and ethnicity.

MUSICAL PRACTICES IN BRAZILIAN NGOS

In a recent study, Kleber (2006a, 2006b) analyzed and interpreted the music-pedagogical process observed between 2002 and 2004 in two NGOs—Projeto Villa Lobinhos (PVL) in Rio de Janeiro and Meninos do Morumbi (AMM) in São Paulo—from a systemic view of the contexts perceived as significant to the understanding of this phenomenon. Both NGOs represent different contexts of teaching and learning music while simultaneously holding important commonalities such as youths at social risk. These contexts are understood as loci of knowledge production whose music-pedagogical process is seen as a "total social fact" (Mauss 2003). To describe the theoretical aspects of this research, Kleber notes four key perspectives:

> First, music is seen as social practice that generates a cultural system that has a substantial foundation that incorporates itself in the socio-cultural structure of groups and individuals. This idea has been proposed by Shepherd and Wicke (1997), Small (2006) and Blacking (1995). Secondly, the music pedagogical process is seen as a "total social fact." This idea derives from Marcel Mauss (2003) who emphasizes the system and complex character inherent within organizations like those of this study. Thirdly, the musical knowledge production in NGOs is seen as a cognitive praxis. This is understood against the ideas of Eyerman and Jamison (1998) who suggest that a social-political force can "open the doors" to the production of new ways of pedagogical, esthetic, political and institutional knowledge. Fourthly, the music pedagogy is seen as both a process that concerns the relationship between people and music and a process of music appropriation and transmission, as proposed by Kraemer and Souza. (Kleber 2006b: 103–104)

According to Kleber (2006a, 2006b) the music-pedagogical process in these NGOs proved to be permeated by the notion of collectivity. The analysis and interpretation of several issues raised by this study points to the understanding of musical practices as sociocultural components of an eminently collective and interactive character.

A Music-Pedagogical Process as a Total Social Fact in NGOs

The music-pedagogical process, seen as a total social fact, covered the physical, institutional, and symbolic dynamics of how music was learned and taught in the observed institutions. The analysis then incorporated interconnections between four dimensions:

1. Institutional: related to bureaucratic, juridical, disciplinary, and morphological dimensions
2. Historical: dimension of the stories told by social actors, protagonists of the construction of the NGO as a physical, material, and symbolic space
3. Sociocultural: dimension of the circulation spaces of symbolic values, meetings, intersubjective and interinstitutional relations, conflicts, and negotiations
4. Music teaching and learning process: focusing on what, where, why, and how music was learned and taught in those spaces

Incorporating the interconnection of these four dimensions has enabled a vision of music pedagogy not only as concerned with teaching and learning but also as a connected multidimensional field. This is the conception of the "music-pedagogical process as a total social fact" (Kleber 2006a: 297) as shown in Figure 8.1.

This model is supported by the fact that the multiple contexts used in the analysis cannot exist in isolation, as a field of knowledge production that can only be thought of systematically. The term "total social fact" was coined by Marcel Mauss,

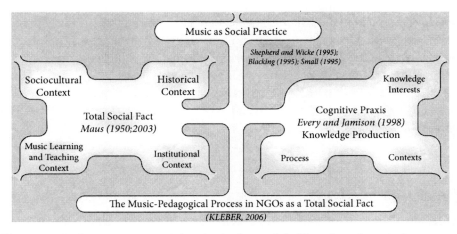

Figure 8.1: Linking concepts and theories in the model of "music-pedagogical process as total social fact" (Kleber 2006a: 297).

who, in 1920, conducted a comparative study on trade and contracts between the various sections and subgroups in archaic societies of Polynesia, Melanesia, and the northwest of America. These social phenomena are considered total because "they express, at once, the most diverse institutions: religious, legal and moral—these being political and familial at the same time, economic—this assuming particular forms of production and consumption" (Mauss 2003: 186). According to Mauss (2003), the social phenomenon seen as "total" does not give room for ruptures or antagonisms between social and individual but rather seeks to reconstruct the whole.

According to Kleber (2006a: 295) the socioeducational proposal for institutions such as NGOs catalyzes the need for recognition that cultural diversity brings different forms of knowledge, experiences, values, and human interests. These aspects are related to the sociocultural dynamics and, therefore, are deeply connected with our own human existence. This is an important issue since it is connected to a refined process of cultural and social exclusion and shows two sides of the same coin, the institutionally taught and valued culture and other cultures (Web Figure 8.2 ⊙).

Projeto Villa Lobinhos

The NGO PVL was created by Walter Moreira Salles, a banker, lawyer, and ambassador, and his son João Moreira Salles, a filmmaker, and institutionalized in 2000. PVL is coordinated by the violinist and teacher Turíbio Santos and aims to promote music education for young people between twelve and twenty years old who come from poor communities in the metropolitan area of Rio de Janeiro. They attend musical perception classes, instrumental practice, ensemble, and computer classes for a period of three years and receive educational support for their regular school classes, with the idea that, after three years, students can follow a musical career. All of the participants—about forty young people in PVL—recorded CDs with varied repertories, preferably Brazilian music, to show their work in a range of settings.

PVL set up a network with several other social projects and institutions, presenting shows in theaters, schools, slums, and companies, achieving a synergy when merging these contexts. Most of the students interviewed live with their families in one of three slums of Rio de Janeiro: the Dona Marta and Rocinha communities and Grota do Surucucu. They were between sixteen and nineteen years old and most of them were boys, only one was a girl.

The Family Network

In the testimonies, the family is represented as a social core whose function is to protect and stimulate the development of the children. It is a social representation that is pluralized beyond the traditional model (father-mother-children). The area of security that surrounds the family also includes situations of conflict, absences, and violence. The family is seen, both by coordinators and students, as an important interlocutor, a partner who will involve children and young people in good projects. A majority of those interviewed indicated that the support and stimulation of their family was significant to their musical studies. Many of the students already have a relative who plays by ear or is otherwise familiar with music, either through participation in musical groups or in community samba schools.

Ademar, seventeen years old, said that he has the support of his father who is a musician and plays the trumpet. According to him, the incentive to be a musician comes from the family:

> My family has always given me support for music. My dad has always come to me and [said], "No, [if] that's what you want, go for it, I'll give you support, go after it, really do it" … and nowadays he even jokes about it, "Brother, if I were you I would not let go of the music. Go for it with the saxophone, because if I put a trowel in your hand, you're out of luck, I know nothing but music." (Ademar in Kleber 2006a: 114)

The first class Ademar attended at PVL was deeply exciting to him because he had never seen so many musicians playing together and had never participated in an orchestra. At the first meeting, he saw eight people together and thought, "WOW!! It has a good crowd down here" (Ademar in Kleber 2006a: 99). This report shows how the social relations that fall into the everyday life promote meetings that may have a meaning to broaden social and aesthetic experiences, allowing the repositioning of a new standard in individual and social identity.

Carla, a flute student who graduated in 2004, lived in the Rocinha Slum and began to study music in her own community at the School of Music when she was nine years old. She is now eighteen years old and considers her family to be her emotional support and her motivation to continue studying music. Her parents are proud of her performances as a student at PVL:

> My mother loved it; my mom and dad give me great support. They loved it and if I ever want to leave this place, they won't let me … they want me to go to the university to do music and become a professional. My grandfather was an Italian singer. … My dad plays a little guitar … and he is very proud and tells everybody every time there is a performance … the environment is very good … it's a family atmosphere that everybody likes everybody, no quarrel with anyone, it is very good. I feel very comfortable. (Carla in Kleber 2006a: 115)

Families see the study of music as important and positive support, as an alternative to an idle life that is often imposed on the youngsters who live in the suburbs and slums. These social projects often appear as an alternative social representation of the family, materialized in the recognition of the physical and symbolic space of PVL as a second home. The role of PVL in dealing with dysfunctional families is shown by the life story of Marcos da Silva. Marquinhos, as he is called by friends, is a multiinstrumentalist who plays trumpet, ukulele, guitar, tambourine, and percussion. He lives at Favela Dona Marta and reveals that before starting his musical training he was not into music: "I did not like any kind of music...I didn't know what music was, I did not like anything, I only listened to funk because the neighbors would play it very loud, so I would just hear it" (Marquinhos in Kleber 2006a: 102).

He says that his horizons got broader and he started noticing that music was more than just funk: there was "Brazilian popular music (MPB), rock, pop, different styles such as folk, samba, many things...music is a completely different world...different from the neighbors" (Marquinhos in Kleber 2006a: 102). His testimony shows how the network of socializing contributed to the construction of his familial and aesthetic-musical references and how the social actions replaced both his mother and the social care that were the guarantee of his survival. Memories of his family embody the disintegration and violence created by the vulnerable environment where he used to live. His life history presents his struggle for survival and reveals the affective, ethical, and cognitive dimensions that a child needs to grow with dignity. He lost his mother when he was three years old and was raised at a day care center in the slum. People who do not have a family often experience this as a vacuum in their lives, leading to the recognition that the actions of the social projects replaced maternal and social care to some extent.

> Since I was a child...my mother and I...didn't starve, but we lived on the streets. My mother would beg for food so I could have something to eat and she always got some and then I grew up in this atmosphere....My mother died when I was three so I stayed with my grandma [who] took me to different places. Then, in the day care center, where Rodrigo met me...I was like...not abandoned...how am I going to put it....I didn't have something for me, it was vague, and everything was vague. I used to wander there in the sports court, there in the slum. Then, with the music, then I started having something to do and then I started seeing that it was totally different with music, totally different from what I lived before; the feeling that music gives you...I felt the music! I don't know, it's something...don't know how to say this; I only know that it changed very much, very, very, very much. (Marquinhos in Kleber 2006a: 102)

There are many stories that reveal a multiplicity of experiences and contexts accomplished by PVL that acquire a meaning beyond music teaching and learning, since they value social representations such as family, friendship, leisure, and the profession. Marquinhos exemplifies the meaning of music in his life, in the construction of his music identity, focusing on issues related to his ethnic condition—being Black—and living in the slums and in love with music:

> And then my music opened the possibility of all that I have now in my life...and without the music my life would be a mistake, this is my aim, I always talk to myself...face things with a clean mind. These are discriminations that most people have to face. And we will always have obstacles in life, and we will face them with a clean mind...when I go to bed, I always think and reflect on what I could have gone through without music....*Chorinho*[1] is so wonderful, I can't even explain it; *Chorinho* comes from inside, from the soul, it moves the body, the blood...a swing, it moves everything! (Marquinhos in Kleber 2006a: 133, 162)

As music in Marquinhos's life played an important role by keeping him away from criminal activity, so too the role of music can be seen as an alternative that can replace violence, criminality, and drug use. Moreover, it is a potential element for the construction of social identity and a way the young can follow in order to distance themselves from the marginalization, violence, and criminality.

A Second Home: The Family Extension

Students cite the lack of family relations as something that constitutes a gap in their existence. Therefore, the opportunities given by social projects are considered a social representation that minimizes this absence. PVL as a second home is a metaphor associated with a cozy, safe, and harmonious environment, in which feeling well is essential. For Marquinhos, PVL is that second home, where he can do his homework, play, chat, and so on: "This place is like your home, a second one here, because in our home one can do anything, like here, but with some rules, but you can do anything" (Marquinhos in Kleber 2006a: 101). The recognition that living in a communal space requires the observation and compliance with rules reflects the awareness of rights and duties, values related to the construction and exercising of citizenship through microrelations.

Performance

Instrumental music was always performed in a group using amplifiers and a microphone with students playing on drums, guitar, bass, and keyboard and Marquinhos on trumpet. The atmosphere was of excitement; they were very comfortable and happy. The arrangements were discussed, and changes of rhythm, harmony, instrumentation, and tonality agreed on, setting up the arrangements and at the same time providing for repetition and improvement. Kleber (2006a, 2006b) captured many moments of musical knowledge exchange between students and the process of communicating musical ideas through processes of orality and imitation. The performance emerged as the axis of the musical pedagogic process, and they enjoyed themselves learning and teaching music among themselves. In the NGOs, the

> performance of musical groups is understood as the product of the music pedagogical process. Evidencing the music performed is a way of presenting the participants musical identities, choices and values.... [through the musical practices] presented demonstrating integration of processes that are related to citizen's values and articulate not only several types of knowledge but also generation, gender, race and social class groups. (Kleber 2006b: 108)

The stories reveal a multiplicity of experiences and contexts accomplished by PVL that acquire a meaning beyond music teaching and learning, since they value social representations such as family, friendship, leisure, and the profession. According to Kleber,

> Aspects, such as the stigma of skin color, the place where people live, and poor origins appear in the reports on the students' identities. The participants reveal that they lived in situations of misery and from this carried much stigma. What is interesting when we compare them after involvement with the NGOs is a clear change of perception to such issues. Such experiences can be considered a very meaningful factor to the reconstruction of new notions of personal and social values. (Kleber 2006b: 106)

These are references that contribute to the construction of the identity of these youngsters. The PVL students circulate in the different spaces and activities performing different musical styles in different venues: philanthropic activities (schools, nursing homes), merchandising (the places the sponsors request), parties, and concerts, among others. The interactive character of the circuits that the members of PVL have contact with and their leisure activities are important in building experience. One notices that in this interactive environment, the musical performance becomes the unifying axis. These examples reflect the role that work of this nature can play in the life of youngsters who are deprived of social care. It reveals that lives can change for the positive, a concrete transformation when the music is a determining factor.

Associação Meninos dos Morumbi

Created in 1996 by Flavio Pimenta, the musical work developed by Associação Meninos dos Morumbi (AMM) (Web Figure 8.3 ◉) includes the Banda Show (BSMM), which is composed of the Grupo de Percussão (Percussion Group), the Grupo Vocal Feminino (Female Vocal Group), and the Grupo de Dança (Dance Group). This is the result of the work done in singing, dancing, and percussion classes for children and adolescents that integrate the community with the Association. The band has five weekly rehearsals, with 300 participants at each rehearsal. A recording can be found at http://www.meninosdomorumbi.org.br/frames/principal.html (go to Banda>CD).

AMM is an NGO, constituted according to its own statute that has its headquarters in Morumbi, a middle class neighborhood in the city of São Paulo. There are about 3,500 participants, most of whom live in poor neighborhoods with the common characteristics of a low HDI (Human Development Index), a high violence index and a poor educational, healthcare and social infrastructure. The AMM mission statement is to "promote a multidimensional learning context for children and youngsters through the construction of positive values that are connected to art and culture, in this way broadening the circuits of inclusion in a participative and entrepreneurial form" (www.meninosdomorumbi.org.br 2010). One of the most important goals is to develop the capacity for teamwork. The project is socioedu-cational and seeks to find alternatives for access to material and symbolic assets, which are the basics for the exercise of citizenship.

The AMM as Part of the Family

The AMM families are assisted through different means: individual interviews, family meetings, thematic forum, assistance in crisis situations, and referrals to a group of volunteer professional psychologists who use different strategies, such as community therapy, sociodrama, group meetings, focal groups, and other methods to tackle problems. The goal is to create an exchange space that provides opportunities for these families to work out positive solutions when facing the challenges of raising their children, in this way increasing family resilience.

All of the interviewed participants were proud and thankful to belong to AMM: "Whenever I hear someone saying *Meninos do Morumbi*, I feel proud of being part of it, and this is the best part" (Cintia in Kleber 2006a: 230). Their testimonies reveal the positive influence that the physical and symbolic presence of the AMM repre-sents in their lives. The feeling of belonging to AMM is also revealed when stu-dents refer to the social locations such as family, work, profession, second home, and friendship as important values in the construction of their identity. Although, most of them come from dysfunctional families, they refer to their families as a structure of safety and affection, as well as of conflicts. In their testimonies, they attribute great significance to AMM, which also appears in the testimonies of the participants interviewed about the psychosocial structure and support through the socialization with the group, as illustrated by Cintia: "Here we are practically a fam-ily, we are a team here. So...if I am going through some difficulty, I come to some-one in my group to talk and they will try to help me....we are a team and always try to help each other here" (Cintia in Kleber 2006a: 231). When asked about the role of music in his life, Pavilhão reports, "Today it is almost everything, because in addition to playing, I work with the sound, I operate a table and this has changed my life completely, thanks to the project I managed to get a family" (Pavilhão in Kleber 2006a: 231).

Metaphors of home and family were used by interviewees to communicate about situations in the everyday life of AMM. Silvinha, a pretty girl aged twenty-one who worked in the administration of the Project, summarized:

> I consider *Meninos do Morumbi* as my second home; my friends are here, my work is here, I grew mature here because...everything that I am today is thanks to this place, because today I work here in a position of trust. Friendship, union, pride and a dream accomplished both in the beginning and now, because it has grown, evolved and whoever has lived this is part of life. It's part of life and I consider myself part of *Meninos do Morumbi* and my life is here and that's it. (Silvinha in Kleber 2006a: 231)

Performance

As with the other NGOs, analysis reveals that performance is a conductor of the teaching and learning process:

> It can be seen as the result of social practices motivated by NGOs and by the sociocultural context of its participants. Collective rituals, classes, rehearsals, games, jokes and informal meetings are moments of synthesis of relationships and experiences provided by music. Leisure, learning how to play, taking care of instruments, executing a musical production and meetings with friends are part of the context of pedagogical and musical process. Audio and video records of the performances from the two selected organizations (Web Figures 8.4, 8.5, and 8.6 ●) are understood here as a result of this process. They are fragments of the repertoire they play, built along the work done in different places already mentioned in this work: the classroom, tests, presentations, music games. Highlight the music they perform is a way to present them through the music making—"musicking" (Small 1995)—which carries traces of their musical identities, steeped in their choices and values that were shared and where they structure themselves as musicians, groups and individuals. (Kleber 2006a: 299)

In regard to the NGOs, Kleber emphasizes that they "are spaces historically built through sociomusical practices and the notion of belonging and the concern for issues of human dignity emerge as features that identify the children and young of both institutions.... [Therefore,] the collective process can be seen as a paradigm in the socio-musical interactions of NGOs. Thus, the sense of belonging is pursued through the educational and joyful activities related to relevant musical practice for those young people involved" (2006b: 107).

Escola Porto Alegre

The Escola Municipal Porto Alegre (EPA) is a municipal public school in Porto Alegre, Rio Grande do Sul, for homeless children and adolescents between ten and eighteen years old. It has a flexible organization, with classes containing mixed-aged students, with different levels of literacy, socialization, and cognitive development. Furthermore, students' attendance is not compulsory.

EPA is considered an open school that, unlike the majority of the educational institutions, maintains a nonhierarchical and nonformal relationship with knowledge. The school values experience and practical knowledge as a starting point for its concept formation, including objective and subjective themes collected from the everyday demands of the students. Therefore, the curriculum includes themes such as sexuality, ethnicity, work, drugs, violence, AIDS, power, and citizenship, to name just a few. These themes connected various areas of knowledge (Müller 2000: 14–15). The new pedagogical dimension of the school provides flexibility and differentiation of the curriculum organization and tries to implement a different logic of inclusion, allowing access to formal learning even for those children and adolescents living on the streets.

In research with children and adolescents from EPA, Müller (2000) has revealed the senses attributed to music and considered the ways in which they relate to it. The specific questions were Where was music located in the school's life? What was the relationship of the students with music? To what extent did the school's political-pedagogical project, reflected in its time-space, determine the relation between its students and music?

Although, at that time, music was not part of the school curriculum, a group of twenty children and adolescents expressed great interest in music and had some kind of musical activity at school almost daily, either by listening to music on a sound system on the school patio or in the classroom or by playing percussion instruments in the *pagode* and samba gatherings, which occurred spontaneously or because of some scheduled presentation. Also, they would rehearse with the Sabedoria de Rua rap group composed of six boys and three girls, who presented group or individual choreographies in or outside of the school environment. Other forms of musical activity were singing in the dining hall when waiting in line for their food to be served; singing and tapping the walls, doors, or school pillars; or singing and dancing in the hall on the way to the classrooms.

MUSIC AS A SOCIAL FACT

When discussing the concept related to music, Anne-Marie Green states, "Music as a total fact is understood from the experiences of a social group, considering that this society is the result of the musical acts by singular actors in relationships that connect one to another" (2000: 34). This means that the musical fact is constructed from the experiences of subjects that belong to certain social groups, as well as individuals. Green thinks of music as a complex object since it is considered a total social fact that combines technical, social, cultural, and economical aspects. From this model "that seeks to have a vision of the relations that are woven, in other words, understanding music as a social reality with its multiple aspects," Green believes that we can have a more acute, sensitive, and thorough comprehension of the musical facts. Green writes that the presence of music in our daily life is so important that we can consider it a social fact to be studied (1987: 88). This is an aspect to which music teachers still seem to give little attention. The works that have a more sociological bias, for example, refer to "the social construction of musical meaning." According to Green,

> There is no musical object regardless of its constitution by a subject. Therefore, there is not, on the one hand, the world of musical works (which are not universal entities and developed in particular conditions linked to a given cultural order) and on the other hand, individuals with acquired conditions or musical conditions

that are influenced by societal norms. Music is, therefore, a cultural fact inscribed in a given society. (1987: 91)

This broader understanding of the social meaning of music is useful for the comprehension of the different musical practices of groups of students in the school or other areas. According to Green, it is more important to define the type of relation that the adolescents, for example, have with music than "limit oneself to the music practice or musical consumption just for its preferred content or genre" (1987: 95). This is explained by the fact that the musical preferences of adolescents would be associated with a musical genre that expresses freedom and change. In other words, the relation that adolescents maintain with music represents the manifestation of a cultural identity characterized by both age and social environment (Green 1987: 100).

The testimonies collected from children and teenagers talking about their musical experiences in their families and communities reveal how these identities are constructed. This process confronts personal and collective expectations with symbolic, aesthetic, and political values. The musical socialization that is built through family and community is also developed at school or in social projects. The music is part of a socialization process through which children and adolescents create their social relations.

Functional and Dysfunctional Families and How Music Helps

For homeless children and adolescents, the family does not function as a mechanism of social protection. In other words, the role of the family is nonexistent as "a mediator between the individual and the society" that operates "as a space of production and transmission of agendas and cultural practices" or as an "organization responsible for the daily existence of its members, producing, gathering and distributing resources to satisfy their basic needs" (Carvalho and Almeida 2003: 109). Almost all students assisted by the EPA live in hideouts that are located under the bridges of the river that flows through the city of Porto Alegre. The students interviewed by Müller chose to refer to the place where they lived as "bridge." Under the bridges, ten hideouts were located, each of them with two to six children or adolescents (2000: 82–83). The spatial proximity allowed them to follow each other's daily lives, controlling their attendance "in the house," the kind of activities that they were doing at certain moments, and their health conditions (Müller 2000: 81). The friends and neighbors from the bridge were their family:

> The fact that most students lived under the same bridge as neighbors, created in these children and adolescents a group identity. This self-image of a group made

them feel proud, since they consider themselves as different from the "homeless children," and in this way avoiding that designation. (Müller 2000: 82)

In spite of the lack of basic material elements necessary for human life—home and food—the music was always present:

> The music seemed to reveal the dimension of this big group because it provided a connection between the children and adolescents from the two sides of the same bridge and when they got together on the same side of one of the bridges in order to sing, dance, and play the cans and buckets that were used to wash cars on the streets. (Müller 2000: 83)

Informants also listened to the radio at night and while they were sleeping, preferring rap mostly. The music would gather them into a big group, "in the same hideout, in order to sing, play and dance to the music that they knew from the radio" (Müller 2000: 84). During these moments, they would also rehearse the songs from their friends who composed raps—something that could also happen collectively, through the *rap de hora* (last-minute rap), a combination of improvised phrases, as Rogerio described in an interview:

> I make a verse, then if I don't know how to sing the other verse, he already has the other verse in mind and then I can include his verse and mine; then he stops in another part that he doesn't know and I invent, others invent, and so forth...that's why the result will be a big, bigger song. Because if I sing, I will sing only one piece, if he sings, he will sing only one piece, or if others sing, they will sing one piece, so now we have a whole song. (Müller 2000: 84–85)

As highlighted by Müller (2000: 117), the students seemed to find cohesion in the practice of rap because, as a group, they recognized themselves as one more participant of the hip-hop movement. A sense of legitimacy in a life of exclusion could be experienced by them in this culture. Their discourse claimed social rights and denounced the difficulties of life in the suburbs, with the objective of mobilizing society.

The hideouts are located relatively close to the school, which helps improve the students' school attendance. The common experience lived by the homeless children and adolescents helps them to "know" the songs created outside the school, as Rogerio explained:

> There, where we live, most of us stay.... in the group, you know, like us. We stay in the group. To sing, we form a group of more than five, six, like in a circle, then start singing...then each starts singing just a little piece, keeps listening and...so on, then when we come to school everybody knows. Then, if one sings there...then, "this song I know ..." then, sings together, another person sings over there...then, that's it. (Müller 2000: 84–85)

The musical performance of these children and adolescents, especially in the improvised rap gatherings, can reveal a lot. According to Small (1998), the people involved in a performance would be celebrating their established relationships, and the quality of the performance would be determined by the quality of the relationship generated at the moment of the performance.

INSTITUTIONS AS IDENTITY BUILDERS

The students at EPA consider making music together a form of celebration that helps them create links with the school and strengthens their personal relationships with certain teachers, which was observed in the field research conducted in 2009 when we returned to the school. At that time, the school had a music instructor with a degree in sociology, who stated that this had given her ideas to deal with the problems present in the school.

One of the primary reasons for making music was the effect of a percussion workshop that was held for a week. The participants were between fourteen and twenty-two years old, had no family, and were mostly involved with drugs, drug dealing, or other types of criminal offences (sometimes the school would experience episodes of violence caused by students' drug withdrawal symptoms or even by their involvement with drug dealing).

The organization of a music workshop was a complementary activity to the classroom, a time for socializing that would be a pleasurable moment in school. This project allowed the students to interact with other musicians and people who were not homeless. It was also a time of celebration, when, at the end of a week of work, the students played a repertoire for percussion instruments with other invited groups, participated in rap gatherings, and organized capoeira performances, and the girls danced in the schoolyard.

The identification with rap is related to the "ethnic" question, since the vast majority of the children and adolescents who attend this school are of African origin. Therefore, this is not simply an area for youth sociability, as stated by Andrade (1999) but an opportunity for them to be with their peers in ethnic groups that cope with the same social and economic difficulties. Music as a possibility of inclusion has a direct effect on the identity of homeless children and adolescents. At EPA, music seems to serve not only to celebrate their ties but also to reveal them in a way that "brings out" social relations, making them visible at times (Müller 2000: 89). It is as if their musical performance is not a mere amusement but gives them a place in the world and among relationships with other people.

CONCLUSION

In this chapter, we have discussed music socialization through family and communities and how it can be developed in other areas, such as school and social projects. With a comprehensive approach, based on three case studies, we have focused on everyday musical practices. In this way, we wanted to study music education facts with tools that could analyze the specifics of music as a social fact. Both in NGO social projects and in the school environment, the students are at social risk, and many of them are involved with drug trafficking and other unhealthy practices.

The interviews with these social actors showed that the possibility of gathering systematic music education process, beyond the frontiers of the community, becomes itself part of the relational capital of individuals and social groups. It means that any transformation depends on existing networks between individuals of the community and those belonging to other social groups—the social capital of the community. It means that, like any other capital (human, financial), investment in social capital also has a return or benefit.

The implications for the epistemological field of music education of this view recognize that the production of musical-pedagogical knowledge should consider multiple contexts of the social reality, dissolving hierarchical categories of cultural values. Furthermore, it is necessary to reexamine the relationship between the knowledge of popular culture and the knowledge established by the universities, as music educators have already proposed.

The contextual perspective of an empirical field reflects the complexity that is present in music-pedagogical processes and is understood as a field that offers the possibility to learn, simultaneously, different aspects of social reality. The two specific spaces join groups, becoming a laboratory of collective experiences that have as their focal point music as social practice.

What is the role of music education processes and culture in these contexts? This question can be understood as ways that produce knowledge from other meanings, incorporating questions that seem to be inherent in the learning and teaching process of any area. But, they are deeply overlaid in guides and decisions. They require reflection, analysis, and commitment because they are the factors that can involve new physical and sociocultural spaces, connecting cognitive, social, ethical, aesthetic, and political aspects to a perspective of social transformation.

Music education in these three case studies was revealed as a positive factor that can change the individuals and groups socially, mainly if the sociocultural patterns in musical practices present in the students' daily lives are considered. The notion of belonging and the concern for issues of human dignity emerge as a feature that identifies the young musicians from these institutions. When we tried to understand the choice made for music education by the children and adolescents from the suburbs of São Paulo, Rio, and Porto Alegre, we realized that many factors are being mixed with immediately explicit variables, such as, "willingness to study music." We realized that the answer could only be found in a deep study that would reveal that the relations are established between youngsters at social risk and music education, that relationships are established between these students and the social projects environment or even away from it, and that there is a relationship between music classes and other school subjects.

These perspectives were aimed at contributing to the reflection and practice about the role of music education in the politically aware process of social movements and social projects in NGOs and schools. These institutions seek transformation and social justice, minimizing poverty, inequality, and social exclusion in favor of human dignity.

ACKNOWLEDGMENTS

Magali Kleber thanks the participant coordinators of Projects Meninos do Morumbi and Villa Lobinhos for their having shared the value of music in their precious life stories, making possible this research.

NOTES

1 *Chorinho* is a genre created from the mixture of elements of European ballroom dancing (like schottisch, waltz, minuet, and especially the polka) and the popular music tradition, with elements of African music.

REFERENCES

Blacking, J. 1995. "Music, Culture and Experience." In *Music, Culture and Experience: Selected Papers of John Blacking*, edited by P. Bohlman and B. Nettl, 223–242. Chicago: University of Chicago Press.

Carvalho, I. M. M. de, and P. H. de Almeida. 2003. Família e proteção social. *São Paulo em perspectiva* 17 (2): 109–122.

Eyerman, R., and A. Jamison. 1998. *Music and Social Movements: Mobilizing Traditions in Twentieth Century*. Cambridge: Cambridge University Press.

Green, A. M. 1987. "Les comportements musicaux des adolescents" in *Harmoniques, Musiques, Identités* 2: 88–102.

Green, A. M. 2000. *Musique et sociologie: enjeux méthodologiques et approaches empiriques*. Paris: L'Harmattan.

Kleber, M. O. 2006a. "Music Education Practice in Non-Governmental Organizations: Two Case Studies in Brazilian Urban Context." PhD Diss., Universidade Federal do Rio Grande do Sul. Accessed August 13, 2010. http://www.lume.ufrgs.br/handle/10183/9981.

Kleber, M. O. 2006b. "Music Education in Practice in Non-Governmental Organization: Two Case Studies in Brazilian Urban Context." In *Creating Partnerships, Making Links, and Promoting Change:*, edited by D. Coffman and L. Higgins, 102–110. Proceedings from the International Society for Music Education (ISME) 2006, ISME Seminar of the Commission for Community Music Activity.

Kraemer, R. D. 1995. "Dimensionen und Funktionen musikpädagogischen Wissens." In *Musikpädagogische Forschung*, edited by Georg Maas, 146–172. Essen, Germany: Verlag de Blaue Eule.

Mauss, Marcel. 2003. "Ensaio sobre a dádiva." In *Sociologia e antropologia*. Translated by Paulo Neves, edited by Marcel Mauss, 185–318. São Paulo: Cosac and Naify. Originally published as *Sociologie et anthropologie* (Paris: Presses Universitaires de France, 1950).

Müller, V. 2000. "'A música é, bem dizê, a vida da gente': um estudo com crianças e adolescentes em situação de rua na Escola Municipal de Porto Alegre—EPA." Masters dissertation, Universidade Federal do Rio Grande do Sul, Porto Alegre.

Small, C. 2006. "Musicking: A Ritual in Social Space." Cielo, TX. April 1995. Accessed May 31, 2010. http://www.musekids.org/musicking.html.

Souza, J., and A. Dias. 2009. "Música, escola e sociabilidades juvenis em situação de risco social: a experiência de investigação no estágio pós-doutoral." In *18º Encontro Anual da Associação Brasileira de Educação Musical*. 800–806. Londrina: Associação Brasileira de Educação Musical.

Souza, J. 1996. "Contribuições teóricas e metodológicas da sociologia para pesquisa em educação musical." In *5º Encontro Anual da Associação Brasileira de Educação Musical*. 11–40. Londrina: Associação Brasileira de Educação Musical.

9

GEORGIAN (CAUCASUS) CHILDREN'S POLYPHONIC CONCEPTION OF MUSIC

POLO VALLEJO

THIS chapter focuses on the unique musical culture of Georgia, a nation located in the Caucasus region at the nexus of Eastern Europe and western Asia, between the Black Sea and the Caspian Sea. With its unique musical language and the originality and richness of its vocal polyphonies in both secular and religious forms, it is a living and dynamic musical treasury. Georgian history and traditions have been transmitted since time immemorial through collective singing. It is one of the most important ways Georgians reaffirm their identity, even in existentially difficult times. As in all oral traditions, the entire community, including wizened elders and young children, share circumstances in which music functions as a link between material and symbolic life and is the main vehicle for transmitting basic thought and sentiment. Although music may appear to be performed most frequently by adults, children also are observed to participate in musical events—without feeling like "outsiders" within a musical system whose harmonic language is per se complex. On the contrary, children assimilate the music they hear and are able to

Figure 9.1: Three generations of Georgian singers: Anzor Erkomaishvili, Girogi Donadze, and his son Erekle, singing polyphonies during a *Supra* banquet at Anzor's home. Tbilisi, September 2008 (Photo: Polo Vallejo).

follow along, singing with adults, without barriers or a sense of struggle, as can be seen in Figure 9.1. This chapter is intended as an initial exploration of the phenomenon of vocal polyphony in Georgia as it is experienced by children, with attention to the particular pieces described. As it is a first examination of children's music in Georgia to be conducted, it should not be considered definitive.

FIRST ENCOUNTERS IN THE MUSIC OF GEORGIA

My first contact with Georgian music performed live dates back to September 2006, when Simha Arom and I were invited by the Folklore Research Center at the State Conservatory of Tbilisi to participate as speakers at the third international symposium on traditional polyphony. When attending the evening concerts at the conservatory, I was astonished by the numerous examples of Georgian polyphonic music that were performed by vocal ensembles coming from every region of the country. As we were so impressed by the beauty and complexity of these polyphonies, Arom and I decided then to undertake research together in hopes of understanding and decoding the features that characterize the vocal music, particularly its harmonic aspects. We are now quite familiar with the culture and system of Georgian music, but we are still immersed in an ocean of questions for which we have no answers. We want to identify the typological classification of modal scales and their variants and the simultaneous intervals and constitution of chords and to analyze the harmonic syntax. The results of our initial investigations have been extensively discussed with recognized Georgian musicologists and other colleagues (see acknowledgments). In order that I might learn more of the vocal music and its harmonic matter, I sought to determine the experience of Georgian children and to study firsthand the relationship between their repertoire and that of their elders.

I considered the hypothetical possibility that if children are able to sing polyphonic songs with features that are similar to those of adults' songs, then it should be possible to find in the children's repertoire more "rudimentary" chords and/or simplified harmonic syntax processes. My aim was to determine whether children, in performing polyphonically, might use less complex harmonic structures that would then provide us with the key to better understanding the complexities of Georgian music, even as children's polyphonic sounds might also be a way of providing "access" for foreign ears. The chapter's title refers to the fact that the ability to sing within a polyphonic context seems to be acquired by children of Georgia in an unconscious way, as it corresponds to polyphonic oral traditions that are alive and well in the culture at large (especially as performed by adults).

Following my personal experience among the Wagogo children of Tanzania (Vallejo 2004), through which I discovered an extraordinary universe of children and their music, I imagined that similar circumstances of children's music making might materialize in Georgia. To this end, I scheduled two field trips in Georgia in order to establish a direct contact with particular children and to "test" their polyphonic abilities. My idea was to begin by limiting myself to the Tbilisi area, which, besides being the location of the majority of the Georgian population, is also characterized by the loss of traditional music due to the omnipresent urban influences of media and technology; my Georgian colleagues informed me of the striking difference in the musical scenes in urban and rural areas. Extracts from my field notes at Tbilisi, Georgia, contextualize the research undertaken on the music that Georgian children make.

The Last Field Notebook: Tbilisi, Monday, March 22, 2010

I've just arrived at the Tbilisi State Conservatory, where I will be giving some workshops to Music Education, Ethnomusicology, and Composition students. As Rusudan Tsurtsumia, Director of International Research Center for Traditional Polyphony, suggested, we phoned Giorgi (Gigi) Garaqanidze (G.G.), a researcher, the leader of the Ensemble Mtiebi, and heir to his father's musical legacy. Edischer Garaqanidze, G.G.'s father, was a renowned scholar of Georgian folklore.

The main purpose of my trip is to visit the Children's Folklore-Ethnographical Studio, "Amer-Imeri." G.G. directs this studio in Tbilisi, where children's learning is nurtured through the practice of traditional folk songs, games, and dances. Components of Georgian history, ethnographies of Georgian citizens, mythology, folk literature, and church chanting are included for children to experience and know at the Studio, in order to "get closer to the customs of the ancestors." This visit and venue is an ideal source for obtaining data and, while the experience is brief, it will be revealing. Because of his interest in my research, Gigi Garaqanidze journeyed from his home outside of Tbilisi to personally chaperone me on my visit; this is a mark of the exquisite hospitality of Georgians!

In order to be time-efficient, G.G. organized a group of children to perform some samples of Georgia's traditional songs for me. He asked me, "What kind of songs are you interested in?" and I responded, "Please do not prepare anything, as I want to listen to the children singing spontaneously." G.G. was willing to experiment with me, so that on our arrival at "Amer-Imeri" School, a group of about fifteen children between 6 and 11 years old, accompanied by adults from the Mtiebi Ensemble, was waiting for me.

After the opening greetings, both the children and adults start singing a traditional song together, and this is what I am hoping for—to be able to hear the multipart organization of their voices. G.G. then accepts my proposal, though not without curiosity and wonder, that the adults be invited to a sing a song that is unfamiliar to the children, so that we can note how the children respond (and whether they could sing the new and unfamiliar song). The adults begin to sing, and the children listen attentively with ears and eyes wide open. As the adults are repeating a ritornello section, G.G. encourages them to continue without interruption. So it was, that as the adults sing a song that could only be described as "purely Georgian in style" (with plenty of harmonies that may be called "dissonant," but which are not perceived as such by them), the children listen until they are gradually "babbling" and articulating a text which for them seemed to be more difficult than making the music.

The collective singing continues naturally until the youngsters are fully integrated into the song with the adults. I am amazed at the moment when, without stopping, each child spontaneously chooses one of three voices to sing—according to his or her own tessitura. (Remember that there is no written notation or words, but just the song's live performance.) Then comes the "miracle," when the children continue singing, in parts, this polyphonic song without the adults! G.G., along with the others who are present (Zurab Tskrialashvili, Ekaterine Diasamidze, Rusiko Tsurtsumia, and Nana Valisvili), show signs of satisfaction and maybe a little pride in the children. This experience confirms my initial hypothesis, that Georgian children, indeed, have a way of understanding polyphonic music, perceiving the harmonies as well as the principal melody and the text, and eventually learning it so well as to be able to sing it. They "inherit" the music almost unconsciously from adults, who are their best singing models.

We repeated the experiment of having the adults sing another, and another polyphonic song, all initially unfamiliar to the children until, by listening, they learned to perform the song themselves. We proceeded to record one of the songs, "Sisatura" (Samegrelo), and while discussing the results with G.G., I also observed that a group of three girls, about 10 or 11 years old, were testing out and synchronizing the different vocal parts. With their permission, we did a multitrack recording using what is called

Figure 9.2: Recording with a multitrack with Gigi Garaqanidze at Amer-Imeri School
(Photo: Ekaterine Diasamidze).

the Playback technique (similar to Simha Arom's use of the technique in 1973, when he recorded the polyphonic music of the Aka pygmies for analysis). The technique will allow me to separate the voices, to transcribe them, and to verify the relationships between them—the points of their connection. The girls sang as if they had done it all their life, as if it were a game. I was quite fascinated, as their attitude further demonstrated that polyphony is for them a very familiar and manageable language.

GEORGIAN CULTURE

Georgia (in the Georgian alphabet საქართველოო, transliterated *Sakartvelo*), known since 1991 as the Republic of Georgia, is a Eurasian country located on the Black Sea coast, south of the Caucasus mountain range. It shares borders with Russia to the north and Turkey, Armenia, and Azerbaijan to the south, its location establishing the undrawn boundary between Europe and Asia. The administrative capital of Georgia is Tbilisi and the country is divided into seventeen different regions that are marked by local features (and musical differences). Today, two of these regions, Abjazia and Samachablo (South Ossetia), have unilaterally declared their independence with Russia's support. They have not, however, been recognized by Georgia or most other Western countries. The regional map of Georgia, its provinces, and vernacular names change depending on the current political situation.

The ancient Greeks and Romans named this area Iberia, and through the centuries of invasions by surrounding empires—Byzantine, Persian, Ottoman, Mongolian, Arabic, and Russian—Georgia's sense of national identity has remained intact. Its roots are profoundly European and it possesses undeniably Mediterranean traits, including a climate that supports ancient and continuing winemaking and gastronomic traditions. The beauty, refinement, and complexity of its vocal polyphonies, both in religious and profane forms, are combined with the use of the vernacular language, მხედრული (transliterated *kartvelian*), whose non-Cyrillic alphabet *Mkhedruli*, used since the eleventh century, is unique in the world.

The Georgian Orthodox Church, founded in the first century AD, is one of the world's most ancient Christian Churches. The liturgy is intensely connected to a community that actively participates in the rite that is centralized around the figure of Patriarch Elias II, and it still provides a strong sense of social cohesion that is part of Georgian national identity. The role of music during Orthodox ceremonies, represented by sacred vocal polyphonies, is key to understanding the transcendence of religious beliefs in Georgia.

Features of Georgian Music

The Georgian experience of material and symbolic life is expressed and reaffirmed through collective multipart singing. The various regions that constitute the Republic of Georgia each possess their own music repertories, styles, and procedures. These in turn are linked to very specific social circumstances: the Orthodox liturgy; epic, historic, banquet (*Supra*), and dedicatory chants; lyric, comic, equestrian, wedding, curative, round, and dance songs; and lullabies, work (harvesting crops, grapes, or corn), and children's songs. Performed for the most part by groups of male singers (occasionally by women's groups but very rarely mixed men's and women's groups), the music includes the use of traditional instruments, of which the *chonguri* and *panduri* (lutes) are best known. These lutes also accompany a highly varied repertory of popular dances, some of which demand great virtuosity from the dancers.

One of the particularities of Georgian choral music is that, unlike most modal music, which is generally monophonic, it is polyphonic. A unique facet is the nature of its constitutive chords and the harmonies that result from their combination. In this sense Georgian music is characterized by sudden changes of color that seem startling and in some cases "strange" to Western ears. In fact, Western theorists provide a hierarchical treatment of so-called consonant and dissonant chords, whereas in Georgian music these chords are on an equal footing and are heard as parts of the harmonic corpus of expressive musical beauty. The sounds of Georgian harmonies may bring to mind harmonies associated with the Middle Ages in Europe or those of the twentieth century, giving the impression of music that is at once religious and profane, popular and "cultured," old and new. Georgian song moves between the popular and the sacred, which, in any case, offers a nexus where folk wisdom, logic, and emotion converge.

PARAMETERS OF GEORGIAN MUSIC

The songs sung by adults and children at the Children's Folklore Ethnographic Studio were recorded; they were then transcribed and analyzed (along with other songs that had been collected earlier). Between continued listening, transcription, and standard techniques of musical analysis, it was possible to elaborate a provisional theory concerning the pitch modes, cadences, and basic harmonic aspects of Georgian song. It became axiomatic that the songs were as much a part of children's musical sensibilities as they were of the adults; these songs could be known and were performed by children and adults.

Georgian Modes

Due to melodic variability in Georgian songs, modal theory in Georgian music is still a matter of musicological debate (as observed at the Fifth Symposium in Traditional Polyphonies that took place in Tbilisi in October 2010). Taking as a reference point the last note on which all voices converge in unison at the end of the song, or when the last simultaneously sounding notes form a perfect fifth (in both cases, the *finalis*), most of the pieces analyzed are based on one of the following modes (A, G, E):

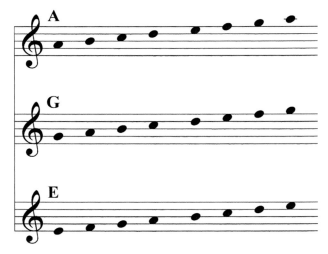

Figure 9.3: Modes.

Sometimes, however, because of accidental alterations, there are temporary "modulations" to neighboring modes, while other pieces that are "harmonically" more complex seem to present more than one mode or another modal syntax. The two upper voices in a three-part song generally proceed by conjunct movement and in parallel motion. Only infrequently is there more disjunct movement (intervals of a third or greater) produced by a change of position of one of the voices within a chord, anticipation of the final note by one of the voices, or repetition of a section. (There are exceptions, such as "escape" notes, the highest voice in B-type cadences [see below], and in the *krimanchuli* voice [*Yodel*] used in some repertoires.)

Cadences

As in adult song repertoires, the songs performed by children showed the presence of three types of cadences, each of which is invariably characterized by the progression of the lowest voice from the seventh degree to the tonic pitch. The interval between these two degrees is always a major 2nd (a whole tone). This cadence can integrate other degrees as well, for example, the sequence of IV-V-VI-VII-I (in C Major F-G-A-B♭ -C).

The first type of song cadence (Type A, Figure 9.4) is characterized by the arrival of the upper voices on the first degree in unison, by way of ascending and descending conjunct motion, respectively, and the lowest voice by ascending contrary motion.

In the second type of song cadence (Type B, Figure 9.5), the voices also arrive on the first degree in unison, but the upper voice does so by way of a jump of a

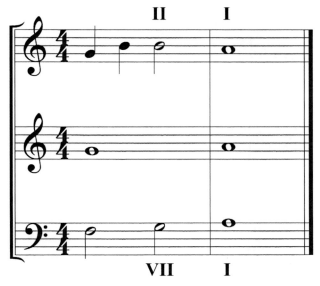

Figure 9.4: "Type A" song cadence.

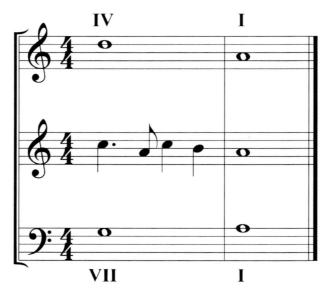

Figure 9.5: V"Type B" song cadence.

descending 4th (from the fourth to the tonic degree), while the middle voice goes from the second degree to the first degree. Meanwhile, the bass makes its characteristic VII-I movement by means of ascending and contrary motion.

The third type of song cadence (Type C, Figure 9.6) is characterized by a final upward turn from the fourth to the fifth degree in the upper voice. The middle voice descends from the second to the tonic degree. The bass voice sounds an ascending VII-I movement, resulting in the interval of a fifth.

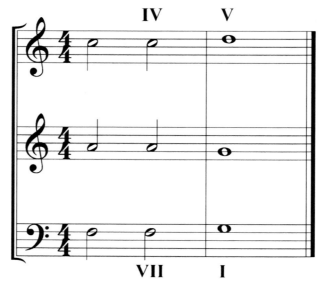

Figure 9.6: "Type C" song cadence.

Homorhythmic Songs Technique

Homorhythmic songs are characterized by all their vocal parts having an identical rhythmic articulation. Some of them, although they exhibit general homorhythmic tendencies, include brief ornamentations such as passing tones, suspensions, anticipations, appoggiaturas, and embellishments between chords, all of which provide more density to the polyphonic texture. The relationship between the voices is predominantly characterized by parallel, but also oblique and contrary, motion. Between the first and second voices we find mainly parallel and oblique motion, with contrary motion between the top two and the lowest voice. In each of the modes (A, G, E), there are various chord syntax possibilities. Certain scale degrees present a greater variety of possible chords than others, with the most frequently used degrees in the A, G, and E modes being the first, sixth, and seventh pitches of the scale.

THE CONTEXT, TRANSCRIPTION, AND ANALYSIS OF THE SONGS

Children were recorded singing traditional Georgian songs at three official music schools located in Tbilisi: the Chokhonelidze School, directed by the Shokholenidze sisters (Tamar and Tiniko); the Rustavi School, directed by Tamar Buadze; and the "Amer-Imeri" School, directed by Giorgi Garaqanidze. Multipart singing was a constant element of the children's repertoires, and they showed great ability and naturalness in assimilating the polyphonic repertoire of adults. The children of the Tbilisi music schools were adept and enthusiastic at singing songs of entertainment, work, and love, as well as lullabies. Two of the songs, "Erejeli" and "Sisatura," are offered in full transcription (See Web Figures 9.7 and 9.8 for recordings ◉ and Figures 9.9 and 9.10 for transcriptions).

Five recordings of other songs are available on the companion website. They are as follows:

Web Figure 9.11 ◉: "Oridili" (Racha): Recorded at the Chokhonelidze School in September 2009. This work song is sung while preparing fire and heating water for cooking.

Web Figure 9.12 ◉: "Khertlis Naduri" (Achara): Recorded at the Rustavi School in September 2009. Sung only by women, the title means "handle" and the subject of the song is a young weaver who injures her hand while working.

Web Figure 9.13 ◉: "Nai Nai" (Achara): Recorded at the Garaqanidze School in March 2010. Most of the words are meaningless; the song is performed as a round circle dance on the day a child is born.

Web Figure 9.14 ◉: "Mokhevis Kalo Tinao" (Khevi): Recorded at the Garaqanidze School in March 2010. This love song is dedicated to Tinao, a young girl from the Tbilisi region.

Figure 9.9: Transcription of "Erejeli" (Samegrelo). This entertainment song was recorded at the Chokhonelidze School in September 2009. The language of this comical story of Erejeli, a young boy, is Magrelian. Three voice parts are articulated homorhythmically, the two highest in absolute parallel motion and the bass with similar rhythmic articulation and mainly on two pitches (except in the cadence). (The pitches of the transcriptions are not absolute. Transpositions have been used to avoid accidentals as much as possible, thereby facilitating a clearer and faster reading of the score.)

Figure 9.10: Transcription of "Sisatura" (Samegrelo). This lullaby was recorded at the Garaqanidze School in March 2010. The intent of the song is to shoo away a small dog, as the text translates "Go away jackal!"

	SONG	REGION	CONTEXT	MODE	CADENCE TYPE	MULTIPART Organization
1	*Erejeli*	Samegrelo	Entertainment	A	B	Strict Parallelism Homorhythmic
2	*Oridili*	Racha	Work song	A	A	Strict Parallelism Homorhythmic
3	*Khertlis Naduri*	Achara	Work song	E	C	Strict Parallelism Homorhythmic
4	*Nai-Nai*	Achara	Circle dance	G	B	Strict parallelism Homorhythmic
5	*Mokhevis*	Khevi	Love song	A	C	Strict parallelism Homorhythmic
6	*Lale-Lale*	Kakheti	Love song	A	C	Strict parallelism Homorhythmic
7	*Sisatura*	Samegrelo	Lullaby	E	A	Strict parallelism Homorhythmic

Figure 9.16: Summary of the social and musical matter of the seven songs of Georgian children mentioned above.

Web Figure 9.15 🔊: "Lale-Lale" (Kakheti): Recorded at the Garaqanidze School in March 2010. A love song starting with nonsense words; it is performed with a dance.

These seven songs are unified in their homorhythmic articulation in the use of a multipart technique in strict parallelism, as well as the use of conjunct melodic motion between the voices. Differences between the songs are in the use of the modal scales (A, G, or E) and in the cadence types (A, B, or C), but the characteristic Georgian polyphony is constant in its use of modal harmonic language, immediately discernible in constituent chords and their combinations (see Figure 9.16 for a comparative summary).

TRADITION AS A PROCESS OF TRANSMISSION

Although the original intent of my fieldwork was to examine the songs of Georgian children's play, including singing games and rhymed chants, this music was not evident among the children with whom I met. Rather, the phenomenon of children singing adult songs in full polyphonic array is an astonishing finding of the project. Georgian colleagues Rusudan Tsurtsumia and Joseph Jordania offered insightful comments on music, children (and other learners), and the music teaching and learning process, as well as remarks as to the "inexplicable [lack of] attention" of scholars thus far to children's music.

Joseph Jordania commented on models of music transmission, teaching, and learning, then and now. He recalled that "in older generations, learning happened in real life—in families and on feast-days." This was not through formal teaching but through the osmotic process by which people hear and learn songs. He described the older model of "learning without teaching" as a slow process, but one that developed song repertoires as well as the possibilities for development and improvisation. Jordania described the newer process of pedagogy as "learning through teaching," in which students are taught a single version of the song by expert singers and singing teachers and are involved in regular rehearsals with a village ensemble. A child will identify with a particular teacher and will say, "I am Erkomaishvili's student" or "I am Kasvadze's pupil" (Jordania and Tsurtsumia 2010).

Rusudan Turstumia analyzed the situation of children's musical repertoire and its transmission and acquisition. He noted that children sing their own songs and singing games, but are constantly engaged with adults singing polyphonically or are within listening range of these songs. Singing is a normal practice in traditional Georgian families, with parents and children sharing songs together, typically from the adult song repertoire, with songs of simpler musical structures for younger children and more complex songs for older children. Traditional processes of oral transmission are observable in Georgian families, so children may start off by identifying the melody as the single part to sing and only subsequently begin to sing other voice parts they have heard adults sing (Jordania and Tsurtsumia 2010).

Turstumia also remarked that there are few places outside the family where Georgian children can receive singing instruction: elementary schools today do not use the traditional repertoire as an educational tool. In secondary schools, children have music lessons but do not learn traditional songs, even though there are some textbooks based on folk songs. Only some music studios, schools, and hobby groups cultivate traditional music. Examples are the Lagidze (choir) Music School of Tbilisi and the "Amer-Imeri," Garaqanidze's school.

The singing of Georgian polyphonic song varies by region, so that it is less strong in urban areas than in rural areas and more likely to be sung by children in mountain regions such as Achara and Svaneti. Polyphonic singing is not to be found in children's playful song repertoire, but rather in folk music and liturgical music, in which children employ such vocal techniques as bourdon, homorhythm, and counterpoint. Turstumia (2010) explained that some melodic alterations are made by children who are comfortable with improvisation (which may rely on their experience in families who hold singing as an important and necessary tradition).

The Previous Field Notebook: September 9, 2009

Since first visiting Georgia in 2006, today will mark my first musical experience with children. In order to listen to the children singing, we made an appointment to visit the music school that the sisters Tamar and Tiniko Tchokhonelidze run in Tbilisi. Before my arrival the teachers asked me, "What are you interested in hearing?" to which I responded, "The repertoire of children's songs." Today, we drive to the studio and are

led to an empty classroom with chairs, a piano, and a stereo. In a few moments a group
of seven girls and one boy, between the ages of eight and ten, enter in a respectful and
somewhat shy manner.

One of the teachers sits at the piano, looks at me, and makes a gesture, showing
me without words that they are ready to sing. I return the gesture silently, indicating
that I am, too. The teacher plays a piano accompaniment that sounds like "cabaret"
music, and the children, with absolute ease and grace, sing in the same cabaret style.
They sing very well, but I am amazed, wondering how I had not accurately expressed
myself.

The song ends, and I applaud, thank, and congratulate them. Then I explain
that I am not interested in music that sounds the same everywhere and ask again for
"Georgian folk music, Georgian children's traditional repertoire." They are surprised
that I am interested in this kind of music, and they tell me that they did not prepare
songs like that. I respond that they should "let the children sing alone anything that
comes to their minds, spontaneously . . . children's songs . . . "

The children look at us strangely, trying to understand. The teachers ask them
for a song that everyone knows. After a moment of doubt, one girl starts singing, and
one by one the rest follow. From this moment everything became clear, as the children
began to sing songs that emerged from a common place in their collective memory:
three-voice songs. Their first choice was "Erejeli."

Conclusion

Until recently, the transmission of musical knowledge in Georgia had regularly followed the process of oral tradition (and aural acquisition), "from mouth to ear."
Since Georgian independence in 1991, and despite the recent circumstances that the
country has experienced since its emancipation from the Soviet Union, Georgians
today live within a time of considerable social, political, and economic development.
Yet music continues to be a social and religious component of Georgian national
identity, and thus far music is not much affected by these changes that are threaded
through the young nation's evolution. The wealth—both quantitatively and qualitatively—of the musical heritage of Georgia and the link between the custodians of
this tradition and the music itself are continually reinforced by singular events that
provide a backdrop for secular polyphony. Among these are the Georgian banquet
Supra, during which everyone shares food, songs, history, and emotions, and the
music linked to the Orthodox liturgy; both phenomena involve the community as
a whole.

The work to preserve the musical treasures of Georgia has been carried out by
the Research Department of the Tbilisi Conservatory, the International Center of
Traditional Polyphony, and various recognized vocal ensembles of Georgia that are
dedicated to the performance and interpretation of traditional music. Efforts have

been advanced in the documentation of exclusively adult repertoire in Georgia, whereas children's musical repertory has received very little attention. Among those whose main mission it is to teach children and youth, knowledge of songs children sing will be useful in assisting the permanence of this repertoire and supporting children's efforts as custodians of their musical treasure.

The traditional music of Georgia has been declared an "Intangible Cultural Heritage of Humanity" by UNESCO. It is more than anecdotal to note that one traditional song, "Chakrulo," known and sung by everyone in Georgia, has become even more widely known. It was one of the musical examples, together with other sound materials, that was sent into space in August 1977 on the space explorer, Voyager, as a musical example that represents the identity and diversity of the planet Earth.

ACKNOWLEDGMENTS

Dedicated to Liselotte Orff and to Gigi Garaqanidze. I would like to sincerely thank all the people and institutions who, directly or indirectly, helped me during the collecting of information on children's music in Georgia.

REFERENCES

Arom, Simha, and Polo Vallejo. 2008. "Towards a Theory of the Chord Syntax of Georgian Polyphony." Proceedings of the Fourth International Symposium on Traditional Polyphony. Tbilisi, Georgia, September 2008.

Chokhonelidze, Kukuri. 2003. Kartuli Khalkhuri Musika. Samegrelo [Georgian Folk Music. Samegrelo]. Vol. 1. An anthology of song transcriptions with annotations. Tbilisi, Georgia: International Center for Georgian Folk Song and International Research Center for Traditional Polyphony at Tbilisi State Conservatoire [in Georgian and English].

Erkomaishvili, Anzor. 2005. Georgian Folk Music (Guria). Artem Erkomaishvili Collection. Tbilisi, Georgia: The International Center for Georgian Folk Song.

Garaqanidze, Giorgi. 2008. Georgian Ethnomusic Theatre and Its Origins. Tbilisi, Georgia: GamomcNemloba "Petiti." Book + DVD.

Jordania, Joseph, and Rusudan Tsurtsumia . 2010. Echoes from Georgian: Seventeen Arguments on Georgian Polyphony. New York: Nova Science Publishers.

Jordania, Joseph. 2006. Who Asked the First Question: Origins of Vocal Polyphony, Human Intelligence, Language and Speech. Tbilisi, Georgia: Logos, Tbilisi State University.

Tsurtsumia, Rusudan, and Tamaz Gabisonia, eds. 2004–2008. Bulletin of the International Research Center for Traditional Polyphony. 1–7.

Vallejo, Polo. 2004. "Mbudi mbudi na mhanga: The Musical Universe of the Wagogo Children from Tanzania." 2 CDs. Madrid. www.polovallejo.com. (Web figure 9.17 ⊙).

10

INTEGRATION IN MEXICAN CHILDREN'S MUSICAL WORLDS

JANET STURMAN

Scenario 1: A Class at the Ollin Yoliztli School in Mexico City

Nine-year-old Teresa[1] strides to the front of the room, untucks her violin from beneath her arm, and raises it to her chin. Standing proudly before her classmates, she glances to her teacher, Maestro Felipe, and they begin playing. Teresa bows a rapid Huastecan melody while her instructor strums the rhythmic accompaniment on the jarana. *Undaunted by her intonation inaccuracies, Teresa plays boldly, without hesitation. Her rhythms are perfect and her phrasing commanding. With equal confidence she stops her bow and in her clear bell-like voice sings the verse of the* son de Carnaval, *"El Pajarito Tordo" (see musical notation in Figure 10.1):*

Pajarito Tordo	Little black bird
Pájaro palomo	Little male dove
Come platanito	Eat a little *plátano* (banana)
y ya no te enojes	And don't get angry anymore

Her delivery is powerful and expressive, and she looks directly into the eyes of her listeners. Alternating instrumental interlude with sung verse, she continues with the same verse in Náhuatl:

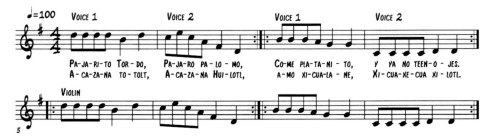

Figure 10.1: Notation for "*El Pajarito Tordo.*"

Acazana totolt
Acazana Huilotl
amo xicualane
Xicuaxecua xilotl

She completes the song and with a satisfied smile accepts the enthusiastic applause of her classmates before returning to her seat.

To someone visiting this traditional Mexican music class at the Centro Cultural Ollin Yoliztli, in Mexico City, Teresa's performance seems extraordinary; such poise is rare in young children, but each of the twenty children in the room will play the same song, with similar poise. In my visit on June 9, 2009, I noted that each took a turn stepping into the character of a commanding performer. Teresa later explained to me, "When I play violin *sones*, I take the job of leader." Envisioning herself a professional, playing alongside an adult as she might at a fandango in a public plaza on a fiesta night, Teresa radiates an air of genuine confidence. Teresa's actions introduce the first important theme that this chapter will explore: how Mexican children consistently, despite very different musical or social contexts, reimagine themselves so that they can perform like, and alongside, specialists.

The song Teresa played is a *son de Carnaval*, a traditional dance song performed during the festivities for the carnival celebration that precedes Lent in the northern region of the state of Veracruz along Mexico's Gulf Coast. Her performance speaks to the principal questions of this chapter: (1) How do Mexican children learn music? and (2) What music fills the life of Mexican children? While there are many answers to these questions, there is a body of music that Mexican children come to know as a shared heritage. The *canciones, sones, huapangos,* and *rancheras* that comprise the repertory of mariachi ensembles represent some of Mexico's best-known music. Since the first decades of the twentieth century, when the mariachi first took hold as the symbol of the nation and as a medium for the integration of regional styles into a shared format, that tradition has eclipsed all other music from Mexico. Nonetheless, the mariachi and learning practices associated with it have been well documented by other authors (e.g., Sheehy 1999, 2005) and will not be discussed here. Instead, this chapter will use selected case studies to indicate the wider scope of musical education for Mexican children, ranging from formal classical instruction to the practice of distinct folkloric and popular styles conventionally associated with particular regions and ethnicities. The music learned by Teresa in her class at the Centro Cultural Ollin Yoliztli offers one example.

"Pajarito Tordo," the song Teresa played, has likely circulated in Mexico for at least 300 years, but what matters to her is that the song is about a bird; she loves animals. The alternation of Spanish and Náhuatl words evokes the defining encounter between Spanish colonizers and the native inhabitants of this land. Náhuatl, the language of the ancient Aztecs, is still spoken in several regions of Mexico and many Huastecan *sones* include lyrics in Náhuatl. Teresa studies the history of the Nahua in school and is proud to be able to sing these lyrics in their language.

Like other cultural expressions from Veracruz, the blend of traditions in Huastecan *sones* also incorporates African elements brought by slaves who came to Mexico with the Spanish (even the *plátano*, or plantain, mentioned in the lyrics is thought to have come to Mexico by way of Africa). The duple meter features two alternating phrases performed in a call and response format (see Figure 1) that repeat throughout the piece. The *jarana* (a small guitar-like instrument, not notated) played by Teresa's teacher Maestro Felipe provides a constant harmonic accompaniment and an additional rhythmic layer. Although not used in the class on the day that Teresa played, a guitar typically reinforces the harmony and rhythm in the traditional Huastecan instrumental ensemble.

The northern region of the state of Veracruz is but one of the regions of the geographic territory in Mexico known as the Huasteca. Situated in the northeast of the country, the Huasteca includes the southern region of Tamaulipas, the eastern portion of San Luis Potosí, the Sierra Gorda region of Querétaro, and the northeast region of the state of Hidalgo. In the past in the Huasteca, females were discouraged from playing instruments and this remains the case in some areas (see Vergara de los Rios and Vargas Mendoza 2007). However, Maestro Felipe explains that today it is quite common to see girls and women playing instruments in native contexts. He also notes that there are now more workshops that offer instruction to both girls and boys in how to perform this traditional music. Young girls comprise the majority of Maestro Felipe's students in his violin *folklórico* classes at the Ollin Yoliztli school, something he cannot explain. One reason may be the poise and confidence they acquire from the experience.

When asked how he is able to instill such confidence in his young pupils, Maestro Felipe outlines the steps he takes. First, he teaches his students the lyrics of the song. He expects his students to master their singing of the song and marching to its rhythm, staying in strict time with the beat. Then, he teaches them the rhythm they will bow on the violin, without using their fingers on the strings. He demonstrates, the students imitate him; notation is not used. Next, they learn the fingering on the strings, now attending to intonation of the pitches of the melody. Finally, they play the song on the violin while singing. It is important that they can sing and exchange verses while solidly playing the violin and coordinating with the rhythmic accompaniment of the *jarana* (Felipe Valle, 2010, personal communication and e-mail exchanges).

Another theme of this chapter is cultural integration, for this process lies at the heart of the modern Mexican experience. How do Mexican children integrate the music they hear and learn into their lives? How do Mexican children's experiences relate to governmental support of music and efforts to integrate diverse cultural practices into a cohesive whole to strengthen the nation? Students at the Ollin Yoliztli school integrate their experience in learning traditional music into their lives in many ways. Few of Maestro Felipe's students will go on to perform professionally or earn a living solely from playing Huastecan music. However, several have formed independent folkloric groups for purposes of their own and for enjoyment. These young musicians travel from one community to another earning money playing for fiestas and giving workshops on the *son huasteco*. Other students find that they can contribute to the financial health of their families with the money they earn by performing traditional music (Felipe Valle, 2010, personal communication and e-mail exchange).

Mexican children quickly learn adult roles. Teresa is proud to be able to lead the ensemble. This role does not seem unusual to her; in many settings Mexican children lead performances and ceremonies and play alongside adults as soon as they are able. Maestro Felipe also teaches adolescent students at the National University in Mexico City, known as UNAM (Universidad Nacional Autónoma de México). Several of these students play the violin as a hobby, and when they have learned four or five songs they play on the public transport buses to earn a few pesos. Most former students move on to other professions; several complement their careers as psychologists, dentists, and biologists by playing Huastecan violin. Finally, for a handful of students, performing *son huasteco* becomes a way of life, even for those who did not grow up in the Huastecan region.

A Study of Flow and Response: Currents of Influence

Mexican leaders recognize music as vital to the nation's identity. From rulers to ordinary people, the ancient ancestors of contemporary Mexicans used music and associated arts as a tool to achieve national unification and cultural distinction, long before the country of Mexico existed as such (León-Portilla 2005). Nahua rulers supported conservatories to train youth as music specialists to lead religious and civic ritual (Meyer et al. 2003; Stevenson 1971, 1976, León-Portilla 2005). Centuries later, after Spanish rule, after independence, and after the revolution of 1910 that established modern Mexico, the role of central authority in musical and artistic life remains paramount. Government directives and educational reforms resulting from the revolution continue to influence modern Mexican musical life and how children build their musical worlds.

Despite the importance of official national policies, resources are distributed unevenly, and citizens, including children, do not respond uniformly to national directives. Cultural life in the country is undeniably shaped by currents of influence that might be considered as conforming to three types: centrifugal (moving out from a centralized source), centripetal (moving toward the center), and decentralized or peripheral (moving within a distinct sphere of action and separated from central activity). Resources, support for the arts, and educational and employment opportunities are most abundant in Mexico's capital and federal district, and that concentration affects activity around the country.

Mexico City is the site for the coordinating offices of the Sistema Nacional de Fomento Musical México (SNFM, http://snfm.conaculta.gob.mx), the central agency promoting musical development and education in the country. SNFM supports performing and training activities, including national and regional choruses, bands, and orchestras, as well as festivals and gatherings (*encuentros*), to promote and exchange regional arts. The pride of the program, and perhaps its best-known ambassador, is the Orquesta Sinfónica Infantíl y Juvenil, founded in 2001. Students and professionals come to Mexico City from across the nation to perform in the national youth orchestra, but also to study, work, and take advantage of many other opportunities. This draw represents a strong centripetal influence shaping music activity and education in the nation. The Centro Ollin Yoliztli, to which we will return, represents another important center for music and arts education in the nation's capital and illustrates the national commitment to promoting a range of formal approaches to musical instruction.

Policy, models, and resources also radiate out from the capital and influence activity beyond the federal capital and district. State-sponsored distributive programs, such as traveling puppet theaters that educate children and introduce them to music and the federally supported Alas y Raíces (Wings and Roots) programs instituted in each state of the nation to embrace and promote instruction in regional arts, represent a centrifugal flow of influence, along with radio, film, and television. These media also play a role in the dissemination and continued popularity of Cri Crí, the most influential character in Mexican children's music since the early twentieth century. Children may learn music from centrally directed media, but as the examples here will show, they adapt that music in practice, play, and drama in ways that reflect regional custom as well as personal experience.

The topic of music making in a peripheral context is considered in this chapter's brief introduction to children's musical activities at the Escuela Albergue Tríbu Pápago (Papago Tribal Boarding School). The case reveals Mexico's paradoxical attitudes and policies regarding its living indigenous population and how isolation affects children's opportunities.

VISIONARY METAPHORS FOR THE SHARED AND THE PARTICULAR

The visions, dreams, and passions of the Mexican people are eloquently expressed in their poetry. Poetic metaphors appear in song lyrics, but also in government slogans. In 1992 the Mexican government began a new program under the auspices of its Ministry of Culture, CONACULTA (Consejo Nacional para la Cultura y las

Artes) to promote local customs and artistic development in Mexican education titled Alas y Raíces (See www.cnca.gob.mx and http://www.conaculta.gob.mx/alas_raices.php). The program Alas y Raíces operates in each state of the country with funds from the National Council for Children's Cultural Development (CNDI), a division of CONACULTA. It differs in scope and mission from the Sistema Nacional Fundación Musical in that it includes a wider range of arts activities, ranging from support of juvenile wind bands in the Oaxaca region to entertaining interactive children's websites for exploring arts in culture. Aimed directly at children, largely in the primary grades, the Alas y Raíces program enacts Mexico's central legislative imperative to honor cultural practices rooted in tradition while also promoting new practices. This dual aim characterizes musical activity in Mexico, including how children learn music and incorporate it into their lives.

The wings and roots metaphor additionally provides a valuable conceptual frame for the complex processes of cultural integration that characterize Mexican children's musical worlds. In *Mexican National Identity: Memory, Innuendo and Popular Culture* (2008) historian William Beezley concludes that despite powerful national directives, the real character of Mexican national identity emerged from the responses of ordinary people to popular arts. Across the nation, Mexicans drew upon the popular arts to enact what we might call a particularized integration, a way of creating common ground that recognizes distinct contexts and overlapping identities and even encourages difference. Children's responses to musical instruction offer excellent examples of particularized integration.

OLLIN YOLIZTLI AND MUSIC EDUCATION IN THE MEGACITY

With a population of more than 8 million people in the federal district and more than 21 million people in the metropolitan area, Mexico City is one of the world's largest cities. The nation's top music schools are located here, and young people and adults come from around the country and abroad to study here. They are attracted to the prestigious programs at the Conservatorio Nacional de Música and the Escuela Superior de Música as well as the Escuela Nacional de Música at UNAM. All offer state-subsidized professional and preparatory training in programs that combine studio instruction with classes in solfege and music literature available without charge or at minimal cost, giving children the opportunity to begin focused music study at an early age. Each has its specialization; the Superior Music School, for example, offers an advanced degree in jazz. Students may also take advantage of specialized programs such as those at the distinctive Casa Escuela de la Música Mexicana (The School House of Mexican Music), which focuses exclusively on traditional music.

The opening scenario of this chapter took place in the foremost school of professional music training for children and youth in Mexico, the Centro Cultural Ollin Yoliztli. It is no accident that the school is named Ollin Yoliztli, which means "life movement" in Náhuatl, harkening back to the ancient Aztecs who believed that music and dance supported the celestial movements that ensured the continuation of human life. Matching the blended worlds symbolized by the Ollin glyph in the center of the Aztec calendar, the curriculum of Mexico City's Centro Ollin Yoliztli combines diverse programs of instruction to initiate children and youth in classical, popular, and traditional Mexican music and dance. Curricula are offered at primary, secondary, and college preparatory levels of instruction, serving pupils from ages six to nineteen years and supporting instruction in folkloric dance, ballet, chorus, and symphonic orchestra. Higher-level instruction is also offered at the school for advanced students seeking the *licenciatura* degree (the standard university degree, basically the equivalent of the bachelor's degree in the United States or Great Britain). Many of the nation's professional musicians began their careers at the School of Life Movement at Ollin Yoliztli.

Conservatories and schools of music elsewhere in the nation increasingly emphasize regional music traditions. Since the 1990s, funding from SNFM has created "instructional nuclei" in various states to promote regional arts. These sites often measure themselves against the national conservatories but also seek to disseminate their own traditions for others in the country to appreciate and accept. The continued support for instruction of Huastecan music and other styles, such as the *son jarocho* taught in the folkloric harp class and the Oaxacan marimba taught to young percussionists as part of the instructional options at Ollin Yoliztli, exemplify such efforts. True integration of folkloric and popular music into the repertory of classical players is a different story. A few students, such as fourteen-year-old percussionist Edgardo, another Ollin Yoliztli student, study both classical and folkloric technique. He does not represent the norm, as Maestro Felipe noted, "*Los clasicos* [the classical musicians] are afraid of losing their technique if they play popular or folkloric music, and the folk and pop musicians are afraid of becoming reading machines." This early specialization is contextually defined; students in each group worry that they will lose their ability to communicate with the community of listeners whose judgment they have come to most value.

MEDIA PARTNERS: CRI CRÍ, PUPPET THEATER, AND THE INTERNET

Mexican children learn plenty of music from radio and television, some of it created just for them. Although this is music created by adults, children adopt this music for their own purposes and hold these songs in their memories the way that

American children retain playful songs like "The Itsy Bitsy Spider." Among the most celebrated are the songs of Cri Crí, the beloved singing cricket created and voiced by the Mexican composer Francisco Gabilondo Soler (1907–1990). His popular radio show on station XEW from 1934 through 1954 aired Cri Crí songs around the country, providing a unifying repertory linking children from one region to another. Children throughout Mexico still sing Cri Crí songs, and the practice links generations as parents and teachers pass them along to children. Reflecting on his education in San Luis Potosí, Luis, now an adult PhD student, told me, "My mother and school teachers sang Cri Crí songs with me; we learned them like folksongs, by word of mouth and sang them at family gatherings." Marisela, a classmate raised in Cananea, Sonora, agreed, "I like 'La patita' [the duckling], 'El chorrito' [the little splash], and 'La muñeca fea' [the ugly doll], all the Cri Crí songs. We sang them a lot and now I sing them with my children." So familiar is Cri Crí (and so iconic of children and childhood in Mexico), that there are even preschools named for the little cricket (Stephens 2009).

Choral arrangements in attractive new publications, such as the set honoring Gabilondo's 100th birthday in 2007, keep the songs of the little cricket in circulation (Figure 10.2). While some songs, such as "El Negrito bailarín" (The Little Black Dancer) may offend modern sensibilities, others, such as "El chorrito" (Web Figure 10.3 **O**), with its poetic lesson about nature's water cycle, seem as fresh as ever. "We used to act out the lyrics, like little plays," said Marisela. Hundreds of primary school teachers, as well as amateur dramatic companies and puppeteers, have drawn upon Cri Crí songs in creating theatrical productions with and for children (Guillermo Murray Prisant, e-mail correspondence with the author, April 25, 2010). Puppet theater, a popular and long-standing medium for engaging children with music in Mexico, goes well beyond Cri Crí as a frame for integrating old and new, modern and folkloric, regional and foreign (Rosales 1997).

Scenario 2: Black Little Red Riding Hood

Children fidget in their seats at the theater as they await the start of the puppet show La Caperucita Negra y Roja[2] *by the Cúcara Mácara Puppet Theater[3] in the city of Morelia. They begin swaying in their seats as the irresistible rhythms of a recording of the Cuban salsa band La Sonora Matancera fills the room with the late Celia Cruz's 2001 hit "La Negra Tiene Tumbao." The show pays homage to the queen of salsa; Celia Cruz is so popular in Mexico that many young people consider her music Mexican despite her Cuban nationality. A hand puppet with a papier maché head has her back turned to the children, while the master of ceremonies welcomes the children and introduces the show. The volume of the recording grows louder and*

Figure 10.2: Cover of a Cri Crí song collection published in 2007. By permission of Sistema Nacional de Fomento Musical.

the puppet whirls around, pulling back the hood of her red cape to reveal her face—surprise! This little red riding hood is a little black girl who encounters a deceitful white wolf in a play intended to raise awareness of racial inequality. As the story unfolds, children continue dancing in their seats while accepting the challenge to decide the fate of the wolf.

The Cúcara Mácara Puppet Theater, one of several puppet companies operating in the state of Michoacán, does not limit its productions to one kind of music or drama, as they might go from Afro-Caribbean salsa music to Indonesian-inspired shadow puppets. The company's directors, Robert Murray Prisant and his wife Beatriz Donnet, know that the puppet theater has a special ability to reach youth, but they view it as a sophisticated art not limited to children. Like puppeteers in Mexico for centuries before them, Cúcara Mácara uses puppets to introduce children to a wide range of music and ideas and to educate them about responsibilities they should or must assume as they mature.

Murray views ancient music as foundational to Mexican identity and his shows, "[It persists] like a murmur in children's songs, [especially] in the lullabies—"El arrullo," "La nana" —and the songs that indigenous mothers sing in their vernacular languages with rhythms inherited over five thousand years ago" (Guillermo Murray

Prisant, e-mail correspondence with the author, April 25, 2010; Turrent 1995). As Murray explained it,

> In the time of the Aztecs there were houses of song, *Casas de Canto* or *Cuicacallis* [in Náhuatl] where young people went, no matter their clan, to learn the mythic songs that established their identity as *nahuas*. Do I use them in my puppet works? Yes, absolutely. (Guillermo Murray Prisant, e-mail correspondence with the author, April 25, 2010)

The book *Piel de papel, manos de palo* (Murray and Iglesias 1995) documents the history of Mexican puppetry, showing how Mexicans integrated international and local practices into their art, including Spanish, French, and Italian puppet traditions imported during the colonial era. Children today play with new interpretations of these traditions in the productions of Cúcara Mácara:

> In one of my works, an adaptation of scenes from *Don Quijote de la Mancha*, the work by Miguel de Cervantes Saavedra, on the occasion of its 400-year anniversary of publication, we employ a game [brought by the Spanish] called *Doña Blanca*. Children in Mexico know this song. But we change a word. Instead of *jicotillo*, we say *Quijotillo*. (Guillermo Murray Prisant, e-mail correspondence with the author, April 25, 2010)

The 1930s began a Golden Age of Mexican puppet theater that allied puppetry with music and education. The celebrated composer Carlos Chávez, then director of the Ministry of Fine Arts, oversaw the content of the dramas produced by the Teatro Guiñol de Bellas Artes, a state-sponsored children's puppet theater offered under the auspices of the fine arts department (*departamento de bellas artes*) of Mexico's Ministry of Public Education (known by its acronym SEP). The Teatro Guiñol began in 1932 as a collection of artists, intellectuals, writers, and bohemians inspired by the socialist aims of the Russian Revolution (Sánchez [1936] 1995). They hoped their dramas would nourish the youth of the new nation by promoting antialcoholism, literacy, political engagement, aesthetic appreciation, a sense of class consciousness, and a desire to promote equity. By 1933 the Teatro Guiñol and its SEP-sponsored affiliate touring companies were presenting as many as four shows a day, traveling to more than eighty-seven schools around the nation.

In her study of children's responses to the Teatro Guiñol productions, historian Elena Albarrán notes that despite considerable governmental control, "children took an active role in their socialization," responding with imagination and their own retellings. Archived drawings of young Mexican children's responses to the popular puppet play *Comino Vence al Diablo* (Comino Overcomes the Devil), document how children in the primary grades imagined themselves vicariously living the capers of the characters on stage, often with results different from the scripted play (Albarrán 2010). Albarrán's findings correspond with the way that children today report responding to contemporary puppet plays.

Music was important in the golden age of puppet plays in Mexico: each started with a musical prelude, others were even built around folkloric or popular musical selections, such as "La bamba," "El jarabe tapatío," and "La bicicleta" (Albarrán 2010). Composer Silvestre Revueltas, who at the inception of Teatro Guiñol was the director of the National Conservatory, composed what may be the most celebrated original piece for Mexican puppet theater: *El Renacuajo Paseador* (The Traveling Frog). Both the story and Revueltas's music remain popular with children today.

El Renacuajo Paseador, based on the poem by Colombian author Álvaro Pombo (c. 1880), warns children to listen to their parents through the story of a disobedient young frog (*renacuajo* is sometimes translated as tadpole) whose love of drink and dance lead to his friend "rat" being eaten by cats and his own demise to a hungry duck. While the story of *El Renacuajo Paseador* may seem a bit grim for school-children, the tale remains popular in Mexico; parents recite the tale to their own children, and contemporary cartoon versions appear on the internet. "It makes me laugh," says ten-year-old Shaleka, writing on a blog dedicated to the story. Modern puppet companies still portray the tale of the hapless frog, including the Cúcara Mácara Puppet Theater. Murray explained:

> We have a production of *El Renacuajo* with a single actress who declaims the text and we play the music of Revueltas beneath her. We've also done a production with hand puppets made from socks, and most recently we've constructed a small production not based on the original designs but on our own design. Do we use Revueltas's music? Yes, of course. (Guillermo Murray Prisant, e-mail correspondence with the author, April 25, 2010)

Revueltas's musical score, which includes symphonic references to *ranchera* melodies, was dedicated to golden age puppeteer Graciela Amador, a respected musician in her own right, whose songs were documented by Vicente Mendoza in his landmark study of Mexican music (Mendoza 1962; Murray and Iglesias 1995: 190). Revueltas's integration of international concert music with regional forms reflected a practice still followed by contemporary puppeteers and one that children readily accept.

The city of Morelia has a strong history of children's drama. In a memoir regarding her school years in Morelia, María, now a music teacher herself, explained the bond that dramatic productions provide and the inspiration she and her class-mates gained in their childhoods from trying to emulate the skilled teacher they so admired:

> [Our shows included puppet theater] and our teacher wrote the script, was the director, the set designer, and the light and sound engineer, but in the end we learned to make the puppets, select the music and do everything like him and we loved him for it. (Martínez Estrada 2006)

Like Teresa in the opening scenario, María enjoyed the chance to "be in charge." She also treasured the chance to travel to faraway lands and experience situations in which "people can fly and animals can sing" in music and drama. She and her friends learned songs and music from these plays, not always as actors but also to help picture themselves in new situations (Martínez Estrada 2006).

SCENARIO 3: *ESCUELA ALBERGUE TRÍBU PÁPAGO*, SONORA

Francisco an eleven-year-old boy from Quitovac, Mexico holds his thunderbird up high and steps forward with the other children. They are learning the skip dance known as chelkona *with an O'odham teacher from the American reservation in Arizona. The girls in the group carry long poles with rain clouds. Thunderbirds sit atop the poles carried by the young boys. Others will carry baskets to catch the rain. Francisco's face is set firm in concentration as he steps lightly, moving softly across the ground, and sings a narrative song in the O'odham language. His classmates shake maracas, rather than the traditional gourd rattles, to accompany their singing.*

At the Escuela Albergue Tríbu Pápago (EATP), a boarding school located in the town of Quitovac in the northern Mexican state of Sonora, the *chelkona* is just one tradition that Mexican children of Pápago (also known as O'odham (pronounced AH ah thum), O'otham in Mexican orthography) ancestry learn (Puente Andrés 2011). Traditionally, *chelkona* is performed at the end of harvest season in thanks for rain and at intertribal games, and it is also thought to embody healing power.

Like other tribal schools, the EATP is sponsored by Mexico's Department of Indigenous Education (Dirección General de Educación Indígena, or DGEI), a federal agency formed in the 1980s to create bilingual schools to promote the learning of Spanish literacy while also retaining indigenous languages. Many of the schools created under this program, like the EATP, are boarding schools where children live during the school week, arriving on Saturday afternoon and returning to their family homes after the school day on Thursday. Music and the arts form an official part of the children's curriculum at the EATP, although this is not always the case in other indigenous schools (Schmelkes 2010). At EATP music and dance are important tools for reinforcing the native language skills and cultural knowledge of a small group of Mexican O'odham children comprising only a third of the student body. The music, ceremonies, and games that all children at EATP learn in the Papago native language are vital to reconstructing the Mexican O'odham culture, which has eroded over time, a process exacerbated by the binational status of the tribe whose homeland was divided between the United States and Mexico by the boundaries established with the Gadsden Purchase of 1853. Interviews with Doraly Velasco, EATP's director, with visiting teachers Bernard Siquieros, of the Tohono O'odham Cultural Center in Sells, Arizona, and Graciela Robinson, a Tucson-based educational consultant who serves as Spanish translator for him and the other English-speaking O'odham teachers who travel the 180 miles across the border to work with EATP children, confirm the extraordinary collaborative effort required to integrate O'odham culture with the rest of the curriculum.

The O'odham speak a Piman language within the Tepiman family, a branch of the Uto-Aztecan language (or Yutonaua, in Mexico; Fitzgerald 2009; Fontana 1987; Steele 1979). Mexico's Commission for the Development of Indigenous Peoples (CDI) reports that the number of Pápago speakers is diminishing in Mexico. In 1949, 15 million Mexican residents were identified as Pápago; by 1982 only 300 were counted in Sonora, with only 125 counted as Pápago speakers (CDI 2006). As ranchers and miners settled the state of Sonora, many Mexican O'odham migrated to the US reservation, where retention of language and customs has been stronger. The push to assimilate in Mexico, where the economic, civic, and mainstream cultural advantages of identifying as mestizo far outweigh retention of native identity, has resulted in a culture and language threatened with extinction (Schmelkes 2010). To combat this problem, teachers and children at the EATP collaborate with their counterparts in native schools on the Arizona O'odham reservation and the children learn music, language, and culture from teachers who live *al otro lado*, on the US side of the border.

Youthful Leaders Matching Tradition with Technology

EATP teacher Leticia Calzada explained that the school aims to train future Pápago leaders who will assume responsibility for maintaining their language in complex and adverse surroundings (CDI 2009). The oldest O'odham musical practices are those associated with religious and spiritual ceremonies, and children assume leadership roles in realizing them.

Much of the music and dance that children learn at the EATP is not ceremonial in nature. Children also learn folkloric Mexican dances, patriotic ceremonies, and songs in Spanish. While English is not a curricular subject, the children have access to popular American and Mexican songs sung in O'odham. The Venito Garcia Library and Archives, on the US side of the border, has released a CD of *Children's Songs and Rhymes in O'odham* (2003) and the Tohono O'odham Cultural Center in Topowa, Arizona has produced two CDs of traditional O'odham songs that EATP teachers regularly use (Siquieros and Velasco, personal communication, 2011). Eight-year-old Marta and her girlfriends like to sing these songs, along with Mexican patriotic and popular songs in the Spanish language, while the boys kick a soccer ball across the dusty courtyard during recess. Soccer, or *fútbol*, as Fernando and his fellow students know it, is hands down their favorite sport. Being able to sing and speak O'odham makes nine-year-old Marta feel proud, but being part of the group at EATP is just as important: "I like learning with my friends," she shyly states, "and I like our school trips." There are only forty pupils at EATP, and the children develop close relationships in an environment where all activities are viewed as integral to the educational mission of training cultural leaders. The students travel to neighboring communities, where they perform for others who know their traditions, participating in community celebrations such as the annual pilgrimage for the Feast of St. Francis in Magdalena, Christmas in Sells, and Easter celebrations with nearby Yaqui as well as civic celebrations in nearby

Caborca and Sonoyta. Like all primary school children in Mexico, children at EATP wear uniforms, sing the *himno nacional* (the national anthem), and march proudly to the recordings of the triumphal march from Verdi's Aida as part of their responsibilities in leading and presenting the Mexican flag ceremony.

At EATP, parents, and local leaders stress the need for self-determination and connection to nature, citing a proverb of the tribe: "Nobody in this world has the right to modify the course of the arroyos [deep gullies formed by streams from infrequent, but intense, rain]" (CDI 2009). Still, in this impoverished territory in the state of Sonora, Quitovac is one of very few towns to have reliable electrical power. Children at EATP live simply, in bare cement rooms with broken windows, sleeping in dormitory-style metal bunk beds, but they have access to technology and are just as eager to learn it as traditional culture. Fernando, a sixth grader at the school, explains, "I want more activities on *Enciclomedia* and the internet" (CDI 2009). He liked using the instructional website, part of a government-sponsored program that was recently discontinued (http://www.sep.gob.mx/en/sep_en/Enciclomedia_program). It includes pages on intercultural activities with titles such as "knowing our culture." Fernando loves watching the digital videos of himself and his classmates on the huge flat panel monitor in the school's office and enjoys learning with the Smart Board situated in the classroom for fourth through sixth graders.

Digital videos, music downloads, and other digitized resources made available for portable players and portable telephones are becoming important tools for Mexican youth, even in impoverished communities. Computers and handheld technology could aid future language and music instruction for the O'odham in Quitovac and in other isolated indigenous communities (Fitzgerald 2009). Children are attracted to these technologies, but the resources to promote indigenous perspectives for them have not received systematic attention from educators. Fernando and his friends may have the chance to use some of the new O'odham language lessons created for computer instruction, but singing and dancing with his classmates and teachers remains most important. Indeed, like other children at EATP, Fernando seems to recognize intuitively the value of the integrative approach to education offered by his school. Singing and dancing in the O'odham language is related to the school's workshops on native nutrition, tending the school's fruit and vegetable farm, and raising domestic animals. In EATP's chicken coop, each child cares for and names his or her own *gallina* (hen), and in the little kitchen building across the yard, each learns to bake traditional tortillas.

MUSIC AND LANGUAGE RETENTION

The efforts of the DGEI to retain indigenous language and customs including music represent a refined position from that expressed by President Lázaro Cárdenas, whose inaugural statement to the first Interamerican Indigenous Congress in

Pátzcuaro, Mexico in 1940 included this statement: "Our indigenous problem is not to conserve 'the Indian' in the Indian, nor to indigenize Mexico, but to Mexicanize the Indian" (Cárdenas del Río 1940).

References to indigenous heritage are rarely absent from formal speech, public architecture, or what historian Luis Edgardo Coronado calls the "national imaginary." Náhuatl words contribute to the Mexican Spanish vocabulary and appear in traditional song texts. Songs in Tarascan (also known as Purépecha), Huichol, and other native languages appear in the children's choral music song collections published by CONACULTA.[4] Still, when it comes to education and socioeconomic opportunity, living indigenous Mexicans stand apart and are left behind, as evident from the uneven support for infrastructure and operations at EATP, where grants provide computers but not paint and windowpanes.

The separation of indigenous people from the much larger mestizo population depends on more than race or phenotype. Most of the children in Quitovac and at EATP have parents who are ranchers and identify as mestizo, the population famously described by the Mexican statesman-philosopher José Vasconcelos (1882–1959) as the raza cósmica—the racially blended who signified new vision and strength born of merged ancestries, the creators of a truly independent Mexico (Meyer et al. 2003).

In Mexico, culture, behavior, status (economic and social), and above all language ability mark identity. There are sixty-two indigenous languages in Mexico, with 288 language dialects. It can be argued that Mexico has the largest indigenous population in Spanish America, and while only 10 percent of Mexicans identify as indigenous, in a nation of 106 million people this exceeds the total in other locations, such as 40 percent indigenous in Guatemala and 25 percent in Ecuador (Schmelkes 2010; Warman 2003 in CDI 2006). Despite all this, indigenous citizens remain largely isolated from the privileges and opportunities associated with full participation in Mexico's civic life. Nonetheless, children at EATP and other indigenous schools are taught, using music and dance as critical tools, to comport themselves as Mexican citizens as well as proud tribal leaders.

While the DGEI does not at present actively promote music in indigenous school curricula, the SEP's Alas y Raíces program does support after-school activities that serve indigenous communities in states with larger populations. Particularly successful are the programs supported by the Sistema Nacional de Fomento Musical promoting bandas juveniles in Oaxaca in which young people learn to play brass and wind instruments and form community bands. More than 100 such bandas juveniles now play popular and folkloric favorites for local audiences and events (Navarette 2008).

CONCLUSIONS

This chapter does not pretend to offer a comprehensive overview of Mexican children's musical activities or of Mexican music in general (see Olsen and Sheehy 1998; Tello 2010). The scenarios and discussions offered here show instead children's responses to contrasting domains of formal musical instruction in Mexico. Children are subject to the dynamics of centralized imperatives, regional perspectives, and separatist strategies, but they are not completely restricted by them. Taking cues from their environments, adults they admire, and their friends, children create space to accommodate the diversity they encounter. Mexican children listen, sing, and dance to the music of Shakira, Celia Cruz, Fergie, and Maná as well as Revueltas and Pedro Infante and perform iconic traditional music such as the *jarabe tapatío*, accepting all as their music. As performers, Mexican children seek opportunities to do things their own way, playing with their peers or integrating themselves into adult contexts.

To teachers and the government, Teresa's success in learning Huastecan violin may represent ongoing centralized efforts to integrate regional folk musics into a shared, and even exportable, national repertory, but to Teresa playing music is fun. It links her to friends, and gives her a feeling of control. In puppet plays and drama children take in music from a wide array of sources without questioning whether or not they are Mexican, allowing musical and dramatic frames to bring together cultures in competition. While Papago teachers aim to combat the disintegration of the isolated tribal culture, Fernando's pride in learning O'odham *himdag* (culture) was greatest when he and his schoolmates were accomplished enough to lead ceremonies on their own.

Like children elsewhere, Mexican children enjoy music for the interactions it promotes with friends, family, and people they admire. It is an added bonus that musical activities provide a means of reconciling the contrasting worlds that shape their lives. From centralized, government-sponsored programs and formal instruction to regional drama and individual play, children learn from a very young age that there are many ways to be Mexican in the modern world. Ultimately, being musical is rarely an isolated activity for Mexican children: it is a way to connect with others, whether playing with a symphonic youth orchestra, a regional *banda*, or a Huastecan trio; leading a tribal ceremony; singing Cri Crí songs and popular *canciones* with family and friends at a festive event; or soaring on the wings of technology while scanning the internet for music downloads on the Alas y Raíces website and elsewhere. Despite new media and technology, the time-honored method of learning music from one's parents or close relatives and performing alongside them in family and community events persists and influences even formal music instruction in conservatory and school settings.

Government programs such as Alas y Raíces and the DGEI are sometimes criticized for not being comprehensively inclusive. There is room for greater integration, as the case of the EATP shows, but perhaps as William Beezley contends, lasting integration resides in the hands of individuals making their own way in the world (Beezley 2010). Mexican children accept this responsibility on their own terms, turning to play, drama, and imagination to create frames for integrating diverse music and culture to suit their particular needs. Such musical play might well inspire government policy.

On the linked website for this volume can be found sources of recordings for the music (Web Figure 10.4 **O**), a list of websites (Web Figure 10.5 **O**), a photograph of Felipe Valle's violin class (Web Figure 10.6 **O**), and a photograph of students at the EATP with singing instructors Matthew Lewis and Verna Enos—photo by Bernard Siquieros (Web Figure 10.7 **O**.

NOTES

1 The child's name, like all others used in this chapter, has been changed.
2 A video clip of this show can be found at http://tu.tv/videos/caperucita-roja-negra.
3 The name of this company comes from a traditional Mexico children's game, akin to "Eeny meeny miny mo" (Salgado 1990: 84).
4 Vol. 3 of the *Antología coral infantil. Cantemos todos* (2006) contains a "Danza de venado" (Deer Dance song, representing Sonoran indigenous tribes), "Nonantzin" (a song in Náhuatl), "Jarana maya" (a Mayan song), and "Ay de Tzamaritum" (a dance song from the Tabasco region) along with patriotic songs of Mexico, songs by famous Mexican classical and semiclassical composers, and songs from Canada, Latin America, Europe, and the Middle East. Examples from the United States, Africa, and Asia do not appear in this volume.

REFERENCES

Albarrán, Elena Jackson. 2010. "*Comino Vence al Diablo* and Other Terrifying Episodes: Teatro Guiñol's Itinerant Puppet Theater in Mexico, 1923–1940." *The Americas: A Quarterly Review of Inter-American Cultural History* 67 (3): 355–374.

Beezley, William H. 2008. *Mexican National Identity: Memory, Innuendo and Popular Culture*. Tucson: University of Arizona Press.

Cárdenas del Río, Lázaro. 1940. "Discurso del Presidente de la República en el Primer Congreso Indigenista Interamericano" [Discourse by the President of the Republic at the First Interamerican Indigenous Congress]. Memoria Política de Mexico [Political Memories of Mexico—a DVD and Web Compilation of Historic Political Texts]. Mexico City: El Instituto Nacional de Estudios Políticos, A.C. (INEP). Accessed July 19, 2011. http://www.memoriapoliticademexico.org/Textos/6Revolucion/1940PCM.html.

Commission for the Development of Indigenous Peoples. 2006. "Lenguas Indígenas en Riesgo: Pápagos. México" [Indigenous Languages at Risk: Pápagos, Mexico]. CDI—Comisión para el Desarollo de los Pueblos Indigenas [Commission for the Development of Indigenous Peoples].

Commission for the Development of Indigenous Peoples. 2009. "Pápagos—Tohono O'otham" [Papago—Desert People]. Mexico City: CDI-Comisión para el Desarollo de los Pueblos Indígenas [Commission for the Development of Indigenous Peoples]. Accessed July 19, 2011. http://www.cdi.gob.mx/index.php?option=com_content&task=view&id=636&Itemid=62.

Fitzgerald, Colleen. 2009. "Language Activism and Revitalization in the Tohono O'odham Community." Keynote address given at the University of Texas at

Arlington Student Conference on Linguistics, March 5–6. Accessed July 19, 2011. http://ling.uta.edu/news/audio/#fitzgerald-activism.

Lago, Roberto. 1987. *Teatro guignol mexicano* [Mexican Puppet Theater]. 3rd ed. Mexico City: Federación Editorial Mexicana.

León-Portilla, Miguel. 2005. *Los antiguos mexicanos a través de sus crónicas y cantares* [Ancient Mexicans through Their Chronicles and Canticles]. Commemorative edition. Mexico City: Fondo de Cultura Económico.

Martínez Estrada, Ana Maria. 2006. "Homenaje al Maestro Alfred Mendoza Gutierrez (1914–1994)." In Honor of the International Day of Theater, Morelia Michoacan, March 2, 2006. [Unpublished, handwritten document].

Mendoza, Vicente T. 1962. *La canción mexicana* [Mexican Song]. Mexico City: Fondo de Cultural Económica.

Mendoza, Vicente T. 1980. *La lírica infantil mexicana* [Mexican Children's Songs and Poetry]. Mexico City: Fondo de Cultural Económica.

Meyer, Michael C., William Sherman, and Susan Deeds. 2003. *The Course of Mexican History*. 7th ed. New York: Oxford University Press.

Murray Prisant, Guillermo, and Sonia Iglesias Cabrera. 1995. *Piel de papel, manos de palo: historia de los títeres en México*. [Paper Skin, Stick Hands: The History of Puppets in Mexico]. Mexico City: Espasa Calpe.

Navarette Pellicer, Sergio. 2008. "Entre la trompeta y el baritono hay un refifi que sólo la tuba puede acompañar" [Between the Trumpet and the Baritone There Is a Competition That Only the Tuba Can Accompany]. In *Testimonial Musical de México, 50 (1964–2009)*, edited by Benjamín Muratalla, 97–111. (With a commemorative 5-CD audio set). Mexico City: Instituto Nacional de Antropologia e Historia.

Olsen, Dale A., and Daniel E. Sheehy. 1998. "Mexico: One Country, Many Musics." In *The Garland Encyclopedia of World Music. Vol. 2: South America, Mexico, Central America, and the Caribbean*, edited by Dale Olsen and Daniel E. Sheehy, 547–627. New York: Routledge.

Puente Andrés, María Immaculada. 2011. "Grupos étnicos de Sonora: Pápagos o 'Tohono O'otham; La Gente del Desierto. Los Pápago'" [Ethnic Groups of the Sonora: Pápagos or "Tohono O'odham; the People of the Desert"]. Accessed July 19, 2011. http://www.lutisuc.org.mx/index6184.html?page_id=53.

Rosales, Astridh Franco. 1997. *Cuentos contados con imaginacion a traves de los títeres*. [Stories Told with Imagination via Puppets]. Guadalajara: Gaceta Universitaria.

Sánchez, George. [1936] 1995. *Mexico-A Revolution by Education*. New York: Viking Press.

Schmelkes, Sylvia. 2010. "Indigenous Education in Mexico." Lecture presented at the University of Arizona, March 24.

Sheehy, Daniel. 1999. "Popular Mexican Musical Traditions: The Mariachi of West Mexico and the Conjunto Jarocho of Veracruz." In *Music in Latin American Culture, Regional Traditions*, edited by John M. Schechter, 34–78. New York: Schirmer Books.

Sheehy, Daniel. 2005. *Mariachi Music in America*. New York: Oxford University Press.

Steele, Susan. 1979. "Uto-Aztecan: An Assessment for Historical and Comparative Linguistics." In *The Languages of Native North America*, edited by Lyle Campbell and Marianne Mithun, 444–544. Austin: University of Texas Press.

Stephens, April. 2009. "Children's Musical Experiences in Mexico: Three Case Studies." Unpublished interviews. Tucson: University of Arizona.

Stevenson, Robert M. [1952] 1971. *Music in Mexico: A Historical Survey.* New York: Thomas Y. Crowell.

Stevenson, Robert M. 1976. *Music in Aztec and Inca Territory.* 2nd ed. Berkeley: University of California Press.

Tello, Aurelio, ed. 2010. *La música en México: panorama del siglo XX* [Music in Mexico: Panorama of the Twentieth Century]. Mexico: FCE, CONACULTA.

Vergara de los Ríos, María del Carmen, and Mariana de Jesús Vargas Mendoza. 2007. "La Fiesta de la Santa Cruz: Struggling to Preserve a Tamulipecan Identity." Lecture presented at the meeting of the Southwest Chapter of the Society for Ethnomusicology. Arizona State University, Tempe, AZ, March 30–31, 2007.

CULTURAL IDENTITIES WITH MULTIPLE MEANINGS

11

CELTICITY, COMMUNITY, AND CONTINUITY IN THE CHILDREN'S MUSICAL CULTURES OF CORNWALL

ALAN M. KENT

WITHIN the Atlantic archipelago, Cornwall has a highly distinctive identity that contextualizes our understanding of the children's musical cultures that are operating there. It has a cultural and political identity that is historically attested, yet the territory finds itself "as a kind of half-way house between English county and Celtic nation" (Deacon 2007: 2). Through the past thousand years, the historical process for Cornwall (*Kernow*, in the Cornish language) has initially been a process of "accommodation" by the English nation-state, succeeded by further integration into "Greater" Britain (Payton 1992; Stoyle 2002). Over time, Cornish identity has changed and developed, but there has always been resistance to this process of incorporation, fought along linguistic, cultural, and political lines (Angarrack 1999). While the Labour government was in power from 1997 to 2010, unlike other Celtic territories (Scotland, Wales, Northern Ireland), Cornwall was not granted devolved government. Thus, Cornwall has an "unresolved duality of place" in which Cornish people are actively "working through the cultural negotiations" in order to "understand the ironies and difficulties of being Cornish in the twentieth and twenty-first centuries" (Kent 2002a: 153–172).

Paradoxically, however, it is these very ironies and difficulties that make Cornwall of such interest to musical and cultural scholarship. The territory has a distinctive continuum (or tradition) of musical culture, connected to identity and "difference," matched by an awareness of space, place, and musical performance unlike many other similar territories (both English and Celtic) within the isles of Britain. The hybrid nature of Cornwall has affected musical culture over time, for in effect, it has two musical continua operating there, in Thomas's useful words, as "corresponding cultures" (Thomas 1999)—being both Cornu-Celtic and Anglo-Cornish. Both of these cultures are noticeable in the children's musical traditions of Cornwall, and both show elements of inherent continuity, discontinuity, decline, revival, and fusion over time (Davey 1983; Davey, Davey, and Davey 2009; Gundry 1966). As this chapter will argue, Cornwall is a relatively small territory, though its musical culture is complex, and it has had a distinctive transnational influence on other territories as well. In part, this can be related to the post-1840 great migration of Cornish mine workers, engineers, fishermen, and farmers (the so-called Cousin Jacks and Jennies) to locations such as North America, South Africa, Australia, and New Zealand. The "writing back" of musical culture from these locations formed a significant strand of musical activity in the aftermath of migration and continues to have an influence today.

The origins of children's musical cultures in Cornwall can be observed in its ancient and medieval literatures. The best source of early musical vocabulary comes from the *Vocabularium Cornicum*, often referred to as *The Old Cornish Vocabulary* (BL MS Cotton Manuscript Vespasian A XIV, London). This Old Cornish-Latin thesaurus, dating from circa 1100, was probably compiled by Ælfric, the abbot of Eynsham (Val Tassel Graves 1962). It classifies biblical and everyday terms for Cornish speakers learning Latin. The *Vocabularium Cornicum* contains many references to instrumentation and types of musicians, which may have accompanied or formed part of early performance. These are *corden* (a string), *teleinior* (harper or harpist), *telein* (harp), *barth hirgorn* (trumpeter), *hirgorn* (trumpet), *Piphit* (piper), *Pib* (pipe), *harfellor* (fiddler), *(har)fellores* (female fiddler), *harfel* (viol), *cherniat* (horn-blower), *corn* (horn), *Pibonoul* (pipe, flute, or whistle), *keniat cobrica* (hornpipe player), and *tolcorn* (fife or flute). Alongside these musical terms are the words *mab* (son), *much* (daughter), *flechet* (children), *ach* (offspring), *goscor* (family), and *teilu* (retinue). As can be seen from this list, the community and its lineage was highly significant, and each instrument had its place in the culture. Clearly, younger people were encouraged to enter this world through study and apprenticeship. Within Cornish musicology, the language of *The Old Cornish Vocabulary* is significant, for certainly since the revival of Cornu-Celtic culture in the early twentieth century, such instrumentation—in particular, the "Celtic sound" (Melhuish 1998; Stokes and Bohlman 2003) of harps, pipes, and fiddles—has determined many young people's musical heritage in Cornwall (Woodhouse 1994).

THE MEDIEVAL AND MATERIALIST CONTEXT

The materialist context for children's musical culture in Cornwall derives from the cultural construction of mystery plays in medieval and Tudor (1485–1603) Cornwall (Kent 2010). Unlike other Celtic territories (notably Ireland and Wales), Cornwall's cultural heritage veered away from the literary epic in both poetry and prose and instead concentrated on community, populist theater, with each parish having either a biblical-themed drama or an origin play based on the life of the local saint (Lyon 2001; Spriggs 2004). Here, universal culture was merged with local culture; the plays usually being written by priests at Glasney College in Penryn, Cornwall (Whetter 1988). Thus *Bewnans Ke* (The Life of St. Kea) (manuscript c. 1580 but performed earlier) is a two-day theatrical event in which the Breton saint Keladocus arrives in the parish of Kea near Truro and then negotiates the peace between King Arthur and Mordred (MS 23849D; Thomas and Williams 2007). Another play, *Bewnans Meriasek* (The Life of St. Meriasek; c. 1504), originating in Camborne, culminates in a musical celebration (MS Peniarth 105; Grigg 2008). At the end of the second day, the Earl of Vannes shouts, "*Pyboryon wethugh in scon / ny a vyn ketep map bron / moys the donysa*" (Pipers, blow at once, / We will, every son of the breast, / go to dance; Stokes 1872: 264–265). The play begins with a comic school scene showing the education of Meriasek as a boy practicing his singing.

Such plays had a number of musical motifs and, as already shown, involved children in their respective communities, who would have been apprenticed for particular a musical performance and for singing in the drama. Much understanding of the children's musical culture of the medieval period may be gleaned from study of these dramas (Rastall 1996, 2001). Perhaps the most famous of these is the *Ordinalia* (c. 1480)—a three-day mystery play cycle comprising *Origo Mundi* (The Beginning of the World), *Passio Christi* (Christ's Passion), and *Resurrectio Domini* (The Resurrection; MS Bodl. 791; Kent 2005; Norris 1859). There are numerous musical references in these three plays, which must have involved children of the local community. The play is thought to have been performed around the estuary of the River Fal in south Cornwall, due to the number of recognizable place names in the drama. Given the status of *Ordinalia*—one of the larger cycles—recruitment would have taken place not only in and around Penryn, but also from surrounding parishes. The musical culture of the drama would perhaps have been led from Glasney College, which had a director of music available to train the community. A sequence in *Passio Christi* offers a more definitive picture of actual children's performance, with a depiction of Palm Sunday, when seven boys spread olive branches before Jesus. The Fourth Boy comments, "*Pen ol war pen y dev glyn / a gan yn gorthyans dotho*" (Everyone upon his knees / Will sing in worship to him; Norris 1859: 240–241). The Fifth Boy then observes,

V PUER	FIFTH BOY
hagh a gan th'agan sylwyas	And will sing to our Savior,
bynyges yv map a ras	"Blessed is the Son of grace,
yn hanow dev devethys	Who is come in the name of God." (Norris 1859: 240–241)

In short, clearly there is a moment in the play in which the boys sing chorally in praise of Jesus Christ. Some indication of the content may come from the antiphon "Hosanna filio David" since Jesus has already been called the "Son of David" by the First Boy. Alternatively, these lines might also suggest "a pre-existent Cornish lyric" sung at this point (Rastall 2001: 318). What is certain is that all seven boys sing in the drama. This is confirmed when Pilate has the lines *"ihesu pendrea leuerta / a'n fleghes vs sow cane"* (Jesus, what sayest thou / Of the children who are singing?; Norris 1859: 254–255). Ritual singing is also found in the third play (*Resurrectio Domini*) when the audience encounters the so-called three Marys (Mary, mother of Jesus, Mary Salome, and Mary mother of James). Interestingly, the song performed says much about the hybrid nature of Cornish musicology and language at this point, since although the majority of the play is conceived in Cornish, at this point, the Marys sing in English. This could suggest a wider bilingual culture of performance—and also, of course, the transfer of language in Cornwall, even at this relatively early stage. Having made that observation, we must remember that Cornwall had a number of language groups operating within its communities between AD 1100 and 1500: Norman French, Latin, English, Cornish, and Breton. Certainly, young people would have drawn on a number of these different musical and language traditions. So, even at this time, Cornish children would have been aware of the hybrid nature of their musical heritage. However, this has not stopped some musical revivalists in Cornwall from imagining a fully operational Catholic, Cornu-Celtic culture in which the apparent "Anglicization" of music is disparaged.

These moments, probably celebrated in individual parishes, would have involved children, especially if the festival of the local saint was being celebrated. Such festivals came down through the ages to the "feasten" days of the modern era (Courtney 1980) when children participate in the parish celebrations with song, music, and dance. This musical energy moved across to Methodist chapel anniversaries (often featuring the children of the chapel) during the height of the industrial period in Cornwall, although its roots were much older.

METHODISM AND CHILDREN'S MUSIC

The rise of Methodism in Cornwall in the late eighteenth century had a dramatic effect on the musical culture of the past. Although the "feasten" element of musicality had in part been stopped by the Puritans, the Methodists perhaps unintentionally also sounded the death knell for much traditional Cornu-Celtic culture. Energy was put into the development of chapels within communities, and children encountered hymns and music containing the Methodist message (Shaw 1962, 1965, 1967; Woodhouse 1997). The appeal of Methodism was almost instantaneous in fishing and mining communities, where the Anglican Church had appeared to neglect its rapidly industrializing populations (Probert 1971, 1979). Suffice it to say, the legacy of Methodism's impact on popular musical culture was considerable. Musical cultures associated with sports, theaters, wrestling, fairs, and festivals were probably discouraged (Rule 2006: 162–189). Some preachers tried to offer children alternative attractions, as in the case of Reverend Thomas Collins, who in 1849 took the children of Camborne Wesleyan Sunday School on a seaside trip to remove them from such influences. He composed a special hymn for the occasion:

> We rejoice and, we have reason
> Though we don't attend the fair;
> Better spend the happy season
> Breathing in the fresh sea air
> Happy children!
> What a number will be there. (Rule 2006: 172)

However, Methodism was not always antithetical to children enjoying music and dancing. In mid-Cornwall a fascinating custom developed known as the "snail creep." This is a unique dance, involving a long procession of both adult and child couples following a band, led by two individuals holding up branches representing the eyestalks of a snail. The dancers then form a large circle and spiral back and forth, as if showing the markings on a snail shell. Local Methodists legitimized this activity at tea treats for young people, who would have taken part in the band as well as the dancing. (A tea-treat is a gathering that usually takes place after a Methodist chapel anniversary in which there are large-sized saffron buns and tea served, accompanied by entertainment, games and sometimes dance and music.) A children's song from Camborne has some similar origin to the snail creep:

> Jin-Jorn, Jin-Jorn put out your long horn [a snail is a *bulhorn* in Cornish]
> The cows is eatin' the barley corn
>
> Snail, snail come out of your hole
> Or I will beat you as black as coal (Davey et al. 2009: 42)

The likelihood is that the snail creep was an adaptation of an earlier folk dance, for it has some similarities to Breton-style dancing later adapted in Cornwall for *Noze Looans* (see below). Although neglected for some sixty years, the dance has recently been revived.

Recording and Revival

Much of the traditional legacy of music for children in Cornwall collected in the nineteenth century is to be found in the folkloric collections of Robert Hunt and William Bottrell (Bottrell 1870, 1873, 1880; Hunt 1865). Hunt and Bottrell collected not only folktales and narratives but also songs, nursery rhymes, playground chants, charms (to ward off evil spirits etc.), and fragments of musical heritage that were quickly disappearing as Cornwall modernized. Substantial collecting of musical works was also completed in the late nineteenth and early twentieth century by figures such as Sabine Baring-Gould (Baring-Gould and Sheppard 1889–1891), Ralph Dunstan (Dunstan 1932), Robert Morton Nance (Thomas and Williams 2007), and Cecil Sharp (Boyes 1993). Antiquarian moves in the nineteenth century, combined with a need to revitalize Cornwall after the collapse of hard-rock mining and the pilchard industry, made a number of activists in Cornwall look back to the early and medieval periods of Cornish history to be inspired by past Celticity (Hale 1997: 100–111; Williams 2004). Such activists broadly looked at an unadulterated vision of Cornwall that was Catholic, Celtic, and apparently Cornish speaking, with industrial, modern, and Methodist Cornwall seemingly forgotten. Cornish revivalists first initiated a Cornish *Gorsedd* (meeting of bards) ceremony in 1928 at Boscawen-ûn stone circle in Penwith, where bards would be initiated and join the Gorsedd if they had contributed to the understanding and "manifestation of the Celtic Spirit" of Cornish culture (Miners 1978). The Gorsedd ceremony was based on a combination of the Welsh *Eisteddfod* and some practices of the Anglican Church: an invention of tradition, based on Arthuriana, and ancient British druidry (Miles 1992). Since its inception, the Gorsedd has rewarded the work of young people within the field of music, through competitions but also via the *Esethvos Kernow* (The Cornish Eisteddfod), which is now held annually (Lyon 2008: 32). Because of links to other Brythonic Gorsethow—such as those held in Wales and Brittany (Raoult 2003: 106–128)—there is a sense of pan-Celtic musicality, often seen in performances by children and young people.

The culture of the Gorsedd ceremony itself also involves music and dancing—principally in the *Offryn Frutys an Nor* (The Offering of the Fruits of the Earth), when the Lady of Cornwall gives the Grand Bard these, symbolic of God's gift to humankind. The Lady of Cornwall is accompanied by harp music and a dance performed by flower girls (Gorseth Kernow n.d.). Usually, the Gorsedd ceremony ends with an evening concert in which a number of young Cornish musicians may play. In the late twentieth and early twenty-first centuries, there have been efforts to stage Gorsedd fringe events in which a more radical Celticity is voiced: musically, dramatically, and poetically. Such fringe events have distanced themselves from the perceived conservatism of the main ceremony.

Whilst Cornu-Celtic revivalism continued, the "unrevived" traditional festivals continued virtually unaffected. Of these, perhaps the two with the most famous children's musical elements are Padstow's May Day and Helston's Furry or Flora Day. Held on May 1, Padstow traditionally celebrates with obby osses (grotesque figures portrayed by a human in a hooped black cape wearing a frightening mask) and music. The precise origins of Padstow's May Day are hard to determine, but they are obviously connected to Beltane celebrations and the greeting of summer (Rawe 1971). Fiercely secretive and loyal and, since the initiation of the Peace or blue oss in 1919, Padstow people have tended to align themselves to either the red oss or blue oss, with children following their parents' allegiance (Rowe 1982, 2006). May Day in Padstow is given over to the singing of various songs through the day and night, accompanied by the traditional drums, melodeons, and accordions that are a popular musical pastime of young people in the town. The "Day Song" welcomes the summer:

> Unite and unite and let us all unite,
> For summer is acome unto day,
> And whither we are going we will all unite,
> In the merry morning of May. (Rawe 1971: 6)

There are, in fact, four obby osses present in Padstow. There are two adult versions, as well as two children's osses or "colts." Each oss parades through the streets and symbolically goes through death and resurrection, reflected in the energy of the music. Children indicate their allegiance by wearing either a red or blue neckerchief.

Helston's Furry Day, meanwhile, was originally held on the eighth of May to celebrate the feast day of St. Michael. It is best known for the promenade-style dance performed through the streets of the town accompanied by brass band music (Deane and Shaw 2003: 156–159). This processional dance is known as the "Furry." Children's musical culture surrounds the event; many children play in the brass band, and many more children from the numerous local schools participate in the children's dance, which begins precisely at 9:50 am. An old piece of children's doggerel has survived in the town, which is to be sung to the Furry tune:

> John said to me one day, "Can you dance the Flora?"
> "Yes I can, with a nice young man, around the streets of Trawra"
> John the Bon was marching on when he met with Sally Dover;
> He kissed her once and he kissed her twice and he kissed her three times
> over. (Deane and Shaw 2003: 159)

Music also accompanies another traditional event in Helston: the *Hal-an-Tow*. There is much debate on the origins and significance of this event, but broadly, it is a piece of May drama, a form of mumming play performed by local adults and children (Kent 2008a: 98–152). The present event was revived by the Helston Old Cornwall Society in 1930 but has a much older origin and is performed at various locations throughout the town.

An enhanced musical festival of the modern era is Tom Bawcock's Eve. Celebrated on December 23 each year, the festival tells the story of Tom Bawcock, a Mousehole fisherman, who put to sea in rough conditions to save the village from famine, apparently bringing back seven sorts of fish. The folklorist Robert Morton Nance found a scrap of the song in the 1920s and created a "conjectural description" of it—in effect completely composing a new song (Nance 1932: 7). The song was

Figure 11.1: Notation for "Tom Bawcock."

performed by children in Mousehole in the twentieth century (Figure 11.1), but during the 1990s the festival underwent considerable reinvention. This reinvention was partly brought about by the success of the children's picture book *The Mousehole Cat* (Barber and Bayley 1993), which retold the story of Tom Bawcock through the eyes of his cat. A second impetus was the community intervention of members of Kneehigh Theatre, who reconceived the ethic and design of the event: incorporating withies (willow stems) and paper lanterns, constructions of fish and Tom Bawcock, and enhancing the processional nature of the song. The event is now led by the children of Mousehole (Mouzel in local dialect) school, who sing Nance's version of the song (1932: 7) before reaching the harbor and launching their lanterns out to sea.

The festival is not without controversy. Some older residents of Mousehole believe the present variant of the festival is not "genuine." However, it has been undeniably successful with many people coming to watch the children's lantern procession and singing.

THE CORNWALL MUSIC FESTIVAL

In the postwar period, an important marker of standards was the Cornwall Music Festival, which celebrated both adult and children's musical culture from the territory. The festival was inaugurated in 1910, so has just celebrated its centenary (www. cornwallmusicfestival.co.uk, Cornwall Music Festival 1980). During the 1960s and 1970s, the Cornwall Music Festival grew exponentially, offering a wider range of classes and opportunities to celebrate young people's musicality. The festival is usually held over a week in early March at Truro Methodist Church, in part reflecting the musical ethos of "classic" Cornish Methodism. In general, the festival celebrates the more conservative end of musical culture in Cornwall for young people and, to this extent, may be regarded as representing middle-class musical aspiration. However, there is a wide range of classes in which children can participate. The categories for performance could be found in any Western European music festival, but with space for Cornish musical culture. The Male and Female Voice Choir tradition is given prominence, and some of Cornwall's Celticity is celebrated through categories such as "folk song solo." Both Cornwall's Celtic Christian and Methodist heritage are also given focus with "sacred song or spiritual solo." Notably, coming out of the late nineteenth- and early twentieth-century industrial, working-class culture of the territory, young brass bands, quartets, and ensembles are celebrated (Mansell 2003, 2005; Pearce and Richards n.d.).

With some degree of continuity back to early and medieval Cornwall, instruments such as the violin, organ, and recorder are also examined, but the more overtly "early" or "medieval" instruments such as the dulcimer, pipes, and horns do not feature (perhaps because of few entries). The event also celebrates the fusion of musicality with verse, and in the choral works, Cornish or Anglo-Cornish poets are requested from competitors, giving a somewhat romanticized link back to early bardic culture in Cornwall. One important aspect of the festival is that it encourages children and young people to engage with the continuum of musical composition from Cornwall, with a list of recognized Cornish composers, such as Judith Bailey, Valerie Jewell, Philip Knight, Russell Pascoe, Goff Richards, and Jean Yeandel. At the end of the week, a grand gala concert is held in which outstanding performers are expected to play or sing.

Cornish Music in the National Curriculum for Schools

Music has been a central strand of the National Curriculum in Cornwall, since its inception (Combellack-Harris 1989). Although it has encouraged a degree of engagement with local music, the curriculum is seen by a number of observers in Cornwall as too centralist and anglicized, in that it does not really engage with the specific "corresponding cultures" of the Cornish tradition (Angarrack 2002), and one of Cornwall's largest nationalist parties, Mebyon Kernow, has made successive criticisms of educational policy in Cornwall. At present, in common with the rest of the United Kingdom, children in Cornish schools engage with musical culture at Key Stages 1, 2, and 3, but at Key Stages 4 and 5 the subject is not compulsory. However, there are popular media, music, and music production courses for students aged sixteen and over, in institutions such as Truro College and Cornwall

College at Camborne. The recent development of higher education at centers such as the Combined Universities of Cornwall—bringing together on one campus the University of Exeter, University College Falmouth, and Dartington College of Arts—offers musical study at undergraduate and postgraduate levels that was not available in Cornwall before. At present there is no national curriculum for Cornish, although there are moves by the Cornish Language Partnership to initiate preschool centers and school-based pilot projects with Cornish songs and music forming an essential component. In the past, many language groups have set up children's music in Cornish. Among the most successful was *Planet Kernow*, a combination of a songbook and a recording on CD (Cornish Language Board 2006).

Compared with the Cornwall Music Festival, at the opposite end of the continuum for young people is *Lowender Peran* (the Festival of St. Piran; www.lowenderperan.co.uk). Founded in 1978 and held in October at Perranporth, this long-standing international festival draws on Cornwall's pan-Celtic credentials, celebrating both adults' and children's Celtic music. Since its inception, *Lowender Peran* has relied on a certain style of Celtic musicianship, broadly based on the height of pan-Celticity during the late 1960s and early 1970s (Ellis 1993a, 1993b). Many of the children attending dress in the traditional or national costume of Cornwall or wear outfits based on classic Cornish colors: gold and black, dressing as miners or *bal-maidens* (female mine workers) or *jowsters* (female fish sellers) or using designs based on Celtic knotwork. The culture of musicianship is both formal and informal. For the former, set piece dances are accompanied by musicians—many of them children—while informal sessions are run both at the festival base and around the town. For a number of years, *Lowender Peran* defined Celticity in children's musical culture in Cornwall.

CONTEMPORARY CHILDREN'S MUSIC PROJECTS

Recently, one of the most significant children's musical projects is an organization called Cumpas (an acronym for Cornish Music Projects and a Cornish word meaning "shipshape" or "proper job"). The brainchild of multi-instrumentalist Hilary Coleman and educationalist Frances Bennett, the project seeks to develop traditional (Celtic) and fusionist musical culture for children in Cornwall. The project is much influenced by approaches to music and learning put forward by Tia DeNora (2000) and Lucy Green (2002). Working under the motto "Know your past, understand your present, create your future," Cumpas operates as an advocacy organization for schools, youth groups, and communities. Much of the energy of this work was in linking the Cornish musical continuum to the "English"-determined national curriculum. Thus Coleman and Bennett allowed children access to a previously "hidden" aspect of music in Cornwall, combining much of their work with a young people's dance group called Otta Nye Moaz (Look at us go). This was groundbreaking because they facilitated reengagement with the Celtic tradition without the trappings of the "performance" of Celticity (Kent 2007: 209–247).

The formation of Cumpas matched a wider critique of musical culture in early twenty-first-century Cornwall. Previously Cornish *troyls* (Cornish for "whirl, revolve, or spin" but has come to represent the Cornish equivalent of a *ceilidh*) were conducted along formal, often pan-Celtic lines, with prior knowledge and the learning of steps and musical motifs essential. Taking inspiration from the Breton *Fest Noz* (Festival Night) events, Cumpas and others (Dalla 2004; Sowena 1999) encouraged a more freeform expression of music and dance culture for young people, synthesizing traditional Celtic components with aspects of trance and rave culture (Davey 2004: 23–36), called *Noze Looan* (Happy Night) in Cornish. Young musicians were encouraged to play at such events, learning from more experienced players. There was no need to precisely learn pieces; improvisation and fusion were to be encouraged. Dancers and musicians were asked not to wear "Celtic" dress but normal clothing and to be comfortable with modernity.

Meanwhile, Cumpas was engaging in wider musical work incorporating aspects of Cornish culture for young people. The year 2000 saw a musical event at the Minack Theatre called *Teere ha Mor* (Land and Sea)—a showcase of young people's Cornish music, in collaboration with BBC Music Live. During the next decade, Cumpas also developed events such as *Treiz ha Ganow* (Singing for Dancing) at locations as diverse as the Eden Project and Murdoch Day (celebrating the life of inventor William Murdoch [1754–1839]) in Redruth, where a children's musical and dance parade was first established. Additionally, wanting to develop this genre, Bennett formed a community fiddle group for young people in Cornwall named Bagas Crowd (Fiddle Group). They played at newly developed Breton- and Cornish-linked festivals such as Aberfest in Falmouth on St Michael's Mount (Penzance) and at *Noze Looan* events. Such work also encouraged the formation of new Cornu-centric young people's bands, including the St Day–based The Red Army (formed by the brothers Philip and Steven Burley and featuring fiddle player Richard Trethewey), Pentorr, Pendans, Peskaz, and Scoot. These bands were influenced by the earlier postwar Cornish folk bands but brought new styling and punk rock ethics to the music (Kent 2007: 209–247).

More work was done by CYMAZ (Cornwall Youth Music Action Zone; www. youthmusic.org.uk/Our-Work/Action_Zones/cornwall.html), who targeted Cornish music, language, and dance at weekly after-school clubs for both primary and secondary ages, focusing particularly on towns that had experienced severe deindustrialization. Wider musical festival culture in Cornwall was also benefiting from the work of Cumpas—not least at the revived Golowan festival in Penzance, the newly invented Trevithick Day at Camborne and at Caradon Hill in east Cornwall, where a theme of children's musical culture became "crowders and horners" (fiddles and clarinets/bombards). This project also facilitated numerous crossovers with brass band culture, borrowing and fusing both traditions: the one modernist, Methodist, and industrial; the other ancient, Catholic, and Celtic (Haile 2009). A wider understanding of indigenous Cornish culture, literature, language, and music has also been part of a Cornwall County Council education project (A Sense of Place) headed by educationalist, storyteller, and bagpiper Will Coleman (http://rural.carnegieuktrust.org.uk/the_commission/case_studies). Some of Cumpas's musical work with young people developed an established festival, such as Bodmin Riding (Munn 1975), but elsewhere, for example, at Grampound in mid-Cornwall, a new musical promenade and dance event was developed to celebrate that community. In short, ritual, community, and musicality had gone full circle and young people were once again being encouraged to celebrate difference. Given Cornwall's highly active festival culture (Deane and Shaw 2003; Williams 1987), these were the perfect places to experiment with young people's music. In the course of the research for this chapter, I interviewed a number of young people about their response to children's musical culture in Cornwall and how they felt about issues in both education and their wider ownership of music. Cathy (aged eleven) was particularly lucid in her responses. Here is part of the transcript of my interview with her:

> AMK: As a young person, what do you feel about your Cornish musical heritage?
> CATHY: I'm happy and doing what I like to do. I'm proud of it too. In assembly at school a while ago we had Cornish music on CD playing before it started and a visitor thought it was Irish music and taught us how to say hello in Irish. I was cross because no one told her it was Cornish. We used to have a Welsh teacher and he'd have said, "No, it's Cornish actually," and perhaps he'd have asked me to say hello in Cornish.
> AMK: Do you see your heritage as resisting more widespread popular musical culture?
> CATHY: No, because I like pop music as well and you can incorporate them with each other. Like you could play a pop tune going into a Cornish tune and it would sound good.
> AMK: Do you think Cornish music gets ignored on the TV and on the radio?
> CATHY: Yes, a bit. I've never watched a television station where they have it on.

This brief section of the transcript provides much illumination on the culture of resistance required by young people in Cornwall responding to their musical traditions, but at the same time we note Cathy's engagement with wider popular music. In some senses, however, this insider-outsider contestation is nothing new, and presumably such processes of hybridization are occurring in other children's musical cultures around the globe.

LANGUAGE AND CELTIC HYBRIDIZATION

A concurrent development that assisted the development of this musicality was the standardization and government funding of the Cornish language, with an organization called the Cornish Language Partnership, which since 2006 has also worked to make Cornish a larger part of public and musical life in Cornwall (www.

magakernow.org.uk). One example of this was Saltash's Livewire Cornish Language Project, which facilitated the recording of *Oberenn Ewn!/Proper Job!*, a compilation of young people's rock music from the area featuring use of the Cornish language (Livewire Cornish Language Project 2008). So funding supported the hybridization of surf rock/grunge with Cornish, and numerous other younger bands also entered events such as the Pan-Celtic Song contest with Cornish-language songs to some considerable success.

Many of the issues in this chapter with regard to contemporary music for young people were first noted in a descriptive history of popular music in Cornwall in the postwar period (Kent 2007). Since the publication of that article, Hayward has argued that although it paid due attention to young people's rock, heavy metal, ska, and punk work in Cornwall, less attention was given to techno, positing that a good deal of young people's creativity in Cornwall uses this genre (Hayward 2009: 173–203). Uniquely, he noted that the do-it-yourself flexibility of techno, as well as the cultural history of north Cornwall (in particular, in a surfing, dance, and club center, such as Newquay), offered the perfect conditions of production to synthesize Celticity with contemporary musicality. Experimentation, he posits, suits Cornwall's musical hybridity. In essence, a minority language matches expression in a left-of-center musical genre. In this respect, the rise of techno was the natural successor to the grunge and surf rock of Newquay in the 1990s (Kent 2002b: 208–227; Pengelly 2009: 14–17). In more mainstream ways, young people's musical efforts were also being anthologized according to genre (Songs from the Hill 2004a, 2004b, 2004c), demonstrating nascent talent, which elsewhere was receiving mainstream media attention for young artists such as Alex Parks and bands such as Thirteen Senses, and Rosie and the Goldbug. The guitarist Graham Hart also inspired young musicianship to adapt many classic Anglo-Cornish songs to a rock format, including not only "Camborne Hill" and "Trelawny" ("Trelawny" or "The Song of the Western Men" is the Cornish national anthem; Hart 2004, 2007) but also a version of Village People's "YMCA" adapted to be an anthem of the shadowy "terrorist" organization the CNLA (Cornish National Liberation Army), who ran a series of high-profile campaigns in 2007. In essence, Hart was simply following a long-established path for some Irish punk rock bands; ownership of the musical culture was passed from the rugby terraces and Old Cornwall Societies back to the young. For teenage musicality at least, the political dimension of Cornish music was taking on a new realism.

In terms of a contemporary symbol for young people's musical culture in Cornwall, there is perhaps no better icon than the violinist Joseph Emidy (c. 1775–1835), who was born in Guinea, West Africa and after being taken as a slave, arrived in Cornwall, there becoming a teacher and composer (McGrady 1991). In 2008, BishBashBosh productions toured a play based on Emidy's life, which constructed him as a frustrated composer who was desperately trying to fuse Afro-Celtic music. The drama, titled *The Tin Violin*, toured many Cornish schools and colleges and demonstrated the international relationship Cornwall had to music. Clearly, Emidy is a powerful symbol for young people of hybridity, Celticity, and musical ambition, despite being born into the most difficult circumstances. The fact that Cornu-Celtic and Anglo-Cornish culture and music were fused in such ways actually belies a continuity of musical expression for young people, which as this chapter has shown has lasted for more than a thousand years and shows no sign of compromise or being swallowed by its larger, imperialistic neighbor. In this sense, despite this Celtic nation being labeled an English county—*a'n fleghes v sow cane*—children are still singing for *Kernow*.

ACKNOWLEDGMENTS

This chapter is dedicated to the work of Frances Bennett and Hilary Coleman.

REFERENCES

Angarrack, John. 1999. *Breaking the Chains: Propaganda, Censorship, Deception and the Manipulation of Public Opinion in Cornwall.* Camborne, UK: Cornish Stannary Publications.

Angarrack, John. 2002. *Our Future Is History: Identity, Law and the Cornish Question.* Bodmin, UK: Independent Academic Press.

Barber, Antonia, and Nicola Bayley. 1993. *The Mousehole Cat.* London: Walker Books.

Baring-Gould, Sabine, and H. Fleetwood Sheppard, eds. 1889–1891. *Songs from the West: Folksongs of Devon and Cornwall Collected from the Mouths of the People.* London: Patey and Willis.

"Bewnans Ke." Unpublished manuscript. MS 23849D, NLW, Aberystwyth.

"Bewnans Meriasek." Unpublished manuscript. MS Peniarth 105, NLW, Aberystwyth.

Bottrell, William, ed. 1870. *Traditions and Hearthside Stories of West Cornwall: First Series.* Penzance, UK: W. Cornish.

Bottrell, William, ed. 1873. *Traditions and Hearthside Stories of West Cornwall: Second Series.* Penzance, UK: Beare and Son.

Bottrell, William, ed. 1880. *Traditions and Hearthside Stories of West Cornwall: Third Series.* Penzance, UK: F. Rodda.

Boyes, Georgina. 1993. *The Imagined Village: Culture, Ideology and the English Folk Revival.* Manchester, UK: Manchester University Press.

Combellack-Harris, Myrna, ed. 1989. *Cornish Studies for Schools.* Truro, UK: Cornwall County Council.

Cornish Language Board. 2006. *Planet Kernow.* Cornwall, UK: Cornish Language Board.

Cornwall Music Festival. 1980. *Seventy Years of Music Making 1910–1980.* Truro, UK: Cornwall Music Festival.

Courtney, Margaret A. [1890] 1989. *Cornish Feasts and Folklore.* Exeter, UK: Cornwall Books.

Dalla. 2004. *Hollan Mouy!/More Salt!* Redruth, UK: Dalla.

Davey, Merv, ed. 1983. *Hengan: Traditional Folk Songs, Dances and Broadside Ballads Collected in Cornwall.* Redruth, UK: Dyllansow Truran.

Davey, Merv, Alison Davey, and Jowdy Davey, eds. 2009. *Scoot Dances, Troyls, Furrys and Tea Treats: The Cornish Dance Tradition*. London: Francis Boutle Publishers.

Davey, Neil. 2004. "Kicking Up Our Boots, Getting Back to Our Roots." *Cornish World/Bys Kernowyon* 38: 26–33.

Deacon, Bernard. 2007. *Cornwall: A Concise History*. Cardiff: University of Wales Press.

Deane, Tony, and Tony Shaw. 2003. *Folklore of Cornwall*. Stroud, UK: Tempus.

DeNora, Tia. 2000. *Music in Everyday Life*. Cambridge: Cambridge University Press

Dunstan, Ralph, ed. 1932. *Cornish Dialect and Folk Songs*. Truro, UK: W. Jordan.

Ellis, Peter Berresford. 1993a. *Celt and Saxon: The Struggle for Britain* ad *410–937*. London: Constable.

Ellis, Peter Berresford. 1993b. *The Celtic Dawn: A History of Pan-Celticism*. London: Constable.

Gorseth Kernow. n.d. *Ceremonies of the Gorsedd of the Bards of Cornwall*. Cornwall, UK: Gorseth Kernow.

Green, Lucy. 2002. *How Popular Musicians Learn: A Way Ahead for Music Education*. Aldershot, UK: Ashgate.

Grigg, Erik. 2008. *Beunans Meriask/The Life of St. Meriasek: A Study Guide*. Cornwall, UK: The Cornish Language Board.

Gundry, Inglis, ed. 1966. *Canow Kernow: Songs and Dances from Cornwall*. Dartington, UK: Folktracks and Soundpost Publications.

Haile, Ian. 2009. *The Next Chapter: Cornish Methodism, 1965–2005*. Truro, UK: Cornish Methodist Historical Association.

Hale, Amy. 1997. "Genesis of the Celto-Cornish Revival? L. C. Duncombe-Jewell and the Cowethas Kelto-Kernuak." In *Cornish Studies: Five*, edited by Philip Payton, 100–111. Exeter, UK: University of Exeter Press.

Hart, Graham. 2004. *Camborne Hill*. Camborne, UK: Killivose Music.

Hart, Graham. 2007. *Trelawny*. Camborne, UK: Killivose Music.

Hayward, Philip. 2009. "Jynwethek Ylow Kernewek: The Significance of Cornish Techno Music." In *Cornish Studies: Seventeen*, edited by Philip Payton, 173–203. Exeter, UK: University of Exeter Press.

Hunt, Robert, ed. 1865. *Popular Romances of the West of England: The Drolls: Traditions, and Superstitions of Old Cornwall (First Series)*. London: John Camden Hotten.

Kent, Alan M. 2002a. "In Some State…": A Decade of the Literature and Literary Studies of Cornwall." In *Cornish Studies: Ten*, edited by Philip Payton, 153–172. Exeter, UK: University of Exeter Press.

Kent, Alan M. 2002b. "Celtic Nirvanas: Constructions of Celtic in Contemporary British Youth Culture." In *Celtic Geographies: Old Cultures, New Times*, edited by David C. Harvey, Rhys Jones, Neil McInroy, and Christine Milligan, 208–227. London: Routledge.

Kent, Alan M. 2007. "Alex Parks, Punks and Pipers: Towards a History of Popular Music in Cornwall, 1967–2007." In *Cornish Studies: Fifteen*, edited by Philip Payton, 209–247. Exeter, UK: University of Exeter Press.

Kent, Alan M. 2008a. "Some Ancientry That Lingers: Dissent, Difference and Dialect in the Cornish and Cornu-English Literature of Robert Morton Nance." In *Setting Cornwall on Its Feet: Robert Morton Nance 1873–1959*, edited by Peter W. Thomas and Derek R. Williams, 98–152. London: Francis Boutle.

Kent, Alan M. 2008b. *The Tin Violin*. London: Francis Boutle Publishers.

Kent, Alan M. 2010. *The Theatre of Cornwall: Space, Place. Performance*. Bristol, UK: Redcliffe.

Livewire Cornish Language Project. 2008. *Oberenn Ewn!/Proper Job!* Saltash, UK: Livewire Cornish Language Project.

Lyon, Rod. 2001. *Cornwall's Playing Places*. Nancegollan, UK: Tavas an Weryn.

Lyon, Rod. 2008. *Gorseth Kernow: The Cornish Gorsedd—What It Is and What It Does*. Cornwall, UK: Gorseth Kernow.

Mansell, Tony. 2003. *St Agnes and Its Band*. St Agnes, UK: Trelease Publications.

Mansell, Tony. 2005. *Camborne Town Band*. St Agnes, UK: Trelease Publications.

McGrady, Richard. 1991. *Music and Musicians in Early Nineteenth-Century Cornwall: The World of Joseph Emidy—Slave, Violinist and Composer*. Exeter:, UK University of Exeter Press.

Melhuish, Martin. 1998. *Celtic Tides: Traditional Music in a New Age*. Kingston, Canada: Quarry Press.

Miles, Dillwyn. 1992. *The Secret of the Bards of the Isle of Britain*. Llandybie, UK: Gwasg Dinefwr Press.

Miners, Hugh. 1978. *Gorseth Kernow: The First 50 Years*. Penzance, UK: Gorseth Kernow.

Munn, Pat. 1975. *Bodmin Riding and Other Similar Celtic Customs*. Bodmin, UK: Bodmin Books.

Nance, Robert Morton. 1932. "Tom Bawcock's Eve." In *Cornish Dialect and Folk Songs*, edited by Ralph Dunstan, 7. Truro, UK: W. Jordan.

Norris, Edwin, ed. and trans. [1859] 1968. *The Ancient Cornish Drama*. London: Blom.

"Ordinalia." Unpublished manuscript. MS Bodl. 791, Oxford.

Payton, Philip. 1992. *The Making of Modern Cornwall: Historical Experience and the Persistence of "Difference."* Redruth, UK: Dyllansow Truran.

Pearce, Monty, and Denzil Richards. n.d. *Still Blawnin': The History of Redruth Town Band*. Redruth, UK: Redruth Town Band.

Pengelly, Nigel. 2009. "Newquay: Time for the Party to Stop." *Cornish World/Bys Kernowyon* 69: 14–17.

Probert, John C. C. 1971. *A Sociology of Cornish Methodism*. Truro, UK: Cornwall Methodist Historical Association.

Probert, John C. C. 1979. *Worship and Devotion of Cornish Methodism*. Redruth, UK: John C. C. Probert.

Raoult, Michel. 2003. "The Druid Revival in Brittany, France and Europe." In *The Rebirth of Druidry: Ancient Earth Wisdom for Today*, edited by Philip Carr-Gomm, 106–128. London: Element.

Rastall, Richard. 1996. *The Heaven Singing: Music in Early English Religious Drama*. Cambridge: D. S. Brewer.

Rastall, Richard. 2001. *Minstrels Playing: Music in Early English Religious Drama*. Cambridge: D. S. Brewer.

Rawe, Donald R. 1971. *Padstow's Obby Oss and May Day Festivities: A Study in Folklore and Tradition*. Padstow, UK: Lodenek Press.

Rowe, Doc. 1982. *We'll Call Once More unto Your House*. Padstow, UK: Doc Rowe.

Rowe, Doc. 2006a. *May Day: The Coming of Spring*. Swindon, UK: English Heritage.

Rule, John. 2006. *Cornish Cases: Essays in Eighteenth and Nineteenth Century Social History*. Southampton, UK: Clio Publishing.

Shaw, Thomas. 1962. *Saint Petroc and John Wesley: Apostles in Cornwall—An Examination of the Celtic Background of Cornish Methodism*. Cornwall, UK: Cornish Methodist Historical Association.

Shaw, Thomas. 1965. *The Bible Christians*. London: Epworth Press.

Shaw, Thomas. 1967. *A History of Cornish Methodism*. Truro, UK: D. Bradford Barton.

Songs from the Hill. 2004a. *Volume One—Punk, Metal and Ska*. Camborne, UK: Songs from the Hill.

Songs from the Hill. 2004b. *Volume Two—Acoustic, Eclectic and Electric*. Camborne, UK: Songs from the Hill.

Songs from the Hill. 2004c. *Volume Three—Folk, Roots and Traditional Music from Cornwall*. Camborne, UK: Songs from the Hill.

Sowena. 1999. *A Month of Sundays*. St Agnes, UK: Sowena.

Spriggs, Matthew. 2004. "The Cornish Language, Archaeology and the Origins of English Theatre." In *Traces of Ancestry: Studies in Honour of Colin Renfrew*, edited by M. Jones, 143–161. Vol. 2. Cambridge: McDonald Institute Monograph Series.

Stokes, Martin, and Philip V. Bohlman, eds. 2003. *Celtic Modern: Music at the Global Fringe*. Lanham, MD: The Scarecrow Press.

Stokes, Whitley, ed. and trans. 1872. *The Life of Saint Meriasek, Bishop and Confessor: A Cornish Drama*. London: Trübner.

Stoyle, Mark. 2002. *West Britons: Cornish Identities and the Early Modern British State*. Exeter, UK: University of Exeter Press.

Thomas, Peter W., and Derek R. Williams, eds. 2007. *Setting Cornwall on Its Feet: Robert Morton Nance 1873–1959*. London: Francis Boutle Publishers.

Thomas, Graham, and Nicholas Williams, eds. and trans. 2007. *Bewnans Ke: The Life of St Kea*. A Critical Edition with Translation. Exeter, UK: University of Exeter Press.

Thomas, M. Wynn. 1999. *Corresponding Cultures: The Two literatures of Wales*. Cardiff, UK: University of Wales Press.

Val Tassel Graves, Eugene. 1962. "Vocabularium Cornicum: The Old Cornish Vocabulary." PhD diss., University of Columbia.

"Vocabularium Cornicum: Cottonian or Old Cornish Vocabulary." Unpublished manuscript. BL MS Cotton Vespasian A XIV, London.

Whetter, James. 1988. *The History of Glasney College*. Padstow, UK: Tabb House.

Williams, Derek R., ed. 2004. *Henry and Katherine Jenner: A Celebration of Cornwall's Culture, Language and Identity*. London: Francis Boutle Publishers.

Williams, Douglas. 1987. *The Festivals of Cornwall*. St Teath, UK: Bossiney Books.

Woodhouse, Harry. 1994. *Cornish Bagpipes: Fact or Fiction?* Redruth, UK: Dyllansow Truran.

Woodhouse, Harry. 1997. *Face the Music: Church and Chapel Bands in Cornwall*. St Austell, UK: Cornish Hillside Publications.

12

MISKITU CHILDREN'S SINGING GAMES ON THE CARIBBEAN COAST OF NICARAGUA AS INTERCULTURAL PLAY AND PERFORMANCE

AMANDA MINKS

WHILE children have long been a central object of study in social sciences such as linguistics and psychology, children's musical practices have often fallen into the cracks between humanistic and social scientific research. Folklorists have tended to construct children's music as a world of its own, detached from larger social and cultural currents (Opie and Opie 1985), while most linguists and developmental psychologists set their sights on a universal norm of children's minds and expressions. Relativistic approaches to children's expressive cultures have been developed by innovative researchers in interdisciplinary spaces, especially engaging the interaction between anthropology, social psychology, ethnomusicology, and sociolinguistics. While each of these disciplines included early works focused on childhood and youth, only recently has an interdisciplinary conversation put childhood—and children's expressive practices—at the center of social and cultural processes. Two paradigms emerging from this conversation are particularly important for this chapter: the study of language socialization developed by linguistic anthropologists (Garrett and Baquedano-López 2002; Kulick and Schieffelin 2004), and the study of children's musical play developed by researchers working at the intersection of ethnomusicology and music education (Campbell 1998, 2010; Marsh 2008). A third paradigm, that of *interculturalidad,* or interculturalism, decenters the Euro-American orientation of much cultural theory and research and shows how children's expressive practices are building alternative notions of culture and citizenship in Latin America (García Canclini 2004; Grimson 2000; Minks 2009).

The children's musical practices that I discuss in this chapter come from Corn Island, some fifty-two miles off the Caribbean coast of Nicaragua, which has long been a site of cross-cultural interaction and exchange. This region was informally colonized by England beginning in the seventeenth century and became an economic enclave of the United States in the late nineteenth century. Although the Nicaraguan nation-state forcibly annexed the eastern coast in 1894, communities in this region maintained alternative cultural networks, with close ties to the West Indies and to US port cities. While western Nicaragua was almost exclusively Spanish speaking by the early twentieth century, communities in eastern Nicaragua have continued to maintain indigenous languages (e.g., Miskitu, Ulwa, Sumu/Mayangna) and regional varieties of Western Caribbean Creole English.

Children and youth have become prominent objects of public policy and debate in Nicaragua since the political and cultural changes of the 1980s. The 1979 Sandinista Revolution led to an era of reconceptualizing education and expressive culture as tools of social transformation across the country. Folk and popular musics were reclaimed to supplant elite forms of musical nationalism, challenging the rigid class hierarchy that had characterized Nicaragua since the colonial era (Scruggs 1999). While the revolutionary government initially promoted transformation of the class system as its central project, indigenous and Afro-Caribbean ethnic movements on the eastern coast insisted on the continued relevance of rights to cultural difference and territorial autonomy. These divergent visions of society contributed to a civil war (the "Contra War"), largely fought in and around villages of the Caribbean coast, which were also targets of intervention by the United States (Hale 1994). This conflict sparked tremendous population upheaval and led to many Miskitu people moving from the mainland Caribbean coast to Corn Island.

In 1987, as part of the postwar peace agreements, two autonomous regions—north and south—were established on the Caribbean coast of Nicaragua. The cultural and educational aspects of autonomy came to be envisioned largely through concepts of *interculturalidad*, or interculturalism. This was a transnational discourse oriented toward indigenous education that put children and youth at the center of discussions of cultural difference and alternative models of citizenship. The postrevolutionary transformations led, on one hand, to a revitalization of cultural identities in many communities and, on the other, to a discourse of cultural rights centered on education. Arguably, the advances made in cultural discourses on youth and education, drawing on concepts of interculturalism and regional autonomy, have created new forms of belonging and identification that fuel the ongoing struggle for a democratic distribution of power, resources, and territory.

Children's musical practices enter into discourses of interculturalism in several ways. At the level of public discourse, children's expressive practices (including music and language) are often important symbols of the future—either held up as a utopian ideal or lamented as a sign of deterioration (Cheney 2007). In intercultural education, informal genres of vernacular expression, such as singing games, are a key resource for curricular reform that aims to bring regional folklore into the classroom. Most importantly, in everyday contexts of play and performance, musical practices are central to processes of cultural interaction, exchange, and transformation. This is because children's activities are often oriented toward playful improvisation (Kartomi 1991) and because children are key actors in processes of socialization and adaptation to changing circumstances. Children learn and transform cultural practices and identities through everyday expressive activities that move beyond folkloric concepts of indigenous culture.

The role of children's interaction in processes of social and cultural change leads to another perspective on interculturalism as an everyday practice, which has been developed by Latin American anthropologists. Alejandro Grimson (2000) argues that culture is not a preexisting set of traits differentiating one group from another; rather, culture is an organizing concept forged through interaction and often through conflict. In this framework, expressive practices such as music are dialogic tools through which differences are enacted, through which boundaries are constructed within and between social groups. This Latin American discourse of interculturalism has been further developed by Nestor García Canclini (2004), who examines how aesthetic practices and objects mediate social and cultural relations and how hierarchies of value connect cultural difference with social inequality. These perspectives follow a broader trend in social sciences to view culture as an active construction rather than a passive list of traits; culture is not something people *have* but something that they *do*. By participating in musical (and other) activities, children develop patterns of expression and identity that draw social boundaries between and within groups of people, creating difference through labels such as "our music" and "their music," "our culture" and "their culture." This approach to interculturalism as an everyday practice helps us see how culture emerges from interaction and play and how communication is accomplished using a diverse pool of resources.

MISKITU CHILDREN ON CORN ISLAND

Children's activities are always important sites for tracking cultural processes, and this is particularly true on Corn Island, where social organization and communicative practices are currently in a state of dramatic change. Historically Corn Island was home primarily to Creole people with West Indian cultural ties who spoke a local variety of Creole English (Gordon 1998). The political-economic transformations in Nicaragua during the 1980s led to an exodus of Creole people and an influx of Miskitu people, who moved to the island from mainland coastal villages to escape the violence of the Contra War and look for work in the fishing industries. The 1990s also brought more Spanish-speaking mestizos to the island from the Pacific region of Nicaragua. In 2003, when I was conducting this study, about half the population of 7,000 was Creole, a quarter of the population was Miskitu, and most of the remaining quarter was mestizo. The children of Miskitu migrants on Corn Island grew up hearing and speaking Miskitu, Creole English, and Spanish, with great diversity of competencies and preferences even within the same family. Miskitu people were generally the most marginalized on the island, periodically threatened with expulsion from the land on which they had built modest houses. Yet Miskitu children created a sense of home and belonging through expressive practices that captured their multiple cultural affiliations.

While this chapter focuses on singing game performance, children were also exposed to other forms of musical experience on Corn Island. In Miskitu neighborhoods of Corn Island, musical soundscapes were mostly mediated by radio and recordings, juxtaposing a diverse range of genres including classic country-western (both US and Caribbean varieties), West Indian reggae and soca, Garifuna punta, and popular Christian music in Miskitu and Spanish. Children and youth participated in formal music performances at church, at school, and in civic events such as parades. Sunday school and musical services at church provided opportunities to sing and, for teenage boys, to play electric instruments in the church youth band (including electric guitar, bass, drums, and keyboard synthesizer). While some children did not attend school at all due to poverty and the transience of migrant labor, those who did had opportunities to experience public performance through marching, dancing, and playing percussion instruments in school events and parades; some high school students also played brass instruments in school bands. The most accessible musical experience for children on Corn Island, however, was participation in everyday play activities such as singing games. Especially when children played outdoors in good weather, they launched singing games by calling out to siblings, cousins, and neighbors, "*Kaia pulaia!*" (in Miskitu) or "*Vamos a jugar!*" (in Spanish)—Let's play!

SINGING GAME PERFORMANCE

Miskitu children's singing game performances are everyday musical practices embedded in a discourse about the coordination of vocal and kinetic activity, the evaluation of individual performances, and the rights and responsibilities of performers. Like most quotidian aesthetic production, there is no clear demarcation between the aesthetic form of the singing game and the discourse that enables and interprets its performance. By closely analyzing the intertwining of musical and verbal activity in social interaction, we can grasp more concretely how a performance is negotiated and accomplished and how social and cultural meanings are produced (cf. Feld and Fox 1994).

In Richard Bauman's influential formulation, *performance* is a context of heightened engagement for a social actor—a singer, a dancer, a speaker—that involves accountability to an audience (Bauman 1977; Bauman and Briggs 1990). In singing games and many other expressive activities, participants are accountable to other performers as well as to observers who may constitute an audience. Evaluations and corrections are made by active and onlooking participants and constitute a key arena for socializing aesthetic and communicative practices.

Many children claimed that singing games were "girls' games," and girls were perhaps the most common participants, especially in organizing singing games. Nevertheless, boys as well as girls sometimes participated, revealing how ideologies of performance diverged from the realization of the performance itself (Minks 2008). In the performance that I analyze here, the children enacting the singing game were all girls, but at least one boy participated as an onlooker and commentator.

The children recorded in this performance were siblings and cousins from a large extended family of Miskitu people who had lived on Corn Island for more than twenty years. Some members of the family spoke mostly Miskitu, others spoke mostly Spanish, and others spoke mostly Creole English. Everyone had at least listening competence in a nonpreferred language, which helped facilitate communication. Children often combined languages in their speech and song, using the full range of communicative resources to which they had access. The children in this group sometimes used extensive Miskitu in their play activities, but during this performance they were speaking mostly Spanish and Creole English.

Most singing games performed by children of all ethnic groups on Corn Island were in Spanish. The song texts were rhythmically structured and linked to choreographed movement; some songs were clearly melodic while others were chants with vague high and low contours. The performance of the game Ron Macarón involves a combination of song and chant (see musical transcription in Figure 12.1). The song text includes words in Spanish and Creole English as well as nonsense vocables. In general, the poetics of singing game texts are more important than their referential meaning. Repetition, assonance, alliteration, and parallelism make the song text memorable and pleasurable. Even if some literal meaning can be deduced, it is often irrelevant to the performers. Ron Macarón does include some text that is referentially meaningful in this context: the counting words "*wan, tu, tri*" (one, two, three), which are used in both Creole English and Miskitu (here they were performed with Creole English pronunciation).

In playing Ron Macarón, the children stood in a circle with their hands extended, palms turned up and resting above or below those of their neighbors (see Figure 12.2). The vocal performance of the song was accompanied by a clapping pattern in which each child, one at a time, slapped the hand resting on top of his or her hand, with the clap making its way around the circle. The words "rin tin tin" and "ron ton ton" were performed with three quick claps, one for each syllable. The person whose hand was slapped on the count of *tri* (three) was *fuera*, that is, out of

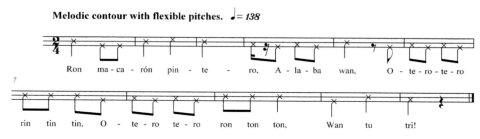

Melodic contour with flexible pitches. ♩= *138*

Ron ma-ca-rón pin-te - ro, A - la - ba wan, O - te - ro - te - ro rin tin tin, O - te - ro te - ro ron ton ton, Wan tu tri!

Figure 12.1: Transcription of "Ron Macarón."

the game. The determination of the unfortunate status of *fuera* was not only due to chance. The children strategized to avoid receiving that third clap, for example, by moving their hand at the last moment or changing their position in the circle. They also debated the action of the game, and through political alignments, the status of *fuera* could sometimes be overturned.

Transcription Key:

Double parentheses (( ))	Explanatory insertions
Repeated colon ::::	Extended utterance
Question mark ?	Upward rising intonation
Hyphen -	Interruption or hesitation
Italics	Spanish
Underlined italics	Nicaraguan Creole English
Underlined roman	Miskitu
Bold	Chanted song text

Figure 12.2: Children playing "Ron Macarón."

The sociolinguistic symbols used in the transcription provide more information about the sound and timing of the spoken, as well as sung, discourse. The speech surrounding song becomes a frame for performance and a means for interpreting its meaning among participants (Fox 2004; Minks 2002, 2008). In the first segment of the transcript, the participants speak in Spanish in addition to performing the poetic song text of Ron Macarón. At the beginning of the performance is a false start, and in line 2 a girl whom I will call Isaura[1] interrupts to say, "*Espera, otra vez*" (Wait, again) in order to coordinate the musical and kinetic activity. After the first full performance of the song text, in line 5, she also corrects one of the players, saying, "You should hit like this, two times," thus socializing the norms of performance. Read through this part of the transcript with an aim to hear the children's voices enacting the game, and then listen to the recording while following along with the transcript (Web Figure 12.3 🔊). The chanted song text is in bold.[2]

1 Group:	***Ron Macarón pin-***	
2 Isaura:	*Espera, otra vez.*	
	Wait, again.	
3 ?:	*Espera, espera.*	
	Wait, wait.	
4 Group:	***Ron Macarón pinte:::ro.***	
	Alaba wan?	
	Otero tero rin tin tin,	
	otero tero ron ton ton,	
5 Isaura:	*Vos debe pegar así, dos veces.*	
	You should hit like this, two times.	
6 Coral:	*Ron ton ton*	
7 Group:	***Wan tu tri.***	
	One two three.	
8 ?:	*Fuera.*	
	Out.	
9 ?:	*Fuera.* ((laughter))	
	Out.	
10 Coral:	*Fuera, Esmeralda. Vos fuera.*	
	Out, Esmeralda. You're out.	

In the crucial moment of the second round of the song text below, Mariana withdraws her hand following some irregularity of the clapping sequence, and in line 13 she protests the status of *fuera*. The controversy over this move prompts the intervention, beginning in line 17, of a bystander, an older cousin, Keiton (a boy), who speaks mostly Creole English, using only the Spanish game term *fuera*. In line 20 Lula responds in Creole, but the others continue speaking Spanish, with evident understanding of the Creole utterances. In spite of Keiton's argument that Mariana should be excluded, she continues to play. At the next point of exclusion, when Isaura is labeled *fuera*, Coral argues in line 29 that the kinetic action of the game had not been properly carried out, and so Isaura has the right to continue participating.

11 Group:	*Ron Macarón pinte:::ro.*	
	Alaba wan?	
	Otero tero rin tin tin,	
	otero tero ron ton ton.	
	<u>*Wan tu tri.*</u>	

12 Coral:	*Fuera!*	
	Out!	

13 Mariana:	*Ha-ah.*	
	Huh-uh.	

14 Lula:	*A ver poner tu mano.*	
	Look put your hand.	

15 Shajaira:	*Para que te pegue.*	
	So she can hit you.	

16 Lula:	*Para que te pegue.*	
	So she can hit you.	

17 Keiton:	<u>*Ah-ah, Mariana* fuera.</u>	
	Uh-uh, Mariana out.	

18 Coral:	*Porqué no me pegó?*	
	Why didn't she hit me?	

19 Keiton:	<u>*Mariana fuera bika yu no hit har, so shi fuera.*</u>	
	Mariana out because you didn't hit her, so she's out.	

20 Lula:	<u>*Yeh, bot shi no hit Mariana, so?*</u>	
	Yeah, but she didn't hit Mariana, so?	

21 Shajaira:	*Fuera, fuera. Andá, andá.*	
	Out, out. Go, go.	

22 Keiton:	<u>*Shi fuera.*</u>	
	She's out.	

23	<u>*Yu haf tu hit Coral bot shi no hit har so shi du har hand so?*</u>	
	You have to hit Coral but she didn't hit her so she did her hand like this?	

24	<u>*Shi shud haf tu stap har hand so?*</u>	
	She should have to stop her hand like this?	

25 Group:	*Ron Macarón pinte:::ro.*	
	Alaba wan?	
	Otero tero rin tin tin,	
	otero tero ron ton ton.	
	<u>*Wan tu tri.*</u>	

26 Shajaira:	*Ah:::::.*	

27 Diana:	*Fuera, Isaura.*	
	Out, Isaura.	

28?:	*Fuera.*	
	Out.	

29 Coral:	*No, también malo porque Ruby no quería que pase a la Isau-*	
	No, that's bad too because Ruby didn't want to pass it to Isau-	

30	*Ella hizo rin tin tin a mi mano.*	
	She did rin tin tin to my hand.	

In the fourth round of the game, which begins in line 36 below, Mariana is again in the unfortunate position of receiving clap number three, and she again withdraws her hand to avoid being slapped. Coral immediately labels her *fuera*, but others argue that it is only valid if her hand is actually slapped and that it was her responsibility to accept it. In line 40, one of only two Miskitu utterances in this game performance, Ruby says, "How did they do that to Mariana!" implying that this argument was not entirely fair. Switching to Miskitu at this point suggests a heightened sense of confrontation, a common technique of code-switching whereby children (among others) create contrasting alignments through change of language (Jorgensen 1998). The increasingly dramatic conflict does not derail the play activity but rather is a central part of the negotiation of rules in the game, and the pleasure of playing the game (Goodwin 2006: 67).

The other performers and the observer Keiton weigh in on the situation, and then in line 47 Ruby's older sister Diana coaches her in Miskitu on strategies to avoid getting labeled *fuera*. Using Miskitu here confirms her alignment and sisterly support of Ruby; Miskitu was also a strong first language of both girls. In lines 39, 44, and 50, Lula speaks in Creole English, following Keiton's speech in Creole English and aligning with his argument. The participants, both performers and onlookers, do not exactly come to a consensus on the rights of participants or the policies of exclusion, but they continue to orient themselves to the common activity of the singing game, which goes on with the prodding of Coral in line 51, "*Rápido pues*" (Hurry, then).

31 Ruby:	*Vamos de vuelta.*
	Let's do it again.
32 Coral:	*Vení de vuelta Isaura.*
	Come again Isaura.
33 Lula:	*Ah, Coral-*
	Ah, Coral-
34 Coral:	*No a ver ella ahí.*
	No, look, her there.
35 Lula:	*Ahí vas a ver.*
	There you're going to see.
36 Group:	**Ron Macarón pinte:::ro.**
	Alaba wan?
	Otero tero rin tin tin,
	otero tero ron ton ton.
	Wan tu? ((pause; laughter))
37 Coral:	*Viste! Viste! Fuera.*
	See! See! Out.
38 Keiton:	<u>*No, no, yu no hit har yet so mek shi put har hand …*</u>
	No, no, you didn't hit her yet so make her put her hand …
39 Lula:	<u>*Yeh.*</u>
	Yeah.

40 Ruby: <u>Nahki Mariana ra baku munan!</u>
             How did they do that to Mariana!

41 Coral: *Tu, tu? Tu? Después va a pegarme <u>tri.</u>*
             Two, two? Two? Then you're going to hit me three.

42 Keiton: *Mariana, Mariana shi gan, shi du har hand so?*
             Mariana, Mariana she went, she did her hand like this?

43   *Al a yu stap yar hand so-*
             All of you stop your hand like this-

44 Lula: *Ah, shi no wan put har hand.*
             Ah, she doesn't want to put her hand.

45 Keiton: *Yu haf tu hit har.*
             You have to hit her.

46 Ruby: ((laughs))

47 Diana: <u>Ruby man mihtam mangkaia ba taim mai prukaia taim man sakaia.</u>
             Ruby put out your hand then when it's time to hit it take it away.

48 Ruby: ((laughs)) *Mentira en tu mano ya-*
             Lie, on your hand already-

49 Keiton: *Ruby if shi so autsaid den.*
             Ruby if she's like that, then she's out.

50 Lula: *Shi no wan put har hand.*
             She doesn't want to put her hand.

51 Coral: *Rápido pues.*
             Hurry then.

52 Group: **Ron Macarón pinte:::ro.**
             Alaba wan?
             Otero tero rin tin tin,
             otero tero ron ton ton.
             <u>Wan tu</u>? ((*pause; final word staggered*)) **<u>tri. tri. tri.</u>**

There is clearly controversy over whether or not a participant should be allowed to withdraw her hand in order to avoid being slapped on "three" and thrown out of the game. The rules of Ron Macarón are not fixed and mechanically followed, but rather open to interpretation and negotiation through shifting social alignments and arguments about rights and responsibilities. As Marjorie Goodwin has described in US children's hopscotch, these kinds of negotiations involve "monitoring the social order" (2006: 72) and enacting moral judgments that involve "how children negotiate rules for behavior within their peer society" (ibid.: 17). They learn, through these activities, that rules are not set in stone but open to interpretation and challenge. The outcome of a challenge can depend on collective negotiation and senses of justice, but it is also dependent on social alignments and access to powerful positions. For example, Mariana was a bit of an underdog in peer group play and was often marginalized in ways that didn't seem objectively fair, but she used the structure of the game, her kinetic skills of strategy, and her capacity for resistance to challenge her vulnerable position.

The singing game is an apt medium for these moments of socializing play because it is an aesthetically shaped, memorable, and pleasurable vocal and kinetic activity. The social productivity of this activity emerges not only from the aesthetic performance itself but also from the spoken discourse in which it is embedded. As George List suggested decades ago, children's expression often involves the inter-twining of speech and song (List 1963). While List drew attention to aesthetic forms of expression that were "in between" speech and song because of their intonational contours, my analysis also shows how speech frames song and shapes its perfor-mance (cf. Fox 2004; Goffman 1974). The play discourse enables, reshapes, and interprets the performance of the singing game.

The poetics and the pleasure of singing games make them mobile and adapt-able across linguistic and cultural boundaries. The singing game performance is an example of interculturalism in practice, because it shows how diverse resources for communication are integrated in a context of interaction. The children used dif-ferent languages according to their preferences and alignments, but they also dem-onstrated common competencies through comprehension of each other's speech and coordination of the singing game. The aesthetic and collective structure of the singing game facilitates desire for collaboration but also involves contestation. Conflictive discourse does not derail the activity but rather enables participants to negotiate their positions within it. Corrections and contestation are means of socializing others into acceptable behavior and of reinterpreting the rules of play.

The singing game and the play discourse create new social positions and rela-tionships as the children take communicative resources from the past and reframe them in the present. These communicative resources do not necessarily come from the same past. The Spanish singing game may not have been part of the repertoires of the children's parents or grandparents, but as people with different histories come together in the same place, a variety of expressive practices come to fill a pool of potential resources for subsequent generations. The performers enacting the sing-ing game were an intimate kin group, and yet the heterogeneity of their expres-sive practices challenges the linking of community and commonality in discourses of identity (Minks forthcoming). The effectiveness of their communication is not predicated on sameness; rather, their communication involves a negotiated compat-ibility, a social relationship that mediates difference (cf. Wentworth 1980: 97).

The political negotiation and struggle over the terms of participation in the singing game also happened, on a broader level, in local discourses of belonging in which inclusion and exclusion were central to the allocation of material and sym-bolic resources. Miskitu people were often viewed by the island establishment as interlopers, as unintelligible strangers, and they were sometimes threatened with expulsion, but Miskitu children made a claim for intercultural belonging through their multilingual expressive practices. They redrew the performative boundar-ies that delineate forms of communication and ethnic affiliation. The multiplicity and variability of expressive competencies facilitated comprehension across forms of communication, especially when they were oriented around a common activ-ity such as the performance of singing games. Young children, even those with limited proficiency in Spanish, acquired aesthetic and "communicative competence" through the formal regularity of the singing game, the pleasure of its performance, and the corrections and guidance of older peers (Hymes 1972).

Miskitu children's creative adaptation of Spanish singing games and multilingual play discourses is not necessarily a threat to indigenous identity and expressive practice. The Miskitu language continued to be a prominent resource for communication among Miskitu children and youth on Corn Island (much more so than is evident in this transcript). Miskitu children's expressive practices on Corn Island reveal the expansion, rather than contraction, of expressive resources and the development of intercultural identities (cf. Jamieson 2007). Speaking about indigenous peoples more broadly, Nestor García Canclini writes, "For millions the problem is not to maintain 'alternate social fields,' but to be included, to arrive at being connected, without trampling their difference or condemning themselves to inequality. In sum, to be citizens in an intercultural sense" (2004: 53). Cultural loss and assimilation are not necessarily the products of contact and interaction. They result from particular alignments of cultural difference and social inequality, in which some expressive practices are ideologically linked to poverty and backwardness, while others are linked to progress. Folkloric projects of cultural revitalization can contribute to the revalorization of stigmatized practices, but if the categories and symbols of belonging are represented as exclusive and primordial, the overall ideological structure remains the same, foreclosing the possibility of indigenous patrimonies that are multiple and heterogeneous.

CONCLUSION

The concept of interculturalism developed in this chapter is not the encounter of two or more fixed, bounded entities or cultures. It is the process of creating meaningful alignments and contrasts in a heterogeneous sphere of practice, often through social and political struggle. Whether the organization of social life is represented in neat cultural compartments, as in a folklore festival, or in densely crossing networks and overlapping frames, as in the singing game performance, the processes of interaction, negotiation, and struggle are equally important in creating ideas of sameness and difference. Music and language are media through which children in many cultural contexts display their affiliation with multiple expressive practices and identities. Norma González's work in the southwest region of the United States provides a similar view of children's negotiation and fusion of multiple cultural frameworks through multiple forms of expressive practice, especially language and music (González 2001). In many postcolonial and immigrant contexts today, multiplicity may be a central feature of children's expression.

John Blacking, one of the few ethnomusicologists of his generation who took children's music seriously, called for a shift from studies of particular musical styles to studies of the musical and social experiences of communities who make and hear music (1977: 18). Turning attention to children's informal musical activities, and the discourses in which they are embedded, is one way of understanding the sociocultural processes that aesthetic practices mediate. While children's lives and voices have particular characteristics that are worth studying on their own terms, the analysis presented here suggests that children's "cultures" are also embedded in histories and structures of power that cross generations. More broadly, Miskitu children's musical practices on Corn Island show us how culture works, and how children are central actors in cultural continuity and change.

ACKNOWLEDGMENTS

The research for this chapter was supported by the Fulbright Institute of International Education, the Social Science Research Council, the Wenner-Gren Foundation, and the Tinker Foundation. I am grateful to all the children and their families on Corn Island who participated in the research and to Angela Abraham and others who helped me with the transcriptions. Revisions benefited greatly from the insightful suggestions of Patricia Shehan Campbell and Trevor Wiggins.

NOTES

1   All the names of children are pseudonyms.
2   See website (Web Figure 12.3 🔊) for audio file; names have been erased in the recording and changed in the transcript.

REFERENCES

Bauman, Richard. 1977. *Verbal Art as Performance*. Prospect Heights, IL: Waveland.
Bauman, Richard, and Charles Briggs. 1990. "Poetics and Performance as Critical Perspectives on Language and Social Life." *Annual Review of Anthropology* 19: 59–88.
Blacking, John. 1977. "Some Problems of Theory and Method in the Study of Musical Change." *Yearbook for Traditional Music* 9: 1–26.
Campbell, Patricia Shehan. [1998] 2010. *Songs in Their Heads: Music and Its Meaning in Children's Lives*. Oxford: Oxford University Press.
Cheney, Kristin E. 2007. *Pillars of the Nation: Child Citizens and Ugandan National Development*. Chicago: University of Chicago Press.
Feld, Steven, and Aaron Fox. 1994. "Music and Language." *Annual Review of Anthropology* 23 :25–53.
Fox, Aaron. 2004. *Real Country: Music and Language in Working-Class Culture*. Durham, NC: Duke University Press.
García Canclini, Nestor. 2004. *Diferentes, desiguales y desconectados: Mapas de la interculturalidad*. Barcelona: Gedisa Editorial.

Garrett, Paul, and Patricia Baquedano-López. 2002. "Language Socialization: Reproduction and Continuity, Transformation and Change." *Annual Review of Anthropology* 31: 339–361.

Goffman, Erving. 1974. *Frame Analysis: An Essay on the Organization of Experience.* Cambridge, MA: Harvard University Press.

González, Norma. 2001. *I Am My Language: Discourses of Women and Children in the Borderlands.* Tucson: University of Arizona Press.

Goodwin, Marjorie Harness. 2006. *The Hidden Life of Girls: Games of Stance, Status, and Exclusion.* Oxford: Blackwell.

Gordon, Edmund. 1998. *Disparate Diasporas: Identity and Politics in an African Nicaraguan Community.* Austin: University of Texas Press.

Grimson, Alejandro. 2000. *Interculturalidad y comunicación.* Bogotá: Grupo Editorial Norma.

Hale, Charles R. 1994. *Resistance and Contradiction: Miskitu Indians and the Nicaraguan State, 1894–1987.* Stanford, CA: Stanford University Press.

Hymes, D. H. 1972. "On Communicative Competence." In *Sociolinguistics*, edited by J. B. Pride and Janet Holmes, 269–293. Middlesex: Penguin Books.

Jamieson, Mark. 2007. "Language and the Process of Socialisation amongst Bilingual Children in a Nicaraguan Village." *Durham Anthropology Journal* 14 (1). Accessed June 28, 2012. http://www.dur.ac.uk/anthropology.journal/vol14/iss1/jamieson.html.

Jorgensen, J. N. 1998. "Children's Acquisition of Code-Switching for Power-Wielding." In *Codeswitching in Conversation: Language, Interaction, and Identity*, edited by Peter Auer, 237–258. London: Routledge.

Kartomi, Margaret. 1991. "Musical Improvisations by Children at Play." *The World of Music* 33 (3): 53–65.

Kulick, Don, and Bambi Schieffelin. 2004. "Language Socialization." In *Companion to Linguistic Anthropology*, edited by Alessandro Duranti, 349–368. London: Blackwell.

List, George. 1963. "The Boundaries of Speech and Song." *Ethnomusicology* 7 (1): 1–16.

Marsh, Kathryn. 2008. *The Musical Playground: Global Tradition and Change in Children's Songs and Games.* Oxford: Oxford University Press.

Minks, Amanda. Forthcoming. *Voices of Play: Miskitu Children's Speech and Song on the Atlantic Coast of Nicaragua.* Tucson: University of Arizona Press.

Minks, Amanda. 2009. "Interculturalidad y el discurso de los niños miskitos en Corn Island." *Wani—Revista del Caribe Nicaragüense* 59: 29–47.

Minks, Amanda. 2008. "Performing Gender in Song Games among Nicaraguan Miskitu Children." *Language and Communication* 28: 36–56.

Minks, Amanda. 2002. "From Children's Song to Expressive Practices: Old and New Directions in the Ethnomusicological Study of Children." *Ethnomusicology* 46 (3): 379–408.

Opie, Iona, and Peter Opie. 1985. *The Singing Game.* Oxford: Oxford University Press.

Scruggs, T. M. 1999. "Let's Enjoy as Nicaraguans: The Use of Music in the Construction of a Nicaraguan National Consciousness." *Ethnomusicology* 43 (2): 297–321.

Wentworth, William. 1980. *Context and Understanding: An Inquiry into Socialization Theory.* New York: Elsevier.

13

EDUCATION AND EVANGELISM IN A SIERRA LEONEAN VILLAGE

SARAH J. BARTOLOME

IT is nearly dusk when the clanking bell echoes through the Sierra Leonean village of Kagbere, signaling the beginning of choir practice. I stand on the porch of the Wesleyan church and watch silently as children emerge out of the dusky evening light from all corners of the village. A small boy in a dirty yellow shirt arrives with a key and unlocks the church, allowing a stream of children to enter. Immediately, they descend upon the drums, and music begins in the darkened room. Even before the director arrives, the choir is practicing, singing call-and-response songs, dancing, and drumming along in the inky darkness. I squint over my field notebook, recording the proceedings unfolding before me even as I keep a peripheral eye out for the plentiful centipedes (*tutus* to the children) that insist on invading my personal space. Ever at my side, Ali, a small boy of eight or nine, holds my flashlight dutifully, aiming it at the rapidly filling blank page and occasionally reaching over to pluck a *tutu* from my hair. When the choir director, Makoti, does arrive, he is carrying an oil lamp that casts a flickering glow on the faces of the young singers. The air is rich with the smell of burning oil as the stragglers file into their pews and wait expectantly for Makoti to take his place in front of his choir. Makoti quietly says, "Let us pray." The children stand silently as Makoti intones a brief prayer. He then takes a drum, announces the song, and the rehearsal begins, a joyful cacophony of sound echoing through the dark and cavernous church.

THE VILLAGE OF KAGBERE

A small subsistence farming village, Kagbere is located in the Magbaiamba Ndonhanhu chiefdom in northern Sierra Leone, West Africa. It is remote, requiring an exhausting eight-hour bus ride through the backcountry of Sierra Leone, and rural, a village without electricity or running water. There are roughly four hundred Landogo (also known as Lokko) people living in the village and working the land under the watchful eye of Chief Kandeh Finoh III. The surrounding countryside is ripe with seasonal fields of swamp rice, groundnuts, and cassava. Within the village, there are three religious institutions (representing Catholic, Wesleyan, and Muslim faiths) as well as three school buildings serving primary and secondary students. A health center has been built at one end of the town, but there were no regular medical personnel staffing the facility during my stay.

One long, red dirt road stretches the length of the village, running from the health center at one end to Chief Finoh's house at the other (see Figure 13.1). Walking the length of the main road from the health center to the chief's abode, you encounter many traditional hut dwellings with mud walls and grass roofs, as well as many modern structures fashioned from mud or concrete bricks with corrugated tin roofs. Along your way, you pass the "UW Village" on your right, a small fenced-in compound featuring a summerhouse for gatherings and three simple, straw-roofed dwellings (built to house visiting University of Washington students). As you continue on your journey, passing houses on either side of the road, the inhabitants might call out

Figure 13.1: The main road in Kagbere.

a greeting to you from their porches. On the left is the mosque and a spur of the road branching off, leading past the school buildings and the Catholic church on the way to several farms and the bush beyond. Just past the mosque, a small shop sells soap, biscuits, beer, and a variety of simple sundries. Across from the shop is the yellow and brown Wesleyan church and, to the right of it, a smaller road leading out to the river where people often bathe and do laundry. Further on from the church is a public gathering space, where the town convenes for community events or elections, and beyond that is Chief Kandeh Finoh's home. The walk from one end of the village to the other takes roughly five minutes, but with no shade along the way and the blazing African sun overhead, the journey often feels much longer.

Each morning, most children are seen making their way down the road to the school in their uniforms. Girls wear a green dress with red trim while boys don khaki-colored shorts and a green button-down shirt. They spend mornings in the classrooms, led by local teachers, then hurry home to help their families with whatever afternoon chores might be required. Other children make their way through the bush to family rice, cassava, and groundnut farms (depending on the season), spending the morning with parents and siblings, planting, harvesting, or tending to crops. In the afternoons, it is common to see children hurrying down the road with large bowls balanced atop their heads as they bring fresh water back to their home from the well in front of the health center. Children are also often seen pounding rice or peppers with sticks in the traditional, large wooden pestles, shelling groundnuts, or chopping greens for a stew. The children of Kagbere are responsible for contributing to the daily work of the family, both in and around the home and in the fields.

Kagbere is also a rich and thriving musical community that embraces a variety of musical traditions, including log drumming, traditional dance, choral singing, ritual music, lamellaphone playing, hand-clapping songs, and childhood chants. While in Kagbere, I saw adults engage in musical activities outside of church only once, when I specifically asked local musicians to play lamellaphones (*gbondoma* and *kongoma*) for me. Following their performance, a few log drums (*kei*) were brought out and audience and musicians danced and sang together for more than an hour. While these instruments (and others) featured prominently in earlier accounts of Sierra Leonean music making (Ottenberg 1996; Turay 1966; van Oven [1973] 1974), I did not witness any spontaneous musicking among adults in the village, aside from the performance I arranged. During my stay in Kagbere, adult, live music making was limited to participation in weekly church services filled with singing, drumming, and dancing, although I was told that music is also integral to seasonal festivals, funerals, rituals, ceremonies, and healing practices. Previous research on Sierra Leonean instruments (Turay 1966; Van Oven [1973] 1974), instrumental musicians (Ottenberg 1996), and masquerade performances (Cannizzo 2006; Siegmann and Perani 1976) supports the notion that music is an important part of the cultural fabric of life in Sierra Leone.

Music also plays an important role in the lives of the children, and they make a significant contribution to the musical life of the community. Every day, children in the village engage in musical play, sing spontaneously in two or more parts, perform hand-clapping songs and games, and dance together. The children also feature in a music and dance troupe that is responsible for performing and perpetuating local traditions. Within the Wesleyan church, the children make up the church choir, leading the congregation through worship services saturated with singing, movement, and instrument playing. It was on this children's choir that I focused my research efforts, hoping to explore the role of the choir in the lives of the children as well as the teaching and learning paradigms that comprised music transmission within this Western-influenced ensemble.

The Kagbere Wesleyan Church Children's Choir

On Sunday morning I dress for church in a simple red skirt and black top—the one semidressy outfit I stuffed into my rucksack prior to departure for Sierra Leone—and make my way to a pew on the women's side of the stifling church. The windows on all sides of the church are open, but there is little breeze and I can feel the sweat dripping down my back as I wait for the Good News Choir to take its place (see Figure 13.2). The choir director, Makoti, places a wooden stool at the front of the aisle separating the pews, perching a small green, plastic basket on top for donations and offerings. He then retreats to his spot in the first choir pew, taking his place alongside the other choir director, Kabi, who will also drum this morning. The members of the Good News Choir file out of their pews and take their places at the front of the church. There are twelve singers today, arranged neatly into two rows. A few girls are dressed in traditional African style, wearing long skirts and tops with matching head wraps in vibrantly colored and patterned brocade fabrics. Several boys are also in traditional dress, sporting short pants and matching tunic topics in equally rich fabrics and colors. Other children are dressed more simply in jeans or shorts, t-shirts, and bare feet. As soon as the two choir directors begin to the play the drums, the choir starts to move together, shuffling their left foot forward, and back, forward, and back in time to the music. The song leader, Fatu, a talented young singer about twelve years old, leads the choir through a call-and-response style song in praise of the Lord, producing a very bright and forward choral sound. I crouch in the aisle with my video camera, grimacing as pieces of grit from the cement floor press into my knees, as members of the congregation file out of the pews and dance forward, dropping coins and small bills into the donations basket. Fatu continues the song until all members of the congregation have filed back to their seats. The choir finishes singing, and with a final flourish of the drum, the choir abruptly stops their shuffle and quietly files back into the pews.

During my stay in Kagbere, I lived with a local family and spent my days interacting with villagers, helping in the cooking hut, working in the rice fields, visiting the school, and learning music and dance from the children. Each evening, I walked

Figure 13.2: The Good News Choir seating.

down the long red dirt road that ran through the village to observe the Kagbere
Wesleyan Church Children's Choir in rehearsal. The choir is divided into two levels,
the Good News Choir, composed of younger children (aged approximately seven
through ten), and the Youth Choir, composed of older children who have earned
promotion. The separation of the choirs into two levels is rooted in issues of development and preparation. The Good News Choir teaches the children not only how
to sing but also the rules and routines of the choir, the standard songs and choreography, and the importance of attendance, discipline, and maturity. Ansu, the choir
president, explained that the choir is divided:

> because the *pikin* [children], they don't learn quick like the big ones. That's why we
> divide the group. We make a Good News [Choir], then we make a Youth Choir, so
> that when the *pikin* start in the Good News, they learn more before going to the
> Youth Choir. That's why we separate.

Kabi, who directs the Good News Choir, insisted, "The children, they are not easy
to groom." Promotion to the Youth Choir is only possible after the child has been
baptized and confirmed and is able to read the Bible, sing and behave well, and
maintain regular attendance at rehearsals. There is also a formal assessment as part
of the promotion process:

> We train them as Good News and we test them if they able to join Youth Choir.
> Like singing, time of practice [attendance]....We assess them. We have many laws
> for choir. We have rules there. When they are able to know these laws, they are able
> to move up. (Ansu, choir president)

When asked about these assessments, Ansu indicated that each child is required to
sing alone to demonstrate her or his ability to sing well.

Although there are two branches of the children's choir at the Wesleyan church, there is no adult choir. Ansu asserted, "We get the choir, but they don't want to join it. We tell them that in a big church, like Makenne, Freetown, the elders are the choir. But here the elders, they do not join the youth." When questioned about the lack of an adult choir within the church, people offered several explanations. Many adults in the village are overwhelmed with family and work responsibilities, leaving no free time to attend practices. Given the evangelical mission of the choir, members are required to travel to other churches and villages to perform and spread their religious message. Often adults are unable to leave the household to complete these minimissions, thereby preventing them from belonging to the choir. Ansu elaborated, "They don't want to move, like from village to village, from Kagbere to Mbenembu. They think it is so far. The youth, they are strong. They can move." Many adults in the village are unable to read, so, as Kabi mentioned, "A major problem is that people are not able to use hymnals." Similarly, there is a language barrier preventing participation in the choir: while many elders speak only Landogo or a bit of Krio, the choir performs in English, Krio, Landogo, Mende, and Temne. The inclusion of unfamiliar languages, paired with a lack of literacy, may be intimidating to adults, thereby discouraging them from joining the choir. Choir member Sarah suggested, "They find it difficult to learn the songs. Especially when in English or Krio. Not all people know how to talk Krio or English." Mabinti, an older song leader, even offered "shame or embarrassment" associated with singing in front of others as possible reasons for the absence of an adult choir. So, despite the fact that the church owns a set of choir robes for adults and traditionally there is a choir for elders, the Kagbere Wesleyan church features only children's choirs. In this sense, the children are primarily responsible for the musical enrichment of the congregation.

Historical Context of the Choir

The very presence of a Wesleyan church in such a small, rural village as Kagbere links back to colonial efforts to "civilize" indigenous populations in Sierra Leone, as well as the primary evangelical and educational activities of the Church Missionary Society (CMS) in the early 1800s. Sierra Leone was established as a colony under the British Sierra Leone Company in 1792. The early settlers "formed the Western foundations of the society, reflected in their Christianity, education, politics, ideals and aspirations, civic pride and high sense of individualism, their mode of dress, their articulateness and their language" (Wyse 1989: 1). When Sierra Leone became a Crown Colony in 1808, it became the base for the British antislavery campaign. The capital city of Freetown was rapidly populated by (in addition to the British settlers) a great diversity of Liberated Africans originally from many parts of West Africa. Paul Richards noted that these ex-slaves "brought into mid-nineteenth-century Sierra Leonean society a rich mixture of technical ideas and social influences from up and down the Western African coast, greatly boosting a process of African 'cultural creolization'" (1996: 37).

In an effort to integrate the Liberated Africans with Westernized Black Englishmen, the CMS began focusing their efforts on the non-Christian settlers in the Freetown area beginning around 1811. The British government subsidized the work of the CMS in an effort to aid the organization in acculturating and Westernizing the Liberated Africans. Not only did the missionaries take on evangelical responsibilities, but they also were committed to utilizing education as a means of civilizing the Liberated Africans in Sierra Leone. Through the construction and staffing of schools, "education for the general mass of people in Sierra Leone was pioneered by the CMS" (Wyse 1989: 33). In this sense, both the colonial government and the CMS were responsible for the spread of Christianity throughout Sierra Leone, and both considered education an important part of their mission to civilize and proselytize both the Liberated Africans and native populations.

It appears that the early evangelical and educational missions of the CMS and the colonial government persist today in the continued efforts of the Wesleyan Church to evangelize and educate. These dual aims are expressed in the organization's mission statement: "To exalt Jesus Christ by: Evangelizing the lost; Disciplining the believers; Equipping the Church; and Ministering to Society" (www.wesleyan.org/about). Today, the children's choir serves as an arm of the Wesleyan Church, adhering to this four-pronged Wesleyan mission through music ministry. The following analysis of the roles of the choir will explore the way the organization achieves each of these missions through its evangelical activities, the education it provides its members, and the services it performs for the church and the community at large.

THE ROLES OF THE CHOIR

Choir as Evangelism

The most important function of the choir, according to its participants, is to share the religious message of the church with others. When asked about the purpose of the choir, Ansu, the choir president, immediately and emphatically declared, "To spread the message, evangelize, spread the gospel to the people in the community." Similarly, Kabi, the director of the Good News Choir stated, "The most important role of the choir is for evangelism, to spread the Good News to the people." These sentiments were echoed by each of the participants interviewed, indicating that evangelism and the ability of the choir to bring their religious message to others is a primary function of the organization. The choir is often asked to perform at other churches in the Wesleyan district, and in this way, they are able to spread their message beyond their own church community to other churches and villages in the area.

As part of its evangelical mission, the choir is responsible for recruiting new members and bringing people into the church. Mabinti emphasized the choir's value in building the church membership through entertainment of the people. She called the choir "the backbone of the church" and asserted that "the church is strong because of the choir." Ellen, a sixteen-year-old member of the Youth Choir noted, "The choir has a great role to play. Without the choir the church does not function. We make people want to go to church when we sing fine songs." Ansu also recognized the role of the choir in encouraging churchgoing: "Sunday we sing in the church fine, and the people are glad to come to church.... [The choir can] draw people's attention more to the church." Indeed, the long Sunday services are filled with music, and the congregation stands and dances as the choir performs, filing down the aisle to make monetary donations in appreciation of the choir's efforts.

The choir even goes so far as to make home visits to nonchurchgoers, encouraging them to join the church. Ansu elaborated on this practice:

> We learn [teach] people God's work, God's way. Because some people, they are not going to church, they are not Muslim, they are not Christian. So the choir moves from house to house and preach the gospel to them.... We say, "Let's go there." We go sing for them and preach.

Makoti also mentioned the unique power of a children's choir to draw adult members, as parents will often attend church to see their child sing or get involved with the church if a child has expressed an interest in singing in the choir. Through entertainment, recruitment, and church and community performances, the choir seeks to spread the Good News and recruit members into the Church as part of their primary evangelical mission. This is in alignment with the Wesleyan Church's overarching mission "to exalt Jesus Christ by evangelizing the lost."

Choir as Community Service

Community service is another of the functions of the children's choir, with members serving both within the church community and within the community of Kagbere at large. Within the church, the choir is responsible for basic maintenance of the church building, including weekly sweeping and cleaning of the altar and pews. The choir is an important part of scheduled prayer circles and crusades, providing music and entertainment as a part of these church events. The children are often called upon to sing at funeral services, provide music for all-night vigils held following a church member's death, and provide assistance for families in mourning. According to choir member Ellen, "Sometimes the choir sings free of charge for Wesleyan funerals in the area." Choir members will often prepare and deliver food to bereaved households and help with basic chores in the home. Similarly, if a church member is in need of assistance due to illness, injury, pregnancy, or financial misfortune, the choir leader will mobilize a team to go to the home and help prepare food, complete household duties, and generally assist as needed. The choir will also pay visits to ailing church members, consoling those who suffer and providing spiritual support. Ellen mentioned, "The choir leader will organize the Good News or the Youth to go help church members who need assistance in the house. People always ask choir members for help." In these ways, the choir is an integral part of the church community, providing services for church members and actively participating in church events that occur outside of regular weekly services.

Within the community of Kagbere, the choir often organizes social events that bring together the church and community members, such as concerts, plays, outings to the forest, and even football games between choir members and community members. These events "build relations between church and community" (Kabi), provide all participants with the opportunity to meet others and socialize, and forward the evangelical mission of the choir. In addition to bringing together the Church and community through social events, the choir often gets involved in projects that benefit the entire village of Kagbere. Mary, the pastor's wife, asserted, "The community, if they need help, they ask the choir." Ellen's father, Stevens, remembered, for example, that when the village was erecting the primary school building, the choir members were responsible for "gathering local materials, like stones and sticks and bringing water for the workers." Through a variety of service activities the choir maintains a presence within the church community and the village of Kagbere, serving church members and community members alike. These varied activities represent choir members' contribution to the Church's mission to "equip the church," as well as "minister to society."

Choir as Education

Another of the major functions of the choir is to teach. The choir teaches both its members and the community and provides education in several, multifaceted areas, including music education, religious education, personal and social education, moral education, and even vocational training. In light of these extensive educational activities, the choir takes an active role in "disciplining the believers," another of the Wesleyan Church's primary missions.

By virtue of its nature as a choir, the children inevitably get a musical education, learning how to sing well through weekly practices and performances and engaging in music listening and composition activities. Indeed, the ability to sing well is a formal requirement for promotion from Good News into the Youth Choir. However, in terms of the major functions of the choir, a musical education is secondary to other, more practical functions. Music is thought of as a means to an end (evangelism, recruitment, education), rather than as merely a leisure activity. Choir members Sarah and Ellen both indicated that their ability to sing was a "gift from God" and they sing in the choir to serve God with the talent they have been given. Music serves God and the Church, and while each member is schooled in the musical arts through participation in the choir, music education is not the primary focus of the choir experience.

In addition to and in support of its primary evangelical mission of educating others in the word of God ("evangelizing the lost"), the choir provides its members with a thorough religious education ("disciplining the believers"). The choir directors strive to "groom them up well as Christians" (Kabi), teaching each choir member how to know God, how to pray, and how to read the Bible. As Mabinti commented, a major goal of the choir is to "teach them God's work, to bring them up as a God-fearing person." Regular Bible study instructs them in the word of God and in how to spread the Good News. This knowledge and understanding then spreads to the family of each child, another form of evangelism. Ansu explained,

> We learn [teach] them how to do evangelism to others, how to preach the gospel. We learn them how to pray, 'cause some of them don't know how to pray. We teach them how to pray. And they teach the family.

The choir maintains its own groundnut farm as a means of teaching members some trade skills. Members are responsible for the maintenance and harvest of the groundnut crops, providing valuable vocational training that will help the children as they mature into adults living in a subsistence farming community. Stevens contends that while some students drop out of school, they may continue to participate in the choir. The choir provides them with an opportunity to learn how to farm even though they may be unable to finish their formal schooling. Stevens went on to say that the choir would like to purchase sewing machines in order to expand their ability to provide vocational training. With several sewing machines, choir members might train to be seamstresses and tailors and develop the skills to manufacture their own choir uniforms. These practical, experiential, skill-building activities extend the function of the choir well beyond religious education and evangelism.

The children also acquire many personal skills as a result of their participation in the choir. Choir members develop social skills, learning how to interact and cooperate with others, making friends both in and through the choir, and learning "to speak to and among people" (Mabinti). They also develop discipline and obedience, becoming aware of the rules of the choir, learning "to respect their elders and each other" (Mary), and making a commitment to regular rehearsal attendance. The children take on leadership roles within the choir, the church, and the community, leading songs, organizing events, and assisting others. According to Makoti, "One of the Youth Choir, they may fill in for the pastor at times," stepping up to lead the entire church for a Sunday service. During rehearsal observations, the choir leader would often step aside as a child took over the solo portion of the song, allowing leadership to pass from the director to the choir member. The choir also fosters reading through Bible study and trains the children in the art of appropriate language. Clearly, choir membership provides a number of personal benefits to those children involved, fostering social, personal, interpersonal, academic, and leadership skills.

The choir's capacity to educate extends well beyond its members, reaching out into the families of the children and into the community at large. The teachings of the church are able to reach the homes of the choir members, as the children take their religious education home to their families. Kabi illustrates: "At times, in the home, parents have conflict. The *pikin* help resolve that conflict by quoting the Bible." In this sense, the religious messages of the church are channeled through the choir members to the parents, allowing the children to educate the adults in the ways and workings of God. Often, the choir will produce plays based on Christian ideals, the dangers of domestic violence, avoidance of abusive language, and other moral issues in an effort to educate parents and the community beyond just evangelism. Choir member Ellen believes "Parents learn much from the plays."

From this analysis, the Kagbere children's choir emerges as a multifaceted culture that reaches well beyond the realm of musical and religious experiences. Specifically, these varied roles and activities allow the choir to achieve the stated mission of the Wesleyan Church and support the institution's assertion that their "ministries emphasize practical Bible teaching, uplifting worship, and special programs to meet a variety of life needs" (www.wesleyan.org/about). While, on the surface, the choir seems to make its contributions through weekly music performances, the choir organization at the Wesleyan Church in Kagbere is actively present in the lives of all villagers, providing an astonishing array of services and benefits to participants, congregants, and community members alike.

MUSIC TRANSMISSION

In examining the choir as a music ensemble, issues of music transmission were explored in an attempt to identify patterns of teaching and learning during rehearsals. All of the participants interviewed outlined virtually the same method of song learning: First, the song leader or choir director performs the song while the choir listens. Then the choir learns the words, repeating each line of text after the leader. Next the melody is taught by rote, with the choir singing each line, then two lines at a time after the leader. Finally, the choir performs the song with the leader and has the opportunity to ask questions. In this way the choir is able to learn words and melody without any written notation, in a strict aural/oral fashion. It would appear that this procedure is locally practiced in other villages as well, as a visiting pastor who attended an evening rehearsal taught two songs to the choir, following almost exactly the pattern outlined above. The singers, having highly developed aural skills from years of learning by rote, were familiar with the routine and picked up the song with astonishing rapidity. Within five minutes, the song leader had taken over the solo portion and the choir was performing the song with impeccable precision and accuracy, while I struggled to keep up.

Within the rehearsal setting, there was a high degree of variability with regard to formal and informal rehearsal techniques. For example, the transitions between pieces were seamless and very few verbal instructions were given. In contrast, physical or dynamic cues were frequently used to signal the musicians. The director physically cued the drum to begin and signaled the end of the song by bringing the volume of the drum way down. There were clear behavioral rules in place, and the leaders occasionally stopped to discipline the choir or ask for silence. The choir leader did not conduct the choir but often took on a leadership role either through singing the call or solo portions or by playing the drum, which indicated the beginning and end of each piece. A typical rehearsal began with an extended, informal "jam" session led by the children themselves. The children spontaneously sang through hymns and selections from their standard repertoire, accompanying themselves on drums and segueing seamlessly from one song to the next. The choir director then took charge, leading the choir in a brief prayer before the rehearsal proper. The rehearsal closed with another prayer and the singing of a hymn: "I Cannot Sing without You." As each of the rehearsals observed adhered to this format, it suggests that the routine of choir rehearsal is rather fixed.

As an aid to examining and deconstructing the complexities of the music transmission process across cultures, Schippers proposed a "framework that provides a solid basis for examining and assessing key elements in teaching music across cultures" (2010: 124). The Twelve Continuum Transmission Framework (TCTF) "can be a powerful and effective instrument for a better understanding of music transmission processes" (ibid.) and encompasses twelve "core" continua that are divided into four categories: issues of context, modes of transmission, dimensions of interaction, and approach to cultural diversity. Each continuum comprises a range of possibilities between two extremes, one representing more formalized, institutionalized music educational settings and the other constituting more informal music-learning environments. Schippers noted that the TCTF may be used as a tool to describe teaching and learning cross-culturally and that "such descriptions of music transmission are preferably based on a full analysis of an observed teaching process, supported by extensive interviews with facilitators/ teachers and learners" (2010: 125). Following my observations and interviews in the field, I applied Schippers's TCTF to the teaching and learning paradigms encountered in Kagbere, focusing on the modes of transmission as manifested in the children's choir rehearsals and in participant comments and behavior.

At the outset, one might assume that the musical behaviors going on in a small Sierra Leonean village in West Africa would gravitate toward the informal side of Schippers's framework: holistic, aural, and intangible. In reality, however, the music transmission occurring in the Kagbere Wesleyan Church Children's Choir rehearsals is surprisingly mixed. On one hand, the tradition is strictly oral/aural. However, the learning process is not entirely holistic and intangible in nature but moves toward analytic and tangible. There is an institutionalized teaching/learning paradigm that is utilized and recognized consistently by participants. This process does not involve repeated listenings of an entire song that is eventually learned over time without formal instruction. In the case of this choir, the leaders break down the piece by line, teaching each line, chunking into larger sections, reviewing these larger chunks, and then performing the song as a whole. The transmission process seems to fall in the middle of the analytic-holistic continuum. While the leaders are not completing a formal analysis of each song, teaching music theory, or utilizing solfege (as would perhaps be expected in Western settings), they are employing some analytic strategies as they teach each song. Similarly, the process itself is more tangible: one can identify how and where and when the learning takes place, despite the fact that the choir is not using printed scores and Western notation. It would seem, then, that the music transmission occurring within the context of the Kagbere Wesleyan Church Children's Choir rehearsals represents a melding of formal and informal elements that mirrors the blending of traditional African and Western religious practices so evident among the villagers.

The relative ease with which Christianity and more traditional African spiritual practices coexist in Kagbere suggests that the two are not irreconcilable for local people. One Saturday afternoon, for example, I learned about the herbs and plants used in witchcraft to heal customers or curse enemies with the help of magic and an appeal to the spirits. The practitioner with whom I spoke greeted me graciously the next morning at the Wesleyan church service, participating enthusiastically throughout the worship event and singing and dancing along in musical praise of the Lord. On the topic of the juxtaposition of Christianity and African religion, Christopher Fyfe noted,

> Though the Creoles [Krios of Sierra Leone] assumed unquestioningly that the Christian religion and European customs and morality were superior to indigenous African religion, customs, and morality, they still retained an African identity. As officials and missionaries, they practiced and preached the alien doctrines they had grown up to believe. Yet they remained Africans, proud of the community they had created and ready to transplant its idiosyncratic ways wherever they went. (Fyfe 1974: 50)

In discussing the emerging Krio society in the early 1900s, Cole contended, "Even among those who had become converted to Christianity and Islam, there was widespread embracing of traditional practices and customary ritual ceremonies" (2006: 44). This blending of Western and African traditions is also evident in the relatively mixed pedagogical strategies employed in music transmission among members of the Kagbere Wesleyan Church Children's Choir as well as in its mixed body of repertoire that features both Western hymns and tradition African selections.

Issues of Repertoire and Performance Practice

The repertoire performed by the children's choir is quite varied, encompassing traditional Western hymns in English (e.g., "I Cannot Sing") and Krio as well as more African-style call-and-response pieces in English, Landogo (see excerpt, "Nuunga," Figure 13.3), Krio, Temne, and Mende. An examination of the printed hymnal reveals mostly English hymns but also a couple of hymns in Krio, including one song that I heard performed frequently outside of the church setting, "Tell am Tenki." Music permeated much of the church service, as the choir led the congregation in the singing of hymns and traditional songs, mostly in Western-style unison. Singing was invariably accompanied by drumming, clapping, and dancing, with congregants standing up in the pews or dancing their way to the front of the church to make monetary donations.

Figure 13.3: Transcription of Nuunga by Sarah Bartolome.

Translation:

My people, Let's work for God.

My people, Let's walk in God's way.

My people, Let's worship God until he comes.

He will take us to heaven. He will take us to heaven.

With the exception of the Western-style hymns, the choir's performance repertoire and vocal sound were decidedly African in style, frequently making use of call-and-response structure and employing a bright, forward timbre. The choir's sound is very much in line with previous descriptions of vocal singing in northern Sierra Leone: "Singers from the country's northern regions frequently tighten their throats to produce the forceful tone and 'metallic' resonance usually associated with North Africa" (Van Oven 1970: 27). When the choir was performing at the front of the church, they customarily had choreographed movements that were perfectly in sync, including simple shuffling steps as well as basic arm and body movements to act out the story of the song.

As one would expect, the themes of the choir's repertoire were overtly religious in nature, encompassing such topics as biblical stories, perseverance in the face of adversity, humility, and thankfulness to the Lord. While I was in the village, I only heard one politically charged song performed by the choir; it was titled "We Jus De Run." The song depicts the arrival of soldiers of the Revolutionary United Front (RUF), the rebel organization that began Sierra Leone's eleven-year civil war in 1991 and frequently employed violence and terror as means of recruiting supporters (Richards 1996). Overall, the choir's repertoire is focused on praise and worship.

Given the aural nature of music transmission and the absence of written notation within this choral culture, one area of interest was how the choir found new music to introduce into their repertoire. Makoti explained that in order to learn new songs, he listens to local African gospel cassettes made by his cousins in Freetown. After repeated listening, he then teaches the new song to the choir. Mabinti mentioned that she often attends different churches in other villages to learn new songs, staying after the services to talk with and learn from other song leaders. She stated, "If I go to Freetown, I go visit so many churches, sometimes a good person sings a song and I like it. I go to the person and I say 'Can you teach me this song? I like it.'" She then returns home to Kagbere and shares these new songs with the choir. Similarly, the choir often learns new songs from other choirs during annual youth camps, five-day-long events in which Wesleyan Church choirs from all over the district come together to share music and compete for prizes. Composer and choir director, Kabi said, "At times, I write the songs myself, from the Bible." None of the musicians/composers interviewed read Western musical notation or utilize staff notation in their creative processes.

Interestingly, several of the participants described a process of collective composition whereby the choir members themselves worked together to write new songs. Makoti indicated that during September and October, the Youth Choir often composes songs. Usually, the group reads the Bible together and identifies verses that they would like to set to music. Then, the song leader "picks" the tune and teaches it to the choir. Ansu explained the process: "First we find a chapter and we read one by one. We study inside the Bible and practice it. Mabinti [the song leader] then can pick the tune. Others follow." Alternatively, the choir members take the verses and go home to make up the tune. The choir then reconvenes and performs their compositions for each other and collectively chooses the best song for inclusion in the repertoire. It seems that this process of facilitated creativity has naturally emerged out of the desire and need for new music in an environment where printed music is inaccessible and, more importantly, impractical.

CHILDREN AS PRIMARY CULTURE BEARERS

Sierra Leonean youth have long been valued as having much to offer society and have historically had a prominent role both culturally and politically. Within the oral storytelling tradition of two distinct tribal groups, there is evidence of the value and power attributed to youth. Finnegan noted a common theme in Limba stories depicting "the younger brother...spurned by his elders, who in the end saves them by his cleverness or insight" (1967: 56). Similarly, among the Mende, Musa Wo is an imaginary, rebellious youth character from oral tales whose exploits "serve to remind Mende elders not to neglect the energy and cunning of the young," challenging them to "harness these skills for the greater social good" (Richards 1996: 59). In Kagbere, the children are indeed employed to serve the greater good of the village, through community service both within the church community and throughout the community of Kagbere at large.

Elsewhere in Sierra Leone groups of boys perpetuate a tradition of a masquerade depicting the *Alikali* devils (Cannizzo 2006). Such a performance by a self-governed group of children "confirms the artistry of the boys as childish, not in the sense of being immature, but in its fuller meaning of being unblemished by time and struggle, of having the stronger power that comes from youth" (Cannizzo 2006: 174). This serves to illustrate more generally the importance of youth in Sierra Leone's cultural arenas. In the village of Kagbere, children and youth are primary bearers of musical culture and the evangelical message of the Wesleyan Church, serving an important role as agents of community service, religious education, and musical preservation.

While this examination of the Kagbere Church Children's Choir represents only a snapshot of a complex and multifaceted musical culture, it is apparent that the children within this society feature prominently in the musical enrichment of the community. Choir members benefit personally, socially, and musically from the education they receive through choir membership, acquiring a wide range of knowledge and skill as part of the choir experience. The church community and the community of Kagbere both benefit from the array of services provided by the members of the children's choir, and the church itself benefits as musical emissaries go forth into the world to advance its evangelical mission. Historical and cultural streams of influence emerged with regards to both the roots of missionary work in Sierra Leone and the utilization of youth within the culture. Despite the historical influences, the covert educational benefits, and the primary evangelical purpose, the children of the Kagbere Wesleyan Church Children's Choir are, at the most fundamental level, part of a rich musical tradition that brings joy to their community. And each night at 7:30, the bell clangs, the children gather, and the voices of these young musicians echo through the darkened village of Kagbere once again.

ACKNOWLEDGMENTS

This chapter is dedicated to the members of the Kagbere Wesleyan Church Children's Choir, who so graciously welcomed me and shared their remarkable musical talents.

REFERENCES

Cannizzo, J. 2006. "The Alikali Devils of Sierra Leone: Play, Performance, and Social Commentary." In *Playful Performers: African Children's Masquerades*, edited by S. Ottenberg and D. A. Brinkley, 167–180. New Brunswick, NJ: Transaction Publishers.

Cole, G. R. 2006. "Re-thinking the Demographic Make-Up of Krio Society." In *New Perspectives on the Sierra Leone Krio*, edited by M. Dixon-Fyle and G. Cole, 33–52. New York: Peter Lang.

Finnegan, R. 1967. *Limba Stories and Story-Telling*. Oxford Library of Africa Literature. Oxford: Clarendon Press.

Fyfe, C. 1974. "Reform in West Africa: The Abolition of the Slave Trade." In *History of West Africa*, edited by J. F. A. Ajayi and M. Crowder, 30–56. Vol. 2. 2 Vols. London: Longman.

Ottenberg, S. 1996. *Seeing with music: The lives of Three Blind African Musicians*. Seattle: University of Washington Press.

Richards, P. 1996. *Fighting for the Rain Forest: War, Youth, and Resources in Sierra Leone*. Portsmouth, NH: Heinemann.

Schippers, H. 2010. *Facing the Music: Shaping Music Education from a Global Perspective.* Oxford: Oxford University Press.

Siegmann, W., and J. Perani. 1976. "Men's masquerades of Sierra Leone and Liberia." *African Arts,* 9(3), 42–47, 92.

Turay, A. K. 1966. "A Vocabulary of Temne Musical Instruments." *Sierra Leone Language Review* 5: 27–33.

Van Oven, C. 1970. "Music of Sierra Leone." *African Arts* 3 (4): 20–27, 71.

Van Oven, C. [1973] 1974. "The Kondi of Sierra Leone." *African Music* 5 (3): 77–85.

Wyse, A. 1989. *The Krio of Sierra Leone: An Interpretive History.* Washington, DC: Howard University Press.

14

CHILDREN'S URBAN AND RURAL MUSICAL WORLDS IN NORTH INDIA

NATALIE SARRAZIN

IT is a typical afternoon in a New Delhi suburb. More than half a dozen children gather in the narrow strip of unpaved parking lot of their four-story concrete apartment building. Six girls and two boys within an age range of four to eleven years play daily after school. After some informal chasing, the children begin playing *poshampā*, a Hindi game chant. The older and taller girls, Manya and Apoorva (ages nine and seven, respectively), hold up their arms to make a bridge while the other children pass underneath. Ayush and Vishu, both five years old, enjoy getting "caught" when the children lower their arms on the last line (*āb to jel jānā paṛegā*), and they repeatedly request to play the game.

Children's Game Chant: *Poshampā*

poshampā bhai poshampā	Posampa, brother posampa
lāl kile¹ me˜ kya hua?	What happened in the Red Fort?
sau rupiye ki ghaṛī churāī	I stole a 100-rupee watch
ab to jel jānā paṛegā	Now you'll have to go to jail
jel kī kichaṛī khānī paṛegī	In jail you'll have to eat *kicheri*²
jel kā pāni pīnā paṛegā	You'll have to drink jail water
āb to jel jānā paṛegā	Now you will have to go to jail

It is typical to find children engaged in play across gender and age boundaries, with younger inexperienced children assigned insignificant roles that enable them first to learn as apprentices (Oke 1999: 216). This type of play is in keeping with the Indian *guru-shishya* apprentice method of learning music, in which the inexperienced musician initially enters the master's house merely as an onlooker to absorb the rules of the music.

After an hour or so of play, the children make their way upstairs to do their homework, spend time with their families, and eat dinner before heading off to bed. Many schoolchildren work before school. Manish, twelve, for example, sells newspapers in front of a milk stand from 5:00 to 7:00 am to earn a few rupees to help his family. Children feel tremendous pressure to have a successful career and earn money for their families. Given these constraints, what role can music play in these children's lives?

CULTURAL VALUE OF MUSIC

Children in India are surrounded by reminders of the value of music found in Indian history and religious philosophy. Children may hear *bhajan-s* (Hindi devotional songs) each morning and evening broadcast from a local temple nearby. In Hindu mythology, the goddess Saraswati rules over learning and the arts, underscoring the belief that the arts make us human. Hindu temples, gods, and goddesses depict instrumental music and dance in keeping with a religion that encompasses the sacredness of sound (*aum, nāda*) and the importance of *sangīt*—a two millennia-old concept combining vocal music, instrumental music, and dance found in the *Nātyashāshtra*, an ancient treaty on the performing arts, (200 BC–AD 200). Indian classical musicians claim an illustrious and unbroken lineage to the present day, flourishing through centuries of invasions and rulers, such as the Mughals, many of whom strongly supported the arts. In the South Indian state of Kerala, children still learn drumming and dance according to ancient oral tradition techniques.

Indian culture is steeped in ritual, religion, and kinship and music is communal and accessible. Children are exposed to live performances without having to buy tickets and are able to participate in a vast array of religious, social, and family events underscored by music. The average child will hear dozens of songs (women's *gīt*) required for the many wedding rituals. They will also hear religious songs for daily worship, such as *ārtī* for *pūjā* and *azzan* (the call to prayer); songs for both Hindu and Muslim festivals, such as *Diwālī, Holī, Ramadan* (*īd*); devotees (professional and amateur) in neighborhood temples or mosques singing *bhajan* and *qawwālī*; and folk and devotional music to accompany religious promenades and festivals, such as *Ganesh chaturthī* and *Kṛiṣna Janmashtamī* (birthdays of Lord Ganesh and Krishna) and *Navrātrī* (nine nights worshipping female divine goddess power). While many of these songs and occasions are not necessarily specific to children, they comprise a large part of their musical enculturation within the community and family.

There is even evidence of India's social and musical values in children's play. The ancient and nationally played game called *kabaddī*,[3] for example, requires a child ("it") to repeat the word *kabaddī* in a continuous and rapid chant-like stream requiring a controlled exhalation of breath as she or he tries to tag another child. When the repetition of the word is broken, the child is out of the game. The attention to breath and sound in the *kabaddī* game highlights long-standing cultural beliefs.

Through a traditional culture and historical continuity, most of India maintains its strong connection to its regional roots, language, rituals, and music. With increased urbanization and globalization, however, these roots are beginning to shift. Children in cities are removed from their family's regional musical identity, with local songs and games supplanted by popular film songs, accounting for the majority of India's popular music consumption.

Given these streams of influence, what might a north Indian urban child's musical repertoire look like? How might the repertoire differ from their rural counterpart? What is the impact of the media on traditional repertoires? To discuss this, I will consider two groups of children in North India—one in an urban area on the outskirts of Delhi (India's capital city region of more than 18 million people) and one in a rural village in Bihar (India's poorest and most illiterate state)—and the musical life of a child domestic servant in North India. These examples represent a cross sample of children's urban and rural experiences and will illustrate the impact of this media on children's repertoires and musical worlds.

CHILDREN IN AN URBAN MUSICAL WORLD: INDIRAPURAM, GHAZIABAD

Indirapuram, Ghaziabad is a city on the eastern border of Delhi and is cited by *Newsweek* as being one of the ten fastest growing cities in the world (Foroohar et al. 2006). Far from being an established Delhi suburb, Indirapuram has sprung up overnight. Since 2001, hundreds of new apartment complexes line crowded neighborhoods in this National Capital Region (NCR), providing an affordable, commutable residential area for government workers. Apartments are considered reasonably priced at twenty to thirty *lakh*[4] rupees (₹), US$40,000–US$60,000. A family must earn more than ₹50,000 per month (US$1,000) in order to afford housing and private school tuition here. Most fathers are higher-level government workers, engineers, newspaper reporters, or schoolteachers earning ₹30,000–50,000 per month. A few mothers also work, contributing a smaller second salary, around ₹20,000 per month (US$400). Indirapuram's exponential growth in the past few years has yielded dozens of public, private, and religious schools, a vibrant and sprawling shopping district, two supermarkets, and six major malls with air-conditioned movie theaters, paid parking, and boutiques, including the world-class high-end Pacific Mall—the first in Eastern Delhi to have an IMAX movie theater.

The glut of shopping malls greatly affects the lives of children in the area. Children now have access to CD and video stores, video arcades, movie theaters, mall-constructed play areas (with battery-operated cars, trucks, and bouncy rides), fast food chains, and stores selling computer games. Mall-sponsored activities are now commonplace. Pacific Mall, for example, regularly stages indoor teen fashion and talent shows in its atrium, featuring singing, dancing, games, and teenaged MCs all set to the latest Hindi film music.

MEDIA CULTURE AND PLAY

Popular music in India is dominated by its many film industries, with Mumbai's Bollywood leading in film production. Since the majority of Indian films contain songs, popular music in India *is* film music—comprising more than 80 percent of the music market. Indian cinema is accessible through cinema halls, cable television, VCDs (video compact discs), CDs, and cassettes tapes. The cultural influence of what is shown on the screen is second to none. Television is also a primary vehicle for film. In a typical cable lineup of more than eighty channels, twelve or more are dedicated to film, with half a dozen channels showing old and more recently released Bollywood films and another five to seven channels dedicated to showing song and dance sequences culled from decades of films. The cinema, India's primary mass medium, creates the closest thing to a shared national identity in a country of local and regional languages and subcultures.

The film world's musical and subject matter affect children's imaginations, as can be seen in an after-school dialogue among children at play on an apartment rooftop in Delhi. Roopa, seven, Sonya, nine, and Myra, six, play with their (Barbie-type) dolls enacting a wedding, modeling the adult world they see and experience (Das 1989: 263). They sing wedding songs from films as they play. The girls are shy, and they stop playing as I arrive for a brief chat with them.

> NS: Why are you on the roof?
> SONYA: Our parents don't want us to play with dolls, so we come up here.
> NS: What are you playing?
> ROOPA: These dolls are getting married.
> MYRA: We're singing wedding songs.
> NS: Do you know where the song is from?
> GIRLS: No.
> NS: What other games do you play with dolls?
> GIRLS: We dress them up as models, too.[5]

The parents of these girls restrict media viewing, limiting the number of films they see as well as the hours spent watching television, listening to radio, and playing video games.[6] Computer gaming and television watching is curtailed by these parents to one hour per day in exchange for study time. Limiting children's film viewing, however, is not just a matter of avoiding movie theaters, as evidenced in this continuing dialogue.

> NS: Do you see a lot of films?
> ROOPA: Yes, but our parents only let us see a few films in a month.
> NS: Where do you see films? Do you go to the theater?
> GIRLS: No, we see them at home on VCDs from the market.

Bootleg VCDs are available on the street at makeshift tables and from itinerant sellers. Most sell high-volume discs with up to six current movies on them for under US$1, giving children access to the latest films and songs at home. They are acutely aware of not only each new film as it arrives but also its songs, actors (such as Shah Rukh Khan), and actresses (such as Katrina Kaif), and they often become instant fans.

With such a dominant industry, it is small wonder that Bollywood film songs influence the children's activities, songs, games, and play. According to Oke, in a study of children's play in urban India:

> Children pretend to be film stars and use dialogues from the films, interspersed with songs. Even while enacting festival rituals like *Ganapati* (in honor of the elephant-headed god), and *Navrātrī* (invocation of the goddess Durga for nine nights), they sing fast beat cinema songs to contrast the lyrical traditional songs." (1999: 211)

The cinema not only influences children's play but also creates it. The widely known singing game *antāksharī* (literally end letter) is predicated solely on knowing large numbers of film songs. The game consists of two teams that compete by singing lines from film songs. The goal is for one team to begin a new film song by using the last consonant in the word that ended the previous song. Adults enthusiastically play this game, and it is popular in extended families with intergenerational participation.

Urban Children's Musical Culture: Home

Recent urban migration affects children's access to an entire layer of their cultural (and musical) identity, removed from the regional areas where their extended family most likely still lives. These regions have their own spoken languages, rituals, customs, and vast repertoires of religious and folk songs. India is a country with more than twenty-two officially recognized regional languages and hundreds of unofficial ones. Children in urban settings might still speak their parent's regional language at home but now have less exposure to rhymes and folk songs in the local dialects. Only a few of the children I spoke with knew their parents' regional language (Maithili from Bihar, Garhwali from Uttaranchal) or any songs from these regions, while several did not even know their ancestors' origins.

Instead of regional language songs, urban children learn a Hindi repertoire for group play. Songs, chants, and games such as *poshampā* (see above) and *Akkar bakkar* (below) are popular across urban North India, where children's mother tongue is Hindi.

Children's Game Chant: *Akkar Bakkar Bombay Bho*

akkar bakkar bombay bho	(nonsense words about Bombay)
assi, nabbe, pure sau	Eighty, ninety, full 100
sau mẽ lagā dhāgā	One hundred has a string
chor nikalke bhāgā	The thief ran away
mem khāye biskut	Madame eats biscuits
sahib bola very good	Master says very good

English words and phrases such as "biscuit" and "very good" as well as the terms *mem* and *sahib* are reminiscent of colonial British rule in India.

Urban Children's Musical Culture: School

Most of the Indirapuram children attend either government (public) or private (religious and secular) school, and all of the schools have some type of formal music class. I spoke with several children about their school music experiences and the songs they knew. The songs most easily remembered were those incorporated into the structure of the school day. Ayush, Vishu, Apoorva, Manya, and Smirti explained that they sing country or national songs (*rastriya gīt*) every day at the morning assembly, especially "*Jana Gana Mana*" (the national anthem of India) and "*Vande Mantaram*."

Apoorva began to sing "*Jana Gana Mana*" ("Thou Art Ruler of the Minds of All People"; See Web Figure 14.1 ◑), whose text was written by the poet Rabindra Nath Tagore, and all of the children joined in.

Manya, a fourth grade student, then sang the refrain *itnī shakti hume denā data*, which she learned at her government school. The song, it turns out, is a *filmi bhajan* (spiritual song) composed for the 1986 film *Ankush*, and it contains uplifting lyrics that encourage moral behavior. The lyrics reference a generic higher power rather than a specific god, and its general meaning is "O Giver, give me strength so that I don't leave my beliefs or convictions and go astray."

When I asked what other songs they sing at school, Vishu, a six-year-old first grader at an Indirapuram private school, was able to impressively sing an entire verse of Vedic chanting in Sanskrit. "We sing this song every day," he said proudly. Children in religious institutions sing a number of songs and prayers. Apoorva, a seven-year-old enrolled in a private school in Indirapuram, sang the song "Make Me a Channel of Your Peace" with lyrics attributed to St. Francis of Assisi. Both Ayush and Smirthi, an eleven-year-old fifth grade student at St. Paul's (see below), knew Hindi and English Christian prayers and songs such as "Father We Thank You for the Night and the Present Morning Light."

These children all received regular music instruction in school. The frequency of music classes ranged from once a week for the older children to two and three times a week for the younger ones. Music classes consisted primarily of choral singing, as few schools have instruments. Choral singing is typically unison singing, as there is no tradition of harmony in India. Most schools have their own part- or full-time music teachers, who focus on learning songs that will be sung primarily during assemblies and performances. Year-end performances showcase classical and folk song and dance. Lip-synching and dancing to film songs are sometimes allowed, but neither is encouraged in most schools.

While music performance has a long and illustrious tradition in Indian culture, economic realities make it almost impossible for children to seriously pursue taking lessons as anything more than a hobby. Currently, schools with eleventh and twelfth grade classes (ages seventeen and eighteen) require students to take a concentration in a field of study in engineering, math, or the sciences. The societal pressure to succeed economically is palpable and is felt by parents and children alike. When I asked one of the parents, a physician from Delhi, about the importance of having music education in schools, he scoffed, "Well, of course you can't regularize a music curriculum now, can you?" Students themselves recognize the economic futility of selecting music or the arts as a career choice, and in one group interviewed, not one child claimed an interest in becoming a musician "when they grow up," though several desired work as a doctor or an "air hostess" (flight attendant). Likewise, a career as music teacher appeared unrealistic to students, perhaps partly because music teachers are paid about half the salary of a core subject teacher.

Music at St. Paul's School

Two of the children I spoke with earlier, Smirthi, eleven, and Ayush, six, attended St. Paul's—an expensive private religious institution in Indirapuram. St. Paul's provides one of the most comprehensive music programs available in the area and thus merits further discussion.

More than 2,800 students attend St. Paul (nursery school through twelfth class), paying tuition and fees of ₹10,000 per month, (US$200). Each day, the entire school participates in a fifteen-minute morning assembly, with songs led on alternate days by the junior and senior choirs. One of the two full-time music teachers accompanies the music on harmonium or electronic keyboard. The assembly begins with morning prayer, followed by several songs, such as a Christian hymn, national song, or Christmas carol. The principal then offers a "thought for the day" followed by announcements and some general knowledge questions.

Further performance opportunities include monthly music and dance competitions. The top thirty to forty students are allowed to perform for outside adjudicators, brought in to avoid favoritism. The final performance of the year is the annual function, which is attended by more than 10,000 people and includes dancing, singing, a variety show, and theatrical performances. The school collects an additional ₹250 (US$5) from each student to support it.

The two full-time music teachers at St. Paul are Shri Devi, who teaches the lower school (up to class five), and Mr. Quereshi, who teaches the upper school (classes five through twelve). Additional part-time music teachers on staff include a guitarist, a drummer, and a sitarist. Both lower and upper school choirs rehearse in the first period after assembly. St. Paul's upper school choir is often called upon to perform outside of the school and regularly wins competitions. On one recent Republic Day (January 26), the choir sang for a gathering at Gandhi's memorial in front of the prime minister of India.

There are no chairs or desks in the music rooms of St. Paul's, and children sit on the floor in rows with legs folded (see Web Figure 14.2 🔘). Traditional music learning culture in India is aural, and no notation is used, even in music class. Students in both Sri Devi and Mr. Quereshi's music classes copy lyrics from the blackboard into their notebooks. All songs are sung in unison, and music teachers stress pitch accuracy, vocal strength, and lyric memorization.

Mr. Quereshi's upper division choir of forty to forty-five students warms up with a few basic *rāga* exercises and then rehearses half a dozen religious and morally uplifting songs in unison to keyboard accompaniment. Individual students also learn more challenging pieces. Anoushka, fifteen, Madhu, sixteen, and Priya, sixteen, are able to sing in the classical north Indian classical *khayāl* tradition.

While traditional music is stressed at the school, students with sufficient family income and leisure time are able to listen to Indian and Western popular music on their home computers. One girl from Mr. Quereshi's choir, Maya, fifteen, stopped me in the hall after choir and asked if she could sing me a song. She revealed that she would not want to sing in front of Mr. Quereshi, knowing that he would disapprove. She then launched into two songs: a soaring rendition of a Hanna Montana song that she had memorized from a download online and the song "My Heart Will Go On" from the film *Titanic*.

School music is seen as a tool for motivation, for character and moral development, and for creating a sense of community within the school and nation. Prayer and worship are woven into children's repertoires in religious schools, where children sing religious songs and songs of moral support, tolerance, and peace. A passion for music runs deep among children here. Several girls in Shri Devi's lower school music class (class five) wrote this tribute to music in English:

> Music is worship
> Music is the voice of God
> Music is a tonic for brain, heart and soul
> Music is a noble art, and real enjoyment of life
> Music is a source of, and direct link with God
> And provides peace of mind

While there is no question that media and film songs influence urban children's musical repertoires, school-going children are exposed to a wide range of song repertoires and performance experiences. Schools play an increasing role in providing a musical canon, as children receive less exposure to traditional regional songs and rituals. Mediated music is widespread, and the influence of computer, video, and film enhance accessibility and awareness of the latest film songs at home and even abroad.

SOUNDSCAPE OF A RURAL BIHAR VILLAGE

Deorhi is a small village of only a few thousand people located in the state of Bihar, in eastern India. According to the government of Bihar website, Bihar is the least literate state in India, with just 60 percent of the male population and 33 percent of the female population being literate. It is also one of the poorest states in India, with a 41 percent poverty rate, according to the World Bank.

The 2001 census states that only 2.0 percent of rural Bihar village households have electricity, only 5.5 percent own a television, and 26.0 percent own a radio. With only a few households able to get electricity, mediated entertainment such as television, videos, and computers is minimal. Infrastructure is extremely poor, with no drainage system for rainwater. Street flooding during the monsoon season brings mosquitoes and other diseases from the standing water. Drinking water is accessed through pump wells in people's courtyards.

The nearest market for food, supplies, jewelry, and clothing is a fifteen-minute walk from Deorhi. The closest movie theater and major train junction is thirty km away in the larger town of Chhapra, but as there are few private family cars and the road is in disrepair most of the year, travel is difficult and requires a hired jeep or local bus. The state capital, Patna, is a three-hour jeep ride and a world away. Most families in the village survive through agriculture, farming small plots of land and tending animals. A few Brahmins take care of the small temple at the entrance to the village. Several families earn money by converting their homes into makeshift shops or selling food. Children mostly work in the family fields or help in the shops, while some attend the government school. For younger children and mothers, an *āngan bārī* (government program) is also available to help feed and care for children and conduct basic tutoring.

A main thoroughfare runs right through the center of Deorhi, one that is large enough for transport trucks, jeeps, and buses of all sizes to pass through on the way to the larger cities. There is little in the way of automobile traffic or auto rickshaws due to financial constraints and poor road conditions. The lack of electricity and absence of car noise in the village foregrounds human and animal sounds (birdcalls, cow and buffalo bellows, goat bleats, etc.). Because of this, the few oncoming larger vehicles can be heard from quite a distance. Buses, jeeps, and trucks blast Hindi film and Bhojpuri popular music from sound systems that are clearly audible for nearly thirty seconds from the time the vehicles enter one side of the village until their departure on the other.

Rural Children's Play

A brightly painted blue brick one-room house is situated just a meter from the edge of the busy village road. Scattered straw covers the small patch of dirt in front, where six-year-old Sunita dances to the sound of a workman pounding out a steady beat with a hammer (See Figure 14.3). Her twelve-year old sister, Anita, meanwhile, knits a hat for their baby brother Manish, who plays nearby. Sunita sings a Bhojpuri popular song as she dances, and Manish joins in. Children here do not speak Hindi, but Bhojpuri, the major regional language of Bihar and part of Uttar Pradesh.

On the rooftop of the house across the street, eleven-year-old Muniya, a domestic servant, spreads new rice out in the sun to dry. Roopa, a neighbor, classmate, and friend, helps her. Even though she is a servant, Muniya attends school, as the family she lives with encourages her education. The two girls play on the roof for a while after work is complete, and soon other neighboring children hear them and run up the stairs to join in. No adult permission is needed, and the children freely enter the house to play.

In keeping with Indian culture in general, play is interactive and social, with children remaining close to home and neighboring extended families. Unlike urban areas, children here are highly aware of and play in accordance with social boundaries such as caste and religion. Untouchables and Muslims live on the outskirts of the village, and these delineations make it unlikely that upper-caste Hindu children will wander

Figure 14.3: Sunita sings and dances.

even a few meters away to play with them. Play occurs in the street, in courtyards, or on rooftops (see Web Figure 14.4 ⏺). Rooftops are flat and large, and many types of ball play, cricket, chasing, and circle games take place there along with regular household tasks such as drying clothes, chilies, and rice. There are very few store-bought toys available, and so children create toys from found objects. When they do have dolls, village girls role-play marriage with them and are more likely to sing local marriage songs than film songs during their play. Gender roles are prominent in terms of play and song repertoire. Play is limited for children who attend school or have other duties. Boys, for example, are more likely to attend school regularly, and many of the girls are responsible for the care of younger siblings or other relatives.

Rural Children's Musical Culture at Home

Music learning in the village occurs through an enculturation process, with vast repertoires of songs related to social, seasonal, and sacred occasions. Not only are village girls exposed to the songs of older women, but they actively learn their songs as they participate in ritual occasions such as weddings and *chhat pūjā*, a Hindu festival to Surya, the sun god. This allows them to learn the melodies and lyrics slowly over time until they are able, in turn, to lead the songs themselves for their friends' weddings and sacred occasions.

Traditional children's repertoires include seasonal celebration songs. In the monsoon season (*sāvan/shrāvan*), children sing *kajari* songs about the joy, pleasure, and emotions brought by the rains. *Kajari* is a Hindustani semiclassical genre known in Uttar Pradesh and Bihar, but at the folk level, it is a girls' genre, usually sung when swinging on rope swings hung from high tree branches. Many songs are age and gender specific, and married girls will no longer swing or sing these songs. I asked the girls most involved in singing and dancing what songs they knew. Muniya, Roopa, and Sunita knew several *kajari* songs, including this *jhūlā* (to swing) song (see Figure 14.5).

Religious songs are also important, particularly those in homage to the goddess. Pilgrimage sites abound in India, with temples of deities that heal and give boons to devotees such as fertility and marriage. The girls knew a song and dance praising the attributes of Devi Mata, a local goddess in the form of Durga, whose temple is in Thawe, around fifty-five km from the village.

Figure 14.5: *Jhula* song.

Bhajan to Devi Mata

sukwā somarwā ke bhir lāge baṛā	On Monday and Friday it is crowded
hamrā utāre ke bā babuwā ke bhāṛā	And I also have to offer for my baby (son)
thāwe mandirwā ke kirpa masahur bā	The blessings of this temple are famous
māi ke darsan ta kayal zaroor ba	It is necessary to do *darsan* of the goddess

As the girls began the song, their dance movements and gestures narrated the lyrics, a common approach to the performance of Indian folk and classical genres. For example, they performed gestures of offering gifts to the goddess during the last line of the *bhajan*. This type of local devotional song is a mainstay with popular Bhojpuri artists, who write and record them for sale on CDs, cassettes, and videos.

Village children's game and song repertoire is extensive, as this is a primary form of entertainment. When I asked the children to sing game songs, they began with "*Nadī kināre*," in which children hold hands and circle around one child sitting in the middle (see Figure 14.6). At the end of the verse, the child in the middle rises and picks another "friend" who takes her place.

Children's game chant: "*Nadī kināṛe*"

nadī kināṛe ek larkī thī	On the banks of a river was a girl
baithī baithī ro rahī thī	Sitting and crying
utho sahelī utho mūh hāth dho lo	"Get up, oh friend, wash your face,
khānā pīnā khā lo apnī sahelī dundh lo	eat and drink something, and go and find your friend"

The children's favorite, however, is "*Okā bokā*," a complex six-part action game in chant and song (see Web Figures 14.7 and 14.8 for a transcription and

Figure 14.6: Village children play *nadīkināre*.

translation 🔘). Children begin by sitting in a circle and placing their fists in the middle. One child then taps the back of each hand to the beat of the chant. On the word *puchūk*, the child's hand is flattened and is "out." This continues until all hands are flat. Second, the phrase *chiuntā leba ki chiuntī* is repeated as the lead child pinches the back of each flattened hand and lifts it on a pile of all of the hands in the middle of the circle. Next, the leader places her hand on top of the hand pile and alternates slapping her hand palm up and palm down to the beat of the rhyme. A song follows as each child grabs the earlobes of the child seated next to him in the circle and everyone sways back and forth to the beat. Eventually this dissolves into the next section—chaos, in which children all kick their feet rapidly in the middle of the circle touching soles with other children. Finally, children create a tower of fists with thumb extended up, each child grabbing the upturned thumb of the child's hand beneath. The leader makes a sawing motion to cut down this fist tower, "chopping" off a hand or two from the top as they say *chhap*.

Rural Children's Popular and Film Song Repertoires

Eight children ranging from a six-month old infant to a thirteen-year-old boy gather on the roof to play in the late morning. We begin a dialogue about Hindi songs they know.

> NS: Can you sing me a song? [Some of the children are a bit shy but quite interested in singing and come closer]
> NS: Do you know any Hindi songs?
> MUNIYA AND ROOPA: No, we don't know any Hindi songs.
> NS: Any film songs?
> MUNIYA: No, we don't know any film songs.
> NS: Do you see any films?
> MUNIYA: No, we don't see any films.
> AMISH ([THIRTEEN-YEAR-OLD BOY): I saw a film.
> NS: Which film was it; do you remember the name?
> AMISH: I can't remember. Oh, I know, *Namak Halal* (an Amitabh Bachchan film from 1982)
> NS: What song would you like to sing?
> MUNIYA: We can dance and sing a song.
> NS: OK, let's see your dance and song.

Muniya beckons Roopa to join her, and Sonya joins in as well. After overcoming their shyness, the girls began to sing and dance a popular Bhojpuri song (see Web Figure 14.9 🔘):

kesiyā bhī jhār leni, penh leni sāṛī	I fixed my hair, put on a sari
lāli lagāy lenī, rūpwā sawārī	Put on lipstick/makeup
ego ho tā te pichwā se cuk rājā jī	One thing is missing from the back, O my love
lagā dīhī choliyā ke hook rājā jī	Hook up my *choli* [sari blouse], O my dear

A second, similar song followed, sung and danced by Sunita. The dance moves appear choreographed and are rather seductive, so I asked where they learned them. The three girls confessed to spending quite a bit of time practicing their performance from dance moves they have seen on VCDs at neighbors' houses (those that have generators). The girls made no distinction between folk, popular, and film song genres, but they noted their preference for Bhojpuri language songs. Bhojpuri popular songs are melodically patterned after Bhojpuri folk tunes, and thus they sound familiar to them. While the rather suggestive lyrics may seem out of place in children's repertoire, popular song lyrics are also based on Bhojpuri folk songs, known for their thinly veiled sexuality, which is often disguised in agricultural and rural metaphors.

Rural Children's Musical Culture at School

Children who are able to attend either the village government school or the convent school. Both schools contain only a few rooms and are mostly open to the elements due to limited funds for infrastructure. Just a few teachers are employed and, like many such rural schools, they must teach multiple subjects and grades. There is no music teacher or formal music classes during the school day. Saturdays are reserved for school assemblies with an opportunity for children to perform different arts such as poetry and music, but this does not happen regularly. Rajesh Singh, an elementary school teacher in Deorhi, took it upon himself to add music to the curriculum. He eventually stopped teaching music, however, because parents were upset at the presence of organized musical activity within the school day and were worried that he was taking time away from more important studies such as math and science. He explained, "I wanted to continue music in the school, but I couldn't do it with my students, so I started teaching music and dance to students in the upper school whom I don't teach."

While there is no formal music teaching in the village school, songs are a regular part of the school day. Amish, a thirteen-year-old boy who attends the government school, recalled the same morally uplifting *filmī bhajan* "itnī shakti hume denā dātā" as did Manya in New Delhi. Children of the government school in this rural area of Bihar also knew another *bhajan* with a theme stressing India's pluralism and religious inclusivity (Hinduism, Islam, Sikhism, and Christianity).

> *Filmi bhajan: "Tuhī Rama"*
> *tūhī rama hai, tū rahim hai, tū karīm, krishna khudā huā*
> You are Rama [Hindu form of Vishnu] and you are Rahim [synonym of Muslim
>   God], and you are Karim [blissful one, Muslim], Krishna, and Khuda [Allah]
> *tūhī wāhe guru tū yasū masi har nām meˉ tū samā rahā*
> You are all the gurus [of the Sikhs], you are Jesus, you are in each name of God
> *tere jāt pāt qurāna meˉ terā daras ved purān meˉ*
> Your caste is in Qur'an and your philosophy is in the Veda-s and Purana-s
> *guru granth ke bakhān meˉ tū prakāsh apnā dikhā rahā*
> And even in the reading of Guru Granth your light is there

Children's repertoires in this rural area consist of age-appropriate games and songs as well as Bhojpuri folk and popular songs. Despite a lack of electricity, children in villages are increasingly influenced by popular music primarily from commercial Bhojpuri language singers. While the families of these children do not have electricity, they are exposed to mediated music through television, radios, VCDs, and CDs from neighbors who have access to power supplies.

The amount of time that the village girls devote to practicing dance movements that they see speaks to the increased prevalence of song and dance sequences available through VCDs and television. For these girls, the songs now seem to be an accompaniment to the dance moves, reflecting the primacy of the visual over the aural.

Music in the Life of a Child Domestic Servant

Educated children represent only part of the story of India's children. The nation's population of 1.1 billion contains 360 million children from birth to age fourteen. Only half of these children, however, actually attend school. According to the 2001 census in India, at least 12.6 million children work (Wikipedia 2012), with some estimates reaching 60 million child workers (Friends of Salaam Baalak Trust, 2012). While many of these children work in agricultural or family business settings, there are more and more cases of children working as domestic servants. What happens to the social and musical lives of these children?

Raju is a thirteen-year-old domestic servant boy living in a Delhi apartment. He is uneducated, having only a year of schooling in a small village in Bihar. His father was a general laborer who died when Raju was young. His mother is emotionally unstable and cannot properly take care of him or his two siblings. The children came under the care of a Brahmin family as servants. When members of the family needed help, Raju was sent, at the age of six, to a city about three hours away from the village. Raju was then sent to Delhi when one of the men of the family relocated. His mother, sister, and brother remained in the village, and he sees them only occasionally, mostly at weddings when he accompanies the family for which he works. Raju does not know his caste, nor does he know his mother's name, although that is not uncommon in India. He has no memory of playing with friends in the village, though he recalls spending time with his brother and sister many years ago. He has no opportunities for play now, nor is it really appropriate for him to do so. He does not play with any other children in the apartment building or with the children of laborers or *dhobi wallahs* (washermen). When I asked Raju about music, he remembered playing some of the more popular village rhyming games as a child, such as "*Okā bokā*" and a few others, but has found no occasion in which to play them since and has forgotten most of them. His main source of enjoyment is when he can watch films on television or hear the film songs played on the stereo in the house, but he has neither time nor occasion for active musical engagement.

CONCLUSION

The musical lives of most middle class urban and rural children in India remain rich, as schools and social rituals provide musical experiences and repertoires derived from an amalgam of traditional and modern influences. Classical, folk, and national songs form the core of the public and private school canon, but the deeply entrenched traditional and regional musics now survive alongside a seismic cultural shift toward mediated popular musics. Many schools, for example, utilize film songs for their moral and pluralistic messages. India's film industry is tremendously influential and sometimes provides the only music available for children who have an inadequate social structure, have inadequate education, and lack a supportive social environment. Children have long incorporated film songs into urban play, according to Oke et al. (1999) in both sedentary singing games, such as *antāksharī*, and when engaged in other activities (movement and dance, imaginary social play, enacting festival rituals, etc.).

As we have seen here, rural children are no less influenced by popular music culture. Attention to dance in both urban and rural children's lives speaks to the increased influence of video and access to the compelling visual component of songs. While rural children are still exposed to a more traditional repertoire, the gradually improving infrastructure and technology is providing greater access to song videos in villages. Girls in both urban and rural India regularly study and imitate film dance movements, preparing for social rituals such as wedding receptions. Songs are now seen as well as heard.

The internet has increased accessibility to performing arts and artists, opening up new musical territories. Children with computer access download and memorize songs and dances, lip-synching dreams from an increasingly powerful mass media promoting a star-studded film world hyping personalities, soundtracks, and competition shows.

However, as Das observed, "The child is not a passive recipient of the world" (1989: 264). Perhaps as the Indian economy expands, children will find democratizing aspects of technology and the media, allowing them to pursue the arts as a realistic livelihood rather than a fantasy. What advantages a growing India promises its children remains to be seen. India's traditional roots, meanwhile, continue to emphasize the importance of sound and music in this continually globalizing culture.

Two video clips of children's games can also been seen on the linked website as Web Figures 14.10 and 14.11. ▶

ACKNOWLEDGMENT

To the Dwivedis who make all of my research possible.

NOTES

1   The Red Fort is a famous landmark in Delhi, but children will often substitute a familiar, local road name instead.

2   *Kichaṛī* is a boiled mixture of *dāl* (lentils) and rice.

3   India even has *Kabaddī* Federation, complete with a standard set of rules. The game is played as a contact sport between rival teams.

4   100,000.

5   Emphasis on model culture is relatively recent, driven, in part, by a rise in the middle class's expendable income, a more aggressive advertising culture, and Indian cinema's latest penchant for bringing in newer, younger, and highly photogenic actors.

6   In the past, films were seen as decadent, and children were only allowed to see "mythologicals"—films based on the lives of gods and goddesses or saints or retellings of the sacred *Ramayana* and *Mahabharata*.

REFERENCES

Das, Veena. 1989. "Voices of Children." *Daedalus: Another India* 118 (4): 262–294.

Friends of Salaam Baalak Trust. "Children in India." Accessed June 16, 2012. http://www.friendsofsbt.org/statistics.

Government of Bihar. "National Informatics Centre." Accessed March 30, 2010. http://gov.bih.nic.in.

Ministry of Labor, India. "Government of India, Ministry of Labour." Accessed March 30, 2010. http://labour.nic.in.

Oke, Meera, A. Khattar, P. Pant, and T. S. Saraswathi. 1999. "A Profile of Children's Play in Urban India." *Childhood* 6 (2): 207–219.

Sarrazin, Natalie Rose. 2008. *Indian Music for the Classroom.* Lanham, MD: Rowman & Littlefield, Music Educators National Conference.

Wikipedia. "Child Labour in India." Accessed June 16, 2012. http://en.wikipedia.org/wiki/Child_labour_in_India.

World Bank of India. 2006. "Development Policy Review." May 29. Accessed March 20, 2010. http://web.worldbank.org/wbsite/external/countries/southasiaext/0,,contentmdk:20980493~pagepk:146736~pipk:146830~thesitepk:223547,00.html.

15

ENJOYMENT AND SOCIALIZATION IN GAMBIAN CHILDREN'S MUSIC MAKING

LISA HUISMAN KOOPS

Nursery school near "Baatiikunda," The Gambia; July 2005
   The school balafon musician, sitting at his instrument, leads a group of about 175 nursery school students in singing a Balanta-language song about the balafon. The students, wearing brown uniforms with the emblem of their school proudly displayed, sing joyfully and take turns dancing during the song. Later the musician explains the meaning of the lyrics in English:

   The melody of the balafon, the sound of the balafon, I cannot sleep.
   The singer man, the balafon singer man, I cannot sleep because of the sound.
   The moment I hear the sound of the balafon, I wake up.
   I enjoy it very well.

   This song captures a common theme in Gambian music making: enjoyment. The lyrics speak of the enjoyment and invigoration that come from the sound of the balafon.
   During another portion of the performance, the teacher leading the singing pauses to ask the children, "Are you happy?" "YES!" the children shout in response. Again, the teacher asks them, "Are you happy?" The children's emphatic answer is "YES!"

"Ndax yaangi noss?" *(Are you enjoying?) asked one woman at a* Sabar *(community dancing and drumming) event.* "Ñungi noss!" *(They are enjoying), laughed a mother as she observed children playing* Kiribang *(a Chinese jump-rope-type game). A girl, telling me about her involvement in singing and dancing, said simply,* "Ñungi noss" *(We enjoy ourselves).*

This word, *noss* (Wolof for "enjoying"), arose repeatedly during fieldwork on children's musical practice within a multiethnic suburban community in The Gambia, West Africa, in summer 2005 and emerged in interviews and observations as one of the prominent meanings for children in their music making. I also observed music as a vehicle for socialization in a variety of situations by the children. In this chapter I will explore the interaction and interweaving of socialization and enjoyment throughout the forms, meaning, and transmission of children's music making in home, school, and community settings.

The Gambia is the smallest country on the mainland of Africa, with an area of 4,363 square miles (11,300 square km). During the colonial period, The Gambia was at various times under the rule of Portugal and Britain, with Britain holding The Gambia as a colony until 1965 (Central Intelligence Agency 2010; Charry 2000). Since that time, the country has experienced a number of relatively peaceful government changes and currently enjoys the tourist slogan "Your Haven in Africa," indicating its peaceful status in relation to some of its neighboring countries. The Gambia is a democratic republic under the rule of Dr. Yahya A. J. J. Jammeh (Central Intelligence Agency 2010; Else 1999).

The Gambia is home to 1.82 million people (July 2010 estimate), 95 percent of whom come from five main ethnic groups: Mandinka 42 percent, Fula 18 percent, Wolof 16 percent, Jola 10 percent, and Serahuli 9 percent (Central Intelligence Agency 2010). Of the remaining population, 4 percent identifies with other African ethnicities, and 1 percent is of non-African origin. Although the official language of The Gambia is English and schools are expected to teach students in English, many other Gambian languages are predominantly spoken in homes and in the community (Gordon 2005). Islam is the predominant religion in The Gambia, with a minority (between 4 percent and 9 percent) practicing Christianity and a smaller percentage (1 percent) claiming indigenous beliefs alone; indigenous beliefs are commonly mixed with both Muslim and Christian religious practices (Central Intelligence Agency 2010; Else 1999; Johnstone 1993).

The vignettes and observations shared in this chapter are drawn from fieldwork in "Baatiikunda" (a pseudonym to protect participant anonymity). Baatiikunda is a densely populated, multiethnic, suburban area about thirty km from the capital city, Banjul. The participants in this study included the families and children who lived on the compound at which I stayed, along with their friends, as well as an extended family of professional *sabar* (drum) players who lived on several compounds throughout the community and their friends and neighbors. I also completed fieldwork in the local primary school for children in grades one through six, Baatiikunda Lower Basic School, interviewing teachers and observing classes and recess.

Throughout observations and experiences with children making music at home, at school, and in community settings, enjoyment arose as both a motivation and an effect for the children as well as those around them. Enjoyment in music making comes in part from the opportunity to participate, the compelling nature of the music, and the chance for children to exert agency—power, control, and authority—within music making (Russell 2006); this fits closely with the use of music for entertainment. Music is also used for education, including religious and social education as well as in-school learning, and communication of cultural, religious, and historical knowledge. In all of these ways, music helps children to better understand and affirm their place in their family, community, and school; to acquire the knowledge necessary for participation in their culture, from religious traditions to courting rituals; and to join in an enjoyable and prevalent part of cultural expression: music making.

Family compound of professional drummers; Baatiikunda, The Gambia; July 2005

Lamin, age nineteen months, has just awoken from his afternoon nap. His mother dresses him in a shorts outfit of Gambian cloth made by his uncle, a tailor. She sets him on the floor of the living room of the house they share with her mother and her three brothers, Lamin's uncles. Lamin begins passing a ball back and forth to me but quickly gives this up when he spots an emery board sitting on the coffee table in one corner of the room. Standing next to the table, which is an ideal height for him to drum on, Lamin begins waving his arms. On his left wrist is a metal bracelet that clunks with each hit; his right hand holds the emery board the way he sees his uncles and cousins hold the gërëm (stick) when playing ndënd (drums). As Lamin experiments with the sounds produced by his bracelet and the emery board on the table, his mother chants encouragingly and claps: "Waaw! Waaw!" (Yes! Yes!) Lamin moves his left and right hand independently, with control, to produce varying rhythms. Occasionally he hits both hands at the same time, but he typically alternates. After several minutes he returns to playing with the ball; several more minutes pass, and he is back at his drumming station. His mother chants the vocables for a popular drum rhythm and says, "Féccal! Féccal!" (Dance! Dance!) Lamin bends his knees to his mother's beat.

We move outside to observe a play session with the other children who live on Lamin's compound. As the eight- to twelve-year-old girls clap and chant, "When I Went," Lamin stands, watching intently and clapping along. The girls switch to Bopp, a game in which they chant and touch head, shoulders, waist, knees, and foot. Lamin tries to copy them as they touch the different body parts. When they begin to play Play Akkara, a competitive clapping and stomping game, Lamin closely watches the feet of his neighbors and bounces along as the girls jump and stomp.

The next week I return to the compound to observe a larger group of children playing and singing. Throughout the two-hour observation, more and more children arrive. After many rounds of clapping games and a few songs, one of the child leaders suggests dancing. The group mobilizes in preparation: two boys grab tall yellow buckets to serve as drums; one of the older girls, about thirteen years old, climbs a mango tree to get a few gërëm (sticks) for the drummers to use. The boy drummers play a few warm-up licks, then settle in to a familiar drumming "track," one they hear their older cousins, uncles, and fathers play at community dancing and drumming events called Sabars *and* Zimbas. *The other children form a circle, similar to the circle formed by women at a* Sabar, *and begin to take turns dancing. Those around the circle clap along and encourage the solo dancer in the middle with verbal affirmation. Each child takes a turn, the younger children bouncing to the beat, the older girls using characteristic Wolof dance movements* (Web Figure 15.1 ▶).

Gambian children like Lamin and the other children on his compound grow up in a rich musical environment (Blacking 1967; Campbell [1998] 2010). Family members or neighbors may be specialized musicians, as are Lamin's uncles and cousins, who are professional drummers. Children living on drummers' compounds hear the drumming patterns from infancy, watch the adults as they play at practices and performances, and internalize the rhythms by learning the accompanying dances. While playing together on their compounds, seven- and eight-year-olds play *ndënd* (drum) rhythms on buckets while their age-mates dance; Tang has noted this occurrence in families of *sabar* players in neighboring Senegal, and the gatherings of children are called "'kiddie' *sabar* groups" (2007: 82–83). At around age twelve, boys begin to take part in the adult-centered performances, playing during the warm-up time at a *Sabar* or *Zimba* or near the end of the performance if another drummer wants a break. They learn to drum through a sequence of listening, observing, and doing (Koops 2006, 2010), similar to a musical learning process described by Kreutzer (2001) among children in Zimbabwe. Even as the children are enjoying their play and participation, they are being socialized to take their places as specialized musicians within the community.

Music Is for Everyone: "It Entertains, Educates, and Communicates"

For children serving in specialized music roles and those children participating more informally, music was tied closely to enjoyment as well as education and communication; all three were important facets of socialization in my observations. The belief that music is for all people in The Gambia, not only the *jalis* or *géwëls* or other specially trained people, was spoken by both children and adults, including the teacher who expressed it this way: "Music is not for only those who are [specialized] musicians, music is for every good person. It entertains, educates, and communicates" (TC, personal communication, July 5, 2005). He reemphasized this belief when asked whether all children are musical: "All of them can either sing, or dance, or clap. It is important to some in one way [or another]. All have musical ability; it entertains, informs, educates, and communicates." I will use the three categories of music as entertainment, education, and communication to organize the observations below about the interplay of music, enjoyment, and socialization in Gambian children's lives.

Music Entertains

Music as entertainment is linked to enjoyment: the musicians enjoying what they are doing, the audience enjoying what they are hearing and observing (Ebron 2002). Entertainment also helps children to pass time while waiting, enables people to forget their troubles, and functions as an aspect of tourism, a major industry in The Gambia. Children seem to enjoy music because of the opportunities it brings for participation and interaction and for expressing their enjoyment through participation; the compelling nature of the music adds to children's enjoyment; the opportunity to exert agency contributes to the enjoyment, as well. Evidence of music's power to evoke response was evident each time I heard drumming and saw children streaming to join in dancing or clapping; each time I heard singing at a Protestant church on our compound and saw children and adults join in with their voices as well as with dancing; each time I saw children walking to school pause to dance to recorded music being played at a business or household along the route. Music was an integral part of their lived experience, and children responded to music in many ways. The enjoyment of children's music making was not limited to the children. One group of adults, watching the children of their compound dancing and singing, smiled and laughed with enjoyment. One woman joined in the dance, modeling the movements for the younger children.

The joy and excitement of musical participation was also evident during a children's drama troupe performance at Baatiikunda Lower Basic School; in addition to enjoying the music through participation, the children enjoyed the music because it was compelling to them. As the drummers started warming up, it seemed as though they were calling the audience through their drumming patterns. Answering the call, more and more children came, and they danced by themselves here and there around the schoolyard. There was such a feeling of joy and excitement in the air. Later one of the school deputies commented to me, "Yes, it has impact on people, on the life of the people. This [drama performance] really motivates the children to come out … children would come out, and you see how happy they are, how they dance. They really appreciate [it]" (MJ, personal communication, June 13, 2005).

There was a similar charge of excitement in the air at the Army Band concert at the school on June 10, 2005, as children gathered to sing, dance, clap, and enjoy the band's music. The Army Band is a touring band that plays Gambian popular music. The school hosted the concert and charged a small admission fee in order to raise funds to repair the corrugated roof of a classroom before the rainy season started. As the musicians set up their equipment, the children gathered around, watching. When the musicians began to play, children who had been playing around the school courtyard ran, jumped, and danced over to the stage. There were around 500 children there at the beginning of the concert, and by the end of the evening, 2330 students had bought tickets. The students closest to the musicians jumped and danced along with the music, responding heartily when the musicians asked them a question or called for a response. The musicians spoke to the children in Wolof, rather than in English, which may have contributed to the audience's feeling of control of the event. Some children stood on chairs to see better and danced on the chairs as they enjoyed the concert. Farther back, small groups of girls danced together. Boys walked past, jumping and dancing as they traveled. A group of girls toward the middle of the courtyard, farther from the band, was playing a jumping game called Ten Zi. The dancing was varied, with some girls lifting their feet as in the jumping-clapping game Play Akkara, some twisting and some jumping. The concert lasted for about two and a half hours, and the children were reluctant for it to end.

Children play many forms of musical games at school and at home, including clapping games, dances, and circle games. Play Akkara and Bopp were the most common games. There are many different versions of Play Akkara, but they all require at least two players to clap and jump a rhythm. In the version most often played at school, a group of about five girls stands in a horizontal line, and the leader faces the first player (challenger). They clap, jump, and stomp, and if the challenger stomps the same (mirrored) foot as the leader three times, she becomes the new leader; if the challenger stomps the opposite foot, her turn is done and the leader moves to the next player. I observed girls from first grade through sixth playing Play Akkara; it was one of the games that was played by the older girls in fourth, fifth, and sixth grade when some of the other clapping games had begun to fade. At school the girls tended to play in same-age groups of about five players each, while at home they played with cross-age groups according to who was available. In home settings I observed a version in which two teams faced one another. This video also shows a common musical learning practice: a group of smaller children off to the side of the main play who are watching and trying out the moves together, working on the coordination and figuring out how the game works (Web Figure 15.2 ▶).

Play Akkara is similar to the rhythmic competitive game *ámpé* or *ampe* played by children in multiple regions of Ghana, as documented by Agawu (1995) and Wiggins (2013). The children and adults I spoke with in The Gambia did not explain where the game came from or how it came by an English name; perhaps it was shared by immigrants to The Gambia from Ghana and given an English name because English is a common language between the two countries. *Akkara* is a popular snack food made of fried black-eyed peas sold by women at stands outside the schoolyard for children to purchase for lunch. The mothers said they knew Play Akkara as children; a woman from Ghana who lived on our compound also reported playing it in Ghana and demonstrated the differences in her version. Girls played it with varying speeds and numbers of opponents. They played it on the sand, standing on the cement porches, and standing on a waist-high cement sign at the front of the school courtyard.

Sometimes they formed two teams and kept score; other times they took turns being the leader. In some versions, the leader chanted a number as she jumped: "Te-en, te-en, twen-ty, twen-ty,..." increasing by ten with each successful standoff; in some games children counted by ones. When the leader lost her leadership and returned to the line, she remembered how high she had gotten and picked up where she left off when it was her turn again.

In mid-July 2005, a variant of Play Akkara, called Bopp, appeared in Baatiikunda and spread quickly at the school and in the neighborhood (see Figure 15.3). When playing Bopp, the set-up is the same as with Play Akkara, with one leader and a line of challengers. The leader and challenger say together "One, two, three" while clapping, then Bopp (and touch their heads), three claps, "*mbagg*" (shoulders), "*ndigg*" (waist), "*òom*" (knees), "*tank*" (foot), touching each part and clapping three times in rhythm between. Throughout this process, the players also jump or bounce. When they finish "*tank*," they shift to a stomping competition such as Play Akkara. Advanced players also spin while doing the opening movements with head, shoulders, and so on. As the game spread across the Baatiikunda community, I observed players at varying levels, some who had mastered the basic game and began to add turns for added complexity, others, often younger, who were still working on coordination of the basic game. In Web Figure 15.4 ◐, following a lull in the games, one girl, behind the camera, says "1-2-3 Bopp?" and invites her friend to the game. The friend responds with a broad smile and "*Kaay!*" (Wolof for "come"). The organizer pauses play to incorporate other players and continues the game. This free-flowing

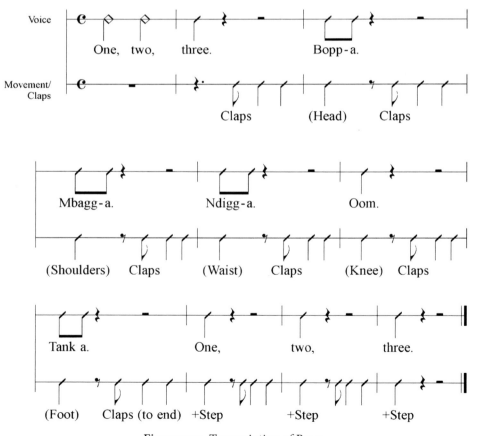

Figure 15.3: Transcription of Bopp.

and child-directed process was common in the observations of musical play and serves as an example of the leadership opportunities provided by such play (Gaunt 1997a, 1997b; Merrill-Mirsky 1988).

In both Play Akkara and Bopp, players demonstrate their skill through competition. These games are most often played by girls and provide a competitive counterpart to the boys' football (soccer) games. The players monitor one another's turns, acting as referees and controlling the outcome of any disagreements about who wins, free from adult intervention. This opportunity to monitor and enforce rules may help prepare children to apply these skills later in life.

Another popular game was Kiribang, a form of Chinese jump rope in which two players stood as "posts" with a thin elastic band stretched around their ankles. Players took turns jumping in and out, twirling, pausing, and chanting according to various levels. With each successful turn the elastic was raised from ankles to knees, then hips, then waist, increasing the difficulty of play. When a jumper made a mistake, she took her turn as one of the "posts" and attempted the failed level again when her turn came back around. Kiribang provided another arena in which children monitored and enforced a complex set of expectations.

Musical play can be entertaining for the children who are playing and it can help to pass the time. Girls often played Play Akkara or clapping games while waiting for the morning assembly at school to start, waiting for class to start, waiting for their teachers to arrive, waiting for the ball to come their way in football (soccer), or waiting for their turn at Kiribang. Playing was a way to pass the time while waiting. The formal structures of the games also provided an arena in which children could learn to monitor and enforce guidelines or rules, another form of socialization.

Music Educates

Enjoyment was evident in the aspects of music as entertainment described above; enjoyment was also at play to varying degrees in school settings involving music. While there was a clear dichotomy between music inside and outside of the classroom at school, children exhibited varying levels of enjoyment and participation in the forms of music making in both venues. Children engaged in music during classroom singing times, at morning assemblies, during a games session, at a drama troupe performance, at an Army Band concert, and during playground play. Throughout these experiences, the children tended to participate more enthusiastically when they had greater control over their situation. In classroom settings, children had little control over activities and repertoire, and their lack of agency was reflected in their attitude and level of participation. On the playground, however, the children exerted agency by controlling the play (what to play and who was playing), controlling the music during play (setting or changing the tempo, adapting lyrics), and demonstrating competitive skill or expressing emotions through play. In activities that occurred outside of either sphere, children exhibited varying levels of control; these findings are similar to those of music education researchers studying children's music making in many areas of the world (Campbell [1998] 2010; Dzansi 2004; Harwood 1992; Marsh 2008; Riddell 1990).

Baatiikunda Lower Basic Schoolyard; July 2005

A group of nine third-grade girls gathers in a circle on the playground, sitting comfortably on the coarse reddish sand. After eating a simple lunch of bread (mburu) and beans (akkara), purchased from a vendor's booth just outside the schoolyard, the girls congregate to play games until their break time is over and they return to sit, crowded three to a desk, trying to learn to read in a language that is not their mother tongue. On the playground today they begin to play a circle game with one who walks around outside the circle, drops a sandal, and then races around the circle while another grabs the dropped sandal and chases the first. The first drops into the vacated seat in the circle as the group sings a tune that contains familiar elements. After several repetitions I realize with some surprise that the words and tune they sing are derived from a circle game I know myself—"I Wrote a Letter to My Love"—not a Gambian music game as I had first assumed.

Teaching in the primary school at Baatiikunda Lower Basic School is challenging. Primary school teachers are responsible for teaching "all the subjects . . . that is, math, English, science, social and environmental studies, physical education, verbal, quantitative, population, and family life education" (AJ, personal communication, June 8, 2005). There are also nine Koranic/Arabic teachers at the school who provide Koranic instruction for the students in daily lessons. Music is scheduled for half an hour in the weekly timetable for each grade level, and rhymes and "games" are added for the lower grades (one through three). Whether these lessons actually occur is based in part on the individual teachers and their interests; there are no music specialists who provide music instruction for all students.

Inside the classroom, students are expected to sit quietly and speak only when the teacher calls on them; children's control over their learning process is minimal. I observed classes laboring over math and reading lessons, with students' heads resting on their hands, paging listlessly through books, as the teacher sat at his desk. This quiet lethargy gave way to joyful running, shouting, jumping, and playing during the break times 11:30–12:00 and 3:30–4:00 each day. The school courtyard pulsated with life as children ate their lunches purchased from vendors, played football (soccer), hopscotch, tag, clapping games, Play Akkara, and roamed about, socializing. Through playground musical play, children learned leadership, creativity, competitive skill, and social awareness (Addo 1996; Dzansi 2004; Marsh 2008).

Schoolteachers are required to teach in English, even at the lower levels; this leads children to have less control over verbal and written communication, as most primary-aged children are not yet fluent in English. The English emphasis carries over to the repertoire sung in the classroom. One morning I visited five first grade classes and asked them to sing for me. In some classes the teachers chose the songs, and in others the children directed the process; when teachers were in control there tended to be pauses between songs, while songs flowed from one to another more naturally when children were in charge. The repertoire was similar in both leadership situations. Almost every class I visited sang the English-language counting song "One Little Finger" for me. They knew many English songs, mostly learned from their nursery school teachers. "Baa, Baa, Black Sheep" was another favorite, with an extended coda. Classes also chanted as part of lessons, repeating what their teacher said or memorizing facts. Including the popular "One Little Finger" and "Baa, Baa, Black Sheep," I heard about twenty-five English songs and chants, five local language songs, and two Arabic songs. When the teacher asked the students to choose a song in a local language, the children often could not think of one to sing or asked for an English song, only to be told by the teacher, "That's English, not local language!" One child, when a teacher asked for a volunteer to sing a song that was not in English, proceeded to sing a song in English. I suspected that she did not realize the song was in English; perhaps she was imitating the words and sounds she had heard, or perhaps she misunderstood the teacher's directions. When I asked children about the origins of specific local language songs they were able to identify Wolof, Mandinka, Fula, and other languages. On the playground, the children could sing many songs in local languages, but in the classroom they had been taught to focus on English-language songs.

A possible reason for the emphasis on English-language songs in the classroom, in addition to the language issue, is that most local language songs for children are intended to be accompanied by dance or play rather than sung sitting in a crowded classroom. When the children did sing local language songs, they often got up and tried to dance in the cramped quarters. Although they could not execute all of the dance movements, they worked in modified movements, and the rest of the class showed appreciation for classmates' dancing with clapping and cheers.

Children's performance of English-language songs inside the classroom and during morning assemblies was different from their use of English-language repertoire during the school breaks. Inside the classroom, many students showed an attitude of boredom or fatigue when asked to sing some English-language songs, contrasted with their energy and enthusiasm for local languages songs. Children sang other English-language songs, including "One Little Finger," enthusiastically, but with less accurate tonal contours and less musical expression than I heard in performances of local languages songs. This could be due to a lack of connection between the musical material of the songs and the music of their cultures, a difference in the tonalities, a language barrier, the manner in which they learned the songs, or other factors.

Outside, the children chose to include several English singing games in their break time repertoire. They adapted the games and lyrics and enjoyed them on their own terms, exercising control over the material by changing it to fit their linguistic and rhythmic interests, such as the version of "I Wrote a Letter to My Love" (also known as "A-Tisket, A-Tasket"). I also observed children playing this game in their home compounds. A research assistant gave these words, apparently a combination of English, pidgin English, and local language text:

Three three dom si
Ah sama letter du ma ansa
Bay ba leka dom si
You will pick in pick it up
And take it in your pocket (SJ, personal communication, July 20, 2005)
   (Web Figure 15.5 ◖)

Perhaps their choice to play this English-based game, modified with their own words, was a subtle form of resistance to the pressure of using English in the classroom. For another example, the version of "Sally Walker" I heard in Baatiikunda contained the phrase "Fly da, fly da, coconut tree," possibly meaning "fly to the coconut tree" (see Web Figure 15.6 ◖.) Although many of the fifty-six variants of "Sitting Sally Walker" listed by Riddell (1990) contain flying themes, none refers to a coconut tree, which is one of the trees well known to Gambian children.

Rhythmically, the girls I observed added a chant to the performance of "Slide, Slide, Slide" as compared with the versions in Riddell (1990), adding rhythmic interest and energy. Much of the English-language repertoire children chose for the playground consisted of chants, rather than songs, which allowed them to focus on rhythmic expression and performance rather than melodic material. This focus on rhythm over melody has been observed in the context of children's play songs in other global contexts, as discussed by Marsh (2008: 16).

Patriotic, religious, and behavior education occurred during the assemblies that took place on Mondays and Fridays. Assemblies began with Muslim prayers led by one of the teachers; children echoed the leader's gentle duple phrases at the same pitch level, with similar contour and melismas, using a light head tone. Their hands were in prayer position. The gathering then recited the national pledge and sang the national anthem. The principal or deputy gave announcements, and then students sang a marching song as they returned to their classrooms and began their day: "We're going to our classes…with paper and pencil…and do what we are told. For learning is better than silver and gold." The assemblies were not geared toward music learning, as the students who know the songs sing them and the others try to listen. This is difficult, however, with 1,800 students in an open area with no microphones. The students near the front of the assembly (fourth to sixth graders) participated, but the younger students at the back just stood and waited. Through reciting the national pledge and singing the national anthem, children learned some of the values of the government. Other songs praised the president, bringing name recognition. These activities were part of socialization as citizens of The Gambia, accomplished through the enjoyable medium of music.

Aspects of competition also are learned through musical play and performance. Many of the children's music games featured competition, most notably Kiribang and Play Akkara. These games gave the girls an opportunity to enjoy competing with one another or outdoing their own previous personal best, and most of them enjoyed the challenge. In most situations, when playing a competitive game, the children competed wholeheartedly. They were careful to watch one another and quick to call "Fail!" (in English) if someone made a mistake. The rules were important to them, and, if someone was not playing by the rules, the group often stopped playing due to frustration.

Other musical play emphasized cooperation, such as the dancing and some of the clapping games. Gambian children live in close quarters with their extended family and neighbors; learning to get along is essential. According to Maranz, one of the metathemes of the worldview of people from The Gambia and Senegal is "personal, transcendent peace" (1993: 61), which includes being at peace with family, friends, and neighbors. This emphasis on peace is demonstrated in musical play that focuses on cooperation rather than competition. Musical performances, such as the drama team's performance, emphasized cooperation through the dance routines and singing.

Performing can be a source of pride and confidence for children. A teacher described the self-growth that occurs when a child sings a song for the class:

> Yes, it helps them to actualize themselves. Because if a child is satisfied, doing certain things, music is inclusive. Now if a child is able to sing a song of any nature, whatever song the child can. You say, "Can you sing it?" "YES!" The hand is straight up in the air. And then, the next moment is "Come!" The child will walk majestically towards where he or she is to stand, and will do it just as she has learned it. So thereby that satisfaction is in her, she has carried out a full song. Because of that, music means a lot to the child. (LJ, personal communication, June 2, 2005)

Students who performed songs in one fourth grade class received affectionate cuffs on the side of the head and the words "Bravo! Thank you!" from their teacher.

Music Communicates

Children communicated joy, ideas, and relationships through their music play and music making. In and outside of school, at adult-centered music events, and during play, children engaged in music activities that told stories, related to current events, and contained cultural ideas and values. Children communicated with one another as musicians during games, songs, and dances that they performed together.

Baatiikunda Lower Basic Schoolyard; July 2005

About thirty children gather around to listen as one of their peers sings "Under 17," looping through the sections of the song and adding a few embellishments along the way. The song, composed by the Gambian rappers Black Acoustic in honor of the Under 17 Gambian Football (Soccer) Team, celebrates the Gambian team's spectacular (albeit controversial) win over opponent Ghana in the final match of the Africa Cup Under 17 championships on May 22, 2005. The song has been in the air since Black Acoustic released it; we hear it on the radio, as ringtones for cell phones, and in sung performances by children and adults. As the main singer of the schoolyard rendition concludes his singing, several youths link arms around one another's shoulders and sing the song again—full of the youthful enthusiasm and exuberance that comes with a memorable song tied to a popular national event. Even children as young as three years old sing phrases of "Under 17."

Some repertoire is distinctly children's music and is only used in children's play or at school. Other songs belong to all age groups, and children use them to dance to or play with. The song "Under 17" was owned by the children in a powerful way. They learned it, sang it, and adapted it on their own, unmediated by adults. They sang with great power and pride. While learned through technology (recordings), it became part of the oral narrative of the children's music culture in summer 2005.

In Baatiikunda, children learned to understand cultures other than their own through music as well as by learning their languages. Through sharing music, Gambians learn one another's songs, traditions, and cultures. One teacher demonstrated this belief by responding to the question at the close of his interview, "Is there any way that I could help while I am here, in teaching individual children, or anything you would like?" He replied,

> Yes, here we would like to have, let's say, songs from people like you, from Irish people, from American people, from British people. To be able to pass your culture to the African way of life, so we can have a taste of white man's cultural and traditional and religious ways of life, comparing it to the African ways of life, especially the Gambian way of life. We would be very happy. You can call upon us on any time. . . . Songs, rhymes, and your culture, tradition. [It] is very important. (AJ, personal communication, June 8, 2005)

This teacher was suggesting that one way for his students to know "about" me and my culture was for them to learn our music. This pathway to knowledge is not a valued one in some contexts, but here it was emanating from the perspective of a Gambian classroom teacher—that a culture's music can help individuals more fully know and understand the people of that culture.

The children, too, were aware of the cultural knowledge shared in music. At the conclusion of one interview with six fourth graders, after I had asked them questions about their favorite songs and games, music at home, school, community, and places of worship, and why they enjoy various kinds of music, I thanked them for their time and prepared to take them back to their classroom. One of the students stopped me and said "Would you teach us a song?" There was a sense of exchange here; they had shared many of their songs with me, and it was only right that I shared one with them. I taught them an Orff-based poem with body percussion that they delighted in learning, especially as they imitated the stomping, clapping, and slapping along with the singing.

Children's involvement in musical activities, so often accompanied by signs of enjoyment, was often also linked to socialization into the expectations, activities, and values of their culture. For all children, both those who were receiving specialized training and those who took part in general music activities, music was a vital thread in daily activities, a powerful and meaningful force in their lives. Their impressive musical skills were borne of their rich musical environment and the many opportunities for musical expression, from home to school to community.

ACKNOWLEDGMENT

Dedicated to the children of "Baatiikunda" and to my beautiful daughters, Linnea Joy and Julia Grace, with gratitude.

REFERENCES

Addo, Akosua O. 1996. "A Multimedia Analysis of Selected Ghanaian Children's Play Songs." *Bulletin of the Council for Research in Music Education* 129: 1–28.

Agawu, Kofi. 1995. *African Rhythm: A Northern Ewe Perspective.* New York: Cambridge University Press.

Blacking, John. 1967. *Venda Children's Songs: A Study in Ethnomusicological Analysis.* Johannesburg, South Africa: Witwatersrand University Press.

Campbell, Patricia Shehan. [1998] 2010. *Songs in Their Heads: Music and Its Meaning in Children's Lives.* Oxford: Oxford University Press.

Central Intelligence Agency. 2010. "The Gambia. CIA—The World Handbook." Accessed June 7, 2010. https://www.cia.gov/library/publications/the-world-factbook/geos/ga.html.

Charry, Eric. 2000. *Mande Music: Traditional and Modern Music of the Maninka and Mandinka of Western Africa.* Chicago: University of Chicago Press.

Dzansi, Mary. 2004. "Playground Music Pedagogy of Ghanaian Children." *Research Studies in Music Education* 22: 83–92.

Ebron, Paula A. 2002. *Performing Africa.* Princeton, NJ: Princeton University Press.

Else, David. 1999. *The Gambia & Senegal.* Melbourne, Australia: Lonely Planet Publications.

Gaunt, Kyra D. 1997a. "Translating Double-Dutch to Hip-Hop: The Musical Vernacular of Black Girls' Play." In *Language, Rhythm, and Sound: Black Popular Cultures into the Twenty-First Century*, edited by J. K. Adjaye and A. R. Andrews, 146–173. Pittsburgh, PA: University of Pittsburgh.

Gaunt, Kyra D. 1997b. "The Games Black Girls Play: Music, Body, and 'Soul.'" PhD diss., University of Michigan.

Gordon, Raymond G. Jr., ed. 2005. *Ethnologue: Languages of the World.* 15th ed. [electronic version]. Dallas, TX: SIL International. Accessed November 18, 2005. http://www.ethnologue.com.

Harwood, Eve. 1992. "Girls' Handclapping Games: A Study in Oral Transmission." *Bulletin of the International Kodály Society* 17 (1): 19–25.

Johnstone, Patrick. 1993. *Operation World.* Grand Rapids, MI: Zondervan Publishing House.

Koops, Lisa Huisman. 2006. "Children's Music Making in The Gambia: Pathways to Culturally Informed Music Pedagogy." PhD diss., Michigan State University.

Koops, Lisa Huisman. 2010. "'Deñuy jàngal seen bopp' (They Teach Themselves): Children's Music Learning in The Gambia." *Journal of Research in Music Education* 58 (1): 20–36.

Kreutzer, Natalie J. 2001. "Song Acquisition among Rural Shona-Speaking Zimbabwean Children from Birth to 7 Years." *Journal of Research in Music Education* 49 (3): 198–211.

Maranz, David E. 1993. *Peace Is Everything: World View of Muslims in the Senegambia.* Dallas, TX: International Museum of Cultures.

Marsh, Kathryn. 2008. *The Musical Playground: Global Tradition and Change in Children's Songs and Games.* New York: Oxford University Press.

Merrill-Mirsky, Carol. 1988. "Eeny Meeny Pepsadeeny: Ethnicity and Gender in Children's Musical Play." PhD diss., University of California, Los Angeles.

National Centre for Arts and Culture. 2004. *Ceremonies of The Gambia: Tradition in Transition.* Banjul, Gambia: National Centre for Arts and Culture.

Riddell, Cecilia. 1990. "Traditional Singing Games of Elementary School Children in Los Angeles." PhD diss., University of California, Los Angeles.

Russell, Joan. 2006. "Inuit Student Teachers' Agency, Positioning and Symbolic Action: Reflections from a Qallunaat on Music Teaching in the Canadian Arctic." *International Journal of Music Education* 24 (3): 231–241.

Wiggins, Trevor. 2013. "Whose Songs in Their Heads?" In *Oxford Handbook of Children's Musical Culture*, edited by P. S. Campbell and T. Wiggins, 590–608. New York: Oxford University Press.

16

CHILDREN'S MUSICAL ENGAGEMENT WITH TRINIDAD'S CARNIVAL MUSIC

HOPE MUNRO SMITH

There's a brown girl in the ring,
Tra la la la la
There's a brown girl in the ring,
Tra la la la la la
There's a brown girl in the ring,
Tra la la la la
For she looks like a sugar and a plum, plum, plum

WHEN Alan Lomax encountered the above song he made the following observation, "This was the refrain of the summer I spent in 1962 recording folk songs in many of the small islands of the West Indies as, one by one, they moved away from British control into independence. The children sensed something was in the air and—as only children can do—summed up the whole situation in a song" (Lomax 1998: ix). In the song, "sugar" and "plum" refer to the beauty of the dancer in the ring, and perhaps Lomax was comparing this to the vitality of the newly independent nation. The song "Brown Girl in the Ring" was also in the air during my fieldwork in Trinidad in 1998. This time one could hear it on the radio, on the local music television channel, and at Carnival fêtes, because it had been adapted as the refrain for "Brownings" by the soca artist Tony Chow Lin On (stage name, Chinese Laundry).

About a month after Carnival, I attended a lecture and book launching celebrating the publication of *Brown Girl in the Ring: An Anthology of Song Games from the Eastern Caribbean*—the highlights of the material that Alan Lomax, Bess Lomax Hawes, and J. D. Elder had collected during that summer in 1962 and the source of the above quote. The event featured a performance by local schoolchildren, whose teacher had used the book to recreate these singing games for this occasion. Clearly, the students were well acquainted with "Brown Girl in the Ring," and this was the most enthusiastically performed song game that evening, as each child went into the center of the circle to "show me your motion."

Whenever I engage in fieldwork in Trinidad or encounter Trinidadians in North America, I am continually reminded of the importance they place upon self-expression, the opening of space to display one's self, whether verbally, musically, or kinesthetically. In terms of interpersonal communication, Trinidadians are passionate about speaking up in the presence of an audience who can appreciate and participate by adding their voices. Even though this has happened to me a number of times, I am always amazed when Trinidadian children and youths, particularly if their peers are close by, are quick to approach me and engage in conversation or to display their interpretations of their favorite songs and dances. Measured by the Anglo-American standards in which I was raised, West Indian children are lively and animated and value making themselves heard in exuberant and flamboyant ways. I see this as a natural outgrowth of a society whose colonial overseer demanded silence and obedience and brutally enforced laws that restricted the "noise" its people made. Thus making "noise," whether that is some form of musical expression or "merely" conversing with peers, is a critical way to share experience and observations that empowers the performer and engages his or her audience.

Music and expressive forms that depend on music, such as dance or festivals such as Carnival, play a pivotal role in the lives of Caribbean people and are often central to their discussions about what makes them distinct from other peoples of the world. Regardless of their class or ethnicity, I found that Trinidadians are keenly interested in music and culture and are proud of the local music that has emerged from their nation and the Caribbean as a region. With very few exceptions, most Trinidadians I spoke with were proud of what made Trinidad unique culturally, and they expressed personal opinions about what mattered most to them: Carnival mas, calypso tents, soca or chutney fêtes, steel band and Panorama, and so forth. While each person had individual preferences and did not enjoy every cultural expression Trinidad had to offer, each voiced strong opinions about the quality of the things that mattered most to them and were quick to critique bad music or performances.

Since Lomax's time, very little has been written about children's expressive culture in the eastern Caribbean. Despite the copious amount of scholarly material written about Trinidad Carnival, there is little attention paid to the role that the nation's young people play in Carnival music, such as calypso, soca, and the steel pan orchestra. One exception has been Shannon Dudley's discussion of school steel bands and Junior Panorama in *Music from behind the Bridge: Steelband Aesthetics and Politics in Trinidad and Tobago* (2008). However, in the nearly fifty years since Trinidad and Tobago's independence, a number of initiatives have been created to foster interest and participation among young people in the musical expressions that originated in Trinidad and Tobago. In addition to activities supported by various government entities and the public school system, there is also considerable support from nongovernment organizations as well as private enterprise and entrepreneurship. Each Carnival season, there are a number of competitions in calypso, soca, and steel band that involve hundreds of school-age children and young adults. Students participate in competitions at their schools and later move on to national competitions. Musical training and coaching is incorporated within the school curriculum, although this varies from one school to another based upon funding and other resources.

The purpose of this chapter is to detail the historical influences that have led to children's participation in the expressive traditions related to Trinidad's annual Carnival celebration and to analyze the various institutions and strategies that foster music education in relation to Carnival music, including the Carnival competitions mentioned above. The conflict between local music and imported cultural strands, particularly those from North America that are received via satellite television and the internet, are also part of this debate. Even though life in contemporary Trinidad is very different from that described by Lomax, children and youths still have venues for the display of personal creativity in various musical settings.

Trinidad and Tobago

Childhood in the Caribbean probably looks idyllic to outsiders: it is after all, a region associated with relaxation, comfort, warm temperatures, and friendly people. While the children of Trinidad and Tobago do have access to lovely landscapes and beaches, the average day is filled with activities similar to those of their peers in other countries. Children rise early to prepare for school—many have long commutes to get to the classroom—and many hours afterward are devoted to music lessons, tutoring sessions, and homework as well as team sports and athletic activities. Weekends are taken up with chores, worship services, Sunday lunch, and other family-oriented activities, which may include an excursion to the beach, river, or mountains. Gender roles tend to be somewhat conservative. Girls are expected to help their mothers with household tasks such as dishes, laundry, cooking, and assisting in taking care of younger siblings. Boys may be given chores, such as yard work, but usually have more freedom to go out with their friends. There are of course differences in one's childhood based on ethnicity, religion, and economic status, but most children in Trinidad and Tobago have experiences shaped by the historical circumstances described below.

The Republic of Trinidad and Tobago is an island nation located at the south-ernmost end of the Lesser Antilles of the Caribbean. Trinidad, the larger and more heavily developed of the islands, lies seven miles off the coast of Venezuela. Tobago, whose topography is allegedly the inspiration for Daniel Defoe's *Robinson Crusoe,* had little connection to Trinidad until the two were united as a British Crown Colony in 1889. During the first half of the twentieth century, Trinidad and Tobago moved toward self-rule. The country became a parliamentary democracy mod-eled on the United Kingdom, with the People's National Movement (PNM) led by Prime Minister Eric Williams, who assumed full control of the government in 1956. Trinidad and Tobago became an independent nation in 1962 and a republic of the British Commonwealth of Nations in 1976.

As of 2010, the literacy rate in the republic was 98 percent, a result of a system of free and compulsory public education from age five to sixteen. Thus, even young children can tell you that the indigenous peoples of Trinidad referred to it as "the Land of the Hummingbird" and that Christopher Columbus christened the island "La Ysla de la Trinidad" (Land of the Trinity) for the three mountain peaks visible along the northern coast. Trinidadian children learn and speak many words that are of Spanish and French origin, but their native tongue is Trinidadian English. The early Spanish settlers named the towns they built and the geographic features of the territory, but the island became largely French speaking during the late eighteenth century, a time when the kings who ruled Spain were the descendants of Louis XIV of France. The Cédula de Población issued by Charles III in 1783 granted free lands to anyone willing to swear allegiance to the Spanish monarch. In less than a decade, the population of Trinidad swelled with planters and their slaves from French West Indian colonies, who were later joined by a number of Scottish, Irish, German, Italian, and English families. In 1797, the Spanish governor relinquished governance to naval commander General Ralph Ambercromby; thus Trinidad became part of the British Empire.

Due to its history as an international crossroads, Trinidad and Tobago is prob-ably the most ethnically diverse nation in the Caribbean. As with other Caribbean colonies, Trinidad and Tobago grew into a plantation-based economy, made possible by the importation of African slaves. Following emancipation in 1838, indentured laborers from China, Portugal, and India were contracted to replace the Afro-Creoles who had left the plantations to pursue employment in the capital city, Port of Spain, or on plots of land in the countryside. The majority of the indentured came from India, with approximately 144,000 migrating to Trinidad in the period 1845–1917 (Brereton 1981: 103). New arrivals from other regions also resettled in Trinidad dur-ing the nineteenth century, including immigrants from other islands in the eastern Caribbean, as well as Christian Syrians and Lebanese who sought relief from the religious persecution of the Ottoman Empire by resettling in the Americas.

Young Trinidadians are keenly aware of the nation's diverse population, and they usually find a way to convey the details of their personal ethnic heritages to visitors to their country. Often I was surprised as someone who to me appeared

Afro-Trinidadian told me about his Indian grandmother. Another young person I assumed had Chinese heritage said her ancestors were Carib-Amerindians. As of 2010, of the nation's 1.3 million citizens, 40 percent are Indo-Trinidadian, 37.5 percent are Afro-Trinidadian, 20.5 percent are of mixed ancestry, and the remaining identify themselves as "other" (including of European, Syrian, and Chinese ancestry) or "unspecified." Approximately 96 percent of the republic's citizens live on the island of Trinidad; of that, 13 percent reside in urban areas (Central Intelligence Agency 2010).

However, Trinidad feels far less rural than official statistics would suggest. Numerous roads and highways were built during WWII, when the US military occupied the island. Thus, for many years, even those living in remote villages have been able to make frequent trips to larger towns and cities on the island. Like Venezuela, Trinidad's south coast is rich in oil and natural gas. Government investments, funded by state-controlled oil and natural gas enterprises, have included the building of new schools and the expansion of existing educational programs, low-cost housing projects, and infrastructure improvements. As a result of its economic base, Trinidad and Tobago has one of the highest standards of living in the Caribbean. Most homes have electricity, and Trinidadians place a priority on having access to news and entertainment. Radios tuned to local stations, televisions tuned to the local music channel Synergy TV, and cable stations MTV and BET provide a constant soundtrack to a home's daily activities. Children and youths have easy access to North American musical expressions via radio, sound recordings, cable television, mobile phones, and the internet.

In the face of imported music and entertainment, cultural critics have expressed concern about its effects on the nation's youth, particularly their knowledge about their own heritage. According to such experts, steel pan and calypso have been "dying" for many decades, and every year there are articles and panel discussions assessing the vital signs of the nation's art forms. The violence and moral indecency depicted in imported movies and television programs have been blamed for the more serious social problems currently facing the people of Trinidad and Tobago, which include gang-related crime and violence, kidnapping and extortion, drug trafficking, domestic violence, teen pregnancy, and HIV/AIDS. One answer to such social problems has been encouraging children and youths to participate in various forms of national culture. During Carnival, and occasionally other times of the year, state organizations, nongovernment organizations, and private entrepreneurs sponsor calypso competitions in which children and youths are able to sum up these situations in song. In the case of junior steel bands, these are seen as an important intervention in the lives of young people, giving them an alternative to negative influences that they may experience, particularly in poorer urban environments. Music both fills time and offers a way for young people to take pride in their accomplishments. It also affords a way to earn prize money that can go toward school expenses and, in some cases, offers a career path to young people with exceptional talent.

Children and the Educational System

Traveling the main roads of Trinidad in the early morning hours of the week, or passing through the bus terminal in Port of Spain, I would see flocks of school-children patiently awaiting public transportation to school. School affiliations are apparent from the subdued colors and insignia of school uniforms—something that I found somewhat conservative for a country internationally known for its tropi-cal beaches and lively annual Carnival. These sentiments were echoed by a neigh-bor's daughter, who wished that she could exchange her drab daily costume for the brightly colored fashions she saw on her favorite US television program, "Saved by the Bell." Younger children will usually attend a primary school close to where they live, but unless they are lucky enough to have a family member drive them, it may take an hour or more to get to the secondary school in which they are enrolled.

The most prevalent forms of public transportation are privately run "maxi taxis," whose drivers are infamous for the loud soca and reggae music they play along their routes. Parents often express their concern in letters to the editor of the local newspapers, requesting that authorities put controls on the "rude" music that might corrupt their children's moral values. Others have suggested that the maxi drivers play socially relevant calypso and steel pan music exclusively so that young people have a better sense of their culture and its history. Maxi drivers, on the other hand, are more concerned with attracting business. Youths say they want to hear soca and dancehall because the music is more "alive" than old-fashioned calypsos, and the lyrics are more relevant to their experience of both Carnival and everyday life.

Children typically enroll when aged three at an Early Childhood Care and Education (ECCE) School and are expected to acquire basic reading and writing skills by the time they begin primary school at age five. During the seventh and final year of primary school, students sit the Secondary Entrance Assessment (SEA), for-merly known as the Common Entrance Examination. These examinations deter-mine which secondary school a student is allowed to attend, and the standards for receiving government assistance to support their attendance at the more prestigious institutions are rigorous and competitive. This is typically a very stressful time for young people with high aspirations. Students from the upper strata of society have distinct advantages, including tutoring in SEA subjects as well as admission to pri-vate schools (with tuition fees) for students who do not perform well on the SEA. Such things are obviously unattainable to those lacking the necessary financial resources.

Secondary school consists of forms one through five and most secondary schools are single sex rather than co-ed. In form five, students take the Caribbean Secondary Education Certificate (CSEC) examinations, which are the equivalent of the British General Certificate of Secondary Education (GCSE) examinations taken at the age of sixteen. Students who are academically qualified may opt to continue secondary school for another two years, at which point they may take the Caribbean Advanced Proficiency Examinations (CAPE), the equivalent of British A-levels taken at age eighteen. Students are then eligible to enroll in tertiary education, typically with government assistance. As of 2010, tertiary education at the University of the West Indies, the University of Trinidad and Tobago, and the University of the Southern Caribbean as well as several other accredited institutions was fully subsidized by the government for academically qualified students (Government of the Republic of Trinidad and Tobago, Ministry of Education 2010a).

Before 1962, schoolchildren would have learned little about local music and culture in the classroom. There was no formal system for transmitting knowledge about Carnival and its music: newcomers learned by watching veteran performers sing calypso, and pan was learned by rote in the panyard. While informal learning still tends to be the norm rather than the exception, there is more integration of Carnival traditions in the classroom. During the first years of Trinidad and Tobago's independence, the PNM, through the guidance of its first prime minister, Dr. Eric Williams, brought about vast cultural change and transformation within the new nation, as well as retention and renewal of the country's inherited complex of cultures. Williams, whose own career potential was realized through educational opportunities, placed great importance on improving access to all levels of the school system as well as self-betterment through a "reenculturation" in local ways and customs, most of which had been diluted under British colonial rule. Williams was keenly interested in the African origins of Caribbean music and folklore and encouraged the research of both local and foreign scholars, such as Alan Lomax, Beth Lomax Hawes, Beryl McBurnie, and J. D. Elder. During the 1960s, the National Carnival Commission was established, and government support for various aspects of the festival was increased. This was both to enhance support for the PNM among the working classes and to attract tourists to Trinidad and Tobago. For both purposes, Carnival had to be improved further via the establishment of events such as the Calypso Monarch and Panorama competitions. The result of the efforts of Dr. Williams and the PNM was a tremendous change in how local arts and culture are perceived by the average Trinidadian (Smith 2004: 39).

However, by 1970, lack of progress regarding development, ending racial discrimination, and the establishment of employment opportunities for the working-class Afro-Trinidadians, brought about massive strikes and organized marches in protest. This period was also one of considerable educational reform. As noted on the Ministry of Education website, "Since the 1970s primary education has undergone a number of curriculum changes. Content and learning experiences meant to be more responsive to the social and cultural experiences of students in Trinidad and Tobago, and to changing understandings about developmentally appropriate curriculum, have been included" (Government of the Republic of Trinidad and Tobago, Ministry of Education 2010b). Thus, students read stories that are set in Trinidad and Tobago, such as the novels of Merle Hodge. Their textbooks refer to local flora and fauna, rather than apples and grapes, and they learn local folk songs such as "Brown Girl in the Ring" rather than "London Bridge Is Falling Down." Due to the media-saturated environment noted above, young people are still exposed to a great deal of "foreign" music, particularly from North America. However, on several occasions I saw young people using these outside influences in distinctly West Indian ways. One example I remember during my fieldwork was children playing a ring game while singing Celine Dion's "My Heart Will Go On," which was enormously popular in the region due to the success of the movie *Titanic*. In general, children and youths engage with both local and foreign music in unpredictable and exciting ways.

Contemporary efforts to include young people in Carnival are attempts both to create a sense of pride in local cultural expressions and to counteract imported cultural strands that are received via satellite television and the internet. While it may be rather extreme to worry that local culture will die out as result of external influences, instruction in Trinidad's musical heritage is officially part of the visual and performing arts curriculum mandated by the Ministry of Education. In addition to general musicianship, students engage in activities that teach them aspects of calypso composition and singing, steel pan manufacture, and arranging for calypso bands and steel orchestra as well as the historical aspects of these various musical genres that originated in Trinidad and Tobago (Government of the Republic of Trinidad and Tobago, Ministry of Education 2010c). Additionally, several local radio and television stations provide educational programming that surveys the history of Carnival and its expressive traditions. The same is true of newspaper coverage, particularly during the Carnival season, which takes up most of January and February of each year.

Playing Mas (Masquerade)

One of the most popular parts of the Carnival season in Trinidad and Tobago is the "Kiddies Carnival," when children and youths are given the opportunity to create their own spectacle separate from the bacchanal of the adult celebration that takes place on Carnival Monday and Tuesday. Bands of young people fill the streets with every imaginable color, dressing as fancy Indians, sailors, folk dancers representing the nation's diversity, and stylized versions of the flora and fauna of Trinidad and Tobago. The same "big trucks" that accompany the adult masqueraders follow the junior masqueraders through the streets, providing the soundtrack of soca music that fills the air throughout the Carnival season. Vendors along the route supply the youngsters with ice cream, snow cones, cotton candy, popcorn, juices, and soft drinks. Although it is a contest with winners for best costumes, most youths are there to take part in the various treats the day has to offer, whether they are in an official mas band or on the sidelines watching the parade pass.

Trinidad's Carnival is one of the oldest in the Americas, dating back to the settlement of French Creoles on the island in the eighteenth century. As the nineteenth century progressed, working-class Carnival bands became increasingly wild, noisy, and violent, with masqueraders portraying lewdness in costume, gesture, and song lyrics and cross-dressing by both men and women. Violent clashes between mas bands frequently resulted in police intervention. By the late nineteenth century, local businesses began to award prizes to well-organized, well-dressed costumed bands, thus encouraging good behavior and decency and suppressing rioting and obscenity (Cowley 1996: 104–106). Various improvements to Carnival over the years have allowed different groups to participate who, in earlier generations, would have been discouraged because of the festival's association with lower class revelry and licentiousness. Community organizations were among the first to sponsor Carnival activities specifically for children, such as the Red Cross Children's Carnival. In contemporary Trinidad, Carnival channels the energy of many creative people of all ages, most of whom do it for love rather than financial gain.

The most visually stimulating aspect of Carnival is the colorful displays of the many mas bands that flock to the streets during Carnival Monday and Tuesday. Those viewing Carnival from abroad, particularly the "bikini mas" of the Carnival bands patronized by adult Trinidadians and tourists, might be surprised at the efforts to include children and youths in the art of playing mas during the Carnival season. Appropriately, the Junior Parade of Bands (affectionately known as Kiddies Carnival) usually takes place one week before Carnival weekend, on Saturday and Sunday, to give young people a stand-alone parade that is separate from the bacchanal of the adults' Parade of Bands. The Junior Parade of Bands receives sponsorship from the National Carnival Bands Association of Trinidad and Tobago, various community organizations such as the Red Cross, and local businesses.

Designers find "Kiddies Carnival" rewarding, and for the children it is an extension of their sense of fantasy and play. It allows them to bring to life the images of West Indian folklore they experience in folktales and in school as well as to engage with contemporary Trinidadian popular music in their own Carnival mas bands. There are, of course, restrictions on the Junior Parade of Bands: costumes must not be offensive or sexual in nature, and children are discouraged from "wining" or dancing suggestively. However, in newspaper and television interviews, designers have commented that they switched from designing for adult mas bands to Kiddies Carnival because they can be more creative, have more freedom of expression, and be less likely to receive negative criticism from masqueraders. Some designers for junior carnival strive to express the cultural diversity of Trinidad and Tobago. Afro-Creole expressions tend to dominate during Carnival. However, children of East Indian, Chinese, and Middle Eastern descent told me they really enjoyed displaying their ethnic heritage in the Junior Parade of Bands. Traditional mas characters such as Dame Lorraine, Fancy Indians, and Sailor Mas are common in Kiddies Carnival, but designers will also find ways to relate local flora and fauna to the images in Disney movies and other familiar aspects of children's popular culture.

While a professional designer will create a theme for the mas band to portray, the parents and other family and friends of the young participants are essential in making the event a success. Some may help to assemble costumes at the mas camps that are the designer's headquarters. During the Junior Parade of Bands, adults act as coaches to guide the choreography of the masqueraders as they pass the judging stands that are stationed along the parade route. Adults also coordinate the movement of children through the streets and ensure their safety during the three-mile parade route. Each band has a king and queen; these individuals also compete for junior king and queen of Carnival at a separate staging area. Mas bands are divided into sections of masqueraders, each portraying an aspect of the designer's concept. DJs play the popular soca tunes of that season. By Anglo-American standards, soca songs may seem to be too focused on Carnival's party atmosphere, but in Trinidad I have heard a number of fans and newspaper columnists comment on how soca is more "wholesome" than the music coming from North America and Jamaica. Like their adult counterparts, junior masqueraders are judged not only on their costumes but also for their ability to move along with the music in a joyful and enthusiastic manner. Thus, Kiddies Carnival joins families and community members together in a colorful and exciting celebration of local music and culture.

JUNIOR CALYPSO AND SOCA COMPETITIONS

Historically, the calypsonian has been portrayed as a "man of words" who acts as a mouthpiece for the underclass, a performer who through his skillful use of wit and wordplay brings to light issues that concern the nation. However, women and children have played an increasingly important role in calypso, and their numbers have been growing over the past four decades. As with mas bands, calypso artists compete against each other in various contexts, the most prestigious being the Calypso Monarch finals, held on Dimanche Gras (Carnival Sunday) and the Soca Monarch competition, held on the "Fantastic Friday" that leads up to Carnival weekend.

Calypso competitions for schoolchildren were organized beginning in the 1970s, with the first nationwide Junior Calypso Monarch taking place in 1976. The Junior Soca Monarch competition (also known as the Schools' Soca Monarch competition) has been held off and on since 1999.[1] The difference between the two competitions is that the Calypso Monarch competitors usually perform topical songs and social commentaries, while Soca Monarch competitors focus on party songs that celebrate Carnival itself. Several different government and nongovernment entities have overseen these competitions. As of 2010, the sponsors who supported these competitions were the Trinbago United Calypsonians Organization (TUCO)—which also oversees the Dimanche Gras Calypso Monarch competition—and the Caribbean Prestige Foundation—which also sponsors the International Soca Monarch competition.

Each competitor must perform a new and original composition on a topic of his or her choice. Children work hard on crafting their lyrics and melody, but as is the case with the Junior Parade of Bands they get help from their family as well as their teachers. Veteran calypsonians often coach younger artists: some as volunteers, while others charge a fee for one-on-one coaching sessions. A common arrangement is for established calypso and soca artists to coach their own children in the junior competitions. I personally know several families who are on the third generation of calypsonians in the family. The adjudication of Junior Monarch competitors is similar to that for senior calypsonians. Contestants are judged on lyrics, which carry a maximum of thirty points, melody (thirty points), rendition (twenty points), originality (ten points), and presentation (ten points). During their preparations for the various rounds of competition, students learn the art of "packing the calypso"—rehearsing it to the point at which lyrics, melody, rhythm, phrasing, and body language cohere into a seamless performance and the finished calypso is identified with the personality of the singer.

The issues that junior calypsonians cover are quite diverse, though they must avoid the vulgar and defamatory lyrics that are present in the calypso songs performed by some of their elders. One common theme is reminding classmates about good behavior. For example, the 2010 winner presented "Don't Waste It." The young boy's lyrics described his mother telling him not to waste food, water, and toothpaste because there are children all over the world who don't have these things:

> Water running too long, in the bath, you just start, boy don't waste it
> Your sister want to bathe, have a heart, son don't waste it
> You know how many people don't have running water in their place
> Son, you watch so much of it, right in front your face
> Ever since she begging me, Aaron boy don't waste

Other junior calypsonians have sung about the pollution of city streets ("Don't Litter"), children's addiction to video games ("They Silent"), and the negative images and violence in the media ("TV Control"). Another common theme is extolling the benefits of a good education. In songs such as "Golden Opportunities," "Success," and "Educate Yourself," classmates are encouraged to study hard; other songs convey the dangers and consequences of school delinquency ("Fool Games").

Junior calypsonians also have created songs that deal with the more negative aspects of life in Trinidad and Tobago, such as crime, HIV/AIDS, and child abuse. Since a majority of the competitors in the Junior Calypso Monarch are girls, the topics that pertain to their gender are prevalent. Songs such as "You Name Woman" and "Pain" warn young women about the consequences of having relationships too early in their lives, consequences such as teenage pregnancy and sexually transmitted diseases. Other female junior monarchs have chosen to critique absentee fathers ("Remember Me Not") as well as the tremendous stress on both mother and children when a father abandons his family, as in the calypso "Since You've Been Gone":

> Since you've been gone, life's no longer the same
> Since you've been gone, Mom hardly ever call your name
> She losing weight, she hardly sleep
> In the dead of night, she takes a peep
> Checking all the doors and windows
> Making sure they are still closed
> Cause in this bandit world today
> A Mom alone is easy prey
> A strong male figure, this family lack
> Please tell me Dad when you coming back?

Like their adult contemporaries, some youths choose to sing on topics other than moral lessons. Many songs celebrate the nation's African heritage; express pride in a singer's ethnic heritage, local customs, or art forms; or pay tribute to elder calypsonians who inspired a singer. There are numerous songs that are humorous observations about daily life. Recent examples include "They Confusing Me," which humorously highlights the idiosyncrasies of the English language. The young lady who won the 2007 competition sang "School Bag Dilemma: Lord Have Mercy, Me School Bag Is Too Heavy," dramatized with the enormous school bags that children have to carry even in primary school grades. The eight-year-old girl who won the 2005 competition created the calypso "Barking Beef," repeating the rumors about local vendors using dog meat in local delicacies like stew beef and roti, punctuated by the young singer's barks and howls:

> My Daddy one day driving to Grande, tell the whole car load he feeling hungry
> My Daddy one day driving through the country, decided to buy himself a roti
> The boss man ask him, "What you having chief?"
> He tell the man he would take a beef
> But after a few bites he heard a barking sound
> Daddy get worry and start to look around
> Then he bawl out, "Oh gosh, I shoulda buy shark,
> First time I get a beef roti that could bark!"
> Barking beef, causing me father grief
> Barking beef, to this day he's in disbelief

The winners from each primary and secondary school go on to compete at the national level, continuing in separate primary and secondary school categories. The finals of the competition combine the fifteen best singers from both the primary and secondary levels. While it might be assumed that older students would prevail, primary school students often win the crown. In 2010, the winner was a six-year-old boy, setting a new record for the youngest Junior Calypso Monarch. As with the adult competitions, there are financial incentives for students to compete. In 2010, the cash prizes for the Junior Calypso Monarch competition were TT$25,000 for first place, TT$20,000 for second place, and TT$15,000 for third place.[2] In recent years, laptop computers have been awarded to the first six finishers. While cultural preservation and survival are on the agenda of the organizations that sponsor competitions by junior calypsonians, the benefits for the young people involved include recognition among peers and financial rewards. Additionally, there are a number of successful calypso and soca artists who began in the junior competitions, thus making this a potential career path as well as an educational pursuit for young people.

Junior Panorama

In 2010, it is difficult to imagine that pan was ever disdained by the elite of its country of origin or that the panyard was once a dangerous place even for the members of its own steel band.[3] When I arrived in my band's panyard for rehearsal, groups of neighborhood children were challenging each other to learn the melodies of the tune the grown-ups would rehearse that evening. Some would ask the "tourist lady" for chewing gum and sweets, but others wanted me to bring them pan sticks so they did not have to wait for a chance to play the music. If I arrived in the late afternoon, I would typically see the students from the local secondary school rehearsing for Junior Panorama. The more experienced members of the school steel band joined us later in the evening; some were so talented that they proudly took their places in the front line of the band's lead pan section.

The story of the steel band movement typically stresses how the working-class "panmen" who developed the instrument overcame the adversity of colonialism and gradually won the support for the steel pan with the middle and upper classes and elevated it to the position of national instrument. Today there are many pannists from young schoolchildren to adult players, arrangers, and adjudicators. Along with the mas and calypso, the steel band has become an important musical expression for the nation's youth and often is touted as a solution to problems such as juvenile delinquency. The roots of the steel pan and its music in working-class culture make it particularly viable for those who do not have the financial resources or industry connections required for other types of artistic expression in Trinidad. Pan is an activity that allows them to, to paraphrase the national motto, "aspire and achieve" within the context of communal cooperation.

During the 1960s and 1970s, various educators, many of them young women, were influential in creating various contexts for steel band instruction and performance for schoolchildren. One of the earliest school steel bands was established in 1974 at St. François Girls college in Belmont; this school also set the precedent of forging ties with neighborhood steel bands to provide instruction to students and to share instruments. There were enough school bands by 1976 to hold the first Junior

Panorama competition. There has been such a competition at Carnival nearly every year since then, as well as a separate Music Festival for the performance of classical repertoire on the instruments of the steel band. Steel pan training in schools and ties between school and community bands has greatly changed how musical knowledge is transmitted in this musical context. Whereas in earlier generations pannists learned by rote from more experienced players, it is more likely that young people will first learn how to play pan in school and then "graduate" to a community steel band (Dudley 2008: 249–250).

It is common for single-sex schools in the same neighborhood to join forces to ensure an adequate number of players for the Junior Panorama competition. Many school bands have arranged to use the instruments of the community steel bands that are established in the neighborhoods closest to the school. This makes things more affordable for the junior bands, as their school does not need to purchase and maintain the number of instruments required for a full band arrangement. Some of the junior steel bands are not associated with a particular school but act as the junior arm of the community steel band. There have also been junior steel bands that are affiliated with private music academies. As of 2010 there were three age categories for the junior orchestras: thirteen and under, sixteen and under, and twenty-one and under (When Steel Talks 2010).

Typically, local music teachers and other music professionals are hired to write arrangements for the junior steel bands although the musicians do not play from notation. Most arrangements are learned orally, one phrase at a time, from the band's arranger and his or her assistants, as is the convention with the neighborhood bands. The more experienced members of the band act as section leaders for each instrument type, assisting the arranger and musical director in teaching the parts to less experienced musicians. Learning and memorizing the musical arrangement requires hours of daily practice during the weeks leading up to competition, and the discipline necessary for this after-school activity is an extension of the rigidity of being a schoolchild in Trinidad and Tobago's school system. Often, teens will play in both their school band and adult steel bands, which means learning several complex musical arrangements. While I often struggled to learn the arrangement for the adult Panorama competition, youths quickly absorbed it and I often found myself consulting teenagers on how to play the more difficult passages our arranger had composed.

Once the music has been learned and the arranger is satisfied with the group's ability to perform it, children are allowed to be more playful and show their enthusiasm. Musical improvisation is not typically allowed, but movement, display, and drama are all part of the evaluation of a band's interpretation of a musical arrangement (Dudley 2008: 181–183). The music is well rehearsed by now, so all the musicians are encouraged to add physical display and flash, or as they describe it "gallerying" and "antics" to the presentation, much like the "packing" done in the sung form of calypso music. It is common to see young musicians dancing in place while playing or spinning around and waving when they have rests or breaks in the arrangement. In preparing to take the stage for competition, each child or youth is encouraged to show the excitement of participating in the event by adding visual interest to the band's appearance. For the performance, players must wear matching jerseys, financed by the band's community supporters and local businesses. However, each individual can, within limits, add his or her own flair to these outfits. Depending on the standards set by the band director, such flair can include jewelry and accessories, sunglasses, shoes, nail polish, glitter, and face paint.

As with the junior masquerade bands, the parents and other family members and friends of the young participants are essential in making the event a success, and many hands are necessary to design and create jerseys and costumes, as well as to enhance the visual impact of the band by building racks, stands, and canopies for the different sections of the steel band, painted with elaborate and colorful designs. Flag wavers and banner carriers also add color and movement to the band's presentation; typically women whose children or nieces and nephews are performing in the steel band perform these roles during the Junior Panorama competitions. Most important are the supporters from the players' schools and neighborhoods, who fill up the seats at the competition and wildly show their enthusiasm for their favorite bands. As with Kiddies Carnival and the Junior Calypso Monarch competitions, Junior Panorama joins families and community members together in a colorful and exciting celebration of local music and culture.

CONCLUSIONS

Children and youths are central to contemporary Carnival arts in Trinidad and Tobago, and among them are the future innovators in mas, calypso, soca, and the steel band. Carnival is, by definition, a time of bacchanal and unabashed play, for both young people and adults. While the contributions of adults to bacchanal are more widely discussed by various scholars and commentators, it is clear that the play of children and youths has an important role in the Carnival culture of contemporary Trinidad and Tobago. Of course, the nationalist impulses that support the various Carnival arts may at times take the form of an intervention in the lives of children and youths to counteract negative influences and societal problems. However, they also provide a way to channel the playfulness of children and youth into creative and artistic endeavors. Another debate that often emerges from this context is the inclusiveness of various Carnival activities. After all, Carnival events are seasonal activities, and Carnival has its basis in a Roman Catholic religious cycle of permissiveness and repentance. Thus there are religious critiques of Carnival even in its domesticated form, particularly from Trinidad and Tobago's evangelical Christians and fundamentalist Muslims. While mas and steel band have become more inclusive of Trinidadians of various ethnic and religious backgrounds, particularly East Indians, it is unusual to see junior calypsonians who are not Afro-Trinidadian. These debates are too complex to resolve in this chapter, but they do act as a counterpoint to nationalist discourse about local music and culture.

What continues to amaze me is the unpredictable nature of the engagement of all ages of Trinidadians with local music and culture as it faces continuing influence from abroad. During my fieldwork, young people would follow up my questions with their own about then-popular rappers such as Puff Daddy and The Notorious B.I.G., about whom I embarrassingly knew very little. I had lengthy discussions with friends and acquaintances of various ages about styles as disparate as hip-hop, alternative rock, country and western, heavy metal, mainstream pop, and gospel. At times I felt that I was an especially poor representative of "American" music, while in contrast, most people I met, regardless of their age, knew details about the local music scene, the lives of important calypsonians, who invented the steel pan, and so forth. As this chapter demonstrates, contemporary life in Trinidad and Tobago fuels the creative spirit of the nation's youth and often provides the material for songs, dances, and other expressive presentations in various performing contexts.

On the linked website with this volume can be found a list of websites that have videos of Carnival (Web Figure 16.1 **O**) and two photos of junior carnival (Web Figures 16.2 and 16.3 **O**).

NOTES

1 These dates are based upon the recollections of musicians and promoters I have talked with, as well as various newspaper accounts that I have gathered since I began doing fieldwork in Trinidad in 1998.

2 In 2010, the exchange rate was US$1 to TT$6. Average wages in Trinidad and Tobago at this time were TT$2,000–5,000 per month.

3 The first pan players were working-class men. The yards where they rehearsed also had various hustlers engaging in illicit activities. Players from competing yards fought each other when they met on the road during Carnival. Over time the band members discouraged these activities to make panyards more respectable places for people to play or listen to music.

REFERENCES

Brereton, Bridget. 1981. *A History of Modern Trinidad 1783–1962*. Oxford: Heinemann Educational Books.

Central Intelligence Agency. 2010. *The World Handbook*. Accessed August 16, 2010. https://www.cia.gov/library/publications/the-world-factbook/geos/td.html#People.

Cowley, John. 1996. *Carnival, Canboulay and Calypso: Traditions in the Making*. London: Cambridge University Press.

Dudley, Shannon. 2008. *Music from behind the Bridge: Steelband Aesthetics and Politics in Trinidad and Tobago*. New York: Oxford University Press.

Government of the Republic of Trinidad and Tobago, Ministry of Education. 2010a. Accessed August 16, 2010. http://www.moe.gov.tt/gate.html.

Government of the Republic of Trinidad and Tobago, Ministry of Education. 2010b. Accessed August 16, 2010. http://www.moe.gov.tt/pri_curriculum.html.

Government of the Republic of Trinidad and Tobago, Ministry of Education. 2010c. Accessed August 16, 2010. http://www.moe.gov.tt/curriculum_pdfs/Visual%20 and%20Performing%20Arts/Visual%20and%20Performing%20Arts.pdf.

Lomax, Alan. 1997. *Brown Girl in the Ring: An Anthology of Song Games from the Eastern Caribbean*. With J. D. Elder and Beth Lomax Hawes. New York: Pantheon Books.

Lomax, Alan. 2000. *Caribbean Voyage: Carnival Roots: The 1962 Field Recordings*. With J. D. Elder and Beth Lomax Hawes. Rounder Records 1166117252. Compact disc.

Smith, Hope Munro. 2004. "Performing Gender in the Trinidad Calypso." *Latin American Music Review* 25 (1): 32–56.

When Steel Talks. 2010. "Panorama 2010." Accessed August 16, 2010. http://www.panonthenet.com/tnt/2010/news/selectionsNationalJuniorPanorama.htm.

PART 2

PERSONAL JOURNEYS IN/ THROUGH CULTURE

17

MUSICAL CHILDHOODS ACROSS THREE GENERATIONS, FROM PUERTO RICO TO THE USA

MARISOL BERRÍOS-MIRANDA

IT is a Friday evening, circa 1960. Family and friends gather in my house in Jardines de Caparra, Puerto Rico to listen to recorded music, converse, play dominos, eat, and dance. In the kitchen my mother cooks delicious food such as "*arroz con gandules*," "*carne al caldero*," and fried plantains. My aunts and other women friends of the family help in the cooking. My father sits at the domino table with my uncles and godfather; other males take turns to play. Children run around, play street games, and come inside the home. The record player provides a constant musical backdrop to all this activity, and sometimes the backdrop becomes the foreground. When El Gran Combo's song "Acángana" begins, some people move into the living room, grab a partner, and dance. Always music and dance are the soul of these frequent gatherings.

Before I ever took an instrument in hand or had a music lesson in school, I learned music through gatherings like this one in my home. I learned that music was fun, that it was for dancing, and that it was an integral part of social interaction between people of all ages—an understanding of music that was really quite similar to that of my grandmother, who grew up in the Puerto Rican countryside with no electricity and who never learned to read. In the transition from her generation and her world to mine, the technology of radio, recordings, and television came to represent an important difference in the way music is experienced; and yet music's fundamentally social context and function persisted.

In this chapter I will offer glimpses of the musical childhoods of three generations, represented by my mother, me, and my children, and ranging from the community of Santurce, Puerto Rico, where I was born, to Seattle, Washington, where my children have grown up. From my own perspective as an immigrant to the mainland United States, the continuities between these generations have helped me to survive and prosper far from my island home. Music in this perspective is a source of cultural security, a marker of my identity and a mode of interaction that helps me know where and with whom I belong. Reflecting on my musical childhood has also helped me to understand some of the more broadly human dimensions of musical experience, such as the social conversation and negotiation that happens in the act of dancing. Perhaps most importantly, my experience has taught me that the world of my living room overlaps with the world of movies, radio, and television and that community music making and popular music inform one another. This may be somewhat distinctive of the place and time I grew up in, but it points to the possibility of holding on to music's community-building function in a world where so much culture is electronically and commercially packaged for us.

BACKGROUND ON SANTURCE, PUERTO RICO

To the extent that my own musical childhood represents Puerto Rican experience generally, it is important to review the musical history of Puerto Rico and of the community of Santurce where I was born (for a more complete version of this history, see Berríos-Miranda and Dudley 2009). Historical dynamics that have shaped music making in Puerto Rico include (1) its political status, first as a colony of Spain and then, after the 1898 Spanish American War, as a territory of the United States; (2) the exchanges of people and culture with the broader Caribbean and Latin America; (3) the intersection of community music making with the commercial music world; and (4) diasporic connections between Puerto Rico and the US mainland, especially New York.

Santurce is a working-class community to the east of the fortified city of San Juan that was founded by people of African descent. It was a community of free blacks for two and a half centuries before dramatic political and economic changes expanded and transformed it in the early 1900s. In 1663 the Spanish Crown issued a royal *cédula* decreeing that slaves who escaped from English, Dutch, and Danish Caribbean islands would be given asylum in Puerto Rico and granted land outside the walled city of San Juan. This area was known as "Cangrejos," named after the land crabs that abounded in the sandbars, lagoons, and mangrove swamps. With the arrival of farmers and fishermen in Cangrejos, San Juan acquired a closer source of food supplies and a supply of labor for bridge building, killing stray dogs, and other tasks that the San Juan residents were unable or unwilling to do (Berríos-Miranda and Dudley 2009: 42–43). Cangrejos also played an important role in the island's defense, particularly during the English attack of 1797. Throughout the eighteenth and nineteenth centuries, Cangrejos (as well as other parts of Puerto Rico) continued to attract immigrants from many parts of the Caribbean. They worked not only as agricultural laborers but also as artisans who did various kinds of building, metalworking, textile work, milling, and other trades (ibid: 94–95). Most of them were coloreds (people of African or mixed race descent), a testament to the relative scarcity of whites in the Caribbean before 1850, especially in the artisan class.

One place where the musical traces of this West Indian immigration can be seen clearly is in the complex of Puerto Rican drum dances known as *bomba* (see Barton 2002: 183–198). While the evidence pointing to French Caribbean influences is most abundant, other foreign influences can be seen in the names of *bomba* styles such as *holandés* (Dutch) and *danué* (Danish; Barton 2002). In Puerto Rico these mixtures took different forms in different places, but the traveling of musicians and dancers between regions also sustained a shared Afro-Puerto Rican musical culture. The music called *plena*, for example, which is thought to have been pioneered in Ponce around 1900 by immigrants from British islands (Flores 1992: 59–68), was popularized as early as the 1930s through recordings (Glasser 1995: 169–190) but took root even earlier in Cangrejos and other black communities through networks of community music making (Pedro Clemente, personal interview in Piñones, Puerto Rico, May 15, 2007).

In the late nineteenth century Cangrejos experienced accelerated urban development, and its name was changed to Santurce. As late as 1910, black and mulatto residents were still a majority in Santurce (Damiani 1997: 344), but immigration from other parts of the island was creating rapid demographic change. The shift to monocultivation of crops such as sugar and coffee in the late nineteenth century displaced rural farmers (Sepúlveda and Carbonell 1987: 29). The US occupation that began with the 1898 Spanish American War further accelerated Puerto Rico's transition to a more urban economy. Between 1899 and 1930 the population of Santurce increased from 5,840 to 81,960 (ibid.: 29) and the growth of housing and businesses was similarly rapid. With immigration from Puerto Rico's interior to Santurce came the music of mountain farmers, called *jíbaros*. Afro-Puerto Rican *bomba* and *plena* were performed in Santurce house parties alongside *jíbaro* music genres such as *seis*, *aguinaldo*, and *mazurka*.

The 1917 Jones Act, which granted US citizenship to Puerto Ricans, inaugurated a period of extensive emigration to New York and other US cities and made Santurce a way station for people en route to the United States. From the 1930s through the 1950s there was a high rate of turnover in Santurce's neighborhoods, as new residents arrived and others departed for the United States. The United States launched "Operation Bootstrap," a program of investment in the tourist industry, pharmaceuticals, banking, and other businesses in Puerto Rico, which helped to make Santurce the financial and—importantly for music—the entertainment capital of the island. By the 1950s Santurce was a magnet for people from all over Puerto Rico who dreamed of new opportunities, whether in Santurce itself or in the United States, and it was an important stop on the touring circuit for famous musicians from Cuba, Mexico, Argentina, and elsewhere.

The history outlined here has several implications for the way I grew up experiencing music in Santurce. First of all, the diverse immigration from abroad and networks of exchange within Puerto Rico have produced a musical culture in Cangrejos that is inclusive, flexible, and attuned to the wider Caribbean. Second, the proximity of this vibrant community music scene to radio stations, hotels, and theaters meant that local bands often shared the stage and the radio waves with international musicians. In this way community music making and professional music making often resembled one another. Third, Puerto Rico's colonial relationship with the United States has made music an important marker of identity. The ease of emigration to the United States has created professional opportunities for musicians from Santurce and led to much cross-fertilization between Caribbean and mainland music genres; but Puerto Ricans have also resisted incorporation into the United States by their attachment to Puerto Rican genres and styles and by affirming their musical ties to the Caribbean and Latin America.

My Mother's Musical Experience

El sábado, en todas las casas en Puerto Rico, ese día era de limpiar. Limpiar pisos, limpiar las ollas, sacar tizne porque se cocinaba con leña y carbón. El Septeto Puerto Rico empezaba a tocar a las 12:00, y ya nosotros habíamos limpiado por lo menos la mitad de casa, limpiado la cocina y eso. Y entonces poníamos el radio, que era un radio Motorola chiquito.... Se salía todo el mundo a bailar a la sala... íbamos haciendo nuestros deberes en los anuncios. Cuando venían los anuncios nosotros parábamos de bailar. Pero se bailaba son, se bailaba guaracha, danza, se bailaba vals.

Saturday was the day for cleaning in all the houses in Puerto Rico. Clean the floors, the pots, clean out the ashes because people cooked with firewood and charcoal. The Septeto Puerto Rico began playing at 12:00 noon, and by that time we had already cleaned at least half the house, the kitchen, and whatnot. So then we turned on the radio, which was a little Motorola radio.... Everyone came into the living room to dance...we kept doing our chores during the commercials. When the commercials came we stopped dancing. But we danced *son*, we danced *guaracha, danza*, we danced waltz. (Juanita Miranda and Sylvia Miranda, personal interview, Seattle, November 16, 1999)

The first radio station in Puerto Rico was WKAQ, founded in 1922, and my mother was born seven years later, in 1929. When she was a young girl her father bought a small Motorola radio, and from that day her musical childhood was shaped by listening to radio music programs while doing chores, as well as by children's play and games. Mami (as I call my mother) and her siblings also heard live music performed by small ensembles at house parties, and in their teenage years they got to hear professional ensembles in live performances at radio studios, theaters, and school dances. The experiences of recorded music, live performances by professionals, and amateur music making in the community were connected, however, through shared repertoire and instrumentation. Ambitious young musicians honed their skills performing in guitar trios and other small combos in homes and street corners, hoping for a chance to enter a radio or TV talent show or to get invited to perform with a professional group. Some of the same performers and songs that my mother heard on the radio were also heard at house parties and other community events. Moreover, whether she was listening to music on the radio or at a house party, her active participation in the form of singing along and dancing created a connection between those experiences.

People in Santurce also made great music that could not be heard on the radio, of course. Santurce's carnival, for example, was still a predominantly Afro-Puerto Rican festival in the 1940s. Organized by members of the Club de los Artesanos, a brotherhood of primarily black masons, carpenters, and other artisans, the carnival featured African masking and *bomba* and *plena* music—but also *sones, guarachas, valses*, and even *danzas* played by small ensembles. After the parade, there was a dance that lasted until early morning, attended by people of different races and classes. The *reina de carnaval* (carnival queen) was chosen not only for her beauty and grace, but also for her black skin, a tradition that continued until the Santurce carnival merged with the San Juan carnival in the early 1940s (Juanita and Sylvia Miranda, personal interview, Seattle, November 16, 1999). My mother told me that she thought the tradition of the black carnival queen was "*como una protesta*" (like a protest), a defiance of the racism that kept blacks out of many of the exclusive clubs and cultural venues and a pointed contrast to the rich white carnival queens of San Juan (Juanita Miranda, personal telephone conversation, November 24, 2008).

As a young child in the 1930s, my mother attended carnival parades with her father. Much of the music she heard there was also played at dances and spontaneous "*rumbones de esquina*"—street corner jams with conga drums, bongos, claves, and bells, and other percussion instruments, in which the dancers and drummers challenged one another and singers improvised in call-and-response with a chorus. As a young girl, she was not permitted to attend such events, but she could often hear the music from her house. Through her active listening, many songs were imprinted in her memory, and some were later reinforced by recordings that helped her reconstruct childhood musical experiences and pass them on to her children. My mother's memory is an archive of Puerto Rican music, from lullabies to folk songs to commercial recordings.

In addition to her participation in the musical world of her community, my mother learned and performed the special repertoires of children. Her knowledge of children's songs was an asset when, at the age of eleven, she began to tutor neighborhood children at her humble family home at Calle Bilbao, #159. On Saturday mornings at 8:00 am, eight to ten children would pay ten cents each to learn the alphabet (in Spanish and English), mathematics, and social history. At the end of each class they sang songs like "Mambru" and singing games like "Dona Ana," whose lyrics are provided as Mami remembers them to sound in about 1940.

"Mambru"
Mambrú se fue a la Guerra,
que dolor que dolor que pena,
Mambrú se fue a la Guerra
no se cuando vendrá,
que do re mi que do re fa,
no se cuando vendrá.
Mambru went to the war,
such a pain, such a pain, some sorrow,
Mambru went to the war don't know when he'll come back,
so do re mi, so do re fa,
don't know when he'll come back.

"Dona Ana"
Doña Ana no esta aquí,
ella está en su vergel,
abriendo la rosa y cerrando el clavel,...
¿Cómo está Doña Ana?;
Doña Ana is not here,
'cause she is in her garden,
opening the rose and closing the carnation,...
How is Doña Ana?
Call:
A Mamá que le mande una cebollita (Send Mama a little onion,)
Response:
dile que coja la mas Chiquita. (tell her to take the smallest one.)

MY CHILDHOOD MUSICAL EXPERIENCE

Like the students my mother tutored, I learned these and other children's songs, which I absorbed in the 1960s through countless repetitions in my home, the homes of my aunts, and with my playmates. Lullabies, of course, were another early repertoire I learned from my mother and grandmother. I also have vivid memories of a song my older sister Angie invented to comfort me when she heard me crying in my crib. She was only three years old herself, but she would stand by my crib looking up at me and singing, "*Maritol te pata ella?*" (*Marisol, que pasa a ella?* Marisol, what is happening to her?). Angie also sang me songs from television commercials, including, "*Siga los tres movimientos de FAB, remoje, enjuague, tienda!*" (Follow the three movements of

FAB [a laundry detergent], soak, rinse, hang!) My family tells me that I used to dance to this and other commercial jingles in my crib as a baby. These are ways that we children invented or adapted songs that then became part of family folklore. To this day, my cousins and aunts and uncles greet me by saying, "*Maritol te pata ella?*"

Some children's songs were used to teach us the musical skills that we would need as adults, especially dancing. One of my favorites was "Shaky Morena," which my aunts would sing to me while I danced with my hands on my waist, swinging my little hips flirtatiously from side to side.

> *Shaky Morena, Shaky*
> *Shaky Morena hué,*
> *A dónde está ese ritmo caramba*
> *Del merecumbé, hué*
>
> *El Juez le dijo al Cura*
> *El Cura le dijo al Juez*
> *Que a dónde está ese ritmo caramba*
> *Del merecumbé, hué!*
>
> *Un pasito alante*
> *Otro para atrás*
> *Y dando la vuelta*
> *Dando la vuelta*
> *Quién se quedará? Fuá!*
>
> Shake it, Morena, shake it
> Shake it, Morena, hey
> Where is that rhythm, *caramba*
> Of the *merecumbé, hué*
>
> The judge told the priest
> The priest told the judge
> Where is that rhythm, *caramba*
> Of the *merecumbé, hué*
>
> A little step forward
> Another back
> Turning around,
> Turning around,
> Who will get left? *Fuá!*

They would also lift my sister and me onto the table to show off our dancing skills while listening to songs on the radio. In this way we were constantly encouraged to dance and to participate in the musical repertoires of adults as well as children. The musical skills and tastes that we developed at this early age stayed with us for the rest of our lives.

My sister Angie, for example, can sing all the improvisations of Ismael Rivera, Puerto Rico's greatest *sonero*, who began his career with Cortijo y su Combo in the 1950s when she was still a toddler. Most of Cortijo's musicians were from the same neighborhood in Santurce, and when they came out with their modern arrangements of *bomba* and *plena* on the radio and then television, it took the sounds of our neighborhood to listeners all over Latin America. When she was two years old, Angie would run to the TV whenever "Maelo" appeared, kiss him on the screen, and tell him, "I love you, Maelo." Once when Angie spotted Maelo at Luquillo beach, she ran after him, and my mother had to catch up and explain to Maelo that this little girl was her daughter and that she was totally in love with his singing. Later, Angie met Maelo again at parties at her godfather's house. Other musicians from Cortijo's combo were friends of my father whom he brought home from time to time. Here again, therefore, the boundaries between community music and commercial music were not always apparent to us as children, and we lavished affection on media personalities and imitated them just as we did to beloved friends and family members.

My Teenage Years

As I was born in 1955, my teenage years coincided with the countercultural revolution of the 1960s and all of its music. Since the people who knew English were usually of a higher economic class, to listen to American popular songs was a sign of status. Therefore, Puerto Rican children and teenagers strove to learn all the lyrics of American songs that played on the radio. When we did not understand the English words we just made them up to fit the music. When Chubby Checker sang, "Let's twist again, as we did last summer," my sister Angie sang, "Let's twist again, as American boogle." Angie, who is the clown of the family, has kept this family folklore alive, and we still laugh today when she sings "the twist song." By the time I graduated from high school my friends knew as many American pop songs as most teenagers in the United States, even if we sang the wrong words sometimes. But I also continued to listen to the music of my parents, and especially to an exciting new style of Caribbean dance music that was developing in New York, called "salsa."

Salsa was the music of my generation, but it was more than just a new style for us. It was a response to the social and political predicament of Puerto Ricans and our own soundtrack to the counterculture of the 1960s and 1970s. Strongly rooted in the Latin Caribbean dance genres of preceding generations—mambo, cha cha cha, *guaracha*, and *son montuno*—salsa was also innovative and modern, featuring new sounds like the trombone, diverse Caribbean rhythms—such as *bomba*, *plena*, *cumbia*—and exciting instrumental improvisations. Many of the pioneering salsa musicians who recorded on the FANIA record label—Willie Colón, Eddie Palmieri, Ricardo Ray, Ray Barreto, and others—were Nuyoricans (Puerto Ricans born in New York), and their music reflected the gritty tension of their urban experience. When the FANIA All Stars released a live video recording of their concert at the Cheetah nightclub in 1971, it captured the imaginations of working-class people in urban centers all over Latin America. Dressed in bell-bottoms and dashikis and playing with a new kind of freedom and desire, these musicians seemed to represent the hardships and the hopes of people struggling to make it in a chaotic and often hostile urban environment. For young Nuyoricans, especially, salsa provided an "expressive liberation" from the racism and poverty of their expatriate experience (Berríos-Miranda 1999, 2002, 2004), connecting them both to their Caribbean roots and to contemporary social movements such as black pride and civil rights.

For those of us living in the island these meanings were also important, and salsa had a special appeal to young *independentistas* who were angry over political repression and police abuses. Tension around Puerto Rico's position as a US territory or its possible independence had continued throughout much of the twentieth century. A new cultural and political line was drawn in Puerto Rico between *rockeros,* who identified with English-language rock, and *cocolos,* who identified with Spanish-language salsa. Even the *cocolos* enjoyed rock music and managed to improve on dances such as the mashed potato and the twist, among others, to the point that Puerto Rican youth became better dancers of these forms than many Americans. But salsa music was the soundtrack of our social lives, the rhythm to which we danced.

In the long run, dancing to salsa was probably the most politically significant thing we did. Salsa's musical and textual references to Latin American and Puerto Rican identity appealed to our developing political consciousness (Berríos-Miranda 1999), but it was in the much less self-conscious act of dancing that we affirmed a Puerto Rican way of being through music. Salsa was an extension of the dance music of our parents and grandparents, and we danced salsa as easily and as often with them as we did with our peers. My mother tells me stories about lying to her father so that she could attend dances. At the age of eighteen, when she had already been working at Plaza Provision, (one of the most influential food distributors in San Juan, Puerto Rico), Mami used to tell my grandfather that she had to go to work. That was her excuse to escape to dances with local or international orchestras. Her love for dancing was so great that she was ready to risk a lot in order to be able to go dancing. Luckily, she was never caught! I could relate so much to her passion for dancing, because it was my favorite thing to do also. But even better, I could dance with her to the same music I danced to with my friends! I learned new/old dance moves from my parents and aunts and uncles, and they delighted in the new dance styles we did, such as *pachanga* and *jala jala.* It was all part of a common language of music and dance, evolving with the young people but understood by the old, a language of sound and movement that bound all the generations of my family in joyful communion at house parties, concerts, weddings, and anywhere else we gathered. Even as I explored the new possibilities and styles of my generation, therefore, I stayed grounded in the lessons I had learned in my crib.

Reflecting back on my childhood learning experience and comparing it to the way I have seen other people learn to dance since then, I have come to appreciate *bailando en la sala* (dancing in the living room) as an important mode of enculturation in which we internalized complex principles of social relationships. In learning how to move one's body to the rhythms of the music, I achieved an experience of solidarity and unity, a joyous feeling of being connected and in sync with others. Dancing fostered the feelings of trust and belonging that were fundamental to my participation in a community.

Related to this function of community building, another principle I learned through dancing is the recognition of individual talents. On the living room dance floor, every individual has the opportunity to shine, to be celebrated, and to belong to the group. Adults exhort children to participate in the dance, to demonstrate their talents, and encourage the timid or shy to join because she or he belongs. This signals that all present are special in one way or the other. Everybody has a chance to shine and everybody belongs in the group. It is not even essential that one have good rhythm, although to "dance in sync" with the music is highly appreciated and greatly supported. I observed adults encouraging children and learned to pass this on to my own children. I learned to enjoy watching people dance, which to this day is one of my favorite entertainments and a great way to learn about people. I learned to give room to anyone who had something to show when dancing.

These values of communal bonding and individual expression apply equally to people of all ages. My grandmother walked with painful care late in her life, but she could shed her years for a moment dancing with a graceful swing of her hip or a well-timed shake of her shoulders. At the same time, youngsters who have not yet mastered the rhythm of the dance steps are still applauded for their spirit. When my father-in-law first visited Puerto Rico and attended family gatherings in our house, he marveled at how comfortable teenage children were conversing with elders, very different from what he was used to seeing in the United States. One of the big reasons for this is that teenagers and elders dance with each other, engaging playfully in a game of rhythm, movement, and display that they all enjoy. We never had birthday parties that were just for five-year-old girls or eight-year-old boys; in our home everyone, from newborn to great-grandma, joined in the dancing when there was something to celebrate.

Dancing also taught me how to relate to men. In our culture, men view dancing as an opportunity to advance toward more intimate corporal relations, and as women we have to be aware of these advances and protect ourselves from improper male behavior, even from relatives or friends. Because partner dancing brings a female and a male body in close physical contact, and it is traditionally the job of the male to propose more intimacy, it is the female who decides how far to go. In dancing a woman develops a sense of self and personal security, a control over males in courtship that enhances self-esteem. The woman decides if the man deserves another dance according to his behavior on the dance floor.

Along with a sense of belonging and security, my experience of dancing has also helped me be a better leader. Dancing has given me a strong sense of self that has permitted me to teach others with security and enthusiasm, the same way I was taught to dance since I was two years old. This confidence in helping and teaching others has made me a more effective leader in all areas of my life and professional work.

My Children's Musical Experience

My children have grown up in Seattle, Washington, far from Santurce, Puerto Rico in a home where music and dancing is a frequent occasion. Even before my son Gabriel could walk he used to sit on the floor and push with his feet to spin round and round on his bottom when music played. My daughter Agueda took ballet classes for a while when she was little, but she got bored because dancing at home was more fun. They dance with us and they dance with each other (see Figure 17.1).

When other families come to our house for dinner or a party they dance, too, and for many of them it's one of the only places where parents and kids dance together. On Christmas Eve we have friends over to share good food and sing carols, and then, as I always did in Puerto Rico on *Noche Buena*, we roll up the carpets and dance to salsa music.

Figure 17.1: Babies dance with each other.

Occasional trips to Puerto Rico have also helped my children to understand and appreciate the importance of dancing. One Christmas when Agueda was five and Gabriel was three we spent a month in Puerto Rico, and I especially remember a party at the house of my friend Ligie where there was dancing. Agueda was dressed in a precocious purple pantsuit that her Titi (aunt) Angie had given her. She was already a graceful dancer, with an impeccable sense of rhythm, and my friends and family were amazed to watch her. She started with her father, but pretty soon she wore him out and moved on to other partners—me, my sister, Ligie, my friend Peri. I'll never forget the image of little Agueda standing there in the middle of the room in her purple pantsuit, sweating, looking around to see who was going to dance with her next.

Between dancing and speaking Spanish at home and attending a bilingual school in Seattle, Agueda and Gabriel have grown up feeling comfortable and proud of their Puerto Rican culture, for which I am so grateful. A few years ago they also had a chance to spend a half-year's sabbatical leave with us in Puerto Rico, where they attended school (sixth grade and fourth grade, respectively), studied in Spanish, and made new friends. At school dances they discovered that they knew how to dance salsa as well as or better than their classmates, and this helped them take a new pride in their dancing skills. Most of their friends were more into *reggaetón* than salsa, though, so they learned to dance *reggaetón*. This genre is some distance from the music of my generation, a mix of hip-hop and reggae, whose electronic effects would be hard to reproduce in a *rumbón de esquina*. But this music was still

Figure 17.2: Agueda dancing with her grandmother—*Que dicha!*

inseparably tied to social experience, as the kids practiced dance steps, sang along together, or challenged one another to recite the lyrics. Gabriel, especially, became attached to *reggaetón* as part of his Puerto Rican culture and social style. He has continued to listen to *reggaetón* since we returned to Seattle, and his favorite shirt is a tank top with the design of the Puerto Rican flag.

Music and dance have helped my children stay strongly connected to me, to my family, and to an experience of community that I cherish and try to hold on to. It may take a village to raise a child, and sometimes I am a little shocked at how different my children's world is from the one I remember as a child, but Agueda and Gabriel can dance happily with their grandmother (Figure 17.2). *Que dicha!* (What joy!)

CODA

So now it is Saturday afternoon in our Greenlake neighborhood in Seattle, Washington. Shannon is coaching Gabriel's soccer game and Agueda is at her soccer practice (if they had grown up in Puerto Rico they probably would have played baseball). I stay home to clean the house, turn on the CD player, and listen to the music of El Gran Combo de Puerto Rico. With vacuum in hand I begin singing and dancing to the glorious music, and mentally I travel between my homes in Santurce, Jardines de Caparra, and Seattle. Tears run down my cheeks, I sob, remembering and living this ever-recurring moment of connection with music that has sustained me for so long, especially in my home away from home. Once again in my living room with my salsa playing, I dance, I remember, I survive, I belong, I am happy.

ACKNOWLEDGMENTS

My deepest gratitude goes to my husband and principal editor, Shannon Dudley, who has devoted many hours to the editing of this chapter, and to my mother, Juanita Berríos, and my sister, Angie Berríos-Miranda, for their unbelievable memory.

REFERENCES

Barton, Hal. 2002. "The Challenges of Puerto Rican *Bomba*." In *Caribbean Dance: From Abakuá to Zouk*, edited by Susanna Sloat, 183–198. Gainesville: University of Florida Press.

Berríos-Miranda, Marisol. 1999. "The Significance of Salsa Music to National and Pan-Latino Identity." PhD diss., University of California, Berkeley.

Berríos-Miranda, Marisol. 2002. "Is Salsa a Musical Genre?" In *Situating Salsa: Global Markets and Local Meaning in Latin Popular Music*, edited by Lise Waxer, 23–50. New York: Routledge.

Berríos-Miranda, Marisol. 2003. "Con sabor a Puerto Rico: The Reception and Influence of Puerto Rican Salsa in Venezuela." Pp. 47–68 in *Musical Migrations: Trans-nationalism and Cultural Hybridity in Latin/o America*, edited by Frances Aparicio and Cándida F. Jáquez. New York: Palgrave McMillan.

Berríos-Miranda, Marisol. 2004. "Salsa Music as Expressive Liberation." *Journal of the Center for Puerto Rican Studies* 16 (2):158–173.

Berríos-Miranda, Marisol, and Shannon Dudley. 2009. "El Gran Combo, Cortijo, and the Musical Geography of Cangrejos/Santurce, Puerto Rico." *Caribbean Studies* 36 (2): 121–151.

Colón, Willie. 1972. *Asalto Navideño*. FANIA SLPF 399.

Colón, Willie. 1972. *Cosa Nuestra*. FANIA.

Cortijo y su Combo. 1955. *Cortijo y su Combo Invites You to Dance*. Seeco SCLP 9106.

Cortijo y su Combo. 1958. *Baile con Cortijo y su Combo*. Seeco SCCD-9130.

Cortijo y su Combo. n.d. *Fiesta Boricua*. Rumba 5519.

Damiani, Julio. 1997. "Santurce, Puerto Rico: Morfología urbana y estructura social de un suburbio 1894–1910." PhD diss., University of Puerto Rico.

El Gran Combo de Puerto Rico. 2004. *Aquí estamos y… ¡De verdad!* Sony Discos, 95481.

18

THE MUSICAL WORLDS OF ABORIGINAL CHILDREN AT BURRULULA AND DARWIN IN THE NORTHERN TERRITORY OF AUSTRALIA

ELIZABETH MACKINLAY

TRY to imagine that you are an Aboriginal child in the remote community of Burrulula in the southwest gulf region of the Northern Territory, Australia. Each day you wake up hungry, not sure if you will eat today, and watch the school bus drive past your house. You know from experience that the day ahead will mean sitting in a whitewashed classroom, learning about whitefella business, in a language and way of being that are not familiar to you. All of the messages you get remind you that you don't belong, and you decide in the same instant as the school bus beeps impatiently, that you are going to run and keep on running away from that whitefella place. You spend the day instead dodging the foul language and breath of the grog drinkers in the town camp; sitting and watching your grandmother play *coon can* (a card game, known as *conquian* elsewhere); getting growled at for making too much noise and humbugging for food; and listening to stereos, televisions, and portable boom boxes blasting the latest music hits on MTV or the nostalgic sounds of country and western music. The day passes and the dark of night comes. You huddle close to your grandmother to keep warm and safe, trying to block out the sounds of drunken people roaring with laughter and anger and desperately hoping for a brighter day tomorrow.

Imagine now you are someone different. You are a young Aboriginal boy who lives in Darwin but with family links back to Burrulula. You are "light-skinned" but feel at ease with your identity. Words like "ceremony," "dreaming,"[1] "traditional country," "native title," "land rights," and the "stolen generations" are part of your vocabulary. You've been to Burrulula many times; members of your Aboriginal family from Burrulula visit your house all of the time, and you've heard all of the old ladies sing in language a lot with your mum too. Your mum is a music teacher, your dad loves to play guitar, and there is music everywhere in your life. Today at school, you are dancing on stage with all of the other Indigenous kids at the weekly assembly. This past week you've been going to dance workshops with Deadly Darren, a hip and cool recent graduate from the NAISDA (National Aboriginal and Islander Skills Development Association) Dance College in Sydney, and have you've had an absolute blast grooving and dancing ("deadly" is used by many Aboriginal people to mean "excellent," "very good," "fantastic," similar to "wicked" used by other English speakers or "bad" by African Americans). A part of you isn't sure whether you really belong on stage; you don't look the same as the "darker-skinned" Aboriginal kids, don't normally hang out with any of them at recess, and you don't have to show up early to school just to eat breakfast like some of them do. You know you are different from them and it makes you feel…shame. You are torn between wanting to hide yourself away and forget about your Aboriginal identity and getting up on stage to groove proudly exactly as you are—just an ordinary kid with an Aboriginal dad and a white mum.

Imagine now you are a dark-skinned Aboriginal child at an urban school in Darwin. You know you are Aboriginal because your skin is dark, your mum and dad are both Indigenous, and you have a huge extended family with lots of grannies, aunties, uncles, and cousins. Your friends at school are mostly Indigenous and you take part in all of the Indigenous-focused educational and extracurricular programs at school. Your family is proud of who they are, but sometimes you are not really sure what that means, especially when teachers and others around you keep talking to you about your country, ancestors, and language. You don't know where your family is from, what your clan is called, or even if you have an Aboriginal name. You decide that it doesn't matter; those traditions are for the old people, not for your generation.

These three contexts have something important to say about the musical, cultural, and "raced" worlds of Aboriginal children today. They are used deliberately to demonstrate that life for Indigenous Australian children is a sometimes happy, sometimes uneasy, mix of all three contexts as they try to sustain a strong and positive sense of self, family, and community amid a society that continually seeks to marginalize, dominate, and silence them. Recognizing the shifting nature of Aboriginal identities in contemporary Australian life and the dynamic relationship between Indigeneity, music, and place, this chapter presents two case studies: the musical lives and experiences of Yanyuwa and Garrwa children living in the remote Aboriginal community at Burrulula in the southwest gulf of Carpentaria, and the musical worlds of urban Aboriginal children in Darwin. Aboriginal children in Australia negotiate the tensions and flow in, across, and between their Indigenous identities and mainstream Australia, and this is lived, experienced, and reflected in their musical cultures.

LITTLE CHILDREN ARE SACRED: CONTEXTUALIZING THE LIVES OF ABORIGINAL CHILDREN IN THE NORTHERN TERRITORY

"The Aboriginal people are likely to disappear within a generation: A report called *Little Children Are Sacred* highlights the blight of alcoholism and child abuse in Australia," writes Sturcke (2007). Commissioned by the Northern Territory government, the inquiry was undertaken by Rex Wild QC (Queen's Counsel) and Pat Anderson, an Indigenous woman well known for her work in Indigenous health and well-being. The inquiry sought to investigate the level of child sexual abuse in Aboriginal communities in the Northern Territory and to suggest measures to protect Indigenous children. Speaking publicly about the "Little Children Are Sacred" report, Wild and Anderson comment, "Put simply, the cumulative effects of poor health, alcohol, drug abuse, gambling, pornography, unemployment, poor education and housing and general disempowerment lead inexorably to family and other violence and then on to sexual abuse of men and women and, finally, of children" (in Sturcke 2007). Their words take me back immediately to a conversation I had with two young girls at Burrulula almost ten years ago while we were out bush digging for yams. Lucy was limping and when I asked her if she was alright, she replied, "Yeah, Mum flogged me on the knee with a *nulla nulla* (hard wooden fighting stick) a few weeks back and it's all swelled up." I looked down and saw the painful swelling and bruising around her knee. The bruises didn't stop there though, they continued right up her skinny leg, across her bony back and onto her thin arms. Lucy saw me looking at her and nodded, "That's from Mum too." Jenny, who had been quiet until now, jokingly pushed her cousin aside, trying to make light of the conversation. "That's nothin' *banji*! Check out the scars on my *binji* (stomach) here!" I watched in horror as the two girls spent the next half an hour comparing bruises, scars, old injuries, and wounds that had all been inflicted upon them by family.

The inquiry found that child sexual abuse is serious, widespread, and often unreported in both urban and remote settings. Wild and Anderson maintain,

> The Inquiry has always accepted the assertion that sexual assault of children is not acceptable in Aboriginal culture...any more than it is in European or mainstream society. But there is a major difference between the two branches of society. A breakdown of Aboriginal culture has been noted by many commentators. A number of underlying causes are said to explain the present state of both town and remote communities. Excessive consumption of alcohol is variously described as the cause or result of poverty, unemployment, lack of education, boredom and overcrowded and inadequate housing. The use of other drugs and petrol sniffing can be added to these. Together, they lead to excessive violence. In the worst case scenario it leads to sexual abuse of children. (2007: 12)

The report paints a bleak picture of what childhood is like for Aboriginal children growing up in the Northern Territory, and perhaps what makes the whole situation even worse is that this is not the first such inquiry into family violence in Aboriginal communities. I begin to count them in my head: Bolger (1991), Mow (1992), Aboriginal Women's Task Force and the Aboriginal Justice Council (Western Australia) (1995), Office of Women's Policy (Northern Territory) (1996), Aboriginal and Torres Strait Islander Women's Task Force on Violence, (Queensland) (1999), Blagg (1999), Memmott (2001), Gordon, Hallahan, and Henry (2002), Aboriginal and Torres Strait Islander Social Justice Commissioner (2006), and Rogers (2006). Now we have Wild and Anderson (2007) to add to the long list.[2]

I turn back to the newspaper, wanting to believe that something has changed, but phrases such as "this deeply disturbing issue," "great pain and unhappiness," and "not enough has been done" begin to blur together on the page as social commentators, politicians, human rights advocates, and Indigenous activists from all over the country buy into the game of naming, shaming, and blaming. These kinds of descriptions and framings of Aboriginal children's lives have flooded the media, research agendas, and community meetings for more than twenty years, and it is hard to find counternarratives. I become lost in my own thoughts about the many Aboriginal children I know, including my own children, and what their lives as children are like. Without doubt, there is not one Aboriginal child in the Northern Territory who is not touched by violence, poverty, and ill health. For some children this script is the dominant scene of their daily life, and for others it remains hidden in the background some distance away. I drop my head into my hands and sigh deeply. Part of the problem is that there is very little research that reports on something other than poor health, child abuse and neglect, or poor educational achievement in relation to Aboriginal children. How on earth am I going to write about Aboriginal children and stay positive when this is what life is like for many children in the Northern Territory? I am torn between wanting to "say it like it is" and "wearing my rose-colored glasses" to paint a prettier and more palatable picture. I realize that I am terribly confused and not at all sure of what I am going to say in my chapter, and all I can hope is that I can at least say *something* about the worlds of the Aboriginal children I know and love at Burrulula and in Darwin.

I realize I have not yet considered the important body of work by ethnomusicologists in relation to Aboriginal children's worlds. For many Indigenous Australian peoples, the tape recordings and field notes of early ethnographers are sometimes the only remaining records of Aboriginal performance culture. These "paper songs and frozen assets," as R. Moyle (1998) once described them, become the bones from which the flesh of songs can find new life for Aboriginal communities today. I immediately turn to the work of the grandmother of Australian Aboriginal ethnomusicology, Catherine Ellis. I can remember my PhD supervisor and mentor, recalling with a huge smile on her face traditional songs made by and for Aboriginal children in the Western Desert, in particular the Andagarinja children's bullock *corroboree* (see Ellis and Ellis 1970). She described this open and public ceremony as "pantomimic," with children variously playing the roles of both human and animal characters, and discussed the potential of such a performance for musical development. In 1969, Margaret Kartomi (1980, 1981, 1999) visited the Pitjantjatjara Aboriginal community at Yalata in South Australia and concluded that children are not small adults but rather have unique musical attitudes and preferences of their own. She wrote, "The typical sound of children at play is a rather chesty, forceful sound, characterized by ragged entries, uneven texture, energetic and even raucous dynamics, and a vigorous animated atmosphere. Children's music is a continual process of change [and] creativity is an ever-present factor" (1999: 71).

Academic literature remained silent on Aboriginal children's musical play practices until the recent work by Kathryn Marsh (2002) appeared. Marsh undertook an ethnographic study of Warumungu, Jingili, and Mutpurra Aboriginal children's music in two Aboriginal communities in the Northern Territory in 2001. Significantly, Marsh's work is situated within, rather than in denial of, the context of colonization and those "social forces which have irrevocably changed the lives" of Aboriginal people, and it reflects on her own role as neocolonial music educator. Marsh's research work and writing attempts to describe the situation as "it really is," and I recognize the hope that she holds for changing the transmission process of traditional and popular songs from one generation of Aboriginal people to the next to become "one which goes both ways" between nonAboriginal and Aboriginal culture (2002: 11). Following in the footsteps of Marsh, I would like to also "bear public witness" (hooks 2003: 116) to the social, cultural, and musical worlds of the Aboriginal children who enter in and out of my own, so as to "engender hope" (hooks 2003: 116) that little children always hold a sacred place in our communities.

KEEPING SONGS IN THEIR MOUTHS: MUSIC AND CHILDREN AT BURRULULA

We sat underneath the shade of a mango tree at the Sandridge, an outstation located on Yanyuwa traditional country approximately thirty km west of the remote town of Burrulula in the southwest gulf country of the Northern Territory. The sun was no longer high in the sky, but the afternoon shadows had not yet lengthened to usher in the dark night. I sat and listened to my husband's maternal grandmothers Nancy and Linda McDinny talk in and around the stories of their lives as selves, sisters, singers, and strong women in their community. I have been working with Nancy, Linda, and other Aboriginal women from Burrulula since 1994, and my relationship with them interweaves my love of music with my family and my academic life. I was interviewing Nancy and Linda as part of an Australian Institute of Aboriginal and Torres Strait Islander Studies project called "Big Women from Burrulula" in association with the Papulu Apparr-Kari Language Centre at Burrulula. During the filming process, many women we worked with chose to tell aspects of their life stories, experiences, and knowledge through song. They spoke often about how much things had changed—even in their short lifetime—in relation to the ways they were taught to perform the songs, dances, and ceremonies of their Yanyuwa and Garrwa cultures and the ways that the current generation is educated about such things. At times a sadness so deep it could only be experienced as grief colored their words as they thought of the songs, the dances, and the ceremonies that—for a set of very complex reasons linked to the capacity of Indigenous peoples to maintain and nurture their cultures in a colonized world—their grandchildren would never experience or know. In our interview, however, Nancy and Linda asserted very strongly that one of their main concerns as Yanyuwa/Garrwa women was to teach their young children about song, dance, and culture. Nancy proudly told us how all of her children and those who had grown up at her father's outstation nearby had "proper *mingkin* (good) legs," they were not "shame" to paint up and dance, knowing how to sing and dance for their country and culture.

Nancy and Linda spoke passionately about the centrality of song and dance to their lives as Aboriginal women, as Aboriginal people, and as an Indigenous Australian community, but they also told of their desperate struggle to teach their children and keep culture strong amid the many obstacles that face people in their community (see Mackinlay and Bradley 2003). Without wanting to paint too bleak a picture but also not wanting to "whitewash" how things are, Burrulula is not unlike many remote Indigenous communities where a family of ten live in a tin shed of two rooms; where it is cheaper to buy a bucket of french fries than to purchase one apple; where health problems such as diabetes, heart disease, obesity, and tuberculosis affect everyone in some way. In a place like Burrulula, alcohol and substance abuse dramatically affect the quality of life for young and old people; domestic violence against women, men, and children has become a normal fact of life; and a community of around a thousand Indigenous people attend a funeral at least three times a month. It is this complex set of issues that negatively influences the attendance of children at school, but it is more than that. For some time now in Burrulula, the Aboriginal community has experienced increasing cultural dislocation from the school. The languages of the four main cultural groups in the region—Yanyuwa, Garrwa, Mara, and Kudanji—are not currently taught at the school. The inclusion of senior women and men as people with authority and knowledge of value has ceased, so the school is not seen as an educational space that is culturally inclusive. Indeed, the entire township of Burrulula privileges whitefellas and whitefella business.

"Nah, *ngabuji* (paternal grandmother)," she tells me quietly. "I don't go to white-bala school—me just stay home la camp with family. When that bus bin come to pick us up, we bin scatter into the bushes and wait tillim all gone." I look down at her and cheekily reply, "Yeah, except on the days when you've got a *mutaka* (car) and you can come out bush for hunting with me!" We are sitting quietly together on the banks of a lagoon, some sixty km out of Burrulula. It is midday and the water is cool. Our feet are knee deep in mud and we are playing dodge ball with the tiny fish swimming in and out of our toes. "What im that song you bin singim, *ngabuji*? Tharrun on the CD in the Toyota?" I stop and look across at my granddaughter. "What you mean? Beyoncé? Or Snoop Doggy?" Rosie looks at me and raises her eyebrows. "Well, I don't know, *ngabuji*." I reply, "Do you want to hum some of it for me?" She bursts into a fit of giggles. "I can't sing im, *ngabuji*! But you can—I bin listen to you sing all the time!" Our shared laughter dies down and we are silent for a moment before Rosie shyly asks, "You reckon you could teach me some songs, *ngabuji*? You know, the ones you bin learn im those other kids in school?" I pause, trying to think of the songs she is talking about, and then it dawns on me. Rosie wants me to teach some of the clapping and singing games I use in my music education classes in Darwin. I smile back at her and take her hands in mine. "Sure, *ngabuji*! Stand up now and let's go!"

Rosie holds my hands and we walk around in a large circle as I sing, "Circle to the left, my friend, circle to the left, my friend." My sister Jemima (Rosie's other paternal grandmother)[3] begins to stir from her sleep and she sits up to watch us dance. When we have finished she calls out excitedly, "Yu! Proper deadly one that song!" Rosie grins from ear to ear. I watch the exchange of pride and pleasure between Jemima and Rosie, and all of a sudden an idea grabs me. "*Baba* (sister)?" I ask Jemima. "Can you help me translate those words into Yanyuwa?" Jemima squints her eyes as she thinks, "Mmm, like this I think; '*a-lukuluku aya, a-lukuluka aya a-lukuluku a-lukuluku aya mara*.' Go on, try im like that." Rosie and I join hands again and carefully keep our eyes locked on to each other's face so that we can remember the Yanyuwa words. We are trying our best to get all of the pronunciation right and to make sure the language matches the melody and the moves we are making. We make it to the end and hug one another in congratulations of our achievement. I look over at Jemima for approval. It is then that I notice she is crying. I rush over to her. "I'm sorry *baba*! I didn't mean to upset you! I won't put the Yanyuwa there again in that song!" Jemima shakes her head and sniffles, "No *baba*, that's not it. To hear my *ngabuji* sing in language; that's it, that's the song. Can you makim some more for us?" Rosie, Jemima, and I spend the rest of the afternoon putting Yanyuwa language to English songs, laughing at both the ease and awkwardness it takes to make the cross-cultural translation. Afternoon shadows begin to fall and we decide it's time to head back to town. We all crawl back into the Toyota to begin the long drive home. As the car rattles along the corrugated dirt road, I can hear Jemima softly singing the songs of her mothers, grandmothers, and other ancestors beside me—the dreaming songs of her childhood and those of her life as a senior Yanyuwa woman today. Rosie smiles as she listens to her grandmother sing and whispers to me, "I love it, *ngabuji*, when she sings like that."

Yanyuwa women, like Jemima, do everything they can to ensure that their children and grandchildren know the songs of their dreaming, their country, and their ancestors. When asked, Jemima and other senior Aboriginal people provide "culture" lessons at the Burrulula School, children are taken on excursions out to sites of cultural significance, and girls and boys participate in both public and restricted ceremony, whenever and wherever they can. However, it is not easy, and at times the obstacles seem insurmountable. Access to vehicles and money for food and fuel is scarce. Access to classrooms and an hour in the school time-table is limited and wavering and dependent upon the political commitment of the school principal to Aboriginal education. The rate of rapid change in a place like Burrulula as a direct result of the ongoing devastation and traumatic effects of colonization on the Aboriginal community in this region cannot be underestimated. Early contact with white people was violent, and recollections of shootings, beatings, murders, and the brutal treatment of Yanyuwa, Garrwa, Mara, and Kudanji people remain within living memory today. The increased presence of white people in the southwest gulf region from the turn of the twentieth century culminated in the "rounding up" of Aboriginal people from their traditional country and relocation into the township of Burrulula (Baker 1999; Roberts 2005). This government-sanctioned removal of Aborigines from their traditional homelands during the 1950s was carried out by the welfare branch under the Welfare Ordinance Act (1956). The stated policy of the welfare branch was that "aborigines in the Northern Territory... will become indistinguishable from other members of the Australian community in manner of life, standards of living, occupations, and participation in community affairs" (in Baker 1999: 95). Aboriginal people at Burrulula call this era in the history of white contact "welfare times"—seen by many Yanyuwa people today as the major catalyst to irreparable social and cultural change. Before her death, senior Yanyuwa performer Mudinji a-Karrakayn Isaac often remarked, "We came into Borroloola [*sic*] welfare time, we sat down and people died... *kanu-wingka, kanu-yibanda kulu kaninyamba-mirra* [translating]" (in Baker 1999: 95). The grief and despair associated with such deep and traumatic cultural loss and upheaval is evident in her words and reflects a sense of powerlessness. Yanyuwa, Garrwa, Mara, and Kudanji people were without choice and were completely reliant on the white government for survival—they had to work for white people, talk the language of white people, and learn to become just like white people. While at one level Burrulula became the major and permanent center of life for Yanyuwa, Garrwa, Mara, and Kudanji people, a number of very important things were lost, "things such as close and active relationships with country, the full articulation of Law and its maintenance in regards to human and non-human kin... certain genres of performance either ceased, such as some of the very sacred ceremonies, or secular song compositions of the men" (Mackinlay and Bradley 2003: 231).

It is within this context of violent, traumatic, and enforced change, the cultural breakdown emphasized in the "Little Children Are Sacred" report, that Yanyuwa children's musical worlds then must be viewed. Jemima, her granddaughter Rosie, their family, and the entire Aboriginal community at Burrulula fight daily to survive against the contemporary realities of historical legacy, social upheaval, and cultural fracturing and dispossession. Children like Rosie struggle to draw links between the songs her grandmother sings while out bush with the harsh reality of town camp living where people are hungry, poor, and unhealthy. A child finds it hard to see the value in the songs of her grandmothers when all of the people around her in positions of power—the white teachers at her school, the white people working at the ration shop, the white authorities from the government who fly in and out—place little value on the song knowledge her grandmother holds. Children like Rosie want to be able to sing like her grandmother in language, to dance to the rhythms of her ancestors on country, but the contexts for her to learn from Jemima according to Yanyuwa systems of teaching, learning, and knowledge are few and far between. The gap between her Yanyuwa Aboriginal culture and mainstream Australian culture sometimes seems too wide to even contemplate closing, but children like Rosie are unsure which side they belong to.

A Snapshot in Time: Darwin Mob Talk about Music in Their Lives

I would like you to meet Jack, Taina, Zetta, and Sage—four Indigenous children at a primary school in the northern suburbs of Darwin. School hasn't started yet and they are sitting together in the classroom, which doubles as a space to run the breakfast program at 7:00 in the morning for Indigenous children at the school. This morning they are eating pancakes, and all four are quiet as they eat. Sage is the first to finish and begins talking. In this narrative, the children's voices are in plain text and my ethnographic or interpretative voice appears in italics. Pseudonyms have been used for the name of the primary school and also the name of each Aboriginal child represented in this chapter to protect the children's identity and confidentiality.

SAGE: So how old are you all? You don't look the same age as me. I'm eleven and I'm in Grade 5. *(Sage is new to the school and interested in finding out where everyone fits.)*

ZETTA: Well, I'm in the same grade as you but my age is ten.

JOEL: That's funny. I'm the same age as you but I'm in Grade 4.

TAINA: I'm eight and right now I'm in Grade 3.

SAGE: Where did you say you were from Taina?

TAINA: Well I grew up in Darwin; I was born in Darwin *(Taina pauses)*. Every holidays we go to my country in Thursday Island...we don't really go down south much.

SAGE: Hey, what about that? I grew up in Darwin too! But my mum's family are from Perth.

ZETTA: *(She has been sitting quietly thinking.)* I *think* I'm from Queensland; I'm not really sure.

JACK: Not me! I'm all the way from Alice Springs—my Nana's family are in Katherine.

SAGE: Well, we're going back to Perth soon, and we will be down there for a whole year.

ZETTA: When my dad gets back from East Timor, we're going back to Cairns or Townsville, I think.

TAINA: We've got family in Cairns too! We go down to Cairns to go swimming in the open sea, and it's really fun because we get to meet people there.

SAGE: My family is a bit different to most others *(Sage pauses)*. I have a disabled brother. He is epileptic, he's blind, and he's autistic. That's why I like music—it calms me down. It blocks out all of the other sounds—my house is pretty noisy. My dad screams at my mother. My brother just screams, flaps his arms, hits his head against the wall, bangs his head, and breaks the wall.

Everyone is very quiet as they listen to Sage's story. As I look at Sage, I can see an incredible amount of pain and grief on his face. His words are matter-of-fact, but I can sense the reality is much more.

SAGE: Music—mostly pop and rock—lets me escape from all of that for a little while. I reckon I listen to it at least two or three hours a day.

ZETTA:*(She nods in understanding and agreement.)* Same. I listen to music about that many hours—some in the morning, and some in the afternoon.

TAINA: You're just like me! Except I'm only allowed to listen to music in the afternoon when it's time for dinner and my mum is making tea. I just lie in the room, put the air conditioner on, and listen to the music and read my books and then I have dinner.

JACK: You're lucky! I only listen to it on Thursdays.

ZETTA: What? Are you serious? Just on Thursdays?

JACK: Yep. Only on Thursday on TV.

SAGE: What?!!

JACK: You know, on the music channel, but then I have a CD player in my room.

TAINA: We don't. We only have one that we all share, and it stays out on the patio.

SAGE: What! You've got a CD player that you share?!!! I have an iPod docking station, which has big speakers, and a white iPod Nano.

ZETTA: I've got an iPod too! It's a little pink one and I get my music for it from the internet with an iTunes credit card.

SAGE: I get my mum to get it for me from Dick Smith's or JB Hi-Fi. I've got some cool bands on my iPod—mostly rock and a bit of pop. I've got the Veronicas and Kasey Chambers is on my iPod.

ZETTA: But she's country!

TAINA: My mum and dad listen to country music all of the time. Slim Dusty, Billy Bob—I guess I don't mind him too much.

ZETTA: I hate country! I love bands like 50 Cent, Akon, Flo Rida, Rhianna, Beyoncé, and Taylor Swift—I think that's about it.

I smile as I listen to the children speak—I used to feel the same way about my parents liking for "country" music. What surprises me though is that the country music they are talking about is whitefella country music. Slim Dusty is one of Australia's most famous country singers, and others such as Tex Morton are familiar names in remote communities. As documented by Walker (2000) and Dunbar-Hall and Gibson (2004), country music—whether by black or white performers—holds a special place in many Aboriginal and Torres Strait Islander people's lives because of its association with the bush and the outback.

> JACK: Are you sure?!!!
> ZETTA: Yep! They're funky; they've got heaps of beats and SO good to listen to! They make me feel all kind of—tuney! *(She giggles.)*
> JACK: My mum loves country music too. I don't like rap though—I listen to pop and old rock bands like Kiss and Skyhooks.

I wonder what kind of rap Jack is talking about—does he mean African American rap or Indigenous rap? I know that many Indigenous children in Australia are big fans of American rap artists—the children at Burrulula even have a gang named after Tupac Shakur! I am more familiar with Skyhooks (the famous 1970s Australian rock band) and Kiss (the glam rock band of the same era). However, Jack's liking for their music tells a story about the limited access to contemporary music by many Indigenous families then and now.

> TAINA: I don't like Slim Dusty, but Hannah Montana is kind of country, and I like her. I even still have some Wiggles CDs on my shelf!

Everyone bursts into loud and raucous laughter. The Wiggles are a famous Australian children's music group that formed in Sydney in 1991. Marketed as "your child's first rock band," the Wiggles have achieved international success through their children's music albums, videos, television series, and concert appearances.

> SAGE: *(He is keen to change the subject.)* I play the flute. I started two or three years ago, and I am still only up to my Grade 1 exam.
> ZETTA: I am going to learn the violin next year, 'cause I have got one at home but I just need to learn how to learn it.
> JACK: Where'd you get it from?
> ZETTA: Um we got it at a garage sale in Townsville. It probably only cost about $50 or so and it was just lying there so …
> SAGE: So?
> ZETTA: Mum just thought it was a good thing to buy me so I can learn something on it. I've tried to play but not really…it's not really working out. I probably need a couple of lessons with someone.

Zetta is a little bit hazy on the fine details of how she might actually learn the violin. She may be able to access violin lessons through the Northern Territory Music School program and its involvement in her school or privately—but neither of these options is free.

> TAINA: Next year I am learning guitar, and when I went to Thursday Island I learnt how to play tapping sticks. My Nana has some old ones and my aunty—because

she is full Aboriginal—she makes them out of wood and we just play it. My sister Hayley uses the old hard ones, and the ones I use are soft ones.

The tapping sticks Taina is referring to are one of the most common percussive instruments used in Aboriginal performance traditions across Australia. First documented by Alice Moyle (1981) in her well-known publication Aboriginal Sound Instruments, *tapping, "concussion," or clapsticks are made from hard wood (such as Mulga wood) so as to produce a clear resonant sound. Their primary use is as accompaniment to song and in some areas of Indigenous Australia to didgeridoo playing.*

ZETTA: You mean like traditional music?
TAINA: (*Nods*) Sort of.
ZETTA: Yeah, I heard some on TV—there was a didgeridoo and people singing in language.
JACK: It would be cool to be able to do that. I don't listen to Aboriginal music, but I heard some in Tennant Creek. They were men singing in language. They were dancing painted up, and they had grasses here (*He points to his legs*) and they had feathers. (*Jack points around his head.*)

Tennant Creek is the fifth largest town in the Northern Territory of Australia, servicing an enormous region made up of million-acre cattle stations and Aboriginal communities. The Warumungu people know Tennant Creek as "Jurnkurakurr," and the town is situated in the middle of the Northern Territory on the traditional country of Warumungu, Warlpiri, Kaytetye, and Alyawarra Aboriginal people. Approximately 3,000 people live in Tennant Creek today, and the Warumungu, Warlpiri, Kaytetye, and Alyawarra communities are well known for their Aboriginal arts and culture practice. Julalikari Arts, Nyinkka Nyunyu Aboriginal Arts and Culture Centre, and Papulu Aparr-Kari Language Centre are the three main organizations in town that support Indigenous arts, language, and cultural traditions.

SAGE: Were they singing in English?
JACK: No, in Aboriginal.
ZETTA: I wish I knew more about Aboriginal music.

The others turn to look at her.

ZETTA: Well, it's just that I could feel more proud if I did.
JACK: Like when we did those dance workshops with my Uncle Darren. When I was dancing, I felt like those mob in Tennant—they way they looked when they were dancing—happy.
SAGE: Well, my music says nothing about me as an Aborigine. I don't even know how to really talk about myself as an Aborigine. I know it comes from my grandfather—my mum's dad—but my mum doesn't know a lot about him because she was little when he died. She was like six.
TAINA: (*She looks at Sage, confused, and then speaks strongly*). I am Aboriginal mostly and only a tiny bit of Thursday Island. I love that song "Taba Naba"—I've got it on CD. It's about the beach and everyone having fun on the beach. It makes me think of home.
ZETTA: What about Jessica Mauboy? She's a Darwin girl!

Everyone nods.

> TAINA: Oh, I love her! I reckon she's deadly!
>
> Zetta: She's got a good voice.
>
> SAGE: Have you met her?
>
> ZETTA: Oh, there was one time a couple of years ago and she was at Casuarina *(a local shopping center)*. There was a big lineup so some people had to stay downstairs, and we went up to get some T-shirts and that, and we went up there and she gave us a CD and signed it.
>
> SAGE: Cool!
>
> JACK: If I could do something with music, I'd like to be a singer.
>
> TAINA: I'd like to write songs. I would write about me going somewhere or about a girl going out somewhere in the open and listening to the waves in the sea.

Although Taina is not speaking about a uniquely Indigenous form or tradition of song writing, the topic of her song reminds me of many Indigenous songs I have heard that are about a longing for the sea and saltwater. The song "My Island Home," written by George Rrurrambu and made famous by Torres Strait Islander performer Christine Anu at the opening ceremony of the Sydney Olympic Games in the year 2000, is one such example (see Barney 2005).

> ZETTA: I'd love to hear that song if you write it one day.

The warning music for school to start begins to chime. It's a "muzak" version of Tchaikovsky's 1812 Overture. The four children scrape their chairs backward as they stand up to go to class. Sage waves at the others as they leave the room and sings out, "I wish they'd play some Jessica Mauboy on the gammon PA system instead of this crappy music!"

A SUBJECTIVE SOUNDSCAPE: ABORIGINAL CHILDREN AND THEIR MUSICAL WORLDS

In this chapter I have attempted to provide a snapshot of the musical lives of Aboriginal children in two sites in the Northern Territory of Australia today—the remote Aboriginal community of Burrulula in the southwest gulf region and a primary school in the urban landscape of Darwin. It has been a difficult conversation, partly because I am concerned to paint as accurate a picture as possible while also acknowledging that it is not perhaps the kind of ethnographic portrait that readers expect or, indeed, want to see. The picture presented here is also smudged because of my own positioning as a non Indigenous academic, albeit one with close family ties and relationships with Indigenous peoples in both places, and further blurring occurs when the diversity of Indigenous life histories, experiences, and contemporary realities is taken into consideration. From this discussion, however, there are some things we do know about Aboriginal children's musical worlds. The ongoing conflict of trying to be Aboriginal in a mainstream society that is *not* Aboriginal is one of the biggest challenges that children in Burrulula and Darwin face. Their musical choices, activities, and understandings in many ways reflect this tension. Rosie wants to be able to sing in Yanyuwa like her grandmother, but she is not sure about the relevance of a tradition that sits on the margins of the mainstream culture that dominates her life. For now, both Yanyuwa musical traditions and mainstream popular music cultures can be heard in her Aboriginal soundscape, but she is not sure what it will mean for her as a Yanyuwa child when one drowns out the other. Sage, Jack, Zetta, and Taina are urban Aboriginal kids and the music of their worlds is the "same but different"⁴ from the sounds that Rosie hears. Their location in a large city, with greater access to facilities and technology through schools, community organizations, and council services, opens up a wide array of opportunities to experience an equally broad selection of music: iPods, CD players, and MTV are major performers on their musical stage, and their movement between locations across Australia adds diversity to their musical experiences. One of the common threads in the narratives of Aboriginal children's musical worlds highlighted in this chapter relates to their identity as Indigenous Australians—an identity that is highly politicized, contested, and debated in academic and public settings. Rosie, Sage, Jack, Zetta, and Taina all struggle with the same question: should they be "shame" to be Aboriginal or should they be proud? Should they listen to Aboriginal music because that's who they are? Or should they listen to the music that has meaning for them in their lives as children? Do these necessarily have to be different, and what would happen if they weren't? The answers to these questions are unknown, but what is certain is that all five children dream of a world where they, too, can be "deadly" as Aboriginal people, proud of themselves, their families, their musical heritage, and the music they choose to listen to.

Acknowledgments

I would like to extend my heartfelt thanks to the five Indigenous Australian children, my family, and my friends who shared their lives, thoughts, and ideas about music with me and whose voices I have written into this chapter. You are my inspiration for continuing to research and write about children's understandings and experiences in and around music, and working together I hope that we can change the world.

Notes

1 For Aboriginal people, "the Dreaming" refers to the creation period (a time beyond human memory), when ancestral beings are said to have spread across the continent, creating human society and its rules for living, language, and customs and laws as they went (Pascoe 2008: 10).
2 Soon after publication of the "Little Children Are Sacred" report, the federal government formulated "Northern Territory National Emergency Response 2007" (also

referred to as "the intervention"), which put in place a number of measures to address the claims of sexual abuse and neglect. However, the "intervention" has been heavily criticized by non Indigenous and Indigenous activists, academics, and observers as an imperial and neocolonial imposition on the rights of Indigenous people to be self-controlling and self-determining. Four years after the implementation of the intervention, early reports suggest the levels of sexual abuse and neglect appear to remain largely unchanged and have indeed increased for many Indigenous children (e.g., Jones 2011).

3 The Yanyuwa kinship system is often referred to as "classificatory" by non Indigenous people and is based on affiliation by blood, marriage, spiritual, and other social practices to moieties, semimoieties or clans, and subsection or skins. In everyday life, this means people will usually have more than one relative of any one kind, which explains why Rosie can have more than one "paternal" grandmother. For further information, see Kirton and Timothy (1977).

4 The phrase "same but different" is something that a senior Yanyuwa woman used frequently to help me understand the equality within differences across boundaries that the West assumes to be oppositional and hierarchical.

REFERENCES

Aboriginal and Torres Strait Islander Social Justice Commissioner. 2006. *Ending Family Violence and Abuse in Aboriginal and Torres Strait Islander Communities— Key Issue: An Overview Paper of Research and Findings by the Human Rights and Equal Opportunity Commission, 2001–2006.* Canberra, Australia: Human Rights and Equal Opportunity Commission.

Aboriginal and Torres Strait Islander Women's Task Force on Violence, Queensland. 1999. "The Aboriginal and Torres Strait Islander Women's Task Force on Violence report." Brisbane, Australia: Department of Aboriginal and Torres Strait Islander Policy.

Aboriginal Women's Task Force and the Aboriginal Justice Council. 1995. *A Whole Healing Approach to Family Violence.* Perth, Australia: Aboriginal Justice Council.

Baker, R. 1999. *Land Is Life: From Bush to Town, the Story of the Yanyuwa People.* Sydney, Australia: Allen and Unwin.

Barney, K. 2005. "Celebration or Cover Up: 'My Island Home', Australian National Identity and the Spectacle of Sydney 2000." In *Aesthetics and Experience in Music Performance,* edited by E. Mackinlay, D. Collins, and S. Owens, 141–150. Newcastle, UK: Cambridge Scholars Press.

Blagg, H. 1999. *It Breaks All Law: Crisis Intervention in Aboriginal Family Violence.* Perth, Australia: Domestic Violence Prevention Unit.

Bolger, A. 1991. "Aboriginal Women and Violence: A Report for the Criminology Research Council and the Northern Territory Commissioner of Police." Casuarina, Australia: Australian National University, North Australia Research Unit.

Dunbar-Hall, P., and Gibson, C. 2004. *Deadly Sounds, Deadly Places: Contemporary Aboriginal Music in Australia.* Sydney, Australia: University of New South Wales Press.

Ellis, C. 2004. *The Ethnographic I: A Methodological Novel about Autoethnography.* Walnut Creek, MA: AltaMira Press.

Ellis, C. J., and A. M. Ellis. 1970. *Andagarinja: Children's Bullock Corroboree.* Port Moresby, Papua New Guinea: Papua Pocket Poets.

Gordon, S., K. Hallahan, and D. Henry. 2002. *Putting the Picture Together: Inquiry into Response by Government Agencies to Complaints of Family Violence and Child Abuse in Aboriginal Communities.* Perth, Australia: Department of Premier and Cabinet.

hooks, b. 2003. *Teaching Community: A Pedagogy of Hope.* New York: Routledge.

Jones, G. 2011. "Aboriginal Intervention Plan Failing, Report Finds." *The Daily Telegraph.* Accessed June 29, 2011. http://www.dailytelegraph.com.au/news/national/aboriginal-intervention-plan-fails/story-e6freuzr-1226080221686.

Kartomi, M. 1980. Childlikeness in Play Songs—A Case Study among the Pitjantjatjara at Yalata, South Australia. *Miscellenea Musicologica* 11: 172–214.

Kartomi, M. 1981. "Songs of Some Aboriginal Children's Play Ceremonies." *Studies in Music* 15: 1–35.

Kartomi, M. 1999. "Play Songs by Children and Their Educational Implications." *Aboriginal History* 23: 61–71.

Kirton, J., and N. Timothy. 1977. Yanyuwa Concepts Relating to "Skin." *Oceania* 47 (2): 320–322.

Mackinlay, E. 2001. "'Same but Different': Musical Behaviour, Gender Roles, and the Transference of Power in Yanyuwa Society." *Kulele: Occasional Papers on Pacific Music and Dance* 3: 65–78.

Mackinlay, E., and J. Bradley. 2003. "Many Songs, Many Voices, and Many Dialogues: A Conversation about Yanyuwa Performance Practice in a Remote Aboriginal Community." *Rural Society* 13 (3): 228–243.

Marsh, K. 2002. "Observations on a Case Study of Song Transmission and Preservation in Two Aboriginal Communities: Dilemmas of a Neo-Colonialist in the Field." *Research Studies in Music Education* 19: 4–13.

Memmott, P., R. Stacy, C. Chambers, and C. Keys. 2001. *Violence in Indigenous Communities: Full Report.* Barton, Australia: Crime Prevention Branch, Attorney-General's Department.

Mow, K. E. 1992. *Tjunparni: Family Violence in Indigenous Australia: A Report and Literature Review for the Aboriginal and Torres Strait Islander Studies Commission.* Canberra, Australia: ATSIC.

Moyle, A. M. 1981. *Aboriginal Sound Instruments,* recorded and edited by Alice M. Moyle. Canberra, Australia: Australian Institute of Aboriginal Studies. Sound recording.

Moyle, R. M. 1998. "Paper Songs and Frozen Assets: Text and Traditions." *Musicology Australia* 21: 28–36.

Office of Women's Policy. 1996. "Aboriginal Family Violence." Occasional Paper No. 12. Darwin, Australia: Northern Territory Government.

Pascoe, B. 2008. *The Little Red Yellow Black Book: An Introduction to Indigenous Australia.* Canberra, Australia: Aboriginal Studies Press.

Roberts, T. 2005. *Frontier Justice: A History of the Gulf Country to 1900.* St. Lucia, Australia: University of Queensland Press.

Rogers, N. 2006. *Inquiry into the Protection of Aboriginal Children from Sexual Abuse.* Darwin, Australia: Northern Territory Government.

Sturcke, J. 2007. "The Aboriginal People Are Likely to Disappear within a Generation." *The Guardian,* June 12. Accessed May 12, 2010. http://www.guardian.co.uk/world/2007/jun/21/australia.

Walker, C. 2000. *Buried Country: The Story of Aboriginal Country Music*. Annandale, Australia: Pluto Press.

Wild, R., and Anderson, P. 2007. "Little Children Are Sacred: Report of the Northern Territory Board of Inquiry into the Protection of Aboriginal Children from Sexual Abuse." Darwin, Australia: Northern Territory Government.

19

REFLEXIVE AND REFLECTIVE PERSPECTIVES OF MUSICAL CHILDHOODS IN SINGAPORE

CHEE-HOO LUM AND EUGENE DAIRIANATHAN

Impetus

As teachers, children's musical cultures—expressed *to* and *by* children—have been our major preoccupation, driven by a need to make music lessons meaningful, interesting, and engaging for them. As academics facilitating teacher education, speaking with, listening to, and observing children in their musical pathways, like global colleagues in music education and ethnomusicology (e.g., Campbell 1998, 2010; Emberly 2009; Marsh 2008), have precipitated a deeper understanding and appreciation of their complex musical worlds. This has inevitably caused a reconsideration of pedagogy and practice as reflective music educators and researchers. Bartleet and Ellis aptly point out, "In music learning and instruction, teachers are reflecting on themselves as learners and critiquing the values and relationships they embody in the classroom with their students and subject matter" (2009: 7).

The following thoughts on a series of interviews with and observations of Clara, a seven-year-old musical child in Singapore, open up a parallel dialogue between a young aspiring learner's pathways toward attaining expertise and experience in musical proficiency and poignancy in triggering childhood memories of one of the authors (Lum, hereafter: me, I, etc.) of this chapter and of his pathways as ethnographer and autoethnographer.

Habitus and *Coiffure*

Clara's and my childhoods are inextricably woven into practice through, first, the Euro-American art-music tradition in Singapore and, second, the dispositions and processes emergent in their pathways. The opus operatum and modus operandi of Clara's and my lived and living practices are prefaced by the writings of Pierre Bourdieu, particularly a central mechanism in his understanding of practice, *habitus* (Bourdieu 1977). Since *habitus* is contingent upon living and lived activity, it involves persons, reciprocal relationships through agents and agency, modes of informal exchanges, and processes of solidification of practice emergent in products that are a function of systems and convention.

As will be exemplified later in Clara's and my lives, *habitus* for this chapter is situated as an enigmatic phenomenon. On the one hand, *habitus* is a "matrix of perceptions, appreciations and actions" and, on the other, "an objective event which exerts its action...demanding a determinate response on those endowed with a determinate type of dispositions" (Bourdieu 1977: 83). Contradictory objectives notwithstanding, we begin with the most notable propensities of the *habitus* such as *body hexis,* which articulates individualized (yet expressive of a collective) ways of assuredness of practice (Bourdieu 1977: 87). This emerges through apprenticeships and curricula that develop personal and collective competences and competencies. The development of *body hexis,* however, is qualified by Bourdieu in the informality of practice "as long as the work of education is not clearly institutionalized as a specific, autonomous practice, and it is a whole symbolically structured environment, without specialized agents or specific moments which exerts an anonymous, pervasive pedagogic action" (Bourdieu 1977: 87).

Where the work of education is decidedly institutionalized in spirit and structure, Bourdieu suggests that there is a reliance on an "orchestration of habitus" (Bourdieu 1977: 80), of a plethora of thoughts, emotions, and actions (Bourdieu and Passeron 1990: 32). To reinforce its inculcation of legitimacy, Bourdieu argues that the mandate to reproduce "is measured by the degree to which the *habitus* it produces is transposable, i.e., capable of generating practices conforming with the principles of the inculcated arbitrary in a greater number of different fields" (ibid.: 33).

Eventually, Bourdieu's *habitus* acquires a complexion and complexity associated with life-giving and life-perpetuating properties:

If the habitus is the analogue of genetic capital, then the inculcation which defines the performance of pedagogic action is the analogue of generation, in that it transmits information generative of analogous information. (Bourdieu and Passeron 1990: 32)

If *habitus* acquires genetic capital, the practice attached to such a *habitus* is extended to the sociopolitical level, making the *habitus* not only practice oriented but also, by virtue of its orchestrator, driven more by extrinsic rather than intrinsic motivation. Bourdieu posits that

If all societies and significantly, all "totalitarian institutions"...seek to produce a new man through a process of "deculturation" and "reculturation," set such store on the seemingly most insignificant details of dress, bearing, physical and verbal manners, the reason is that treating the body as a memory, they entrust to it in abbreviated and practical, i.e., mnemonic, form the fundamental principles of the arbitrary content of the culture. (Bourdieu 1977: 94).

Thus far, Bourdieu's *habitus* informs us of the ways agents, agency, and systems converge—through processes of orchestration—upon a *coif*. This "orchestration of habitus" entails "the production of a commonsense world endowed with the objectivity secured by consensus on the meaning of practices and the world" (Bourdieu 1977: 80). The practice of *coiffuring* (to suit the *coif*) a culture with arbitrary yet predetermined form results in "the homogeneity of habitus...[which] causes practices and works to be immediately intelligible and foreseeable, and hence taken for granted" (Bourdieu 1977: 80).

This homogeneity has an unfortunate consequence for the *body hexis*. The less restrictive pathways available in competences and competencies through informal means are positioned against or outside of institutional imperatives. The consequence of such imperatives are to be found in what Bourdieu refers to as symbolic violence that is to be found not only in sociopolitical structures but also in "all pedagogic action (PA) [that] is, objectively, symbolic violence insofar as it is the imposition of a cultural arbitrary by an arbitrary power" (Bourdieu and Passeron 1990: 5).

But perhaps the most telling of the symbolic violence, as too the *coiffuring*, is the way it permeates every field of the *habitus*—even the familial environment for a learner's education through music.

Childhood Musical Memories as Points of Departure and Recollection

Encountering Clara (aged seven) and her parents made me feel a sense of déjà vu. Taking field notes and recording her playing on the piano and singing, I saw in Clara's ritualized behaviors a glimpse of my musical childhood—daily practice, weekly lessons, and annual practical examinations. Each time I tried asking Clara a question about her musical preferences, she would deflect it to her parents to answer (who were always quick and eager to respond). Armed with current thinking on child agency and child-centeredness in educational philosophy (Cannella and Kincheloe 2002; Prout 2005), I was adamant that Clara should speak her mind so I would be clear about what she really thought and felt. But it then occurred to me that when I was a child, I did the very same thing; I deferred to my parents and preferred that they spoke on my behalf any time. In fact, I spoke so little during my early childhood that the preschool principal embarrassed my parents by enquiring if I had speech or developmental impediments or had been abused at home. I was a quiet but contented child, brought up to respect and obey my teachers and elders at all times in keeping with the tradition of our family who were of Chinese-Cantonese ascription.

Our Version of a Musical Childhood

> Music lessons [in school] happens once in six months and she [music teacher] is grouchy!(Clara, seven years old, 2009)
>
> One of my music teachers in primary school was also my math teacher. I have absolutely no memory of music lessons but remember the immense fear I had of him in shaming us if we did our math calculations wrongly!(Me, eleven years old, 1983)

School (more specifically music classes in school) has not been a hospitable avenue for Clara's musical exposure, nor was it for my own musical development. I begin at this juncture to emphasize the significance of our parents in the formation of "an education through music" for us during our formative years.

Clara (aged seven in year 2009) and I (aged nine in year 1981), both of Chinese ascription, belong(ed) to the thousands of children in Singapore, then as now, who came to know a critical musical experience each year. This was a practical instrumental (piano) examination lasting from fifteen to sixty minutes that transpired in a tiny air-conditioned room with no windows. The examination was conducted by a strange Caucasian woman or man peering unnervingly and writing furiously as we struggled through this frosty environment, playing out of our comfort zones while wearing oversized sweaters. We strained to listen; trying to decipher English pronounced and enunciated in ways to which we were unaccustomed, slightly fearful we might not have understood what was asked of us; plowing through sight-reading and aural exercises; sometimes forgetting in our nervousness the so-we-thought crucial "Thank you, sir/madam" our piano teachers had warned us not to forget, thinking we'd be penalized for such lack of courtesy. Our teachers' advice to us echoes Kok's recollection of childhood experiences of taking Associated Board of the Royal Schools of Music (ABRSM) examinations in Malaysia: "Be submissive, play the colonizer-colonized scenario, and you will be fine" (Kok 2006: 90). Months later, we would get to see that same comment sheet, struggling to decipher unfamiliar remarks and writing styles. But the comment sheet did not hide the fact that our results informed an object exercise in numeral currency: Did we get a pass, a merit, or a distinction?

The quantitative evaluations were reliable indications of each candidate's worth and degree of "Anglicized eurocentricity" in activities ranging from beating time to playing pieces from the Euro-American art-music canon (Kok 2006: 96). Thirty years on, as part of my assignment as an assistant professor within the music department of a teacher-training college, when I am tasked to be one of the examiners for teacher-trainees' instrumental recitals, I preside over a majority of students who play their Euro-American art-music repertoire, mainly on the piano, with a sprinkling of students performing on their Chinese traditional instruments (e.g., *erhu*, *sheng*, and *yangqin*) and the occasional classical guitarist or electronic organist. This setting still reminds me of the "ambience" of my ABRSM piano examination in my childhood except that I have now assumed the role of the "curious white other," writing furiously on my comment sheets while the next Beethoven or Mozart piece or movement is being feverishly executed by the anxious teacher-trainee.

The ABRSM had local representation in Singapore as early as 1948 and enrollment for this music examinations body has grown ever since, now totaling at least 40,000 students a year with total annual revenue of 8 million Singapore dollars (ABRSM 2010). During the "examination season," all music studios at many private music centers would be fully booked with students practicing and rehearsing their set pieces and piano teachers checking on the conditions of the pianos while parents hovered protectively around the studio spaces.

Musical achievement for Clara and me translated crudely into certificates and competition with peers as to who would be the first in a circle of friends to complete the eight grades in the prediploma benchmarking series. This led to an almost religious reliance on what the ABRSM symbolized as "homogeneity of *habitus*" together with officializing strategies that imposed ABRSM certification as evidence of competence. Summarily, Clara and my musical childhoods were *coiffured*. We were chauffeured around by our parents to piano lessons once or twice a week and kept under parental surveillance as we practiced our instruments at home. But the *coiffuring* also took place musically; the three mandatory examination pieces were practiced "ad nauseum" until the day of our practical examination. In most cases, repertoire building comprised no more than a diet of three "carefully selected" options from the list of examination pieces year-on-year until the eighth grade. The ABRSM eighth grade acted as a passport for accessing higher musical worlds. One could gain entry to local music colleges, using these musical qualifications to gain access to undergraduate music programs at institutes of higher learning, including the National Institute of Education, Nanyang Academy of Fine Arts (NAFA), La Salle-SIA College of the Arts, Yong Siew Toh Conservatory, and, more recently, the School of the Arts (SOTA; which accepts students from ages thirteen through eighteen and prepares them for the Swiss International Baccalaureate). Students wanting to offer music as an O-level subject had to satisfy prerequisites such as a minimum ABRSM Grade 5 (theory and practical) certification (or the equivalent from the other examination syndicates, such as Trinity, Guildhall, London College, and Australian Board).

Clearly, therefore, subscription to the ABRSM or one of many other examination syndicates was, and still is, a serious endeavor and an industry of sorts involving a spectrum of stakeholders: music learners, instrumental music teachers, music examiners, examination syndicates, music schools, music book and instrument vendors, and the Singapore Symphonia Company, a government-backed private company that runs the ABRSM operations in Singapore alongside the business of the Singapore Symphony Orchestra.

A Brief Background of Our Colonial History in Singapore

Most academics and writers have regarded the history of modern Singapore as beginning with its founding as a trading settlement by Thomas Stamford Raffles for the East India Company in 1819 (Phan 2004: 18–20). By 1824, the East India Company had control over the entire island, and Britain's sovereignty in Singapore was acknowledged. Between 1873 and 1913, Singapore's trade increased eightfold and its activities expanded to include preliminary processing, such as tin smelting and rubber processing. From probably only around 1,000 inhabitants on the island, who were mainly indigenous people known as "*orang laut*" (sea gypsies), Malays and Chinese arrived around 1819 and increased the population of the island to 226,842 by 1901. By the end of the nineteenth century, Singapore became regarded as the most cosmopolitan city in Asia, comprising nearly three-quarters Chinese and sizeable minorities of Malays, Sumatrans, Javanese, Bugis, Boyanese, Indians, Ceylonese, Arabs, Jews, Eurasians, and Europeans.

Geographically, Singapore's location in Southeast Asia, its unrivalled "fortuitous juxtaposition of deep-water berthing with a position on a growing world-trade route" (Joo-Jock 1991: 12), proved instrumental to its development as a port. All this ensured Singapore's status as one of the world's wealthiest and busiest ports, with its economic growth also attracting increasing numbers of immigrants. When the King George VI dry dock opened in 1938, Singapore's significance in the British Empire was summed up as "The Gibraltar of the East...the bastion of British might." It was that overwhelming sense of impregnability that must have prompted Winston Churchill to call the surrender of Singapore to the Japanese army in February 1942 the "worst disaster and largest capitulation in British history" (Elphick 1995: 4). After World War II, Singapore became a separate Crown Colony in 1946, obtaining self-government in 1955 and internal autonomy in 1959. In 1963, it gained independence as part of the new Federation of Malaysia but was expelled in 1965, following unrest between political parties and individuals in Singapore and Malaysia, to become a fully independent nation from then on (Phan 2004: 18–20).

According to statistics as recent as late September of 2009, about one-quarter of nearly 5 million people living in Singapore are neither citizens nor permanent residents. Demographics still indicate the amalgamation of all Chinese dialect-speaking groups to comprise 74.2 percent of the population while the Malay and Indian communities comprise 13.4 percent and 9.2 percent, respectively. An odd description for a community of citizens, *Others* (anyone not of Chinese, Malay, or Indian ascription) comprise 3.2 percent of the remaining citizen/permanent residence population (Statistics Singapore 2010).

Clara and I can trace our ancestry/cultural provenance back to Southern China: Fujian and Canton, respectively. Clara is fourth generation while I am a second generation Singaporean. We both grew up (and still are growing up) in an educational system driven by an economic model that favors English as the primary medium of instruction while our mother tongue is designated as a second language. We grew up with nursery rhymes such as "London Bridge," "Twinkle Twinkle Little Star," "Old King Cole," and "Humpty Dumpty" but also "Liang Zhi Lao Hu" (Two Tigers) and "Ke Ren Lai" (The Guest Is Here). Our favorite Mandarin "folk nursery songs" featured melodies taken from "Frère Jacques" and were harmonized with I-IV-V chord progressions.

We were brought up with our parents' interpretation of Confucian ethics, which impressed upon us to always respect and obey our elders and to have a sense of filial piety. This code of conduct made us perfect candidates for a constructed musical childhood. Our parents, like many Chinese parents, saw our childhoods as a phase of human development that is not valued for its own merits. They viewed childhood as a time for development through education while inculcating a deep reverence for the intellectual and moral of elders, of tradition, of enculturation of the potential of the child through education (Kinney 1995). And yet this is almost antithetical to what Confucius actually suggested, "Respect the young. How do you know that they will not one day be all that you are now?" (Beck 2010).

COIFFURED MUSICAL CHILDHOODS

Clara

I met Clara through an international research project (Young et al. 2010) in which I was studying the daily musical lives of seven-year-old children. Clara's parents were most excited and delighted when I called to introduce myself as I sought permission from them regarding audio/video recording of subsequent house visits and interviews.

Clara proudly proclaimed that her favorite song was "Danny Boy," a ballad of English/Irish origin. In probing further, I realized that "Danny Boy" was one of the set pieces from the ABRSM examination syllabus in singing. I listened to Clara as her father accompanied her at the piano. I was at first amazed by her sense of pitch accuracy and how she tried to clearly articulate and enunciate the lyrics of the song. Midway through the performance, I began to wonder why this song would even be remotely appealing to Clara, as the lyrics could not have remotely resonated with her current experiences living in a tropical cosmopolitan Asian city:

> Oh Danny boy, the pipes, the pipes are calling
> From glen to glen, and down the mountain side
> The summer's gone, and all the flowers are dying
> 'Tis you, 'tis you must go and I must bide.
> But come ye back when summer's in the meadow
> Or when the valley's hushed and white with snow

Perhaps it was the musical dimension, of a haunting melody and/or her father's impeccable accompaniment as well as parental affirmation (in contradistinction to authoritarianism) that fueled Clara's love for the song. She continued to sing it repeatedly over the next few months for her private singing coach leading up to her singing examination.

As I spoke further with Clara's parents about her musical experiences, I learned that there were several video clips of Clara's spontaneous singing and playing and of various performance events in which she had participated. Many of the video clips were recorded on her mother's cell phone (e.g., when Clara was singing in the car) and handheld video camera recorder (e.g., especially the church and kindergarten graduation performances and solo singing during school assemblies). These clips were clear indication of the commitment and enthusiasm Clara's parents have for her musical development.

Clara's parents were very proud that Clara seemed to have been equipped with or perhaps had acquired absolute pitch and that she was able to memorize melodies aurally and quickly as well as to display a love for both singing and playing the piano. Clara's singing repertoire beyond the ABRSM examination syllabus included songs such as "Tomorrow" from the musical *Annie,* "It's a Small World" among other Disney songs, and songs learned from her children's opera chorus. Her piano repertoire stemmed mainly from the ABRSM examination syllabus. Clara's parents seemed to have taken an active role in her experiences in the Euro-American art-music tradition. They constantly played CD tracks of her graded examination pieces for piano and voice; they tuned in to the local Western classical music radio station (Symphony 92.4 FM) each time they traveled in the car; they played DVDs of concerts by famous Western classical pianists at home as well as a range of musicals such as *Annie, Pocahontas, My Fair Lady*, and *The Sound of Music*, and even Christian songs in Mandarin. They provided for her external instruction in voice while piano lessons were taught by her father. They enrolled her in children's opera choruses and found opportunities for her to perform in school, church, and public spaces. Through Clara's parents, there is an active "technologizing" of the child toward an appreciation and learning of a predominantly Euro-American canon via an effective system of maintenance, surveillance, encouragement, and support. An alternative reading of this technologizing is found in later Bourdieu as "symbolic violence" through PA in at least two senses: first as "the establishment of a relation of pedagogic communication...by an arbitrary mode of imposition and inculcation" (Bourdieu and Passeron 1990: 6) and second by "imposing and inculcating certain meanings, treated by selection and exclusion and becoming worthy of being reproduced, reproduces (in both senses) the arbitrary selection" (ibid.: 8).

Could Clara have resisted such cultivation of a predominant Euro-American canon? Bourdieu makes the observations that "practical estimates give disproportionate weight...through the economic and social necessity...which become in turn the basis of perception and appreciation of all subsequent experience...practices are always liable to incur negative sanctions when the environment...confronted is too distant from that to which they are objectively fitted" (Bourdieu 1977: 78).

For the moment, however, Clara is content with her immersion in a selection of Euro-American musical experiences. But such immersion cannot escape the consequences of subscribing to expertise and proficiency in these musical experiences as acquiring currency in "the culture of the dominant sector...[which] contributes to the reproduction of the position of dominance of the dominant class" (Reed-Danahay 2004: 47). Whether or not her parents are conscious of this hidden agenda, they have essentially invested heavily, if not solely, in this cultural capital, situating Clara's musical growth and development no differently from any other activity, such as bonsai cultivation.

Interlude: And What of Our Chinese Ascription?

Clara's parents are of Chinese Hokkien provenance, while my parents are Chinese-Cantonese. While I am comfortable conversing with my parents and grandparents in Cantonese, Clara (like many current generation Singaporean children) does not speak or understand the family's Chinese dialect. This is a consequence of the launch in 1979 of the Singapore government's "Speak Mandarin Campaign," with the objective of encouraging the speaking of Mandarin as a common language among the Chinese population.

In 1991, Goh Chok Tong (then prime minister) explained the rationale in the launch of the campaign:

> For the Chinese community, our aim should be a single people, speaking the same primary language, possessing a distinct culture and a shared past, and sharing a common destiny for the future. Such a Chinese community will then be tightly knit. (Tong 1991)

While I still have musical memories of my grandparents and parents singing Cantonese lullabies, chants, and children's songs to me, Clara's musical childhood does not include this particular strand of children's traditional or common repertoire. Instead it encompasses only what her parents have *coiffured* for her: a focused musical identity through technological gadgetry and media. Clara's musical repertoire at childhood, as sanctioned by her parents, seems to have been a function of publicly performing musical groups she participated in. Even the popular music selections have been drawn from the Tin Pan Alley tradition of the early twentieth century without any representation from contemporaneous popular musics. Clara's musical childhood is a poignant reminder of my own *coiffured* musical identity despite the variety and diversity of unexplored exposure available and accessible to me as a child. Clara's musical identity may seem less complicated than mine but as Gould points out, "As difference is devoured, both the master and the Other are lost" (Gould 2008: 37).

Clara's Musical Childhood as Poignant Reflection of Self

My father used to work as a carpenter/polisher in an old piano shop, while my mother worked as a hairdresser, trying to make ends meet as they provided the best they could for me and the family. Private music lessons were then a privilege, in stark contrast with the more affluent for whom it was a staple. In providing for my musical education, my father was often chastised by his peers and relatives for not living within his means and spending unnecessarily on my "idle" (in contradistinction to his ideal) pursuits.

The ritual every Saturday afternoon consisted of my taking a public transport bus to my father's workplace then on the back of his motorcycle to my weekly hour of piano lessons while he patiently waited in the vicinity for me to finish. Every day after work, my father would always check with my mother to ascertain if I had practiced at the piano for at least two hours. If I didn't, he would always remind (read as reprimand) me of how expensive piano lessons were and the sacrifices he had had to make to provide me with this "luxury." The sense of guilt in me was strong whenever I missed practice and that motivated my urgency to practice as I progressed rather swiftly through the piano grades.

My father's rationale was clear for my musical training, as well as choice of music for "training in." It comprised a lifeline to a possible future career in case I did not succeed in more prestigious academic pursuits such as the sciences, law, medicine, or business studies. But I reasoned my father had always wanted to prove to others (and to his relatives in particular) that his son was capable of achieving as much as other children did despite our less-privileged socioeconomic status and even more so in an area (such as Euro-American art-music) that was considered the purview of those who not only were wealthy but also possessed the cultural "savoir faire." But I always wondered why my father—who was a Mandarin conversant speaker, had studied Mandarin as a first language, and was proud of his Chinese cultural provenance and rich tradition—did not encourage me to pursue studies on Chinese traditional instruments such as the *guzheng, yangqin,* and *erhu* instead.

Private piano lessons began with Wang Lao Shi (Teacher Wang), a well-mannered but strict Chinese gentleman who came to the house for an hour each week. I remember going through the John Thompson piano series and was particularly fond of playing a young learner's version of the "Song of the Toreador" from Georges Bizet's opera *Carmen*. Subsequent piano teachers were all from China and ensured that my techniques were firm and my progression steadfast, playing through a standard and standardized repertoire of Mozart and Beethoven piano sonatas, Bach preludes and fugues, and Chopin mazurkas, waltzes, and etudes, with a touch of Bartok's *Mikrokosmos*. My father had no objections to the strict manner in which my piano teachers disciplined me at the piano. A few slaps and some teary moments were not uncommon, but I do not recall feeling resentment of any form or sort. This is because I had been "cultivated" to feel indebted to my parents for all they had sacrificed for me. To reciprocate through successful outcomes not only embodied but also fulfilled the essence of my filial piety.

At the recommendation of my piano teacher, my father would buy tickets for symphony orchestra concerts (particularly if an international pianist was featured). He promptly brought me to these concerts at the Victoria Concert Hall on weekends, preceded by a ritual incentive: a plate of our local hawker cuisine at the food center (demolished today), a short walk from the concert hall. This also supported his exhortation (strong suggestion actually!) that I listen to the Western classical music radio station at home. It should have come as no surprise that by my teens, I had no knowledge or listening experiences of popular music culture and therefore had to remain silent whenever friends talked about their favorite popular songs. As an appropriate countermeasure, I actively elected to avoid any other musical genre and became very insular and selective in my musical choices. My musical preferences were clearly directed toward the Euro-American art tradition, and I embraced that preference wholeheartedly.

Music education in school, which consisted of general classroom music in my primary school and the music elective program in my secondary school, further affirmed that my musical choice was a preferred, if not prestigious, one. I felt on top of the world and even had a sense of arrogance during general music classes in school. I expended little or no effort to play the recorder or read notation while my classmates struggled to read, to get correct finger positions, and to achieve an acceptable tone quality. This assured musical ability bolstered my self-esteem, cutting right through the "disability" of a less-privileged socioeconomic background. I felt empowered by this "gift" that my parents had bestowed upon me through my private music lessons; this feeling further fueled my immersion in the Western classical music genre.

Coiffured Connection

Eventually, my initial pursuits in Euro-American art-music landed me in an academic position as a music education assistant professor in a teacher education college in Singapore. I am grateful for all that my family, particularly my father, constructed during my musical childhood and for choosing the *right* musical genre for me, as I realized how significant my Euro-American art-music background was, from the primary school right up to graduate-level entrance examinations. My family environment prepared me for the right type of schooling that "inculcate[d] a secondary habitus, the 'cultivated habitus,' which privileges the cultural capital (which includes world views, linguistic codes, certain types of knowledge, and material objects, such as books) of a particular social class, the dominant social class" (Reed-Danahay 2004: 47).

Foucault explains this cultivation of a practice as that belonging to a colonial power that

> can be analyzed as more complex, as produced by human beings, while at the same time producing privilege for particular groups, naming (labeling and limiting) other particular groups, and reproducing itself...can be invisible, masked in discourses of freedom...can emanate from multiple locations, from unquestioned societal assumptions to marginalized positions of resistance. (Cannella and Viruru 2004: 61)

Since both colonial and postcolonial discourse allows for the merger between power and knowledge and is rooted in human ideas, institutions, and actions, subscription to Euro-American art-music practice-as-tradition traps individuals within and makes it difficult for them to think outside its frame (Cannella and Viruru 2004). Within the Singaporean context, Euro-American art-music is deeply rooted within its institutions and actions. The music curriculum in primary and secondary schools is prescribed by the Ministry of Education, and while recently moving toward a greater awareness of culturally diverse musical practices (Ministry of Education 2008), it is still heavily set within the structure and code of Euro-American art traditions. Moreover, the ABRSM syllabus and certification continues to supplement this dominant view outside the mainstream school system. Thousands of children continue to flow through their graded system, with parents thinking that this ABRSM system validates, if not officializes, their children's musical development.

To exacerbate this *habitus*-of-benchmarking—of which ABRSM is but one source—students in Singapore schools wishing to select music as an elective subject at the secondary and postsecondary levels (Cambridge examination syndicate O- and A-level) must possess a minimum of a practical and theory certification of Grade 5 (ABRSM or equivalent examination board certification). The Cambridge examination syndicate and syllabus remains the most crucial form of benchmarking for the O- and A-level examinations in Singapore, albeit with a Singaporean slant on subject matter and modes of examination. Prior ABRSM qualification is not a general requirement for the international GCSE O- and A-level examinations, which makes ABRSM certification as prerequisite to offer O-level music in Singapore schools a localized phenomenon (see Cambridge 2010).

But is this access to offering music as an elective subject available—in policy and practice—to students who are trained in Chinese orchestra, North or South Indian

classical genres, Malay traditional music, wind ensemble, jazz, or popular musical practices? Our undergraduate students at the National Institute of Education
(NIE; the only teacher education institution in Singapore) have acknowledged,
albeit anecdotally, that in their secondary and postsecondary schooling, they were
permitted to select music as O- and A-level elective subjects only if they possessed
ABRSM, Guildhall, Trinity, or London College certification, put in another way, if
they possessed collateral that was Euro-American art-music.

What of music in the primary and secondary school classroom? Clara and I agree
upon our impressions of a less-than-adequate quality of music lessons in the school
music classroom that continues to this day, albeit with varying levels of engagement. It should not be surprising that the dearth of quality musical learning in the
school music classroom serves not only to attract subscription to Euro-American
art-music practice as collateral for musical development and competency but also
to service the offering of O- and A-levels music study as currency.

At a governmental level, Euro-American art-music practice was confirmed in
its national status when the Singapore Symphony Orchestra (SSO) was instituted
in 1979 as a professional orchestra supported from public funds by the Singapore
Totaliser Board funds (Singapore Totaliser Board 2010). The patron of the SSO,
the late Dr. Goh Keng Swee (then defense minister, later senior minister), initiated
the establishment of a symphony orchestra in Singapore in 1973 when he lamented
publicly the absence of a professional symphony orchestra:

> It strikes me as...a minor scandal that Singapore does not have a symphony
> orchestra.... I trust something will soon be done to establish a symphony orchestra
> in Singapore...it is important that the members are full-time professionals. It costs
> money to maintain an orchestra—the labourer is worthy of his hire and this applies
> to...good musicians. (Singapore Government 1973)

The formation of the SSO in 1979 represented an unprecedented commitment
on at least three fronts. First, funding for the SSO came from public funds, marking
the initiation of "flagship arts companies nurtured by the Government...to enrich
the local culture scene, serve as a bridge between the musical traditions of Asia and
the West, and provide artistic inspiration, entertainment and education" (Singapore
Totaliser Board 2010). Second, funding for the SSO by the Singapore government
was tantamount to nationalizing Euro-American art-music practice as Singaporean
property, or perhaps recolonizing its tradition and practice. Third, the SSO was
set up as an arts company to "provide inspiration, entertainment and education."
Consequently, national education could not have avoided education *of, about,* and
through Euro-American art-music practice.

The SSO performances are now housed within the iconic Esplanade Theatres
on the Bay (Esplanade 2010). Select educational institutions are further examples
of the government's push toward a particular form of arts education in Singapore.
One example is the Yong Siew Toh Conservatory of Music (housed within and vali-
dated by the National University of Singapore), which operates as an international/
external franchise of the Peabody Conservatory based at Johns Hopkins University,

Baltimore-Washington (Yong Siew Toh Conservatory 2010). Another example is the SOTA housed in the Arts Belt in the heart of the city under the auspices of the Ministry of Information, Communications, and the Arts (SOTA 2010).

If I were twelve again, I could flourish in my musical development even better in this present setting than that at the time of my own childhood. More than at any time before, if and when it is her conviction and commitment, Clara has the local opportunity and support to pursue her passion in the Euro-American art music tradition. It would seem that artistic practice as interpreted by the residual source of colonialist power works seamlessly into the entrepôt fabric of the city-state of Singapore.

But the esteem of a version of the Euro-American art-music tradition in Singapore, with its alignment with Euro-American political, economic, and educational structures, offers a powerfully attractive appeal to all stakeholders concerned. These circumstances create "a form of domination...exercised in an unrecognized manner because it is fully normalized within the sociohistorical setting" (Bourdieu and Loïc Wacquant 1992: 167). For Clara, *coiffured* in the Euro-American art-music practice-as-tradition, structure and system are already in place for her to pursue a career in music locally. But moves toward an informal musical practice or something different from the established *coif* would render her *hostage* to a bumpier journey toward formal recognition. Inevitably, musicians will have to conform, to some extent and level, to the code of solidified convention or leave disenfranchised and demoralized, drained and dissatisfied. It may not be far-fetched to consider Bourdieu's notion of symbolic violence in this context, as "censored, euphemized, i.e., unrecognizable, socially recognized violence" (Bourdieu 1977: 191).

REFLECTIONS

Clifford Geertz reminded us that "one of the most significant facts about us may finally be that we all begin with the natural equipment to live a thousand kinds of life but end in the end having lived only one" (Geertz 1973: 45). Ethnomusicologist John Blacking believed "music is the result of intentional interaction, of processes of decision making in society, and both the music and the social interaction are parts of systems of shared communication, or cultures" (Blacking 1981: 190). From Geertz and Blacking, we come to understand the holistic education of a young beginning learner, in and through music, that affects not only that young learner but also the systems and persons enabling the learner reciprocally. From Geertz, we understand the choice of one life from many options, never forgetting how the eventual singular pathway is weaved through the processes articulated by Blacking.

What would be the effect of being excluded from a rich array of musical cultures around the world that exist in a single concentrated location such as Singapore? Our concerns surround the privileging of one among many systems of symbols as *the* system. This universalizing potentially imputes particularized expectations and value judgments on ways of knowing and learning in the multitude of cultures around the world, and nowhere else is this more painfully evident than in Clara's and my pathways to musical learning.

In her chapter on the music curriculum discourse, Janet Barrett noted the calls for change in curricular practice in at least four areas: (1) challenge longstanding views of musicianship and musical understanding, including more comprehensive views of musical behaviors, a wider array of musical styles, an integrated sense of music as an embodied experience, and greater depths of musical understanding; (2) situate the music curriculum as a dynamic social practice; (3) relate developments in the music curriculum to broad arenas of educational policy that enable or inhibit change; and (4) foster views of teachers as primary agents of change in curriculum work (Barrett 2007: 147–161).

The recently revised General Music Programme for Singapore schools identifies six objectives for engaging in music creating, performing, and responding, of which two are particularly pertinent for this discussion: the ability to discern and understand music from and of various cultures and genres; and the ability to understand the role of music in daily living (Ministry of Education 2008). The coincidence of these recent developments in the General Music Programme learning objectives in Singapore and Barrett's challenges in curriculum discourse are not fortuitous. Together, they reiterate an inclusion in the music curriculum for music as lived and living space.

Juxtaposing two lived and living musical pathways in this chapter makes it possible, through parallel ethnographies, to interrogate the dynamics between them serving to "highlight their commonality as mediated representations" (Minks 2006: 215). As such, "childhood experiences and the practice of remembering do not determine identity, but they are crucial tools in its construction" (Minks 2006: 214).

A corollary to this juxtaposition is the correlation between construing and constructing of identities in lived and living reality. Anthropologist Tim Ingold suggests that "life-activities" that occur in the course of a musical education "are themselves not generative of personhood but ways of bringing established identities into play... it is not what you do... but the received attributes that you import through these various projects" (Ingold 2002: 46).

Clara's and my predicaments, from socioeconomic backgrounds through musical affinities and propensities, provide compelling descriptions about the irrelevance of ascribing ability and proficiency to nature or nurture arguments; they are about a balance of *both*. Canella and Viruru point out that postcolonial research, especially for education and the social sciences, should be conceptualized as "the pursuit of social transformation for liberation, which includes contesting political and cultural identities through collectivity, rather than coercion; generating critical specific activism as collective transformational power; and challenging the will to truth and power that legitimizes control for particular privileged people(s) and places 'others' in the margins" (Cannella and Viruru 2004: 148–149).

The content of these parallel reflections raises serious questions about the importance of ensuring that musical apprenticeships in both nature and nurture domains are not impoverished in their delivery and engagement. *Coiffured* musical learnings not only bear the consequences in *coiffured* repertoire and musical person but also reveal the complicity, not to mention currency, of systemic coercion in an educational system: *habitus.* Interrogating *coiffured* musical learnings is much less about uncovering a particular truth than generating multiplicities of thinking and enacting by observing learning experiences of a young child, while reflecting on the realities of my own lived and living pathways. Such parallel questioning situates my lived and living identities: as musical learner, music educator in teacher education in Singapore, and musical protagonist, working with and against the enduring discourse of a situated version of the Euro-American art tradition made dominant.

The power of Bourdieu's *habitus* is a painful reminder of its derivations from issues of endogamy among the Kabyle in Algeria (Barnard 1994: 801). The right of every child is the right to access and opportunities in a diversity of musical worlds as to diversity through explorations in and among them. My pathways—predispositions notwithstanding—were subjected to impositions of a *habitus* of a local version of the Euro-American art-music world with attendant sociopolitical motivations orchestrated through education. The endogamous practices (in contradistinction to exogamous principles espoused in our General Music Programme) were encountered in part through my undergraduate curriculum, which made me discover not only a world of diverse musical practices other than my *coiffured* early-learning experiences and expectations. But that encounter was partly a meeting of my predispositions fueled possibly by Cantonese-Chinese-Singaporean-Southeast Asian ascriptions.

Occasionally, I wrestle with my homegrown musical identity and announce to people I'm going through a "classical music rejection phase," engaging for instance in my graduate school days with the Balinese *gambus* ensemble, the *guzheng,* and gospel choir. At the same time, I have withdrawal symptoms as I listen to Schumann and Rachmaninoff piano concertos and my beloved Chopin nocturnes and etudes on my iPod using my earphones. I am constantly mindful of the caveat "Don't bite the hand that feeds you." This is more for the fact that I am sitting comfortably in my office chair, having the freedom to think and write about this reflection, which makes me grateful for all the benefits of a constructed musical childhood targeted at the "right" musical genre, even at the "right" time. The well-structured musical system and organization that pervades from micro- to macrolevels disguises itself well as the norm and claims its inclusivity of other musical systems. The possibilities and feasibilities of change always seemed miniscule given its strong foundations anchored with significant stakeholders.

This chapter began with an examination of *habitus* through two lived and living realities. It now serves to alert us to unintended consequences of *habitus* as impoverished musical nourishment or an overly narrow musical diet when the right of every child's musical beginning is to celebrate the diversity and variety of all that is before them. But the *habitus* is also an ironic reminder of its power to perpetuate musical impoverishment by colluding with agents and agencies through "systems of durable, transposable dispositions"—ultimately at the expense of the musical learner.

REFERENCES

Associated Board of the Royal Schools of Music. 2010. "The Growth of ABRSM."
  Accessed February 4, 2010. http://www.abrsm.org/regions/en/singapore/singapore.

Barnard, Alan. 1994. "Rules and Prohibitions: The Form and Content of Human
  Kinship." In *Companion Encyclopedia of Anthropology*, edited by Tim Ingold,
  783–812. New York: Routledge.

Barrett, Janet. 2007. "Currents of Change in the Music Curriculum." In *International
  Handbook of Research in Arts Education*, edited by Liora Bresler, 147–161. Dordrecht,
  Netherlands: Springer.

Bartleet, Brydie Leigh, and Caroline Ellis, eds. 2009. *Music Autoethnographies.*
  Queensland: Australian Academic Press.

Beck, Sanderson. 2010. *Attitudes of Confucius.* Accessed February 4, 2010. http://www.
  san.beck.org/CONFUCIUS2-Attitude.html. Accessed February 4, 2010.

Blacking, John. 1981. "The Problem of 'Ethnic' Perceptions in the Semiotics of Music."
  In *The Sign in Music and Literature*, edited by Wendy Steiner, 184–194. Austin, TX:
  University of Texas Press.

Bourdieu, Pierre, and Jean-Claude Passeron. 1990. *Reproduction in Education, Society
  and Culture,* London: Sage.

Bourdieu, Pierre, and, Loïc Wacquant. 1992. *An Invitation to Reflexive Sociology.*
  Chicago: University of Chicago Press.

Bourdieu, Pierre. 1977. *Outline of a Theory of Practice.* Cambridge: Cambridge
  University Press.

Cambridge International Examination Syndicate. 2010. "Cambridge O-Level Subjects."
  Accessed May 31, 2010. www.cie.org.uk/qualifications/academic/middlesec/olevel/
  subjects.

Campbell, Patricia Shehan. [1998] 2010. *Songs in Their Heads.* New York: Oxford
  University Press.

Cannella, G. S., and Radhika Viruru. 2004. *Childhood and Postcolonization.* New York:
  Routledge Falmer.

Cannella, Gaile S., and Joe L. Kincheloe, eds. 2002. *Kidworld: Childhood Studies,
  Global Perspectives, and Education.* New York: Peter Lang Publishing.

Elphick, Peter. 1995. *The Pregnable Fortress: A Study in Deception, Discord and
  Desertion.* London: Hodder and Stoughton.

Emberly, Andrea. 2009. "Mandela Went To China … and India Too: Musical Cultures
  of Childhood in South Africa." PhD diss., University of Washington.

Esplanade. 2010. "Esplanade Theatres on the Bay." Accessed February 5, 2010. http://
  www.esplanade.com/index.jsp.

Foucault, Michel. 1980. *Power/Knowledge: Selected Interviews and Other Writings
  1972–1977.* Edited by Colin Gordon and J. M. Marshall. Brighton, UK: Harvester.

Geertz, Clifford. 1973. *The Interpretation of Cultures.* New York: Basic Books.

Goh, Chok Tong. *Speak Mandarin. Are You Game?* 1991. Accessed February 7, 2010.
  http://www.mandarin.org.sg/current/about-the-campaign/history-background.
  html.

Gould, Elizabeth. 2008. "Devouring the Other: Democracy in Music Education."
  Action, Criticism & Theory for Music Education 7 (January): 29–44.

Ingold, Tim. 2002. "Between Evolution and History: Biology, Culture and the Myth
  of Human Origins." In *The Evolution of Cultural Entities,* edited by M. Wheeler, J.

Ziman, and M. Boden, 43–66. Proceedings of the British Academy. Oxford: Oxford
    University Press.

Kinney, Anne Behnke. 1995. *Chinese Views of Childhood*. Honolulu: University of
    Hawaii Press.

Kok, Roe-Min. 2006. "Music for a Postcolonial Child: Theorizing Malaysian
    Memories." In *Musical Childhoods and the Cultures of Youth*, edited by S. Boynton
    and R.-M. Kok, 89–104. Middletown, CT: Wesleyan University Press.

Marsh, Kathryn. 2008. *The Musical Playground*. New York: Oxford University Press.

Ministry of Education. 2008. *General Music Programme: Primary/Secondary*. 2008.
    Accessed February 11, 2010. http://www.moe.edu.sg/education/syllabuses/aesthetics
    -health-and-moral-education/files/general-music-programme.pdf.

Minks, Amanda. 2006. "Afterword." In *Musical Childhoods and the Cultures of
    Youth*, edited by S. Boynton and R.-M. Kok, 209–218. Middletown, CT: Wesleyan
    University Press.

Phan, Ming Yen. 2004. "Music in Empire; Western Music in 19th Century Singapore
    through a Study of Selected Texts." MA diss., Nanyang Technological University.

Prout, Alan. 2005. *The Future of Childhood: Towards the Interdisciplinary Study of
    Children*. New York: Routledge Falmer.

Reed-Danahay, Deborah. 2004. *Locating Bourdieu*. Bloomington: Indiana University
    Press.

School of the Arts. 2010. Accessed February 5, 2010. http://www.sota.edu.sg/
    TheSchool/tabid/36/Default.aspx.

Singapore Government Press Statement. 1973. Speech by Dr. Goh Keng Swee, Minister
    of Defence, at the opening of the SEIWAEN (Japanese Garden); February 16, 1973.

Singapore Totaliser Board. 2010. "Singapore Symphony Orchestra." Accessed February
    5, 2010. http://www.toteboard.gov.sg/donations_grantstories.html.

Statistics Singapore. 2010. "Demography." Accessed February 4, 2010. http://www.
    singstat.gov.sg/stats/themes/people/hist/popn.html.

Yong Siew Toh Conservatory of Music. 2010. Accessed February 5, 2010. http://music.
    nus.edu.sg.

Young, Susan, Beatriz Ilari, Chee-Hoo Lum, and Elizabeth Andango. 2010. "My Place:
    My Music." Accessed February 12, 2010. http://www.myplacemymusic.com/index.
    php?title=Main_Page.

20

THE MUSICAL CULTURE OF AFRICAN AMERICAN CHILDREN IN TENNESSEE

MARVELENE C. MOORE

AFRICAN American children are known for their ingenious, inventive, and highly rhythmic singing and chants, jump rope, hand clapping routines, and line dances. Each day they generate, perform, and pass on these games to their family, friends, and others who listen, watch, and may join them in their performance (Gaunt 2006: 1). The children preserve, invent, and reinvent these forms of expression for reasons that include sheer pleasure and enjoyment, the social interaction that they provide, and the release of energy that these songs allow. These children's musical forms also serve a historical purpose as a vital link to a rich African American music heritage that has been transmitted from generation to generation. They reflect the rhythmic complexities of jazz, the sliding and bending notes heard in spirituals and the blues, and the fervor of gospel music, poetic verse, and the rhythms of rap. In the Southern region of the United States, one of the main vehicles for transmission of African American music and culture has been through children's games. The games are often learned by the children from adults and preserved through playful interactions.

Children on the playground of Red School (a pseudonym), an urban elementary school in Applesville, Tennessee take ownership of their musical games as well and describe them in vivid ways that emphasize their personal, mutual, and communal interests and identities with them. Listen to the children as they describe the musical games they play:

MM: What is the name of your game?
CHILD: "Apple on a Stick."
MM: How did you learn to play the game?
CHILD: My sister taught me.
MM: Will you show me your games?
CHILD: Yeh!!!!!!
MM: Are these your games or do other children play them?
CHILDREN: Our games!!!!

Children value their singing games. They regard them as their own African American songs, games, and lore and derive pleasure from playing, showing, and sharing them with others. The history of African Americans in the United States provides insight into the struggle of a people to find their identity and maintain a sense of pride and community, and music was often present to assert identity and to enhance lives. Often, it was through the hand clapping routines, jump rope chants, and singing games of African American children that issues of identity and status were addressed, particularly within the historic communities of the American South. For example, the folklorist Harold Courlander examined the song "See See Rider" and found it functions as a children's ring game, one that expresses discontent with young lives that were created by a historically dominant white society and displeasure with a double standard that exists among elder generations within their own community.

> Version I (Discontent)
> See see rider, *satisfied!*
> What's the matter? *Satisfied!*
> I got to work, *satisfied!*
> And I am tired, *satisfied!*
> And I can't eat, *satisfied!*
> Satisfied Lord, *satisfied!*
> Version II (Double Standard)
> Mamma Mamma, *satisfied!*
> Leave me alone. *Satisfied!*
> When you were young, *satisfied!*
> Were you in the wrong? *Satisfied!*
> Papa Papa, *satisfied!*
> You the same, *satisfied!*
> You the one, *satisfied!*
> Give Mamma's name. *Satisfied!* (Courlander 1963: 152)

NATIONAL AND CULTURAL IMPERATIVE: HISTORICAL PERSPECTIVE

Upon arrival to the United States from mostly sub-Saharan Africa, former citizens of African kingdoms and cultures were forced into servitude, in the North primarily as indentured servants and into slavery in the South. The treatment of African arrivals to the Southern United States was most severe, immediately and continuing for generations. There, attempts were made to strip Africans of dignity and identity with their homeland. The Virginia General Assembly was the first to legalize slavery in December 1662, as reflected in Act VI, Laws of Virginia (Hening Statues at Large 1662). Later, the General Assembly published the following declaration on slavery, "All Negro, mulatto and Indian slaves within this dominion...shall be held to be real estate. If any slave resists his master...correcting such slave, and shall happen to be killed in such correction...the master shall be free of all punishment...as if such accident never happened" (Virginia General Assembly Declaration 1705).

News of the declaration passed through the American South, and soon similar laws were enacted for the enslavement of Africans in Alabama, Arkansas, the Carolinas, Florida, Georgia, Kentucky, Louisiana, Tennessee, and Texas—and parts of the border states Maryland and Missouri. According to the 1860 US Census, of the 31.4 million people in the United States, 4.4 million were African American, and 90 percent of African Americans were slaves in the South. Due to their physical and social treatment, these slaves were made to feel that being black was a "problem" and that their blackness made them inhuman. In 1863, after the emancipation of the slaves, African Americans faced further challenges in a very slow transition to their roles as freed men and women in a predominantly white society and in developing their own free communities and creating their personal identity.

Throughout their history, music was a primary source for realizing an African American identity. Vibrant musical expressions were a constant presence within African American life—as created by adults and as adapted, expanded, and created anew by children. In the Southern states, African American culture developed separately from white society and created unity within their communities. Song, instrumental music, and dance were performed regularly for many occasions, much of it reminiscent of the African cultures they had been forced to leave. Despite their roots in various African regions and nations, there were pan-African facets and features that they remembered and fused into the African American music genres that were emerging. These genres have permeated American music and have become known and influential throughout the musical world, even while they maintain their uniquely African American character.

Children's songs and singing games were important vehicles for transmitting essential elements of African American musical culture, learned from adults and preserved, reinterpreted, or even transformed through the children's playful interactions. While the children learned the rhymes from their elders, they also improvised and created other versions in their street and playground games and often regarded those taught to them by their parents as inaccurate (Harwood 1998a: 114). In true African American style, these hand clapping games were passed on to other children: friends, playmates, and classmates. These games served as a basis for the later creation by children of jump rope chants, including a "double Dutch" repertoire of tunes and moves, as well as hip-hop and rap music. Planet Rock illustrates the somatic historiography of the children's chants to transmission of African American music culture (Gaunt 2006: 182–183).

Much contemporary repertoire of American children's songs was created by African American children living in poverty and within societal circumstances that delivered messages of their inferiority to white culture. However, these songs mirror the resilience of the children, the song makers whose joy and hope were evidenced in their songs and games. For example, when I was a young child during the era of segregation (a period lasting until the mid-1960s), I accompanied my Mom uptown for a shopping trip in a Southern city. It was a hot summer day and while shopping in a department store, I became thirsty. I ran to the water fountain and my Mom immediately ran after me because she knew the conditions for getting a drink from the fountain. When we arrived at the fountain, we were faced with a sign that stated, "Negroes drink from the cup," a cup that was chained to the water fountain for all African Americans to drink from. My Mom read the sign to me and, needless to say, she would not allow me to drink from the cup. She attempted to explain why I could not have a drink, but I really did not clearly understand until some years later after remembering that a white adult had immediately gone to the water fountain after we were there and was able to have a drink from the free flowing water that bubbled forward. My Mom informed me, years later, that after I arrived home that day, I created a rhythmic chant and hand game from the incident that she heard me playing with my friends:

> No water for me,
> No water for you,
> But I won't cry,
> Boo hoo, hoo hoo!

This was my way of dealing with the disappointment of not being able to drink from a water fountain.

Often African American children in the South created games that served to confirm their self-image and worth, especially when white oppressors treated them as less than human. I recall an incident on another occasion in which I turned my personal hurt and shame into a playful game. At that time, all public facilities were segregated and designated as "Negro" or "White" with areas in the front reserved for "Whites" and those in the back for "Negroes." This meant that when African Americans rode public transportation, they rode in the back of the bus while special areas in the front were designated as "white only." My mother and I boarded a bus to travel uptown to buy me a special dress. How excited I was with the prospects of that trip, such that I did not pay attention as my mother proceeded to the back of the bus, but instead I sat on the front seat, with thoughts of getting my new dress. The bus driver yelled to my mother, "You better get this *N-word* child to the back of the bus," causing me to recoil, infuriating my mother, and resulting in an exchange of words. She then took me by the arm and forced me to sit in the seats reserved for "Negroes." The bus driver's words were so hurtful and penetrating, that with tears streaming down my face I suddenly broke out in a chant, creating a body percussion on the back of the seat in front of me (Figure 20.1).

Somehow I had managed to combine words from one of my father's sermons about how much God loves us and my feelings about the bus driver's actions toward

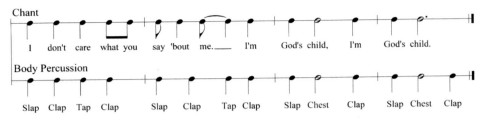

Figure 20.1: Notation of rhythmic chant, "I Don't Care."

me into a chant to reaffirm my worth. This became MY hand clapping game that I taught and played with my friends. They in turn taught it to their sisters and cousins, and it was passed around to children within the community.

African American children's play reflects the music-making principles found in popular genres of African American music, as it also underscores the oral-kinetic mode of learning music characteristic of the culture (Gaunt 2006: 1). As Harwood points out, this style of learning supports not only acquiring and sustaining a standard repertoire of hand clapping games but also "learning how to learn music" (Harwood 1998b: 54).

THE MUSICAL ENGAGEMENT OF AFRICAN AMERICAN CHILDREN

Charles Keil observed the physicality of children in their musical engagement, noting that, "It's about getting down and into the groove, everyone creating socially from the bottom up" (Keil 1995: 1). African American children make music for enjoyment and the pleasure of social interaction. Their music is rooted in the musical qualities of African American genres, which recalls old-world African musical characteristics as well. In other words, the music of African American children is an integral component of who they are as descendants of African society and as members of the greater community of African Americans whose adults help to transmit, nurture, encourage, and applaud their musical efforts.

In a gathering of African American children at play with their singing games, most of the players are girls. They are fully focused and engaged in their play and they smile, laugh, and encourage each other with expressions such as "Bring it on down," "Take it to the lap," and "You go, girl." They clap, snap, stomp, and jump up and down as the games reach a climax, after which they often fall into each others arms, laughing from sheer exhaustion. As well as encouraging each other during play, the children can be very free with voicing their criticism to each other when the games are not played with precision and accuracy, an important ingredient to the children (Harwood 1998b: 56). They can spend hours playing the games with the numerous repetitions providing opportunities for learning all aspects of them. I remember that when I played games with my friends, we would often play until we fell down to the ground, totally drained of energy, at which point someone would say, "Oh-o-o, child, I'm so tired, I've got to go home." ("Oh-o-o, child" was an adult expression that we echoed in our play.) Participation in playing singing game creates a sense of bonding and belonging among the girls, helping to sustain them as individuals when they depart from the group, as it also assists them in establishing identities that are unique yet reflective of their playgroups. As Gaunt recounted, the games serve as "ethnic cohesion and solidarity despite the national, geographical, and socioeconomic differences among African American across time and place" (2006: 57).

Common features of adult music emerge in the musical expressions of African American children, including (1) call-response forms, as found in spirituals and work songs (many of which are still performed today); (2) the bending and sliding of notes, as heard in blues and gospel music; and (3) the presence of syncopation, present in assorted jazz styles as well as other genres of African American music (Gaunt 2006: 2, 58). One of the children's games that I recall playing with friends illustrates a clear example of the use of the sliding notes. We made "Mary Mack" our very own song as we sang it with our stylized melody (see Figure 20.2).

In addition to displaying specific features of adult music, "Mary Mack" relates a personal reaction to the difficulty of combing African American children's hair in its natural state. Many combs have been broken by mothers and girls while attempting to comb and braid the hair. Further, the expectation of a whipping, a common punishment awaiting African American children (certainly in the 1950s and 1960s)

Figure 20.2: Author's childhood version of "Mary Mack."

for breaking a valuable item like a comb, or for misbehaving, was a worrisome thing to young girls. The texts of children's songs are reminders of African American life, as they provide a historical perspective on experiences and modes of expected behavior within the community—all preserved and passed on to generations of children through play. Gaunt similarly observed, "Black girls" musical play offered insight into the learned ways of being that foster and reflect individual and group identity within the African American community" (2006: 13).

One of the troublesome issues of identity in African American society, especially among young girls in their childhood and adolescence, was body image—what it meant to be pretty and how to achieve it. In the singing game "East Coast Line," there are references as to how pretty a child can be if she (or he) has "good food" available to eat. The message is directed to the necessity of having adequate food for the health and balance of children's development and of the community (Wharton-Boyd 1983: 47). That the message sounds through the song of African American children is yet again an example of how culture is transmitted through children's playful musical interactions.

African Traditions in American Music

When African Americans arrived in the United States, they were initially permitted to perform their music, especially in the South, which contributed to the preservation of African traits within the music. Although the landowners were uncomfortable with the drums because they suspected them of carrying messages, other forms of music were encouraged by the owners as a form of entertainment, especially when guests were present (Brooks 1984). There is strong evidence to confirm the retention of the African cultural legacy in music and the memories of the past (Maultsby 2005: 326). Although surrounded by European traditions and artistic forms, African Americans were able to retain basic African perspectives and create new expressive forms relevant to their situation. Levine supported this probability when he concluded, "Culture is a product of interaction between the past and present. Its toughness and resiliency are determined not by a culture's ability to withstand change... but by its ability to react creatively and responsively to the realities of a new situation" (1977: 5).

There is continuing evidence of the African legacy in the music and dance of African Americans in the pre- and post-Civil War periods, as well as throughout the twentieth century and into the present time. Prior to the Civil War, African Americans of the Southern states lived on plantations, where they were forced to rely on the slave owners to provide for them. While working, music and dance were central to their existence. In the fields they often expressed themselves through cries, calls, hollers, and spirituals—ways that lightened their loads as they communicated with one another; this practice dates back to their African ancestors. The spirituals they sang were generally performed in the call-response expression of African forms, which allowed the delivery of information by one individual as well as a response to it by another (or by many within earshot who had heard the delivery). This traditional musical form provided opportunities for improvisation in the solo (call) and a repetitive phrase in the refrain (response). Call-response is a frequent characteristic in the songs and musical games of African American children.

Following their emancipation, the former slaves faced a social system that denied them equal access in American society when compared to their white counterparts. They were forced to perform strenuous labor in order to provide for their families, and they often worked long hours in gangs and groups. From their labors emerged work songs, with workmen singing in call-and-response form, which provided opportunities for solo improvisation of melody and text and group affirmation. The subjects of work songs ranged from humorous to sad, from community gossip to social commentaries. Singers communicated their views of their bosses, their preachers, their neighbors, and almost any other subject they encountered in their lives (Courlander 1963: 89). African American children's games and songs exhibit a connection to work songs in their frequent call-response form as well as the commentaries on aspects of everyday African American life and the individuals—teachers, friends, neighbors—that fill them.

By the late nineteenth century, a new African American musical expression was developing especially for singing voices and guitars. With texts that were secular in nature, the blues featured the flatted third and seventh notes, called "blue notes." These tones lent the songs a sad and mournful sound, which was conducive to expressing sorrow (or hope for a better life). Blue notes are frequently heard in children's songs. "Mary Mack," for example, supports the children's worry for "Mama's" discovery that one of her children had broken a comb—and what sort of "sad event" that would bring for them.

Ragtime was another African American musical form of the period, created alongside and flourishing in the period of the early blues (Cohn 1993: 16). Peaking in popularity from 1896 to 1917 (Brooks 1984: 65–67), ragtime was distinguished from other genres of African American music in two important ways: it was dance music, and it was played on the piano. It accompanied popular dances such as the cakewalk and the two-step. Ragtime did not retain the practice of call response, but it was known for its employment of syncopation throughout. Ragtime employed the use of accents that were performed on the weak beats of the rhythm; the second and fourth beats in the treble pitches of the right hand played over an even rhythm in the lower pitches of the left hand (Brooks 1984: 67). These features can be seen in African American children's games as they employ the interacting of syncopated rhythms in their chant and complementary rhythms in their body movements.

As one of the most improvisatory musical forms, jazz was developing in African American communities of the early twentieth century alongside blues and ragtime. While ragtime's popularity rose and then waned, the flexibility of jazz (and jazz musicians) allowed it to sound new and fresh from its beginnings through its considerable developments and interpretations. Jazz is notable for its extensive improvisation by wind, string, and percussion instruments. It employs textures based on heterophony and exhibits form that is not structurally fixed (Brooks 1984: 83–91). Jazz is reminiscent of African music in its use of multilinear rhythms and melodies, polyrhythms, and polymelodies. Extensive syncopation, polyrhythms, melodies consisting of blue notes, and improvisatory performances are jazz features that also appear in the hand clapping, foot stomping, chanting, and singing of African American children's songs and games.

Gospel music was central to African American religious life in the early twentieth century and has continued in popularity as a contemporary religious expression that is carried by the media. Gospel music is unique in its juxtaposition of religious text to elements of blues melodies that employ the flatted third and seventh degrees and that use syncopated jazz rhythms alongside vocal (and instrumental) improvisation. A common feature of gospel music in live performances is the use of vocables sung by the soloists and singers to add intensity to the music and create a heightened sense of fervor among the singers and the listeners. This technique can frequently be heard in the performances by African American children of their singing games as well, especially after many repetitions of the songs and singing games or sections of a melody. Shouts of encouragement, support for continuing certain motions within the games, are features of gospel music that can be heard in the children's songs, too, as they play (Burnim 1988).

Since the middle of the twentieth century, American popular styles like R&B, soul, rap, and hip-hop have taken in the African American components of syncopation, blue notes, and improvisation. Hip-hop is an outgrowth of the frustrations of many African Americans over the discriminatory practices they have experienced in housing, education, health, and other social services (Rose 1994). Rapidly spoken and highly rhythmic, with punctuations, accents, and syncopations of every sort, rap takes speech to new levels of expression. The language of rap is frequently abrasive and offensive, yet it conveys the realities of harsh experiences and provides a platform for young African Americans to express what they feel. When listening to African American children play hand clapping games, I am reminded of rap as they chant their spoken language in intricate rhythms and fortify their words with the rhythmic density of hand clapping, slapping, snapping, and intricate body movements at an almost unmanageable speed.

Components of African American music are notable in the music in the children's songs, games, and body movements, evidence that adult expressions and mediated forms have been woven by children into their own expressions. Maultsby (2005) pointed out that specific African songs and genres no longer exist in the music of African Americans. However, "Africanisms do exist in the old and new forms of African American music in that [new songs were] created in the style of the tradition, using its [African] vocabulary and idioms, or in an alternative style which combined African and non-African resources" (Nketia 1981: 82–88). In African American genres, including spirituals, work songs, blues, ragtime, jazz, gospel, and rap, these musical features have been retained, as well as in the music that children make.

AFRICAN AMERICAN CHILDREN'S SONGS
IN A TENNESSEE COMMUNITY

Children of the third-grade class at Red Elementary School in a Tennessee community showed themselves to be active agents in the preservation and transmission of an African American musical heritage. The school, located within the city of Applesville in eastern Tennessee, is uniquely named after an African American educator, Louise Red, the granddaughter of a former slave. Red rose to prominence in the Applesville community in the 1940s because of her visionary teaching and curricular development in the establishment of her own kindergarten (when it was not popular for African Americans to do so). Later, Ms. Red served on the Applesville school board and was influential in politics and in the education of all children, especially African American children in the city. She lives in Applesville and celebrated her centennial birthday in 2010.

Applesville, Tennessee shares a similar history with other African American communities in the Southern United States in that the predecessors of its citizens today were resident workers on large white-owned plantations. These African Americans lived together in small houses with limited land space. After their emancipation, children and their families were permitted to live in a certain community but only in accordance to the laws of segregation, which declared them "separate but equal." Other African Americans migrated to the North and elected to live together in their urban neighborhoods, creating the phenomenon of the "inner city" (Hahn 2003: 455–456).

African American Children in Applesville and Red School

Applesville, Tennessee has a population of 600,000, and the inner city citizens are predominantly African American. Children attend the community's schools and are joined by small populations of children from adjacent white and Mexican American communities who are bused to the schools. African American children attend the same churches, play at the same community centers, and shop within the same stores. Many of the African American children who attend Red School enjoy playing singing games and are eager to share their music with each other and interested visitors like me. They are articulate and protective of their songs and games, which they identify as their very own, to pass them on to younger sisters and brothers. In listening to the children, ten third-grade girls, eight to nine years of age, gathered on the playground of Red School during their recess period one day, and they revealed to me, through a conversation, an understanding of their musical and socially interactive activities.

> MM: What is the name of your singing game?
> CHILD: "Apple on a Stick."
> MM: Who do you think gave it this name?

CHILD:[Giggling] Applebee's Restaurant [the name of a family restaurant chain].
MM:How did you learn to play the game?
CHILD:My sister taught me.
MM:How did she teach it to you?
CHILD:First, she taught me the song [the chant], then she taught me how to do the
    hand thing.
MM:Do you think that children other than African American children play these
    games?
CHILDREN (TOGETHER):NO!
CHILD:Yes, other children play them.
MM:What other children do you think play the games?
CHILD:Korean, African, and probably Chinese.
MM:Do you think they play them in the same way?
CHILD:No.
MM:What makes us play our games differently?
CHILD 1:Because, like, where 'cause they are a different type of person that learn in
    different ways and we are a different kind of person that learns different ways.
CHILD 2:Because we speak different languages.
MM:Have you taught this game to anyone else?
CHILD:Yes.
MM:Who?
CHILD:My little sister.
MM:Did she learn it well?
CHILD 1:No, she hit me in the face [while playing the hand game].
CHILD 2:My baby sister.
MM:How old is she?
CHILD:Three.

The explanation by one girl that their singing games might be played by children outside their immediate circle is noteworthy. She was attempting to articulate
that she and her friends were unique and that they learned in distinctive ways.
While some children's songs have spread throughout the world, including African
American songs such as "Mary Mack," there are those that belong principally to the
children who invent and reinvent music that is uniquely theirs to hold.

THE MUSIC OF CHILDREN'S GAMES

An examination of two singing games performed by children at Red School and
another singing game (in ring, or circle, formation) from my childhood shows
African American musical features and gives weight to the argument for Africanisms
in the music making of African American children. The girls who immediately
yelled out "Apples on a Stick" and "Down by the River" as their first choice songs
were willing to show and share them with me. They later demonstrated a jump rope
game, too, and the enthusiasm of one girl for "Ice Cream" was visible in the unusual
height of her exuberant jumps (see Figure 20.3).

Figure 20.3: Jump rope game, "Ice Cream."

Singing games can be viewed musically through the lens of Mellonee Burnim, who proposed that "time, text and pitch are the three basic components that form the structural network for interpretation of black music" (1988: 115). In Burnim's system of analysis, time refers to the structural and rhythmic aspects of the music and includes illustrations of repeated words, phrases, sections, and cadenzas; layers of hand clapping; rhythmic complexity: syncopation; and change in tempo: speed. When considering the text, the qualities of call-and-response form and local dialect emerged. Melodic features of bending tones, sliding tones, and melismata were notable, as the particularities of many African American genres were apparent: blue notes, syncopation, improvisation, vocables, and the rapidity of syncopated rhyming lines (see Web Figure 20.4 ⊙).

As they sang "Apple on a Stick," the girls clapped hands in partners that faced one another (see Figure 20.5).They chanted in one rhythm while clapping in a second rhythm and swaying from side to side in yet a third rhythm, crossing the rhythms in their integrated performance of music and movement. The words of their chant contained snippets of African American slang, for example, "two forty six", perhaps indicative of the tempo of the heart beat, although this would be considered very fast, since the maximum heart rate for a healthy young adult is just 200 beats (see Figure 20.6). The technique of bending pitches was also in play at the same phrase "two forty six." Further, within the same chant, sliding tones were in evidence, most obviously in their articulation of "boyfriend."

As in "Apple on a Stick," there were no boys in the ring for the performance by the Red School group of "Down by the River." The girls were considerably animated in their performance, vigorously tapping each other's hands as they chanted. (See

Figure 20.5: Red Elementary School girls performing "Apple on a Stick."

transcription on website, Web Figure 20.7 **◐**.) Their regular and intricate movement continued unabated, even as they appeared to change the grouping of the song's rhythm from duple to quadruple meter, with accents shifting from every two pulses to once every four pulses. As they approached the end of the game, the girls became more animated and increased the speed of their performance. The girls stood in circle formation, each one placing her right hand atop the hand of the girl standing to her right, with her left hand underneath the hand of a girl to her left, tapping the beat. A single collective "tap" was passed from one hand to the

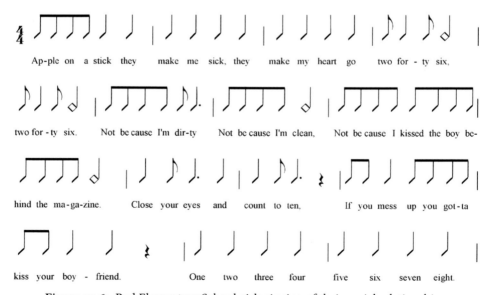

Figure 20.6: Red Elementary School girls singing of their social relationships
with friends and boyfriends.

I do love___ short-nin' bread I do love___ short-nin' bread Ma - ma___ loves

short nin' bread Pa - pa___ loves short nin' bread Ev - 'ry bod y loves short nin' bread.

Figure 20.9: Alabama version of "Shortnin" Bread."

next all around the circle. As the hand-tapping gesture progressed similar to a wave around the circle, the tempo increased until it became too fast to manage, after which the girls would step out of ring formation in boisterous laughter that ended the game. They would then commence to tap and chant in playing the game again. (See photo, Web Figure 20.8 ●.) The African American (and African) musical features described previously were present in the performance.

From my own childhood comes the singing game "Shortnin' Bread," popular among my friends in the early 1960s. We would stand in a circle facing inward, clapping our own hands while lifting our left foot and placing it to our left side while rocking. Next, we would turn our backs to the center of the circle and lift our right foot, placing it to the right side while rocking. We continued to alternate our positions of facing in to the circle, and then out of it, while clapping and singing, to the end of the refrain. Then on the verse, each person improvised a gesture simultaneously, depicting certain words in the text before returning to the refrain. Nine features of African American (and African) music are identifiable in this ring game: syncopation; call-response; African American dialect; tone bending; tone sliding (in the refrain); the presence of blue notes on "lo-ove," "ma-ma," "pa-pa," and "every-body"; improvisation in movements to the text and at the song's end (when each person invents a phrase to chant); vocables (such as "yeah," "do tell") that operate as interjections; and the increased speed of the spoken chant (see Figure 20.9).

THE IMPACT OF TECHNOLOGY ON AFRICAN AMERICAN CHILDREN'S MUSIC

From the prominence of music in African American culture, historically and in current times, music appears as vital to African Americans as breathing is to life. While African Americans have established unique sonic features in their music that come from within their community, they are not immune to outside influences that have helped to shape their characteristic ways of creating and making music. For adults, African and European features converged in the design of musical forms and expressions. Certainly, African American children have found themselves between two music worlds, too: that of a first culture that is handed to them by their parents, grandparents, and other family elders (which is grounded in the essence of all that constitutes African American music) and that of popular culture that comes at them through technology and the media.

The global reach of technology, including satellite television, mobile devices, and the internet are influential in restructuring children's media practices (Drotner 2008: 1). The music of popular culture is readily accessible by African American children, and they are active in their incorporation of facets of song texts, rhythms, and melodies in their musical play. This blending of family and mediated music cultures is exemplary of "transculturation," a process that occurs, according to Wallis and Malm (quoted in Lull 1992: 18), when aspects of one musical culture merge with a second musical culture. This process gives way to the development of "hybrid" musical forms. The new, or visiting musical culture, is accepted but is actively shaped and manipulated to suit the musical tastes and needs of those who listen to or perform it. Lull (1992: 17) observed the tendency of pop and rock bands to incorporate new material into their own more familiar musical expression. Another example of transculturation is rap music in Russia, in which African Americanisms are musically present even when traditional instruments such as the balalaika are played as music accompaniments.

Transculturation may also occur as two musical genres from a single culture come together, as is the case when African American children's singing games sound "rap-like" in quality. Verses may be chanted at high speed and with spoken (and underlying tracks) of rhythms that consist of complicated syncopations. In rap, these tracks are instrumental or technologically produced synthesized rhythms, while in children's songs the rhythmic layers appear in the sounds of clapping, slapping, and snapping. As well, children's song texts may point to the tough realities of living in a poor, urban setting, which may approximate or approach the harsh realities to which rappers refer. The hand clapping game "Mission" makes reference to the experience of incarceration in a prison referred to as a "mission."

> I don't want to go to mission no more, more, more.
> There's a big old watchman at the door, door, door.
> He'll make you want to hollar, make you pay a dollar.
> I don't want to go to mission no more, more, more.

Children who perform this song may not be fully aware of the text's expression of how it feels to be profiled and jailed, but the embedded meaning is definitive of a very real experience.

Technology transmits African American children's music to listening communities throughout the world where their music and games are not part of the ethnic culture. Through sonic and musical media, the music games reach children in world cultures who speak a language different from the African American children but perform the games in their play. Within the United States, technology has played a major role in preserving and making African American children's games available initially through field recordings, Smithsonian Folkways Recordings, and recordings housed at the Library of Congress and other public-access archives. Later, for financial reasons, the games appeared in commercials on radio and television that depicted African American girls singing and playing (Gaunt 2006: 56). Consequently, many young listeners were exposed to the lively rhythms and driving sounds that emanate from African American children's songs such as "Mary Mack," "Apple on a Stick," "Down, Down Baby," and "Shortnin' Bread."

Rap music is typical of African American genres that reflect the adoption of African American children's handclapping games and utilize technology in a revolutionary way. Tricia Rose supports this in her reference to rap as fundamentally literate and deeply technological. She describes rap as lyrical, with musical texts that echo features in African American music (including children's hand clapping games) of oral traditions and postliterate orality with advanced technology (Rose 1994: 95). The technological advancements made in rap were the unique uses of the drum machine and samplers to duplicate a sound and play it back on any pitch or in any key. Prior to rap, sampling was used primarily to add an instrumental section to an existing piece of music on a specific instrument/voice or as vocal backup. However, with the advent of rap music, the break beat was invented, which allowed all sounds in a piece of music to "rupture" (to be suspended) so that individual rhythms could be isolated and heard, for example, drums (Rose 1994: 73)—after which all rhythms and sounds could be layered one on another and presented as a total sound. This technique mirrors the sounds heard in African American children's hand clapping games, in which chanting and body movements are layered but heard and performed as a whole. Famous rap artists have used sampling and other electronic devices to arrange and reproduce children's playground songs to create new renditions of classic children's songs. One rapped rendition by Little Richard (the rock-and-roll artist from the 1950s) in 1991 features chanting in rap style of "Itsy Bitsy Spider." Other examples are Kanye West's "Family Business," in which he incorporates a syncopated African American children's version of the traditional rhyme "Rain, Rain Go Away" and Nelly's use of "Down, Down Baby" and "Shimmy, Shimmy Ko-Ko Pop" in his recording of "Country Grammar." Technological means, as well as mediation to listeners through recording, radio, television, and the internet, provide young listeners with fresh renditions of the continuing traditions of African American children's music.

SUMMARY

African American children mirror their environment in the various games, songs, and dances they play. The games and songs are important because they serve as a homogenizing agent in stabilizing issues of race, poverty, and social injustice that concerns African Americans within their communities. Further, the games contribute to forming and maintaining personal and group identity, survival (Gaunt 2006: 14), socialization, solidarity, cooperation, and strength within the group (Wharton-Boyd 1983: 52–53). Although, the songs and games of their African ancestors no longer exist, the structure of African music remains within the music culture of the children. In addition, the songs of African American children exude features of African American adult music that have emerged over the decades. Young girls, especially those in their middle childhood years of seven to ten, are protective of their singing games, maintaining them and shaping them to their needs. The enthusiasm of African American children for their singing games ensures the continuation of long-standing beliefs and values that belong to them and to the spectrum of musical expressions within African American culture at large.

ACKNOWLEDGMENT

Special thanks is extended to the third-grade girls in "Red School," a public elementary school in Tennessee, for sharing their African American games with me.

REFERENCES

Brooks, T. 1984. *America's Black Music Heritage.* Englewood Cliffs, NJ: Prentice Hall.
Burnim, M. 1988. "Functional Dimensions of Gospel Music Performance." *Western Journal of Black Studies* 12 (2): 112–121.
Cohn, Lawrence. 1993. *Nothing but the Blues.* New York: Abbeville Press.
Courlander, H. 1963. *Negro Folk Music.* New York: Columbia University Press.
Drotner, K., and S. Livingstone. 2008. *The International Handbook of Children, Media and Culture.* Los Angeles: Sage.
Gaunt, K. 2006. *The Games Black Girls Play.* New York: New York University Press.
Hahn, Steven. 2003. *A Nation under Our Feet.* Cambridge, MA: Harvard University Press.
Harwood, Eve. 1998a. "Go On Girl! Improvisation in African-American Girls" Singing Games." In *In the Course of Performance: Studies in the World of Musical Improvisation*, edited by Bruno Nettl and Melinda Russell, 113–125. Chicago: University of Chicago Press.
Harwood, Eve. 1998b. "Music Learning in Context: A Playground Tale." *Research Studies in Music Education* 11 (1): 52–60.
Hening Statues at Large. 1662. Laws of Virginia, 2:167.
Keil, C. 1995. "The Theory of Participatory Discrepancies: A Progress Report." *Ethnomusicology* 39 (1): 1–19.
Levine, L. 1977. *Black Culture and Black Consciousness.* Oxford: Oxford Press.
Lull, J., ed. 1992. *Popular Music and Communication.* Newbury Park, CA: Sage.
Maultsby, P. 2005. "Africanism in African American Music." In *Africanism in American Culture*, edited by Joseph E. Holloway, 326–355. Bloomington, IN: Indiana University Press.

Nketia, J. H. Kwabena. 1981. "African Roots of Music in the Americas: An African View." Report of the 12th Congress of the American Musicological Society, London, 1946.

Rose, Tricia. 1994. *Black Noise: Rap Music and Black Culture in Contemporary America*. Hanover, London: Wesleyan University Press.

Virginia General Assembly Declaration. 1705.

Wallis, R., and K. Malm. 1992. "The International Music Industry and Transnational Communication." In *Popular Music and Communication*, edited by J. Lull, 1–32. Newbury Park, CA: Sage.

Wharton-Boyd, Linda F. 1983. "The Significance of Black American Children's Singing Games in an Educational Setting." *Journal of Negro Education* 52 (1): 46–56.

PART 3

MUSIC IN EDUCATION AND DEVELOPMENT

21

CHILDREN'S AND ADOLESCENTS' MUSICAL NEEDS AND MUSIC EDUCATION IN GERMANY

ALEXANDRA KERTZ-WELZEL

> Luckily, teachers do not know a lot about children, because
> most of the time, they are only interested in what children
> do not know. (Segler 2003: 200)

THE German music educator and ethnomusicologist Helmuth Segler (1914–1992), who became famous for listening to children's voices by collecting their songs and dances, criticized German music education from the 1960s to the 1980s because of its focus on teaching instead of exploring children's musical cultures (Segler 2003: 197). The fact that scholars and teachers know little about children's musical cultures is one important aspect contributing to the fact that music education in German schools is often perceived by children and youth to be the least popular subject. If teachers do not know their students' musical cultures, it becomes challenging to offer music education lessons that can be meaningful to them.

This chapter explores the musical cultures of children and youth in Germany, including their musical and aesthetic needs. The voices of children are heard and honored alongside the views of scholars in order to understand what impact the

German tradition of music education has had on children's lives as well as to find new ways for more effective music education theory and practice.

BEING A CHILD OR ADOLESCENT IN GERMANY

> Music means a lot to me and I could not imagine a life without music. (Jan, age twelve)

It is commonly accepted by scholars in the educational sciences that today's childhood is a "changed childhood" (*veränderte Kindheit*) in that many matters in young people's lives are not the way they used to be (Fölling-Albers 2005: 19–34). Different family structures, the impact of the media, and changing perspectives on education and schooling have changed the situation in which children grow up. While these aspects are often seen as signs of the decline of German society, putting at risk children's development, German children seem to view this situation in a different way. According to the World Vision Kinderstudie (Hurrelmann and Andresen 2007), which investigated how German children between the ages of eight and eleven live and what they think about family and school, children rate poverty, their parents' unemployment, and the lack of friends as far more problematic to them than the impact of new family structures. In general, most German children are happy with their family life (Fölling-Albers 2005: 23). They experience their family as a place of safety and love, although parents' separation or divorce often destroys this happiness. Many German children—as many as one in three—experience parental unemployment at some point in their young lives, particularly children of immigrants, children of single parents, children in the former East Germany, and children in poor families. While 53 percent of all children think that they have what they need, 13 percent consider themselves living in poverty (Hurrelmann and Andresen 2007: 13). Dennis—an eleven-year-old student in a school for children with special needs, who lives in an old skyscraper in Berlin, and whose parents are separated—said that if a fairy would grant him three wishes, he would like to live in a different apartment, to have a happy family, and to own a cool car. He confided that he would ask King Kong to help him to change the world and also "to torment some people" (Hurrelmann and Andresen 2007: 13). While Dennis did not name which people he would like to annoy, it is most likely that at least some of them are in schools, as this is the place that most German children do not like (Fölling-Albers 2005: 25). This is particularly true for children in the first two grades of elementary school, when many are confronted for the first time with aggression and social hierarchies. Surprisingly, children are not afraid of their teachers, as was the case some decades ago, but rather find some of their peers unsettling to them. Up to 10 percent of students experience some kind of violence during their school years, often undetected by teachers (Hurrelmann and Andresen 2007: 16). The German school system, in its traditional version, is generally the cause of considerable problems since it is focused on the support of students from wealthy families and is typically less attentive to children and youth from lower socioeconomic backgrounds. A successful life in Germany very much depends upon the socioeconomic background of the family one is raised in. According to the 2007 OECD (Organisation for Economic Co-operation and Development) study, children from parents of lower social classes are less likely to go to college in Germany than in any of the other eight European states investigated. Children of wealthy parents are twice as likely to go to college as children from poorer families (OECD Briefing Notes 2007: 14). The lack of support and opportunities to learn in lower social class families and in families with a non-German background are problems that neither kindergarten nor school are able to compensate, particularly because the German government does not spend as much money as other European countries on education (OECD Briefing Notes 2007: 18). This also affects the kind of college degree students aspire to. Most students in German high schools, the *Gymnasium* (formerly the only way to get into university programs), are from families of middle or upper social classes. Students from lower classes aim at schools and degrees that offer them fewer and less well-paid job opportunities. These students are not interested in going to a university and therefore decide to go to schools such as the *Hauptschule*, which does not offer the highest high school degree (*Abitur*). Eleven-year-old Kevin, who is a student at a *Hauptschule*, wishes he were "smarter" because he knows that with his education he will never have a chance to get a good job (Hurrelmann and Andresen 2007: 19). This overall tendency of having few students educated at the highest quality secondary schools also shows in the graduation rate from universities in Germany, which is only 20 percent or less, compared to more than 40 percent in Australia, Finland, and Italy (OECD Briefing Notes 2007: 2).

Outside school, leisure time is another important part of children's lives, and the differences of ethnic background, money, class, and education are also obvious here. Group activities such as sports and music classes are attended by 77 percent of the children of German origin, but only 63 percent of children with a non-German background, and only 47 percent of children with a lower class background. Children who do not participate mostly watch TV or play computer games (Hurrelmann and Andresen 2007: 20). Children of the lower classes often do not have access to sports clubs or private music instruction because their parents do not consider these activities to be important (Hurrelmann and Andresen 2007: 21–22). Another significant aspect of children's lives is the feeling of well-being, which, according to Hurrelmann and Andresen (2007: 23–25), in Germany depends significantly on social integration, the city where children live, their nationality, and family structure. Most children (88 percent) like the way they live and the freedom their parents grant them. They also think that their opinion is valued in their own family and that the schools and other places where they spend time do not acknowledge them in the same way (Hurrelmann and Andresen 2007: 27). Fear of the future, of bad school grades, or issues like climate change are not as significant for children as for adolescents, but the fear increases with age (Hurrelmann and Andresen 2007: 28).

Childhood and adolescence in Germany are also very much influenced by the media. Many children spend considerable time watching TV, playing computer games, and listening to music. While the media's impact on children's lives can be troublesome in that they shape them as dangerously passive recipients who rely emotionally on the media and substitute them for real relationships, they also offer information, enabling young people to organize their private and musical life more independently. A survey regarding the media's impact on German students' lives (Krebs 2008: 5) asked what they would take with them to a deserted island. Young people made interesting statements: a thirteen-year-old boy responded that he would only need the internet because he would then have everything; an eleven-year-old boy preferred his cell phone, because he would be able to call everybody, including people who could rescue him; a ten-year-old boy preferred the TV; another thirteen-year-old boy would take the internet and maybe the radio because of the music they offered him. These statements are evidence of the media as a constant companion and that music plays an important role in young people's lives.

CHILDREN'S AND ADOLESCENTS' MUSICAL CULTURES IN GERMANY

Music means a lot to me. Because I play piano, I could not even imagine a life without music. I almost always listen to music. Without it, my life would be boring. Music makes you happy, comforts you, and gives you energy. (Tatjana, age thirteen)

While trying to explore children's and adolescents' musical cultures in Germany, one is confronted with a terminological dilemma. There is no literal translation of the English "children's musical cultures" but only some words that come close to its meaning, such as *Kinderkultur* or *musikalische Lebenswelt*, which also exemplify the more general problems German music education has regarding young people and their musical worlds.

The term *Kinderkultur* (children's culture) can have two different meanings, one regarding children's culture in general, defining music or art that adults think appropriate for children, the other one aiming at the "culture" or musical world children select or create for themselves (Bullerjahn 2005: 128–130). The first meaning of *Kinderkultur* is based on a notion of childhood most common since the seventeenth century regarding children as rather helpless creatures who need instruction in order to become moral, self-responsible, and musical human beings. The second meaning of *Kinderkultur* in terms of the music or art that children choose or create for themselves is based on the idea of self-socialization. According to this concept children act as independent members of the society and choose the information, roles, and music they are interested in. While this notion of *Kinderkultur* seems similar to the English-language meaning of children's musical cultures, in fact, there are differences. According to Bullerjahn (2005: 129), many German music educators agree that children's use of music should be subject to discussion or at least a more conscious selection that is guided by adults because children should not use music only for pure pleasure or for escaping into a world of dreams.

These doubts concerning children's choices might be surprising in view of the fact that since the 1980s, the term *Jugendmusikkultur* (youth music culture) and its notion of adolescents creating their own musical cultures have been widely accepted by educators and researchers. Youth cultures are generally seen as adolescents' specific reactions to their situation in society in terms of searching for their own place. They offer young adults important opportunities for developing their personal and musical identities through adapting certain musical styles and concepts of living that offer them emotional and social stability (Müller 2005: 121). Being an active member of a musical youth culture such as hip-hop or punk also involves developing the musical competencies and knowledge that is part of this culture.

Another German term that is often used regarding the musical world of children and adolescents is *Lebenswelt* (life-world). Originally introduced in philosophical discussion by the German philosopher Edmund Husserl in 1936, it characterizes the pregiven, self-evident background of individuals in terms of real and nonscholarly perceptions and experiences, contrasting with the experiences offered by the sciences. The life-world is the basis for all epistemological inquiries. While the meaning of life-world is not completely clear either in Husserl's writings or in Sartre's or Merleau-Ponty's thinking, the German educational sciences nevertheless adopted the term in the 1980s, using it to describe students' everyday life experiences as opposed to those they encounter in schools. The implicit idea was that teachers would try to connect their lessons to the experiences that students know outside of schools. While there have been scholars arguing for a clear distinction between school and life-world—often justified by the tradition of *Bildung*—in music education, the life-world approach became popular in the late 1980s and early 1990s. It would seem that the German term for musical life-worlds of children, *musikalische Lebenswelten von Kindern*, would be the most appropriate translation for the English-language phrase "children's musical cultures."

Apart from the terminological issues, children's musical cultures do exist in Germany, and there are various ways of approaching them. One of the most extensive research projects is a study conducted by Günter Kleinen and Rainer Schmitt in 1991. They collected and analyzed more than 5,000 drawings by German students from age six to fifteen from the northern German cities of Braunschweig, Bremen, Bremerhaven, and Hannover. Analyzing the content of these drawings, Kleinen and Schmitt were surprised about the variety of illustrations and the significance of music in young people's lives. The analysis of content led to eight different areas in which students pictured music's meaning in their lives. These areas are making music, movement and dance, music on stage, listening, dreams and wishes, music and nature, political dreams, and music as picture. Drawings often showed students in the act of performing, frequently in front of an audience. Eleven-year-old Arend drew a picture of himself playing piano while his parents watched and supported him (Kleinen and Schmitt 1991: 16). Ten-year-old Almuth pictured the weekly rehearsal of a school choir and orchestra (Kleinen and Schmitt 1991: 18) and said that she enjoyed most being with other children and making music. Children also drew a variety of situations in which they danced, from the little second grader Janine who pictured herself as a "dream dancer" (Kleinen and Schmitt 1991: 32) to older students who depicted themselves as ballet dancers, break dancers, or dancers in discos. Students who drew situations exemplifying music on stage appeared to be influenced by the media, often picturing themselves as singing stars or players in rock bands. While twelve-year-old Patrick made a drawing with the Beatles on stage, ten-year-old Sandra drew a picture of her class performing on stage with classroom instruments (Kleinen and Schmitt 1991: 48). Drawings regarding the topic "listening to music" were mostly concerned with the various ways students use music in the privacy of their daily lives. Children created pictures in which they appeared alone in a room, with headphones or their stereos. Concerning dreams and music, there were many stereotypical illustrations, such as images of an island with palm trees, or flying human figures, or things in nature such as birds, water, and trees that were their symbolic renderings of paradise. Fourteen-year-old Carmen drew a picture of a boy and a girl dancing in a room under a cloud, illustrating her perception that music is a way of escaping into a world of wishes and dreams (Kleinen and Schmitt 1991: 83). Twelve-year-old Erdal drew a picture of himself on a secluded island with palm trees listening to music, exemplified by a huge stereo (Kleinen and Schmitt 1991: 88). Pictures belonging to the section "music and nature" showed similar stereotypes. Waterfalls, singing birds, the sea, trees, the sun, clouds, and rainbows were the most common ways of picturing the connection between music and nature. Drawings such as twelve-year-old Sahrie's "Music at a Waterfall" showed the waterfall splashing a white froth of fast water with notes drawn as if coming from the water (Kleinen and Schmitt 1991: 102). A Turkish student, Kimon, claimed that "nature is like music in my ears" and drew a person riding a bike close to beautiful mountains, flowers, and meadows. Making music, celebrating, and dancing with friends in a meadow were also important topics of the drawings (Kleinen and Schmitt 1991: 106).

Although Kleinen and Schmitt's study was conducted from the late 1980s to early 1990s, it still functions as a point of reference for research on the meaning of music in young people's lives. It offers a framework for how they make music meaningful in their lives. In order to examine how today's students would describe the meaning of music in their lives, I invited students ten to thirteen years of age enrolled in grades 5, 6, and 7 of a German high school (*Gymnasium*) in the southwestern part of Germany to draw pictures regarding the topic "*Ich und die Musik*" (Me and Music). Although this small and informal study is not representative of students at large, it offers timely insights in children's musical worlds. Not surprisingly, the results did not differ greatly from Kleinen's and Schmitt's research. Many students in the fifth grade drew musical instruments, rehearsals, musical situations at home, or a band on stage; many others created a poster featuring their favorite bands and singing stars. Two little girls with Turkish backgrounds, Aisha and Shirin, both eleven years of age, offered different drawings: One picture showed the girl by herself, weeping, with notes circling around her, and the topic "Me and Music" written above the picture. On the back of the drawing, she says that she only listens to music when she is sad, because music makes her happy. On Shirin's drawing (see Figure 21.1) there is the title "Music Is the World" and a girl in the center who is surrounded by various real and imagined musical instruments; in the background there is a plane, a sunrise, clouds, and birds, all of which are intended to symbolize the world.

Johanna, a twelve-year-old student, concentrated on the meaning of music in various situations. In the left corner of her picture (see Figure 21.2), she drew a person playing the saxophone, while in the right-hand corner a person is depicted lying on a bed in her room, listening to music and dreaming. In the upper part of the picture, there are people dancing or performing on instruments, and in the middle, the German word *vielseitig* (versatile) points to all corners, signifying the various meanings that music can have.

While drawings exemplify children's ideas and imaginations about music, it is useful to know what children and adolescents in Germany have to say about music in their personal lives. A study conducted by a group of researchers at the University of Hildesheim between 1998 and 2001 examined self-initiated musical activities of German third- and fourth-grade students in order to determine their involvement in musical activities (Badur 2007). The study revealed that children participate in more self-initiated musical activities and learning (58 percent of all musical activities) than in activities that were guided by parents or teachers. One-fifth of children's musical activities were "frame activities" (*Rahmenaktivitäten*), such as obtaining musical information or material, looking for musical situations, or reporting musical activities (Badur 2007: 61). Children are interested in the newest music trends,

Figure 21.1: Shirin's drawing for "Me and Music."

Figure 21.2: Johanna's drawing for "Me and Music."

popular hits, dance styles, and CDs. They read stories about their favorite musicians or bands and share information with each other about it. Furthermore, they sing, dance, and imitate their stars and enjoy talking together about music, for example, about organizing a band or learning how to dance. Their musical experiences are often connected to games such as role-playing and karaoke singing. Children also enjoy improvising and inventing songs that feature the characters they know from TV shows or books (Badur 2007: 65).

Research regarding the meaning of music in the lives of elementary school children in the 1990s, including their musical needs (Weber, Bullerjahn, and Erwe 1999), supports earlier findings but also led to some unexpected results: primarily that children's concept of music is very much influenced by the media, particularly rock and pop music and musicians. While it is commonly understood that popular music is important to adolescents, it appears that rock and pop music is also important for younger children. However, it is not, as for adolescents, part of their individual identity but a way of playing, improvising, or managing their mood. In one research project, the children were told a story about a government minister who wanted to ban music in order to regulate the economy (Weber et al. 1999: 117). Third graders were asked to write letters to the government minister expressing their feelings (which were mostly outrage and anger) about this decision, underlining music's vital importance for their own lives and the lives of other people. Later, fifth graders at a German high school were invited to respond to the situation as well, and their letters did not vary much from those of the original study: many students wrote that it would be wrong to ban music, because it makes their lives meaningful, helps them to relax, and makes life more fun. "Without music," ten-year-old Max states, "the world would be very sad pretty soon." Jenny (age eleven) wrote this example (Web Figure 21.3 ⬤):

> Dear Mr. Minister,
> Please do not ban music, because children and adults want to have fun. Music calms you down if you are sad or angry.... For many people, music is their life, and if you take away music, they will not have a real life anymore.... Music is vital.... Do you want to destroy people's lives? (Translation by K.-W.)

Because of the importance of music in their lives, students in German schools are often disappointed by their school music classes because they do not address their musical interests and needs. Knowledge of formal music education in Germany, and how the content and processes fall short of student expectations, is useful in a discussion of more relevant and effective music instruction for German children and youth.

German Music Education and Students' Musical Needs

> Music means for me that I can listen to it and feel better afterward, particularly when nobody understands me. (Katharina, age thirteen)

Music education is the least popular subject in German schools (Deutsch 2008: 32), particularly at German high schools. While there might be many reasons for this, for example, the quality of instruction or the lack of equipment in a music room, it is also significant for the traditional German music education approach, which is a general music education. It seems that student needs and the knowledge and skills music education has to offer them simply do not match.

Why do students not like music education in German schools even when music is such an important part of their lives outside of schools? Studies conducted by Schulten (1980), Bastian (1985, 1992), and Harnitz (2000) suggest the following reasons:

1. Students are not able to understand the meaning and goals of music education in schools, particularly as related to their own musical cultures.
2. Students often do not like traditional lesson content such as reading and writing notation, studying Western European art music, drilling on matters of music theory or group-singing of school music repertoire.
3. Methods are often teacher-centered instead of action- or student-oriented.
4. Teachers frequently rely too much on the power of words for instruction and thus they talk about music instead of offering students various

opportunities for making music, exploring it or playing with various kinds
of sounds.

5. The difference between student expectations and teacher intentions is a
   permanent source of tension. (Krämer 2004: 230)

These various issues lead to serious classroom management problems in
German schools, which then makes music education one of the most challenging subjects to teach. In interviews regarding their experiences in music education, many young people stressed the rather annoying methods of instruction and
the questionable reactions of students. A sixteen-year-old male student stated that
"nobody was interested in music education, so students threw things around and
ignored the teacher's instructions" (Bastian 1989: 338). An eighteen-year-old female
student reported that "nobody wanted to sing in music education or to listen to
classical music." Students reported that other students sang wrong intentionally or
made paper planes when they should have been attending to lessons (Bastian 1989:
338). Particularly in German high schools, the main emphases in music education
are theory, listening, and information giving, with little attention to various exploratory and participatory musical activities (as is much more the case in elementary
schools). A nineteen-year-old female student said that fifth-grade music class at a
German high school was mostly concerned with "completing worksheets, reading
texts and getting to know the basic musical elements," which matched the curricular
description (Funk 1990: 99). Students also preferred not to focus on listening activities, "music appreciation," which led to testing of information on styles and works.
Furthermore, students who received private music instruction outside of school
were bored by their school classes, because they already knew the content.

This ill-matched connection between students' musical needs and German
music education might be partly the result of the specific German tradition of education in terms of *Bildung* and *Didaktik*. These two words stand for two important
educational concepts that aim at ambitious ideals of education. *Bildung* is a term
that became important during the eighteenth century, describing a kind of formation and cultivation of individuals that goes beyond the learning of useful skills and
knowledge. It particularly concerns the development of students' self, their personality, and their identity, regarding both self-determination, responsibility, and
autonomy and cognitive, aesthetic, and moral aspects (Kertz-Welzel 2004: 278).
The idea of *Bildung* in its original version led to a domination of the humanities
and the liberal arts, lesson content that has often been far away from the life-world
of students. This also fostered a distinction between high and low culture, the first
being for cultivated people who reached the goal of *Bildung*, the second for people who do not live in the realm of the liberal arts and therefore go to vocational
schools, aiming at more practical professions. The idea of *Bildung* also fostered an
elite understanding of talent, promoting the ideology of "the musically gifted few,"
while other students were viewed as listeners rather than musicians.

Another important term for the German tradition of education and music education is *Didaktik*. This is an umbrella concept for the theory or science of teaching

and the practice of organizing lessons by offering certain models of instruction. These models provide a theory of educational content and aims. *Didaktik* concepts that have been important are the focus on music as art, the development of auditory perception, polyaesthetic education, music as aesthetic experience, and the life-world approach (Kertz-Welzel 2004: 280). These various models emphasize different meanings of music, music education, and teaching. While polyaesthetic education tries to foster a reunification of the different arts through improvising and creating theatrical scenes, the life-world approach is much more oriented toward students' everyday musical experiences. The artwork approach underlines the aesthetic power of Western European art music, mostly relying on listening and analyzing music. All *Didaktik* concepts offer a pedagogical or aesthetic foundation as well as categories for selecting educational content or methods. However, *Didaktik* is also a theory that puts the teacher into an authoritative position, conceiving what might be useful in order to make students into musical people, to foster their musical formation (*musikalische Bildung*). While child-centered and action-oriented approaches are certainly common in Germany, the tradition of *Bildung* and *Didaktik* implies an emphasis on the teacher, often not paying as much attention to the abilities and skills students already have because the main interest is on instruction and "cultivating" students. Furthermore, the *Didaktik* tradition in terms of enabling teachers to be professionals in educational models has led to underestimating the impact of methods for successful music education instruction. Distinct pedagogical methods such as those proposed by Orff, Kodály, and Dalcroze have never been fully exercised in German schools.

Does the German tradition of music education have to result in students' lack of interest? Is there no overlap between the goals of music education in Germany and students' interests? Certainly, there are commonalities. Particularly through knowledge about children's musical cultures, it would be possible to create a more successful music education practice. Renate Beckers (2004: 165–174) emphasized that there is not much difference between the musical life-worlds, wishes, and needs of children between ages four and ten and what music education is supposed to offer, according to the music curricula of some states. She compared the music education curriculum of elementary schools in Nordrhein-Westfalen, the largest of the German states, to the musical cultures of students in Germany between ages four and ten years. There are many similarities, such as making music, listening, movement, and talking about music.

- Singing: Students are able to perform their favorite pop songs by heart, even when they are rhythmically difficult. It seems that children do not need age-appropriate, easy music (as has been suggested by music educators). Children simply need to love the music, and then they are willing to learn what it takes to perform it. Music education curricula also propose singing as important but often in different ways from children's musical cultures.
- Listening: For children, listening seems to be a way of being actively involved with music, whether it is background music or music for specific

situations. Children are experts in their specific kind of music, particularly pop music, and they enjoy moving to it and talking about it. This approach to listening offers a valuable overlap between music education curricula and children's musical cultures that can be useful.

- Movement: Movement and dancing are, for children, the most natural ways of perceiving music. While children often move intuitively, a school program can be constructed to consist of various musical activities that invite children to move in musically sensitive, eurhythmic, and dance-like ways.
- Notation and musical terminology: The music curriculum for elementary schools dictates studies in notation and musical terminology in order to develop the musical understanding of students. Children like to gather information regarding the music they love and to talk about it, but they often do not know the right terminology. Music education can offer certain concepts for making music and talking about it.

Music educators can learn from the commonalities between children's musical worlds and the music education curriculum in order to create successful school music programs. In fact, music programs in German elementary schools are succeeding (Gaul 2009: 241) where secondary school music is not. In question at the secondary school is whether music education should always be connected to students' own musical interests or whether there are ways to bring adolescent students into a study of various musical expressions that include popular music, participatory music making and classical music, music theory, and music history.

German youth often criticize the lesson content as well as the methods teachers use (Schulten 1980). They want "creative methods" that enable them to be actively engaged. Students prefer working in small groups as well as exploring and trying out various things and sounds, and they enjoy planning music lessons by themselves, selecting their own topics of study, and giving presentations. When I invited seventh- and ninth-grade students at a German high school to present the music they like or were interested in, they chose different topics. Seventh-grade students who liked punk and rap picked both international music performers, such as Lady Gaga, 50 Cent, The Black Eyed Peas, T.I., David Guetta, Linkin Park, and German bands, such as Culcha Candela, Peter Fox, Wise Guys, Die Toten Hosen, and Die Ärzte. Students also chose popular music "classics," including Nirvana and Michael Jackson. Ninth-grade students chose similar musical groups and styles, with particular interest in performers such as Rise Against, Tenacious D, Billy Talent, Kanye West, and Marit Larsen. They claimed they were not as influenced by the media as younger students, and there was greater mention by ninth-grade students of popular music classics such as ACDC, Bob Marley, Carlos Santana, and Red Hot Chili Peppers. The time and energy students in both grades spent on creating presentations and posters of their music was an indication of their interests in describing and discussing music as well as in their need for the guidance of teachers in helping them to grow their descriptive vocabulary (see Web Figures 21.4, 21.5, 21.6 🔘).

Students frequently mention their interests in making music. While singing and playing classroom instruments are components of the German approach of general music education, choirs and orchestras have traditionally been extracurricular activities. However, in recent years, there have been attempts to introduce orchestral and band instruments into schools. The most widely known project is the JeKi (Jedem Kind ein Instrument: An Instrument for Every Child) initiative. At the core of one well-documented JeKi project was that young first- and second-grade children in Bochum were introduced to musical instruments in addition to the regular vocal music and listening program. During the first year of this two-year study, children were introduced to various kinds of instruments and became acquainted with them, allowing them to choose their favorite instrument. During the second year, they participated in group lessons based on their choice of instruments. The results are unsurprising: children were enthusiastic about learning to play an instrument and enjoyed their school music instruction (Beckers and Beckers 2008: 123–137).

Apart from the JeKi project, there are attempts to introduce instrumental music education in German schools, for example by offering string classes for fifth- and sixth-grade students. But instrumental music education is certainly not the only way to connect music education to the musical worlds of German children and youth. There are many more ways, which depend upon the extent of knowledge of the musical needs and interests of young people.

Conclusion: The Meaning of Children's and Adolescents' Musical Cultures for Music Education in Germany

Without music, life would be boring. (Marvin, age twelve)

An examination of the musical cultures of children and adolescents in Germany offers new perspectives for their musical education. After all, students as well as teachers have musical expertise in various areas (Hofmann 2011). Even if music is already an important part of children's lives, in order to become musically more proficient, they need the help of their parents and teachers. Formal systems of music education should certainly take into account children's genuine interest in music and specific kinds of musical activities—although it should not be solely focused on what children prefer but also on what they need to know. In this way, music education can offer opportunities to broaden the musical perspectives of young people and to develop new abilities and skills.

Renate Müller posited that it cannot be music education's goal to meet every musical need of every student (1990: 227–228). Rather, music education should aim at various means of musical engagement that can be enthusiastically received by students. Helping children and youth to become more musically skilled and knowledgeable, with the ability to use music effectively in their lives, are important aims. Music education in Germany will be successful when it addresses the musical needs of students and when it develops pathways for them to become self-determined musical individuals who use music the way they need it.

Accepting children as musicians in their own right and as creators of their musical cultures will develop music's place in the curriculum of German schools. Then, the challenge will be not only facilitating the content of curricula but also helping children to learn how to meet their own musical needs, particularly regarding mood management and self-expression, and to develop their creativity (Segler 2003: 206–208). The educationalist Hans Aebli (1997: 164) stated that we are only successful teachers as long as we know students' worlds and the things that are important to them in order to connect lessons to their experiences. This is certainly not an easy task, particularly not in German music education with its tradition of *Bildung*. But this underlines the basic dialectical nature of teaching, particularly teaching music: music education has to be related to students' musical cultures and meet their musical needs, but it sometimes has to go beyond their wishes and comfort zone in order to initiate learning. The German music education scholar Heinz Antholz (1984: 124–133) proposed that, while taking into account student needs in terms of a student-centered approach in music education, it is also often necessary to refuse some of their preferences. Particularly then, the teacher can plan and deliver meaningful lessons that lead young people into the musical unknowns. This does not invalidate the meaning of young people's musical cultures but emphasizes the need for getting to know their musical worlds in order to be able to facilitate meaningful musical experiences and musical learning. German music teachers will do well to take into account students' musical cultures while also going beyond the borders of what music they know so that music education can be more meaningful and fulfilling, both for German students and teachers.

REFERENCES

Aebli, Hans. 1997. *Grundlagen des Lehrens*. 4th ed. Stuttgart, Germany: Klett-Cotta.

Antholz, Heinz. 1984. "Der Schüler—der findet gar nicht statt." In *Musikpädagogische Konzeptionen und Schulalltag. Versuch einer kritischen Bilanz der 70er Jahre*, edited by Friedrich Ritzel and Wolfgang Martin Stroh, 124–133. Wilhelmshaven, Germany: Heinrichshofen.

Badur, Imke-Marie. 2007. "Selbstinitiierte musikbezogene Aktivitäten von Kindern im Grundschulalter." In *Musikalische Sozialisation im Kindes- und Jugendalter*, edited by Wolfgang Auhagen, Claudia Bullerjahn, and Holger Höge, 54–70. Musikpsychologie no. 19. Göttingen, Germany: Hogrefe.

Bastian, Hans Günter. 1989. *Leben für Musik. Eine Biographie-Studie über musikalische (Hoch) Begabungen*. Mainz, Germany: Schott.

Bastian, Hans Günter. 1992. "Musikunterricht im Schülerurteil—Ergebnisse und Konsequenzen aus qualitativer und quantitativer Forschung." In

Schülerbild—Lehrerbild—Musiklehrerausbildung, edited by Ulrich Günther and Siegmund Helms, 112–137. Essen, Germany: Blaue Eule.

Beckers, Erich, and Renate Beckers. 2008. *Faszination Musikinstrument—Musikmachen motiviert.* Berlin: LIT.

Beckers, Renate. 2004. *Die musikalische Lebenswelt 4- bis 10-jähriger Kinder.* Münster, Germany: LIT.

Bullerjahn, Claudia. 2005. "Kinderkultur." In *Lexikon der Musikpädagogik*, edited by Siegmund Helms, Reinhard Schneider, and Rudolf Weber, 128–130. Kassel, Germany: Gustav Bosse.

Deutsch, Karl Heinz. 2008. "Kinderweltenstudie 2008. Basisdaten Kinder & Eltern." Paper presented at the Kinderwelten Fachtagung, Frankfurt am Main, Germany, May 27, 2008. Accessed June 24, 2011. http://superrtl.de/Portals/0/Mediadaten/01_Deutsch_Basisdaten.pdf.

Fölling-Albers, Maria. 2005. "Nicht nur Kinder sind verschieden." In *Musiklernen im Vor- und Grundschulalter*, edited by Jürgen Vogt, 17–36. Essen, Germany: Die Blaue Eule.

Funk, Anja. 1990. "Wie Schüler den Musikunterricht erleben." *Musik und Bildung* 2: 99–100.

Gaul, Magnus. 2009. *Musikunterricht aus Schülersicht.* Mainz, Germany: Schott.

Harnitz, Matthias. 2000. "Lehren und Lernen im Schatten von Konflikten. Ergebnisse einer empirischen Studie zum Musikunterricht." *Musik und Bildung* 3: 22–27.

Hofmann, Katja. 2011. *"Ein Esel galoppiert durchs Paradies …" Musikalische Hörfähigkeiten von Kindern im Grundschulalter.* Augsburg, Germany: Wißner.

Hurrelmann, Klaus, and Sabine Andresen. 2007. *Kindsein in Deutschland aus Sicht der Kinder: Ergebnisse der I. World Vision Kinderstudie.* Friedrichsdorf, Germany: World Vision Institut. Accessed June 24, 2011. http://www.kinderschutzbund-nrw.de/kinderstudie2007.pdf.

Kertz-Welzel, Alexandra. 2004. "Didaktik of Music: A German Concept and Its Comparison to American Music Pedagogy." *International Journal of Music Education (Practice)* 22 (3): 277–286.

Kleinen, Günter, and Rainer Schmitt. 1991. *Musik verbindet: Musikalische Lebenswelten auf Schülerbildern.* Essen, Germany: Blaue Eule.

Krämer, Rudolf-Dieter. 2004. *Musikpädagogik—Eine Einführung in das Studium.* Augsburg, Germany: Wißner.

Krebs, Carola. 2008. "Kinder im Netz: Zur Rolle des Web 2.0 im Medienbudget der 8- bis 14-Jährigen." Paper presented at the Kinderwelten Fachtagung, Frankfurt am Main, Germany, May 27, 2008. Accessed June 24, 2011. http://superrtl.de/Portals/0/Mediadaten/05_Krebs_Web20.pdf.

Müller, Renate. 2005. "Musikalische Jugendkulturen." In *Lexikon der Musikpädagogik*, edited by Siegmund Helms, Reinhard Schneider, and Rudolf Weber, 122–123. Kassel, Germany: Gustav Bosse Verlag.

Müller, Renate, Patrick Glogner, Stefanie Rhein, and Jens Heim, eds. 2002. *Wozu Jugendliche Musik und Medien gebrauchen.* Munich, Germany: Juventa.

OECD Briefing Notes für Deutschland. 2007. Accessed June 24, 2011. http://www.oecd.org/dataoecd/22/28/39317467.pdf.

Schulten, Marie-Luise. 1980. "Schülerwünsche zu Unterrichtsmethoden im Musikunterricht." In *Musikpädagogische Forschung. Band 1: Einzeluntersuchungen*, edited by Klaus-Ernst Behne, 96–111. Kassel, Germany: Laaber.

Segler, Helmut. 2003. "Kritik an einer Pädagogik des Kindgemäßen." In *Musik und Kind*, edited by Günter Kleinen, 197–208. Kassel, Germany: Laaber.

Vogt, Jürgen. 2001. *Der schwankende Boden der Lebenswelt. Phänomenologische Musikpädagogik zwischen Handlungstheorie und Ästhetik*. Würzburg, Germany: Königshausen und Neumann.

Vogt, Jürgen. 2005. "Lebenswelt." In *Lexikon der Musikpädagogik*, edited by Siegmund Helms, Reinhard Schneider, and Rudolf Weber, 140–141. Kassel, Germany: Gustav Bosse.

Weber, Rudolf, Claudia Bullerjahn, and Hans-Joachim Erwe. 1999. "Musikbezogene Bedürfnisse und die Bedeutung von Musik für Kinder der 90er Jahre." In *Kinder— Kultur*, edited by Claudia Bullerjahn, Hans-Joachim Erwe, and Rudolf Weber, 107–129. Opladen, Germany: Leske und Budrich.

22

THE INTERWEAVING THREADS OF MUSIC IN THE WHARIKI OF EARLY CHILDHOOD CULTURES IN AOTEAROA/NEW ZEALAND

SALLY BODKIN-ALLEN

IT is after lunch at the Fernside Early Learning Centre[1] and the children and teachers are all outside. A group of children are playing in a wooden rowboat while their teacher Anna makes up different verses to the tune of "The Farmer in the Dell" about who is in the boat. Over in the sandpit, three-year-old Caleb is singing, "Happy Birthday" as he makes a mud pie birthday cake. Inside, the babies are being settled for sleep time and teachers are singing "Moe Moe Pepe" (Sleep, Sleep Baby), a Māori lullaby, as they gently rock them back and forth in their prams, or rub their backs. At Fernside and in similar centers for the education and caretaking of young children in Aotearoa/New Zealand, music is woven throughout the experiences that young children have alone, at play with their peers, and under the direct influence of a curriculum that is enacted by their teachers.

Early childhood education in Aotearoa/New Zealand plays a vital role in the development of young children who participate in some kind of formal early childhood education before they begin school on their fifth birthday. In 2008, for example, 94.7 percent of all Year 1 schoolchildren had attended an early childhood education service before enrollment at school (Ministry of Social Development 2009). This chapter will focus on the musical experiences of children attending early childhood provision and the connections to home and family, locality, community, and nationhood.

Early childhood education in Aotearoa/New Zealand operates within a complex social framework that is both bicultural (between *Pākehā* [New Zealanders of European descent] and Māori [indigenous New Zealanders]) and multicultural (predominantly Pacific Island communities and more recent Asian immigration). The Treaty of Waitangi, a document signed in 1840 between Māori and *Pākehā*, is Aotearoa/New Zealand's founding document and because of it, biculturalism lies at the heart of the country's national identity and education system. The national curriculum framework acknowledges the value of the Treaty of Waitangi and of New Zealand's bicultural identity and multicultural society (Ministry of Education 2010). While the official state-led policy of biculturalism is "of vital importance to the construction of New Zealand identity as the primary vehicle for the reaffirmation of the indigenous culture of New Zealand" (Bendrups 2010: 30), at the same time the present-day context of Aotearoa/New Zealand is one of "cultural hybridity where there is an interplay between cultures in a postcolonial environment" (Johnson 2010: 6). In Aotearoa/New Zealand "bicultural" is political and about power sharing, while "multicultural" is descriptive (Jenkins 2009; Stuart 2002).Children are educated within a society that is officially bicultural and, in reality, often multicultural.

This chapter focuses on four contexts of early childhood education operating within this framework—kindergartens, childcare centers, *aòga amata* (Samoan immersion centers), and *te kōhanga reo* (Māori immersion centers)—and the musical threads woven throughout. It draws on ethnographic fieldwork carried out in several different early childhood centers throughout Aotearoa/New Zealand from 1998 to 2002 and my continuing involvement in the early childhood sector both as educator and mother. Starting from a belief that all children are inherently musical (Blacking 1973; Campbell 1998), the early childhood education environment provides a setting for this musicality to be explored more than any other time in a child's education. It provides opportunities for spontaneous music making, as well as music during group gatherings and improvised dancing. While *kōhanga*, *aòga amata*, childcare centers, and kindergartens all differ from each other in philosophy, they have similar threads running through them.

BACKGROUND AND CONTEXT: EARLY CHILDHOOD EDUCATION IN AOTEAROA/NEW ZEALAND

Aotearoa/New Zealand is a unique sociocultural setting with significant historical streams of influence in operation that help to shape children's musical cultures today. These influences have also shaped the course of early childhood education.

The historical background of Aotearoa/New Zealand is grounded in bicultural-ism between the indigenous Māori people and *Pākehā*. The singing of the nation's national anthem in both English and Māori, which often occurs in early childhood centers throughout the country, is indicative of this biculturalism. The presence of particular Pacific Island communities throughout Aotearoa/New Zealand and, since the late 1980s, an increase in Asian immigration has led to the development of a more culturally diverse country that transcends the longstanding bicultural char-acter of the nation.

Due to the sociohistorical context, early childhood education in Aotearoa/New Zealand is marked by its diversity (May 2002; Smith 1992), offering a plethora of choices to parents: kindergartens, childcare centers, *kōhanga reo*, language groups, and several others. Kindergartens are the oldest form of early childhood education, with the first being established in 1889 (Smith 1992), and generally provide a ses-sion-based program, with three-year-olds attending afternoons and four-year-olds attending mornings. Traditionally, kindergartens have been the most common type of early childhood education, but with more mothers entering the workforce, the session-based hours are not always suited to meet families' needs. This has caused an increase in the number of children attending childcare centers, which cater to children from birth to five years and have flexible hours. *Te kōhanga reo* were established in 1982, many on *marae* (traditional meeting place), and provide Māori immersion early childhood education in both language and culture. The belief underpinning *kōhanga reo* is that total immersion in Māori language (*te reo*) and culture (*tikanga*) will revitalize *Māoritanga* (Māori culture) and ensure its survival. *Aòga amata* provide Samoan early childhood immersion. They are often operated as part of a church or community group and aim to use the Samoan language and cultural beliefs within an early childhood program and to preserve both language and culture in this way. A Samoan language group curriculum does not limit chil-dren to *faàSamoa* (the Samoan way) but tries to bridge the gap between the chil-dren's environment in Aotearoa/New Zealand society and the importance of their cultural heritage (Tanaoilelagi 1988; Utumapu 1998).

Kindergartens and childcare centers reflect the nation's British roots and heri-tage, while *kōhanga reo* arose out of the indigenous culture, and the Pacific Island language groups reflect the evolving diversity of the nation. This has implications for children growing up in Aotearoa/New Zealand, for there is no one universal experience of early childhood education; instead, there are many different experi-ences of early childhood and, consequently, of musical cultures. While all early childhood education services are governed by the early childhood curriculum, *Te Whāriki* (Ministry of Education 1996), and all acknowledge biculturalism and the Treaty of Waitangi, they are able to interpret the curriculum document in their own way:

> The early childhood curriculum was envisaged as a Whāriki, translated as a woven
> mat for all to stand on. The Principles, Strands and Goals provided the framework,
> which allowed for different program perspectives to be woven into the fabric of
> the weaving. There were many possible "patterns" for this depending on the age

and interests of the children, the cultural, structural or philosophical context of the particular service, or the interests of parents and staff. (May 2002: 11–12)

This metaphor of a woven mat is pertinent to use when discussing and describing children's musical cultures in Aotearoa/New Zealand. There are musical connections between the early childhood education center and the child's community, home, and family and to the nation and the wider world. These are the musical threads that will be explored in this chapter through focusing on specific settings.

ON THE MAT

Ana and Mikayla are singing "Happy Birthday" as they cut pictures and paste them onto paper. A small argument develops over who should have possession of pictures that Ana has just found in a magazine of the stars from *High School Musical*. The call to assemble in the music room for mat time interrupts this, and they join the other children where they sit in a circle with their teachers for the morning *karakia* (prayer) and *mihimihi* (ritualized self-introduction). A *waiata* (song) is sung after each child's *mihimihi*, emulating the protocol of the *marae*, and is accompanied by a teacher playing the guitar. Each child selects the *waiata* that follows his or her speech, and everyone joins in the singing. In this way the group shows their support to the child, and they all become one group or *whanau* (family). Ariana sings a *waiata* that is unknown to her teachers and that they guess has come from her *marae*. Later in the morning *kaiako* (teacher) Cathy sings a *karanga* (call) to summon the children to lunch.

Mat time, a part of the day when the children and teachers gather as an organized group, occurs in most early childhood educational contexts in Aotearoa/New Zealand. Mat times involve the singing of songs and finger plays, stories, and other activities. In *kōhanga reo* (literally "language nest"), the morning mat time is usually based on the *karakia* and *mihimihi* session. The *mihimihi* process is an established part of *kōhanga* protocols (Tangaere 1997b). The singing of *waiata* after a speaker is an established code of behavior in Māori culture. The *waiata* is regarded as *kinaki*, or relish to complement the speaker's words (Tangaere 1997a). Thus, by following these processes in the early childhood education environment, children are absorbing the practices of their culture.

Kindergarten and childcare center mat times involve all of the children and are usually led by one teacher who takes responsibility for choosing the songs of the day, although children might contribute choices as well. Most often these songs are sung along with a recording, although teachers occasionally accompany the singing with a guitar. Songs sung at mat times often include what teachers refer to as the "old favorites": songs, such as "Who Stole the Cookie from the Cookie Jar" and "Tena Koe, Hello to One" (see Figure 1), and finger plays, such as "The Beehive" and "Incy Wincy Spider."

Figure 22.1: "Tena Koe, Hello to One."

My observations of these mat times is that there is often a limited range of songs used by teachers and that they tend to fall back on those they know well and are familiar with. Gharavi (1993) found a similar scenario in a study of preschool teachers in Tennessee, who also made use of a very limited song repertoire. At one kindergarten I observed the use of a single song, "When I Was One I Kissed My Mum," in every mat time over the course of one week.

Children in the *a'oga amata* gather on the mat with their teachers several times during the day. These gatherings are usually signaled by a teacher or a child playing the *pate* (traditional Samoan wooden drum made from a hollowed log and played with a wooden striker), and this is an example of the maintenance of a musical tradition. In Samoan villages, the *pate* is used as a signaling device and is closely associated with announcing the start of school (Moyle 1988). In this way a connection with life and culture on the islands is established.

All of the children and all (or most) of the teachers attend the mat times, and singing is the mainstay of the activities, often accompanied by teachers playing guitar, and/or simple percussion instruments. Unison singing is rarely heard in the *a'oga* when the group gathers on the mat, because as the children are singing a single-line melody the teachers are singing one or several harmonies alongside them. This multipart choral singing is typical of Samoan (and other Pacific Island) culture. Nearby Samoa, Fijian children are socialized from childhood into the musical languages and practices of the surrounding culture, and Russell posits that part singing provides an environment where singing flourishes as it "provides places for all voices and...lets every voice sing" (Russell 1997: 107). So the part singing that occurs in Samoan *a'oga amata* makes connections to the singing of *fa'aSamoa*, includes every voice, and embodies a cultural attitude to music and musicality.

WEAVING THE *WAIATA*/SONGS

It is a sunny morning at Mountainview Kindergarten and children are busy outside at different activities. Poppy skips past, singing, "drawing, drawing" to sol-mi as she gets some more felt pens to draw with. Davey, who is making fairy bread for the shared morning tea, is singing, "sprinkle, sprinkle, sprinkle" in an ascending scale as he shakes the colored sprinkles over the bread, and Natalie sings, "I'm going high, I'm going higher than you," also using sol-mi while swinging on a rope in the play area. Hamish rushes past her singing, "I Just Can't Wait to be King" from the film *The Lion King* as he chases after a group of girls. Inside, teacher Sonia is singing the Māori color song "Mā Is White" with Jessica as they sit and work on a color puzzle together. Later in the morning at mat time, all the children are sitting with their teachers singing Hirini Melbourne's beautiful *waiata* "E tu Kahikatea."

Research in Aotearoa/New Zealand into early childhood teachers' perceptions of biculturalism in early childhood education recognizes the importance of partnership, equity, and sharing (Jenkins 2009: 104–105). The teachers in Jenkins's study acknowledged that an appropriate way to honor the Treaty of Waitangi is through using the Māori language in the early childhood setting. Indeed, the well-being of the Māori language has been the focus of the efforts toward making a bicultural society (Doerr 2009). This can be seen through many of the songs that are sung in early childhood settings. The greeting song "Tena Koe, Hello to One" (see Figure 22.1), for example, is effective in teaching children appropriate greetings in the Māori language, whether to one, two, or a group of people. These vary from songs that are adaptations of English-language songs to include Māori words, such as "If You're Happy and You Know It *Pakipaki*" (to *pakipaki* is to clap) and "The Hanikani" (a version of the traditional movement song "The Hokey Pokey," generally known as "The Hokey Tokey" in Aotearoa/New Zealand), to songs that have been specifically composed for use in early childhood settings to develop basic Māori language skills. The Māori color song "Mā Is White" (Figure 22.2) is one such song.

Although some versions of this song have several verses that give names for many colors as well as numbers and weather/temperature,[2] it is the first verse that is most commonly sung. This song is significant because not only does it teach Māori language but also the vowels at the end of the verse illustrate the correct pronunciation of the vowels in the Māori language. Other songs similar to this are "Tāhi, Rua, Toru, Whā" (One, Two, Three, Four), a Māori counting song, "Pākipāki Tāmariki Ma" (Clap Clap, Children), which has a range of verses that introduce different actions (*kanikani*/dance, *rere, rere*/fly, *peke, peke*/jump, etc.), and "Māhunga, Pākihiwi" (Head, Shoulders), which teaches the words for different parts of the body. In the *aoga amata*, children experience Samoan adaptions of Māori children's songs such as "Pakipaki," which becomes "Patipati" in Samoan, and the Māori counting song "Tahi, Rua, Toru, Wha," which becomes "Tasi, Lua, Toru, Wha" in Samoan.

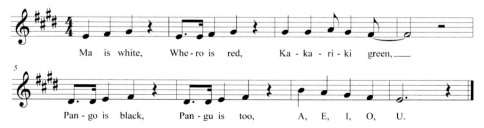

Figure 22.2: "Ma Is White."

Children attending *aòga amata* are growing up within the bicultural framework of both *Te Whāriki* and Aotearoa/New Zealand, and Māori songs are part of the way that biculturalism is acknowledged. It is common for Māori and Samoan versions to be sung in succession. These songs are woven throughout educational settings for children, so that children sing Māori songs alongside traditional Western nursery rhymes, such as "Twinkle, Twinkle Little Star," or traditional Samoan songs, such as "Pusi Nofo."

Notable Māori educationist Greg Tata has written of the place of music within Māori culture. He posits that for Māori, music is seen as being a living entity with spiritual and functional qualities just like a body and soul:

> Māori music has a far deeper meaning than just sound. It is seen as a natural part of life because it represents how people think and feel about situations they have experienced in grief or enjoyment. Māori music deals with real situations which it records in musical expression, thus preserving the taonga or treasure of te iwi or tribe's people. (Tata 1998: 15)

In early childhood education, *waiata* have an important role to play in children's learning. Through the singing of *waiata,* children not only gain an understanding of musical values and beliefs but also begin to learn the stories and values of their culture. The knowledge that is imparted through *waiata* is significant. All *waiata* have a purpose, to pass on the history, *whakapapa* (genealogy), events, and stories of the *iwi* (tribe) and are not just for entertainment (Tangaere 1997a). As Woodward (2005) noted, it is through the indigenous music of their cultures that children obtain the stories of their people and their past as well as others that are contemporary and reflect new customs. *Waiata* sung in *kōhanga reo* might be traditional songs from the *iwi* of particular children or from the surrounding area of the *kōhanga,* or they might be new *waiata* composed in more recent years for early childhood settings, such as Hirini Melbourne's "E Tu Kahikatea" (see Figure 22.3).

This *waiata* features in the first of the *Ngā Pihi* series (Universal Children's Audio 1995), a collection of *waiata* designed for use in educational settings to promote *te reo* that features *taonga pūoro* (traditional Māori instruments) played by Hirini Melbourne. The words of "E Tu Kahikatea" are particularly appropriate for young children, as they describe standing tall like the *kahikatea* tree, and the underlying message is of supporting each other and becoming strong through that support. The meaning inherent in the text of this song illustrates the point above: that

Figure 22.3: "E Tu Kahikatea."

the importance of *waiata* extends beyond the song itself. The text makes connections to the other children in the *kōhanga* in which it is sung and to the wider world beyond the center, the natural world. It embodies philosophical concepts of Māori culture, in which it is acknowledged that empowerment comes from the group rather than the individual.

In a discussion about the sources of others songs used in the *kōhanga*, Cathy, a teacher, suggests that in the early days of *kōhanga* there were many songs that were translated versions of English early childhood songs in Māori (Bodkin-Allen 2009: 61). Some of these are still around today: "Twinkle, Twinkle Little Star/Kapokapo whetu iti" and "Flick—I'm a Little Fire Engine/Ko Flick ahu ingoa."[3] Songs such as these have been described to me by the teachers as throwbacks to the early days of *kōhanga reo*. Some of the songs have stayed around and become old favorites. Another common source of songs was for a *kaiako* to take a preexisting tune and put words to it. "Tohora Nui," a song about a whale that uses the tune of "Making Whoopee," is such an example. The borrowing of tunes is a feature of contemporary Māori music and was used to popularize action songs (Katene 1989). The use of preexisting tunes still happens today in *kōhanga*, but to a lesser extent.

This also happens in Samoan language groups. However, while Samoan versions of English songs are often seen in the *aʻoga amata*, this is not the case in the *kōhanga*. This same teacher, Cathy, ascribed this to the fact that the *kōhanga* had been around for a little longer than the Samoan groups (the first *kōhanga reo* opened in 1982, whereas the first Pacific Island language groups opened in 1988): "I think that's because we've just had a little more time, and we actually had and we still have the strong base, the common knowledge we have, we say 'oh we're not going to use that material, we'll use our own', that's how it happens" (Bodkin-Allen 2009: 61). Another significant element to consider is the changing political situation from an earlier time to the present day. Māori in Aotearoa/New Zealand have had to struggle to reclaim their *Māoritanga* and for their right to be recognized by the state. The phasing out of songs that have connections to *Pākehā* New Zealand can be seen as an assertion of Māori identity. As Cathy explained, "They have their own songs that they can sing and they do not need to borrow from a European tradition." In contrast to this, Pacific Island communities in Aotearoa/New Zealand have no Treaty issues, and no history of intense political struggle. The use of songs that are part of a *Pākehā* tradition in the *aʻoga amata* does not have the same meaning as it does in a *kōhanga*. Kaemmer (1993) posited that music can be used in a political symbolic sense. In this instance music works in this way; in the *kōhanga* the use of Māori *waiata* is symbolic of Māori *tino rangatiratira* (self-determination), whereas the use of traditional European songs represents *Pākehā* dominance.

Teachers also readily make up songs when the need arises. "Glue ear," or *otitis media with effusion*, is an inflammation of the middle ear that often affects young children in New Zealand, particularly those of Pacific Islands ethnicity (Paterson et al. 2006). A teacher at one *aʻoga amata* had written a song to teach the children about the importance of blowing their noses correctly in order to combat the incidence of glue ear. The children enjoy singing this song immensely, as it involves lots of movement and ends with them all blowing their noses on tissues and putting them in the rubbish bin.

THREADS OF FAMILY, COMMUNITY, AND PLACE

The walls of the Brookside *Aoga Amata* are decorated with *siapo* (tapa cloth) and a display about *Te Whāriki*. Under the heading "Communication" are the words "Singing" and "Cultural Identity, Dancing, Sense of Self." Next to these are photographs of the children and teachers at the center playing musical instruments, singing, and dancing wearing traditional Samoan dress. Kiri is sitting at the Play-Doh table, singing "Happy Birthday." Next to her, two-year-old Tom starts to sing, "Tami o li ti" as he squeezes the dough through his fingers. Maria, Silei, and Tavita, who are also playing at the dough table, join in with him. Toni, a teacher who is at a table nearby with a group of children and various percussion instruments, starts to sing the same song. Lisa, a teacher who is walking around the room, also sings the song. Before long most of the children and teachers in the room are singing the song that began with two-year-old Tom. Later in the morning the children and teachers do an exercise/dance session to a CD of pop songs, brought into the *aoga amata* by one of the children.

One of the principles woven through *Te Whāriki* is the concept of family and community/*whānau tangata*. There are many musical pathways between *kōhanga* and the wider community. Sometimes these occur through teachers' connections with *kapa haka* (Māori performing art involving singing and dancing) groups. Tania, a *kaiako* in an Auckland *kōhanga*, sometimes brings in songs she has learned through from *kapa haka*, after seeking permission from the group. Connections to a child's *whānau* and *iwi* can be seen musically. When children start at *kōhanga*, the teachers will often approach the parents and ask if they know of *waiata* that are associated with the child's family. Another example of connections to the wider community can be seen in the process that occurs when a child makes the transition to school. As well as the singing of "Happy Birthday" in Māori (and perhaps English also) at a special group time, children might have a *powhiri*. Kate, another teacher in an Auckland *kōhanga*, outlines what happens when a child turns five: "We ask the parent to arrange a *powhiri* and we take a small group of children from here to support that child and go there for a *powhiri*. And they are welcomed on and we say look after them and pass them on" (Bodkin-Allen 2009: 138). A *powhiri* is a ceremony of welcome that involves both *korero* (speeches) and *waiata*. Kate is describing a rite of passage, from the *kōhanga* to the school; the music and the speeches make a bridge between the two settings.

Another way connections occur between the early childhood setting and the home is through children teaching songs they learn at the *kōhanga* to their parents. Tangaere (1997a) has discussed this in a study of her daughter Rangi's Māori language acquisition focusing on the two settings of *kōhanga reo* and home, and she acknowledges the role of singing and sharing *waiata*, Māori chants, and songs. Of particular significance was Rangi's role in teaching her mother and other members of her *whānau* songs that she learned at *kōhanga reo*. In Māori culture there is a specific name for this type of teaching: it is the *tuakana/teina* principle, by which the child can become the "teacher" and shift roles from child to teacher once they acquire the expert knowledge. Again, this illustrates what Tata (1998) was referring to: that music, for Māori, has a far deeper meaning than just sound.

There are strong connections to community made apparent by the locations of the *aōga amata* referred to here: one was physically located in a community church hall, and the other was attached to a school. These connections were reinforced musically as well, with the children who attended the church-based *aōga* singing songs during their time at preschool that they also sang when they attended church. One of these was "God's Love Is So Wonderful," the words of which were written in both Samoan and English on a wall poster. The children at the *aōga* located on the school site regularly attended the school assembly, singing songs with the school-children and performing traditional Samoan songs and dances at assembly once a month. The school itself had both Samoan and Māori bilingual classes, and the children from the preschool were sometimes taken by a teacher to the Samoan class for stories and singing together.

Connections to the children's homes also occur when parents attend special events. This generally happens only on special occasions, such as birthdays, end-of-year concerts, and Christmas parties. These connections tend to be rather fleeting and often consist of parents observing the musical processes rather than participating. When approached and invited, parents will become musically involved. For example, I have observed a father who is a musician singing a mix of pop songs ("I'm a Believer" and "Mamma Mia") and children's songs ("Rock a Bye Your Bear," popularized by the Australian children's rock band The Wiggles) with his guitar at a childcare center. A childcare center in Auckland that had a special "cultural day" invited the sister and mother of one of the children at the center to perform a traditional Bengali dance to Indian classical music. However, these links between parents and centers are limited, most probably due to parents being just too busy in their working lives to get greatly involved.

More common are musical pathways that spread between teachers. Teachers moving between centers in relieving capacities can be a source of music, and some-times the songs that are transmitted reflect the diversity of Aotearoa/New Zealand's multicultural society. Lina, a teacher at an *aōga amata*, says that when the teachers do relieving in *Palagi (Pākehā)* centers, not only do they learn new songs in English that they bring back to their center and translate to Samoan, but they also teach the children at the *Palagi* center Samoan songs. She was delighted to discover on a subsequent visit to the preschool that the children still remembered and sang the songs that she had taught them (Bodkin-Allen 2009: 95). "Siva Siva" is one song that fits into this category, which I observed being sung in a preschool in Wellington and which illustrates the musical connections that occur between the center and the wider community that the children are growing up in. As both Wellington and Auckland have significant Pacific Island communities, this song is one example of how these links manifest themselves in early childhood music.

Pop songs also sometimes make their way into early childhood education settings, reflecting the wider environment and the presence of the mass media in children's lives. The songs of groups such as the Spice Girls and Abba seem to resurge at centers periodically, as does other popular song material. Most often these recordings are used as background music during the day, for exercise sessions, or improvised dancing when children will request a certain CD to be played so they can create their own dance moves. Teachers relate this incorporation of pop songs into the early childhood setting as being a part of acknowledging the child who brought it. As Joan, a kindergarten teacher, informed me, "We only use them for movement things...to make them feel they're contributing, everything that comes from home we try and acknowledge" (Bodkin-Allen 2009: 118). This also relates to *Te Whāriki*, the early childhood curriculum, as one of the aims that is woven throughout is "belonging" (Ministry of Education 1996). Thus, by having the music from the children's homes at the kindergarten, the two environments are connected and children can feel a sense of belonging in each setting.

Western pop music might also have a place in *aòga amata* because the *aòga amata* is about bridging the gap between Samoan culture and identity and the children's location in Aotearoa/New Zealand. Pop songs were used for aerobics-style exercise sessions at the Brookside *Aòga Amata*. I observed Spice Girls' songs, Aqua's "Barbie Girl," and music from the *Barney* television program being used in this way. The use of music such as this, from the world outside the early childhood education setting, recognizes that the role of the center is not to confine the children to *faàSamoa* but to adapt programs so that the children learn to live happily in their new environment as well as hold on to their cultural values and language (Tanaoilelagi 1988).

Two songs from the American television program *Barney* are very popular. Both children and teachers sing "I Love You" often; on one memorable occasion a teacher sang it to comfort a child who was distressed about making the transition from the under-two to the over-two area. The *Barney* "Clean Up" song is another that is encouraged by teachers and that children often sing as they join in cleaning and tidying play areas. Just like the children outlined by Campbell (1998: 36), who sang songs and chants as they wiped down tables in the school cafeteria, preschool children in Aotearoa/New Zealand often sing as they clean.

Newly composed songs for early childhood centers in Aotearoa/New Zealand often reflect a distinctly local identity, such as "You've Got to Put on Your Hat" and "I Went Down to the Beach," both by the Auckland-based Kids Music Company.[4] The first is a didactic song that stresses the importance of wearing hats, sunblock, and sandals during summertime, and the second uses a clever integration of natural materials from the beach as percussion instruments: shells, rocks, and sand (in shakers). These two songs make connections to the outdoors environment, which is an inherent part of the lives of young children growing up in Aotearoa/New Zealand.

Figure 22.4: *A Kiwi Jingle Bells.*

Christmas songs are another part of the early childhood center repertoire, in which a distinct sense of identity can be seen. "Christmas on the Beach," a song that appears on the *Kiwi Kidsongs Collection* (Ministry of Education 2000) and is a musical resource created for primary schools throughout Aotearoa/New Zealand, has filtered down to preschools. Christmas in the Southern Hemisphere occurs in summertime, and so many of the traditional Western carols are not particularly relevant for children here. "Christmas on the Beach" refers to having a barefoot beach picnic under a *pōhutakawa* tree, an image far closer to home than snow and mistletoe. Other traditional songs might be adapted. One such example is *A Kiwi Jingle Bells* (Morrison and Hinde 2006), a book/CD set in which the traditional carol has been reworked with lyrics that reflect a distinctly local Christmas. The verses refer to hokey pokey ice cream, pavlova, chocolate fish, and Anzac biscuits, all "cracker Kiwi *kai* (food)" (ibid.: 15), in telling the story of a family's beach Christmas. The chorus retains half of the original text but has been modified as well (Figure 22.4).

Songs such as these make connections to the environment and nation that the children are part of. Images and themes that pertain to growing up in Aotearoa/New Zealand are another thread that is woven throughout early childhood music experiences.

The Interweaving Threads

Brief insights on the different musical circumstances of young children growing up in Aotearoa/New Zealand suggest differences based on cultural identity as well as overlapping ideals that are threaded into the national attention that is given for the healthy development of young children in early childhood education settings.

Kindergartens and childcare centers are resonant of specific values of *Pākehā* culture, *kōhanga* with Māori, and *a'oga amata* with Samoan, even while all follow the early childhood curriculum, *Te Whāriki* (Ministry of Education 1996). The national intent is that children and their families will experience an environment where connecting links with the family and wider world are affirmed and extended, where they can discover and develop different ways to be creative and expressive.

The presence of pop songs and music from the mass media is prominent in all centers devoted to the education of young children. Connections to nationhood can be seen in the singing of songs that feature the Māori language and reflect Aotearoa/New Zealand's bicultural status. Songs such as "Mā Is White" teach children basic Māori language, while songs such as "E Tu Kahikatea" make connections to wider concepts of Māori culture. Also woven throughout this discussion are traditional English-language nursery rhymes, contemporary children's songs, and songs that reflect Aotearoa/New Zealand's growing multicultural society.

Many of the songs discussed in this chapter originate from locally produced resources in Aotearoa/New Zealand. Music compilations such as these are significant for a number of reasons: the songs provide a distinct sense of place though the use of particular "Kiwi"- flavored language and concepts, and they contain traditional children's songs sung with New Zealand accents. In the case of the *Ngā Pihi* series they feature *taonga puoro*, instruments that are part of the indigenous culture. Early childhood education in Aotearoa/New Zealand is noted for its diversity. Between kindergartens, *kōhanga reo, aoga amata,* and childcare centers, teachers and children engage in spontaneous and organized music making that reflects the complexities of the society they live in. Not only is early childhood education diverse, but this is matched by the variety of the songs that are woven throughout those centers.

Notes

1. The names of all centers, teachers, and children have been changed.
2. See, for example, http://www.waiariki.ac.nz/documents/events/ Ma_is_White-Complete_Song.pdf.
3. Many of these can be found on the New Zealand Folk Song website http://folksong.org. nz/kids_waiata/index.html#100. Some have audio samples as well as text.
4. http://www.kidsmusic.co.nz has many resources for early childhood educational settings as well as running workshops for teachers.

References

Bendrups, Dan. 2010. "Migrant Music in New Zealand: Issues and Concepts." In *Many Voices: Music and National Identity in Aotearoa/New Zealand*, edited by Henry Johnson, 30–38. Newcastle upon Tyne, UK: Cambridge Scholars Publishing.

Blacking, John. 1973. *How Musical Is Man?* Seattle: University of Washington Press.

Bodkin-Allen, Sally. 2009. *Being Musical: Teachers, Music, and Identity in Early Childhood Education in Aotearoa/New Zealand*. Cologne, Germany: Lambert Academic Publishing.

Doerr, Neriko Musha. 2009. *Meaningful Inconsistencies: Bicultural Nationhood, the Free Market, and Schooling in Aotearoa/New Zealand*. London: Berghahn Books.

Gharavi, G. 1993. "Music Skills for Preschool Teachers: Needs and Solutions." *Early Childhood Arts Education* 94 (3): 27–30.

Jenkin, Chris. 2009. "Bicultural Meanings: What Do Practitioners Say?" *New Zealand Research in Early Childhood Education Journal* 12: 95–108.

Johnson, Henry. 2010. "Introduction." In *Many Voices: Music and National Identity in Aotearoa/New Zealand*, edited by Henry Johnson, 1–19. Newcastle upon Tyne, UK: Cambridge Scholars Publishing.

Kaemmer, J. 1993. *Music in Human Life: Anthropological Perspectives on Music.* Austin: University of Texas Press.

Katene, T. P. 1989. *Māori Music: An Interaction between the Community and the Experts in Cultural Survival.* Christchurch, New Zealand: ISME Commission on Community Music.

Macpherson, Cluny. 1996. "Pacific Islands Identity and Community." In *Ngā Patai: Racism and Ethnic Relations in Aotearoa/New Zealand*, edited by Paul Spoonley, Cluny Macpherson, and David Pearson, 124–143. Palmerston North, New Zealand: Dunmore Press.

May, Helen. 2002. "Early Childhood Care and Education in Aotearoa—New Zealand: An Overview of History, Policy, and Curriculum." Accessed January 13, 2010. http://www.aeufederal.org.au/Ec/HMayspeech.pdf.

Ministry of Education. 1996. *Te Whāriki.* Wellington, New Zealand: Learning Media.

Ministry of Education. 2000. *Kiwi Kidsongs Collection: Twenty-two Favourite Songs from Kiwi Kidsongs 1–8.* Wellington, New Zealand: Learning Media. Book and compact discs.

Ministry of Education. 2010. "The New Zealand Curriculum Framework." *Te Kete Ipurangi: The Online Learning Centre.* Accessed June 30, 2010. http://www.tki.org.nz/r/governance/nzcf/foreward_E.php.

Ministry of Social Development. 2009. "Participation in Early Childhood Education." *The Social Report/Te Purongo Oranga Tangata 2009.* Accessed March 23, 2010. http://www.socialreport.msd.govt.nz/knowledge-skills/participation-early-childhood-education.html.

Morrison, Yvonne, and Deborah Hinde. 2006. *A Kiwi Jingle Bells.* Auckland, New Zealand: Scholastic.

Moyle, Richard. 1988. *Traditional Samoan Music.* Auckland, New Zealand: Auckland University Press.

Paterson, J. E, S. Cater, J. Wallace, Z. Ahmad, N. Garrett, and P. A. Silva. 2006. "Pacific Islands Families Study: The Prevalence of Chronic Middle Ear Disease in 2-Year-Old Children Living in New Zealand." *International Journal of Pediatric Otorhinolaryngology* 70: 1771–1778.

Russell, Joan. 1997. "A 'Place' for Every Voice: The Role of Culture in the Development of Musical Expertise." *Journal of Aesthetic Education* 31 (4): 95–109.

Smith, Anne. 1992. "Early Childhood Education in New Zealand: The Winds of Change." In *International Handbook of Early Childhood Education*, edited by Gary Woodhill, Judith Bernhard, and Lawrence Prochner, 383–398. New York: Garland.

Stuart, I. 2002. "Māori and Mainstream: Towards Bicultural Reporting." *Pacific Journalism Review* 8: 42–58.

Tanaoilelagi, Iole. 1988. "What Would a Pacific Island Curriculum Look Like?" *Childcare Quarterly* 17 (4): 10–11.

Tangaere, Arapera Royal. 1997a. *Learning Māori Together: Kōhanga Reo and Home.* Wellington: New Zealand Council for Educational Research.

Tangaere, Arapera Royal. 1997b. "Māori Human Development Learning Theory." In *Mai i Rangiatea*, edited by Pania Te Whaiti, Marie McCarthy, and Aroha Durie, 46–59. Auckland, New Zealand: Auckland University Press.

Tata, Greg. 1998. "Māori Music in the New Zealand Classroom." *Fanfare* 48: 15–16.

Universal Children's Audio. 1995. *Ngā Pihi 1: Māori Songs for Children*. Compact disc.

Utumapu, T. 1998. "O Le Poutu: Women's Roles and Samoan Language Nests." PhD diss., University of Auckland.

Woodward, Shelia. 2005. "Critical Matters in Early Childhood Music Education." In *Praxial Music Education: Reflections and Dialogues*, edited by David Elliott, 249–266. New York: Oxford University Press.

23

BALANCING CHANGE AND TRADITION IN THE MUSICAL LIVES OF CHILDREN IN HONG KONG

LILY CHEN-HAFTECK

I loved singing and sang all the time when I was little. At the age of four, I told my mom that when I grew up, I wanted to become a famous pop star—just like the ones I saw on TV. I stopped singing when I went to secondary school because my music teacher didn't choose me to join the choir. Since then, I always heard her in my mind saying, "You are not a good singer! You can't sing!" At the same time, I lost confidence in myself and became shy after a classmate teased me for being spontaneous and responsive whenever the teacher asked a question, unlike my other classmates. "Don't you have shame?" These words stayed with me for many years. My experience in learning the piano was no better. When I was six, my mother told me that music is good for children and so I started my piano lessons. I was all excited at that time, but, unfortunately, it didn't last long. I lost my interest, as my teacher only wanted me to learn to read music and practice the assignments she gave me. She discouraged me from improvising and playing by ear. I wasn't motivated to practice, and my mother put a stick on the piano to warn me of the consequence of not practicing. That was the stick she used to beat me and my brother when we were naughty!

THIS is my own description of my musical life as a young child growing up in Hong Kong. Although this was many years ago, I hear similar experiences from current university students living in Hong Kong: their love of music since an early age; their directive teachers; the pressures from their parents, teachers, and peers in suppressing their individuality; and their strong parental involvement in education. Such experiences are typical for Hong Kong Chinese children, now and then. My experiences were challenging, and yet I continued to study music, leading me to my professional development as a music educator. I was able to eventually express my inherent love of music at a later stage of my life despite the difficulties of growing up as a child in Hong Kong.

In this chapter, the musical lives of children in Hong Kong will be explored through an examination of the influences of the city's unique (1) culture, (2) environment, and (3) education (see Web Figure 23.1 ⊙). I base my discussion on my personal experiences, the research literature, and the recent interviews I have collected. This encompasses both the past and present situations, thus exploring issues of tradition and change as well as the balance between the two. The structure of the discussion ahead is outlined in Web Figure 23.2 ⊙.

CULTURE

Ma-mi, 我要食 Lunch 啦！
(Mommy, I want to eat lunch!)

This is the way that children in Hong Kong often speak. The mix of English words into Cantonese conversation is a common phenomenon among not only children but also adults, and it offers a view of the extent to which Chinese and Western influences are intertwined in Hong Kong. Early experiences in such a stimulating multicultural environment can provide children with an open-minded and receptive view of their sociocultural situation, including how they experience music. Hong Kong children are familiar with a variety of traditional and popular genres of Chinese and Western music.

Tradition: Cultural Beliefs and Values of the People

Chinese people are proud of their long history, with civilizations dating back to ancient times. This same sense of history is reflected in their unique cultural beliefs and values, deeply rooted among Chinese people for many generations. Thus, despite the diverse cultural influences, Chinese culture still remains at the core of the Hong Kong people and exerts strong influences on the development and socialization of Hong Kong's children.

Chinese Personality

Like many Asian cultures, the concept of *interdependent self* is prominent among Hong Kong people. It emphasizes harmonious connectedness with other people and the importance of "fitting in" as a member of society. It is in contrast to the *independent self* of Western cultures, in which individuals maintain their independence from others by attending to their own individual needs, interests, and responsibilities and expressing their own unique opinions and sentiments (Markus and Kitayama 1991: 224). The concept of interdependent self is particularly important for enabling children to adapt socially to the environment in Hong Kong, where they will live and work closely with many people around them. As a result, Chinese children have been taught to conform to what is expected from the group rather than to express their individuality and personal creativity. Moreover, they learn to be humble and are taught that they should never say or feel that they are "good" (or "good at" something); acting proud is regarded by the Chinese as a negative attitude. This is supported by the findings that Chinese students have lower self-esteem (Brand 2004) and seem to be more shy (Xu 2005) in comparison to American and other Western students.

The Chinese Concept of Learning

Chinese people value the utilitarian function of diligent study and learning. Play is regarded as trivial and a possible barrier to learning (Liu 2004). The Chinese conceptualization of learning is related to "seeking knowledge" and "achievement" (J. Li 2003: 263). Terms used by Chinese students to describe learning included "diligence," "hardship," "steadfastness," and "concentration" (ibid.). This is in contrast to the American conceptualization, which relates to "learning process" and "learning content" (ibid.: 262). Chinese attitudes are evident in the learning of arts subjects, too, as Hong Kong students have indicated that they need to work hard in order to do well in music and visual art (McPherson et al. 2005).

This structured attitude toward study is further amplified by the examination-oriented system that is pervasive in Hong Kong. Children must pass through numerous in-school and public examinations throughout their years of schooling. There is a strong emphasis on performance excellence, which is determined by examination, as indicative of academic success. Even for preschoolers, admission to primary school often requires an entrance examination. Therefore, Hong Kong children constantly live under tremendous pressure for their high academic achievement, to the extent that they are led to believe that the goal of education is to achieve strong examination marks.

The Role of Parents in Children's Education

In Chinese families, parents play an important role in the upbringing and education of their children. They often have high expectations of their children because they believe that their offspring should bring prosperity and glory to the family. Moreover, for Chinese parents, it is an important achievement in life if they have raised successful children and a shame if their children are not successful. Stevenson and Lee (1990) reported that Chinese parents are highly devoted to helping their children succeed, doing so by assisting with schoolwork and providing a home environment conducive to learning. Furthermore, mothers of Chinese students were less satisfied with their children's grades in comparison with mothers of American students (Stevenson, Chen, and Lee 1993). Chinese children's achievement is viewed as a collective goal that requires the parents' active participation. Stevenson and Lee (1990) found that in contrast to American culture, in which the individual is expected to be responsible for his or her achievements, in Chinese and Japanese cultures, members of the family, teachers, and peers in the classroom all assume partial responsibility. According to Confucian ethics, everyone has to fulfill the functions of their respective roles in society. This is important for ensuring interpersonal harmony and unity and for maintaining social order (Chan 1963). Parents are superior to their offspring and so children must be submissive and respectful of their parents. Chinese parents can often be restrictive, controlling, and authoritarian (Chao 1994), with little attention to the emotional needs of their children (Porter et al. 2005).

Interestingly, the relationship between parenting style and children's achievement was found to be culture specific. Authoritarian styles of parenting correlated with poor academic performance among American children but showed the opposite effect on Chinese children (Leung, Lau, and Lam 1998; Pearson and Rao 2003; Stevenson, Chen, and Lee 1993). This is because in Chinese culture, the parental control and authoritarian parenting style is one of the "culturally meaningful dimensions of socialization" (Chen 2007: 20) that is widely viewed as reflecting parental love and concern. Therefore, parental control is seen as a positive attitude that motivates Chinese children to attain academic excellence.

Change: The Political, Economic, and Sociocultural Evolution

Located on the southeastern coast of China, Hong Kong is a special administrative region of the People's Republic of China. It operates with a high degree of autonomy and maintains a system of government and economy that differs from the rest of China. It became a British colony in 1842 and returned to the sovereignty of China in 1997. The British rule of more than a century had profound influences as Hong Kong developed from a small fishing village into an international financial center. Now, Hong Kong has a population of 6.9 million (Hong Kong SAR Government 2006) and is densely populated. Children study both Chinese and English languages, sing Chinese and English songs, and celebrate both Chinese and Western holidays and festivals.

Balance: Children's Musical Lives Supporting the Cultural Experiences

"I feel comfortable when listening to music." (Yu Yan, aged six)
"Feel good." (Chun Hei, aged twelve)
"Fun, relax." (Ka Hei, aged thirteen)
(Conversations translated from Cantonese)

The views of these three Hong Kong children on music can provide a glimpse of the role played by music in their lives. The positive experiences that children derive from listening or making music seem to be universal, no matter how old they are and where they live. To the children, music makes them feel good and comfortable, and it is fun and relaxing. The function of music in soothing children emotionally is especially important for the children in Hong Kong, who undergo tremendous pressure in their lives with respect to their social development and academic achievement.

Children in Hong Kong face many challenges. They live in a densely populated city and, thus, must learn ways of socializing with people. Because of high expectations from their parents to achieve academic success, they put aside their playfulness as young children to study seriously at school. Thus, musical activities that provide children with positive experiences are important in helping them balance their lives and maintain their emotional equilibrium. The musical lives of Hong Kong children reflect their unique cultural experiences.

ENVIRONMENT

Cantonese is the native language of most of the Hong Kong Chinese population. Children sing songs in both Cantonese and English languages and listen to both Chinese and Western music in their environment. As a result, the musical environment in Hong Kong has been described as "an intercultural activity framed by Western, traditional Chinese and local Hong Kong cultures" (Ho and Law 2009: 72).

Tradition: Language and Music

The Relationship between Text and Melody in Cantonese Songs

Cantonese is one of the nine main groups of dialects in China. It is a tonal language in which pitch is used as a syllable-differentiating agent, like vowels and consonants (Yung 1989). Thus, besides expressing emotions through intonation, pitch can also determine the meaning of words in the form of linguistic tones. There are nine tones in Cantonese: high falling/constant, high rising, middle constant, low falling, low rising, high clipped, middle clipped, and low clipped (Chao 1947). A syllable means different things when spoken in different tones. The characteristics of the linguistic tones include pitch properties, such as the relative pitch levels, the contour of pitch movement, and the duration of pitch, within each syllable. Figure 23.3 shows the pitch relationships of the Cantonese tones following Chao's (1947) five-point scale.

Since each Cantonese word has its restricted relative pitch level, there are certain limitations on the setting of Cantonese words to music. To make the text sound most meaningful in songs, the pitch relationship between text and melody must be observed; otherwise, it sounds like singing songs with nonsense texts. I have previously investigated Hong Kong preschoolers' singing in relation to different degrees of the text-melody relationship (Chen-Hafteck 1999a). No significant difference was found in the overall pitch accuracy between singing the Cantonese tone-matched (linguistic tones in the text match the melodic contour) and tone-mismatched (the two do not match) songs. However, when the text-melody relationship was closer, the linguistic tonal articulations were manifested more clearly (e.g., rising tones were exhibited in singing the tone-matched songs but not the tone-mismatched song), and the text was learned and recalled more efficiently. Clearly, the text-melody relationship found in Cantonese songs is an influencing factor on the singing of songs by children in Hong Kong.

The Influence of Cantonese Language on Children's Musical Abilities

Given the complicated tonal system of Cantonese language, a much more precise pitch discrimination ability is required in speaking Cantonese than in nontonal languages like English. It stands to reason that the tonal characteristics of Cantonese might offer an advantage in singing accuracy to children who speak this language over children who do not. Findings from comparative research showed a significantly higher pitch accuracy in the singing of the Cantonese-speaking children over English-speaking children (Chen-Hafteck 1999b; Trollinger 2004). It is conceivable that native English speakers who also learn to speak a tonal language while young may develop vocal skills that may enhance their pitch-matching and singing skills (Trollinger 2004).

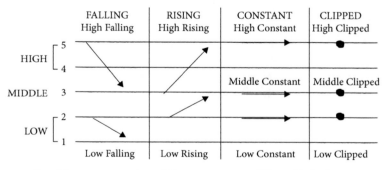

Figure 23.3: Graphic representation of Cantonese tones (Chen-Hafteck 1998: 19; Used by permission © 1998, International Society for Music Education, www.isme.org).

The musical quality of the Cantonese language is widely understood, such that Cantonese poems and rhymes consisting of words only are nonetheless considered a type of song. Most traditional Cantonese children's songs are rhymes with no music set to them, yet they are supposed to be "sung" in the natural pitch and rhythm of the lyrics. Mang (2001) found that English monolingual children displayed clear distinctions between speech and singing, whereas Chinese bilingual children did not. This further supports the close relationship between language and music among Cantonese-speaking children. With such a relationship, the musical potential of Cantonese children can be reinforced by the early focus on pitch discrimination that is required by their language. Educators who are aware of such potential can work in developing pitch discrimination from an early age (Chen-Hafteck 2010).

Traditional Cantonese Children's Songs

Traditional Cantonese children's songs serve the function of transmitting societal values to the young. However, unlike many English nursery rhymes, which have a simple melody and rhythm to facilitate young children to learn them easily, a majority of the Cantonese children's songs have complicated and long texts. They are not expected to be sung by the children themselves but by adults to children while they listen and follow along. The dominating role of adults over children in Hong Kong society is thus reinforced through this practice.

The famous Cantonese lullaby "Yuet Guang Guang" (月光光; Moonlight) is a typical example (see Web Figure 23.4 **◐**) that illustrates the functions and characteristics of these songs. Its soothing melody is intended to be performed at a slow tempo, and it is sung to a child at bedtime. The song text reflects the life of Chinese people living in an agricultural society. Through this song, children learn about the roles played by various members of the family within Chinese society and note the song's prominent theme of the importance of a strong work ethic. The lyrics translate to "Under the moonlight, my son, you will sleep. Tomorrow your mother has to go to the field and your grandmother has to bring the cows to the mountains." This Cantonese-language song demonstrates the close text-melody relationship found in other such traditional songs known by children in Hong Kong, as the linguistic tonal inflections of the lyrics are clearly built into the melodies.

Today, such traditional Cantonese songs are no longer commonly sung in children's homes. Children no longer easily understand these songs culturally because the subject matter is not relevant (present-day Hong Kong society is urbanized, and farm life is a thing of the distant past), and the song features an archaic form of Cantonese language that is no longer spoken. Fortunately, there are a number of Hong Kong musicologists and composers who see the significance of these traditional Cantonese-language songs as their cultural heritage and are trying to preserve them. "Yuet Guang Guang," for example, has been arranged by composers and is often performed by famous local children's choirs and singers.

Change: Music in Modern Hong Kong Society

Hong Kong society has undergone drastic changes over the past century. The rapid development of Hong Kong from a rural town into a modernized urban city has changed the lifestyle and family structures of the people. Advancements in technology have greatly affected children's access to information. As a result, the music that is present in the children's environment has also been transformed. During the 1960s, Western culture, including its artistic practices, was favored by the citizens of Hong Kong. Parents of this period did not feel the need to sing traditional, "old-fashioned" Cantonese songs to their children. At school, children learned to sing English nursery rhymes in translated Cantonese words that were tone mismatched and that were thus neither authentically English nor Chinese.

With an increasing number of Hong Kong families in which both parents are working, parents have limited time to play, sing, and share stories with their children, and so the singing tradition of Hong Kong people has sadly diminished to the extent that family singing has vanished altogether in some homes. However, with the rise of easily accessible recorded music and videos for children, music is readily available through home recording collections and by way of internet sites such as YouTube and various others from which music can be downloaded. Today, children can access music through the use of technology, including the computer, MP3 players, and electronic keyboards (see Figure 23.5). While older children prefer to use computers to access music, younger children are more likely to receive their musical experiences via television. The increase in accessibility to music has also led to an increase in the variety of musical genres that are present in children's environment. Most parents report that their children listen to both Western classical music and Hong Kong–styled Cantonese pop music. Religious music is also an important

Figure 23.5: Two Hong Kong girls experiencing music through technology.

experience for children who are Christians and who often sing and listen to hymns in church.

It should be noted that in Hong Kong, most working families hire maids from Southeast Asia, particularly from the Philippines, to help parents in caring for their children. In interviews I have conducted, parents have reported that the Filipino maids like to sing while they are working. Some of them sing English nursery rhymes and hymns with the children. Thus, these Filipino maids also play a role in providing musical experiences to Hong Kong children.

Cantonese pop songs can be heard in the everyday life of Hong Kong citizens through multimedia and are much loved by a majority of the population. The lyrics are everyday spoken Cantonese, attendant to the common themes of people living in Hong Kong. While Hong Kong children study formal written Chinese, spoken Mandarin, and English at school—none of which is their native language—they connect and identify more easily with Cantonese songs. Furthermore, the singers of Cantonese pop songs are often pretty or handsome youngsters who are easily idolized by children and youth. While admiring and enjoying the musical performances of these idols, children also find a means for expressing their feelings and establishing their identity. Within conservative Hong Kong society, the lyrics of Cantonese pop songs are nonviolent, nonpolitical, non–cult oriented, and nonsexy, so parents do not have to constrain children from listening to such music. In fact, Cantonese pop songs are welcomed by adults and parents, and some parents even enjoy this music with their children.

Despite the popularity of Cantonese pop music, children and parents are still receptive to Western classical music. Many families actually reported that they listen to both styles. As most Hong Kong children learn to play Western musical instruments from an early age, they grow up listening and playing a Western classical music repertoire. Evidently, Western music has been embraced by Hong Kong people as part of their culture more than they embrace traditional Chinese music. Just as the English language has been fused into everyday Cantonese conversations in Hong Kong, Western musical features have also seeped into Cantonese pop music. Consequently, Western music is never considered foreign to Hong Kong children.

Balance: Environmental Experiences Shaping Children's Musical Lives

The rich and diverse musical experiences of Hong Kong children and the inherent musical abilities that are acquired due to the musical qualities of the children's native language (i.e., Cantonese) contribute to the musical lives of Hong Kong children. However, it should be noted that although such environmental influences are evident, children may be unaware of them. One five-year-old boy, Enzo, told me that he enjoyed sharing the music they made with others: "It's fun and enjoyable, especially when people are listening [to my music]" (conversation translated from Cantonese). This is a clear indication that the social influences that children know are more obvious to them than anything else. The positive feelings that arise from the social interactions happening in music are mutually beneficial. Parents report that they enjoy sharing musical experiences with their children, finding that such sharing develops a positive relationship between them and their children.

Education

Tradition: Formal and Informal Music Education

Educational Experiences in Music at School

Music has long been a subject in the official government curriculum of Hong Kong, and thus music programs are well established. Hong Kong schools provide a comprehensive general music program at all levels, with many schools also offering music ensemble activities such as choir and orchestra. The general music curriculum is important for all students, whereas the ensemble activities are often directed toward those students who seek additional performance opportunities and are naturally competitive.

The annual Schools Music Festival is a significant event within the realm of Hong Kong's formal music education. It offers an array of music competitions, including solo and ensemble groups on various instruments in both Western and Chinese repertoires. Most schools in Hong Kong participate in this competitive festival every year, and music teachers are expected to involve their students. (In some schools, the teachers have been told from the day of their hiring that their aim should be to assist students in winning prizes and places at these competitions.) Competition, however, can exclude many children from the music education experience, particularly those who may be seeking music for its social and recreational (and not competitive performance) purposes. My own experience was a good example. Although I have always enjoyed singing, I was not selected to join my school choir because the teacher wanted a certain level of singing skill from choir members so that the choir could compete successfully at the festival competition.

The distinction between music heard inside and outside school in Hong Kong is obvious (Hargreaves and North 2001). It is a common trend that music in school is considered serious music, in contrast to the familiar music that students enjoy listening to outside school. Children's view of school music is illustrated in Campbell's interview data from children: "The only music you can listen to in school are classical and kids' music" (2010: 265). This is true in Hong Kong schools too. Cantonese pop music dominates the commercial music market in radio, television, and internet and is heard everywhere but in school (although it has now been recommended in school, too, in the recent education reform).

Educational Experiences in Music outside School

In traditional Chinese culture, music and its effects on people are viewed as very positive. The Chinese word for music, *yue*, means enjoyment and happiness. Confucius himself believed that music unifies hearts in shared enjoyment and that music serves the function of joining people together in harmony (Yeh 2001). Adding to this traditional belief is the recent advocacy efforts based on the "music makes children smarter" rhetoric that has emerged from research on the "Mozart effect" (Rauscher et al. 1997). Thus, Hong Kong parents are highly supportive of music education for their children.

Most children in Hong Kong are enrolled in music lessons and ensemble experiences in the after-school hours. They take private lessons on piano, violin, flute, and a host of other instruments and may also join choirs, bands, and other instrumental groups. There are several renowned children's choirs and youth orchestras in Hong Kong that have a long history and are well organized. Parents put their trust in them as enrichment for their children. For young children, there are classes such as Kindermusik, Gymboree, and the Orff-based experience in music and movement. For children who are learning a musical instrument, there is a continuing series of performance proficiency examinations. Every year, private instrumental teachers prepare their students for the examinations that are organized by the Associated Board of the Royal Schools of Music, based in the United Kingdom and well established in Hong Kong. These examinations set the standards for children's achievement. Hong Kong children prepare their examination pieces during their private lessons. The achievement-oriented characteristics of Hong Kong education are thus reinforced again.

Musical competence, in particular the mastery of skills in playing an instrument, requires hard work and patience in practice, and parents want to support this (see Figure 23.6). Children typically dislike practice, as illustrated by Emmanuel, age fifteen, who said, "I do love music, just not practicing for it. It [music] pleases my ears" (conversation translated from Cantonese). Parent-child conflicts may arise during music practice because parents, who intend only to show their support, push

Figure 23.6: A mother providing support and encouragement to her son in
his music practice.

their sometimes uninterested children. Today, my mother still believes (and rightly so) that it was her strict disciplinary measures in pushing my piano practice when I was young that brought me to a successful career as a music educator.

Change: Educational Policies and Practices

Education has always been highly valued by the Hong Kong government. The fact that the government has allocated one-fifth of its annual budget to education in recent years, the largest allocation to any policy priority, indicates its commitment to education (Chen 2007). Since 2000, there have been major reforms in educational policies that are a result of the trend toward a more global view of education. The slogan of the 2000 reform is "Learning for life, learning through life," indicating the aim of education to lay a foundation for lifelong learning and whole-person development (Curriculum Development Council 2001). There is an emphasis in Hong Kong education on the learner-focused approach, an educational methodology imported from the West.

Arts education has been identified as one of the eight key learning areas (Curriculum Development Council 2002) and is viewed as the entitlement of every student. It is recognized as one of the most effective means for nurturing creativity. The new curriculum calls for changes in the learning and teaching processes, with the declaration "Teachers should develop students' creativity, critical thinking and communication skills as far as possible through a balanced arts curriculum" (ibid.: 4). In addition, the curriculum stipulates, "Teachers should develop a range of approaches such as integrative learning in the arts, project learning and using IT [information technology] for interactive learning" (ibid.: 5). In fact, the initiative to incorporate a creative approach in music education has been in place for several decades, although it has never been formalized as such.

The need for reform in music education is evident from the majority of both primary (Cham, Cheung, and Mak 2006) and secondary (Leung 2000) school music teachers in Hong Kong, most of whom have indicated the importance of creative activities in their classrooms. Yet there was little confidence that such a goal could be successfully implemented. At the preschool level, teachers face a number of concept, ability, and self-image barriers in putting into practice the "learning through play" approach (West and Chiu 2007), and they perceive firm traditional instruction—instruction that is characterized by an "emphasis on planning, preparation and external judgment" (Y. L. Li 2003: 28)—as an indicator of good teaching. Leong (2010) reported that six years after the start of education reform, the focus on the practical applications of creativity in music education was still absent in both primary and secondary schools. As a result, young music students have considered assessment through singing or instrumental performance, or by way of written examinations, as more important than creative activity; this is in contrast to visual art students who had learned mainly through creative activities and preferred evaluations of their creative work. Leong logically concluded, "Music education in Hong Kong has some way to go in achieving the reform goals" (2010: 89).

In terms of the music repertoire, educational reform promotes the inclusion of Chinese culture in arts education (Curriculum Development Council 2002). Besides singing and listening to folk songs from diverse regions of China and playing Chinese musical instruments, the 2003 music curriculum guide (Curriculum Development Council 2003) also includes the study of Cantonese popular songs with its cultural and historical contexts. A recent study (Ho and Law 2009) indicated that while more than 92 percent of the instrumental students played Western musical instruments (and Western classical music), their listening preferences ran counter to this music. In fact, pop songs, Western folk music, and music of other cultures were preferred by young students, and Chinese folk songs, Cantonese opera, and Beijing opera were preferred the very least (Cheung 2004; Ho and Law 2009).

The need to introduce Chinese music to the curriculum arose following the political change of hands, when Hong Kong became part of China in 1997. However, because Chinese music was greatly ignored in Hong Kong's formal education for many years during British rule, the Hong Kong Chinese (including music teachers) are still unfamiliar with it. Although there is a recent increase in the number of Hong Kong students learning Chinese traditional instruments, it will still take some time to see the effects of the current effort in incorporating Chinese traditional culture into school music programs.

Balance: Educational Experiences Shaping Children's Musical Lives

As a result of Chinese cultural beliefs, Hong Kong Chinese children are generally not nurtured for their expressivity, creativity, or individual ideas and opinion. Instead, they are directed to compete and to achieve musical success as performers. The integration of both Chinese and Western perspectives into the curriculum will continue to challenge teachers, children, and their parents. Although children are highly adaptable and the government is pressing for a student-centered curriculum, the maintenance of tradition is strongly valued when it comes to educational content and process and in the realm of the parent-child relationship.

MUSICAL EXPRESSION OF HONG KONG CHILDREN: BALANCING TRADITION AND CHANGE

A major task of childhood is learning socially and culturally acceptable ways of behavior. Children are successful in doing so, as they also look for outlets and opportunities for expressing themselves artistically and creatively. The fulfillment of children's developmental needs is an essential task of caring adults, including what they learn and how they learn it. Music is important for children's achievement of such a balance, a point that was brought home to me when I was traveling on a bus in Hong Kong.

> A little girl was sitting with her mother behind me, singing very loudly and repeatedly a short melody that she had invented. The mother stopped her little girl and berated her for being too noisy. I turned around to look at the little girl and thought of the pressure that she faced in learning to behave in a socially accepted manner. In order to maintain the balance of her interdependent self and meeting the social requirements of "quiet behavior," she would need to be submissive to her mother and give up on her playful and musically expressive act! Very soon, I saw the girl start to move rhythmically, albeit more quietly than before. Thus, she had found another form of musical expression that was culturally acceptable and approved by her mother. Children seem to find a way to adjust and balance themselves and to make music, despite social and cultural constraints.

In addition, a classroom observation I made in Hong Kong also brought me to an understanding of children's creative selves.

> Twenty preschool children were gathered in a small and brightly colored music room. When the teachers asked half the class to dance, the girls crowded in a cramped circle and followed the teacher's directions in dancing: As the music slowed down, the children lifted their hands up and down, and as the music quickened, they danced in a circle. My first impression was that these young children followed the teacher's instructions well. But then I started to notice their individual creative interpretations of the music within the framework of the dance movements set by the teacher. Even though they danced in a circle, one girl was nodding her head from side to side, another was shaking her whole body, while others were stamping their feet or jumping to the rhythm. I noticed that the boys who sat in a corner of the room by themselves were still following the movements of the children in the circle, and some were dancing by themselves.

The unique musical expression and creativity of Hong Kong Chinese children is evident where Chinese and Western influences and attitudes coexist with one another. The Hong Kong children described above offer certain proof of this statement. Thus, Chinese educators who wish to incorporate the new curriculum can proceed gradually rather than to drastically replace the traditional approach to children's musical education. Current Chinese beliefs and practices can be continued even while new ideas, often from the West, are studied and adapted.

The musical lives of Hong Kong children are obviously a demonstration of a complex balancing act between tradition and change and Chinese and Western cultural and educational practices. When I speak with Hong Kong Chinese children about music, they exclaim delightedly and with heartfelt enthusiasm of the exuberant fun and sheer pleasure that music brings to them. Children's artistic expressions cannot be curtailed or squashed. Music helps Hong Kong Chinese children to achieve a balanced and healthy development.

ACKNOWLEDGMENTS

I am grateful to the parents and children of the ten families in Hong Kong for participating in this study and Dr. Jennifer Chen, Ms. Ruth Chung, Dr. Wai Chung Ho, and Dr. Marina Wong for sharing their experiences and opinions with me.

REFERENCES

Brand, M. 2004. "Collectivistic versus Individualistic Cultures: A Comparison of American, Australian and Chinese Music Education Students' Self-Esteem." *Music Education Research* 6 (1): 57–65.

Campbell, P. S. 2010. *Songs in Their Heads*. New York: Oxford University Press.

Chan, W. 1963. *A Source Book in Chinese Philosophy*. Princeton, NJ: Princeton University Press.

Cham, E., J. Cheung, and C. Mak. 2006. "Report on the Study of Creative Music-Making in Primary Schools—2005/06." Hong Kong: Education Publishing House.

Chao, R. K. 1994. "Beyond Parental Control and Authoritarian Parenting Style: Understanding Chinese Parenting through the Cultural Notion of Training." *Child Development* 65: 1111–1119.

Chao, Y. R. 1947. *The Cantonese Primer*. New York: Greenwood Press.

Chen, J. J. 2007. *How the Academic Support of Parents, Teachers, and Peers Contributes to a Student's Achievement: The Case of Hong Kong*. New York: Edwin Mellen.

Chen-Hafteck, L. 1998. "Pitch Abilities in Music and Language of Cantonese-Speaking Children." *International Journal of Music Education* 31: 14–24.

Chen-Hafteck, L. 1999a. "Discussing Text-Melody Relationship in Children's Song-Learning and Singing: A Cantonese-Speaking Perspective." *Psychology of Music* 27 (1): 55–70.

Chen-Hafteck, L. 1999b. "Singing Cantonese Children's Songs: Significance of the Pitch Relationship between Text and Melody." *Music Education Research* 1 (1): 93–108.

Chen-Hafteck, L. 2007. "Children, Music, and Culture: A Cross-Cultural Perspective on Musical Development." In *Listen to Their Voices: Research and Practice in Early Childhood Music*, edited by K. Smithrim and R. Upitis, 140–160. Toronto, Canada: Canadian Music Educators Association.

Chen-Hafteck, L. 2010. "Enhancing the Development of Pitch Perception and Production through Learning a Tonal Language." In *TIPS: The Child Singing Voice*, edited by M. Runfola and J. Rutkowski, 75–81. 2nd ed. Lanham, MD: Rowman & Littlefield.

Cheung, J. 2004. "Mapping Music Education Research in Hong Kong." *Psychology of Music* 32 (3): 343–356.

Curriculum Development Council. 2001. *Learning to Learn—the Way Forward in Curriculum Development*. Hong Kong: Hong Kong Government Printer.

Curriculum Development Council. 2002. *Arts Education—Key Learning Area Curriculum Guide (Primary 1–Secondary 3)*. Hong Kong: Hong Kong Government Printer.

Curriculum Development Council. 2003. *Arts Education Key Learning Area: Music Curriculum Guide (Primary 1–Secondary 3)*. Hong Kong: Hong Kong Government Printer.

Hargreaves, D. J., and A. C. North. 2001. "Conclusions: The International Perspective." In *Musical Development and Learning: The International Perspective*, edited by D. Hargreaves and A. North, 220–234. London: Continuum.

Ho, W. C., and W. W. Law. 2009. "Sociopolitical Culture and School Music Education in Hong Kong." *British Journal of Music Education* 26 (1): 71–84.

Hong Kong SAR Government. 2006. *Hong Kong Yearbook 2006*. Hong Kong: Hong Kong Government Printer.

Leong, S. 2010. "Creativity and Assessment in Chinese Arts Education: Perspectives of Hong Kong Students." *Research Studies in Music Education* 32 (1): 75–92.

Leung, B. W. 2000. "Factors Affecting Hong Kong Secondary Music Teachers' Application of Creative Music-Making Activities in Teaching." *Asia-Pacific Journal of Teacher Education & Development* 3 (1): 245–263.

Leung, K., S. Lau, and W. L. Lam. 1998. "Parenting Styles and Academic Achievement: A Cross-Cultural Study." *Merrill-Palmer Quarterly* 44: 157–172.

Li, J. 2003. U.S. and Chinese Cultural Beliefs about Learning. *Journal of Educational Psychology* 95 (2): 258–267.

Li, Y. L. 2003. "What Makes a Good Kindergarten Teacher? A Pilot Interview Study in Hong Kong." *Early Child Development and Care* 173 (1): 19–31.

Liu, Y. 2004. *The Multi-Perspectives of Cultural, Psychological, and Pedagogical Research on Children's Play*. Beijing: Beijing Normal University Press.

Mang, E. 2001. "Intermediate Vocalizations: An Investigation of the Boundary between Speech and Songs in Young Children's Vocalizations." *Bulletin for the Council of Research in Music Education* 147: 116–121.

Markus, H. R., and S. Kitayama. 1991. "Culture and Self: Implications for Cognition, Emotion, and Motivation." *Psychological Review* 92: 224–253.

McPherson, G., R. Yu, B. W. Leung, K. S. Ma, and H. S. A. Ng. 2005. "Factors Affecting Primary and Secondary School Children's Motivation to Study the Visual Arts and Music." Full Report, Quality Education Fund, Education Research Project No. 2002/0978. Hong Kong: The Hong Kong Institute of Education.

Pearson, E., and N. Rao. 2003. "Socialization Goals, Parenting Practices, and Peer Competence in Chinese and English Preschoolers." *Early Child Development and Care* 173 (1): 131–146.

Porter, C. L., C. H. Hart, C. Yang, C. C. Robinson, S. F. Olsen, Q. Zeng, J. A. Olsen, and S. Jin. 2005. "A Comparative Study of Child Temperament and Parenting in Beijing, China and the Western United States." *International Journal of Behavioral Development* 29 (6): 541–551.

Rauscher, F. H., G. L. Shaw, L. J. Levine, E. L. Wright, W. R. Dennis, and R. L. Newcomb. 1997. "Music Training Causes Long-Term Enhancement of Preschool Children's Spatial-Temporal Reasoning." *Neurological Research* 19: 2–8.

Stevenson, H. W., and S. Lee. 1990. "Contexts of Achievement: A Study of American, Chinese, and Japanese Children." *Monographs of the Society for Research in Child Development* 55 (1–2).

Stevenson, H. W., C. Chen, and S. Lee. 1993. "Mathematics Achievement of Chinese, Japanese and American Children: Ten Years Later." *Science* 259 (5091): 53–58.

West, L., and A. Chiu. 2007. "Hong Kong Teachers' Perceptions of Children's Learning through Play." Paper presented at the 15th International Conference

Reconceptualizing Early Childhood Education: Research, Theory, Policy and Practice, Hong Kong, December 13–17, 2007.

Xu, Y. 2005. "Understanding Shyness in Chinese Children: Temperament, Physiological Reactivity, and Psychosocial Adjustment." *Dissertation Abstracts International* 65 (9-B): 4878.

Yeh, C. S. 2001. "China." In *Musical Development and Learning: The International Perspective,* edited by D. Hargreaves and A. North, 27–39. London: Continuum.

24

TRADITION AND CHANGE IN THE MUSICAL CULTURE OF SOUTH KOREAN CHILDREN

YOUNG-YOUN KIM

JIYONG, Dijay, Jihun, Youngi, and Sumi sit together in a circle on the living room floor of Dijay's home. It is a Saturday, and they are gathered to celebrate Dijay's ninth birthday. Beyond the structured games, activities, and obligatory refreshment time, they have gathered to play a singing game of their own choosing. They sing-song together the story of a rabbit and the moon, and the Korean vocalizations sound out loud and clear, *Sse-sse-sse*. One song leads to another, as the children race through their repertoire of traditional tunes—some whose melodies sound diatonic and others that feature a minor quality in tonality, also tilting in the direction of a Korean rhythmic sound with its swinging in triple meter. The children clap the beat of the songs and decide that as one song finishes, the next child is immediately to introduce another. Four songs are sung and clapped with enthusiasm until Sumi declares that she is bored, at which point the collective of children follow Sumi to the piano to hear her play the songs of their singing games and her favorite Mozart piece.

The contemporary realities that surround Korean children in the developing years of their childhood are reflected in the music they make and prefer to listen to. At the same time, the philosophical frameworks of Korean society and its schools determine the content and approach of the music that children learn in school and in which some are trained through formal study outside of school. Children come to know the music played at them from the media and from the technology-inspired toys and gadgets that fill their homes. At the same time, the school music curriculum offers them a balanced diet of Western art music, traditional Korean music, and music of the world's cultures to sing, play on classroom instruments, and move to. In some families, Western art music is so highly valued that children are provided with instrumental lessons from an early age—on piano, violin, and flute, especially. The mixed and varied musical experiences and training of Korean children will be explored and contextualized through a description of Korean social settings and educational priorities, the scope of Korean children's daily lives, and children's musical involvement and environments.

KOREA AND KOREANS

South Korea is tucked into the northeastern corner of the Asian landmass, and its children only gradually become aware of their rich history and culture. In the second or third grade, they discover their proximal location in a nation lying east of China, across the East Sea from Japan, with three sides of their nation's land area surrounded by the sea. Korea has a recorded history of more than 4,000 years, from 2,333 BC to the present. It consists of the Old Korea, the Three Kingdom Period (57 BC to AD 668), the United *Silla* dynasty (668–907), the *Koryo* dynasty (907–1392), and the *Yi* dynasty, which was continued into the early twentieth century. Korea was annexed by Japan in 1910 but was freed after World War II and divided at the thirty-eighth parallel into North and South Korea in 1953. Now Korea remains as the last divided country in the world. There is no national state-mandated religion (Choe 1996), although Christianity and Buddhism are the principal religions practiced today.

In this small and beautiful mountainous peninsula of 99,538 square kilometers live 48 million South Koreans, one-third of them located in the capital city of Seoul. However, a low birthrate (1.15 children per family in 2009) is seen as a serious current social problem in Korea. The government is encouraging population growth; for example, the third and additional children of families are guaranteed free education through primary school and the family is offered financial incentives on taxes and utilities such as electricity, mobile phone, internet, and transportation (Korean Ministry of Health and Welfare 2011; Statistics Korea 2011). Since the 1960s, the economic development of South Korea has markedly increased, and today the country is known as one of the largest exporters of products such as cellular phones, computers, televisions, home appliances, and automobiles (Korea Trade-Investment Promotion Agency 2011). One of the "Asian Tiger" nations, the shift toward high-technology industries that include developments in aerospace, bioengineering, and microelectronics is balanced with continued activity in automobile and ship production.

Historical evidence of musical activity has been found in several places in Korea. For example, there is a mural in a tumulus in Chipan of Koguryo that was painted during the period of The Three Kingdoms and another in a tomb in Anak, north of the Yalu River. In these murals, three female and two male dancers are portrayed, accompanied by a zither, a lute, and a long vertical flute (Chosunilbosa 1995; Lee 1981). References to music have appeared in literature and paintings through the ages, indicating the value of music in Korea as long lasting and continuous.

In Old Korea, there was a rigid caste system of *Yangban* (aristocrat) and *Ch'unmin* (commoner) families until the mid-twentieth century. *Yangban* families did not approve the involvement of their children in musical or artistic activities (Choe 1996). In particular, boys were strictly prohibited from engaging in artistic activities in public and were steered toward the study of literature and away from engagement in artistic work. Both boys and girls from *Yangban* families were prohibited from singing and playing musical instruments, so they listened to the music performed by *Ch'unmin* commoner artists. Traditional music was gradually and quite recently brought into the schools as an identity marker of South Korean-ness, such that all children have been invited to listen, sing, and play music—regardless of socioeconomic circumstances. Children of today learn the traditional Korean singing style (*P'ansori*) mostly in the southern part of the peninsular and traditional instruments such as the *Tanso* (bamboo flute) and the *Changgo* (hourglass-shaped drum) in school. Also, traditional Korean musicians are welcome today in many places in and beyond Korea and actively work as performers and teachers.

Music plays a prominent part in the lives of South Koreans at home and in their families. When they gather for birthday parties and holidays, Koreans enjoy singing standard songs, including folk, traditional, and popular songs and dancing. At home, grandmothers and mothers often sing songs to soothe or amuse their children. At bedtime, children are frequently lulled to sleep with traditional Korean children's songs such as "Kumjadonga okjadonga" (My Beloved Baby)[1] or the onomatopoeias of "Chajang chajang," sung while softly tapping the child's back. Even young mothers unwilling to sing in front of others will regularly sing to their baby. Mothers are seen in public, too, singing to their babies on buses and trains, although nowadays this is seen much less often than it was at an earlier time.

THE PLACE OF MUSIC IN CHILDREN'S LIVES

Although the South Korean Ministry of Health and Welfare has announced that daycare centers must accept children from infancy, about 75 percent of Korean children are raised at home from birth to three years, with grandparents and mothers who do not work outside the home tending them during the day (National Archives of Korea 2011). Songs such as "Chajang chajang uri aga" (a lullaby) and "Kon'gi,

kon'gi" (a playful song featuring nontranslatable vocables) are well known and associated with grandmothers at home with the children.

The story of my own acquisition of children's songs dates back to 1960. At that time,
I was a five-year-old girl, the second child among four siblings. My family belonged
to a middle-class Christian family, and I took weekly private piano lessons from a
college music student. My mother frequently took me to choir concerts and piano
recitals. From the 1960s to the 1980s, the period of my childhood, youth, and young
adulthood, Western art music performances were numerous while Korean traditional
music concerts were rare. My mother, a devout Christian, asked me to sing solo in
the church choir at Easter and Christmas. After I graduated from elementary school,
however, my parents turned their attention only to my academic success. As in other
middle-class families in Korea, my entering a highly ranked college was important to
my family. Yet after I entered college, I often chose to attend music concerts and sang
in my church choir. I enjoyed hearing touring musicians who visited Seoul, including
the New York Philharmonic Orchestra as well as soloists and chamber groups from
Berlin, Chicago, and Boston. Music made me happy, and I continued my own piano
practice too, playing alone in a small, dark, and cold room.

In contrast to my own Western-centered musical experiences, today's children
have options that include Korean traditional music, Western art music, and popular
music. Some children learn Korean traditional vocal and instrumental music, as well
as Korean traditional dance, from the age of five onward. Concert performances of
Kayagum, Changgo, and *P'ansori* abound (Figure 24.1). Recordings, video performances, and downloads of a vast spectrum of music is now easily accessible to all.

Figure 24.1: Children playing the Korean instrument *Puk* (big drum).

However, as was my own experience, most families direct children to put aside their musical interests after childhood so as to focus their attention on their studies for college entrance examination (Korea Arts and Culture Education Service 2008).

Since education is highly valued among the South Korean people, most children finish their private music lessons as early as ages eleven or twelve, although a few children who are seeking entrance to a tertiary institution for musical study may continue. Yet about one-fifth of the average middle-class Korean family's income is allocated for children's private education (Statistics Korea 2011). Parents provide after-school and weekend opportunities for their children to learn music, dance, visual arts, math, writing, computer skills, science, and Tae Kwon Do. Most children in Korea go to a specific learning center, called a "Hagwon," or to culture centers and take private lessons on piano or another instrument prior to their entrance to elementary school. Piano is the most popular instrument for Korean children at age five, while violin and flute are preferred by slightly older children (Kim 2002).

FEATURES OF KOREAN CHILDREN'S SONGS

The songs that Korean children sing include orally transmitted traditional songs that have been known for several generations or more, although contemporary songs composed for children by adult musicians have also joined the ranks of familiar music. From their earliest childhood, children hear songs sung to them by family members or on recordings, until they enter into their own active engagement in music as singers and students of various Western instruments.

Traditional Korean Children's Songs

According to Kim's (1998) analysis of traditional Korean children's songs, which were collected from women who were children between 1900 and 1930, many songs predate the Japanese occupation or withstood its influences. These older songs for children are set principally in pentatonic mode, and their melodies consist of phrases that feature major seconds, minor seconds, perfect fourths, and perfect fifths. Their rhythms fall into a sense of triple meter. Since the melodies of traditional Korean children's songs are simple and repetitious, they are frequently sung by both children and adults and are orally transmitted from generation to generation (Doosan Ch'ulpansa 2006). Some songs have call-and-response structures, and many of the songs are associated with circle games. Songs such as "Urijibae we wanni" (Why Are You Coming to My House?) and "Maengkkong" (the sounds of croaking frogs) are representative of call-and-response songs within traditional Korean children's songs (Figure 24.2).

In the past, traditional Korean children's songs were often heard in the alleys when children played outdoor games, but these are gradually disappearing with

Figure 24.2: Notation of "Maengkkong."

social modernization, which has brought various changes in daily life. For instance, people now prefer wearing Western style apparel instead of a Korean *Hanbok*, apartments are more common than houses for single residence, children go to school instead of to *Sodang* (a private tutoring place), and so on. However, Korean cultural heritage has been revaluated and become respected by Korean people nationwide, with governmental endeavors to retrieve intangible treasures such as traditional music found in many places. The collection and dissemination of traditional children's songs has been given governmental support since the middle 1980s, and traditional Korean children's songs are now included within school music textbooks. Radio programs are an additional medium for the transmission of folk tunes and traditional Korean children's songs. Thus, it is not unusual to hear snippets of traditional Korean children's songs sung by elder women over the public airwaves.

Contemporary South Korean Children's Songs

In contrast to traditional Korean children's songs, there are contemporary South Korean children's songs based on diatonic scales that contain melodic patterns suited to the application of various I, IV, V, and V7 harmonies that are frequently featured in Western, traditional, and popular art music. The vocal range of the melodies, from A2 to D4, spans a larger register than that of traditional children's songs. Contemporary children's songs are often sung by Korean children and grown-ups, mostly those who sang them in their own childhood. Songs such as "Yonnaligi" (Flying a Kite), composed by Han Susong, and "Hanul nara tongwha" (A Fairy Tale from the Sky), composed by Lee Kangsan, have been enjoyed by children since the 1980s and are still popular today. Lim and Kim (2004) examined the appropriateness of children's songs preferred by Korean preschool teachers from the perspectives of children's musical ability and concluded that composers of children's songs need to give more careful consideration to children's vocal development.

In 1983, a South Korean television broadcasting station initiated the first children's song festival in order to encourage and distribute newly composed children's songs to Korean children. This was followed by additional broadcasting stations and organizations such as the YMCA, which continues coverage of this song festival even now (Han 2000; Jung and Kim 2008). In an examination of the songs composed for this event, Jung and Kim (2008) reported that common features included 4/4 meter, a vocal range of A2 to D4, an average song length of twenty-four measures, fast tempi, and rhythmic syncopation. These contemporary songs are distinguished from traditional songs in their use of meter, range, song length, and syncopation (see Web Figure 24.3 ◉). Major topics of the composed Korean children's song texts were hopes and dreams, family, and nature, while traditional children's songs focus attention on animals, plants, and other nature topics, with less attention to family and nearly none to hopes and dreams.

MUSIC IN THE FAMILY

South Korean children experience music all the time, everywhere they go, especially within the family and at school. Even though a career as a professional musician is seldom recommended by parents, music is deemed a valued engagement for children. Until the 1980s, South Korean children often played singing games and sang hand-clapping and rope-jumping songs and chants in the alleys and yards of their family homes (Kim 1998). However, social and economic development in South Korea after the mid-1990s, including a significant downturn in the export economy for the next fifteen years, was such that families of three generations of grandparents, parents, and children began to live together in high-rise apartment complexes. Children adapted to playing inside rather than outside, just as grandparents gathered together in specially designated community rooms while their children worked and grandchildren went to school (Huh 2008). The small apartments kept children in close contact with their parents and grandparents (and the media), and so influences were considerable and constant.

Today, the song repertoire of South Korean children is extensive, ranging from traditional children's songs to popular adult material from TV and the internet. Children easily learn these songs and then modify them variously into their own styles. Song texts and rhythmic and melodic patterns may be changed and games created to fit these songs. Girls are more active than boys in this creative process, playing with the many musical possibilities of songs (Marsh 1997, 2008; Marsh and Kim 2006).

In recent years, children have begun to go to after-school programs to learn traditional Korean instruments such as the *Changgo* (drum) and the *Tanso* (flute). A piano (or keyboard) is available in many homes and is often played by mothers, who provide music for their infants and young children and a musical model for their children to emulate. Occasionally, mothers sing with and provide singing lessons for their children; for these mothers, singing raises self-confidence in their children and is a source of amusement and parent-child bonding (Jang 2007; Jung and Kim 2008). Children enjoy music in after-school programs, often because that is an acceptable activity in which their peers are also involved, so that musical involvement is a means of "belonging" to a social group (Kim et al. 2010; Korea Arts and Culture Education Service 2007).

MUSIC IN SCHOOL

The educational system of South Korea consists of preschool for three- to five-year-olds, six years of elementary school, three years each of middle and high schools, and two-, three-, and four-year colleges. In 1961, the Korean Ministry of Education established the first curriculum for the primary grades, and music became a formal subject in the national curriculum at this time. A preschool curriculum was established for Korean children in 1969, and this early education is deemed as highly desirable by families throughout the country (Korean Ministry of Education 1993). The Ministry of Education has revised and refined the elementary and secondary curricular several times since then (Korean Ministry of Education and Human Resource Development 2007; Korean Ministry of Education, Science, and Technology 2008).

Music in South Korean preschools and the primary grades of elementary schools is taught by classroom teachers who trained not only in early childhood education but also in music. Some preschools invite music specialists for extra music classes, in addition to the standard curriculum in music (Lee and Lee 1997). Specialists teach young children the Korean traditional percussion instruments such as the *Changgo* and the *Puk* (big drum). Teachers may add to these drums the performance techniques for *KKaengwari* (a small gong) or *Ching* (a large gong). When these drums and gongs are performed in ensemble, it is called *Samul* (literally, four materials) *nori* (play or performance). Children's *Samulnori* performance has become popular, and many elementary schools boast one or more *Samulnori* ensembles. During the *Samulnori* playing, children recite *Changdan* (traditional Korean rhythmic patterns, based on grouping rather than on time; Lee 1980) with the onomatopoeic syllables of *dong, duk,* and *k'ung* (Kim 2002).

Music is a mandatory school subject for children from the first through ninth grades. Music in the first and second grade is frequently an arts-integrated subject, called "*chulgoun saenghwhal*" (joyful life), which includes music, visual art, and physical education (Kim 2007). Music teachers typically teach music theory and performance in "general music classes" for children in the intermediate and middle school grades and lead children in learning to sing Korean folk songs and traditional children's songs. Often, children learn in school to play the *Tanso* and the recorder as well.

Since the 1970s, when curricular attention was turned toward globalization in South Korea, the elementary and secondary music curriculum expanded to include Korean traditional music and music from other cultures. Kim (2009) reported that there were fifty-four pieces of music in the current *Chulgoun saenghwhal* textbook. Among them are thirty-nine pieces of traditional Korean music, most of which are children's songs, such as "KKwongkkwong changsobang" (a song about "Mr.

Peacock"). Also, songs from the neighboring East Asian countries of Japan and China are featured in these elementary school music textbooks.

Multimedia instruction is frequently featured in the school music instruction of South Korea. Often, elementary school classroom teachers may not play the piano; instead, they teach children through the use of the computer. Contemporary music education depends more upon the computer knowledge of teachers than on their performing ability. Through computers, children learn to read rhythmic and pitch notation as well as about instruments, composers, and traditions—none of which is necessarily tied to performance.

There are regional differences in the music educational content of schools, and of the quality of music instruction, throughout South Korea. For example, the well-known vocal genre known as *P'ansori* is rooted in the Cholla Province of southeastern Korea and is very much alive in its periodic performances (Lee 2002). *P'ansori* is a form of traditional musical theater that features a solo singer and a barrel drum player, whose repertoire consists of satires, folktales, and love stories. Frequently, there is an exchange of verbal interaction between performers and audience members. Singing *P'ansori* requires extraordinary vocal virtuosity and techniques such as glissando, with frequently changing melodic fluctuations and various changes of *Changdan*. The singer's voice is typically husky, and both masculine and feminine vocal styles are presented. *P'ansori* singing involves long and intensive training, and while children are exposed to it in their music classrooms and through the media, its performance techniques are far beyond the reach of classroom instruction. However, due to the governmental effort to preserve and distribute to the next generation traditional Korean music, which was especially developed in the artistically distinguishable place known as the Cholla Province, children learn *P'ansori* singing in school (Kang 2011). The number of *P'ansori* child singers is steadily increasing. Among the favorite *P'ansori* are songs titled "Simch'ong jon" (Simch'ong's story) and "Ch'unhyang jon" (Ch'unhyang's story). Despite the difficulty of this singing technique, segments of these *P'ansori* have become more popular among children in Korea (An 2006; Choe 2001). Thus, the number of children taking private *P'ansori* lessons is sharply increasing in the Cholla area, although this is not the case in the capital, Seoul. Recently, however, some elementary teachers in Seoul began to include *P'ansori* in their music teaching materials. They encourage children to sing in *P'ansori* style with the modified libretto quoted from children's fairytales such as *Pyoljubujon* (a story about a turtle). Parts of *P'ansori* are rearranged by music teachers for children's classroom use (Jin 2008).

Music in the Community

Children's music classes are provided by culture centers, which are associated with department stores, with newspaper companies, and through TV and radio. Often, colleges and universities provide music programs for children and parents as a part of their effort to accomplish lifelong education in music. There are many private music institutes and venues for instrumental lessons at the community level. Cultural centers attached to shopping places are welcomed by young parents, who drop their children off when they go shopping for groceries, clothes, and household items. Classes utilizing Dalcroze eurhythmics (a movement-based music course) or Edwin Gordon's audiation instruction (an orally and aurally based early music experience) are top rated by the mothers of infants, toddlers, and preschool children (Figure 24.4). Orff and Kodaly methods are interwoven in the music sessions designed for lower grade elementary school children, so that they play xylophones, engage in singing games, and learn to read music while their mothers shop.

In many cases, the culture center is the first experience for children in their formal musical education. Some programs offer children instruction in violin and flute, too, or an experience in choral singing. Sometimes, grandmothers will attend music classes in culture centers in order to learn the songs and singing games that they will later practice at home with their grandchildren. Further, some grandmothers may work as storytellers for children in community centers. According to a new law announced by the Korean Ministry of Health and Welfare in 2008, elderly women who have a good memory of traditional Korean songs, games, and stories are invited to the preschools and elementary schools as guest teachers (Kim 2009).

In other community venues, the aforementioned festival of contemporary, composed children's songs is evident. This festival is aimed at celebrating Korean Children's Day in May and is continued for the purpose of distributing newly composed children's songs by several organizations (Han 2000; Jung and Kim 2008). Some popular festival songs that every child knows are featured, such as "Agi yomso" (A Baby Goat), composed by Lee Sunhyong, and "Talmumkkol kajok" (A Look-Alike Family), composed by Yunhwan Chung. Many of the festival song composers are elementary school teachers, those who know children through their daily interactions with them. Although these festival songs are composed for elementary school students, younger children sing them as well and continue to sing them later

Figure 24.4: Toddler and mother in music learning center.

as college students. Jung and Kim (2008) examined the repertoire of festival songs originally intended for older children and found that despite the more sophisticated nature of the musical structures of the songs, young children were motivated to learn and to sing them repeatedly; this finding is supported by the research of Stradler (2000).

Children's choirs are common in South Korea, even as teachers' choirs (in which teachers gather to sing together) are also evident. Private elementary schools often have a children's choir as well as orchestra classes for young string players. Wind bands and performance instruction on woodwind and brass instruments are quite rare in schools and in the community, however. Religious organizations, especially Christian and Catholic churches, provide venues for children's musical education and performance activity (Kim 2005) as children play handbells, ocarinas, and harmonicas in church. Occasionally, through their internet communications, children will find others who want to sing together, so they get together instantly and sing in a place such as a community center or a church. Children in the upper elementary grades and on into secondary school may be skillful in computer sound control techniques, and thus they enjoy creating their own songs on the computer, which they distribute online by uploading and posting their songs on their own blogs and websites (Korea Arts and Culture Education Service 2007).

CHANGES IN CHILDREN'S MUSICAL ENVIRONMENTS AND PREFERENCE

In South Korea, there is a specific place for singing called *Noraebang*. This is a compound word; literally, *norae* means "to sing," or "songs," and *bang* means "room." *Noraebang* is quite popular and is found throughout South Korea as a musical engagement for Koreans of various ages, including children (Kim 2004). A *Noraebang* space is well equipped with an electronic audiovisual system similar to the phenomenon of Japanese karaoke. Many families visit *Noraebang* with their children, who look forward to such outings. Sometimes, children will sing in imitation of adult popular singers' singing styles. There are various types of songs, such as traditional and composed Korean children' songs, songs from televised cartoon programs, hymns, and Korean art songs, in addition to Korean commercial songs. Furthermore, in the song selection book to which people refer in *Noraebang*, there are numerous songs from Japan, China, and North America, thus allowing children opportunities to experience foreign culture through music.

Due to the continued economic development of South Korea, where families typically have access to electronics of various sorts, many elementary school children have their own cellular phones and MP3 players, and they save their favorite popular songs on these devices, listening to them whenever and wherever possible (Han 2000, 2009; Kim 2004). MP3 players are a preferred gift item among children, with cellular phones and accessories also popular toys for many. Since these phones have multiple functions for music listening, it is possible for Korean children to access music with ease. Thus the electronic devices are not separated from the Korean children's daily life. Besides electronic devices, the internet contributes to children's access to music and helps communication with their friends on musical styles and artists. Korean children are familiar with computer and internet games from their early childhood forward. South Korean schools of every level are equipped with computer facilities in their classrooms (Kim 2009; Yang 2001), so that it is easy for children to access music alone and together with friends at school.

Popular singers and movie stars are objects of children's attention. The mass media, including MTV and Korean music videos produced in South Korea and in North America, are strong influences on children's musical preferences (Han 2009). Children enjoy singing popular songs sung by a popular idol. For example, there is one commercial television advertisement that uses a melody from Verdi's opera *Rigoletto*, "La donna e mobile." Since the onset of this commercial use of the music, children have been heard singing the aria's melody in and out of school. This was followed by melodies from other operas' arias, such as "Brindisi" from *La Traviata,* which also became a popular tune. Children switched the aria song texts, giving the melody their own words, and parodies of the arias abounded.

As pop singers are appealing to South Korean children, they imitate their adult styles of singing and dancing. Children find that some popular song texts match well their own thoughts and feelings of self, relationships, and goals. Because they like a fast tempo with frequent beats, Korean hip-hop is preferred by Korean boys. There are several teenage singing groups that are idolized. Groups named H.O.T. and Tong Vfang Xien Qi (known as TVXQ, an acronym that means mysterious energy from the East) are the famous boys groups, while Sonyosidae (literally girls' generation) is a girls group, and BoA is a well-known solo girl singer in Korea and further afield. Representative examples of their music can be found on YouTube, including "Candy" by H.O.T., "Before U Go (monologue)" by TVXQ, "Tell Me" by Sonyosidae, and "No. 1" by BoA. Many Korean children like to sing these songs, so some parents may take their children to professional singing teachers or to television and music studios so that they may learn pop vocal style in order to prepare them for a debut as a pop singer—or at least to pave the way for their children to sing in choirs that are featured on pop songs, TV, and radio.

SUMMARY

The children of South Korea have access to music of many styles and often know rich musical environments in their developmental years. Both at home and in school, mothers and grandmothers sing to babies and toddlers. Music is a mandatory subject in South Korean schools, and parents are supportive of the children's music learning in their early years of schooling, even as they look for community and church opportunities for their musical education as well. By adolescence, such attention to music wanes, as families turn toward the support of their children's studies in preparation for successful college entrance examinations. Children find music wherever it may be, including at home, in shopping centers, in public spaces, and in community venues. Their musical environments are changing rapidly, and the ubiquitous technologies are critical sources of children's listening pleasure. They are learning to play traditional Korean music instruments in greater numbers than ever before, and exposure to *Changgo* and *Tanso*, *P'ansori* music, and *Samulnori* are on the increase, in addition to the long-standing lessons in piano, violin, and other Western instruments and genres. Children in Korea are showing themselves to be musically flexible in their listening activity, and through the support of their families and the Korean Ministry of Education, they have fairly intensive experiences in music all through their childhood.

NOTES

1 *Kumjadonga* and *okjadonga* are composite words of four syllables with different meanings. As single words, they are used when the adults call for their babies. *Kum* means "gold" and *ok* means "jade." *Ja* is frequently used as the second syllable of someone's name; *dong* means "little" and *a* is an ending syllable when you call someone's name.

REFERENCES

An, K. 2006. "The Reconstitution and Instruction Guidance of P'ansori Soogunga for an Effective Appreciation Study." Master's thesis, Kyong'in National University of Education.

Choe, C. 1996. *An Old History of Korea and Japan*. Seoul: Korea text Publishers.

Choe, J. 2001. "A Study of Teaching Singing of the P'ansori for Elementary School Students." Master's thesis, Wonkwang University.

Chosunilbosa. 1995. *Chipan Koguryo Pyokhwa* [Mural paintings in *Chipan* of *Kogury*]. Seoul: Daily Chosun Publishing Company.

Doosan, Ch'ulp'ansa. 2007. *Doosan Encyclopedia*. Seoul: Doosan Publishers.

Han, C. 2000. *MP3 Music World*. Seoul: Youngjin Tat Com.

Han, U. 2009. "Research on Contemporary Music's Effect on Youth." Master's thesis, Kyongsang University.

Han, Y. 2000. *Han'guk ui umak sasang* [Philosophy of Music in Korea]. Seoul: Minsogwon.

Huh, M. 2008. "Educational Environment for the Children from Multicultural Families." *Journal of Early Childhood Education* 28 (1): 265–281.

Jang, E. 2007. "Music Education Model for Early Childhood Teacher Training." PhD diss., Ewha Women's University.

Jin, E. 2008. "Characteristics of Created P'ansori for Children." *Journal Research of P'ansori* 25: 281–301.

Jung, S., and Y. Kim 2008. "An Analysis on Musical Structure of the Songs: Selected from Children's Song Writers Competition and Taught in the Early Childhood Educational Institutes." *The Journal of Korea Open Association for Early Childhood Education* 13 (6): 195–218.

Kang, B. 2011. "Research on the Method of Teaching *P'ansori* as a Juvenile Education—Focused on Cho Sang-hyun's Simchung-Jun." Master's thesis, Chungang University.

Kim, H. 2004. "A Study on the New Model of 'Idol' Group in K-Pop." Master's thesis, Tanguk University.

Kim, H. 2009. "The Current Collection of Folk Songs in Elementary School Textbooks and Improvement Measures." *Journal of Korean Folklore* 25: 35–70.

Kim, U., U. Choe., and H. Cho. 2010. "Research of after School Curriculum Activation Policy for Preschoolers." Report 2010–2015. Seoul: Korea Institute of Child Care and Education.

Kim, Y. 1998. "Korean Traditional Children's Songs: Collection, Analysis, and Application." PhD diss., University of Washington.

Kim, Y. 2002. *Yua umak kyoyukron* [Introduction to Early Childhood Music Education]. 2nd ed. Seoul: Hakjisa.

Kim, Y. 2007. "Music an Integrated Subject or a Part of Art Subject." Proceedings of the Asia-Pacific Symposium on Music Education Research, Bangkok, Thailand, July 25–27, 2007.

Korea Arts and Culture Education Service. 2007. *Arts and Culture Education.* Seoul: Korea Arts and Culture Education Service.

Korea Arts and Culture Education Service. 2008. *Arts Education: Looking through Video Recording.* Seoul: Korea Arts and Culture Education Service.

Korea Institute of Child Care and Education. 2011. "Child Care Policy Research." Accessed July 31, 2011. http://kicce.re.kr.

Korea Trade-Investment Promotion Agency. 2011. "KOTRA." Accessed July 31, 2011. http://www.kotra.or.kr/wps/portal/dknew.

Korean Ministry of Education. 1993. *The 5th National Preschool Curriculum Guide.* Seoul: Korean Ministry of Education.

Korean Ministry of Education and Human Resources Development. 2007. *Revised 7th National Preschool Curriculum.* Seoul: Korean Ministry of Education and Human Resources Development.

Korean Ministry of Education, Science, and Technology. 2008. *Teacher's Guide of Preschool Curriculum I, II, III.* Seoul: Korean Ministry of Education, Science, and Technology.

Korean Ministry of Health and Welfare. 2011. "Make a Lifelong Friend, Health and Human Services." Accessed July 31, 2011. http://www.mw.go.kr/front/index.jsp.

Lee, B. 1980. "Korea." In *The New Grove Dictionary of Music and Musicians*, edited by Stanley Sadie, 192–208. Vol. 10. London: MacMillan.

Lee, E., and S. Lee. 1997. *Teacher's Guide to Children's Musical Activity* Seoul: Kyomunsa.

Lee, H. 1981. *Essays on Korean Traditional Music.* Translated by R. Provine. Seoul: Seoul Computer Press.

Lee, H. 2002. *Music Education for Feeling And Intuition.* Seoul: Sekwang umak ch'ulp'ansa.

Lim, H., and Y. Kim. 2004. "Research on the Appropriateness of the Children's Songs Preferred by Korean Kindergarten Teachers." *Journal of Early Childhood Education* 24 (6): 193–211.

Marsh, K. 1997. "Variation and Transmission Processes in Children's Singing Games in an Australian Playground." PhD diss., University of Sydney.

Marsh, K. 2008. *The Musical Playground*. London: Cambridge University Press.

Marsh, K., and Y. Kim. 2006. "A Tale of the Three Cities: Children's Musical Play in Australia, Korea and USA." *Asia-Pacific Journal for Arts Education* 41: 3–20.

National Archives of Korea. 2011. "National Archives of Korea" Accessed July 31, 2011. http://content.archives.go.kr/next/content/viewMain.do.

Statistics Korea. 2011. "Research/Statistics." Accessed July 31, 2011. http://kostat.go.kr/portal/index/survey.jsp.

Stradler, S. 2000. *Spiel und Nachanhmung: Uber die Entwicklung der elementaren musikalischen Aktivitaten* [Play and Imitation: About the Development of Basic Musical Activities]. Aarau, Switzerland: Npomulk.

Yang, O. 2001. "An Epistemological and Ethical Categorization of Perspectives on Early Childhood Curriculum." *International Journal of Early Childhood* 331: 1–8.

25

PERSPECTIVES ON THE SCHOOL BAND FROM HARDCORE AMERICAN BAND KIDS

CARLOS R. ABRIL

THE band room sits silent until the school bell rings, marking the start of a new class period. Soon after, about eighty high school students squeeze through the main entrance, quickly filling the space. Most are engaged in conversation; a group of girls arrives laughing; several boys use hand gestures to greet one another; some walk in clusters; others walk alone. Once in, students scatter to different places around the expansive room, which is decorated with awards, band photos, memorabilia, and posters. Some students go on to the instrument storage room, while others, with instruments in hand, walk directly to their chairs. Without direction or supervision, they find music folders, move music stands to their seats, assemble instruments, and begin playing.

There is a general dovetailing effect, from the sounds of adolescent banter to instrumental play. Among other sounds, a trombonist is playing an excerpt from *West Side Story*; a piccolo player is practicing scales; a snare drummer cuts through with a complex rhythmic pattern played repeatedly; and two trumpet players are discussing something sitting on their music stand. Amid the cacophony, the band director walks in from her adjacent office. Students seem oblivious to her arrival, but when she steps on the elevated podium at the center of the band and raises her arms, the room falls silent. The ensemble begins with a series of musical exercises created specifically for the woodwind, brass, and percussion instruments that comprise the American concert band (see Web Figure 25.1 ⬤).

On my first visit, the band played through several pieces from their marching band repertoire, including arrangements of Led Zeppelin's "Immigrant Song," The Who's "Pinball Wizard," and Survivor's "Eye of the Tiger," in preparation for an upcoming recording session. On subsequent visits, I heard them rehearse pieces from their concert band repertoire, including original works, such as Eric Whitacre's "Ghost Train" and arrangements for band, such as tunes from Leonard Bernstein's *West Side Story*. Typical band classes included a period of playing warm-ups followed by rehearsing the pieces of the day. Bands like this one are a common sight in schools across America and represent one unique landscape and soundscape of adolescence. Links to further information and views of bands can be found in Web Figure 25.2 ⬤.

BAND IN AND AS CULTURE

Almost a century after they made their way into schools, American band programs capture the interest of a large number of adolescents (Elpus and Abril 2011) and are the most commonly offered music elective, found in an overwhelming number of schools (Abril and Gault 2008). Courses such as beginning and intermediate band serve as training grounds for the concert band, the pinnacle of the band program. More specialized courses, such as jazz and marching band, are also fairly common.

Band is an institution that has been referred to as an American folk art (Kourlas 2009), a symbol of America (Humphreys 1989), and an "expression of the community's unity and its future generation of good citizens and leaders" (Foley 2001: 25). It is embedded in popular culture, where it has been depicted in movies, novels, and music videos. As a typical component of community celebrations and sporting events, bands function as a socially and physically unifying force (Lindquist 2006). Evidence abounds that bands are a prominent and valued part of schools and communities, although some argue that large ensembles lack a strong connection with a real world of music in our time (Kratus 2007). Such arguments prompt the question: why does participation in large ensembles remain such a valued and meaningful part of the educations and lives of so many adolescents in the twenty-first century? In this chapter I seek to examine the role adolescents play in the American school band and bring into focus the meaning and value they derive from participation. This examination will require stepping back to consider the intricacies of band in the context of the American high school.

High school is a complex culture, characterized by a unique set of values, beliefs, structures, and social groupings (Firestone and Louis 1999). Within that culture resides a number of inclusionary and exclusionary subgroups, some of which are constructed, regulated, and maintained solely by students, such as cliques. Other subgroups, such as band, are structured around school-sponsored activities (Adler and Adler 1995).

Kastenbaum (1997) argues that all subcultures share three characteristics: (1) they are associated with a recognizable lifestyle, or a series of values and patterns of behavior; (2) they are "separated from the larger culture only in terms of this life-style" (ibid.: 491); and (3) they develop in parallel but remain distinct from the lifestyle found in the broader culture. Morrison (2003) frames school band as a culture, providing many examples of the ways it is a unique social structure within school yet distinct from the greater culture in which it resides. To further build the case, he illustrates how band is characterized by distinct rituals, language, and behaviors. Stereotypical views of band members, exemplified by commonly used labels (e.g., band fags and band geeks; Foley 2001; Kinney 1999), suggest that band members are perceived as sharing a particular lifestyle that is distinct from the larger culture (i.e., school) or even other subcultures (e.g., jocks). Morrison (2001) also situates band within a greater music culture, claiming that they have "long since moved away from re-creating or emulating the performance medium that was so popular in the past [in the United States]" to create their own musical rituals and traditions (ibid.: 25). Many of these facets of band culture suggest that it is a subculture of school.

Adolescents in band (Web Figure 25.3 ⊙) feel connected to one another in part through shared interests and the sheer number of hours they spend together (Adderley, Kennedy, and Berz 2003). They characterize band as a "home away from home," a place where they create strong social bonds with peers and adults through the music experience. As in many other large social groups, smaller subgroups take shape, with distinct characteristics that are regulated and shaped by its members (Adler and Adler [1995] 1998). Within band, there are subgroups divided along various lines, including grade level, instrumentation, performance ability, and years of membership, with student-regulated hierarchies of power (Adderley 2009; Laine 2007).

A characteristic of band culture is the belief that the collective is of utmost value and importance. In a study of a high school band, Laine (2007) noted that band directors were so focused on ensemble achievements that they only focused on individual growth if they believed it would benefit the collective. Even at the middle school level, bands have been found to be primarily product oriented and centered on competition to the exclusion of artistic goals (Scheib 2006). Allsup and Benedict claim that band members "are individuals submerged by the rules of its practice and are thus likely to embody class situations that are bound by its discourses: belief in strong leadership, belief in commitment to a larger collective, belief in meritocracy" (2009: 157). If these claims and observations are valid, they bring up another question: how do subgroups of band contribute to the collective goals and at what costs?

McNeill helps us understand the impact of humans working together toward a common goal. He suggests that "human beings desperately need to belong to

communities that give guidance and meaning to their lives; and moving rhythmically while giving voice together is the surest, most speedy, and efficacious way
of creating and sustaining such communities that our species has ever hit upon"
(1995: 152). A commitment to the collective might be characterized as a loss of self,
something McNeill called "boundary loss." He refers to boundary loss as "collective
way of looking at the same thing: a blurring of self-awareness and the heightening
of fellow-feeling with all who share in the dance" (1995: 8). In other words, when
one is participating in some activity involving rhythmic movement, a level of social
bonding occurs. Groups of people who move or play in time create experiences
of synchronization that help them envision themselves as being part of a collective (Linquist 2006; McNeil 1995). Through playing and moving together in time,
band may offer the prime sociomusical space in school for some students to develop
strong group identities, which are both valuable and meaningful to adolescents.

ADOLESCENCE

Adolescence can be viewed as a phase of life marked by a synthesizing of childhood
(Marcia 1980) and transitioning into adulthood (Graber et al. 1996). It can be seen
as a part of childhood in that individuals continue to be closely connected to family
and school (Dornbusch 1989). In Western culture, it is a time to seek independence
from within the family unit (Dunphy 1969) and to define one's self "by trying different identities on and off" (Dimitriadis 2003: 6). This extension of and transition
from childhood is marked by increased associations outside the family, with peers
who share similar values, interests, and behaviors (Dornbusch 1989) and who have
great influence on one another (Adler and Adler [1995] 1998).

Music plays a central role in the lives of adolescents, serves to mediate peer
group relations, and contributes to the formation of identity (Campbell, Connell,
and Beegle 2007; Tarrant, North, and Hargreaves 2002). Davidson and Burland
noted, "The transition from adolescent to young adults involves the individual
identifying and pursuing what seems necessary to fulfill his/her idealized personal
identity" (2006: 487). They believe music "must be at the core of this identity" and
claim that music is "a key identity construct, relating to self-expression, must be at
the core of this identity" (ibid.: 487). School music programs are thought to help
students gain a sense of group identity and to also come to recognize differences
among groups (Lamont 2002). As a school-based activity and subculture of high
school, band may offer a valuable social space (Web Figure 25.4 ⊙) whereby adolescents develop personal and musical identities alongside peers with similar interests
and pursuits.

This chapter seeks to build upon but also move in a new direction from many
of the reviewed large ensemble studies by examining a subset of the band culture—
the hardcore band kids. These are the adolescents who form the social and musical

nucleus of band. Giving them voice will provide insight into the meaning and value they find in participating in band and understanding of the ways such participation relates to the musical, personal, and social realms of their lives. Specific questions guided this study: (1) How do adolescents characterize their role and the role of others in band? (2) How do they describe the meaning and value of participating in band? and (3) In what ways do their musical worlds outside of school intersect with school band? To answer these questions, I made my way to a Chicago high school with a band that had earned a reputation of excellence in the city.

THE HARDCORE BAND KIDS

Washington High School is situated between a city park and a residential neighborhood, within view of Chicago skyscrapers. Given the multimillion dollar homes, the upscale shopping district, and the people walking in the community, one would think that the school serves an affluent student body, yet other neighborhoods within the school boundaries and special enrollment efforts diversify the population along ethnic and socioeconomic lines. According to district figures, more than two-thirds live outside of the school neighborhood boundaries. Neighborhood students are automatically qualified to enroll; students from outside the area can apply for a magnet program. Students are socioeconomically diverse yet more than 50 percent come from low-income households. Students identify as African American (35 percent), white (30 percent), Hispanic (18 percent), Asian/Pacific Islanders (11 percent), and other (6 percent). The students participating in the study were culturally and socioeconomically diverse. Between the ages of seventeen and eighteen, these seniors were identified by the school music directors as being hardcore band members, as defined by multiyear participation and significant dedication to band. The five band members (who participated in the study) and the band director estimated that there were between ten and twelve hardcore band members. The attitudes and understandings of three representative students will be presented here. Pseudonyms are used to protect the identity of these students.

Raymond has a stocky build, medium-brown skin tone, and facial hair and appears older than his senior-year status would suggest. Yet while adult in appearance, his behavior is adolescent and admittedly "a bit goofy at times," a characterization echoed by others. In contrast, when playing trumpet he consistently appeared serious and focused. Raymond was born in Mexico and immigrated to Chicago with his family at the age of three. Although he considers himself "somewhat Americanized," he still feels distinctly Mexican. He is enrolled in four music classes (concert band, jazz band, orchestra, and piano) and claims to practice between two to three hours daily. He also attends the government-subsidized City Music School on Saturdays, where he participates in ensembles and applied lessons. He hopes to attend college to become a band director upon graduation.

Micheline described herself as a "social butterfly," and this was evident from her energetic interaction with peers before and after rehearsals. She is one of the more talented flute players in the band, having played as first chair in the concert band since her sophomore year and currently serving as flute section leader. She has danced ballet outside of school since her preschool years. She is unsure if she wants to study music professionally but wants to continue being involved in the arts throughout her life. She identifies as "mixed race," with a "black father" and "white mother."

Baccus has a mature way about him. He describes himself as someone who is "very good at playing the trumpet, talented, and a leader." His father is Greek born and his mother is American of Greek descent. He is enrolled in the same music classes in school as Raymond and claims to be his good friend. They attend concerts together and "hang out during and after school." Baccus is also enrolled in the City Music School and has been selected to play in the all-state band for three consecutive years. He hopes to study music upon graduation.

On Roles and Hierarchies

Adler and Adler ([1995] 1998) studied the roles of children within the social system of school. They found that children organize themselves into social groups composed of people with whom they can relate and identify. These groups are found to be hierarchal in nature, with four main strata: popular (most exclusive group), wannabe (aspire to be included in the exclusive group), middle (smaller friendship groups), and social isolate (individuals who are usually alone). In discussing the roles in band, students shared their experiences, beliefs, and perceptions, which revealed the social intricacies of band.

Roles

All the students contributing to this study see themselves as leaders in the band, both official (peer vote and teacher recognition) and unofficial (self-determined). Raymond is the drum major, a role that involves conducting and serving as the top student leader of marching band. Micheline is flute section leader, a role involving being the primary leader of an instrumental section of the band. Other students are leaders based on their perceptions and behaviors, not their titles. All students maintained that an effective leader in the band had to earn the respect of peers. This was a struggle for Raymond when assuming the role of the "top student leader." He soon learned that he would have to modify his attitude and behaviors in order to gain the respect and trust of the band he would be leading as drum major. When discussing leadership, some students focused on the nonmusic skills: organization, socialization, dedication, and respect for others. Baccus believed that musical skills were paramount: "You have to know what you're doing on your instrument and be really good. People start to look up to you when you are and that's the only way you can gain respect here."

Students explained how leadership roles are negotiated and less fixed than they might appear. Micheline sounded protective of her position as leader: "Raymond tries but he's not really much of a boss for me. I just do my part and he doesn't say anything. I'm pretty much the boss of the flutes. He knows I've got it under control." In discussing the role of the section leader, Baccus believed that there are people who are the official leaders but that responsibilities should be shared: "Sure there is a section leader, but really… we all just help each other because that's the way to get things done."

Most also spoke about the need to mentor less-experienced or -able members. Raymond said, "I think to be a good band member you have to be someone who is helpful to others and that means you first have to be a master of your instrument." Raymond sees himself as a teacher, which he believes requires the ability to "be patient," "communicate well," "listen," and "have ideas for making something better." Micheline claims that her most important leadership task is to listen to her peers play so she can offer suggestions for improvement. A few explained that they felt a responsibility to help others because it was in the best interest of the group and would lead to a stronger band. Student leaders in this ensemble function as support systems for the teacher directors; they allow for more microlevel monitoring, management, and assessment. Most agree that student leaders need a combination of leadership and music skills. Students' perspectives on leadership were reflective of and seemed limited by their roles.

Hierarchies

When discussing roles, all students spoke of a sociomusical hierarchy. In the upper stratum were the hardcore members, who were essential to the band's success. They attained their status through a combination of musicianship, positive dispositions, and leadership/social skills. Baccus called them "hardcore guys." Raymond said, "The people who make the band are the ones who are the most dedicated to the band and the people. These are the people you notice practicing during their free time, during lunch period, or after school. They bring out the band the most." Micheline also spoke of a top group of band members, referring to them as the "cool band guys." These are the members who "are not only good at their instrument but people admire them… we socialize and people want to be around us…. We're just cool that way…. We are also the people who love music to our core… and we're usually trying to make sure everybody's doing what they need to do too. We love what we are doing and others respect us for it." Another student spoke of the way this group clumps together: "We share a common interest and a passion for music so we group together and we hang out. Everyone knows who we are." A subset of the core group is the "jazz clique," so labeled by Micheline; "They are the ones who have a passion for jazz... they act different than the rest of us... they are just really hard core about jazz. You can't just be a part of them if you want... you have to belong." Raymond spoke of his membership:

> We jazz guys always stick around each other... I guess because we are the better players, instrumental-wise; we're the top guys in the other ensembles [e.g., concert band]. I don't think we exclude people on purpose. We talk to people across the board but we usually are together because we have the most in common with each other. I mean, I sit down with them and we talk about music, like things we just got on our iPod, mostly jazz stuff.

Baccus characterized himself as "one of the jazz guys" because most of his close friends were in that group and because of shared interests in jazz music.

One notch below students in the upper stratum were those who were somewhere in the middle—the "middles." Baccus said, "It's hard to put your finger on them; they're not *that* bad but not *really* good either. They are just in between... somewhere in the middle." Raymond described them as those who are "less dedicated" and "don't really hurt the band but don't do so much to make it great... but they aren't really with us." They were thought to represent the largest number of people in the band and to belong to cliques outside of band and/or friendship circles in band. Some students in the middle were thought to be close to becoming hardcore but needed more "seniority in band," "proof of their dedication," and/or "friends at the top."

At the low end of the hierarchy were "the slackers," said to comprise a minority in band and thought to actually "hurt the band." Hardcore members believed that the slackers lacked responsibility to the band in "not preparing their music," "not having their uniforms," or "just not showing up." Micheline said they just "don't hold up their end of the bargain" and noted their lack of cohesiveness: "They really aren't socially together though... we just know who they are because of the way they do things in band... I'm not sure some of them are part of any group at school. I'm not sure why they stay here."

Various exclusionary tactics seemed to be used by hardcore members. Baccus claims that some members ostracize or even embarrass the slackers. "Sometimes we make sarcastic remarks or are in your face and say, 'What the hell are you doing? Shape up, man!'" He went on to explain how members of his sociomusical group stay distinct: "We never mix or hangout with the bottom group. *Never!* If we mix with anyone it would be more with the middle group. They understand us a little better." Raymond explained that some students were ignored but thought the leaders should not overlook them in the interest of the collective. "People give them a hard time but I know we need them so I try to help." Interestingly, Baccus believes many slackers see him and other hardcore members as being "odd.... They look at us sometimes and say, 'Man those guys are dorks... geeks... they're going to be so weird.'" Students believed that it was possible for members to move up or down from one rank to another. For instance, three used Raymond as an example of someone who was a "complete slacker" at one point and later became the top student leader. Baccus explained that going down was quick and easy, yet going up could take years.

Of the three strata noted, the "hardcores" (the term used by students in the study) were the only ones that formed a traditional clique, as evidenced by their use of various exclusionary/inclusionary tactics as characterized by Adler and Adler (1995). What makes these findings different from prior research is that artistic skill/ achievement has a significant amount of social capital in the clique, and the loyalty and dedication is directed to the band, not to the clique itself. For them, the band was not so much a class or a course in school but a sociomusically uniting activity. Findings support prior studies that reported the formation of subgroups in large ensembles along lines of instrument, seniority, and expertise (Adderley, Kennedy, and Berz 2003; Laine 2007). For these students, band was "a family," "a home," and "*the* place to be in school." Hardcore students I interviewed clumped the next group of band members into one group, which I call the "middles." It was interesting to note the distinction they made between the middles, who seemed about ready to move to the hardcore group, and how others were thought to clump into smaller friendship circles. These findings are strikingly analogous to the "wannabes" and middle groups described in prior research (Adler and Adler [1995] 1998), although students in the current study only clumped them into one group. The "slackers" did not form a cohesive peer group but were categorized based on their behaviors, which were perceived to be harmful to the collective. Baccus's comment that slackers view hardcores as "geeks" and "dorks," reminds us that the notion of being a popular or exclusive social group in high school is only relative to those making the judgment. Band was considered a "cool" activity by students interviewed, yet this view is unlikely to be shared among band members, let alone others in the school.

On Meaning and Value

All students found meaning from actively making or responding to music. They focused on the sheer enjoyment they experience in performing for themselves, with each other, and people outside band. Some spoke of performing as being connected to their identities. Micheline said, "I love my instrument; I love playing it. I love how it feels and how it makes me feel.... It is an amazing feeling when the music sounds so great. Music is such a life force for me...it's pretty much like my soul. It's part of who I am; it is me. When I play it, it gets even deeper into me." Baccus simply stated, "Playing my trumpet is when I really feel alive...because it's who I am."

Some spoke of the ways performing music in band influenced or educated their emotions. Micheline described how performing music helped her to develop greater emotional awareness and self-regulation: "Both ballet and music help me to be more in tune with emotions and with controlling my emotions, too." She also claimed that her experience in band has helped her convey emotions through music performance: "I have to know the feeling and then find ways to produce that feeling through sound...it's harder to make the people listening share in that feeling. I love music because it affects the people around you and it requires you to be capable of controlling it. Band has helped me improve that."

Micheline described how playing in band helped to mediate her emotions during the time her mother had been diagnosed with cancer.

> I was not feeling well a long time but one day I woke up and was like "you know, you've got band" and that one thought helped me. I felt good to be doing something where I didn't have to feel obligated to worry. Instead I could focus on doing what I had to do for band...I mean it was hard but making music took me some place else emotionally.

Baccus also used band as a temporary escape:

> I've gone through a lot of stuff these four years.... My father opened a business [that] went bankrupt. So despite that going on, being in band is something that I can look forward to. It is both fun and a lot of hard work but that keeps me focused. Music gets you to feel different from the stuff of the everyday.

Hardcore members value working with peers to meet common goals. Raymond: "I love being with other players constantly. We motivate each other to do better and better." Baccus: "[In band] you're with people who also enjoy making music...there's something about that that's different from in other places in the school.... We are working together to get something accomplished." All students described the social dimension of the band experience as being important. Micheline: "[Band] kind of feels like a family because we are pretty tight with each other. We've grown up together...we've shown each other that we can do this and that brings us together. It gives us respect for each other. I feel so good when I am playing with everyone." Baccus: "You make great bonds and friendships...even so many [romantic] relationships in band." The importance of the social aspects of band was also reported in prior research (Adderley, Kennedy, and Berz 2003). It would be interesting to know if these findings would hold for the "middles" and how the experiences of the "slackers" would differ.

Various themes arose from our conversations about the meaning and value of band in these students' lives. Like younger children (Campbell 1998), adolescents in this study placed significant value on being actively engaged in the music experience through performance. It was a theme that resonated throughout the interviews. Related to performing music, they spoke about the value in learning challenging music or unfamiliar music and the meaning they constructed from having something deeper to ponder. Students' conversations about meaning arising from performance zoomed in and out between the personal and social dimensions.

Discussions about emotions and feelings were also notable. Some found that performance gave them a way to connect with and control emotions and to express emotions through music in ways that might affect others. It was interesting to note how performing in the band seemed to serve as therapy for some, where they could be transported to "someplace else emotionally," "feel different stuff from the everyday," or "clear the mind." The perceived therapeutic and emotional benefits of music participation have been documented in prior research (Campbell 1998; Campbell et al. 2007).

On Connections

Band's meaning and value extends and intertwines with life outside the band room.

One summer Raymond was hired to play in a mariachi band. This opportunity arose after a neighbor heard him practicing. He explained that the neighbor "was impressed with what he heard and asked me if I played mariachi. I said 'no' but he said I would be able to learn...I knew mariachi because I heard it a lot but had never played it." This was the first time Raymond had ever been paid for playing and explained how band made this opportunity possible: "Everything I had learned here [in band] really was paying off for me...we never play mariachi [in band] but I had learned the technique I needed."

His dedication to music has come at a cost.

> I really don't have any time to relax [and] sometimes feel overwhelmed with all the things I have to practice for and try to get better.... I don't spend as much time with friends as I used to because I'm usually in a practice room or listening to music. Well, I have friends in the band so when we are playing, we're together.

On the flip side, Raymond viewed his busy schedule as being a positive thing:

> I live in a community where there's gang influence and violence. It's difficult and dangerous.... If I wasn't in music, because I used to hang out with these kinds of people, they would still be my friends today and I would probably be with them instead of playing my trumpet.

Raymond has a voracious appetite for music, which is mostly focused on "classical, jazz, and Latino music." He attributes his taste for classical and jazz to his experiences playing music in school. "I love listening to music, especially classical trumpet players like Maurice André or jazz trumpet like Freddie Hubbard. I mostly have stuff like that in my collection. I do have a lot of Latin stuff too, so like mariachi, Latin pop, Latin rock, and other Latin stuff." Raymond claimed that his parents exclusively listened to Latino music and were puzzled by his interests in classical and jazz because they seemed so foreign to other family members.

Raymond hopes to study music upon graduation but was concerned because his parents could not "see music as a profession or a career." He explained, "They think that musicians are drug addicts and alcoholics, people who don't get paid well." He spoke of the tension between family and personal goals, rationalizing them on cultural terms:

> My family doesn't really support me, music-wise. I guess being from Mexico, we struggle coming to the USA. While I was born there, I have learned a lot from

being here most of my life. My parents have a different perspective on life, and sometimes it brings me down.... I know Latinos come from a background of hard work and my parents think that music isn't hard work.... Sometimes I have troubles, thinking to myself, "Why am I doing music if my family isn't supporting me?" but at least my friends are. It's hard because my family is the number one priority in my life.

Micheline ruminated on music from her perspective as a dancer. She says, "When I am playing it, I am dancing to it, even when I am not really dancing. That is the way I feel music, through my body. I live to feel music and dance to it. I mean you have to move with it, you know?" This illustrates how her personal experiences outside of school shape her way of responding to music in band and elsewhere.

Micheline's interests embraced various styles of music; she claimed to be an "alternative rock type" but also one who listened to "bluegrass, movie sound tracks, and easy listening." Despite her affiliations with alternative rock among her peers, she says that she enjoys jazz and classical music more than other styles. Her interest in jazz comes from her father: "My dad introduced me to it and we listen to jazz together." Her mother developed her love of classical music. She says that classical and jazz are "two halves of me... it's all kinda all one thing for me... they're in different places in my life but they are connected to who I am."

Baccus primarily identified as a "jazz guy." His interest in jazz arose from initial experiences in the school jazz band but he claims flourished as a result of experiences outside of school, including the City Music School and excursions into the Chicago jazz scene. He also possesses a sizable collection of jazz music on his iPod and proudly noted that there is no popular music on his playlist.

His father plays the bouzouki, a stringed instrument with a lute-like body. He says that his father "loves Greek music." Baccus's father seems to have made several efforts to teach his son the music and culture of his homeland, enrolling him in Greek school and involving him in music and dance lessons. "The only thing I remember is that we did the Zorba dance and all that stuff.... It was cute but I had to move on." He also hummed part of a Greek song he learned as a child but couldn't remember it all or recall the name. He said that his father "just gave up after a while because I had no interest." Baccus generally speaks of Greek music as if it resides outside the worlds of jazz and classical. He explained, "The stuff we play here is sometimes kinda weird. It's contemporary and more advanced. But the music that my dad listens to is 'old school.'"

The connections between band and music outside of school varied among members of the same clique. The connections were strong and focused for some: Raymond and Baccus were fully immersed in and committed to music. The lines between school music and music in their lives were blurred in some respects and separate in others. Their music study, in and out of school, seemed to shape their musical preferences, their attitudes toward other musics, and the musical opportunities they were afforded. This full immersion, however, came at the expense of other aspects of their lives: friendships outside of music, narrow musical preferences, lack of other school experiences, and disconnects with family culture.

Davidson and Burland's (2006) research might suggest that Raymond's strong sense of a musical identity made him more resistant to pressures he felt from friends in his neighborhood and family away from music. The tension between Raymond and his parents speaks to the challenges students face when familial perceptions and expectations conflict with those of schools or with the process of findings one's identity. Adolescence is a phase of childhood characterized by a search for personal and group identity (Dimitriadis 2003); this may be especially challenging for first- and second-generation immigrants, like Raymond.

For others, less fully immersed in music both in and out of school, band was discussed in relation to their other interests and identities. Dance informed Micheline's way of talking about performing music and coming to understand it. Her need to move to music both inside and outside her body echoes younger children's engagements with music (Campbell 1998). It should come as no surprise that all students' music preferences were closely connected with their musical and cultural identities (Tarrant et al. 2002), yet it was interesting how they aligned those preferences to their varied experiences in band and family (Web Figure 25.5 ⊙).

ON LESSONS LEARNED FROM
HARDCORE BAND KIDS

The insights and personal narratives from the hardcore band kids provide us with a unique perspective from which to consider the inner workings of band and the important role it plays in their lives. One interesting finding from this chapter is the notion that there are three major hierarchical strata in the band, with only the hardcores forming a true clique. The differentiations between these strata may or may not hold if this study had included a wider sampling of band members. Future research might give voice to members of large ensembles whose voices might offer vastly different perspectives—those who have little interest in music, those considered "slackers," or those who discontinue their participation in band.

The question of relevance must also be addressed, given recent calls to reconsider large ensembles in music education. While it is healthy to interrogate common practices, we must also pause and listen to those who currently find great value and meaning participating in school bands and choirs. The adolescents in this study spoke passionately and sincerely about the importance of music in general and band in particular. They characterized band as a social learning space where they could find identity, lose themselves in performing, and work with peers to meet goals more ambitious than they could ever accomplish individually. In an era of high stakes testing and a continued focus on individual accomplishments in schools, large ensembles such as band may fill a lacuna in the school curriculum. The hardcore band members' relentless focus on the collective recalls McNeill's (1995) notion of boundary loss, in which humans become less aware of self and instead heighten their awareness of the efforts of the social collective. Humans have a need to belong and contribute to some community; for some, like the hardcore kids in this study, band offers that space.

ACKNOWLEDGMENTS

The author gratefully acknowledges Jennifer Shuck, Tina Yao, and David Schwartzer for their invaluable assistance with various aspects of this project.

REFERENCES

Abril, C. R., and B. Gault. 2008. "The State of Music in Secondary Schools: The Principal's Perspective." *Journal of Research in Music Education* 56 (1): 68–81.

Adderley, C. 2009. "Music in Motion: An Overture to the Student Experience in the High-School Marching Band." In *Musical Experience in Our Lives: Things We Learn and Meanings We Make*, edited by J. Kerchner and C. R. Abril, 239–253. Lanham, MD: Rowman and Littlefield.

Adderley, C., M. Kennedy, and W. Berz. 2003. "'A Home away from Home': The World of the High School Music Classroom." *Journal of Research in Music Education* 51 (3): 190–205.

Adler, P. A., and P. Adler. 1995. "Dynamics of Inclusion and Exclusion in Preadolescent Cliques." *Social Psychology Quarterly* 58 (3): 145–162.

Adler, P. A., and P. Adler. [1995] 1998. *Peer Power: Preadolescent Culture and Identity.* New Brunswick, NJ: Rutgers University Press.

Allsup, R., and C. Benedict. 2008. "The Problems of Band: An Inquiry into the Future of Instrumental Music Education." *Philosophy of Music Education Review* 16 (2): 156–173.

Campbell, P. S. 1998. *Songs in Their Heads.* New York: Oxford University Press.

Campbell, P. S., C. Connell, and A. Beegle. 2007. "Adolescents' Expressed Meanings of Music in and out of School." *Journal of Research in Music Education* 55 (3): 220.

Davidson, J. W., and K. Burland. 2006. "Musician Identity Formation." In *The Child as Musician: A Handbook of Musical Development*, edited by G. E. McPherson, 475–490. New York: Oxford University Press.

Dimitriadis, G. 2003. *Friendship, Cliques, and Gangs: Young Black Men Coming of Age in Urban America.* New York: Teachers College Press.

Dornbusch, S. M. 1989. "The Sociology of Adolescence." *Annual Review of Sociology* 15: 233–259.

Dunphy, D. C. 1969. *Cliques, Crowds and Gangs: Group Life of Sidney Adolescents.* Melbourne, Australia: Cheshire.

Elpus, K., and C. R. Abril. 2011. "High School Music Students in the United States: A Demographic Profile." *Journal of Research in Music Education* 59 (2): 128–145.

Firestone, W. A., and K. S. Louis. 1999. "Schools as Cultures." In *Handbook of Research on Educational Administration*, edited by J. Murphy and K. S., 297–322. San Francisco: Jossey-Bass.

Foley, D. E. 2001. "The Great American Football Ritual: Reproducing Race, Class, and Gender Inequality." In *Contemporary Issues in Sociology of Sport*, edited by A. Yiannakis and M. J. Melnick, 23–40. Champaign, IL: Human Kinetics.

Graber, J., J. Brooks-Gunn, and A. Petersen. 1996. *Transitions through Adolescence: Interpersonal Domains and Context.* Mahwah, NJ: Erlbaum.

Hebert, D. G. 2001. "The Tokyo Kosei Wind Orchestra: A Case Study of Intercultural Music Transmission." *Journal of Research in Music Education* 49 (3): 212–226.

Humphreys, J. T. 1989. "An Overview of American Public School Bands and Orchestras before World War II." *Bulletin of the Council for Research in Music Education* 101: 50–60.

Humphreys, J. T. 1995. "Instrumental Music in American Education: In Service of Many Masters." *Journal of Band Research* 30 (2): 39–70.

Kastenbaum, R. 1993. *Encyclopedia of Adult Development.* Phoenix, AZ: Oryx Press.

Kourlas, G. 2009. "Just like Dancing, with Sousaphones." *New York Times*, December 27, AR1.

Kratus, J. 2007. "Music Education at the Tipping Point." *Music Educators Journal* 94 (2): 42–48.

Laine, K. 2007. *American Band: Music, Dreams, and Coming of Age in the Heartland.* New York: Gotham Books.

Lamont, A. 2002. "Musical Identities and the School Environment." In *Musical Identities*, edited by R. A. R. MacDonald, D. J. Hargreaves, and D. Miell, 49–55. Oxford: Oxford University Press.

Lindquist, D. C. 2006. "'Locating' the Nation: Football Game Day and American Dreams in Central Ohio." *Journal of American Folklore* 119 (474): 444–488.

Marcia, J. E. 1980. "Identity in Adolescence." In *Handbook of Adolescent Psychology*, edited by J. Adelson, 159–187. New York: Wiley and Sons.

Mark, M. L., and C. L. Gary. 2007. *A History of American Music Education.* Lanham, MD: Rowman and Littlefield Education.

McNeill, W. H. 1995. *Keeping Together in Time: Dance Drill in Human History.* Cambridge, MA: Harvard University Press.

Morrison, S. J. 2001. "The School Ensemble: A Culture of Our Own." *Music Educators Journal* 88 (2): 24–28.

Scheib, J. W. 2006. Lindy's Story: One Student's Experience in Middle School Band. *Music Educators Journal* 92 (5): 32–36.

Tarrant, M., A. C. North, and D. J. Hargreaves. 2002. "Youth Identity and Music." In *Musical Identities*, edited by R. Macdonald, D. J. Hargreaves, and D. Miell, 135–150. Oxford: Oxford University Press.

26

THE NATURE OF MUSIC NURTURING IN JAPANESE PRESCHOOLS

MAYUMI ADACHI

ACROSS the world, children sing. Music making is universal and uniquely human, and spontaneous song is a child's first creative act, one that comes from within and without the assistance of an external tool (e.g., Tafuri 2009). It is the role of music education to enhance and broaden this attribute: to turn the aural corollary of stick figure drawings into finer craft, and ultimately into art. Musical expression is an essential human craving, the desire to wander in melody (and/or rhythm). Music educators seek the means for nurturing the development of children's musical expression and recognize that some instructional techniques are inefficient and even stifling to the creative process.

Nowhere is this more the case than in Japan, where regurgitation is the norm and creation of original song/music the exception. In one fine day of "open school," which is an annual school festival, preschool teachers presented their pupils neatly lined up for group singing in front of their parents and grandparents, many who were proudly holding video cameras to record the well-trained performances of their little boys and girls. Everyone smiled, including the children themselves, while I wondered how many hours of potentially creative time were jeopardized for the preparation of children for this specific show. No one seemed to question what this preschool tradition of song performance could be doing to young children's musical minds and to the long-term goals of their musical education. It is from this cautionary tale that the chapter proceeds, with the intent of responding to questions of young children's music involvement in early childhood programs in Japan.

Japanese preschoolers sing many songs during free play, just like those from other cultures (Campbell [1998] 2010; Opie and Opie 1973). However, unlike Australian children, who primarily sing invented songs (Whiteman 2001), the content of Japanese preschoolers' spontaneous schoolyard singing primarily consists of the enculturated Western-style songs or Japanese traditional child songs— *warabe-uta*—invented by former generations of Japanese children (Ogawa and Imagawa 2008). Six months of observations of Japanese children in a nursery school, ages one to four years (e.g., Fujita 2002; Fujita and Nakakura 1996), revealed that more than 75 percent of their spontaneous singing consisted of these standard Western-styled and *warabe-uta* songs.

A similar contrast was found between children in an English-speaking location and those in Japan when each child was explicitly asked to make up a happy or a sad song (Adachi and Trehub 2011). Although 80 percent of Canadian preschoolers created songs of original quality (i.e., either completely original songs or variations of familiar songs with new words), only 20 percent of Japanese children did so. Japanese children generally chose to sing a song they knew rather than to create one. This tendency was also apparent in Japanese first graders but not in older children when they were given the same task. The Japanese first graders who failed to provide original songs were nonetheless able to express their feelings by telling stories. It was the task of singing that constrained young Japanese children from showing their creativity. Why would this be?

An answer to this question may be paradoxical. Music plays an important role in Japanese early childhood education (Japanese Ministry of Education, Culture, Sports, Science, and Technology 2008). Unlike the early childhood specialist training in the United States (Nardo et al. 2006), music courses are compulsory for prospective preschool/nursery schoolteachers in Japan (Yamamoto, Fukunishi, and Miyake 2007). Musical activities are thought to provide shared positive experiences among classmates and to develop a sense of unity, facilitating young children's socialization. In particular, singing songs is the most commonly practiced musical activity in early childhood education in Japan (Miyake, Fukunishi, and Yamamoto 2004). The absolute majority of singing activities led by a teacher are the reproduction of standard songs and *warabe-uta*. Exploratory or creative singing is limited (Fujita 2002; Fujita and Nakakura 1996; Miyake et al. 2004). Modifying the lyrics of a familiar song can be considered wrong, and improvising call-response patterns is also scarce. This balance in singing activities between reproduction and creation may be reflected in Japanese children's tendencies to sing familiar rather than invented songs both in the schoolyard (Fujita 2002; Fujita and Nakakura 1996) and in laboratory experiments (Adachi 2001, 2011; Adachi and Trehub 2011). These tendencies are culturally led.

According to the thirty-four preschools and nursery schools from which the Japanese first graders in Adachi's study (2001) graduated, children sang familiar songs every day and learned many new songs throughout the year, while they rarely had opportunities to be involved in creative activities or free musical expression. On the other hand, children's verbal expressions (such as telling of their own experiences) were encouraged and practiced throughout the school year—which could explain why Japanese first graders could generate emotionally laden personal stories but not original songs.

The findings of the above survey appear to imply that Japanese preschoolers' musical experiences may be musically rich but creatively poor. Yet before making such a statement with confidence, a larger sampling of preschools in Japan was examined. The goal of this chapter is to reveal Japanese children's musical lives in preschool, including the music they are taught and the musical activities in which they are encouraged to participate, based on survey responses about the nature of young children's engagement in music from 121 preschools in Japan.

JAPANESE CHILDREN'S MUSICAL LIVES IN PRESCHOOL: A SURVEY

A survey of preschools was conducted in three prefectures in Honshuu (the main island), Japan. Populations of those prefectures at the time of the survey ranged from 0.6 to 3.0 million people, that is, small to medium-sized for Japan. There were 126 preschools that replied, and one teacher in each school provided information on the class taught in the year before the survey (i.e., April 2001 to March 2002). All respondents were female, and teaching experience ranged from one to more than thirty years, with a median of sixteen to twenty years. Twenty-three respondents described a classroom for three- and four-year-olds (the youngest, or *nenshou,* grade), twenty-five for four- and five-year-olds (the younger, or *nenchuu,* grade), and seventy-three for five- and six-year-olds (the kindergarten, or *nenchou,* grade). Five responses from classrooms of mixed grades or a classroom in a nursery school (whose goals were different from a preschool's) were excluded from data analyses, which resulted in the final sample of 121.

The questionnaire used in Adachi (2001) was devised to capture children's overall preschool experience, rather than a musical one per se. Questions about the overall setting included the number of children in the classroom, the number of teachers involved in the classroom activities, the school hours, the origin of the classroom policy, the availability of equipment and material in the classroom, and the accessibility of such to the children. Questions about musical activities included the type and the frequency of activities in which children were engaged throughout the year, the number of songs sung in the classroom, titles of songs children particularly liked, and titles of songs unpopular with children. In addition, free description spaces were given for the teacher's comments about particular efforts to improve her classroom management and those about challenges she had to face. Preliminary analyses showed no differences among responses across grade levels.

Overall Preschool Setting

In Japan's preschools, classroom sizes are generally large, so that individual teachers tend to work full days—often alone and with a large group of children. The median class size for each grade level was sixteen to twenty children for the youngest (*nenshou*) and twenty-one to thirty children for the older grades (*nenchuu* and *nenchou*). The majority (74 percent) of classrooms were taught by one classroom teacher, and the rest by a classroom teacher and one or more assistants. Children spent an average of 5.72 (*SD* = 1.25) hours during weekdays and 2.61 (*SD* = 1.28) hours on Saturday in their preschools. Most preschool teachers (76 percent) determined their classroom activities cooperatively with other teachers, whereas some (11 percent) were autonomous. The rest followed school policy.

In general, preschool classrooms are equipped with both music-related and non–music-related material. Figure 26.1 summarizes equipment available in at least 25 percent of preschool classrooms. It shows that a variety of music-related material was available in the majority of preschool classrooms, including music recordings and playback equipment, songbooks, a piano, and castanets. Preschool teachers appear to make considerable use of recorded music and musical instruments, such that they can lead children's singing, moving, and playing rhythms. While the access to these musical materials for young children's voluntary use was limited, access to nonmusic materials (e.g., picture books, crayons, color markers, craft paper) was high. Because almost all preschool classrooms equipped with handmade music instruments (14 percent) allowed children free access to them, preschool teachers may feel more comfortable with children's playful maneuverings using materials that can be perceived as consumable.

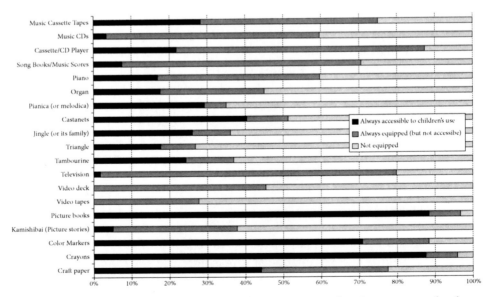

Figure 26.1: The material equipped in at least 25 percent of 121 Japanese preschool classrooms and its accessibility to children.

Preschool Classroom Activities

The most typical activities in Japanese preschool classrooms are free play, singing, and "storybook listening," that is, the teacher's reading aloud of a storybook and sharing illustrations of the book while children listen and look. Figure 26.2 summarizes how often children were engaged in each of twenty activities, ordered according to the frequency of engagement. *Free play in classroom* or *in playground/gym* was the activity of greatest classroom engagement, followed by *listening to a storybook reading, singing a familiar song,* and *learning a new song.* The four least frequently engaged in activities involved either highly creative thinking (*creating a new song/music, modifying lyrics, creating a story*) or memory-oriented practice (such as *acting a drama*). These overall tendencies were in line with earlier research by Adachi (2001).

Looking more closely at the eleven musical activities (shaded in Figure 26.2), *singing a familiar song* was the most frequent: 68 percent of classrooms sang a familiar song every day, and 97 percent sang one at least once a week. Children *learned a new song* at least once a month (99 percent), while 27 percent learned a new song at least weekly. Despite the popularity of singing as a classroom activity, *modifying lyrics* (31 percent, never, and 71 percent, every six months or less) or *creating new music* (58 percent, never, and 87 percent, every six months) were rarely seen.

Children in 88 percent of classrooms *listened to a music CD/tape* at least once a month, with 56 percent listening at least once a week, including 19 percent every

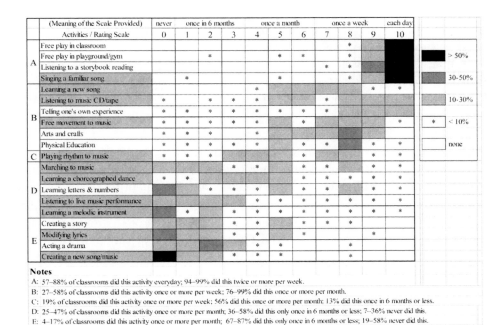

Notes

A: 57–88% of classrooms did this activity everyday; 94–99% did this twice or more per week.

B: 27–58% of classrooms did this activity once or more per week; 76–99% did this once or more per month.

C: 19% of classrooms did this activity once or more per week; 56% did this once or more per month; 13% did this once in 6 months or less.

D: 25–47% of classrooms did this activity once or more per month; 36–58% did this only once in 6 months or less; 7–36% never did this.

E: 4–17% of classrooms did this activity once or more per month; 67–87% did this only once in 6 months or less; 19–58% never did this.

Figure 26.2: The frequency distribution of twenty classroom activities reported by 121 Japanese preschool teachers.

day. Teachers in more than one in four classrooms (27 percent) had children *listen to live music performance* at least once a month (with 14 percent once or more per week), but children in 53 percent of classrooms had this opportunity at most once in six months.

While listening to music, young children readily move, clap, play a rhythmic instrument, or march to it. *Free movement to music* was incorporated at least once a month in 87 percent of classrooms (with 43 percent at least once a week). Children in 56 percent of classrooms *played rhythm (or clapped the beat) to music* at least once a month (with 19 percent at least once a week), but those in 13 percent of classrooms did this only once in 6 months or less. *Marching to music* was conducted in 48 percent of classrooms at least once a month (with 24 percent at least once a week), but for 36 percent of the classrooms this occurred only once every six months or less (while no marching occurred in 12 percent of the classrooms). Children in approximately 30 percent of the preschool classrooms *learned a choreographed dance* at least once a month (with 12 percent at least once a week), but another 30 percent did this only once in six months or less. While children in one in four classrooms (24 percent) *learned a melodic instrument* at least once a month, those in 35 percent of classrooms never experienced this.

Both *learning a choreographed dance* and *learning a melodic instrument* are typically associated with children's performances for a school event. Other activities related to such special occasions may be *acting a drama, playing rhythm to music, singing a familiar (or a newly learned) song,* and *arts and crafts.* From the frequency distribution of these activities, *learning a choreographed dance, learning a melodic instrument,* and *acting a drama* appear to be solely for performances in the annual special event. For the majority, *playing rhythm to music* is a year-round activity along with *singing a song* and *arts and crafts.*

These findings reveal that music is an important part of preschool activities in Japan. Classroom teachers' free descriptions also indicate their sincere efforts to provide children with a *musically rich* environment. For example, one teacher "tried to incorporate live performances of piano, cello, voice, flute, etc. with special occasions such that children can experience 'real' music." Another teacher "tried constructing a nice atmosphere for singing" so that she could enhance children's love of singing. On the other hand, some preschool teachers expressed how challenging it is to have all children in their classrooms engage in musical activities, because "some children were interested in music and rhythm activities while others were not" or because "[some children] do not want to sing or to move to music." Japanese preschool teachers have good intentions in having children experience "how fun music can be," but regrettably, not all children appear to enjoy singing, moving to music, or playing rhythms, that is, the music activities typically offered in their classrooms.

In examining relations between the content of preschool teachers' free descriptions and their classroom activities, interesting patterns emerged. Thirty-three preschool teachers described efforts to facilitate children's individuality or creative minds (whether or not it relates to music). For example, "I tried acknowledging each child's own expression and improving his or her confidence"; "I tried respecting individual children's own images, intuitions, and ideas, and incorporating them with classroom activities"; and "I tried encouraging children to discover and to realize things for themselves." In the classrooms led by the teachers who provided similar comments, children tended to be engaged in *modifying lyrics* and *playing the rhythm to music* at least once a month (which was much more frequent than the average teacher, especially for *modifying lyrics*). In other words, the preschool teachers who value children's individuality and uniqueness tend to feature greater creative music activity within their program, including such experiences as stimulating children's playful capacity to modify song lyrics and to engage in the playing of various rhythmic instruments. As well, teachers who reported their efforts *both* in music and in the development of their children's individuality incorporated not only Western music but also Japanese traditional music such as *kagura* (a traditional dance dedicated to the *Shintou* God), *yosakoi-sooran* (a modernized version of traditional folk dance), and island music such as *eisaa* (folk music from Okinawa, Japan). Thus, the preschool teachers' awareness of children's individuality appears to influence the kind and the frequency of music activities that they lead in their classrooms.

Songs Sung in Preschool Classrooms

The distribution of classroom activities (Figure 26.2) clearly indicates that singing was as valued as the provision of free playtime for children by Japanese preschool teachers. The importance of singing was reflected not only in the frequency of singing but also in the number of songs sung in their classrooms. The total number of songs sung throughout the target year ranged from 10 to 100. More than three different songs were sung per month in each preschool classroom, for a grand average of thirty-eight songs per year in the preschool classrooms.

To explore the style of singing in Japanese preschools, I asked teachers to list the titles of songs that children appeared to enjoy. A total of 380 different titles were listed by 121 preschool teachers. Of those, each of 225 titles was listed only by one teacher, whereas the rest were listed at least by two teachers. Only 3 out of 380 song titles were classified as *warabe-uta*: "Genkotsu-yama no Tanuki-san" (Mr. Raccoon Dog in Mt. Fist), "Saita Saita" (Bloomed, Bloomed), and "Momo-ya" (Dear Peach). (These *warabe-uta* titles were listed only once, by three different teachers.) The remaining songs listed were Western-style composed songs.

Figure 26.3 shows the top forty of children's favorite songs, with English equivalents of their titles. The list includes songs originating from the media, such as those introduced in animated films: "Tonari no Totoro" (My Neighbor Totoro) and "Sen to Chihiro no Kami-kakushi" (Spirited Away) (indicated as "Animation" under "Original Source" in Figure 26.3); in television programs for children, "Okaasan to Issyo" (With My Mom) and "Hirake! Ponkikki" (Open! Ponkikki) (indicated as "TV-Child"); and in the NHK daily five-minute television program called "Minna no Uta" (Everyone's Song) (indicated as "TV-Song"). In addition, there were Japanese adaptations of

Rank	Japanese Title (No. of Classrooms)	English Equivalence [Additional Information]	Original Source
1	Sanpo (39)	Stroll [The opening theme song of "My Neighbor Totoro"]	Animation
2	Awatenbou no Santakuroosu (27)	Careless Santa Claus	
3a	Karendaa Maachi (15)	Calender March	
3b	Yakiimo Guu Chii Paa (15)	Baked Sweet Potato, Rock, Scissors, Paper	
4a	Sekai-juu no Kodomo-tachi ga (14)	Children All Over The World	TV-Child
4b	Matsubokkuri (14)	A Pine Cone	
5a	Ookina Furu-dokei (13)	Grandfather's Clock [by H. C. Work, with Japanese lyrics]	Foreign/TV-Song
5b	Chiisana Sekai (13)	It's A Small World [A Disney song with Japanese lyrics]	Foreign
5c	Ho! Ho! Ho! (13)	Ho! Ho! Ho! [Nothing to do with Santa Claus.]	TV-Child
6a	Kinoko (12)	Mushrooms	
6b	Chuurippu (12)	Tulips	
6c	Donguri Korokoro (12)	Rolling Acorns	
7a	Tonbo no Megane (11)	Dragonfly Glasses	
7b	Niji no Mukou ni (11)	Over The Rainbow [Nothing to do with the musical]	TV-Child
7c	Basu Gokko (11)	Playing The Bus	
8a	Obake nante Nai-sa (10)	There Are No Such Things As Ghosts!	TV-Child
8b	Tokei no Uta (10)	Clock Song	
9a	Kita-kaze-kozou no Kantarou (9)	Kantaro, The Northwind Boy	TV-Song
9b	Makka na Aki (9)	Bright Red Autumn	TV-Song
10a	Ichi-nen-sei ni Nattara (8)	When I Become The First Grader	TV-Child
10b	Uchuu-sen no Uta (8)	Spaceship Song	
10c	Tomodachi ni Naru-tame ni (8)	To Become a Friend	
10d	Minna Tomodachi (8)	We're All Friends	TV-Child
10e	Yama no Ongakuka (8)	Musicians In The Mountain [A German folk song with Japanese lyrics]	
11a	Ai-ai (7)	Aye-aye [An endangered primate from Madagascar]	TV-Child
11b	Ame-furi Kuma-no-ko (7)	A Cub In The Rain	TV-Child
11c	Omoide no Arubamu (7)	A Memorable Album	TV-Song
11d	Kaeru no Uta (7)	A Frog Song [A German folk song with Japanese lyrics]	Foreign/Shoka
11e	Koinobori (7)	Carp Streamers [A symbol of a family, typically found around May 5, the Child Day]	
11f	Doki-doki-dokin! Ichi-nen-sei (7)	The First Gradesr, You'll Be Okay!	TV-Child
11g	Mori no Kuma-san (7)	Mr. Bear In The Forest [adapted from an American folk song "Sippin' Cider Through A Straw"]	Foreign/TV-Song
11h	Ganbari-man no Uta (7)	Mr. Eager Beaver's Song	
12a	Aisukuriimu no Uta (6)	An Icecream Song	TV-Song/TV-Child
12b	Itsumo Nandodemo (6)	Always With Me [The closing song of "Spirited Away"]	Animation
12c	Ohisama ni Naritai (6)	Wanting To Be The Sun	
12d	Sensei to Otomodachi (6)	Be Friend With My Teacher	
12e	Te-no-Hira o Taiyou ni (6)	The Sun Looking Through My Palm	TV-Song
12f	Te o Tatakimasyou (6)	Let's Clap Hands	
12g	Hajime no Ippo (6)	The First Step	
12h	Yuki (6)	The Snow	Shoka

Figure 26.3: The list of the forty favorite songs of Japanese preschool children based on the classroom teacher's free descriptions.

foreign songs and *Shoka* (songs to be taught in school music education, assigned by the Japanese government) included in the top forty favorites list. All songs except "Spirited Away" (the ending theme of a popular animated film released in 2001) were older songs, the majority of which had been in educational use in the period of 1960 to 1990, with a few songs dating from the early 1900s. Considering that the survey was conducted with one teacher per preschool and the responses for the favorite songs were all *free* descriptions rather than those for multiple choice questions, the probability of even two teachers reporting the same song title is quite low. The songs in Figure 26.3, listed by six or more different teachers, may be considered a good representation of the songs Japanese preschoolers sing in their classrooms.

Features of the Top Forty Favorite Songs

The top forty list of songs named by teachers reveals that Japanese children tend to sing songs with repeated syllables and words, composed in a major mode and in a duple meter. All the songs are written in a major mode (including a major-type Japanese pentatonic scale). Only three songs (11c, 11e, 12b) flow in triple meter, while the remaining songs are in duple meter. Dotted or syncopated rhythms are dominant in sixteen of the forty songs, whereas isochronous rhythms are dominant in the rest of the twenty-four songs, indicating no particular preference for either rhythmic feature. The majority of songs feature lyrics describing animate or inanimate characters (or figures) that can elicit images of scenes, events, emotions, and atmospheres. Onomatopoeia or mimesis, characterized by repeated syllables in the Japanese language (Jorden 1982) such as *rin-rin-rin* (a bell ringing), *gero-gero* (the sound of a frog), and *doki-doki* (the heart pounding) were observed at least once in the lyrics of twenty-four songs. There were seven lyrics without onomatopoeia or mimesis that had repeated words, such as *saita, saita* (bloomed, bloomed), *naranda, naranda* (lined up, lined up) in "Chuurippu," *makka-da-na, makka-da-na* (bright red, bright red) in "Makka-na Aki," and *zutto zutto* (forever and ever) in "Te-no-Hira o Taiyou ni." In total, thirty-one of the top forty songs have lyrics with some form of repeated syllables or words.

One teacher commented that "[Children] like nicely fast songs with fun actions." In the top forty list, only a handful of songs are associated with commonly known actions: "Yakiimo Guu Chii Paa," which includes hand gestures for rock (*guu*), scissors (*chii*), and paper (*paa*) while singing; "Matsubokkuri"—making a pinecone's rolling actions with both arms; "Basu Gokko"—bouncing to the beat and acting out the content of the lyrics as a bus passenger; "Yama no Ongakuka"—pretending to play the corresponding instruments portrayed in the lyrics as animal musicians; "Sensei to Otomodachi"—shaking hands with friends; and "Te o Tatakimasyou"—clapping, stamping, pretending to laugh, pretending to glare. However, as some of the action-free songs have onomatopoeia or repeated words to which children can clap or play rhythm instruments, it is quite possible that such rhythmic engagement might also be considered "fun actions." One such example may be seen in a popular stage performance of "Awatenbou no Santakuroosu," portraying funny episodes of Santa Claus.

Some of the song lyrics carry symbolic messages that cannot be fully understood by preschool children. Instead, they may be accompanied by playful repeated sounds that attract the attention of preschoolers. In *Ho! Ho! Ho!*, for example, a yodeling-like sound dominates the song, and the message in the lyrics probably does not matter to preschoolers:

> When we want to make the yesterday's tears disappear,
>> Let's call the tomorrow's sky [i.e., Let's look to the future].
>>> *Ho! Ho! Ho! Ho! Yodelehi, yodelehi, yodelehi, yodelehi! Ho! Ho! Ho! Ho! Yodelehi,*
> *yodelehi, yodelehi, yodelehi!*...(original lyrics by Akira Ito)

In "Tomodachi ni Naru-tame ni," the word phrase *kimi to* (with you) is repeated seven times in the middle of a verse and again three more times before closing it with *kimi to tomodachi* (be friends with you), as illustrated below.

> *Ima made deatta takusan no* [Those whom I have met so far]
> *Kimi to kimi to, kimi to kimi to, kimi to kimi to kimi to,* [With you, you,...
> and you,]
> *Korekara deau takusan no* [And those whom I will meet in the future]
> *Kimi to kimi to, kimi to,* [With you, you, and you,]
> *Kimi to tomodachi.* [I will be friends with you.] (lyrics by Toshihiko Shinzawa)

The song with the most difficult lyrics is "Itsumo Nandodemo" the ending song of the Oscar-winning animated film *Spirited Away*. The first verse of the English subtitle starts as follows (Miyazaki and Wise 2002):

> Somewhere, a voice calls, in the depth of my heart
> May I always be dreaming, the dreams that move my heart
> So many tears of sadness, uncountable through and through
> I know on the other side of them I'll find you....(original lyrics by Wakako Kaku)

This English subtitle portrays the poetic and abstract nature of the Japanese original lyrics. There are no repeated words, and the melancholy melody is not easy for preschoolers to sing either. Yet the song landed in the top forty list, quite possibly due to the fact that preschool teachers themselves preferred it. One teacher rather myopically remarked, "Children enjoy songs that the teacher likes," reinforcing this view. From another teacher's point of view, the inclusion of this popular song repertoire was simply "good teaching" that sought to avoid children's boredom. A third teacher reported the use of sign language while singing the song, thus offering children the additional enhancement of gestures. While the young children did not understand the meaning of the lyrics, singing it may have reminded them of the pleasure of viewing the film in which the song was featured.

Features of the Unpopular Songs

Along with favorite songs, the questionnaire asked for songs *unpopular* with children—only twenty-six teachers listed such songs. The list of unpopular songs consisted of 40 titles, much shorter than the 380 favorites. Of these, twenty-one titles

Figure 26.4: The last phrase of "Tomato" (Tomatoes), lyrics by Takeshi Shoji, melody by Megumi Oonaka, JASRAC No. 055–0318–3.

were also favorite songs, with more positive than negative responses, except the following three songs: "Oshougatsu" (New Year) (four teachers found it to be *unpopular*, while two listed it among the *favorites*), "Tsuki" (The Moon), and "Tomato" (both with three *unpopular* and one *favorite* votes). These three songs are composed using Japanese pentatonic scales: the first two with *Yonanuki* (do-re-mi-so-la) and the last one with *Min'you* (re-fa-so-la-do). This does not mean that Japanese preschool children do not like songs using Japanese pentatonic scales, as some of the favorite songs in the top forty list also use the *Yonanuki* scale (Figure 26.3: 4b, 6b, 7a, 9a, 11e). The melody of "Tomato," however, does sound quite different from those of other songs. In addition to having the sound of *Min'you* scale, the ending of the melody does not provide a proper closure to the ears to one accustomed to a Western scale (Figure 26.4). This peculiarity may have affected children's reaction to this particular song.

ANALYSIS OF RESEARCH FINDINGS

The findings of this research indicate that Japanese preschools offer a musically rich program of education in many ways. Preschool classrooms are equipped either with a piano or with an electric organ, played by classroom teachers who lead their children's musical activities (although they are typically not musically trained specialist teachers). By contrast, only one-third of preschools or similar institutions in the United States have a keyboard available for use by teachers and only three-quarter of classroom teachers lead their children's musical activities (Nardo et al. 2006). This evidence alone highlights how musical activity is valued and practiced in early childhood education in Japan. In fact, one might observe that preschools may serve as a cultural foundation for generating children's musicality and for launching the development of young talented musicians with superb techniques but who possess little individuality in their music-making activities.

The most prominent musical activity in Japanese preschool classrooms is singing, similar to the American preschool setting (Nardo et al. 2006), but classroom singing in Japanese preschools is usually led by the teacher's piano accompaniment while singing in American preschools tends to be unaccompanied. The overwhelming majority of songs sung in Japanese preschool classrooms appear to be Western style rather than *warabe-uta*, although some preschools are intent on emphasizing *warabe-uta* more than Western-style songs (e.g., Akiyama 2000). One of respondents in the study was also positive about using *warabe-uta*: "I tried incorporating as many *warabe-uta* as possible to develop children's social skills among peers.... I want to use *warabe-uta* through which children can have positive experiences in playing with their peers." If the current study's survey had been conducted with only such preschools (or teachers), a quite different list of children's favorite songs would have resulted.

From the frequency distribution of various activities, the present research reconfirmed a paradoxical aspect of the Japanese preschool environment. Young children are encouraged to explore their own ideas and to try alternative actions through free play, providing them with opportunities to construct something new, to reconstruct something memorable from their own past experiences, and to share these constructions with their friends. Such high respect for free play reflects one of the overarching goals of early childhood education set up by the Japanese government: to facilitate children's healthy development in body and mind through spontaneous, active, independent engagement in play (Japanese Ministry of Education, Culture, Sports, Science, and Technology 2008).

Since the appearance of the 1989 guidelines for early childhood education, the subject area noted as "expression," to which music belongs, has been implemented to facilitate creativity through children's own expressions of their thoughts and feelings. In this study, *telling of one's own experience* and *arts and crafts* were relatively frequent activities. In the first of these, children must reconstruct their experiences in their *own* words, which is qualitatively different from reproducing lyrics in song. The category *arts and crafts* also involves creative processes in which children choose their own materials and colors as well as their own brush strokes. In music, on the other hand, the majority of preschool children appear to be simply encouraged to listen to music, to reproduce songs from their memory, or to learn new songs to add to their repertoire. The only musical activity involving a form of creative expression in which children are engaged relatively frequently is *free movement to music*, which may be considered a creative activity with greater attention to movement than to music. It appears that music is the only expressive domain that tends to lack structured instructions for creativity in Japanese preschool education.

A clue to the musically-rich-but-creatively-poor paradox in Japanese preschools may be found in the image of music for preschool children held by college students who majored in early childhood education: more than 70 percent believe that "singing" is necessary, because it offers an opportunity for children to have fun by expressing themselves and communicating with peers (Konishi and Miyake 1996). Considering that the majority of these students become preschool teachers, it is possible that in-service teachers also conceive of group singing as a medium of *self*-expression, which could explain why singing familiar songs is incorporated as frequently as free play.

The very idea of group singing as a medium of *self*-expression may derive from a long history of Japanese culture that values individuals as a group rather than individuals themselves. Moreover, the primary music training for early childhood education has been focused on piano and voice training so that classroom teachers can sing songs while playing a piano accompaniment (Yamamoto et al. 2007). This kind of training can develop a stereotype in prospective teachers that children's singing must be accompanied by the piano, evident in the comment of a student teacher, "I was surprised when I saw children singing joyfully even without the piano/organ accompaniment" (Miyake 1999: 127). The overwhelming piano and voice training may prevent prospective (and later in-service) preschool teachers from realizing a higher degree of freedom in sung expression without an accompaniment. Thus, the paradox of children's musical experiences in Japanese preschool classrooms appears to reflect their teachers' own musical training: musically rich but creatively poor.

The necessity of including creative music training has been acknowledged and practiced in an early childhood education program (e.g., Miyake 1999; Toyoda and Miyake 1998). In some cases, music specialists visit a preschool to stimulate and provide support for children's creative music making during free play (e.g., Tsubonou et al. 2005) or as a classroom activity (e.g., Bae 2008), which, in turn, helps preschool teachers learn how to play a musician's role in children's creative activities (Furuyama et al. 2010). Some preschool teachers have been aware that they can create an environment in which children can experience more than group singing and playing Western-style instruments, for example, by using bamboo growing on the school campus as sound-making toys/instruments and placing various ethnic instruments in a corridor for children to play (e.g., Iguchi 2004). However, the majority of preschool teachers tend to stay within perceived expectations (e.g., Miyake 2003). One teacher in the present study confessed, "I wonder what I should say to those who do not want to sing or to move to music. Every year I wonder how I could convince these children how much fun music can be." Perhaps exposing children to creative music making will bring a long-awaited "Aha!" moment to this teacher.

Preschool teachers' attitudes and what they do in their classrooms can affect what children do outside the classrooms. For example, preschool children bring home musical activities they engaged in at school and either share them with their family members or review them by themselves (Adachi 2012). The proportion of children who repeat preschool activities during spontaneous musical play at home appears to double in the second half of the school year, particularly using songs with a character and/or an action (Adachi 2012). Indeed, "Kinoko" (6a in Figure 26.3, see also Figure 26.5), one of the top ten songs, was sung by a five-year-old girl in the schoolyard during free play, repeating softly an onomatopoeic portion of the lyrics portraying growing mushrooms *noko noko noko noko* while making all kinds of actions, such as stretching up, shrinking down, and kicking sand; soon after, other children playing nearby joined her as well (Miyake 2003: 36).

When preschool children share what they learned with their family or friends, they often reconstruct the entire episode of the learning process by pretending to be their teacher (Adachi 1994, 2012). This means that if the teacher simply sings a song, children will sing that song as it was presented, whereas if the teacher incorporates singing with some kind of a creative activity, children will also internalize the song in that way. In other words, what preschool teachers do in their classrooms and how they do it can affect what and how children review what they have

ki ki ki no ko   ki ki ki no ko   no ko no ko no ko no ko   a rui ta ri shi na i

Figure 26.5: The first phrase of "Kinoko" (Mushrooms), lyrics by Michio Mado, melody by Shoji Kurakake, JASRAC No. 024–7164–7.

learned during play, determining *what will be reinforced* outside classrooms, which can shape Japanese preschool children's musical culture.

CONCLUSION: THE KEY TO NURTURING JAPANESE PRESCHOOLERS' CREATIVE MUSIC CULTURE

In the 2008 revision of the governmental policy for preschool education, the word "creativity" was included officially in a goal for the subject "expression": "To facilitate creativity by nurturing sensitivity and expressiveness through having children express their own feelings and thoughts with their own terms" (Fukunishi, Yamamoto, and Miyake 2009: 84), "music making" was officially implemented along with singing and playing instruments. On one hand, officially using the words "music making" and "creativity" in the policy may guide preschool teachers toward offering more balanced music curriculum between reproduction and creation. On the other hand, Japanese music education tends to practice "slow change," which has prevented the majority of elementary schoolteachers from implementing creative music making in classrooms for more than ten years, even after *that* concept was introduced in the governmental policy and an abundance of workshops and handbooks for creative music activities became available for teachers (e.g., Adachi and Chino 2004). It is possible that preschool education will follow the same path taken by elementary schools.

Just as "children enjoy songs that the teacher likes," they would be more likely to enjoy any musical activity that the teacher likes. If teachers can show their enjoyment in creative music-making activities, children will internalize this enjoyment. For example, children learned how to create a simple melody by manipulating patterns in their weekly music class in their preschool, then created their own songs at home (Figure 26.6; see also Adachi and Chino 2004: 324). These children, a minority, live in a different musical culture from that portrayed in the present chapter.

According to Honjoya (1982), the majority of Japanese traditional child songs, *warabe-uta*, are not children's original creations but are songs created by adults for them. By definition, however, *warabe-uta* is child song, owned by and shared among Japanese children. Perhaps, Japanese children's *warabe-uta* culture may be seeded by adults and nurtured by children themselves. Similarly, Japanese preschool children's musical culture may be seeded by their teachers but could be nurtured during

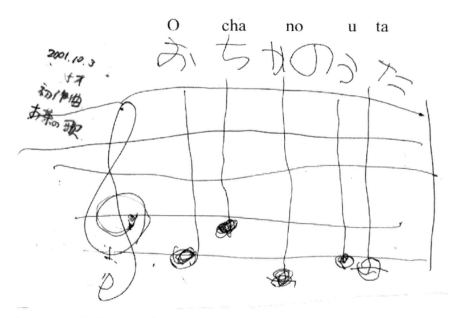

Figure 26.6: "Ocha no Uta" (Tea Song), created by a five-year-old girl during her play at home. Her mother's memo on the upper left side reads "3 October 2001, [the girl's name] age 5, the first composition, *Ocha no Uta*." The ascending two-note stepwise motif is repeated in sequence, the kind of pattern manipulations she was experiencing in her weekly music program at her preschool.

free play at school and/or at home by friends, teachers, and parents, who serve as practice partners (e.g., Adachi 1994, 2012; Whiteman 2001).

The teacher is the key to the extent and quality of music in preschool education in Japan. While parental influence, peer esteem, sibling competition, and other internal motivations can be factored into children's use of music, without a well-trained teacher who inspires and seeds musical creativity, the richness and joy of music can be forever lost. The playful nature of music (e.g., Adachi and Chino 2004) and children's inherent creativity (e.g., Adachi 1994, 2012; Adachi and Trehub 2011; Campbell [1998] 2010; Omi 1994; Tafuri 2009; Whiteman 2001) can easily be suppressed by a well-intentioned but misguided teacher. Japanese preschools' rich musical environment has great potential to offer a rich creative environment if the preschool teachers can develop their musical activities to include a broad palette of possibilities for children's musical inventions.

Acknowledgments

This research was supported by JSPS Grant-in-Aid, Exploratory Research (1999–2001) and Scientific Research (2002–2004). Thanks to Yoko Ogawa and Hajime Takasu for their assistance in the survey.

REFERENCES

Adachi, M. 1994. "The Role of the Adult in the Child's Early Musical Socialization: A Vygotskian Perspective." *The Quarterly: Journal of Music Teaching and Learning* 5 (3): 26–35.

Adachi, M. 2001. "Why Can't Japanese First Grade Children Make Up Songs?" In *Proceedings of the Third Asia-Pacific Symposium on Music Education Research*, edited by Y. Minami and M. Shinzanoh, 49–50. Vol. 2. Nagoya, Japan: Aichi University of Education.

Adachi, M. 2011. "'Happy' to 'Sad'—Kodomo wa dou uta ni takusu no ka?" In *Warai-ryoku—Jinbungaku de wahhahha*, edited by K. Chiba, 91–122. Sapporo, Japan: Hokkaido University Press.

Adachi, M. 2012. "Incorporating Lesson Materials into Spontaneous Musical Play: A Window for How Young Children Learn Music." In *Musical Childhoods of Asia and the Pacific*, edited by C. H. Lum and P. Whiteman, 133–160. Charlotte, NC: Information Age Publishing.

Adachi, M., and Y. Chino. 2004. "Inspiring Creativity through Music." In *Creativity: When East Meets West*, edited by S. Lau, A. N. N. Hui, and G. Y. C. Ng, 305–340. Singapore: World Scientific.

Adachi, M., and S. E. Trehub. 2011. "Canadian and Japanese Preschoolers' Creation of Happy and Sad Songs." *Psychomusicology* 21: 69–82.

Akiyama, H. 2000. "Kodomo no kanjou no hattatsu o unagasu *warabe-uta*." In *Proceedings of the 2000 Meeting of Japan Society of Research on Early Childhood Care and Education*, 716–717. Tokyo: Japan Society of Research on Early Childhood Care and Education.

Bae, M. 2008. "Kodomo-shuudan ga kyoudou-shitsutsu souzou suru ongaku-hyougen—Tomo ni tsukuru hanpuku to sokkyou no ongaku." *Japanese Journal of Music Education Practice* 6 (1): 40–49.

Campbell, P. S. [1998] 2010. *Songs in Their Heads: Music and Its Meaning in Children's Lives.* New York: Oxford University Press.

Fujita, F. 2002. "Rizumikaru na kotoba no sousaku o tanoshimu: Hoikuen 3-saiji kurasu no kodomotachi no ongakukoudou no kansatsu-kiroku kara." *Proceedings of the 2002 Meeting of Japan Society of Research on Early Childhood Care and Education*, 76–77. Tokyo: Japan Society of Research on Early Childhood Care and Education.

Fujita, F., and M. Nakakura. 1996. "Kodomo ga utaihajimeru toki: Hoikuen 1-saiji-kurasu no ongaku-koudou no kansatsu kara." *Proceedings of the 1996 Meeting of Japan Society of Research on Early Childhood Care and Education*, 74–75. Tokyo: Japan Society of Research on Early Childhood Care and Education.

Fukunishi, T., A. Yamamoto, and K. Miyake. 2009. "Hoiku-genba to rendou shita youseikou no ongakukyouiku-naiyou/houhou no arikata (2)—Kodomo no souzouteki na ongakukatsudou o sasaeru kiso-ginou-shuutoku o mezashite." *Takada-Tanki-Daigaku Kiyou* 27: 83–96.

Furuyama, R., K. Koma, M. Ajifu, and Y. Tsubonou. 2010. "Youji no souzouteki na ongakukatsudou no kaihatsu ni kansuru kenkyuu V—'mivurix' ni yoru jirei no bunseki o tooshite." *Nihon-Joshi-Daigaku-Daigakuin Kiyou (Kaseigaku Kenkyuuka/ Ningen Seikatsu Kenkyuuka)* 16: 99–107.

Honjoya, M. 1982. *Warabe-uta kenkyuu nooto.* Akita, Japan: Mumyosha Shuppan.

Iguchi, Y. 2004. "Watashi no jissen o furikaette—Kodomo to oto no kakawari o tsukuru." *Japanese Journal of Music Education Practice* 1 (2): 8–11.

Japanese Ministry of Education, Culture, Sports, Science, and Technology. 2008. *Youchien Kyouiku-youryou Kaisetsu.* Tokyo: Froebel-kan.

Jorden, E. H. 1982. "Giongo, gitaigo to eigo." In *Nichieigo hikaku kouza.* Vol. 4: *Hassou to hyougen,* edited by T. Kunihiro, 111–140. Tokyo: Taishukan.

Konishi, Y., and K. Miyake. 1996. "Hoikusha-youseikou no 'hyougen kyouiku' to gakusei no 'hoiku-ongaku ishiki' ni tsuite—Gakusei no ongaku-ishiki ankeeto chousa o tooshite." *Proceedings of the 1996 Meeting of Japan Society of Research on Early Childhood Care and Education,* 216–217. Tokyo: Japan Society of Research on Early Childhood Care and Education.

Miyake, K. 1999. "Hoikusha-youseikou ni okeru ongakuhyougen-kyouiku no arikata ni kansuru kenkyuu—ongakuhyougen-jugyou to hoikujissen tono kanren o saguru." *Takada-Tanki-Daigaku Kiyou* 17: 123–144.

Miyake, K. 2003. "Kodomo no ongaku-katsudou o sasaeru hoikusha to hoikusha-youseikou no ongakukyouiku no ichikousatsu—Hoiku ni okeru ongaku-katsudou to gakusei no senmonteki-rikiryou no ikusei o mezashite." *Takada-Tanki-Daigaku Kiyou* 21: 33–55.

Miyake, K., T. Fukunishi, and A. Yamamoto. 2004. "Hoikusha no ongakuteki-senmon-rikiryou-keisei ni tsuite (1)." *Proceedings of the 2004 Meeting of Japan Society of Research on Early Childhood Care and Education,* 564–565. Tokyo: Japan Society of Research on Early Childhood Care and Education.

Miyazaki, H., original director, and K. Wise, director for English adaptation. 2002. *Spirited Away.* Burbank, CA: Walt Disney Pictures. Film.

Nardo, R. L., L. A. Custodero, D. C. Persellin, and D. B. Fox. 2006. "Looking Back, Looking Forward: A Report on Early Childhood Music Education in Accredited American Preschools." *Journal of Research in Music Education* 54 (4): 278–292.

Ogawa, Y., and K. Imagawa. 2008. *Ongaku-suru kodomo o tsukamaetai: Jikken-kenkyusha to fiirudowaakaa no taiwa.* Okayama, Japan: Fukurou Shuppan.

Omi, A. 1994. "Children's Spontaneous Singing: Four Song Types and Their Musical Devices." *Journal of Kawamura Gakuen Woman's University* 5 (2): 61–76.

Opie, I., and P. Opie. 1973. *The Lore and Language of School-Children.* Oxford, UK: Oxford University Press.

Tafuri, J. 2009. *Infant Musicality: New Research for Educators and Parents.* Farnham, UK: SEMPRE/Ashgate.

Toyoda, K., and K. Miyake. 1998. "Hoikusha-youseikou no kyouiku-naiyou/houhou no arikata ni kansuru kenkyuu—sono kadai to jugyou-houhou no kokoromi." *Takada-Tanki-Daigaku Kiyou* 16: 41–65.

Tsubonou, Y., M. Kimura, M. Ajifu, H. Ogawa, and M. Bae. 2005. "Youji no souzouteki na ongakukatsudou no kaihatsu ni kansuru kenkyuu—Youji no ongakukatsudou no henyou no bunseki/kaishaku o tooshite." *Nihon-Joshi-Daigaku-Daigakuin Kiyou (Kaseigaku Kenkyuuka/Ningen Seikatsu Kenkyuuka)* 11: 225–233.

Whiteman, P. J. 2001. "How the Bananas Got Their Pyjamas: A Study of the Metamorphosis of Preschoolers' Spontaneous Singing as Viewed through Vygotsky's Zone of Proximal Development." PhD diss., University of New South Wales, Australia.

Yamamoto, A., T. Fukunishi, and K. Miyake. 2007. "Hoiku-genba to rendou shita yousei-kou no ongakukyouiku-naiyou/houhou no arikata (1): Kisoginou-kamoku 'Youji Ongaku' no jugyou-kaizen to sono hyouka-kentou." *Takada-Tanki-Daigaku Kiyou* 25: 79–98.

27

THE COMPLEX ECOLOGIES OF EARLY CHILDHOOD MUSICAL CULTURES

PETER WHITEMAN

Borders and Boundaries

border, *n.* A side, edge, brink, or margin; a limit, or boundary; the part of anything lying along its boundary or outline

—(Oxford English Dictionary. 1989. 2nd ed. 2:411)

Borders are essentials of human existence. From the earliest points in our lives, we engage with an abundance of people, groups, and institutions, each of which is bound by borders. It is the negotiation and renegotiation of these, the establishment of new borders and the cultures that are constructed as a result that make childhood such a rich and complex phenomenon. The cultures of childhood and children's development can be viewed from two broad perspectives: that of childhood as apprenticeship to the world of adults or that of childhood as a valued and valuable construct in itself (see, e.g., Corsaro 2005; Lambert and Clyde 2000; Pellegrini and Blatchford 2000). The former, teleological outlook is manifested in the tradition of the developmentalists. Steeped in the established axioms of the likes of Piaget (e.g., Piaget 1973) and Vygotsky (e.g., Vygotsky 1986), the culture of childhood is all about preparing for adulthood. Often regarded as a smooth unilateral trajectory (Lambert and Clyde 2000), childhood is geared toward achieving what is perceived to be important by the more senior members of a culture. Importantly, children's behaviors and actions are viewed in terms of adults' behaviors. The role and place of early behaviors and actions are to prepare for later behaviors and actions, and success is judged by the distance from the endpoint, whether Piaget's notion of formal operational thought (Piaget and Inhelder 1958) or beyond, as proposed by more recent research (e.g., Labouvie-Vief 1982). Border crossing in this teleological world is clear and businesslike: children move through a series of predetermined stages in a linear fashion on their way to adulthood. In reality, this smooth path is far from absolute.

In the postdevelopmental world of the twenty-first century, the unilateral course has been replaced by acknowledgement of the true complexities of childhood. Humans are perceived as being actively engaged in socially located, collective action and childhood is a period in someone's life that is intrinsically valued and valuable. Lockstep Piagetian-type models have evolved into studies of humans that eschew a single psychological or biological approach (e.g., Rogoff 2003), and border crossing can be reframed as moving backward, forward, through, and around existing borders in addition to the reinvention and coconstruction of new borders. Childhood is no longer a time of preparation for the real thing (adulthood), but rather it *is* the real thing, a bona fide construct in and of itself. This generative view of children and childhoods draws together aspects of education, psychology, biology, sociology, and anthropology. Children are seen as active agents who operate within and coconstruct a range of social contexts; agents who *do* things, rather than have things *done* to them. Two useful lodestars with which to situate current thinking are bioecological systems (Bronfenbrenner 2004) and interpretive reproduction (Corsaro 2005).

Bronfenbrenner's sociocultural view positions children within five environmental systems that influence, and are influenced by, children. The systems range from the most inner (microsystem), where direct action with social agents such as family members, teachers, and playmates occurs, to the broadest (macrosystem), which consists of cultural elements such as beliefs and inclinations of the members of the child's culture. According to Bronfenbrenner,

> To a greater extent than for any other species, human beings create the environments that shape the course of human development. Their actions influence the multiple physical and cultural tiers of the ecology that shapes them, and this agency makes humans—for better or for worse—active producers of their own development. (2004: xxvii)

As children move back and forth through Bronfenbrenner's systems, they cross borders. They actively engage with others and shape their cultures that in turn shape them. This dynamic symbiosis allows us to give weight in its own right to the effort that children devote to shaping their cultures as a result of their childhood endeavors.

Similar is Corsaro's (2005) notion of interpretive reproduction. Corsaro sees children's peer culture "as a stable set of activities or routines, artifacts, values, and concerns that children produce and share in interaction with peers" (2000: 92). He maintains that as children set about constructing these cultures, two primary themes underpin their actions and intent: "*to gain control* of their lives and *to share* that control with each other" (ibid., emphasis in original). As they gain control and share it, children necessarily engage in the creative appropriation of elements from existing cultures in order to incorporate these revisions in the new children's cultures that they build as part of everyday life. Rather than the aforementioned teleological stages, Corsaro conceptualizes children's endeavors as peer cultures that children produce and in which they participate, which are, in turn,

> embedded in the web of experiences children weave with others throughout their lives. Therefore, children's experiences in peer cultures are not left behind with maturity or individual development; rather, they remain part of their live histories as active members of a given culture. (Corsaro 2005: 26)

This "orb web" of experiences is likened to that of spiders, with varying institutional fields (radii) such as family, politics, and community traversing a number of diverse peer groups over time (spirals). This model allows children to be positioned as participants in both adults' and children's cultures, shaped by their memberships in both. As children weave their web from birth onward, they pass through, back, and around a multitude of borders. In shaping their evolving cultures, each of these borders provides opportunity for creative interpretation. An idea here, a role there, a song, perhaps reproduced in entirety, or often reproduced with small yet significant changes and then embedded in the culture as time moves on. It is these interpretive reproductions, children's business on the edge of these borders that form the core of the following stories. Teleology has been abandoned in favor of generativity, and enculturation has been discarded for interpretive reproduction. Children's musics are seen in their own light, rather than cast in the shadow of the adults that went before them.

Exploring Children's Musical Cultures

Early childhood (from birth to eight years) is a time of unmatched growth and development. At no other stage in children's lives will they experience such a rate of change. During this time, children are perennial border crossers. They move in, out, and through a range of musical traditions and customs as they weave new musical cultures with members of their families, schools, and communities. Rather than the reproduction of established musical mores, these rich, sophisticated, and multifaceted musical cultures come about through children's agency in musicking anew and adapting and recasting existing musics and practices. Through the lens of interpretive reproduction, this chapter documents emerging musical cultures of young indigenous and nonindigenous children, their families, and their communities in New South Wales, Australia, and Hawaii, USA.

Unpacking the children's musical cultures through a contemporary lens requires detailed knowledge of how children make music, with whom, and where. To ensure authority and preserve the inherent complexities, it seemed most fitting to seek information from children themselves and their families. The following stories evolved from semistructured interviews with fifty children and their parents (forty in total).

Tailoring the approaches to engage in discussions with participants was critical. I was crossing a range of borders myself as I was welcomed into indigenous and nonindigenous cultures in two different countries. I was a city dweller in remote and rural Australian communities and an Australian in the United States. As a "white fella" (Martinello 2002) in New South Wales and a "*haole*" (Talmy 2010) in Hawaii, I was mindful of the need to engage in research in culturally sensitive ways. The need for culturally sensitive approaches to research with indigenous communities is well documented (see, e.g., Burchill 2004; Hanlen 2002; Tuhawai Smith 1998). Constantly aware of the need to minimize direct questioning procedures, I continually reminded myself of the importance of ensuring that I took time to sit, listen, learn, and share. In Australia, we "yarned up" (Burchill 2004); in Hawaii, we "talked story" or spent time "shooting the breeze" (Bickerton 1991). Conceptually similar, these terms can be used as nouns or verbs and have, at their core, the sharing of knowledge and experiences. In all settings, taking the time to sit in order to know the participants and their communities was of paramount importance. Such undertaking ultimately results in empowered participants and the gathering of thick description advocated by Geertz (1973), who maintains that research is undertaken *in* rather than *on* communities.

As a result of yarning, talking story, and generally shooting the breeze with children and families, I offer the following four bricolages. They do not report on four identifiable children or families but rather form representative images of children's musical practices in four geographically disparate locales and serve as examples of the musical borders that are regularly traversed in early childhood.

Vicki

Vicki is a three-year-old indigenous girl who lives with her mother, Kelly, and four sisters (one younger and three older) in a town of about 1,000 people in the North West of New South Wales, Australia. It takes a little more than ten hours to drive from Sydney, the state capital, to Vicki's country. This part of the world has been in drought for a long time, and driving into the town, the dry, cracked landscape is occasionally punctuated by farmers walking emaciated livestock, attempting to eke out some small morsels of food on the side of the road. When Vicki, her mother, and her sisters walk to the older girls' school, they pass the local café, shop, and hotel, greeting most people in the town's main street by name; many of the towns-people are not permanently employed. The weekday morning ritual is complete when Vicki enters the local preschool and Kelly returns home with her youngest daughter, only to be repeated in reverse when the afternoon school bell sounds.

While at home during the day, Kelly listens to music on the radio and plays CDs. She happily sings along and sometimes makes up dances with her daughter. The music that blasts through the house during the day is a mixture of Top 40 hits on commercial radio, music from children's television shows, and the occasional song from church sung by Kelly without recordings. She reports liking "Britney [Spears] and Shaggy [an American reggae artist]" and thinks that music "is an important part of growth" for her children because it "lets them express themselves." She says that her daughters have always been keen singers and dancers, often learning children's songs through repeated exposure to them on television. "Music," according to Kelly, "is part of our [her] culture; part of expressing ourselves with our singing, our hymns, and our music."

Nowhere is this expression more visible in this family's household than when the children return home from school. Vicki cheerfully regales those within hearing range with information about stories and songs from preschool. She offers snippets of contemporary children's songs by nonindigenous Australian composer and teacher of indigenous children, Wendy Notley, that "honor Aboriginal children and celebrate Aboriginal culture" (Aunty Wendy's Mob 2009) and sings small segments of some songs for older people with her older siblings and mother. These songs come from works recorded by the Stiff Gins, an Aboriginal band of two women who "are through harmony and song, reclaiming a derogatory term for Aboriginal women, instead declaring its meaning as proud, passionate and talented" (Simpson and Briggs 2010). The singing of these folk- and pop-influenced songs continues for approximately fifteen minutes.

Vicki recollects that attendance at weekly church services is an established routine for Kelly and the girls. An inquiry about details of her favorite song gives rise to an energetic, assured performance (see Figure 27.1).

In response, Kelly praises her daughter and remarks that her own childhood was awash with "music of today," bereft of much of the traditional music and language of her heritage. She goes on to explain that she is heartened by the fact that some attempt to resurrect these lost languages and stories is being made with young people in schools and prior-to-school settings, such as Vicki's preschool. She maintains that while the contemporary works by singers such as Archie Roach and the Stiff Gins talk about her people's history, she welcomes the resurgence of some traditional culture for her children.

Figure 27.1 "If I Were a Butterfly" (opening).

Cooper

Entering the gates of five-year-old Cooper's school during autumn is an arresting sensory experience. Trees are beginning to lose their leaves, and birdcalls from the likes of galahs and sulphur-crested cockatoos saturate the airwaves. Cooper began his first year of formal primary school four months ago, in his hometown in regional New South Wales. Situated just more than 200 km (125 miles) northwest of Sydney, the state capital, almost 30,000 people reside in this regional service center that was originally settled in the early 1800s. Cooper attends an independent (nongovernment) coeducational school that enrolls students from kindergarten through high school. This morning, Cooper's mum is attending the primary school assembly, proud to know that her son is singing in the front row of a performing group.

After a greeting from the school principal, all in the auditorium join together in singing the school song. Then, as everyone takes their seat, the primary school choir files onto the stage, launching forth with a powerful rendition of "Shine, Jesus, Shine," a modern worship song (Figure 27.2).

As they reach the chorus, the kindergarten children move to the front: "Shine, Jesus, shine, fill this land with the father's glory; blaze, Spirit, blaze, set our hearts on fire" (Kendrick 1987). Cooper's resonant delivery and glowing smile elicits a similarly agreeable response from his mother. After assembly, with parents returned to work or home, the children's school day continues with normal routine. During lunch, Cooper can be heard discussing the morning's assembly performance with some friends. He talks about how he liked singing the song because of the words, and through the conversation with Katherine and James (also both five), the children start to improvise a riff around the words "Shine, Jesus, shine." Their text is interspersed with beatbox vocalizations that they've heard emanating from the older children's playground and soon mutates into an impromptu performance with some text recognizable from the choir's song, peppered with new words and tunes, accompanied with elementary beatboxing, all bound with dance moves that would not be out of place on a music video.

When Cooper arrives home from the bus, he greets his one-year-old twin sisters with a certain amount of indifference, throws his schoolbag down, and ardently devours the afternoon snack that his mother has waiting for him. A rapid-fire report of the day follows with all manner of detail about in and out of class activities relayed to his mother, who offers praise for the morning choral performance. Sometime into this colloquy, it becomes evident that the twins' diapers need changing and Cooper remains to finish his snack while his mother takes the girls to the bathroom. Soon after, Cooper joins his siblings to the sound of his mother chanting "Miss Mary Mack" to the girls while she changes them: "Miss Mary Mack, Mack,

Lord the light of your love is shin - ing, In the midst of the dark - ness shin - ing

Figure 27.2 "Shine Jesus Shine" (opening).

Mack, all dressed in black, black, black, with silver buttons, buttons, buttons, all down her back, back, back." He begins to sing along under his breath, foot tapping in time, and gradually gets louder until he is singing full voice. The twins, one on the change table, one on the floor, are giggling as their mother and brother sing to them. Cooper continues to sing once his mother stops to concentrate on completing the diaper change, and Rose, the twin on the floor, becomes the object of his refrain: "Miss Mary Rose, Rose, with a great big nose, nose, nose!" Shortly, Cooper loses interest in being with the girls and takes a soccer ball outside.

Sometime later, Cooper runs to meet his father, who is parking his car in the family driveway after work. The car windows are down and clearly audible is the Beatles' "Let It Be." Cooper sidles up to the car beginning to join in with the CD: "Let it be, let it be, let it be, let it be!" he belts, just as he did with the "Shine, Jesus, shine" text earlier in the day. In between welcome hugs, Cooper and his father share the remainder of the song (in various levels of completeness) as they enter the house in readiness for the nightly ritual of family dinner, where Cooper's day will be recounted again for his family.

Iolani

It's 7:00 am on a Friday morning in suburban Honolulu, the state capital of Hawaii, located on Oahu, Hawaii's most populated island. It is only a few weeks until Christmas, and the balmy autumn morning is shattered as the clock radio erupts into life. "You're waking up to Hawaii's bomb music station" the station promo announces, "We are the only station that matters. 1027 da bomb!" This is the way that four-year-old Iolani ("bird of heaven" in Hawaiian) and her family are welcomed to the morning most days. They wake up and breakfast to "Da morning bomb" crew playing a range of Top 40 music, and the announcements, advertisements, and newsbreaks that one expects to hear from a successful commercial radio station. After completing her morning family rituals, Iolani travels to preschool on the bus with her mum. Like about 1,500 other three- to four-year-old children, she attends a Kamehameha Schools preschool for four and a half days each week. Funded by a bequest from the great granddaughter of King Kamehameha, Kamehameha Schools operate schools and preschools that serve in excess of 6,000 students across the state of Hawaii. Preference for admission is given to children with verifiable Hawaiian ancestry, and the schools place high value on Hawaiian cultural values and language. Separating from her mother at the edge of her classroom with ease and confidence, Iolani wafts through the door and joins her friends. She deposits her schoolbag in her locker, quickly and effortlessly joining several children in home corner, and engages vigorously and blissfully in highly intricate dramatic play. Their actions are punctuated with snippets of spontaneous singing. "Change the diaper, baby, change the diaper, baby, change the diaper, baby, 123!" is the chant soon taken up by Iolani and her playmates Kristy and Puanaui. The regular power broking that one would expect to see among a group of three- to five-year-old children playing in proximity

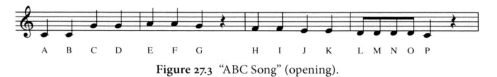

Figure 27.3 "ABC Song" (opening).

accompanies their endeavors to put a clean diaper on their "baby" (a life-sized baby doll). As roles are established, the baby gets a clean diaper, breakfast is prepared for the baby and other dolls, household chores are undertaken, and home corner takes on an air of organized chaos. While Kristy is clearing away the dishes, Puanaui brings a small ukulele back to the group, settles herself on some cushions near the baby, and begins to sing. Strumming her instrument, she looks the baby directly in the eye and begins to sing with island-like calm (see Figure 27.3).

Her "ABC" song is recognizable from many corners of the globe, but in this case, it has a particular Hawaiian quality to it. While she hasn't yet mastered the ukulele (in fact she doesn't know how to play the instrument), she does know that many Hawaiian musicians hold and strum it in a certain way that she emulates quite masterfully. However, the chords emanating from the instrument bear no resemblance to Western or other tonal traditions in that they are clusters of notes seemingly produced by placing fingers at random on the fingerboard. What is notable is the affect that she adopts while singing and playing: the baby is serenaded in a style reminiscent of the late Israel Kamakawiwo'ole, one of the most influential Hawaiian musicians in the past fifteen years (Ho'omanawanui 2006). Puanaui strums gently and performs the "ABC" song with a hauntingly lyrical Hawaiian feel, albeit with dissonant chords that are somewhat harsh to the ears. Once the song is finished, the girls decide that it is time for the baby's morning nap, and they carefully lull her to sleep in a bed improvised from the cushions.

It has been about forty-five minutes since the beginning of the school morning, and everyone has arrived in the classroom. As the children are gathered in a group, their teacher, Lehua, starts quietly humming a song. Eager to demonstrate her memory skills and musical prowess, Iolani raises her hand as high as she can and when Lehua calls her name, she beams with pride as she sings the first four words of the "Rainbow Song." After she praises Iolani, Lehua asks all the children to join together and sing the "Rainbow Song" (Figure 27.4) with hand actions. They launch forth in strident yet controlled voices just as they do when singing with members of their families or at community gatherings such as church.

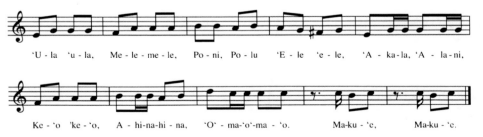

Figure 27.4 "Rainbow Song."

Iolani's mother provided the following translation of the colors in this song, which are also reflected in the hand actions: *ula ula*—red like the volcano; *mele mele*—yellow like the sun; *poni*—purple like a flower; *polu*—blue like the ocean; *ele ele*—black like the night; *akala*—pink like a flower; *alani*—orange like the orange (fruit); *keo keo*—white like the moon; *ahina hina*—gray like the rocks; *omao mao*—green like the trees; *maku'e*—brown like the mountain.

Several children are asked to sing sections by themselves, and it is not long before many are clamoring to demonstrate their ability. Soon, the group singing transforms into singing Christmas carols. This particular year, two of the children's most favorite carols are "Rudolph the Red-Nosed Reindeer" and "Jingle Bells," so it is these that the children sing fervently before Lehua announces that she would like to read them a story. One of the children proclaims that the group *must* sing the ubiquitous "Mele Kalikimaka," the ubiquitous Hawaiian Christmas song that can be heard statewide during the holidays. Eventually the group moves on to their story, and the day unfolds through the normal preschool routine, including mealtimes, other learning experiences, and an afternoon nap.

Now late in the afternoon with postnap learning experiences and snack time over, parents and family members begin to arrive to collect the children. Grinning from ear to ear, Mike (Kristy's father) crosses the threshold of the classroom cheerfully singing "Aloha Friday" (Figure 27.5).

This is a ritual that Kristy and her father established with her teacher and class a short time ago. He says that the song and brightly colored Aloha shirts that many wear to work on Fridays (Arthur 2006) bring a "light mood" to Fridays and a good start to the weekend. Kristy willingly joins with the singing, closing her week with joy and announcing the beginning of a weekend of holiday cheer, island style.

Michael

The North Shore is an area of Oahu famous for surfing, a little more than an hour's driving time north from Honolulu. Four-year-old Michael's local community of approximately 4,000 people has markedly increased in population because it is winter, and the world famous surfing competition season is in full swing. Michael attends the local preschool, and his sister Kayla (seven years old) is in the second

Figure 27.5 "Aloha Friday."

grade. The children's father is a native Hawaiian local, having lived in the area for all of his life, who is active in the local Hawaiian community; their mother is *kamaaina* (a long-time Hawaiian resident).

Michael wakes up on the North Shore of Oahu somewhat differently from Iolani in the city. Da bomb's jolt into the new day is replaced by Michael's mother gently singing a song that she learned from her mother-in-law. Michael's eyes gradually open and his Monday morning starts with calm reverie. After breakfast, Michael walks to school with Kayla and his mother. He enters his classroom after kissing his mother good-bye and greets Malia, his teacher. For a short time, Michael engrosses himself in a box construction that he and some of his friends were working on the previous day. They manage to add a few more "houses" to their "city," when Malia calls everyone to the mat for morning news. As the children take their turn, among other things, the group is told about new people that the children have seen in town because of the surf competition and the upcoming concert on the beach; hears an impromptu version of the song that accompanied a radio commercial in the car on the way to school; is offered a repeat performance of a nonsense song that was sung at home with a father the night before; and listens to a rendition of "I Have a Family Here on Earth" (Figure 27.6).

Malia asks Hanna about where she learned "I Have a Family Here on Earth," and Hanna explained that this is a song she learned at church with the family. Hanna's church is the Church of Jesus Christ of Latter-Day Saints (LDS). The LDS church plays a big part in the local community, as do the Polynesian Cultural Center and Brigham Young University's Hawaii campus, both LDS affiliates. Michael joins in with Hanna and happily recounts the small number of occasions that he and his family have joined Hanna's family for "family night," an evening (often Monday) of gospel study and relationship building (Faust 2003). Michael and Kayla learned some LDS children's songs and shared some of their own songs with Hanna's family during these times. Malia brings the group session to a close by leading a rousing performance of "Incy Wincy Spider," complete with vigorous hand actions. After the song and morning snack, the morning routine continues with some children remaining inside to play while others venture outdoors. The children's morning experiences are anchored in clearly defined local norms. The LDS songs and the traditional finger play of "Incy Wincy Spider" are surrounded by early childhood routines of bidding farewell to parents, participating in the telling of "news," and eating morning snack likely preceded by the ubiquitous packing up of earlier activities and equipment.

Later in the afternoon, walking home, Michael begins to hum the song that Hanna shared that morning, and conversation around songs that the family knows transpires. After some discussion about the time they went to see an LDS choir

Figure 27.6 "I Have a Family Here on Earth" (opening).

perform at the Polynesian Cultural Center (the choir sang Hanna's song among other things), Michael and Kayla reached their front yard, their skipping punctuated with a nonsense song they had recently heard on television. Soon after, the children's father returns home, and the family heads off to the beach to watch the enormous waves that are too dangerous for anyone except the professionals to enter. Floating along the waterline is a mix of live present-day Hawaiian guitar and vocals and 1960s-inspired surf music that would not be out of place in contemporary Southern California.

BORDERS, GAINING CONTROL, AND SHARING

On the surface, Vicki's, Cooper's, Iolani's, and Michael's stories appear unexceptional. Children musicking as part of their everyday lives can be considered a somewhat run-of-the-mill phenomenon. This is especially true of reasoning steeped in teleological tradition. The children all engaged (to various degrees) with musics that surrounded them and were possibly on the path to enculturation into the knowledges, practices, and beliefs that were bound by these. Iolani might become more "Hawaiian" in her musicking, Cooper and Michael might deepen their involvement in their respective church or school, and Vicki might go on to be an aficionado of contemporary, acoustic, commercial music by indigenous performers. This outmoded view of the children and their musics is limited and underrates the complexities of the children's enterprises. Applying a more contemporary lens reveals a different picture.

In his explanation of interpretive reproduction, Corsaro points out that children actively influence and at the same time are influenced by society. This involves children "creatively appropriating information from the adult world" but rather than internalizing existing culture, "actively contributing to cultural production and change" (2000: 92). An important conduit for the realization of this production and change is the notion of "secondary adjustments" (Goffman 1961). Corsaro explains these adjustments as reactions to adult rules and expectations by which children find ways around adults' assumptions. Whether conceived of as an "underlife" consisting of actions that violate existing norms (Goffman 1961), "tactics" to make space within existing power structures (deCerteau 1984), or other forms of creative aversion, children readily "buck the system" in their attempts to reinterpret and reorganize social norms. But a musical underlife is perhaps not as immediately visible as is children finding ways around rules that often dominate daily preschool routines such as packing away, snacks, and nap time.

Vicki, Cooper, Iolani, and Michael acquired knowledge of norms and expectations of existing musical cultures through experience. These norms were manifested in home, school, community, and commercial music. Iolani's friend Puanaui reproduced a traditional children's song (the "ABC" song) but added some local flavor to her performance. She took an existing norm and bucked the system by performing it in a manner befitting her social context. Cooper, Katherine, and James reproduced a worship song that formed part of their school ritual but adapted its reproduction with the addition of a beatboxed accompaniment. Similarly, the other children and their friends appropriated, customized, and creatively reproduced musical norms they encountered crossing numerous borders as they traversed the orb web.

These children cross and help shape a number of borders as they gain control of their musics and share them. Involvement in indigenous music, whether in a contemporary, commercial sense or learning songs from community elders, intersects with early music education experiences in prior-to-school settings and in schools. Systemic mandates, whether in the form of standards or outcomes, drive assessment and reporting, but beyond this, there is opportunity for natural interpretive reproduction. Add church into the mix and more borders are created, with as many again modified as part of everyday activity. Parental engagement with music and the manner in which children's resultant dispositions are shaped provide further opportunity for children to appropriate aspects of this musicking and adapt it in the evolution of their own cultures. For these children, the confluence of school, personal, mediated, home, and community musics from a range of heritages makes for complex, multifaceted musical cultures. To shoehorn these into teleological convention is to deny children the application of what is truly part of their day-to-day operations. Contemporary children are valued and powerful social agents (Kjørholt 2002; Lambert and Clyde 2000). Their complex musical ecologies must be acknowledged by educators, education systems, and communities, whose obligations include offering optimal opportunity for the development of responsive, sensitive musical cultures. Continual disregard for young children's musics suspends their opportunity to forge new musical cultures and truly organize their "routines, artifacts, values, and concerns" (Corsaro 2000). Unambiguous approbation, on the other hand, will facilitate the continual evolution of these cultures, empowering children in their ongoing commission of interpretive reproduction in the musical niche that is childhood.

References

Arthur, L. B. 2006. "The Aloha Shirt and Ethnicity in Hawai'i." *Textile: The Journal of Cloth and Culture* 4 (1) :8–34.

Aunty Wendy's Mob. 2010. "The Official Website of Aunty Wendy's Mob." 2009. Accessed March 9, 2010. http://www.auntywendysmob.com/index.html.

Bickerton, D. 1991. "Creole Language." In *The Emergence of Language: Development and Evolution*, edited by W. Wang, 59–69. New York: W. H. Freeman.

Bronfenbrenner, U., ed. 2004. *Making Human Beings Human: Bioecological Perspectives on Human Development*. Thousand Oaks, CA: Sage.

Burchill, M. 2004. "Enough Talking—More Walking—Achieving Deadly Outcomes." *Stronger Families Learning Exchange Bulletin* 6: 6–9.

Church of Jesus Christ of Latter-Day Saints. 2010. "Children's Songbook." Accessed March 7, 2010. http://www.lds.org/cm/display/0,17631,8764-1,00.html.

Corsaro, W. A. 2000. "Early Childhood Education, Children's Peer Cultures, and the Future of Childhood." *European Early Childhood Education Research Journal* 8 (2) :89–102.

Corsaro, W. A. 2005. *The Sociology of Childhood.* 2nd ed. Thousand Oaks, CA: Pine Forge Press.

deCerteau, M. 1984. *The Practice of Everyday Life.* Berkeley: University of California Press.

Faust, J. E. 2003. Enriching Our Lives through Family Home Evening. *Ensign,* June 2–6.

Geertz, C. 1973. *The Interpretation of Cultures: Selected Essays.* New York: Basic Books.

Goffman, E. 1961. *Asylums: Essays on the Social Situation of Mental Patients and Other Inmates.* Garden City, NY: Doubleday.

Hanlen, W. 2002. "Emerging Literacy in New South Wales Rural and Urban Indigenous Families." PhD diss., School of Humanities, University of Newcastle, Ourimbah, NSW.

Ho'omanawanui, K. 2006. "From Ocean to O-Shen: Reggae, Rap and Hip Hop in Hawai'i." In *Crossing Waters, Crossing Worlds: The African Diaspora in Indian Country,* edited by T. Miles and S. P. Holland, 273–308. Durham, NC: Duke University Press.

Kendrick, G. 1987. *Shine, Jesus, Shine.* Surry, UK: May Way Music.

Kjørholt, A. T. 2002. "Small Is Powerful: Discourses on 'Children and Participation' in Norway." *Childhood—a Global Journal of Child Research* 9 (1): 63–82.

Labouvie-Vief, G. 1982. "Dynamic Development and Mature Autonomy: A Theoretical Prologue." *Human Development* 25: 161–191.

Lambert, E. B., and M. Clyde. 2000. *Rethinking Early Childhood Theory and Practice.* Katoomba, Australia: Social Science Press.

Martinello, J. A. 2002. "Voids, Voices, and Story without End." *Southerly* 62 (2): 91–99.

Pellegrini, A. D., and P. Blatchford. 2000. *The Child at School: Interactions with Peers and Teachers.* New York: Oxford University Press.

Piaget, J. 1973. *The Child's Conception of the World,* translated by J. Tomlinson and A. Tomlinson. London: Paladin. Originally published as *Représentation du monde chez l'enfant.*

Piaget, J., and B. Inhelder. 1958. *The Growth of Logical Thinking: From Childhood to Adolescence,* translated by A. Parsons and S. Milgram. London: Routeledge and Kegan Paul. Originally published as *De la logique de l'enfant à la logique de l'adolescent.*

Rogoff, B. 2003. *The Cultural Nature of Human Development.* New York: Oxford University Press.

Simpson, N., and K. Briggs. 2010. "Stiff Gins." 2010. Accessed January 18, 2010. http://www.stiffgins.net/www.stiffgins.net/Welcome.html.

Talmy, S. 2010. "Becoming 'Local' in ESL: Racism as Resource in a Hawai'i Public High School." *Journal of Language, Identity and Education* 9 (1): 36–57.

Tuhawai Smith, L. 1998. *Decolonising Methodologies.* London: Zed Books.

Vygotsky, L. S. 1986. *Thought and Language,* translated by A. Kozulin. Cambridge: Massachusetts Institute of Technology Press.

28

THE ROLE OF CONTEXT AND EXPERIENCE AMONG THE CHILDREN OF THE CHURCH OF GOD AND SAINTS OF CHRIST, CLEVELAND, OHIO

SARA STONE MILLER
AND TERRY E. MILLER

UNDERSTANDING the old adage "The proof of the pudding is in the eating," no one who observes the children's choir of the Church of God and Saints of Christ (CGSC) can deny the fact that its members master complex, multipart, chromatic choral music without ever formally studying music systematically, learning notation, or having singing lessons. This they accomplish beginning from when they can walk, finally graduating seamlessly into the adult choir as they reach the late teen years. The system of musical training exhibited in this denomination is as effective as it is invisible. We believe it begins with an assumption that everyone is potentially musical and is therefore to be part of the musical community. We also observe that in this church's system, the children themselves can act as agents of change, bringing to their own choir favorite songs learned elsewhere, some of which might be later adopted by the adult choir as the children age up into the adult choir.

THE CHURCH OF GOD AND SAINTS OF CHRIST

The CGSC is an African American denomination with local churches (called tabernacles) in many North American cities, primarily in the Northeastern and Midwestern regions of the United States, with churches also located in Miami, Toronto, and outside North America in Jamaica, Bermuda, London (England), three areas of South Africa, Zimbabwe, and Mozambique. Tabernacles are normally located in predominately African American neighborhoods and are generally fairly small. Many of the tabernacle locations were established by the founder of the church early in the twentieth century during his years of traveling and preaching, so that there is a historical legacy for each tabernacle.

While the CGSC has a few religious practices and musical traditions in common with other African American denominations, far more of them are unique to the church, most having developed early in the church's history. The CGSC was founded in 1896 by William Saunders Crowdy (1847–1908), known to members as Prophet Crowdy, a former slave who became a cook in a hotel in Kansas City and subsequently homesteaded in Oklahoma. In 1893 Crowdy received a revelatory dream in which he was given the name, tenets, and other information regarding the founding of a new church, which was to be called the Church of God and Saints of Christ (Walker and Walker 1955). Among the important aspects of the church are observance of the Saturday Sabbath, celebration of the major holidays of Passover and the Holy Convocation, a complex structure of governance, the wearing of special church uniforms, and the central place of singing, marching, and the choir in the Sabbath service. Some of this ritual and its accoutrements can be traced to Crowdy's earlier participation in a Masonic lodge.

Most members of the church have grown up within the church, only a few new members joining from outside each year. The church is family-oriented, and extended multigenerational families make up a large part of church membership. The church constitutes a highly structured and central part of the lives of its members and serves as a major cultural and ethical influence in the lives of the children whose parents are members. Children born into the church soon become accustomed to spending extended periods of time in church, especially their entire Saturdays as well as multiple days twice a year for the Holy Convocation and Passover. What they gain is being part of a close-knit community that becomes a virtual family.

Members are to be present in the tabernacle for the entire Sabbath, from beginning of services at 10:00 am (11:00 am daylight saving time) until sundown. After a morning Sabbath service of several hours, members partake of lunch, which is then followed by various other activities, including Sabbath School for the children, choir rehearsal for both adults and children, relaxation, and concluding testimonial service, prior to returning home after the completion of the Sabbath. In addition, a Friday evening Beginning of Sabbath service is held. For the celebration of Passover, the entire church body meets together in a chosen location, usually a large convention center, for one week of services, worshipping up to eight hours a day in two segments. The Holy Convocation, also encompassing full-day services, is celebrated for one week in January within each individual tabernacle. None of the ministers or other officers of the church is reimbursed for their service. Membership in the church requires a significant commitment of time and financial resources but becomes a central element of most members' lives. For children this means spending long hours in services and foregoing the pleasures of playing outside or going to the mall on Saturday. The desire to participate in other activities sometimes increases as they become older, but because most of the children are born into the church, they have learned from the beginning that they are expected to keep the commandment to honor the Sabbath Day.

In addition to an individualized form of service, church members wear special uniforms during services, which differ according to winter or summer seasons. Choir members' uniforms have additional features that make them distinctive. The uniforms were instituted by Prophet Crowdy and still reflect the fashion style of the early years of the church at the turn of the twentieth century. The church colors are blue and brown, and the winter uniforms consist of brown English walking suits for men and blue blouses and long brown skirts for the women. Summer uniforms consist of white suits for the men and white blouses and skirts accented with blue belts for the women. Female choir members wear blouses with 365 tucks representing the days of the year, and skirts with 52 pleats representing the weeks of the year. Members wear rosettes within which a photograph of Prophet Crowdy is placed. Children wear an adaptation of the church uniform; boys wear brown or white suits while girls wear blue blouses and brown skirts or jumpers and white skirts and blouses in the summer. While young children are content with their uniforms, sometimes adolescents question them or wish to make adjustments. As they grow into the later teen years and adulthood, however, they embrace the uniforms. Wearing the uniform becomes part of their identity and reinforces their solidarity with everyone in both the tabernacle and the denomination at large. Even when members travel to church functions (e.g., Passover), they wear special travel uniforms that make them distinctive in the eyes of all who see them.

THE CHOIR AND ITS ROLE IN THE CHURCH

Singing and the choir are central in the life of the church. All singing is a cappella, as musical instruments are not used in the CGSC to accompany singing. The CGSC has a distinctive song style consisting of four- to six-part harmony, often rather chromatic, and often with an independent bass line. The choir was established by Prophet Crowdy, who bestowed on them the name "singers of Israel." The choir is extremely important; in fact, there is no separate congregational singing. Approximately 60 percent of the service is given to singing or to demonstration marches, during which the adult choir marches in complex formations around the tabernacle while singing, followed by a scaled-back version performed by the children.

It is considered an honor to be a choir member, and especially a choir leader, called chorister. The chorister always uses a baton, which has symbolic significance. The baton is considered an extension of the chorister, "who transmits the spirit of singing to the Singers through its use" (CGSC n.d.) and is also described as an instrument of warfare used in directing the choir in singing the word of God. Another important position in the choir is that of the shepherd boy (an adult), who leads the march and gives other signals to the choir with his staff. The staff symbolizes a shepherd's staff and the saving power of Christ and is also considered an "instrument of warfare," its principal use being "for the protection of the Holy and Most Holy place and its personnel." The staff symbolizes the rod of the house of Levi upon which was written Aaron's name and which was placed in the tent of testimony as one of the twelve rods from the twelve houses of the people of Israel. Ribbons attached near the top of the staff symbolize the blossoms and almonds that budded on Aaron's rod to show that he was the man chosen by God (Numbers 17). Each tabernacle has at least one shepherd boy, and there is a chief shepherd boy, who leads the mass choir at general gatherings and instructs the other shepherd boys (Web Figure 28.1 ◉). Being a shepherd boy is a typical entry point for young men, who, upon proving themselves, may be promoted to higher offices in the church's elaborate hierarchy.

Song composition is also an integral aspect of the church; the majority of songs sung in the church are composed by members. Members who compose say they receive their songs from the "song angel" or the "angel of song." They may receive a song in a dream or spontaneously while awake. Most composers do not read music, but they often say that they hear their songs in their minds as if sung by a mass choir. If a song is accepted by choir officials, it is taught to members by rote and usually harmonized intuitively in the church's typical style. Songs are shared among tabernacles, with the Passover Observance being the primary time for exchange of songs, so that there is a denomination-wide repertory.

The adult choir sits arranged by voice part (soprano, alto, tenor, and bass) in a semicircular arrangement with a center aisle on the main floor of the tabernacle in front of the pulpit, which stands on a raised platform across the front. The choir's area is considered an extension of the pulpit and represents sacred ground. The congregation, including children, sits facing the front of the tabernacle.

The structure of a CGSC service is quite formal. It begins with two "trumpet" (actually bugle) calls, the first to call people to order and the second to formally begin the service. The service always begins with the singing of the church anthem, "I Love Thy Church, O God," sung to the tune "Laban" composed by nineteenth-century choral musician and educator Lowell Mason and using a text by Timothy Dwight, the first verse of which is not included in the version sung in the CGSC. This is followed by the Lord's Prayer, a greeting by the pastor, and usually another song. After a responsive scripture passage, there are more songs alternating with words from the pastor. A testimony segment lasting about an hour then takes place, with individual members testifying verbally and by singing songs in which the choir joins. Children are also encouraged to testify from a young age, but their opportunity comes later in the service.

At noon a prayer is said, followed by the demonstration march. During the demonstration march choir members follow the lead of the shepherd boy with his staff as he leads them in complicated formations throughout the tabernacle. The specific formations differ among tabernacles, but the general form entails the choir proceeding to the rear of the sanctuary, where they stand together as they sing a number of songs. During a pause between songs, female choir members don special hats called "crowns." After this they resume singing while being led back to the front of the church (Web Figure 28.2 ⊙.) The shepherd boy, leading the choir, pauses in front of the choir seating area and bows toward the pastors while a trumpet signal is given, and he might perform certain figures with his staff. Then choir members, usually in pairs, stop for a few beats and bow their heads toward the front of the church as well (Web Figures 28.3, 28.4 ⊙). As a chief executive officer explained, they are not bowing to the pastors, but to signify submission to God and the act of being received by God (Stone 1985).

The shepherd boy's use of the staff is one of the more obvious striking and ceremonial aspects of the CGSC service. Even when the choir is singing while seated, he often uses it to keep time with the singing by tilting it forward and back in time to the beat. During the demonstration march he again moves the staff up and down in time to the beat as he leads the chorister and choir in its march. In recent years, some shepherd boys have even devised quite ornamental movements, seen primarily at Passover, including twirling the staff or even tossing it between shepherd boys, usually during a stationary segment of a demonstration march. Another use of the staff is to signal a particular choir movement; for example, sometimes after they have reached their seats, the choir stops singing but continues marching in place. The shepherd boy then taps the staff on the floor at regular intervals, first of four beats each and then of two beats, as each choir member makes a quarter turn on each tap. At times, the sound of the stepping feet, such as at the end of a song, inspires people to "feel the Spirit" or "get happy," which may inspire holy dancing.

Following the march by the adult choir, the children also have a chance to perform their own testimony, songs, and demonstration march. From the time they are able to talk, children are expected to testify, which at first simply entails saying the words, "Please pray for me," when the microphone is held in front of them (Web Figure 28.5 ⊙). From the time they can walk, they are included in the children's march. They are led by a young boy with a staff (imitating the shepherd boy) and a young girl with a baton (imitating the chorister). Adult members sing along, if needed, to encourage and support the children. Older children help the younger with their roles, often holding their hands as they march and sometimes steadying the enthusiastic movements of the shepherd's staff or reinforcing the steady movement of the chorister's baton. An adolescent leads the singing while they stand in place, including giving the starting pitch, starting and ending the song, and keeping the beat with the baton. The songs sung by the children are generally well-known church compositions; occasionally a

child may sing a pop song with a general theme such as brotherly love learned outside the church as a solo. The adults are quite tolerant of the songs chosen by the
younger children, since they do not yet have a sense of what a "church song" should
be. Adolescents often get together and form "quartets" (not necessarily four singers),
and their songs can vary from church songs in their own arrangements to songs from
the broader black gospel tradition. The total time allotted for the children's segment of
the service is perhaps 10 percent of the whole, but throughout the service, the children may sing, clap, and step during the adult choir's songs. Following the children's
demonstration march, the sermon takes place, after which the service concludes with
more singing, announcements, and closing words.

The children's participation in their own choir along with their own demonstration march serves to instruct and induct them into church society at large. Children,
having had ample opportunities to observe the adult musical behaviors, are given
their own chance to perform these same roles in the service. For the children and
adolescents, having the chance to perform their separate demonstration march and
song segment is a way to feel part of the church, emulate adults, learn about their
future roles in the church, and take part in an enjoyable activity that gives them a
chance to burn energy during a service lasting several hours. Their efforts are supported by the adults, who often sing along to bolster them; any song started in the
most tremulous voice is immediately reinforced by the adults. Gender roles are established in that boys are given the role of shepherd boy, leading the procession with a
child-sized shepherd's staff, while girls are given the baton to symbolize the role of
chorister. (Adult males can be choristers also, but women are never shepherd boys.)

The chorister and shepherd boy fulfill important roles, both practical and ceremonial, and this is obvious to young members of the church. Boys who are given
the shepherd's staff during children's demonstration marches or choir rehearsals
enthusiastically move the staff to keep the beat in imitation of the adults. They are
taught to use it with respect, however, and never as a toy. Members recall that when
they were children, the boys all wanted to be a shepherd boy and the girls to be a
chorister, and everyone wanted to sing in the choir eventually.

The trumpet (bugle) sounder also has an important role, as he signals both a call
to order and a call to formally begin the service. In addition, the trumpet is sounded
during the demonstration march, at the point in which the shepherd boy pauses upon
reaching the front as the choir is returning from the stationary portion at the rear of
the church. Finally, the trumpet signals the end of the formal service. In individual
tabernacles, it is not unusual for a young boy to be given the role of trumpet player,
at least for some services. Boys learn to produce a few notes on the trumpet (bugle)
at church; the call during services at local tabernacles is usually quite simple.

Singing in the choir is seen as a respected and valuable part of church membership, and children, seeing this, often aspire to become members. It is also a way for
children and adolescents to "fit in." In addition to participating in their own choir
and demonstration march, children usually sing and clap along with the adult choir,
and often the younger children step or jump in time to the livelier songs. Adolescents
are also encouraged to sing solos or form small groups such as trios, quartets, or
quintets, which helps to validate their learning and talent. One member recalled

singing in such a quartet in his teen years: "We used to all sit down and sing during lunch break. We got in a group before it was time to go down to eat. We'd all sing in a circle. And that's how we learned our different voices, how to harmonize" (Eric Gray, personal interview, July 3, 2010). Another recalled that since the adults had a group called "The Melodious Four," she and several others decided to call their own group "The Melodious Juniors" (Peggy Reed, personal interview, July 3, 2010).

Passing on a Heritage

Cultural imperatives within the church include the necessity of preserving a unique heritage, instructing both children and adults in how to live ethically, and upholding the traditions of the church. The history and doctrine of the church are taught through both formal Sabbath School and song texts. Singing and the role of the choir are integral to the CGSC, and children are incorporated into their own choir from the time they can walk. In addition, observing the adults as they carry out their roles in the church—be they religious, organizational, or musical—has a profound effect on the children. Children even like to "play church" at home, including singing and marching. As one member related, "We used to sing, play church. We used to act like what we saw here. We'd go home and act it out. We acted like we was the shepherd, chorister, preacher" (Eric Gray, personal interview, July 3, 2010). Members also observe children modeling specific adults: "If you look at the younger children you can see who they model. If you really observe them, you'll know who they're trying to sing like. And we just sit back and smile, because they look just like whoever we know they're trying to be. Doing the whole movement" (Eric Gray, personal interview, July 3, 2010).

Finding One's Niche

The organizational structure of the CGSC, both in general and in musical areas, gives great opportunity for members to find a niche. Children learn about these many offices in the church from the beginning, and as they become older, they begin to aspire to hold such positions in the future. It is certainly true that the church provides many of its members with a sense of importance and purpose through these many titles. Outside the church they may live lives of little notice, perhaps holding a menial job, going about their business anonymously within a big city. In the inclusive structure of the CGSC, members are known and addressed as "saint" from birth, and from there numerous additional roles may be filled. Further, there is upward mobility through the ranks. Some may attain high office within the church and take a prominent place both within their own tabernacle and at larger gatherings of the church, especially Passover.

Gender is a determining factor in some church roles and offices. The church is governed by a group of male officers of various ranks and by a Board of Presbytery composed of twelve of these officers. At the top of this hierarchy are the bishops, one of whom is the chief executive officer. Other male officers include evangelists-at-large, a chief evangelist, Grand Father Abraham, evangelists, elders, and deacons. While women are not ordained as ministers, they are chosen or called to fill various offices of considerable importance in the church. The highest rank attained by women is that of chief evangelist—a role appointed by the executive officer. They chair the Women's Board, which is similar to the Board of Presbytery. Other women's officers include sister elders, who are to the women as the male elders are to the church in general. Both chief evangelists and sister elders may preach; chief evangelists may preach at the Passover, and sister elders may preach in their own tabernacles. Further opportunities for women to be officers occur in the women's auxiliary, which has officers in each tabernacle and nationally.

For children especially attracted to singing, there is an elaborate hierarchy of music officials and thus a built-in incentive to participate in the choir, learn the songs, and attain the skills necessary for someone to be noticed and designated "chorister" or beyond. In the musical organization, the two highest music officers are the minister of music and the chief chorister, both appointed by the chief executive officer. Together, they oversee the musical aspects of the church, and the chief chorister leads the mass choir at the Passover. There is also an assistant general chorister and district choristers. These officers visit tabernacles to teach songs and make sure everyone is performing his or her duties correctly. Each tabernacle then has one or more choristers who teach songs and lead the singing within the tabernacle. Choristers and music officers may be either male or female. As previously described, the shepherd boy fulfills a unique and necessary role in the choir by leading the singers during marches at the command of the chorister, assisting the chorister in sustaining order, and seeing that all singers are in the choir in proper uniform; the chief shepherd boy leads the entire mass choir during the Passover Observance. Naturally, the children are witnesses to this elaborate hierarchy and the status, pomp, and circumstance associated with it. They come to understand from a young age that they will someday take the places of the adults presently serving. Just as with singing, the children begin absorbing what they need to know from their first years and gradually move from imitation to participation to actual positions.

Historical and Traditional Influences

The CGSC occupies a particular niche within the history and development of African American churches in the United States. The reverence for Prophet Crowdy and his teachings is an important aspect that helps to shape the outlook of members. Prophet Crowdy taught that black people were the true Jews and instituted the observance of the Passover within the church. Nevertheless, he preached the gospel, and belief in Jesus Christ is central to the doctrine of the CGSC. The basic doctrine of the CGSC is thus similar to that of other Christian denominations, with the addition of belief in the teachings of Prophet Crowdy, the observance of the church's particular religious holidays he instituted, and the reverence for him.

The Passover is the most important holiday of the CGSC year, and one that has a profound effect on all who attend, including children. It is said that it is not a Jewish Passover but the "Lord's Passover." Church members identify with the ancient

Israelites; during the first night of the observance, church members bring their coats to the service and wear them at midnight to symbolize the Israelites fleeing Egypt. At midnight each member is given a serving of lamb and unleavened bread. There is a current of excitement during this evening, which is considered the most holy of the church year, and the ceremony makes a distinct impression on all in attendance, especially children, who are present for the entire service, which can last until some hours after midnight. The remaining seven days of the Passover consist of services from morning to evening, with breaks in the afternoon for lunch and rest. Throughout, the children are expected to attend; there are no separate playrooms or separate classrooms. Various days have themes, such as a day devoted to the women's organization, one devoted to the choir known as "Singers' Day," and "Children's Day," which reinforces the children's role and importance in the church (CGSC 2002).

On Children's Day, along with the usual aspects of the service such as scripture reading, prayer, sermons, communion, and selections from the adult choir, there are special recognitions of the children. Often occurring on the Sabbath, there are Sabbath School exercises; "Children's Moments," including children's testimony and songs, sung by both soloists and by children's choirs from the various tabernacles; and a children's retreat and processional (march). This is led, with help from adults, by various young boys who take turns holding the shepherd boy's staff and young girls who take turns waving the chorister's baton. One member stated that all children love the Passover and look forward to it each year and that Children's Day is thought of as "a special day for them to shine and express themselves. We used to practice and rehearse all year just for Children's Day" (Alan Gray, personal interview, June 3, 2010).

On Singers' Day, the choir from each tabernacle shares new songs composed during the past year with each other. These are recorded and learned by choirs from the various tabernacles, with some songs catching on more than others. The importance of singing, song composition, and the choir actually was established by Prophet Crowdy, who was said to have a powerful singing voice and established the choir and its traditions. In the early years of the church, members sang old hymns such as those by Dr. Isaac Watts, but early on members began composing original songs with texts drawn from the Bible. Song composition is highly regarded within the church, and children become aware of this early on. Members grow up hearing the particular style of song and harmonization of the CGSC, so that this soundscape is part of their sonic heritage.

Music styles from the Caribbean and African branches of the church can sometimes be detected in the songs, as heard during Singer's Day at the Passover Observance. For example, the members of tabernacles in Miami and Toronto are predominately West Indian immigrants or their descendants and bring some Caribbean-style church-related elements to their compositions. Immigrants from Zimbabwe have also performed their particular style at Passover gatherings. Overall, however, there is more influence in the opposite direction, with the North American song style of the CGSC exerting itself on the practices of the tabernacles in the Caribbean and South Africa. While the differences between the two are greater in the case of South African tabernacles, where a distinctive local choral style has developed, there is also little direct contact between the American and South African members. Even so, many CGSC songs from the United States are sung in the CGSC in South Africa, and the song style in the segment of the South African CGSC most closely allied with the church in the United States is often amazingly similar.

Throughout the history of the CGSC, stylistic elements have been introduced from other groups. Old hymns from the Baptist tradition were sung in the early days, but after CGSC singers developed their own style, the chromatic harmonic style they acquired suggests influence from barbershop harmony and other popular styles of the turn of the twentieth century. African American gospel style and some of its repertory have also added to the repertory, but always reconfigured into the a capella, chromatic idiom that makes this church's singing so distinctive.

Impact of Technology and the Media

Outside the church's services the children of the CGSC are influenced by the same technology and media as their peers. They listen to the same radio stations, watch the same television programs, and participate in the same kinds of choir and band ensembles at school, including school-based gospel choirs. Influences from popular song styles find their way into the performance practices of the children and adolescents, and these are most clearly heard when the children perform during the services. One such influence that has audibly changed the church style over the past thirty years is the increasing use of a highly ornamented style of singing often found in African American popular song styles. Ironically, that melismatic style originated in the black Baptist and Methodist-Episcopal churches where African Americans embraced the unaccompanied singing of lined psalms and hymns in the tradition of "Dr. Watts" (Tallmadge 1961).

The advent of recording equipment made it easier for members to learn and remember new songs, since historically most members did not read music. Only song texts were written down, with the melodies and harmonies having to be learned orally and remembered from singing. When inexpensive cassette recorders became available, members began recording the new songs heard at the Passover to aid in remembering them and for practicing them in their home tabernacles. Today members use MP3 voice recorders and iPhones to record songs. Each new generation seems more attuned than the previous one to the current technologies for transmitting musical material. With most of the children attending public schools, many have learned to read notation in choir or band programs, and some have learned to play instruments. We expect that as time goes on, the CGSC music tradition will be better understood by members, who can perhaps begin to harness the evident musical talents of the children even more effectively than is already true.

CONCLUSION: LESSONS ABOUT LEARNING

Many church members credit their propensity to compose songs, sing, and march to the example set by the founder, Prophet Crowdy. Prophet Crowdy was described as having a powerful singing voice and is credited with composing songs and instituting the demonstration march. Early accounts in the church newspaper evidence the fact that singing, song composition, and marching have been important aspects of the church from its earliest days (*The Weekly Prophet* 1908). Because of the central position of the church in their lives and the lives of their family, the importance of and the amount of time devoted to singing and marching during long church services, and the inclusion of the children in their own version of the adult choir as well as the fact that they can sing along with the adult choir at any time in the service, children are surrounded by and drawn into the musical tradition of the CGSC. One composer, speaking of the phenomenon of singing and composition in the church, described the experience this way:

> I think it is a love of music. Music is pushed into childhood, and we just [have] a natural born love of music, and we grow up from children to adults hearing and listening to harmonies. And most of us, even from children, know discord when we hear it. We can't tell you what it is, but we know it. And it is just an appreciation for at least that particular type of music.... I guess it is a good background to learn naturally, because you're surrounded by it. At home, at church, all day long. You're just swimming in it. Music, music, and it is a thing that, in the church service, not only the choir sings, but the whole body sings all the musical parts. So you're just surrounded by it. (John Millerton, personal interview, July 1984)

In speaking of the musical learning of children in the CGSC, the late chief executive officer Bishop James R. Grant stated, "They learn it from infancy, even before they're conceived. It's in their parents, it's in their genes. It's a part of them. Most of these young people that you see were born into the church" (*Marching in Their Footsteps* 1996). This brings to mind the words of Zoltan Kodaly, who when asked at what age music education should begin, replied, "nine months before the mother's birth" (Kokas 1970: 53). Perhaps not surprisingly, some members say that the church anthem, "I Love Thy Church, O God," is the earliest song they remember. "I even notice it with my children. Before they can actually even form sentences they can sing the church anthem. They make a tune. They have it. The first two words that are prevalent in most of the young people are 'I Love'" (Erika Hendricks, personal interview, July 3, 2010).

What can we observe from the CGSC and its effective but nonsystematic pedagogy? To what extent is this way of learning context or culture specific?

First, church members and song leaders assume that all human beings are musical and capable of making music with their own voices. No one—not the "tone-deaf child," not the person with mental or physical challenges, nor the person who has an initial aversion to performing—is excluded. As a result, the children participate freely and without inhibitions because they are encouraged to and because there are no judgments being made about quality. Even preschool age children, if they attempt it, can begin a song that all will pick up and support, so a majority of members actively participate in the church's singing.

Second, growing up in the thick of musical activity for much of each week's Sabbath results in the absorption of the church's style of melody, harmony, and rhythm. Understanding this musical system becomes intuitive. As a result, by the time the children are adolescents, they have acquired the ability to participate in spontaneous harmonizations of newly learned melodies. Along with the adults in the choir, the children become skilled at creating harmonic accompaniments on the spur of the moment. Perhaps the first time through the harmonies are fairly simple, but by the second time the choir is able to begin creating contrasting textures and complex, chromatic harmonies that work within the functional harmony system, a system that they have never studied formally. Because this is the main musical world in which church children grow up, this is what they assume is normal behavior, and over time they too develop a sense of appropriate harmony. Though they cannot name the chords—and sometimes they are of a complexity that challenge musicians—they understand intuitively how they work.

Because the church makes all its own music, never using recorded accompaniments, never depending on instrumental support, the children learn that music is something you do for yourself and for your community, family, and church. Though church members may have their MP3 players for outside church and watch music videos on television as full participants in modern American musical life, the essential music in their life is that of the CGSC, and it is here that they learn that they are capable of creating, performing, and enjoying music entirely of their own making and doing it in the context of a warm and caring community that values each contribution regardless of the skill exhibited. The church exemplifies the view that all children are musical and that the challenge is not to teach it to them but to let it out. No one in the CGSC "teaches" music as we understand that term, but they provide outlets for each child to "musick," as Christopher Small (1998) writes. The results can be clearly seen by anyone who observes the church and its activities.

REFERENCES

Church of God and Saints of Christ. n.d. History of Singers of Israel. unpublished.

Church of God and Saints of Christ. 2002. Milestone International: Passover. Milestone Publication Committee.

Kokas, Klara. 1970. "Kodaly's Concept of Music Education." Bulletin of the Council for Research in Music Education 22 (Fall): 49–56.

Marching in Their Footsteps: The Handing Down of a Musical Legacy in the Church of God and Saints of Christ. 1996. Kent, OH: Advanced Field and Lab Course Video Project. Videotape.

Small, Christopher. 1998. Musicking: the Meanings of Performing and Listening. Hanover, NH: Wesleyan University Press.

Stone, Sara M. 1985. "Song Composition, Transmission, and Performance Practice in an Urban Black Denomination, The Church of God and Saints of Christ." PhD diss., Kent State University.

Tallmadge, William H. 1961. "Dr. Watts and Mahalia Jackson—The Development, Decline, and Survival of a Folk Style in America." Ethnomusicology 5 (2): 95–99.

The Weekly Prophet. Philadelphia, February 14, 1908.

Walker, Beersheba Crowdy, and Elfreth J. P. Walker. 1955. Life and Works of William Saunders Crowdy. Philadelphia: Elfreth J. P. Walker.

29

MUSIC IN THE LIVES OF REFUGEE AND NEWLY ARRIVED IMMIGRANT CHILDREN IN SYDNEY, AUSTRALIA

KATHRYN MARSH

AUSTRALIA is a culturally diverse nation, having been settled through multiple waves of immigration throughout its history. As a result, the Australian population is drawn from more than a hundred birthplace groups. Sydney, the largest Australian city, is the most ethnically and linguistically diverse Australian community, particularly as it is an initial place of settlement for many immigrants, including refugees. This chapter investigates the role of music in the lives of refugee and newly arrived immigrant children in Sydney as a means of developing forms of communication, a sense of belonging and empowerment, and a contribution to cultural maintenance, identity construction, emotional release, and integration within the host culture.

The Broader Sociopolitical and Sociomusical Context

A refugee is defined as "any person who is outside their country of nationality and is unable to return due to a well founded fear of persecution for reasons of race, religion, nationality, membership of a particular social group or political opinion" (United Nations Convention Relating to the Status of Refugees 1951). In the years 2006–2008, Australia granted more than 26,000 humanitarian visas to refugees. Despite the relatively small numbers in global terms, Australia has, at various times in its history of extensive immigration, provided permanent settlement for a large number of refugees relative to population (Bhabha and Crock 2007).

However, the unauthorized appearance of asylum seekers on the shores of Australia has typically led to political unease, particularly when asylum seekers arrive in the highly visible form of "boat people" who reach the island continent of Australia with the assistance of "people smugglers." Although policies of multiculturalism and cultural pluralism have been entrenched in Australian law since the 1970s, elements of xenophobia and racism persist within aspects of Australian society (Vasta and Castles 1996), contrasting with strong coexistent social justice movements. It is within this uneasy sociopolitical climate regarding immigration and refugee resettlement that refugees entering Australia currently reside.

To varying degrees, refugees and newly arrived immigrants may face a range of social, emotional, and cultural challenges related to geographical and cultural displacement and trauma experienced in the country of origin, en route, and in the process of relocation and resettlement (Aroche and Coello 2002; Hamilton and Moore 2004; Jones, Baker, and Day 2004; Sebastian 2008). Reyes characterizes the life of refugees from the time of flight from homeland to resettlement in a new host environment as "an extreme case of decontextualization and recontextualization" (1999: 16). She notes that the "effects of life experiences, particularly when they are traumatic, life threatening, and intensely disorienting" (ibid.: xiii) are long lasting, enduring well into the resettlement period and making the process of resettlement more difficult for forced migrants (refugees) than for voluntary migrants. This is particularly the case for children, who, as well as experiencing trauma, hardship, educational deprivation, and the difficulties of resettlement (including language difference, loss of identity, and cultural adaptation), often have even less choice in their relocation than adults (Bhabha and Crock 2007). Reyes posits that songs, instrumental music, and dance provide an alternative avenue for communication that is often inhibited in speech form for refugees by danger, trauma, and language difference and that the sharing of music with others may facilitate psychological, social, and musical points of entry into new forms of life, as well as maintain links with homeland traditions.

A number of studies have investigated the role of the arts and, more specifically, music activity among refugee populations as a means of developing forms of communication, a sense of belonging, and empowerment, and as a contribution to cultural maintenance, identity construction, stress relief, and integration within the host country (Diehl 2002; Jones, Baker, and Day 2004; Ladkani 2001; Pesek 2009; Reyes 1999; Sebastian 2008). However, there has been less emphasis on the role of music or other arts in the lives of refugee children and young people, despite the UNICEF estimate that global armed conflicts between 1986 and 1996 had traumatized and significantly affected the well-being of 10 million children (Harris 2007). Harris states that "cultural resources, including those associated with creative artistic expression, have been shown to enhance communities' resilience in the face of terror and deprivation, and to cultivate children's capacities in particular" (2007: 135). Heidenrich (2005) notes that music therapy programs have constituted a part of psychosocial therapy with children in postconflict situations in a number of nations, including Sierra Leone, Rwanda, Palestine, and Bosnia-Herzegovina, with aims including the expression of feelings, development of self-esteem and self-respect, and provision of the opportunity to play in a safe environment (see also Osborne 2009; Sutton 2002).

This chapter draws on an ethnographic study of refugee and newly arrived immigrant children engaged in music activity in early childhood playgroups; in school classrooms, playgrounds, music groups, and therapeutic groups; and in community-based youth groups, which commenced in Sydney in 2009. In keeping with other studies of children's musical lives (Campbell 1998, 2010; Marsh 2008), the study has explored different forms of music participation in home, community, and educational settings; the use of mediated music and technology; and the perceived outcomes of music participation for these children. Although there are some differences in attributes and needs of refugees and immigrants who have chosen to immigrate, many of the needs may be similar, at least initially in the resettlement period. Some refugees also do not identify publicly as refugees, fearing that a social stigma attaches to this designation. Therefore, while the emphasis in this chapter is on refugees, participants also included other newly arrived immigrants. This chapter focuses on a case study of children within one of the selected settings: a primary (elementary) school with the highest population of refugees in the state of New South Wales (NSW), in which the city of Sydney is located.

The Microcontext: Fineview Public School

Fineview Public School (pseudonyms are used for all institutions and people) is a state-funded primary school, located 29 km southwest of the Sydney city center. The suburb of Fineview and the surrounding region of southwestern Sydney has for several decades been a major resettlement area for newly arrived immigrants, including refugees. Of Fineview school's 619 students, 90 percent have language backgrounds other than English and sixty different languages are spoken by the school community. The majority languages of Arabic and Assyrian[1] reflect the high percentage of refugees in the school, constituting 26 percent of the enrolled students. Although the largest groups of refugees are from Iraq, there are also a number from Bosnia-Herzegovina, Afghanistan, Sudan, Sierra Leone, the Democratic Republic of Congo, Nigeria, Uganda, Liberia, Iran, East Timor, and Burma.

With such a high level of ethnic and linguistic diversity, in addition to a relatively high degree of economic disadvantage in the local population, the school has instituted a number of programs to help students to develop to their full potential, including specialist English as a Second Language tuition and community language programs in Arabic, Assyrian, and Vietnamese. Newly arrived immigrant and refugee children are settled into the school in special classes as part of the New Arrivals Program, before entering integrated classrooms. Specific initiatives funded by the state and federal government also provide additional literacy and refugee support to students and their families.

The school caters to children aged mostly from five to twelve years of age in stage groupings (Early Stage 1 and Stage 1 from five to eight years; Stage 2 from eight to ten years and Stage 3 from ten to twelve years). This means that most classes have children of more than one age group, facilitating interage friendships. This integrative disposition is continued in the organization of curriculum content, which is clustered in thematic units. Classroom music is taught within this cross-curricular format by generalist classroom teachers. There are also cocurricular special interest groups that include a vocal group, choir, and dance group. The latter two groups perform both at school occasions and outside the school at local events and regional school festivals. As is usual in many NSW primary schools, there is no specialist music teacher, though teachers have acted in this capacity in the recent past.

Field recording at this school took place toward the end of the school year, when all classes were preparing performances for culminating Presentation Days. Many of the performances involved music, and there were many class rehearsals that the research team was invited to observe. We also observed playground activities and

Figure 29.4: Sudanese and Iraqi girls playing hand clapping game Sisilala.

conducted both formal interviews and informal discussions with groups of children, often in the context of their play on the playground or during sessions inside at lunchtime.[2] Here performances of games or favorite songs were elicited from groups previously observed on the playground as shown in recordings available on the linked website (Web Figures 29.1, 29.2, 29.3 ⊙) and Figure 29.4).

Music in the Lives of Children at Fineview

As can be deduced from the description above, music played a part in the lives of virtually all of the children in the school. However, the nature and extent of musical involvement varied according to the setting and the preferences and propensities of different children; it was more or less evident and discussed with varying levels of interest and openness by children. In the following sections some forms of musical involvement occurring in the school, home, and community environments as observed at the school and reported by children and teachers are outlined with reference to their outcomes for children.

Musical Opportunities Provided by the School

It was evident that teachers of both younger and older children recognized some of the benefits that musical activity can provide for the children in their care. Such benefits were sometimes explicitly expressed, while in other instances they were seen to be inherent in day-to-day planning. One teacher with extensive experience of teaching music in the school indicated that refugee and newly arrived immigrant children had an immediate response to music in the classroom. She explained that the daily reiteration of song repertoire and the relaxed atmosphere and ability to join in communal musical experiences encouraged refugee children to participate in music despite a reticence to engage in some other verbally based classroom activities. Children were able to gain a sense of belonging to a group and security in familiarity with known songs that lessened the feeling of risk that might accompany individual verbal responses for children learning English.

Repetition and use of songs with movements that depicted meaning enabled newly arrived children both to take an active part in music experiences and to gain an understanding of the language in song texts through visual and auditory modeling. Songs for Stage 1 children were chosen with language learning needs in mind, in addition to their links with cross-curricular content, and the children in the Stage 1 New Arrivals class were observed enthusiastically participating in performances of action songs along with their age cohort. It was notable that most observed performances of songs taught by teachers at the school were in English.

Music from cultures of origin was not prioritized, but the matching of song and movement content with curricular content provided a common ground between all members of classes at each stage, fostering inclusion. Repertoire could also be used to initiate important thematic aspects of the curriculum for refugees and other immigrants. For children in the early years of school, in particular, singing and movement were a regularly occurring part of the school day, used for enjoyment, transitions, vocabulary development, and managing behavior, providing security through routine.

Security and the invitation to share in both teaching and learning experiences with music also encouraged young newly arrived children to demonstrate both singing and dancing expertise in the classroom, drawing on out-of-school experiences. Break dancing and hip-hop dancing were integral to dance activities both provided by the school and observed on the playground, where several boys demonstrated some quite strenuous hip-hop movements in response to my camera and expressed a preference for this genre. Quite a few of the girls who were interviewed also talked about dancing to popular music at home with friends or siblings. It was clear that dance could provide entertainment, enjoyment, and also a powerful form of release for refugee children, as expressed by a twelve-year-old Sudanese girl, Awek: "I like dancing, because it's fun and it's like when you dance it's like you're free alone."

The school special interest dance group was notable for inclusion of a significant number of refugee children of different ages, both girls and boys, especially those from Sudan and other sub-Saharan African nations. This group performed impressively choreographed and coordinated dance routines to popular songs with verve and considerable prowess and was in demand for school occasions and external performances in the region. Hip-hop was a prominent influence on the movement routines. Despite frequent rehearsals, the members of the dance group appeared to consistently enjoy the routines and were always focused. This was true of some refugee children who were noticeably diffident and distracted in other situations (Web Figure 29.5 ⬤). This enjoyment and dedication could have been partially attributable to the dancing activity itself but was also engendered by the ownership that derived from their active involvement in the choreography. Two refugee girls in the group, one Iraqi and the other Sudanese, discussed the collaborative way in which the choreography for the dance group was devised:

> ARAMINA: Like our people get in groups and then they dance, right, and then she [the teacher who runs the dance group] stops the song and then like you perform in front of her; the group comes and performs it...and show her the dance, and then we can all put it together and make a dance.
> RESEARCHER (R): Oh, so you work out the moves to start off with, do you?
> ARAMINA and AKOI: Yep....
> ARAMINA: And sometimes she starts it and we end....
> R: Where do you get those dancing ideas from?
> AKOI: Like sometimes the teacher and sometimes....
> ARAMINA: You know, *So You Think You Can Dance?*[3] Sometimes we watch it and get some moves from that.

Even though the final decision regarding the content of the dance performance lay with the teacher, the creative collaboration between children and between children and the teacher enabled a sense of agency in refugee children, who have experienced such limited opportunities for agency in their lives prior to arriving in their place of final refuge. Aramina and her Iranian friend Ilham noted that this form of collaborative generation of ideas also occurred in classroom contexts, especially when several classes worked together to create a performance for Presentation Day or other special occasions:

> ILHAM: There are three classes....
> ARAMINA: And it was just interesting singing and dancing with other classes....
> ILHAM: 'Cause you get ideas from one class, then another class, then our class, and you put them all together.

Although the school musical activity toward the end of the year was focused on producing well-practiced performances, other activities that took place throughout the year also utilized children's musical preferences for popular music in a less performance-oriented context. For refugees Aramina and Ilham, a sense of familiarity was extended by child-directed listening activities that linked the classroom with external musical preferences, using common technologies through which preferred songs could be accessed. Such activities were used in their classrooms during spare time and as a reward for good behavior.

> ARAMINA: Sometimes we do it at lunchtime. Like only hearing songs; in the class Miss lets us set up our laptop and get songs out and hear them....
> ILHAM: In our class if we finish our work quickly we have free time. Half of the boys goes to that computer, half of the girls goes to that computer [indicating there is one computer on each side of the classroom], and then we play music, play games, and have fun.

Although these activities did not constitute part of the planned curriculum, they acknowledged children's frequently stated preferences for the popular music that was an important part of their out-of-school experience.

Music in the Public Space: The Acculturative Disposition

On numerous occasions during informal discussions and in more formal interviews, children's musical preferences were mentioned. The form that these preferences took was often influenced by the nature of the audience, the relative length of time that children had been in Australia, and the ethnicities of the children concerned. A number of factors influencing the relative degree to which immigrants adopt the identity of the host culture are outlined in the literature. These include the length of time since immigration along with "visible minority status, language use, religion and the proportion of friends who share the same ethnic identity" (Walters, Phythian, and Anisef 2007: 60). Studies in several countries indicate that integration (involving the maintenance of ethnic identity while simultaneously adopting aspects of identity of the host culture) is the preferred acculturative attitude of many immigrants. However, cultural maintenance may be more difficult for immigrants who are members of very small ethnic communities (where there are insufficient members of their communities to support integration), and in these situations immigrants are seen to be more likely to choose assimilation, in which the host country identity is adopted (van Oudenhoven, Prins, and Buunk 1998). An Australian study has found, "The more the immigrants identified with Australia, the more they were accepted by Australians and the higher was their self esteem [and] self efficacy" (Nesdale 2002: 1501). This acceptance was more likely to increase with time in Australia.

In "public" discussions with Fineview children, where a large number of children from various friendship groups and ethnicities were present, children attested that their favorite songs or artists were "English" or "Australian," despite the fact that almost all of the artists named in these public disclosures were American or recorded in the United States. Two such exchanges are outlined below:

R: Do you have any favorite songs?

ARAMINA: Well not that much. I hear a lot of songs. And some of them are my favorite....

R: So where do you hear the songs?

ILHAM: Radio.

ARAMINA: Um, I hear them sometimes on YouTube, sometimes I hear them on television and sometimes I buy CDs and hear them.

R: Are these songs all in English, or other languages?

ARAMINA: Nah, English.

R: So who are your favorite singers then? Do you have any particular ones?

ARAMINA: Well ... [shows reluctance to say more]

AKOI: Did you ask what's your favorite singer?

R: Yeah.

AKOI: I like Chris Brown, Rihanna, Beyoncé, 2Pac, Shakira.

FORTEE: Lady Gaga.

AKOI: I don't like her.... I like Akon, 50 Cent, Kelly ...

R: Who is your favorite musician?

ALIJA: Mine is Hilary Duff and Miley Cyrus.

R: Hilary Duff and Miley Cyrus. Do you have some CDs of them or do you watch them on TV?

ALIJA: I have a lot of CDs of them because I have a computer.

R: Oh, OK. What about you, sweetheart? [Directed at Karuna] It doesn't have to be an English artist either.

KARUNA: I don't know yet.

R: You don't know? That's OK. That's fine.

MONIKA: I like Ne-Yo and Flo Rida. Oh, and Alicia Keys and Beyoncé.

R: Oh, OK. So you learned that from CDs or ...?

MONIKA: Radio ... and CDs. And TV.

NAJAT: Beyoncé and, um ...

R: Can't remember the name?

NAJAT: No.

R: That's OK. Shamiran?

SHAMIRAN: I forgot.

A number of interesting issues emerge from an analysis of these replies. The two most forthcoming responses were from ten-year-old Akoi and twelve-year-old Monika, both of whom are Sudanese Dinka refugees who had been resettled in Australia for a considerable time (Akoi for five years and Monika for seven years). With the exception of Shakira, their favorite artists were all black—African American, Senegalese American, and Barbadian—and their favored genres were rap and R&B. Recordings of all of the named artists were disseminated by a mainstream popular music industry associated with the host country by linguistic affiliation (English) and by regular promotion on Australian television and radio shows. For these girls there seemed to be a racial identification with named artists and (to a lesser extent) genres but a simultaneous affiliation with music in English that was endorsed by mainstream media in the host country. For Alija, a ten-year-old Bosnian girl who had moved to Australia from Germany (her family's first place of refuge) in 2004, the musical choices were Anglo-American singers who were also promoted by the mainstream media in Australia. Fortee (a Liberian refugee who resettled in Australia in 2005) chose the Anglo-American Lady Gaga, but this preference was quickly rejected by her friend Akoi.

The other girls were quite guarded about their musical preferences, sometimes in very marked contrast to their outgoing conversations when interviewed with one or two members of their immediate friendship group. As a number of these children had mentioned quite diverse preferences linked to their home cultures in other discussions (outlined in following sections), their adherence to the prevailing "English" mainstream idea or to nondisclosure of "forgotten" performers was initially quite surprising. However, there may be several explanations for this. One was a school discourse of English as the dominant language. Although there was first-language maintenance through community language classes in Arabic, Assyrian, and Vietnamese, there was a primary emphasis on developing literacy skills in English for all students in the school. As previously discussed, this was enacted musically through the predominant choice of English language songs throughout the school program. English was also the lingua franca of this very linguistically diverse school, and therefore communication between children with different linguistic and ethnic backgrounds could most easily take place in English.

Possibly both of these attributes of the school environment had an effect on acceptance of other languages by children from different linguistic groups within the school context. This was most evident in a discussion of whether children played playground singing games in their first language with children who spoke a different language. In most instances, children reported that they mostly played games in their first language with siblings or friends with same language backgrounds. The reasons for this were discussed by Malaika (a newly arrived ten-year-old girl from the Democratic Republic of Congo), Karuna (a newly arrived eleven-year-old Marathi-speaking Indian girl), her ten-year-old Gujerati-speaking friend Mitali (also newly arrived), ten-year-old Muslim Iraqi Najat (in Australian since 2007), Sudanese Akoi, and eleven-year-old newly arrived Assyrian girl, Shamiran.

> R: Why do you think that is, like the Indian girls are saying to me they only teach those Indian games to Indian girls? Malaika?
>
> MALAIKA: Miss, because the other people can copy it.
>
> R: And so why don't you want them to copy it? It's because it's something from your country only?
>
> MALAIKA: Yeah....
>
> AKOI: Miss, it might be from your religion. And it's from your country and you can't, like the other people can't say it....
>
> MITALI: ...because like, the language is different and maybe they don't understand. And sometimes they really tease us like, "Err, look at your language."
>
> R: Ah, maybe you're afraid that other people will think that the language is funny. Yeah?
>
> NAJAT: Might think, "Oh what are these songs? They're not nice." Then they tease you....
>
> AKOI: Some people laugh.... Because if you say something in your language they might laugh because they think it's funny and they go spread it around and then everybody comes and say, "What are you singing now?" and you get embarrassed....
>
> SHAMIRAN: Miss, sometimes we play games, Arabic games, some English girls or boys come and they say, "You are swearing to us." ...
>
> R: Do they really think you're swearing or are they just teasing you, do you think?...
>
> SHAMIRAN: Teasing.
>
> R: You reckon they're teasing. Does that make you stop playing it or do you still play it anyway?
>
> SHAMIRAN: Stop.
>
> R: You usually stop, yeah? So do you feel a bit embarrassed or...?
>
> SHAMIRAN: No....I ignore them....
>
> NAJAT: Like some people tease me, they keep following me. I just like go somewhere else and just keep continuing my game.

As can be seen from the foregoing transcript such experiences had a different effect on different children. In the public space of the playground, children from relatively large ethnic groups, including Arabic-speaking Muslim and Assyrian Iraqis and Bosnian children felt free to play games in first or second languages from their home culture, secure in the support of a broadly represented ethnic cohort and in spite of mockery by other children. Such security in ethnic identity for some groups was possibly also promoted by the institutional endorsement provided by the in-school community language classes in Arabic and Assyrian. However, children such as the diffident and somewhat marginalized Malaika would only play clapping games learned in her country of origin with her younger brother, because there were no other friends from her ethnic and linguistic background with whom to play.

> R: Malaika, do you know any games from back in the Congo? Did you learn any games from there?
>
> MALAIKA: Yeah.

R: You did? And do you ever teach these games to Akoi and all [of] them [referring
   to her friendship group, largely Sudanese girls]?

MALAIKA: No. My brother.

R: Your brother and you do these games?

MALAIKA: Yeah....

R: Maybe you can teach Monika or anyone, and then you can show me those games,
   because I'd love to see some of those games too from the Congo.

MALAIKA: Miss, me and my brother.

This seemed to be both because of her wish to avoid ridicule and also because
this was one of the small ways in which she could preserve aspects of ethnic identity
that could not otherwise be shared with like others. Although she was repeatedly
invited by members of the research team to show her games just with her brother,
she could not be persuaded to do so. She was, however, included in "English" playground games by her Sudanese friends, thereby achieving a measure of social integration through the games (see video in Web Figure 29.6 ⏺).

The Sudanese Dinka girls who constituted a small but racially visible ethnic
minority group in the school and who had settled in Australia five to seven years previously, did occasionally play games in Dinka with each other, but seemingly not publicly. They were adept players of games designated as English (even though quite a few
of these had nonsense words) and could be regularly found performing these on the
playground. Over time these girls had adopted an assimilative disposition toward the
host country, playing "English" playground games and taking on the musical preferences promulgated by the local media. New arrivals Karuna and Mitali could be seen
playing Indian games on the playground (regardless of the fact that they spoke different Indian languages). However, for these two girls there had been insufficient time to
develop their knowledge of accepted Australian musical preferences relating to popular music, hence Karuna's reply, "I don't know yet." The Iraqi girls who had arrived
relatively recently and were part of much larger ethnic communities both within and
outside the school had considerably more eclectic tastes regarding popular and traditional music, conveyed in "private" conversations with small friendship groups, but
would not reveal these in a "public" space, fearing lack of acceptance.

The reality of private musical lives for many children, regardless of their public protestations was expressed by Ilham, who, as an Iranian refugee arriving in
Australia many years previously, had almost no other ethnic and linguistic affiliates
in either the school or the local community.

ILHAM: At home everyone has their own language or English music. Like me and
   my sister hear Persian music, or English, or she [Aramina] listens to Arabic or
   Assyrian music.... Like everybody Sudanese, Arabic, Indian, any language that
   he [has] at home. Any song.

Despite her minority status and length of time in Australia, Ilham had developed a very idiosyncratic integrative disposition through a strong friendship with
Aramina and their collaborative use of the media and internet. The role of cross-
cultural and within-cultural friendships and mediated music in maintaining or
developing musical identity is explored in the following sections.

"True Friends": Creating, Sharing, and Belonging in the Private Musical Space

Ilham and Aramina were prolific users of television and the internet, especially YouTube, and their initial discussion of musical preferences when alone with the researchers appeared to be normative. They enjoyed watching YouTube performances and reenacting *Australian Idol*, taking turns to sing and act as judges and printing lyrics from the internet to facilitate learning, their eventual aim being to post their own performances on YouTube. Miley Cyrus (the singer/actor of the Disney *Hannah Montana* television and movie franchise) and Rihanna were named as favorite artists. When asked to sing a favorite song they gustily sang parts of the *Hannah Montana* song "True Friends," with modifications to the chorus:

> We are tru-u-u-ue friends;
> You're here 'til the end....
> Don't need to pretend ...
> You're a true friend.

However, the strong bonds entailed in the girls' friendship enabled them to depart from musical convention in numerous ways that illustrated the fact that they did not "need to pretend" in each other's company. They discussed their joint devising of a wide variety of strategies to creatively combine dance and musical ideas.

ARAMINA: And we like dancing also. Sometimes she comes over, or I go over and we make up our own dance....

ILHAM: And sometimes we get hats.... And we shake it around and everything. There are like three hats, they take each [category] like [for instance] slow; your partner is—Aramina; and we see what song do you pick up. You pick up that song and you try to make a dance with that.

The girls went on to explain that these strategies had been further extended to the creation of songs using different tempi, styles, and languages. These included known languages that they spoke (Arabic, Persian, and English) as well as languages (such as "Indian") that were less familiar but learned from cousins, with assistance from the interpretive dictionary function in Google. Their linguistic abilities were used in even greater creative endeavors, the devising of new languages for use in songs and dances.

ILHAM: We try to make our own language that can make songs and anything.

ARAMINA: Sometimes me and her, we get like a paper ... and for example we'll make our own words, and we make them into a song, but in a different language, not a language—we make up our own language....

ILHAM: First we get a paper, all the alphabets in the different language and then we add them all together.

ARAMINA: But not a language that the world knows—our own language...

R: So what's good about, you know, making up songs in a new language?

ILHAM: It's kind of...fun. Like to do if you're bored, you do something interesting you've never done before. A new language that you can learn, or if you don't know what to learn you can say something like Arabic that no one knows, or English. You can talk with them that can't know 'cause it's private, only you and your friend can know...

Although these creative acts were associated with the formation of a private musical world for these two girls, it transpired that YouTube, far from limiting access only to singers associated with the host culture, provided other models for this syncretic activity. YouTube and similar internet video sites opened up globalized musical reach to well-known popular music performers from the girls' home cultures, singing in their first languages but also in conjunction with performers from other countries in other languages.

ILHAM: Some singers in my language sing with a partner.... Asu's from Azerbaijan and Arash is from Iran. And they sing together.... And there's another one, he sings with an Indian girl. But the Indian girl knows a bit of English and Persian, so they mix together.

The internet was thus a liminal zone containing musical associations with the homeland and those of the host country. Ilham and Aramina's cross-cultural musical creativity resulted in additional forms of liminality: between languages, and musical styles and genres, bridging differences and providing enormous freedoms within the private space of their friendship, a space in which they truly belonged.

Music, Symbiotic Friendship, Emotional Release, and the "Enjoyful"

As Ilham and Aramina's experiences illustrate, refugee children within close friendships could create musical spaces of comfort that were socially and psychologically safe. Within these safe spaces children were free to revisit music of the homeland with all its powerful associations, to provide enjoyment, emotional release, and the emotional support attendant on acceptance of a preferred identity.

Another example of such a friendship in which music played a major part was that of Assyrian refugees Shamiran and Sawrina. Whereas Sawrina had lived in Australia for six years, Shamiran had only resettled in Australia in the previous year and had experienced a particularly traumatic childhood both prior to and following resettlement. As members of a large diasporic community in the region, both girls had frequent opportunities to participate in Assyrian social and religious events involving music and had the endorsement of identity provided both by the community and by community language classes in the school. Unlike many other children in the school, they were particularly keen to demonstrate their large repertoire of playground games in Arabic and Assyrian quite publicly on the playground. They also wanted to share their knowledge of other Arabic and Assyrian songs and dances with the researchers and did so in recording sessions over several hours. Although Sawrina's musical interests encompassed "Australian" popular music and playground games, both girls expressed an avowed preference for Arabic and Assyrian music, which Shamiran listened to and performed virtually exclusively.

As they performed their varied repertoire for us, it became very clear that they had a symbiotic teaching and learning relationship. Because Shamiran had attended school in Iraq more recently, she had a more extensive knowledge of Arabic playground games, but Sawrina had also replenished her repertoire on a recent trip to relatives in Syria. Shamiran tended to have a better knowledge of dances, and their knowledge of songs was sometimes complementary but always shared, as discussed after a demonstration of the Arabic playground game Ani La Lingi (orthography of games and songs provided by the informants).

> R: Did you both learn that from somewhere else?
> SHAMIRAN: No, she learned it from me.
> SAWRINA: No, Miss, she learned it from Iraq and I learned it from her. Miss, sometimes we learn it both from Iraq and Syria. Sometimes she learns it from me, and sometimes I learn it from her.... sometimes we know the same one, and sometimes I teach her and she teaches me.

Both girls frequently consulted each other regarding game movements, dance steps, and song texts and would swap roles in performances based on superior knowledge, with one girl singing while the other danced or drummed accompaniment patterns on the improvised drumming surface of a table top. They took great delight in all of these activities and described how some were learned in community-based social events and through satellite TV.

> R: How do you remember these songs and dances and things? ...
> SAWRINA: Miss, from Iraq there's this satellite dish...and there's this channel called Abuvabi Ashtar, Orange TV...and we hear all that.
> SHAMIRAN: When we go here in Australia, we go to party and they dance there.
> R: And they dance those things as well?
> SAWRINA: Yeah, Miss, we go to weddings.... My mum and my dad, they'll go weddings. I watch them. I watch my parents dance, watch everybody and I learn.
> SHAMIRAN: When I go like wedding, I dance with them 'cause I know everything.
> SAWRINA: Sometimes we dance. Sometimes in our religion, at weddings, sometimes you're allowed to sing, so we know all these songs.

However, at times, elements of traumatic events surfaced in their performances. For example, the game Ani La Lingi contained sinister words and movements:

> SAWRINA: There's a police coming and she has to hit me with her thing [demonstrates police baton]. [More text is translated] And how a soldier does that [demonstrates salute] and how a soldier shakes people's hand [demonstrates rigid handshake].

Although this game may have originated in circumstances not associated with war, it is possible that its enactment enabled the children to express some of the fears attendant on previous experiences of war and oppression through the means of a pleasurable game that verbally disempowered the symbols of violence and repression, police and soldiers. (See full transcription in Figures 29.7 and 29.8. A recording of "Ani La Lingi" can be heard online as Web Figure 29.9 ●.)

The two girls begin the game facing each other, about 2 meters apart.

Figures 29.7: Transcription of "Ani La Lingi."

Figures 29.8: Transcription of "Ani La Lingi."

The use of music as a vehicle for emotional expression was poignantly demonstrated by Shamiran, who spontaneously asked to sing an Arabic song, "Lo Ishotuya," meaning "I wish I lived with my dad." It had been learned from satellite television in Iraq, but to Shamiran it had a special meaning.

> SHAMIRAN: I sing it every day. I sing it every day.... Because my dad die, so I sing it every day.... Every time I sing it, I cry.

In further discussion with teachers, it was revealed that Shamiran's father had been kidnapped and killed and that she spent considerable time at school crying, in great contrast to her delight in performing the playground songs, traditional Assyrian songs and dances, and some Arabic popular songs with her friend and in our company. It was clear that music provided Shamiran and, to a lesser extent, Sawrina with different forms of emotional release. Sawrina said that when Shamiran sang that song she also remembered the death of her own infant sister. However, when asked if there were other songs of emotional significance, she said,

> SAWRINA: Yeah, Miss, but the other ones are enjoyful.
> R: The other ones are joyful.
> SAWRINA: Yeah, Miss, you're good to have a life.
> R: They make you feel good to be alive?
> SAWRINA: Yeah.

To exemplify "enjoyfulness," she and Shamiran performed a well-known Arabic pop song, "A Tap Tap," taking turns singing and drumming (the title of the song refers to the sound of drumming), followed by several other Arabic popular songs jointly performed by both girls and learned from parents, satellite television, the internet, or imported CDs from Iraq.

The comfort derived from music was further shown by Shamiran's fervent singing of two hymns, "Salm Maryam" and "Hallbrini Sanied" from the Assyrian church that both she and Sawrina attended in Sydney.

> SHAMIRAN: Can I sing, how I say for you, like the church song? It's very nice. [She sang with occasional graceful movements, her face transfigured, as if lit from within].
> SAWRINA: It's like a song. It's a song. It's like praying and singing at the same time.

Both girls told us that they sang these hymns every night before they went to sleep as a form of prayer, a way of providing consolation and reassurance in what were still in many ways troubled lives.

CONCLUSION

Music was found in the lives of many refugee and newly arrived immigrant children in this Sydney school. Depending on the length of time since resettlement, individual proclivities and interests, the presence and size of diasporic groups, and institutional endorsement, music had different functions for children in this demographic. Its presence in regular planned activities in the school provided opportunities for host country social integration and language development. Creative involvement with music and dance in both formal school and informal out-of-school settings gave highly disempowered refugee children some form of agency. A variety of technologies, particularly the internet, facilitated children's contact with the music of the home culture as well as that of the host culture, sometimes providing a virtual and extended diasporic musical community in the absence of a real one in the host environment. As an integral part of human experience, music offered important ways for children in the process of resettlement to draw comfort, express emotion, and connect with others, because, in the words of a twelve-year-old Sudanese girl, "Music, it can show you about friendship, love, and all those things."

ACKNOWLEDGMENTS

I wish to acknowledge the assistance of Laura Corney, Samantha Dieckmann, Jwan Youkhanis, and the children and staff members of Fineview Public School. The project was supported by a research grant from the University of Sydney.

NOTES

1 Assyrians are a Christian ethnic minority group that originated in the Middle East. Assyrians from Iraq constitute the largest number of refugees at the school, due to consistent persecution in their country of origin, particularly since 2003.
2 Formal interviews were organized by the school, and children in informal interviews were self-selecting. Most interviewees were girls, and this is reflected in the interview transcripts. However, boys were observed in special interest groups, during in-class activities, and on the playground.
3 *So You Think You Can Dance?* is a popular reality television program in which generally unknown contestants, dancing in a variety of genres, compete to win a major prize.

REFERENCES

Aroche, Jorge, and Mariano Coello. 2002. "Towards a Systematic Approach for the Treatment Rehabilitation of Torture and Trauma Survivors in Exile." Accessed April 29, 2010. http://www.startts.org.au/default.aspx?id=116.
Bhabha, Jacqueline, and Mary Crock. 2007. *Seeking Asylum Alone: Unaccompanied and Separated Children and Refugee Protection in Australia, the U.K. and the U.S.* Annandale, Australia: Themis Press.
Campbell, Patricia Shehan. 1998. *Songs in Their Heads: Music and Its Meaning in Children's Lives.* New York: Oxford University Press.
Campbell, Patricia Shehan. 2010. *Songs in Their Heads: Music and Its Meaning in Children's Lives.* 2nd ed. New York: Oxford University Press.
Diehl, Keila. 2002. *Echoes from Dharamsala: Music in the Life of a Tibetan Refugee Community.* Berkeley: University of California Press.
Hamilton, Richard, and Dennis Moore, eds. 2004. *Educational Interventions for Refugee Children: Theoretical Perspectives and Implementing Best Practice.* London: RoutledgeFalmer.
Harris, David Alan. 2007. "Dance/Movement Therapy Approaches to Fostering Resilience and Recovery among African Adolescent Torture Survivors." *Torture* 17 (2): 134–155.

Heidenrich, Verena. 2005. "Music Therapy in War-Effected Areas." *Intervention* 3 (2): 129–134.

Jones, Carolyn, Felicity Baker, and Toni Day. 2004. "From Healing Rituals to Music Therapy: Bridging the Cultural Divide between Therapist and Young Sudanese Refugees." *The Arts in Psychotherapy* 31 (2): 89–100.

Ladkani, J. L. 2001. "Dabke Music and Dance and the Palestinian Refugee Experience: On the Outside Looking In." PhD diss., Florida State University.

Marsh, Kathryn. 2008. *The Musical Playground: Global Tradition and Change in Children's Songs and Games*. New York: Oxford University Press.

Nesdale, Drew. 2002. "Acculturation Attitudes and the Ethnic and Host-Country Identification of Immigrants." *Journal of Applied Social Psychology* 32 (7): 1488–1507.

Osborne, Nigel. 2009. "Music for Children in Zones of Conflict and Post-conflict: A Psychobiological Approach." In *Communicative Musicality: Exploring the Basis of Human Companionship*, edited by Stephen Malloch and Colwyn Trevarthen, 331–356. Oxford: Oxford University Press.

Pesek, Albinca. 2009. "War on the Former Yugoslavian Territory. Integration of Refugee Children into the School System and Musical Activities as an Important Factor for Overcoming War Trauma." In *Music in Motion: Diversity and Dialogue in Europe*, edited by Bernd Clausen, Ursula Hemetek, and Eva Saether, 359–370. Bielefeld: Transcript Verlag.

Reyes, Adelaida. 1999. *Songs of the Caged, Songs of the Free: Music and the Vietnamese Refugee Experience*. Philadelphia: Temple University Press.

Sebastian, Samantha. 2008. "A Multicase Study of the Ways Music Learning Is Used to Meet the Social, Emotional and Cultural Challenges Experienced by Refugees and Asylum Seekers in Sydney." Honors thesis, Sydney Conservatorium of Music. Accessed April 29, 2010. http://ses.library.usyd.edu.au/handle/2123/2241.

Sutton, Julie P., ed. 2002. *Music, Music Therapy and Trauma*. London: Jessica Kingsley Publishers.

United Nations Convention Relating to the Status of Refugees, Resolution 429 (V), Article 1, 1951.

Van Oudenhoven, Jan Pieter, Karin S. Prins, and Bram P. Buunk. 1998. "Attitudes of Minority and Majority Members towards Adaptation of Immigrants." *European Journal of Social Psychology* 28: 995–1013.

Vasta, Ellie, and Stephen Castles. 1996. *The Teeth Are Smiling: The Persistence of Racism in Multicultural Australia*. St Leonards, Australia: Allen & Unwin.

Walters, David, Kelli Phythian, and Paul Anisef. 2007. "The Acculturation of Canadian Immigrants: Determinants of Ethnic Identification with the Host Society." *Canadian Review of Sociology and Anthropology* 44 (1): 37–64.

30

ENCULTURATIONAL DISCONTINUITIES IN THE MUSICAL EXPERIENCE OF THE WAGOGO CHILDREN OF CENTRAL TANZANIA

KEDMON MAPANA

INTRODUCTION

The location was the Mwenge Secondary School performance hall, known as "Ukumbi wa Mashindano" (Competition Hall) in the town of Singida in central Tanzania, almost twelve hours west of Dar es Salaam by bus. The occasion was the UKWATA (the National Interdominational Christian Youth Organization) National Conference, June 18–23, 2008. Christian secondary school students, ages sixteen to twenty-two, had come to the conference from all over Tanzania, and I was invited to be one of the judges of the choral competition, a featured activity of the conference. Twenty-five choirs had each prepared three songs to perform in the competition. The first song was selected from a hymnbook for all the choirs, while two additional songs were selected by each of the choirs for their performance: one in Western notation to demonstrate the ability of choir members to read music, and the third from the repertoire of traditional music of a Tanzanian cultural group, using appropriate instruments, costumes, and dance. The intent of the third song was to provide the young singers with a means of demonstrating their local cultural identity.

It was stunning to see and hear the mostly student-aged audience shouting, ululating, and clapping their hands following each of the twenty-five choirs' performances of their traditional Tanzanian song selection. The church hymns and notated Western songs, on the other hand, were invariably greeted with polite applause. It was consistently evident that these secondary school students felt deeply the musical traditions of their particular ethnic-cultural group and that they were also inspired and enamored of the traditional musical expressions of the students of other Tanzanian traditional cultures. Following the competition, I spoke with students about how they learned their traditional songs. The majority of them reported that they frequently sang these songs in their homes, their churches, and in the different social contexts of their communities. There was no mention by students of having ever encountered the traditional songs within their curricular studies, as these lively and deeply meaningful songs lived for them far outside the borders of their schools and schoolyards.

The positive responses of audiences to the traditional songs and students' own responses to my queries were telling. They raised questions for me: where is the place of the traditional music of Tanzania's many cultural groups in the curriculum of Tanzanian schools? How do Tanzanian children and youth express themselves musically when left to their own interests and musical decision making? How do they use the music they learn at home for understanding music, culture, and the world?

Further questions developed, too, concerning music learning and transmission, musical identities, and the place of family, neighborhood, and school in the raising of children and youth to be knowledgeable of their cultural roots and the contemporary circumstances of their nation and its regions. What is the continuity (or discontinuity) of Tanzanian children's music learning from home to school? Does the absence of traditional music cultures in schools negatively affect Wagogo and Tanzanian national culture? Is it feasible for Tanzanian children to learn in school the music from their specific ethnic-cultural groups and from selected regions of the country as well as to learn a national musical expression? Could the recognition by teachers of their local musical expressions be an initial step that might eventually lead to the study of music of the world (including the West)? These questions are all interrelated and sit on a sliding scale that extends from informal, in-family enculturation to the formal education of schooling. They form the basis of this chapter.

The development of children's musical skills and understandings is necessarily linked to their first musical experiences (Campbell and Scott-Kassner 2010). Further, it is widely understood that the musical education of children requires their experiences in sound before symbol (Gordon 1993; Orff 1966). However, the practice of music education within Tanzanian schools does not adhere to these principles. How did the present system develop, and what can be done to honor in a systematic education the musical repertoire and learning process that comprise children's enculturation?

Music in Tanzanian Schools

As an academic discipline, the subject of music was introduced into Tanzanian schools during the colonial period. The study of music featured Western music theory and notation, using British concepts and terms (e.g., crotchet equals quarter note). In 1963, only two years after Tanzania's independence, a new all-subject curriculum was agreed on for use in schools nationwide (Edmond and Sefu 1977). However, the substance of the content of the syllabi for subjects such as music did not change, as British-styled content was continued without modification. In fact, even in 2008, when educators sought to revise the 1995 "A-levels" (the advanced-level music syllabus), they were unable to do so in a substantive way because the advanced-level syllabus had to remain linked to the existing ordinal-level syllabus that continues to be supported by the Tanzanian Institute of Education. Western music theory and notation are considered basic knowledge in the primary and secondary schools of Tanzania. As kindergartens and preprimary early learning initiatives are recently emerging in Tanzania, they, too, are following the British-styled curriculum. Even young Tanzanian children are learning symbols before sound, and the songs they sing are not the songs (or the style) of the music they were weaned on. Herein lies the problem first illustrated in the opening scenario of the choral competition at Mwenge. For James Carlsen (1994), a problem is a fact (in this case, Western music dominates the existing Tanzanian national music curriculum), which is a barrier to the perceived need for change. Little music of Tanzania appears in the school curriculum, thus causing discontinuity of children's music learning as well as the inability to focus on the knowledge and skills appropriate for a variety of Tanzanian music cultures. There is no existing curriculum in Tanzania that is based upon the local musical expressions of various Tanzanian ethnic cultures. A solution to the problem, as well as a foundation for further studies, involves closing the knowledge gap that is created by the absence of a curriculum of traditional and contemporary music of Tanzania. The result could be a curriculum that encompasses local, national, and even international musical expressions, an all-African curriculum that is grounded in the first and continuing musical experiences of the family unit and local community.

Julius Kambarage Nyerere, the first president of Tanzania, maintained that "culture is the essence and spirit of any nation. A country which lacks its own culture is no more than a collection of people without the spirit which makes them a nation" (1966: 186). Nyerere was unfortunately using the term "nation" in the way of colonialists, rather than to reflect the perspective of resident indigenous Africans on the sociocultural and political unit that was represented by (then) Tanganyika. Yet Nyerere also argued for music that was Tanzanian and African. He remarked,

> When we were at school we were taught to sing the songs of the Europeans. How many were taught the songs of the Wanyamwezi or Wahehe? Many of us have learned to dance the "rumba" or "chachacha," to "rock n' roll" and to "twist" and even to dance the "waltz" and the "fox-trot." But how many of us can dance or have even heard of the Gombesugu, the Mangala, the Konge, Nyang'umumi, Kiduo or Lele Mama? Many of us can play the guitar, the piano, or other European instruments. How many Africans in Tanganyika, particularly among the educated, can play the African drum? (1966: 186)

Nyerere's reflection here has deep ramifications for the musical education of children of Tanzania's various cultural groups, including the Wagogo of the Dodoma region of central Tanzania.

Raising issues of curricular change may create strong reactions in political and educational circles, yet this conversation is long overdue. It is essential that there be a redesign of curricular content and method in music across Tanzania, one that takes into account theoretical perspectives emanating from the research in anthropology, education, ethnomusicology, and sociology. For the sake of Tanzanian children and youth who grow up in living local cultures, such a curriculum must embrace the musical expressions of local Tanzanian cultural groups as well as the musical treasures of selected other people and places in Tanzania and across the African continent.

ENCULTURATION IN MUSIC AND IN SOCIETY

Enculturation is the gradual acquisition of the characteristics and norms of a family, community, and culture (Herskovits 1948). Through experience, observation, and instruction, children are enculturated from infancy onward into the practices and values of their local environment. Music is one of multiple facets of their culture that they absorb naturally, such that, as surely as they learn to comprehend and speak their mother-tongue language, they also learn the songful expressions of their community. Musical enculturation as a sociocultural process through which musical culture is transmitted and acquired by children has been defined and discussed by Campbell ([1998] 2010) and McCarthy (1999) among others. The teaching and learning process has been studied for its sociocultural contexts, including both family and school, and informal and formal realms by which music is acquired by children (Campbell 1991; Figueroa 1995; Lundquist 1998, 2002; Marsh 2008; Merriam 1964; Nettl [1983] 2005; Szego 2002). The association of enculturation theory with teaching and learning offers a logical framework for the development of a culturally sensitive curriculum that celebrates the music of the family and local community, as well as national, pan-African, and global musical expressions.

As a broader construct linking music to myriad other features of culture, Margaret Mead was fascinated by enculturation in her study of the informal process by which Samoan youth of the southern Pacific Islands acquired a sense of their cultural priorities (1930). As an anthropologist, she examined the process of learning a culture from infancy onward, including the values, attitudes, and beliefs of a culture and all of its corresponding behavioral patterns. Melville Herskovits coined the term, explaining enculturation as the aspects of the learning experience "by means of which, initially, and in later life, [an individual] achieves competence in his culture" (1948: 39). Merriam, a leading scholar in the formative years of ethnomusicology, expanded the anthropologists' definition by saying that the word "enculturation refers to the process by which the individual learns his culture and... this is a never-ending process continuing throughout the life span of the individual" (1964: 146).

Nettl identified ethnomusicology as a discipline that engages scholars who have "grappled most... with the problems of studying music both in its own cultural context and also from a comparative perspective, and with ways of seeing what it is that music does in culture" (1998: 23). The field embraces studies of enculturation and of sociocultural processes of how music is taught and learned, both in general terms (Merriam 1964; Nettl [1983] 2005) and in specific cultures (e.g., McCarthy 1999; Rice 2004). The construct of enculturation as discussed in ethnomusicological terms (Nettl 1998) is an intellectually defensible foundation for the creation of a music curriculum that embraces Tanzanian local musical cultures as well as indigenous cultures across the African continent.

Recent scholarship by educators documents the interest in the connections of home and family activity to formal schooling. Weinreich articulated that "the primary processes involved in identity development are ones of enculturation of cultural elements, not acculturation" (2009: 124). He made the case for both formal and informal learning being deeply connected to an individual's enculturation, referring to schooling situations in which students identify with cultural elements of "influential others" (2009: 127) in the process of enculturation. Weinrich further postulated, "Enculturation references the agentic individual's process of identification with whatever cultural elements of influential others are available to the person" (2009: 127). Questions arise as to who within the culture constitutes the "influential others" and whether teachers who deliver a child-centered and culturally appropriate curriculum would qualify in this role.

Tishman et al. argued for environmentally conscious enculturation, asserting that "learners tend to act in ways cued and supported by the surrounding environment" and then seek to identify an enculturation model of teaching (1993149–150). This model advocates "cultural exemplars, cultural interactions, and direct instruction in cultural knowledge and activities" in a culturally sensitive curriculum, and its qualities are employed in curriculum and instruction in order to "a) provide exemplars of the disposition, b) encourage and orchestrate student-student and teacher-student interactions involving the disposition, and c) directly teach the disposition" (ibid.: 150). In her research of musical learning by young children, Adachi resonated with the presence of cultural exemplars, especially regarding adult cueing and the use of musical signs in "the adult roles of transmitter, practice partner and co-player and...how these adult roles facilitate the musical [enculturation] of the child" (1994: 28). Likewise, Gibson (2009) studied "musical parenting" within a community of married university students and described in considerable detail the songs parents sang to their infants and toddlers.

As a widely revered educationist, Jerome Bruner (1996) championed constructivism in his vision of reality construction as a product of meaning making shaped by traditions and encouraged educators to assist young people in using these to better adapt to the world. While some constructivist theorists support the premise of students as creative agents (Bruner 1996; Dewey 1938) who create knowledge by themselves based on their ongoing experiences (in order that they discover new ideas), it is realistic to assume that students know a fair balance of discovery and sequential learning, the latter guided by the goals and procedures of trained teachers. In fact, this balance is integral to the continuum of enculturation into education. When teachers acknowledge the home and family experiences of their students and offer them further knowledge and tools, they ensure that their students learn though a culturally conscious continuous process. It is this enculturative quality that pays heed to the early (and continuing) learning by children away from school, thus supporting optimum learning and creating an environment that is conducive to the development of young minds.

Osberg and Biesta view enculturation as a collaborative process and acknowledge the challenges of education in contemporary multicultural societies in which preference for "unguided learning" and "planned enculturation" raises the question of "who decides what or *whose* culture should be promoted through education" (2008: 315). They recommend experiences that create a "space of emergence" in which the "singularity and uniqueness" (ibid.: 315) of each student can emerge in interactions with a cultural experience that is shared by teacher and students. Felder and Prince (2007) refer to "the many faces of inductive teaching and learning" that encompasses enculturation as well as inquiry-based learning, collaborative teaching, participatory teaching, student-centered teaching, problem-based learning, and discovery learning, to mention a few. In all of these approaches to learning, the teacher's role is to facilitate the development of student understanding, skills, and values. With a global awareness of the importance of student-centered learning, Tanzania and other African nations are shifting away from the nineteenth-century top-down lecture method in which the teacher is the source of knowledge and the pedagogical task is to feed information to students to absorb. While teacher-dominated direct lecture instruction is effective in certain instructional circumstances, a balance of teacher and student engagement is key (Arthur Ellis, personal communication, April 27, 2010). Likewise, a top-down Western-oriented curricular content (and its inherent delivery systems) does not lead to the achievement of student-centered needs nor to the continued development of local community knowledge even as national and global priorities settle in.

Student-centered learning is of considerable interest to music educators, as are issues of children's early musical development, their natural and unschooled musical interests, and the manner in which musical enculturation evolves (Campbell [1998] 2010; Gibson 2009). Lum and Campbell (2007) examined the musical "surrounds" of an elementary school, noting the playful presence of music in children's free periods and the manner in which classroom teachers of language arts and physical education inherently (and sometimes unknowingly) inserted musical matter into their classes, so that children were regularly experiencing singing, chanting, and "rhythmicking" through the school day. Watts (2009) studied the recollections of the musical girlhoods of four generations of women (and several ten-year-old girls) and found that while none were involved professionally in music as adults, most remembered and valued their extensive engagement in informal listening, singing, dancing, and singing games at school.

Enculturation is powerful and widely evident, and cultural beliefs and practices like music that are present in families and communities are naturally shared by adults with children, thus providing them with their cultural foundations and identities. Friedrich Froebel's use of playful musical activity in the educational program called "kindergarten" (1889), newly evolving at the close of the nineteenth century, is an exemplar of the manner in which local musical and cultural expressions are identified in the natural environment and integrated into school practice. Likewise, contemporary programs in early childhood education provide scheduled times for large group circle shares, small group projects, and free-play time, much of which is threaded with song, movement, stories, poems, and dramatic play (Campbell and Scott-Kassner 2010). The weave of local music into educational experiences is a natural act, and in such a context as a Wagogo village in central Tanzania, this continuation of music and culture from the outside into the curriculum is logical, relevant, and likely to be effective in the development of the knowledge base and cultural identity of children.

Morrison et al. (2008) and Demorest et al. (2008) engaged in systematic study of the impact of enculturation in the retention and valuing of music, thus underscoring earlier work by Campbell (1998), who observed that children entering the music classroom at five years of age are typically steeped in the musical experience they have known at home and in the family. In thumbnail sketches of various American cultural communities, Campbell (2010) offered portraits of musical enculturation in the earliest years of children's development and noted differentiated musical experiences for children of African American, Irish American, and Vietnamese American families. Returning to the lacunae that result from curricular content that falls from on-high dictates of state department officers of education with little interest in the music of local communities, a striking reality is portrayed in this question: What would happen if Anglo-American children (or children of other ethnic-cultural communities), who have been musically shaped by their parents in their familial experience, were expected almost immediately in school to be able to sing Wagogo, or Tanzanian, or other African songs, while they clapped and danced to the rhythms? The challenge would surely be an unreasonable and insurmount-able one, for children would first need to have heard this or other similar music repeatedly in order to know it and to have integrated it into their ears, minds, and bodies. They would need to have been enculturated into this music for them to par-ticipate fully in it from its first formal introduction to them in school. Alternately, there would need to be patient teachers standing by, repeatedly facilitating experi-ences, guiding and monitoring the capacities of students to know music that is not of their own background. Of course, this music could eventually be learned but not without the challenges of acquiring a "musical vocabulary" different from that of children's own earlier enculturation. Thus, enculturational discontinuities arise.

Consider the challenge of Wagogo children and children of other Tanzanian cultural groups and in other parts of the African continent who are led headfirst into the study of Western music theory and notation in Tanzanian schools. While learning can be achieved, children need to contend with musical conceptualizations far from their core experience and to work their way through enculturational dis-continuities. Another way forward is to feature the home and community cultural expressions of children as well as "distant music" in a curriculum, validating them, and building from children's local knowledge to an understanding of people from elsewhere on the globe. The benefits of a tandem of cultural experiences within a system of educating children and youth are many.

Musical Enculturation in a Wagogo Village

A close-up of musical enculturation processes among the Wagogo people of cen-tral Tanzania provides a case for the study of informal learning of culture (and musical culture). The Wagogo are a Bantu ethnic group, one of 120 East African cultural-linguistic groups living within the boundary of the Republic of Tanzania. The Wagogo are located in the center of Tanzania, in the region of Dodoma, Tanzania's national capital. The Wagogo comprise 3 percent (1,735,000 people) of the population of Tanzania. They live largely in rural villages and are primarily engaged in agriculture and pastoral activities. Many are farmers on small plots of family land, growing maize, millet, and sorghum for food and peanuts and sun-flower seeds for trade. Some herd cows, goats, and sheep, traveling to and from their family homes every day to wide-open land where there are low grasses for grazing. Cattle are valuable in Wagogo culture, as they can be seen as a source of finance, trade, or bride wealth (i.e., dowry).

In considering the enculturation of Wagogo children, it is noteworthy that kin-dergarten did not exist in my village of Chamwino during my childhood (and is a recent intervention). I grew up musical, however, because my father and mother were musicians. My father was a drummer, dancer, and singer, playing in the

Figure 30.1: Leah Milimo playing three *muheme* drums at the Wagogo music festival held at Chamwino village, Dodoma, Tanzania. Photo by Chandra Rampersad. July 30, 2011.

church-oriented *mapelembo* music tradition, and my mother was also a singer in St. Peter's (then called Maduma) Anglican Church. My musical participation in *mapelembo* music served the purpose of developing my musical skills and abilities.

A child's musical development begins even prior to birth, with musical behaviors of one form or another evident across the lifespan (Keil and Campbell 2011; Welch 2005). Early enculturation fosters children's musical development and the realization of musical potential. For Wagogo children like me, *mapelembo* provided a head start to knowing music, and of being musical. I recall one song, "Wadala wakulonga" (see Figure 30.2) that was popular in my childhood and remains so, confirming a contention by Campbell (1999) that every child, adolescent, and adult, in various stages of their life course, identifies with music they consider powerful to them personally.

> Translation: The elder women say (with joy) "Our children are late getting to the farms because of Elisha. When the drum of *Maduma* rings, it makes our children be late getting to the farms."

When my father played the drum at the *mapalembo* celebration, adults and children would joyfully dance to his music, sometimes well into the night. Children would forget about bedtime and arrive back to their homes quite late. Consequently, they would also sleep late in the morning, which delayed their work on the family farm. Parents thus tried to convince children not to be involved in this dancing, but the drumming was too appealing to them and they could not stay away.

I was one of the children in our Wagogo village, Chamwino, who loved dancing to my father's music. One day my mother said, "You are singing like your father. You

Figure 30.2: Transcription of "Wadala wakulonga."

have imitated him. You used to go to the *mapalembo* dance late into the night—even when you were not allowed." While there was some admonishment within the comment, it was also meant (and received by me) as a high compliment, in that I had developed my father's musical style. Imitation is a frequent component of the enculturation process, which assumes that attentive listening is also very much in play in order to acquire the subtleties of stylistic tone (Campbell 2001a). In the natural learning process, "imitation involves trying to reproduce the mental images that have been stored in the brain" (Criss 2008: 44). It is sometimes described as mimicking, and is "a natural ability we have when there is a performance model to observe" (ibid.).

In my own early childhood, musical enculturation was in a constantly active state such that music was simply "there," and there was never a day that my father told me to sit down and learn how to sing, dance, or play and make a musical instrument. As in the whole-language approach to learning to read, in which reading is "caught rather than taught" in any formal sense, musical experiences were immediately accessible and all-enveloping. My father would find me singing, dancing, and drumming. Sometimes he would wonder, and also admire, how I managed to learn the songs and the dance movements, and neither of us considered then that it was my own imitation of my father that developed my skills and understandings. This process applies to the Wagogo children in Chamwino today, too, who participate alongside adults in musical events (see Figures 30.1 and 30.4). As is also the case in rural Bulgaria (Rice 2004), among the Wagogo, musical repertoire and skills are imparted through a social processes, as children grow into the music as an integral component of their heritage. Campbell and Scott-Kassner (2010) asserted that as children play with other children and socialize with adults, they acquire music and other realms of cultural knowledge. Children's musical play consists of familiar and new songs that are transmitted intact by adults (and other children) as well as spontaneously created new musical inventions.

Songs of children's musical play are a reality, as in my own experience as a five-year-old child. Under moonlit skies, we children gathered outside the house and played singing games by ourselves, beyond the influence of adults. "Kazuguni" is a song from that time and place (see Figure 30.3).

"Kazuguni" is a backward or lazy child who emerges one day from the back of the class enthusiastic and energized and finds his place at the head of the class. The

Figure 30.3: Transcription of traditional Gogo song, "Kazuguni."

message to us children was that while we might have been behind economically, socially, and educationally, we could overcome these challenges with effort and focus. Through songs like this one, we learned music, movement, and the underlying meanings of the song texts.

A Fitting Curriculum: Local, National, and Pan-African Music

Based upon enculturation theory and the actual experiences of my own Wagogo childhood, I am proposing a tentative framework for the creation of a music curriculum that would remove enculturational discontinuities and help to sustain cultural identity. I am encouraged by Bruner's position, too, that "we need to realize human

Figure 30.4: Wagogo children performing *ngomayamuheme* at the Wagogo music festival, July 30, 2011 at Chamwino village, Dodoma regio n, Tanzania. Photo by Chandra Rampersad.

potential, but we need to maintain a culture's integrity and stability. We need to recognize differing native talents, but we need to equip all with the tools of the culture. We need to respect the uniqueness of local identities and experiences" (1996: 164).

The proposed curricular framework for music in the schools of Tanzania addresses local concerns and national agendas as well as both traditional and contemporary music expressions. Contemporary music is seeded in traditional music, utilizing its instruments, rhythmic material, and melodic features, even as it is fused with features of Western-oriented music of the popular media. In a sense, contemporary music may be an extension of traditional music sensibilities and may have been some of the music in which children are enculturated at an early age through TV, radio, and the internet. If not explicitly local in style, the various rock and popular genres that filter through the media are decidedly national music performed by star musicians claimed by a broad swath of the nation's population.

Traditional expressions, such as Wagogo music, would reasonably be included in schools that serve Wagogo children due to its local significance, even as it would also make an important contribution to the content of a national music curriculum for Tanzanian schools. At the very least, a half dozen local music cultures could be considered cultural features for their specific songs and dance styles. Importantly, national curriculum directives could prescribe the integration of the local music no matter what the cultural composite of the school may be, and various community members could be conscripted by teachers to perform and engage children in music and dance experiences. These local musical expressions would fit neatly alongside nationally recognized genres of Tanzania, and beyond these genres would be a selection of musical expressions from throughout Africa.

Ngoma is a keystone concept of the music of sub-Saharan Africa, and one that could function as a means of introducing students in school to the musical world of Tanzania as well as a common or shared principle that distinguishes music of the nation and region from other parts of the world. It is particularly noteworthy that in precolonial Tanzania, *ngoma* (typically used to refer to traditional dances) was evident in every cultural community. *Ngoma* performances differed from one ethnic group to another in various villages and regions. The word *ngoma* was also differently interpreted and could mean singing, dancing, and playing a musical instrument. In fact, *ngoma* may be a musical instrument as well as an indication of a social function or an event such as an initiation ceremony (Nyoni 1998). Despite its varied meanings, it could be readily employed as a unifying curricular concept in musical study.

In Tanzania, dances and songs are based in people's way of living and are much affected by their physical environment. For example, among the Maasai of northern Tanzania, long rhythm sticks normally accompany dances, as the Maasai are from a pastoral society in which walking sticks are a constant presence. In eastern Tanzania, the music of Wazaramo is often associated with initiation ceremonies, and among the Wagogo musical practices are songs and dances expressive of life as pastoralists in agricultural work. *Ngoma* performances occur at weddings, at work, in initiation ceremonies, and in other rituals with the aim of building social solidarity, and communication and of imparting values and norms from one generation to another. *Ngoma* can be utilized as a way of enculturating children in the values of their community and preserving a culture's continuity.

The national curriculum for primary and secondary school's "O"-level could include Tanzanian traditional and contemporary music from a variety of cultural groups. In the postcolonial era, from 1961 onward, many expressive musical forms emerged in Tanzania, some of them much influenced by "visitors" from within and beyond the African continent. Musical forms meant to educate and sustain musical values through the generations were joined by those based on commerce and entertainment, so that additional musical forms were developed in Tanzania such as *kwaya* (choir) or *muziki wa injili* (gospel choir), *muziki wa mwambao (taarab)*, *muziki wa dansi* (jazz band), and the current "flavor" of hip-hop music known as *bongo flava*.

Of the traditional *ngoma* music of Tanzania's local communities, ensembles that feature drumming have become popular in Dar es Salaam and other urban centers. Electric guitars play with traditional drums in this urban-style *ngoma*, and notable *ngoma* groups in Tanzania include the Muungano Cultural Troup, the Parapanda Theatre Arts, and Sisi Tambala. All feature the use of indigenous rhythms for expressing contemporary sociopolitical issues.

Choral music is widespread among Christian believers, and many large, almost "mass" choirs are found in churches. Two church-based choral practices are distinguished from one another by the presence or absence of instrumental accompaniment. Church singing bands are known as *kwaya* (*Muziki wa injili*), in which Western musical instruments such as electric guitars and keyboards accompany a large group of singers who perform indigenous Tanzanian melodies. Outstanding examples of *kwaya* with instruments are Unjilist (gospel) Kijitonyama, African Inland Church Vijana (Youth) Chang'ombe, and the Nazareth choir Kurasini. A second choral music practice features Western-based four-part a cappella music without the accompaniment of musical instruments. Examples of unaccompanied choirs are KKKT Kipawa and Ubungo Anglican. Characteristic of these choirs is that singing is but one feature of their gatherings, as they function as social groups who study the Bible, raise their children together, play games together, and provide support to each other in times of need. Choirs outside the context of church are few and far between, but their secular nature may focus on issues or political campaigns as in the case of Tanzania One Theatre (TOT).

Taarab is a musical genre found in the Tanzanian coastal region and out on the island of Zanzibar, known also in Swahili as *muziki wa mwambao*. The origin of *taarab* can be traced to Arab and Islamic infusion in the eighteenth century and has been represented by such esteemed performers as Siti binti Saad, Bi Kidude, and Issa Matona. *Taarab* is sung poetry, so the lyrics and vocal features are crucial. Musical instruments such as the *oud* (lute), *qanun* (zither), violin, cello, electric organ, and small drums called *ki-dumbak* are commonly used. *Taarab* exists in two styles: orchestral *taarab* (*taarab asilia*) and modern *taarab*. In the older *taarab asilia* style, singing is performed in unison and while sitting, and there is no dancing, while instruments like *ki-dumbak* drums, violin, *mkwasa* (claves), *cherewa* (maracas), accordion, and *qanum* are commonly played. The Zanzibar Culture Club and Ikhwani Safaa are examples of musical clubs representing the traditional *taarab asilia*. On the other hand, modern *taarab* employs electric guitars, electric keyboard, and drum kit machines, and dancing to this music is a vital component of the experience.

Muziki wa dansi (jazz band) is yet another important form of musical expression in Tanzania, especially in the urban areas, in which bands play weekly in restaurants and clubs. Mbaraka Minshehe was the lead singer, guitarist, and composer of this Tanzanian jazz style in the 1960s, working with the group called Moro Jazz Band. By the 1970s, DDC Mlimani Park Orchestra was formed, famed for the intricate poetry of their lyrics and featuring renowned musicians Hassani Bitcuka and Cosmas Chidumule, while in the 1980s, Hugo Kisima started the International Orchestra Safari Sound. Bands like the Kilimanjaro Band (Njenje), Msondo Ngoma, Sikinde, African Stars (Twanga Pepeta), and FM Academia (Ngwasuma) all play jazz in Dar es Salaam today. *Muziki wa dansi* has contributed a lot to the profound exploration of the beauty of Tanzanian music in a contemporary society.

Bongo flava is Swahili rap from Tanzania. It expresses the thoughts and dreams of East African youth. Unlike American hip-hop, *bongo flava* went unnoticed by the rest of the world initially but has become the best-selling pop music in East Africa. Rappers such as Juma Nature and Professor Jay are loved for their amusing way of tackling social problems through the lyrics in their compositions. Gangwe Mobb is known for creating at least one new slang word in each of their comic-like cartoon rap songs. Their neighbors, LWP Majitu, are popular for their hard-hitting, hardcore lyrics. Mr. Ebbo has become the most popular urban ambassador of the Maasai, giving them a hymn with his song, "Mi Mmasai." While Afande Sele's song "Mtazamo" was chosen as the best Tanzanian rap song in 2004, X-Plastaz, from Arusha, is probably the only Tanzanian rap crew known in Europe and America.

For Tanzanian students pursuing a secondary school "A"-level certification in music, a curriculum replete with traditional and contemporary music of Tanzania, and of the African continent, would be suitably challenging to their intellectual and musical sensibilities. Sub-Saharan African music cultures and those music cultures with roots in Africa (such as Afro-Cuban music) are relevant and fitting components to a broad African-based curriculum. With a wide lens on the musical education of children, youth, and university students, Nketia maintained that "knowledge of traditional African music...is...a prerequisite both for understanding the contemporary musical scene in Africa and for gaining some insight into the music experience as it relates to the African in [both] person and social life" (1974: 30). A compilation of key musical genres of Tanzania is key to a curriculum that celebrates national styles and that can extend outward to other areas of Africa as well as inward to the most local of musical expressions found within home and family.

THE SPIRIT OF THE MWENGE EXPERIENCE

Enculturation is a natural process that need not be dismissed and discontinued as mandatory schooling pulls children out of their families and homes and into the formal learning experiences that they will know and share with one another. The songs, rhythms, and movements that children playfully learn at home—before their schooling begins and in spite of schooling—may constitute their deepest cultural roots. As such, this music need not be abandoned but rather can be noted and nurtured, designed, and delivered through a school curriculum that continues to build upon the local experiences of children's early years. The musical enculturation of children is a baseline and a reference point for them, and further learning of distant musical expressions can be built upon the foundations of their musical sensibilities. Like the choir students at the festival at Mwenge Secondary School, there is every good reason to celebrate the music that is natural to students, that is internalized from their earliest childhood, and that is understood as basic and relevant human expression.

REFERENCES

Adachi, M. 1994. "The Role of the Adult in the Child's Early Socialization: A Vygotskian Perspective." *The Quarterly Journal of Music Teaching and Learning* 5 (3): 26–35.

Barrett, M. 2010. *A Cultural Psychology of Music Education*. New York: Oxford University Press.

Bruner, J. 1996. *The Culture of Education*. Cambridge, MA: Harvard University Press.

Campbell, P. S. 1991. *Lessons from the World*. New York: Schirmer Books.

Campbell, P. S. [1998] 2010. *Songs in Their Heads: Music and Its Meaning in Children's Lives*. New York: Oxford University Press.

Campbell, P. S. 1999. "Pass It On! Our Multimusical Heritage." *Kodály Envoy* 25 (3): 9–11.

Campbell, P. S. 2001a. "Usage Suppositions? Cutting across Cultures on Questions of Music's Transmission." *Journal of Music Education Research* 3 (2): 215–226.

Campbell, P. S. 2011. "Musical Enculturation: Sociocultural Influences and Meanings of Children's Experiences in and through Music." In *A Cultural Psychology of Music Education*, edited by M. Barrett, 61–82. New York: Oxford University Press.

Campbell, P. S., and C. Scott-Kassner. 2010. *Music in Childhood: From Preschool through the Elementary Grades*. New York: Cengage Learning.

Carlsen, J. C. 1994. "The Need to Know." *Journal of Research in Music Education* 42 (3): 181–189.

Criss, E. 2008. "The Natural Learning Process." *Music Educators Journal* 95 (2): 42–46. ERIC Document Reproduction Service No. EJ822502.

Demorest, S., S. J. Morrison, D. Jungbluth, and M. N. Beken. 2008. "Lost in Translation: An Enculturation Effect in Music Memory Performance." *Music Perception* 25 (3): 213–223.

Dewey, J. 1938. *Experience and Education*. Chicago: University Press.

Edmond, S., and M. Sefu. 1977. "The Development of Primary Education in Tanzania." Master's diss., University of Dar es Salaam.

Felder, R. M., and M. J Prince. 2007. "Many Faces of Inductive Teaching and Learning." *Journal of College Science Teaching*. National Science Teachers Association. Accessed August 6, 2009. http://www4.ncsu.edu/unity/lockers/users/f/felder/public/Papers/Inductive(JCST).pdf.

Figueroa, P. 1995. "Multicultural Education in the United Kingdom: Historical Development and Current Status." In *Handbook of Research on Multicultural Education*, edited by J. A. Banks and C. A. M. Banks, 778–800. New York: Macmillan.

Froebel, F., E. Michaelis, and H. Moore. 1889. *Autobiography of Froebel*. New York: C. W. Bardeen.

Gibson, R. 2009. "Musical Parenting: An Ethnographic Account of Musical Interactions of Parents and Young Children." PhD diss., University of Washington, Seattle.

Gordon, E. E. 1993. *Learning Sequences in Music: Skill, Content and Patterns*. Chicago: GIA.

Hanley, B., and J. Montgomery. 2002. "Contemporary Curriculum Practices and Their Theoretical Bases." In *The New Handbook of Research in Music Teaching and Learning: A Project of the Music Educators National Conference*, edited by R. Colwell and C. Richardson, 113–143. New York: Oxford University.

Herskovits, J. M. 1948. *Man and His Works: The Science of Cultural Anthropology*. New York: Knopf.

Keil, C., and P. S. Campbell. 2011. "Born to Groove." Accessed September 1, 2011. http://borntogroove.org/course/view.php?id=2.

Lum, C., and P. S. Campbell. 2007. "The Sonic Surrounds of an Elementary School." *Journal of Research in Basic Education* 55 (1): 31–47.

Lundquist, B. R. 1998. "A Music Education Perspective." In *Musics of the World's Cultures: A Source Book for Music Educators*, edited by B. Lundquist and C. K. Szego, with B. Nettl, R. P. Santos, and E. Solbu, 36–46. Reading, UK: Callaway International Resource Centre for Music Education for International Society for Music Education.

Lundquist, B. R. 2002. "Music, Culture, Curriculum, and Instruction." In *The New Handbook of Research on Music Teaching and Learning; A Project of the Music Educators National Conference*, edited by R. Colwell and C. Richardson, 626–647. New York: Oxford University Press.

Marsh, K. 2008. *The Musical Playground: Global Tradition and Change In Children's Songs and Games*. New York: Oxford University Press.

McCarthy, M. 1999. *Passing It On: The Transmission of Music in Irish Culture*. Cork, Ireland: Cork University Press.

Mead, M. 1930. *Social Organization of Manu'a*. Honolulu: Bernice P. Bishop Museum.

Merriam, A. P. 1964. *The Anthropology of Music*. Chicago: Northwestern University Press.

Ministry of Education and Culture. 2005. *Music Syllabus for Secondary School, Form I–IV*. Dar es Salaam: Tanzania Institute of Education

Morrison, S., S. M. Demorest, and L. A. Stambaugh. 2008. "Enculturation Effects in Music Cognition: The Role of Age and Music Complexity." *Journal of Research in Music Education* 56 (2): 118–129.

Music Syllabus for Advanced Secondary Education of 2009/2010. The United Republic of Tanzania Ministry of Education and Vocational Training. Dar es Salaam: Tanzania Institute of Education.

Nettl, B. 1998. "An Ethnomusicological Perspective." In *Musics of the World's Cultures: A Source Book for Music Educators,* edited by B. Lundquist and C. K. Szego, with B. Nettl, R. P. Santos, and E. Solbu, 23–28. Reading, UK: Callaway International Resource Centre for Music Education for International Society for Music Education.

Nettl, B. [1983] 2005. *The Study of Ethnomusicology: Thirty-one Issues and Concepts.* Urbana: University of Illinois Press.

Nketia, J. H. K. 1974. *The Music of Africa.* New York: W.W. Norton.

Nyerere, J. 1966. *Freedom and Unity: Uhuru na umoja; a Selection from Writings and Speeches 1952–1965.* Dar es Salaam, Tanzania: Oxford University Press.

Nyoni, F. 1998. "Conformity and Change: Tanzanian Rural Theatre and Social Political Change." PhD diss., University of Leeds.

Osberg, D., and G. Biesta. 2008. "The Emergent Curriculum: Navigating a Complex Course between Unguided Learning and Planned Enculturation." *Journal of Curriculum Studies* 40 (3): 313–328.

Rice, T. 2004. *Music in Bulgaria: Experiencing Music, Experiencing Culture.* New York: Oxford University Press.

Szego, C. K. 2002. "Music Transmission and Learning: A Conspectus of Ethnographic Research in Ethnomusicology and Music Education." In *The New Handbook of Research on Music Teaching and Learning; A Project of the Music Educators National Conference,* edited by R. Colwell and C. Richardson, 707–729. New York: Oxford University Press.

Tishman, S., E. Jay, and D. N. Perkins. 1993. "Teaching Thinking Dispositions: From Transmission to Enculturation." *Theory Into Practice* 32 (3): 147–53.

Van Reken, R. E., and S. Rushmore. 2009. "Thinking Globally When Teaching Locally." *Kappa Delta Pi* 45 (2): 60–69.

Watts, S. 2009. "Transgenerational Musical Play: Oral History Accounts of Girls' Musical Engagement." PhD diss., University of Washington, Seattle.

Weinreich, P. 2009. "Enculturation Not Acculturation: Conceptualising and Assessing Identity Processes in Migrant Communities." *International Journal of Intercultural Relations* 33 (2): 124–139.Welch, G. 2005. "We Are Musical." *International Journal of Music Education* 23 (2): 117–20.

31

TINKERING AND TETHERING IN THE MATERIAL CULTURE OF CHILDREN'S MP3 PLAYERS

TYLER BICKFORD

MP3 players are iconic devices of "new" media, which privileges increasingly mobile and unrestricted communication and circulation, and children are iconic users of such technologies, commonly seen as "digital natives" socialized from birth into a digital world (Bull 2008; Palfrey and Gasser 2008). This chapter challenges a view of children's uses of MP3 players that emphasizes wireless connectivity, communication at a distance, and technological expertise. Instead, I consider MP3 players from a "material culture" perspective, working from ethnographic research with schoolchildren at a small public elementary and middle school in rural Vermont. This approach reveals that children emphasized the tangibility of their MP3 players as objects more than as devices for communication or data storage. Music devices were ever-present throughout the school day, slipped into pockets, threaded under clothing, and handled until worn. When friends shared earbuds to listen together, the cables tethered them ear to ear, and they delighted in the bodily challenge of moving in tandem with earbuds balanced delicately between. Kids tinkered constantly with their MP3 players, decorating them with decals, markers, tape, and nail polish, trading unsalvageable ones to save for spare parts, and seeking out charged batteries in a never ending process of "enlivening" (Skuse 2005; also Appadurai

1986) their fragile devices. When they broke, as they often did, kids repaired them or lived with malfunctions. Stories about failed devices were told enthusiastically, and the reasons for their failure were often shrouded in mystery. In these ways, I argue, children's MP3 players have been thoroughly domesticated within a "childish" material culture already characterized by playful physical interaction and portable objects such as toys, trading cards, and dolls that can be shared, manipulated, and held close. Children's emphasis and interest in the materiality of the devices as objects also informed their conceptions of sound, music, and circulation, as they treated circulating songs as resonating sound rather than digital files and swapped songs with each other using the earbuds of one person's device to record through the microphone of another's.

The Community and the Study

Heartsboro is a town of fewer than 800 people in southern Vermont, about a thirty-minute drive from the nearest grocery store. (Note that all names, including that of the locality, are pseudonyms.) Children in prekindergarten through eighth grade (ages three through fourteen) attend Heartsboro Central School (HCS). While I was in residence there during the 2007/2008 school year as a full-time researcher, HCS had fewer than seventy K–8 students. During that period I spent my days observing, talking, and playing with kids in and out of class, with the goal of understanding children's expressive practices and popular music consumption within the broader social context of everyday schooling. For part of the year I taught music classes one day a week, as the school had trouble finding someone to fill the position.

Heartsboro is relatively low income by US standards.[1] Many families go back locally several generations, and cousins and siblings from a few large extended families account for a substantial portion of the student body at HCS. Historically Heartsboro's economy was dominated by small manufacturing and some tourism, but by 2007 little local industry remained, and a chair factory and ski slope had both closed in the past generation. Thus Heartsboro has been a microcosm of a dramatic regional process of deindustrialization in the northeastern United States (cf. Kirsch 1998). Outdoor activities, for example, hunting, snowmobiling, and riding four-wheelers are common pastimes, and NASCAR is a favorite sport. These regional characteristics only partially influence kids' music or media habits, since media and consumer practices can be powerfully deterritorializing forces; even in a relatively isolated location like Heartsboro, children can be remarkably cosmopolitan in their consumption. For instance, at the time of my research, country music did not have a privileged place among adults' or kids' tastes, despite other common markers of White working-class US culture like hunting or NASCAR. Kids' musical tastes ranged widely: from Top 40 pop, rock, hip-hop, and R&B, to more obscure recordings of "hard-core" metal or hip-hop passed down from older siblings or friends, to popular music from the 1970s and 1980s introduced to them by their parents. The uses of MP3 players I discuss in this chapter were widespread enough to be largely independent of musical preferences or taste, though they did, to some extent, vary by age, gender, and peer group.

CHILDISH THINGS: NEW MEDIA, TECHNOLOGY, AND CHILDREN'S MATERIAL CULTURE

Media and communication technologies can seem radically disconnected from the material world of bodies, places, and objects. Hence, common narratives about portable music devices see private listening practices intruding upon and fragmenting public spaces, increasingly partitioning individuals within personalized musical soundscapes that detach listeners from their surroundings (Bull 2008; du Gay et al. 1997). To the extent that such narratives understand portable music listening to involve communication or interaction, it is separated from the immediate act of listening and instead occurs across vast distances online by sharing files and playlists or tagging and rating songs. Anxious or nostalgic narratives of the spread of MP3 players emphasize the disappearance of physical recordings—LPs or CDs and their cover art—and lament the intangibility of digital files.

Challenging this view, recent scholarship argues for understanding new media specifically in terms of "materiality"—recognizing the unmistakable fact of embodied users interfacing with devices (Munster 2006) and the importance of face-to-face social networks in their use and significance (Miller 2010). Vannini points out that in a fundamental sense technology and material culture are inseparably tied up with one another: "Technology is about doing, knowing, and using objects and ... materiality is about the character of those objects or things" (2009: 1). In reference to children, this perspective seems especially salient, as children's own understanding of the meaning and role of new media music devices in their lives seemed to focus especially on the material characteristics and physical utility of such technology. We might even see children's material culture as a more relevant context for understanding their adoption of particular music technologies than their "musical culture," in the sense of the music they make or listen to, though my position here is that children's musical culture is itself inextricably tied up in existing forms of children's material culture.

This argument requires an assertion that there is such a thing as "children's material culture." It seems to me that there is, and that the category of "childish" things has real salience in the lives of children and adults.[2] Children's movements are restricted to "islands" set off for them by adults (Gillis 2008), whether playgrounds (Kozlovsky 2008), stores, or departments of stores (Cook 2003), or even media genres (Banet-Weiser 2007; Bickford 2012) and restricted internet sites (Montgomery 2007). Within such islands, kids have relative freedom; for instance, the movements of kids' bodies in the playground—vertical and horizontal, swinging and climbing, running and crawling—contrast markedly with the restriction and regulation of movement in classrooms. This freedom of movement and activity within confined spaces is often understood in terms of "play"—an activity ideologically associated with children and childhood (Sutton-Smith 1997). Play, of course, is associated with a particular class of things—toys—and the link between play as an activity and toys as objects helps to define the broad outlines of children's spaces and children's things, as, for instance, in drawing boundaries around children's role as consumers (Cross 1997; Fleming 1996; Kline 1993; Sutton-Smith 1986). Children and adults articulate sophisticated taxonomies of "childish" things, as anthropologist Stephanie Melton finds in children's categorization of "kids' food," the boundaries of which are marked by complex intersections of healthfulness, color, packaging, processing, size, and ability to be handled and played with (2010).

Sharon Brookshaw points out that it can be difficult to distinguish the material culture of children from materials made for children (2009). In making this distinction, Brookshaw calls attention to "makeshift" toys that are "designed, made, named, remodeled, used, and reused solely by children; they represent the creativity and imagination of children and the way in which almost anything can be adapted for their amusement or entertainment" (2009: 369). At HCS, for example, school supplies like masking tape, pencils, and paper clips, became the substance for imaginative and never ending creation, especially of medieval weapons like grappling hooks and balls-and-chains. So rather than distinguishing categorically between objects for and objects made by children, I would argue that the affordances of an object for manipulation and activity and its capacity to be repurposed for children's use may be a diagnostic of potential childishness. Melton, for instance, describes an eleven-year-old girl "boxing" a pear as though it were a speed bag, and possibilities for such playful uses suggest why fresh, but not cooked, fruits and vegetables were classified as "kids' food" by the children in her study.

Studies of musical toys produced for children suggest that music, too, needs to be materialized in bright colors, physical manipulability, and interactive potential to be suitably childish. Campbell describes the complex overlapping of visual and sonic stimuli in a large urban toy store, in which electronic sounds are integral (and intentionally designed) elements of the colorful and interactive commercial world of toys (1998). Multicolored and rocking-horse-themed instruments, singing dolls and dinosaurs, and even nonmusical toys that inspire or elicit musicking and movement from children all point toward deep connections between music, movement, and objects in children's culture. Similarly, in a study of the everyday home lives of young children in seven countries (Young and Gillen 2007), electronic toys that make music appear to be incredibly common, and children's everyday activities include dancing to child-themed CDs and vocalizing along with music-making pinball toys. Young writes that "in contemporary media, music is interwoven with images, animations, texts, spoken words and sound effects, and these extend into the material items of musical toys and other equipment" (2008: 43).

On the surface, MP3 players seem *not* to share in this "childish" potential of objects. They are small, yes, and sometimes brightly colored, and increasingly they are marketed to children using recognizable visual cues. I have seen Hannah Montana–themed devices and Lego devices with removable pieces, and the toy company Hasbro has had success selling its iDog series of animal-shaped plastic speakers. But this remains an emerging market. At HCS there were only two iDogs and none of the thematically decorated devices. Most of the MP3 players children had were monochrome, many black or gray, a few red, purple, or blue. The cheaper versions most students owned were lightweight, plastic, and uninteresting to look at; as objects they seemed designed to disappear, to subsume themselves into the sort of transcendent "non-space" listening Bull describes (2005). But nonetheless children constantly saw in their MP3 players the childish potential for exactly the sort of manipulability, interactivity, and movement that characterized the rest of their material culture, reimagining them not in terms of transcendent freedom *from* bodies, spaces, and sociality but as tangible anchors *to* their material, embodied, and spatial surroundings, and especially to one another. In this they amply demonstrate Miller's point that "possessions often remain profound and usually the closer our relationships are with objects, the closer our relationships are with people" (2008: 1).

TETHERING

Alan Prout writes that children's bodies "are inseparable from, produced in, represented by, and performed through their connections with other material objects" (2000: 2). This point was prominently demonstrated by kids' uses of MP3 players at HCS, as objects that were constantly present attached to kids' bodies. A prominent example was sixth-grader Melissa, who got a purple iPod Shuffle for Easter along with a matching pair of squishy purple earbuds. Melissa wore jeans and a baggy sweatshirt to school almost every day, and after she got the iPod it remained clipped to her sweatshirt all the time, except when teachers made her put it away during class (even then it would remain close, in a pocket). She kept it on even after school during the hockey program she attended, clipped to her sweatshirt with one earbud in her ear, the other dangling. The cables tossed around and kept getting tangled in hockey sticks, but even though the coach and I repeatedly asked if she might want to put the device away while she was playing, she always declined. She kept it on even when the batteries died and she couldn't listen to music. Eighth-grader Amber, too, often kept an earbud in her ear even when not listening to music, and kids would keep their MP3 players on their bodies during school, rather than storing them in their bag or lockers. When they entered the classroom the devices would disappear into pockets and sleeves, snug and close, ready to reappear immediately upon leaving class.

Beyond the individual intimacy of the object, MP3 players created close physical connections from one child to another. A near-universal practice was to share the earbuds of their devices, one-for-me, one-for-you, to listen together to music. Kids would move, play, eat, and talk while sharing earbuds. In groups, earbud cables coupled children into pairs even as they looked at and talked to others in the group. Children enjoyed the challenge of moving while tethered together, and they coordinated their bodies to walk, run, and swing with earbuds dangling precariously from each other's ears. Earbud cables traced out social networks by physically linking friends and intimates together in embodied connection (see Bickford [forthcoming] for a detailed analysis of earbud-sharing practices).

BREAKING

Like a lot of objects sold to children, the generic MP3 players that most of the HCS kids had were cheap, even disposable. Devices regularly broke or were lost, and kids' use of them reflected Colloredo-Mansfield's point that "material practice revolves around loss more often than preservation—luster fades, things fall apart" (2003: 246). The $40 or $50 that even the least expensive devices cost was significant enough that kids lived with partially broken devices, scrounged around for replacement parts, and tried to repair cracked cases or wires when they could. Though they were aware of the possibility that the devices would break, they were not careful at all with their devices, keeping them around during active play or sports, and carelessly setting them down where they might forget them. Cranking the volume up to use their earbuds as miniature speakers, they often blew out headsets.

While they worried about breakage, they also related stories about broken devices with bravado, "stake[ing] prestige…on the techniques and materials of consumption and destruction" (Colloredo-Mansfield 2003: 252). Sixth-grader Dan, for instance, told me, "I have [an MP3 player], but it's broken. I can't download songs onto it. I don't have the cable, and I think it has a CD that you need. I got it from my cousin [eighth-grader Erica], and she's stupid. I think she lost the CD." Dan never did get a working MP3 player during the year, and instead he used his portable CD player. But he also never got rid of his cousin's hand-me-down device, even carrying it to and from school in his backpack, and its presence provided a relished opportunity to complain about his older cousin's ineptness in losing the data cable and software disk.

On another occasion, I sat with seventh- and eighth-graders Kathy, Alice, and Amber at breakfast, listening to Jordan Sparks and Taylor Swift on Kathy's iDog. The dog bobbed its head in time to the music, and disco lights flashed on its face. The girls' conversation revealed the delight taken in stories about the failure of devices and also the detailed knowledge these friends had about one another's devices. I asked Kathy if she was happy with the MP3 player she got for Christmas.

She nodded, but my question prompted Alice to complain, "My MP3 player's being retarded."

Kathy elaborated for her: "It doesn't turn on."

I asked, "Still? Did you try resetting it or whatever?"

Amber jumped in, incredulous: "It doesn't have a reset button!"

Alice said, "My dad, literally, went and picked it up, like this, and went"—she mimed dropping the device—"like that, on the floor to try to get it to work. And I did it too! And it won't turn on. I've had it for two weeks, and it's already broken."

Alice and her sister Megan, in sixth grade, had matching MP3 players. I asked Alice, "Your sister's works fine?"

Amber replied for her, "Yeah, except she blew her earphones," and then she bragged, "I've blown two pairs of earphones!"

"How do you do that?"

"It goes too loud and it overblows."

"When you turn up the volume to use them as speakers?"

"No, just as earphones."

"Do you put them real loud in your ear?"

Amber nodded. Alice joined in: "I told Megan not to have hers up cause she's gonna blow them. And she's using my headphones." Since Megan's earbuds were broken, and Alice's device would not turn on, the sisters had consolidated their equipment.

Amber bragged, "I've blown my earphones, my iPod earphones, and my MP3 player earphones. And I traded my mom my dad's earphones—he gave them to me—for my mom's iPod earphones. So I had those, and hers are about to blow, so now I got these, so I have a second pair, my mom's. I blow up earphones very easily," she said with evident pride.

The discussion made Kathy nervous. She pointed to her new iDog and asked, "These could never blow up, right? Could these ever blow up?" Amber and I tried to assure her that the lightweight plastic device should be fine.

Several weeks later the story of the broken device had developed into a routine between Alice and Amber, with a mysterious malfunction providing the narrative lead-up to a ready punch line.

During an interview with both girls, Alice remembered, "I got a sucky MP3 player but—"

Amber whispered, "It broke!"

"—it wound up breaking! It broke the first week I got it! 'Cause, what it was, I had the earphone in my ear, and I had the MP3 in my pocket. What was so weird was that the headphone fell out of my ear and I tried turning it back on and it didn't work after that. After the earphone fell. I didn't even drop it."

Amber asked, apparently for my benefit, "Where'd you get it?"

"A pharmacy," Alice laughed. "CVS."

Amber grinned and delivered the punch line she had set up: "Yeah, don't buy electric things at a pharmacy."

ENLIVENING

As these stories reveal, breaking and loss did not end the social lives of these objects but were rather the impetus for particular "enlivening" practices in which kids continually worked to maintain and enhance their devices' social utility. Enlivenment "is normatively equated both with the appropriation of commodities, but also with a more mundane practice of maintenance, in the sense that certain commodities such as portable radios require a continual economic investment in the purchase of batteries if they are to remain enlivened in the socio-semantic sense" (Skuse 2005: 124–125; also Appadurai 1986). Enlivenment, therefore, continually resists entropy or dispossession, the failure, disposal, or transience of objects (Lucas 2002). When Alice's and Megan's two devices had different failures, the sisters consolidated them and shared. Amber found a seemingly inexhaustible supply of headphones in possession of her family members, and she saw her task as cajoling them into sharing or trading. Dan would later ask me for the USB cable his hand-me-down MP3 player needed to work, and we tried connecting it to one of the school computers, even though he still lacked the necessary software CD. Sometimes students would even break their devices on purpose, as when fourth graders Dave and Brian one morning aggressively snapped one earpiece off of an old pair of headband-style earphones, so they could each listen to one speaker at the same time. Just as the failure of Alice's device was transformed into an occasion for shared storytelling with Amber, in Dave and Brian's case enlivenment was the direct result of destruction that accommodated sharing, manifesting Colloredo-Mansfield's suggestion that "exhausting commodities frequently opens up channels of connectivity, yet it also reduces individual control of them" (2003: 251).

Batteries, which Skuse points to in a very different context, were central to HCS kids' enlivenment of music devices. Economizing battery power was often mentioned as a reason to share the earbuds to one device between friends. Amber and Alice knew every detail of one another's battery usage, because batteries affected how and when they could listen together. They talked about how they navigated different rules at home and the differences between their devices to listen together as much as possible. Amber told me that one of the reasons she and Alice listened together was because "I charge my iPod every day, and she likes to save her battery. I listen to mine a lot, so I have to charge it every day."

Alice agreed, "'cause I'm limited to so many batteries. My mom bought me a four-pack of batteries. And then I find batteries around the house."

"My battery," Amber continued, "as much as I listen to it, could last me about an hour or two. A full battery."

"My battery can last me two, three weeks."

"'Cause she barely listens to hers, and I listen to mine a lot, like every day."

Alice's Samsung took a single AA battery, while Amber's iPod had an internal battery that was easily charged at an outlet at home—without the need for any cash or purchase from her parents. While her dependence on batteries severely limited

Alice's ability to use her device, she and Amber collaborated to avoid Alice's device ever going completely dead. That the girls had such minute knowledge testifies to their closeness and to the important role of these devices as mediators of the girls' friendship. In fact, the MP3 player that Alice had to scrounge batteries for was actually Amber's old Samsung, a device she had before she got her iPod. Alice received this device on indefinite loan from Amber after the player she got at Christmas had broken. So while Amber phrased her explanation in terms of her own frequent listening habits, her ability to listen more than Alice was also structured by her parents' willingness to buy her an iPod and the particular affordances of that device's rechargeable battery. But at school Alice probably listened to music as much as Amber, because Amber would always automatically pass her the second earbud when she took out her iPod.

TINKERING

In addition to such attentive social mediations of battery power, the transience of these devices was tied up in practices of tinkering, repair, and decoration—activities that seemed in most cases to go together—as though the material instability of MP3 players opened up possibilities for kids to interact with them in new ways. Their "cheapness," in this sense, could be seen as a source of constant renewal and interest.

Like Alice, who emphasized the mysterious circumstances of her MP3 player's failure, seventh-grader Randy told me that his old earbuds "just melted! I felt some heat on my arm," he said, "and I looked down, and they were melting up!"

I asked, "Really? Just for no reason?"

"Yeah, really! So I tore them apart to see what's inside." Randy pulled them out of his bag to show me (Figure 31.1)—he carried even such irreparably damaged items around in his bag, reconstituting them as objects for investigation rather than as deconstituted "trash" (Lucas 2002).

Randy told me he got his current pair from the airplane on his family's recent trip to Disneyland. But unlike his old ones, these weren't marked "L" and "R" for left and right. So he showed me how he would listen to Trace Atkins's "Honky Tonk Badonkadonk" to figure out which ear is which—the song starts with, "left, left, left right left," with "left" and "right" panned to alternating channels. Then he went into the office to get a Band-Aid that he could rip up to mark the earbuds so he wouldn't have to keep checking them with the recording. But he couldn't rip the Band-Aid by hand, "because it's thicker than the ones I use at home." Instead he pulled a sheet of decals out of his Game Boy case and wrapped a confederate flag sticker around the left earbud. He marked the decal with an "L," using a permanent marker he also pulled out of his Game Boy case, and said with satisfaction, "That's a good redneck way to do it" (Figure 31.2).[3]

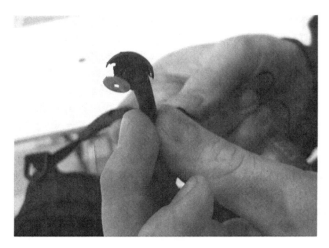

Figure 31.1: Randy tore apart his "melted" earbuds to see what was inside.
Photograph © 2008 by the author.

Like MP3 players, portable gaming devices were also subject to such decoration, as, for instance, eighth-grader Nate cut strips of electrical tape to give his Game Boy Micro tiger stripes. Girls, too, decorated and toyed with their devices, like Kathy, who got an MP3 player for Christmas: by June the screen was held together with tape and she had painted the back case completely with red sparkly nail polish (Web Figures 31.3 and 31.4 ⊙).

Randy was the only kid who even once mentioned the left and right channels of a recording. But, like the rest of the kids at Heartsboro, he never seemed concerned about listening to the full stereo soundscape—which the widespread practice of listening with just one ear, of course, completely devalued. For Randy a new pair of earbuds missing labels presented an opportunity for tinkering and design, more than a difficulty for faithful listening, and even the sonic organization of the audio track was put in service of the object and its decoration, rather than appreciated on its own.

Figure 31.2: "A good redneck way to do it." Randy marked the left earbud with a
confederate flag sticker. Photograph © 2008 by the author.

TINKERING AND TETHERING IN THE
CIRCULATION OF RECORDINGS

Noting Randy's use of the stereo sound of a recording to organize his earbuds on his body, rather than to structure his listening as such, children's material orientations toward MP3 players can provide clues about their conceptions of music and sound. Common understandings of sound and music as uniquely ephemeral, even disembodied, suggest that hearing is especially susceptible to technological or schizophonic mediations. Further, infinite reproducibility—that media files can be transferred and copied without any loss of information, unlike analog recordings or film photographs—is seen as a central feature linking postmodern technological and cultural configurations, the characteristic affordance of digital media. But kids at HCS often ignored or rejected such characteristically "digital" capacities of their devices, instead approaching the circulation of sound recordings in ways that located them within the material world, rather than as placeless and immaterial digital "files." In particular, many used the built-in (and very low quality) microphones in their MP3 players to record and circulate music. They put the microphone up to their television or to computer speakers to record music from a music video, rather than searching for a song on the internet, downloading it (possibly paying for it with a parent's credit card), and transferring it to their MP3 player. Or they placed an earbud to the microphone, to transfer music from one device to another.

At eighth-grade gym class, held outdoors in June, several girls sat out because it was "too hot." Amber listened to her iPod, while Sarah fiddled with her friend's MP3 player and her very new cell phone—a Motorola RAZR. Flipping open the RAZR, she looked at the screen for a bit and then played a song using the phone's speakers. I asked her where she got the music—off of the internet? I imagined she was using one of the new music-downloading services the cell phone companies had been aggressively advertising. She shook her head and held up the MP3 player. "Off of this."

I was puzzled. MP3 players, I thought, did not connect from device to device—you had to use a computer to transfer files.

So Sarah demonstrated for me, holding one earbud up to the microphone on her phone. As she showed me, the music was interrupted by a loud girlish screech, and Sarah said, "Erica was being loud during that part. She ruined it." But Sarah let the song play on despite being "ruined," and she and her friends would continue to listen to this track on the phone over the rest of the school year.

During interviews kids would often place their earbuds up to my recorder to "show" me songs.[4] Notably, they only used their MP3 players to record or share music; they never used them to record one another. My audio recorder would elicit performative talk from kids of all ages, but the kids never seemed interested in listening to themselves later, even when I offered. Younger kids would do funny voices or sing when I took it out, and older kids would say swear words or insults, or call one another gay or stupid. But their own devices were just for songs.

Kids would also record music off of the internet or television, including advertising jingles and TV theme songs. When I asked Randy in an interview, "Would you say you like music?" his immediate response was, "Well, my custom radio says so, yeah!" He went on to tell me about the seven speakers he had attached to an old boom box and wired around his room with strobe lights.

When I asked Randy about what types of music he likes, he said, "Rock, heavy metal stuff, country. And the occasional anime shows. You know like—the show's so awesome I can't even remember the name of it. *Blood Plus* there. That's a good show."[5]

"Yeah?"

"Yeah, they always have cool theme songs. Actually I got like ten of 'em on here," he said, pulling out his MP3 player.

I noticed the white earbuds and asked, "What are these, iPod headphones?"

"No, I stole them from my brother." Randy laughed.

"What's this, like your fifth pair this year or something?"

"I used the ones from the airplane. They sucked." Randy found his song. "This is one of those Japanese anime ones. It's from *Final Fantasy Dirge of Cerberus*. It's a cool song." He held one of the earbuds up to the microphone on my recorder. He whispered to me, to avoid disrupting the recording he was making for me, "That's how I got it on here—I recorded this off the internet [i.e., from one of the speakers attached to a computer]. Off *Dirge of Cerberus*."

We both listened closely to the quiet recording being played on tiny headphones resting on the table. As he transferred music that he had originally recorded from computer speakers from his MP3 player on to my recorder, Randy was executing a fully analog chain of transfers between digital devices, as though this were a completely normal way to move songs around.

Randy listed several other shows whose songs he liked. He described the theme to *Death Note* for me and then remembered, "I still need to record that. I gotta write that down." He told me that he would stay up to watch the shows when they came on late on Saturday night. He would set his TV's timer to remind him, and then hold the MP3 player up to TV speakers and record the song. He picked up his MP3 player to show me how. "See that, that's the mike. What you do is when you turn it on, it takes forever. Here we go. You go like this. And it says 'recorder.' Then it'll be like that," he pointed to a menu on the screen, "and you just go like this and it's recording. See? And if you don't want to save it you'll see an X. You just swap over to that and go *tsiu*." Randy finished with a laser-gun sound effect for X'ing out the songs.

Earlier in the year Randy and a couple of other boys rode with me on a field trip to hear the author Lois Lowry talk, and I let them pick songs on my iPod to play in the car. When "Stronger," the new Kanye West single, came on, Randy pulled his MP3 player out of his bag and stuck it down at the speaker in the door by his feet. Several months later, I was making a CD of songs for him and asked if he wanted that song. He said no, because he already had it: "Don't you remember? I got it when we were on that trip before?"

At our interview, Randy continued through the songs on his MP3 player. He found "Party Like a Rockstar" and said, "That's one of the ones I got from music class"—he had recorded it during the music show-and-tell that was a regular part of my music class. He said, "You'll hear it stop, you'll hear Kathy's voice on there eventually."

I asked, "Does the fuzziness bother you at all?"

"No not really. I know how far to keep them away from the speakers, and sometimes the fuzziness doesn't affect 'em at all. Like this one: this is from *King of Hearts*. This one I need to redo. I mean, it's good, but it's kind of weird."

I suggested, "You might be able to find the actual songs on the internet."

But Randy dismissed this out of hand: "I don't even know the names of them."

Sarah and Randy were from opposite ends of the social hierarchy. Sarah had a large and close group of friends that was widely acknowledged as high status. Randy, on the other hand, had no close friends, and few people even to hang out with. He was widely acknowledged to be a social maladroit. Randy represented an extreme version of this do-it-yourself, tinkering ethos of music listening, and he loved to repair and retrofit his old and broken stereo and his old and broken MP3 player. Sarah and her friends were early adopters of shiny new technology, like Sarah's RAZR phone and Michelle's portable Sirius Radio receiver. Nonetheless, they both moved music around in this remarkable way, from earbud to microphone. My own first reaction to Sarah recording music directly from an earbud was disbelief, and I suggested to Randy that these recorded copies Randy passed from device to device were somehow less real than digital sound files, the "actual songs." It would never occur to me to move songs around like this. The layers of *in*fidelity to high quality digital reproduction represented by such a practice were stacked upon one another: MP3 encoding already represents concessions of quality to portability; cheap earbuds hardly produce decent playback, and with only one earbud transferring music to the microphone, half the original track is lost; the microphones on MP3 players and cell phones are barely suitable even for casual voice recording; and the audio from the microphone is then subjected to further degradation from another round of low bit rate MP3 encoding.

But these practices certainly were faithful to an alternate conception of music, in which sound, songs, and recordings were integrated into the physical, spatial, and embodied world that children and their music devices occupy. Sarah and Randy both transferred music by connecting one physically present device to another with the umbilicus of their earbud cables. As they held the earbuds up to the microphones, they transferred sound from one vibrating membrane to another, in real time. If anything, the recordings they made were composed more of "actual" sounds and music than digitally encoded representations. On the internet, songs would be found by searching for metadata—titles, artist names, dates, etc.—but as Randy pointed out, he didn't know the names of many songs on his device. He did, on the other, hand, know very clearly how the songs sounded. So, just as MP3 players themselves existed as objects as much as media, it seems songs and music existed for HCS kids as sound objects more than as files, and so to move music from device to device the song had to actually resound in physical space.

SOUND AND CHILDREN'S MATERIAL CULTURE

Stephen Connor writes that sound "strikes us as at once intensely corporeal—sound literally moves, shakes, and touches us—and mysteriously immaterial" (2004: 157). In the face of powerful and pervasive discourses of immateriality that surround new media and weigh in forcefully on the latter conception of sound, it takes a certain ingenuity for children to envision the corporeality of sound and to see in MP3 players—these iconic objects of new media—material affordances for circulation, movement, embodiment, and sharing. But these practices fit perfectly within the clear and present demands of kids' social and material environment, in which objects and bodies constantly circulate and interact in immediate, face-to-face settings. To seek out some digital file on the internet would require turning attention away from this rich and solid social world. Sound "constitutes a form of material action" (Witmore 2006: 276), and it is this potential for material action—for play, manipulation, tinkering, investigation—that I argued at the outset is central to the identification of a thing as "childish." The devices stuck in their clothes and tangling among their bodies, and the sounds those devices produced, were thus available to be toyed with, using the sort of immediate agency kids cultivate as they climb in and around their environment and put objects in physical contact. Connor writes about "a restoration of...equilibrium in the face of the extreme disembodiment of hearing, a reclaiming of the proximal tactility of the here-and-now body" (2004: 171). But it appears that children need not "reclaim" anything at all. Their cultures of hearing have retained the "proximal tactility" of their cultures of materiality, grounded among practices that include boxing a pear, climbing on a jungle gym, collecting and trading cards, or building medieval weapons out of pencils, masking tape, and chains of paper clips.

NOTES

1 In 2007, a majority of students at HCS were eligible for government-subsidized lunches, a common measure of family means.
2 I use the term "childish" advisedly, and I am sensitive to Adora Svitak's argument that "the traits the word 'childish' addresses are seen so often in adults that we should abolish this age-discriminatory word when it comes to criticizing behavior associated with irresponsibility and irrational thinking" (2010). But to describe without criticism things identified by children and adults as marked for childhood, I find the adjective "childish" preferable to the now common "children's," which carries a suggestion that children independently claim ownership rather than negotiate the boundaries of their lives with adults and others. Still, I recognize that the term retains valences of trivialness, irrationality, or irresponsibility. I think this usefully highlights the fact that children and childhood remain marginalized and disputed categories and helps to avoid whitewashing the actual discourses and genealogies that come with notions of childhood or childishness.
3 Randy's use of the term "redneck" was unique at the school and in the broader community, as far as I know, and stemmed in part from his interest in comedian Larry the Cable Guy. His interest in the Confederate flag was always directly linked to the "General

Lee," the hot rod car with the flag on its roof from the television show and movie *Dukes of Hazard*. Rather than positioning him within the local sensibility of rusticity shared by his peers, Randy's identification as "redneck" and use of Confederate iconography contributed to his relative social isolation.

4 This turned out to be tremendously useful documentation of what might have been playing on kids devices during recordings when otherwise the microphone would only pick up their talk.

5 Anime is a Japanese animation genre that is increasingly popular globally.

References

Appadurai, Arjun. 1986. "Introduction: Commodities and the Politics of Value." In *The Social Life of Things: Commodities in Cultural Perspective*, edited by Arjun Appadurai, 3–63. Cambridge: Cambridge University Press.

Banet-Weiser, Sarah. 2007. *Kids Rule! Nickelodeon and Consumer Citizenship*. Durham, NC: Duke University Press.

Bickford, Tyler. 2012. "The New 'Tween' Music Industry: The Disney Channel, Kidz Bop, and an Emerging Childhood Counterpublic." *Popular Music* 31 (3).

Bickford, Tyler. Forthcoming. "Earbuds Are Good for Sharing: Children's Headphones as Social Media at a Vermont School." In *The Oxford Handbook of Mobile Music Studies*, edited by Jason Stanyek and Sumanth Gopinath. Oxford: Oxford University Press.

Brookshaw, Sharon. 2009. "The Material Culture of Children and Childhood: Understanding Childhood Objects in the Museum Context." *Journal of Material Culture* 14 (3): 365–383.

Bull, Michael. 2005. "No Dead Air! The iPod and the Culture of Mobile Listening." *Leisure Studies* 24 (4): 343–355.

Bull, Michael. 2008. *Sound Moves: iPod Culture and Urban Experience*. New York: Routledge.

Campbell, Patricia Shehan. 1998. *Songs in Their Heads: Music and Its Meaning in Children's Lives*. Oxford: Oxford University Press.

Colloredo-Mansfield, Rudi. 2003. "Matter Unbound." *Journal of Material Culture* 8 (3): 245–254.

Connor, Steven. 2004. "Edison's Teeth: Touching Hearing." In *Hearing Cultures: Essays on Sound, Listening, and Modernity*, edited by Veit Erlmann, 153–172. New York: Berg.

Cook, Daniel Thomas. 2003. "Spatial Biographies of Children's Consumption: Market Places and Spaces of Childhood in the 1930s and Beyond." *Journal of Consumer Culture* 3 (2): 147–169.

Cross, Gary. 1997. *Kids' Stuff: Toys and the Changing World of American Childhood*. Cambridge, MA: Harvard University Press.

du Gay, Paul, Stuart Hall, Linda Janes, Hugh Mackay, and Keith Negus. 1997. *Doing Cultural Studies: The Story of the Sony Walkman*. Thousand Oaks, CA: Sage.

Fleming, Dan. 1996. *Powerplay: Toys as Popular Culture*. Manchester, UK: Manchester University Press.

Gillis, John R. 2008. "The Islanding of Children—Reshaping the Mythical Landscapes of Children." In *Designing Modern Childhoods: History, Space, and the Material*

Culture of Children, edited by Marta Gutman and Ning de Coninck-Smith, 316–330. New Brunswick, NJ: Rutgers University Press.

Kirsch, Max H. 1998. *In the Wake of the Giant: Multinational Restructuring and Uneven Development in a New England Community*. Albany: State University of New York Press.

Kline, Stephen. 1993. *Out of the Garden: Toys, TV, and Children's Culture in the Age of Marketing*. New York: Verso.

Kozlovsky, Roy. 2008. "Adventure Playgrounds and Postwar Reconstruction." In *Designing Modern Childhoods: History, Space, and the Material Culture of Children*, edited by Marta Gutman and Ning de Coninck-Smith, 171–190. New Brunswick, NJ: Rutgers University Press.

Lucas, Gavin. 2002. "Disposability and Dispossession in the Twentieth Century." *Journal of Material Culture* 7 (1): 5–22.

Melton, Stephanie. 2010. "Food Rules: The Role of Kids' Food in Children's Peer Culture." Paper presented at the meeting Exploring Childhood Studies, Department of Childhood Studies, Rutgers University, Camden, NJ, April 9.

Miller, Daniel. 2008. *The Comfort of Things*. Cambridge: Polity Press.

Miller, Daniel. 2010. *Stuff*. Cambridge: Polity Press.

Montgomery, Kathryn C. 2007. *Generation Digital: Politics, Commerce, and Childhood in the Age of the Internet*. Cambridge: Massachusetts Institute of Technology Press.

Munster, Anna. 2006. *Materializing New Media: Embodiment in Information Aesthetics*. Hanover, NH: Dartmouth College Press.

Palfrey, John, and Urs Gasser. 2008. *Born Digital: Understanding the First Generation of Digital Natives*. New York: Basic Books.

Prout, Alan. 2000. "Childhood Bodies: Construction, Agency, and Hybridity." In *The Body, Childhood, and Society*, edited by Alan Prout, 1–18. New York: St. Martin's Press.

Skuse, Andrew. 2005. "Enlivened Objects: The Social Life, Death, and Rebirth of Radio as Commodity in Afghanistan." *Journal of Material Culture* 10 (2): 123–137.

Sutton-Smith, Brian. 1986. *Toys as Culture*. New York: Gardner Press.

Sutton-Smith, Brian. 1997. *The Ambiguity of Play*. Cambridge, MA: Harvard University Press.

Svitak, Adora. 2010. "What Adults Can Learn from Kids." TED Talk, Long Beach, CA. Accessed April 13, 2010. http://www.ted.com/talks/adora_svitak.html.

Vannini, Phillip. 2009. "Introduction." In *Material Culture and Technology in Everyday Life: Ethnographic Approaches*, edited by Phillip Vannini, 1–12. New York: Peter Lang.

Witmore, Christopher L. 2006. "Vision, Media, Noise, and the Percolation of Time: Symmetrical Approaches to the Mediation of the Material World." *Journal of Material Culture* 11 (3): 267–292.

Young, Susan. 2008. "Lullaby Light Shows: Everyday Musical Experience among Under-Two-Year-Olds." *International Journal of Music Education* 26 (1): 33–46.

Young, Susan, and Julia Gillen. 2007. "Toward a Revised Understanding of Young Children's Musical Activities: Reflections from the 'Day in the Life' Project." *Current Musicology* 84: 79–99.

32

ECONOMICS, CLASS, AND MUSICAL APPRENTICESHIP IN SOUTH ASIA'S BRASS BAND COMMUNITIES

GREGORY D. BOOTH

This study examines the musical lives of two young men, Pappu (b. 1986) and Imran (b. 1994), living with their family in Northern India (see Figure 32.1). It is based on ethnographic research in the world of Indian wedding bands and bandsmen (Booth 2005), which began in 1988. I do not reiterate the results of that ethnography here. This study is also based on my long-term relationship with the boys' family, especially my friendship with their father, bandmaster Muhammad Bachchhan (b. 1956), who owns and leads a brass band in India's still massive wedding band trade. Through these experiences I am able to trace the place and meaning of music over the course of these boys' lives, encompassing their musical engagement as children and adolescents, and to examine the interactions among professional and processional musicianship, socioeconomic mobility, and individual, community, and professional identity on the other.

Processional musicians in India's brass band trade often are (and are invariably understood by their culture as) marginal figures in social, economic, and musical terms. For Pappu, Imran, and other children in this community, professional musicianship and an engagement in this music trade have negative implications. Even though these boys are now effectively young men, the issues addressed here have

Figure 32.1: Pappu and Imran with their father.

structured their musical lives since birth and through their childhoods, and they continue to affect other young boys in the trades (such as their nephew Farhad'deen, see below). The meanings and economic implications of some forms of musicianship as constructed by South Asian culture do indeed make music something to be avoided (Web Figure 32.2 ⊙).

Briefly, Indian bandsmen derive the vast bulk of their incomes from the fees paid to them for their performances (consisting almost exclusively of renditions of popular Hindi film songs) that accompany wedding processions. In the weddings of most Indian families, especially Hindu families, such a procession is one of the important rituals that constitute the wedding. Because most Indian weddings are seasonal, brass bandsmen also work seasonally; many are also migrant workers, moving from their homes in smaller towns and villages to play for other bandsmen in larger cities who own the shops and who handle all the interactions with customers. Bandsmen tend to have low levels of formal education (less than eight years on average) and have generally acquired what musical training they have received from family members or from local music masters in an apprentice system. For sons of band owners, musical training is part of the economic life of the family. However much their families love them, Pappu and Imran (and other children like them) are economic factors in the maintenance of what are effectively family businesses.

In this region of Uttar Pradesh, India, the most obvious aspects of children's music culture are simply part of adult music culture; there are few alternatives that do not involve electronic music media. Certainly, small children play with instruments as toys, for the enjoyment of the noise, but the distinction between music as a matter of personal interest and a source of satisfaction and music as a necessary activity for the feeding of families is at the heart of this study. For Pappu and Imran, involvement in the adult world of brass bands is not a matter of choice, but key to supporting their father in his efforts to maintain his family. This study seeks to untangle the factors that shape these musical lives and that have compelled Pappu and Imran into an increasingly devalued musical profession.

The musical world into which Pappu and Imran were born has been shaped largely by their family and community history, their Muslim identities (which make them part of India's largest and most politicized religious minority), and their community's understandings about music and childhood. The impact of these factors on their lives is best understood in the context of (1) the transitional nature of this community's practices of capital accumulation and transmission, (2) a South Asian socioeconomic context that is changing with increasing rapidity and that renders the older aspects of such practices ever more obsolete, and (3) long-established local understandings about the low status of music and musicians in processional practice in South Asia. Ultimately, for Pappu and Imran and for their father (and for many of their uncles, cousins, grandfathers, brothers-in-law, nephews, and other males in the family), these conditions have made professional musicianship one of a handful of realistic life choices. In a recent conversation on this matter, Pappu offered his version of a distinction that is widely encountered in South Asian Islam between an interest in music and what he explains as life, in this case, the pursuit of music as a profession: "I am not playing music out of interest, this is our life."[1] This distinction is one that has deep roots in South Asian culture. Baily (1988) reports in detail the implications of Afghani distinctions between amateur or even dilettante musicianship and those who display their musical talents and skills in order to make a living. A dependence on music for one's livelihood is something best left to members of low-status social groups in Afghanistan (and in other parts of South Asia). Bourdieu reminds us that

> the share in profits which scarce cultural capital secures in class-divided societies is based, in the last analysis, on the fact that all agents do not have the economic and cultural means for prolonging their children's education beyond the minimum necessary for the reproduction of the labor-power least valorized at a given moment. (1986: 49)

The highly class-divided world of "traditional" India together with their community identity and family's specific history have all imposed constraints on Pappu's and Imran's lives. Those constraints have limited their options (especially in matters of education, as Bourdieu notes) and have made it extremely difficult for them to avoid inheriting their father's cultural and economic position in Indian culture, even though they and he realize that this position has long since ceased to be desirable and is becoming increasingly tenuous economically.

A SOCIAL AND MUSICAL FAMILY HISTORY

In addition to Pappu and Imran, Bachchhan's family includes his wife (b. 1960) and his daughters (b. 1982 and 1991).[2] The family home is in Rampur (Uttar Pradesh State; population approximately 282,000, according to the last available census information in 2001), the former (pre-1947) capital of the Nawabs (princely rulers) of Rampur, descendants of Afghan Rohilla mercenaries who wandered into India in the eighteenth century. Bachchhan asserts that his ancestors were, in fact, Rohillas who came to Rampur with their leaders, who became the Nawabs. In South Asian Islam, Muslims who can claim descent from Arab, Persian, Turkic, Afghan, or other supposed pre- or non-Indian Muslim groups are traditionally understood to be socially superior to those whose must claim descent from groups of Hindus converted to Islam. Bachchhan, for example, is very clear about his social superiority to Muslim bandsmen in some eastern cities (with whom he has worked), whose ancestors were probably low-status Hindus and who converted to Islam in an effort to improve their socioeconomic standing. However, like some other forms of cultural and social capital in which Bachchhan has invested, this distinction is somewhat outdated and less valuable than it was twenty or more years ago.

Since 1947 and Indian independence, although it retains a distinctively Muslim identity, Rampur's position as a regional center of Islamic art and culture has declined significantly. Depending on the perspective of those asked, the city's predominantly Muslim population (sometimes estimated to be as high as 85 percent; the district is officially recognized by the Indian government as a minority concentration district) has either made it harder for the government to undertake change (because of the alleged obstinacy of the local Muslim population) or has made it easier for the government to neglect local development (allegations of Muslim disenfranchisement/ disempowerment are common in Indian politics). Regardless of the realities of this matter, which are beyond the scope of this study, Rampur is distinctly underdeveloped in modern terms, even in comparison to other Uttar Pradesh cities of its size.

Pappu and Imran are of the third generation of an extended family in which cultural and social capital have been embodied (although not exclusively) in musical knowledge and skills, marriage relationships with other musical and band-owning families, the reputations of individual musicians and band shops, and professional relationships with other musicians. For the brass band world, theirs is an especially musical family, but this has proven to be a mixed blessing.

Their paternal grandfather, Abdul Rashid (c. 1925–1989), was a bugler who served as a household musician for the Nawab of Rampur. Their maternal grandfather, Muhammad Guchchhan (c. 1910–1986), was a clarinetist and wedding bandsman who received instruction in classical Hindustani raga from at least two of mid–twentieth-century India's more famous classical musicians, Ustad Wazir Khan (a Rampur court musician) and Ustad Feroze Khan (who performed regularly in Rampur). With this training and in his time, Guchchhan could thus aspire to a musical career beyond the world of wedding bands. In addition to his band and his performances with them, he was employed as a radio artist by the government-owned All India Radio and even played concert programs of classical music. He enjoyed significant regional status in the mid-twentieth century.

Three of Abdul Rashid's four sons (of whom Bachchhan is the youngest) have been engaged in the band trade for much or all of their lives. When Bachchhan was twelve years old, Abdul Rashid apprenticed his youngest son to Muhammad Guchchhan, whose family still lives next door to Bachchhan's family home. As was not uncommon practice among musicians in mid–twentieth-century India, the musical apprenticeship involved not only the transmission of musical and professional knowledge from Guchchhan to Bachchhan but also a more formal relationship when the two families agreed that Bachchhan would marry Guchchhan's daughter (Web Figure 32.3 ●).

The training that Bachchhan received from Guchchhan, in effect, replaced part of the financial obligations that Guchchhan's family would have otherwise incurred as part of the financial exchanges that are a formal part of most wedding arrangements in traditional Hindu and Muslim communities. Whether one calls it dowry (which is illegal in India) or any of its other names, such exchanges inevitably favor the family of the groom over that of the bride. Sons are thus a form of cultural capital on which families can trade. Bachchhan's musical apprenticeship thus took on direct economic value, replacing, perhaps, a set of furniture, cooking utensils, jewelry, or other goods that Guchchhan's family would have been expected to provide. This training would subsequently allow Bachchhan to aspire to a musical career that exceeded the limits of his father's role as court bugler. In the long run, this may not have been the best investment Abdul Rashid could have made for Bachchhan, but at the time, given Guchchhan's reputation and obvious success, an investment in the cultural capital that a classical music apprenticeship represented seemed quite reasonable.

ACCUMULATING AND TRANSMITTING CAPITAL IN LATE TWENTIETH-CENTURY INDIA

The complex interconnections between the families had two structural consequences (in addition to the human consequences of Pappu, Imran, and their sisters, of course). The first was what became a three-generation involvement in the wedding band trade—a growing field in the mid-twentieth century and an expression of Indian modernity. The second consequence was a two-generation connection, increasingly tenuous though it became, to India's classical music heritage.

Like many in his trade (and indeed, like his teacher), Bachchhan spent the early years of his career as an itinerant bandmaster, playing for wedding processions during India's annual wedding seasons in various bands owned by others; by 1995,

Figure 32.4: The Master Abrar Band.

however, Bachchhan had managed to amass enough economic capital to lease his own band business in the market town of Muzaffarpur in Bihar State, the Master Abrar Band. As a commercial enterprise, a band requires the owner to invest in the paraphernalia of a brass band shop, as shown in Figure 32.4: the actual physical space for an office (for bookings and storage), publicity, banners, uniforms, the musical instruments themselves (most of which are owned by the band owner), and so forth. Band owners are effectively capitalist subcontractors; they use their accumulated capital to harness the labor of other less successful bandsmen in the attempt to produce more personal wealth.

Despite the fact that the two towns are separated by 872 kilometers (a distance that takes twenty or more hours to cover by public bus or train), Muzaffarpur has been something of a steady market for Rampur band owners (Guchchhan's band was located there). Rampur's unusually large Muslim population has limited the value of that city as a market for wedding bands because many of the city's Muslim families, following the stricter interpretations of their religion, do not use brass bands or indeed any music in their wedding processions (Web Figure 32.5 ●).

Because music, musicians, and musical instruments are often in their homes, children in band-owning families interact with their fathers' profession almost from birth. This is apparent in Web Figure 32.5, in which Bandmaster Mumtaz leads a rehearsal in the front room of the family home, while his children (and his brother's children as well) cluster around him, with his youngest daughter climbing in and out of his lap. There is often considerable professional, largely preparatory activity as musicians learn songs (aurally), rehearse, and work out arrangements. As soon as they can walk, children wander into the midst of rehearsals or practice sessions or pick up stray instruments. Drumsticks and drums seem to be universal favorites for children, along with other percussion instruments that make noise readily. Musical instruments are toys; indeed, small drums of various kinds are often purchased as toys for children. Playing with the materials of their fathers' professions is also a way for children to imitate adult behaviors and interact with their fathers. This may take place in unstructured and untutored ways, when children imitate the music-producing motions and gestures they observe. As Figure 32.6 illustrates, however, for boys, early experiences with musical instruments may simultaneously be play and the beginnings of their musical apprenticeships, as boys learn the skills and behaviors that will be part of their profession. In this family specifically, Bachchhan also enjoys listening to music cassettes of Hindustani classical music, *ghazals*, *qawwalis*,[3] and other light classical forms. In addition, since the advent of cheap video compact discs around 2000, the boys have been exposed to the music of the American cinema. Although Pappu and Imran are at least familiar with the sounds of a relatively wide musical world, their musical preferences are for the Hindi cinema, especially since they can understand the lyrics.

The family home in Rampur is two rooms facing a courtyard (with a common hand-pumped tube well and latrine, but with two cooking spaces) shared with the families of two of Bachchhan's brothers. The home has become considerably less practical as the children have grown; it will be impossible to continue living there

Figure 32.6: A young Pappu demonstrates children's ability to conflate play and professional behaviors. Rampur, 1994.

when Pappu (to say nothing of Imran) is married. Increasing the difficulties of their living situation is the significant degree of interfamily tension regarding the ultimate fate of this jointly owned property. Bachchhan is slowly building a new house in a newer part of Rampur; until this is completed, the family will continue to spend roughly half their year in living in rented premises in Muzaffarpur.

When Pappu and Imran were young, they stayed home with their mother while Bachchhan traveled and, later, managed his band in Muzaffarpur. Pappu benefitted from this stability in that he was able to attend a government-run school for roughly seven years. He was subsequently, if relatively briefly, apprenticed to a man who ran an electronics repair shop. Imran's educational history has been negatively affected by his father's successful transition from itinerant bandmaster to band owner and the geographical split in the family's yearly existence. It has also suffered from the delayed implementation of the Indian government's Right to Education Act. This response to a 1993 supreme court order will soon make schooling mandatory for all children between ages six and fourteen, but at the time Imran was old enough to begin going to school, the family's bifurcated existence (part of the year in Rampur, part of the year in Muzaffarpur) made it impossible for him to attend school. In consequence, he has had no formal education. All the children can read *devanagari*, the script in which Hindi is written. Pappu can read English script but has little facility with spoken or written English. Bachchhan can also read the Persian-based Urdu script.

Children's musical training in this world takes the form of family-based musical apprenticeship. It inevitably has economic implications, in that it is imparted with the idea that the emerging musician will contribute to a family band. Pappu began learning saxophone, his father's "second instrument," but switched to harmonium, a traditional melodic instrument for much North Indian music. His father taught him the basics of this instrument and some basic raga information; but over the course of Bachchhan's career, amplified electronic keyboards have come to occupy an increasingly central place in the brass band business. In 2004, Pappu acquired his first electronic keyboard, a relatively simple Casio. He has since moved on to more sophisticated and elaborate keyboards, with built-in rhythms and chord features. Pappu has had to work out these technical features for himself by trial and error, or by asking friends, since Bachchhan has no understanding of (or interest in) modern technology and English is the universal language of most instruction manuals.

Like most boys in this community, Pappu was acting as a young adult rather than a child by the time he was twelve. At that time, he began to accompany his father during the wedding season to Muzaffarpur, spending his time practicing keyboard (and saxophone) and learning how to manage the family business. Young boys in band families are often taught to sing film songs that were originally sung by female film singers. They then become featured singers in wedding processions using portable amplification systems to carry their voices above the sound of the band. Pappu and Imran both sang for the family's band when they were younger, but as their voices changed both shifted to instrumental performance. Pappu will sometimes still sing male-voiced songs but more commonly uses the amplification system to lead the band using his electronic keyboard. Because he is the eldest son, Pappu has begun to feel some of the responsibility for his family's survival.

Imran began learning to play clarinet and saxophone around the age of nine or ten and, like his brother, began playing in processions when he was roughly twelve or thirteen years old. Playing a wind instrument in an Indian wedding procession requires more physical stamina than does singing or playing through an amplification system. Processions typically last two or more hours and often require additional hours of travel and waiting before and after the actual event. Wedding processions are loud events in which environmental hazards (noise, fireworks, dancing, sometimes inebriated customers, and pedestrian and motor traffic, etc.) abound. The poor quality of many instruments often means that bandsmen must exert considerable effort to produce the requisite volume. The job is physically taxing, "too much work" as Imran describes it. Bandsmanship, especially in a leadership position, requires a highly flexible sense of musicianship and ensemble and sensitivity to aural and behavioral cues from both other musicians and from processional participants (who are often dancing). The boys now share with their father the musical leadership of the band and the commercial management of the business.

PERFORMANCE MANAGEMENT AND SOCIOMOBILITY IN THE BRASS BAND TRADE

Processional music performance in South Asia carries multiple connotations of low socioeconomic status, whether constructed in modern terms of socioeconomic class or in terms of the older English-Portuguese word "caste," with all its complex religious, cultural, and hereditary implications. In both understandings, however, actual musical performance in processional settings can be a significant factor in confirming the negative social and musical the strength of these assumptions. Bachchhan's family are Muslim, as are many band families, and are thus one step (but only one) removed from the traditional caste-based implications of their trade because these have their origins in Hinduism. Despite their separation from the direct religious implications of processional musicianship that directly affect Hindu bandsmen, Muslims are caught up in the negative associations that come with the processional musicianship.

The widely encountered pattern of upward social mobility in the band world (in which Bachchhan has taken the first two important steps) has been from musicianship to musical leadership to band ownership. At the point of ownership, however, most band owners seek gradually to distance themselves from actual music performance and retain a purely managerial (nonmusical) role. The increasingly marginalized musical role of bandsmen has exacerbated this trend. In a field in which musical performance generates little musical prestige and explicitly negative social connotations, only a very dedicated (or very desperate) musician would continue performing if there were realistic and reasonable alternatives. Bachchhan, however, has never considered disengaging from musical performance. Unlike some of his peers in the trade, much of his sense of self and identity are tied into his long and relatively sophisticated training and his interests in classical music. These make it harder than normal for him to make this transition that is often essential for upward sociomobility.

Many band-owning families who make the shift to management subsequently seek to ensure that their children have nothing to do with their former profession. They also seek to increase their engagement with alternative income streams and forms of cultural and social capital, such as training in other trades, higher levels of English-style education, and marriage relationships outside the band world. Pappu's brief experiences in the world of electronics repair was just such a move on the part of his parents, who did not initially intend for their sons to follow their father into a permanent or full-time commitment to music and the brass band trade. The fact that Bachchhan had no brothers who were willing to help him in his band business meant that these plans had to be altered.

Roughly ten years ago, Bachchhan's eldest daughter was married into a brass band family near New Delhi, owned by her new father-in-law and managed by her husband Feroze (b. 1982). Like Bachchhan and his wife, Feroze and his wife are equally determined that their son, Farhad'deen (b. 2001) not follow his father into the band trade. Feroze's response to the question is an emphatic and immediate "No." Farhad'deen is currently going to a government-run English-medium school, which represents the most widely recognized and easily accessible potential exit strategy for bandsmen's children. Nevertheless, Feroze notes that "changing lines is not easy."

The difficulties involved in leaving the world of processional musicianship behind revolve around the fact that a successful band is rarely a one-man undertaking. If Feroze is going to be successful at keeping his son out of the trade, he will need to ensure that he has other reliable support, preferably from within his family. This is something Bachchhan has not been able to do. The need for musical leadership and performance management, as well as for economic oversight and customer interaction, is more than one individual can undertake. Bachchhan and his sons are forced to maintain their family's investments in the band world simply because it is their only source of income and their only major capital investment.

Furthermore, and for whatever reason, it has often been harder for Muslims than other bandsmen to accumulate the alternative forms of cultural capital necessary for the development of alternative career pathways for their sons. Although this might appear to be due to a greater reluctance among many Muslim families to consider alternative "nontraditional" pathways, my perception is that such reluctance is in fact a result of the broader political challenges that Muslim communities face in India.

The ways that Pappu and Imran behave outside of professional settings and the ways that they describe the role of music in their lives reflect the ambivalence built into their family history and their position. Outside of a procession or the Bachchhan Band premises, one would not necessarily have any idea that either was especially interested in music. Of the two, Pappu is, not surprisingly, the more articulate. Imran, like many fifteen-year-old boys, is still forming his views on many matters and rarely reflects on the conditions of his life. When asked, he will agree that he likes music. His response is, no doubt, the one that he thinks is appropriate, but he is probably also responding to the fact that he is taking on more of a leadership position (as a son of the owner) than he was able to do three to four years earlier. Music is thus allowing him a degree of social and professional status he had previously not experienced (as the youngest member of the family, he is still the one who runs errands for all concerned and is only beginning to emerge from the lowest position in the family's social hierarchy).

Despite Imran's formally expressed liking for music, his behavior suggests a fascination, which is widely recognized in his family, with the items of modern technology, such as mobile phones (he has a collection of old phones that he sometimes tries to revive or take parts from), video players, cameras, and portable electronic games. From his childhood, Imran has been fascinated by such items, which began to appear widely in India just as he was growing up. For many years he has been in charge of the family's succession of audio and videocassette and, recently, DVD players, arranging the cables and learning—largely by trial and error—how things work and which buttons do what. His access to music outside the family is largely through bootleg video compact discs (VCDs), available in local markets throughout India, that offer the latest Hindi films but also the latest Hollywood films (dubbed into Hindi). Imran prefers Hollywood films because "they have better fighting and chases." But he nevertheless realizes that Hindi films are important for the family business; and ultimately, "the songs in our films are better." Although neither boy feels the need to mention something so obvious in their world, their preference for and attention to Hindi film songs has a clear professional basis. As part of the leadership structure in the band, the boys will be responsible for helping to teach the new film hits to Bachchhan bandsmen and for making performance choices during processions.

Although he has no training in such things and cannot read English-language operating guides, Imran is the local technical expert and is constantly reconfiguring the electrical wiring in the house to accommodate the family's collection of mobile phone and camera battery chargers, in the face of limited electrical outlets and limited electricity. Unlike his father, with whom I have lengthy conversations about music and musicians, Imran's questions to me are about computers, disks, and other technological matters. He does not reflect on (and does not seem to recognize) the discrepancies between his behavior and his formally expressed position.

Pappu is twenty-three, however, and the differences in the brothers' positions may simply be one of age or temperament. Although he also expresses interest in music generally, and clearly respects his father's and my knowledge of classical music, he can articulate the distinctions, described above, between music as interest and music as profession. Although both he and Imran are competent band musicians, Pappu is fondly dismissive of his father's musical orientation: "He's always thinking about music." In 2008, when Bachchhan seemed to be in poor health, we discussed suggesting that he take more of a managerial role and leave the hard physical labor of the wedding procession to his sons. Pappu agreed with the logic of the idea but saw little hope of Bachchhan agreeing to such a plan: "For him [Bachchhan], music is all there is." The unspoken implication in his comments, of course, is that music is *not* all there is for him (Pappu). Nevertheless, Pappu is old enough to reflect on the fact that regardless of the success of the Master Abrar Band, if he wishes occupational choices, he will need to make significant changes in his life. As things stand, he has little access to any practical alternative.

Bachchhan has not successfully transmitted to Pappu or Imran his knowledge of classical music, and neither demonstrates any special interest in it. Although both verbalize respect for the classical tradition, they do not listen to it even when their father and I do. They do not know the names of musicians or ragas or possess any of the other information or behaviors that classical musicians (or classical music fans) demonstrate. Pappu is aware, however, of the discrepancy in his lack of this knowledge, especially as the son of a distinctively classically orientated bandmaster. He argues that music in general, but especially classical music, is something that has to be learned when one's mind is at ease and (with complete justification) that this is rarely possible in the band world.

In addition to the difficulties of learning classical music under the conditions Pappu currently experiences, there are other impediments that he does not mention, primarily that even if he and his brother were consummate classical performers, there would be no demand for such music or performances from the consumers of brass band music, who expect nothing but film songs. Although there certainly was such demand when Bachchhan was learning music in the 1960s, India and Indian music culture have changed radically since that point. Bands are expected to play the latest film hits and little else.

MUSIC AND PROCESSIONAL MUSICIANSHIP IN A "NEW" INDIA

The brass band trade is presently almost entirely dependent on the widespread practice of the groom's family processing with music and celebration to the bride's family home. In this, the brass bands are part of South Asia's long-standing practice of the wedding procession, at which bands have been a constant feature for most of the twentieth century. Such processions continue to be part of wedding rituals in the twenty-first century, although there are indications that the practice is becoming more negotiable, especially in the major urban centers. Bandsmen, most of whom must earn a significant portion of the yearly income during the three to six months of the wedding season, are sensitive (and vulnerable) to even minor fluctuations in demand; but men of Bachchhan's generation perceive a general increase in the difficulties of their trade and a general decrease in demand.

Faruq is the father of Feroze (above), who is Pappu's and Imran's brother-in-law, and thus the grandfather of Farhad'deen. He recently pointed out that increasing levels of education and modernization in India are widening the already considerable social and financial distance between themselves and "new" India. Like his son Feroze, Faruq is insistent that his grandson (Pappu's nephew) not join the family business: "The times are changing; this line is no longer any good for us. I think that in some years it will be completely finished." As more bandsmen reach such conclusions, more emphasis will be placed on formal education for more sons and grandsons (daughters will probably take some time yet, at least in some communities). For Pappu and Imran and many of their contemporaries, however, the challenge is managing (or at least surviving) the transition. The success of any such transition is impeded by the necessity of an ongoing source of income, which Pappu and Imran can only generate through the family music business. Any alternative training or jobs they seek cannot remove them completely from musical participation in wedding processions or shop management.

Bachchhan's acknowledged musicality and his investment in classical music actually make the process harder. Classical music training, after all, is a large investment in time and effort and is not easily abandoned. Furthermore, Bachchhan and his sons can see clearly that classical music still has value in India and the world. Indian classical music continues to operate as an economy of symbolic capital and, as Bourdieu (1993) explains, to possess a cultural value in inverse proportion to its economic value, a denial of economic realities that characterizes most classical music traditions. Nevertheless, if individuals in the band trade are beginning to perceive the inevitable change in their trade, changes in the nature and value of Indian classical music were well underway by the time of Indian independence (1947). Those changes made it harder, and ultimately impossible, for clarinetists and bandsmen to maintain a profitable or acknowledged engagement with classical music (Booth 1997). Such changes have made it increasingly difficult (and, again, ultimately impossible) for Bachchhan to participate in the symbolic economy of Hindustani classical music. Indeed, Bachchhan is the only remaining clarinetist/bandsman I know of in India that can make any claim to classical music content and performance practice. In not passing it on to his sons, Bachchhan has effectively acknowledged classical music's devaluation and the changes that have brought that on. For him personally, however, even if there is no economic profit to be had, classical music is a difficult investment simply to abandon. After all, classical music's value has never been a form of economic capital; its continued value as cultural capital at some levels (such as the international concert circuit) remains both quite significant and quite visible.

CONCLUSION: STRATEGIES FOR THE FUTURE AVOIDANCE OF PROFESSIONAL MUSICIANSHIP

As I noted at the beginning of this study, the perspective offered by these musical lives of children offers a rather negative view of professional music activity. Pappu and Imran have grown up in an intensely musical environment, even for the band trade. They have inherited a level of respect and enjoyment for classical and light classical musical styles from their father; the practical realities of their lives, however, which include the nature of their musical livelihood and the changing nature of Indian society, make that respect rather abstract and esoteric. They are coming to understand what their father has realized: however much they may respect or enjoy listening to it, music is an economically uncertain source of income.

The boys have served their musical apprenticeships and are currently working alongside their father in managing and performing in their family's business, which they will inherit when their father retires. In this, they are participants in a long-standing pattern of capital accumulation and transmission in India, one that has (for a range of reasons) characterized their community more than it has some others. The problem for them is to find a way out of their musical profession. The concerns of Bachchhan and his wife for their sons' futures are now slowly merging into the similar, incipient concerns that Pappu and his brother-in-law (Feroze) have for *their* sons' musical (or nonmusical) futures.

These very personal concerns have been framed in terms of the accumulation, transmission, and transformation of various forms of social and cultural capital. The challenges facing both the boys and their parents revolve around the need to divest themselves of the long-term investments they and their parents have made in music (and especially in processional brass band music). In order to do this and survive, they must maintain their investment in music until they are firmly established in some other line while simultaneously (or at least over the course of the next generation) acquiring the means and the access to transfer their investment into a new line.

The (non)musical proclivities of their local environment add an additional barrier in that they must all spend months of the year away from the environment in which they hope to effect this transformation (Rampur). Nevertheless, if they are successful, the lives of Pappu's and Imran's sons will be significantly improved on the socioeconomic level; they will also be considerably less musical. Given that most of their time is devoted to the brass band business and that the excess income the trade generates is limited, the family will need to exploit any nonmusical social or cultural capital they might have or be able to borrow.

With an eye on the next generation Bachchhan has recently taken what may be a considerable risk, although if it pays off (so to speak), it may ultimately prove to be a vital factor in the family's successful transition to a nonmusical future. On my most recent visit to Rampur, we celebrated Pappu's engagement to the daughter of a family from a nearby town. Marriage (especially the marriage of sons) is seen as an inevitable and positive step in this community and a cause for celebration by elders and friends. Although the wedding is at least two years away, Pappu naturally perceives his engagement as a portent of increasing adult responsibilities—especially since the traditional expectation is that his sister's marriage (which will entail considerable financial investment) must be finalized before his own marriage can take place.

Somewhat unusually, the family of Pappu's new fiancée is not a brass band family. More surprising is the fact that the father of the family is a schoolmaster and speaks some English. Still more startling is the fact that the young woman in question has completed not only her secondary schooling but is actually and currently pursuing a bachelor's degree at a local college. The wedding will need to wait at least two more years until she has completed her degree. Although I did not speak to her, it is reported that she speaks English. Such a marriage connects India's future to its past in a very direct way. In arranging this marriage, Bachchhan is taking advantage of almost the only untapped cultural capital he possesses, his eldest son. Like his father before him, he is reducing his financial expectations from his son's marriage in exchange for a form of cultural capital that he hopes will prove more rewarding in the long run. An educated wife/mother significantly improves the chances that Pappu's children will receive substantial education. Unlike his father, however, Bachchhan is investing in something that he hopes will make it easier for his grandchildren to contribute to his family's nonmusical, upward sociomobility.

NOTES

1   All quotations in this study are personal communication from the individuals named, 2008–2010.

2   This study will reflect (but not reflect on) the understandings of gender and gender relations that are part of this community's reality. The subject is well beyond the scope of this chapter, given that women do not participate directly in the musical lives described here. Generally, women (and men) marry those whom their parents choose. Men work to earn money. Women manage the cooking and cleaning and the raising of children but do not work outside the home. Women maintain a casual and largely symbolic form of seclusion from male strangers. Most wear burqas when they go out of their homes, courtyards, and neighborhoods.

3   A *ghazal* is a romantic or philosophic poem, originally and still most commonly composed in Urdu or Persian, often set to music. *Qawwali* is a specifically South Asian form of Muslim (and specifically Sufi) devotional song, traditionally performed at the shrines of Muslim saints (*pirs*) by a male soloist, instrumental accompanists, and a male choir.

REFERENCES

Baily, John. 1988. *Music of Afghanistan: Professional Musicians in the City of Herat.* Cambridge: Cambridge University Press.

Booth, Gregory D. 1997. "Socio-Musical Mobility among South Asian Clarinet Players." *Ethnomusicology* 41: 489–516.

Booth, Gregory D. 2005. *Brass Baja: Stories from the World of Indian Wedding Bands.* New Delhi: Oxford University Press.

Bourdieu, Pierre. 1986. "The Forms of Capital." In *Handbook of Theory of Research for the Sociology of Education*, edited by J. E. Richardson, 241–258. Westport, CT: Greenwood Press.

Bourdieu, Pierre. 1993. *The Field of Cultural Production: Essays on Art and Literature.* Cambridge, UK: Polity Press.

33

CONSTRUCTIONS AND NEGOTIATIONS OF IDENTITY IN CHILDREN'S MUSIC IN CANADA

ANNA HOEFNAGELS AND KRISTIN HARRIS WALSH

AT the start of the twenty-first century in Canada, parents of young children have a plethora of choices for the musical entertainment and amusement of their children. In addition to the highly commercialized materials generated by companies such as Walt Disney and Fisher-Price, not to mention television program–inspired music based on characters such as Dora the Explorer and Thomas the Tank Engine, parents can also choose from children's musicians that include Canadian artists Annie Brocoli, Carmen Campagne, David and Judy, Michael Mitchell, and Charlotte Diamond.[1] While some parents choose not to purchase CDs, DVDs, or other music "consumables" for their young children, others believe that the music, and messages contained in the song lyrics, may nurture their children's musical development while fostering a broad spectrum of other skills and knowledge. For example, many adult performers for children include songs that teach body parts, the importance of kindness and friendships, and information about the world around them. Since adult entertainers create their repertoires for their young audiences, and parents choose which entertainers their children will hear, children often have a lack

of agency in terms of the music they consume. However, the musical sounds, lyrics, and song meanings that children listen to through these performers may shape
their sense of musicality, various aspects of their personal identity, and how they
interact with the world around them.

It is important to make a distinction between the folklore that children create
for themselves and the cultural choices that adults make and impose on children.
Folklorists such as Carole Carpenter (2002–2003), Elizabeth Tucker (2008), and
Jay Mechling (1986) clarify the distinctions between children's own culture and the
increasingly pervasive outside influences from the adult world, particularly since
much of the folklore that children create for themselves challenges and subverts
the adult world around them. These musicking traditions are indeed rich and varied, but in Canada in the 1970s, children's musical worlds experienced a radical
shift as children were introduced to adult-performed music aimed directly at them
as consumers. Of course children's own culture, replete with skipping rhymes and
parodies, continued (and continues) unabated. But children born in the 1970s and
later have had more varied musical influences, largely orchestrated by parents, who
bought albums (and later cassettes, CDs, then digital downloads) and increasingly
brought their children to concerts. The sound of the music created by adults for
children from this period was similar to the music of their parents, and the lyrics
contained messages that parents considered important for their children. The children's musical canon that developed in the 1970s is now in its second generation of
Canadian children and grew out of an idealistic place in the Canadian mindset: one
that embraced the best of folk music, multiculturalism, national pride, and a growing sense of Canadian identity. Although adults both created the music and exposed
their children to it, the hegemonic effort was tempered somewhat by the grassroots
origins of the music itself. As much as the 1970s saw a marked boom in the number
of musicians who performed specifically for children, this increase not only drew
from earlier folksong collections for children but also begat future musical acts for
whom children and families were the target audience.

Canada has a unique history in the children's music industry, largely due to
the efforts of various critical figures in the late 1960s and early 1970s whose output appealed to a broad North American audience. Some performers, such as the
trio Sharon, Lois & Bram and the solo act of Fred Penner, also launched television programs that were successful in both Canada and the United States. The
large number of contemporary children's performers in Canada today is a direct
result of the legacy of children's music performers whose careers began in the early
1970s. Musical entertainment for children has become an increasingly large part
of the Anglo-Canadian music industry, continuing the long-standing tradition of,
and interest in, folk music performance and scholarship in Canada that began in
the late nineteenth century. This chapter surveys the scholarship about and historical context for Anglo-Canadian children's folk music, the development of the
children's folk "movement" in the 1970s, and the resultant Anglo-Canadian children's musical canon in order to explore the relationship between the musicians
and the selection and contents of songs through the repertoire of two musical "acts":

performers Sharon, Lois & Bram, and Raffi. Through our analysis and comparison of the music, performance practices, and song lyrics presented by Sharon, Lois & Bram, and Raffi—some of the most noteworthy trailblazers in children's musical entertainment in Canada—we will demonstrate that although there is great overlap between repertoire, target audiences, and goals, there are significant differences in the particular agendas of these two acts.

FOLK MUSIC SCHOLARSHIP IN CANADA: SETTING THE STAGE FOR A CHILDREN'S MUSIC CANON

The success of Canadian artists in the children's music industry is not surprising when one considers the ongoing interest in folk music scholarship and performance in Canada since the late nineteenth century. Indeed, it is the sociohistorical context in which these performers worked that enabled the children's music industry to develop and flourish. Folk song scholarship in Canada began in earnest in the late nineteenth and early twentieth century, with collectors such as Ernest Gagnon (1834–1915) and Marius Barbeau (1883–1969) in French Canada and W. Roy Mackenzie (1883–1957), Helen Creighton (1899–1989), Edith Fowke (1913–1996), Philip Thomas (1921–2007), and Kenneth Peacock (1922–2000) in English Canada, documenting various folk music and folklore traditions in selected regions and communities in Canada. Different agendas were at play with these scholars. Some collectors, such as Maud Karpeles (1970) and Kenneth Peacock (1965), were interested in documenting the existence in Canada of traditional songs from the British Isles and France, while other collectors wanted to preserve folk traditions before they were "tainted" by "civilization" (Karpeles 1970: 17) or "disappeared" through modernization and urbanization. Still others collected these songs as a means of illustrating a uniquely Canadian repertoire and, by extension, identity.[2] Whether the intentions of the collectors were nationalistic, preservationist, or to document concordances with existing traditions elsewhere, these folk song collectors shaped a musical canon that has come to represent "Canadian" traditional music, with a particular focus on English-texted songs and audiences. The resulting collections served as the source materials for various folk music performers, including those involved in the folk revival of the mid-twentieth century, some of whom would become children's performers in the 1970s. Indeed, some collectors, such as Kenneth Peacock (1965), devoted sections of their publications to materials and songs by and for children, while others, such as Edith Fowke and Barbara Cass-Beggs, researched and published print materials of children's music for use by families and schools, contributing significantly to the available repertoire in Canada. These two women worked in different regions in Canada and had contrasting backgrounds. Both women produced songbooks that were widely used by parents and schools alike to develop musical skills and competencies and to promote a sense of Canadian identity in song. Both were also qualified teachers—Cass-Beggs received pedagogy training at the Royal Academy of Music (London) as part of her formal music training (which included composition, piano, and voice), and Fowke received an education certificate from the Saskatchewan College of Education. This training likely influenced these women's interest in folk music for children; they also collaborated on their review of folk song publications in Canada (Anonymous 1966; M. Cass-Beggs 1973; Fowke 1969, 1970, 1972, [1973, 1978] 1983).

Cass-Beggs was born in England in 1904 and moved to Canada in 1939. As a music teacher in the public school system and with private students, she was interested in collecting folk songs that could be used for teaching purposes, and she is credited with a number of songbooks and instruction books for use in the classroom and by parents alike (Cass-Beggs 1969, 1974, 1975, [1973, 1978] 1990, 1980, 1986a, 1986b). Cass-Beggs's interest in music education for young children is also evident in the two articles she wrote about introducing children to music: "A Unified Approach to Music, as Related to Children Aged Two to Six" (1987) and "How Music is First Introduced" (1991).

Edith Fowke is similarly recognized for her important contributions of folk music materials for children's consumption and for her proliferation of folk music through various radio programs she hosted on CBC (Canadian Broadcasting Corporation) 1950 to 1974. Although Fowke's educational background was in English literature and history, in the 1940s she noticed the scant documentation of English Canadian folklore; this began her quest to find, document, and celebrate English Canadian folklore (Fowke 1972, [1973, 1978] 1983, 1990). Her role as a national promoter of folksong scholarship and performers contributed to the professionalization of the folk by showcasing various singers and songs on her radio programs and identifying the importance of folk song collecting.

The legacy of these and other folksong collectors is clear, as the songs they collected formed the canon of Canadian folk music that many performers would draw upon in the creation of their repertoires, and sometimes featuring children's songs. Indeed, the use of the collections of Cass-Beggs and Fowke in schools further contributed to the canonization of these songs for children, moving folk song creation and performance into an institutional and more formalized setting.

THE FOLK REVIVAL AND FOLK FESTIVALS: SETTING THE STAGE FOR CHILDREN'S PERFORMERS

Complementing the collection and publication of folk song in Canada was the professionalization of folk music performance and the commercialization of the "folk." Following the folk song revival of the 1940s and 1950s, when musicians such as

Alan Mills, Jacques Labrecque, Hélène Baillargeon, and Tom Kines enjoyed successful careers as performers of traditional folk music, the period of the 1960s saw a flourishing of the singer-songwriter tradition and the establishment of various folk festivals, such as the Mariposa Folk Festival in 1961, the Regina Folk Festival in 1969, and the Winnipeg Folk Festival in 1974. The "glory days" for folk music in Canada were amplified further during the period of the late 1960s and early 1970s by the heightened sense of nationalism that permeated arts and culture, as Canada celebrated its centennial year and hosted the World Expo in Montreal in 1967. Moreover, the CRTC (Canadian Radio-Television and Telecommunications Commission) was created in 1968, eventually forcing the promotion of Canadian artists through its Canadian content regulations. These developments and social context affected musicians in the 1970s and shaped various repertoires of music, including music for children. Indeed, 1969 marks the year of the first publication of both Fowke's and Cass-Beggs's collections of Canadian folksong aimed at children, and, as Sheldon Posen has argued in his article "The Beginning of the Children's (Folk) Music Industry in Canada: An Overview," the late 1960s and the 1970s saw a general boom in interest in music for children in Canada.

Perhaps most important for the establishment of the children's music industry in Canada was the development of secondary shows at folk festivals in which the children of the "folkies" were entertained by adult performers. Realizing the value of performing for young children and the positive reception they received from parents, various folk performers reshaped their philosophies and repertoires to suit their new target audience. Complementing the site of festivals for children's music was the development of folk music programming in various schools in the Toronto area; after their success performing for children at the Mariposa Folk Festival (held variously in Toronto and smaller cities outside of Toronto since 1961), many performers became involved in an educational initiative called "Mariposa in the Schools." Launched by the Mariposa Folk Foundation in 1970, the program brought successful folk song performers into children's classrooms, including Raffi Cavoukian; Ken Whiteley; Chris Whiteley; Bill Usher; Eric Nagler; and Sharon Hampson, Lois Lillenstein, and Bram Morison—this threesome later became known as Sharon, Lois & Bram. Although the Mariposa program was based in Toronto, the impact of the CBC and the general trend toward a specialized market for children's products meant that the 1970s was an ideal period for the success for performers for children. Because of the influences from Mariposa in the Schools and the increasingly popular folk music of the 1960s, much of the music that was created by adults for children sounded similar to the music that the parents were listening to. This, then, meant that the music was equally accessible to parents and to their children and enabled new children's artists to grow in popularity since their styles meshed with two generations at once. Indeed, the careers of many noteworthy children's music performers in Canada began in the 1970s and flourished into the 1980s and 1990s, with various performers releasing commercial recordings, initiating television programs, and promoting a sense of Canadian identity and entertainment for children, marking Canada as a forerunner in children's musical entertainment.

Sharon, Lois & Bram: Canada's First "Superstar" Children's Performers

Sharon, Lois & Bram emerged in the late 1970s and developed an international reputation as performers for children in the 1980s and 1990s. Each group member had a solo music career prior to uniting, but it was through their involvement in the Mariposa in the Schools program that the threesome came together as musicians. In their trio, each of the three members sings, while Bram also plays guitar and Lois the piano. Their career as a trio was launched in 1977 when they teamed up to create *One Elephant, Deux Éléphants* (1978), an album that was hugely successful in both Canada and the United States. This, coupled with their first Canadian tour in their show *The Greatest Little Touring Super Show* a year later, catapulted the trio into the spotlight in Canada (see Figure 33.1). After various special concerts and TV shows for national television stations CBC and CTV, they developed the television series *Sharon, Lois & Bram's Elephant Show* in 1984, which aired on CBC and other stations (including some in the United States) from 1984 through 1988. Nine years later their second television series, *Skinnamarink TV,* was aired on CBC in Canada and the Learning Channel in the United States, featuring Sharon, Lois & Bram with some adult-sized "puppet" characters, including CC Copy Cat and Ella the Elephant. The success of this trio is evident not only in the syndication of their television shows in Canada and the United States but also by the extensive number of commercial recordings (almost fifty) released in their twenty-five plus year career, together with ten films and television programs that have subsequently been released in video format and three collections of songbooks (1985, 1989b, and 1991a). Indeed, the

Figure 33.1: Sharon, Lois & Bram live in concert.

group's importance in Canada has been recognized through the granting of a number of awards, including Juno Awards (national music awards in Canada akin to the Grammys in the United States) for best album: in 1980 for *Smorgasbord* (1979), 1981 for *Singing 'n' Swinging* (1980), and 1999 for *Skinnamarink TV Singalong* (1998b); the Estelle Klein Award in 2009 (an Ontario Council of Folk Festival award, granted for their contributions to the province's folk music community); and the Order of Canada in 2002. In 2000 Lois retired from the trio, yet Bram and Sharon continue to perform, demonstrating their continued commitment to their young audiences and their families and the interest on the part of their audiences to continue hearing music performed by this iconic group (Miller 1992; Posen 1993). Two tracks by Sharon, Lois & Bram, "Skinnamarink" and "One Elephant, Deux Éléphants," can be heard on the companion website for this volume (Web Figures 33.2 and 33.3 🔊).

Much of the success of Sharon, Lois & Bram can be attributed to their musical interpretations of a varied repertoire that appealed to a broad audience. While their repertoire drew largely from the traditional English and French folk song repertoire associated with Canada, they also incorporated songs from other cultures (e.g., Jamaican, Ghanaian, German, Trinidadian, North American Aboriginal), musical idioms (e.g., camp songs, playground tunes, popular music), and performance practices (e.g., schoolyard chants, nursery rhymes). Some songs were also specifically composed for performance by Sharon, Lois & Bram, and in other cases, lyrics of existing songs were added to or modified to be more child friendly or to suit the goals of the performers. Throughout their careers, Sharon, Lois & Bram produced music that was engaging and enjoyable for children and adults alike, often showcasing their musical talents through instrumental solos, creative harmonization of melody lines, and a significant level of engagement with children, both on the CDs as performers and as active listeners and consumers of music. Their goals in producing music for children was first articulated on the liner notes of their debut *One Elephant, Deux Éléphants*, and when this CD was reissued in 2002 they recounted their original goals and commented on their musical journey together, writing,

> We wrote this in 1978 when *One Elephant, Deux Éléphants*, our first recording, was released. Now it—and we—are twenty-five years older. We were totally unprepared for the journey that began with "One Elephant." In fact we didn't even know there was to *be* a journey. We just wanted to make a recording of the children's songs, games, and chants we have collected and treasured over the years; to present them in arrangements both original and traditional; to feature children of all ages singing alone and with us; to contain material uniquely Canadian; to entertain and inform; to be for children of all ages, to be enjoyed by the whole family.

Various trends can be detected that illustrate the strategies Sharon, Lois & Bram used to engage children as performers and audiences. Their prodigious recorded output and highly successful career allowed the trio to experiment with different songs and styles while remaining popular with their target audience. While their music is generally aimed at young children (ages two to eight), some songs are geared more for very young children (e.g., "Mr. Sun" from *Sing A to Z* [1991b] and performed by small children, and the Iroquoian lullaby "Ho Ho Watanay" on *One*

Elephant, Deux Éléphants sung by Bram) or to older children with a more developed sense of humor and an ability to substitute words with sounds (e.g., "My Hat It Has Three Corners" from *Silly & Sweet Songs* [1998a]). Similarly, throughout their career, certain albums were marketed to a particular age group (e.g., *School Days* [2004] and *Mainly Mother Goose* [1984]) and for different listening contexts (*Car Tunes for Summertime* [1989a]) and holidays (e.g., *Candles, Snow and Mistletoe* [1993]). The vast majority of their songs are sung in English; however, some songs are sung in French (particularly those that derive from the traditional French Canadian folk song repertoire such as "Sur la pont, d'Avignon") or Spanish ("Cabillito Blanco" from *Great Big Hits* [1992]) or use vocables ("Ho Ho Watanay" from *One Elephant, Deux Éléphants*). Some songs that derive from other cultures and traditions are sometimes sung with "false" Jamaican, Cuban, or German accents. The range of sources for their music, as well as the ways in which these songs are interpreted and marketed, reinforce the broad audience that was targeted throughout their careers as well as their awareness of the movement toward multiculturalism and diversity in Canada during the 1970s.

Sharon, Lois & Bram's repertoire includes songs that are silly ("Do Your Ears Hang Low" from *Stay Tuned* [1987]) and songs that are didactic, teaching things such as the alphabet ("'A' You're Adorable" from *Smorgasbord*), body parts ("Head and Shoulders, Baby" from *Smorgasbord*), counting ("Ants Go Marching" from *Singing 'n' Swinging*), and animals and their sounds ("Grandpa's Farm" from *Sing A to Z* [1991a]). Other songs develop a sense of musical performance and an awareness of musical instruments ("Ha Ha This-A-Way" from *Mainly Mother Goose* and "One Man Band" from *Silly and Sweet Songs*). As they often draw on the Canadian folk music canon, some of their pieces have references to Canadiana, through the use of original folk songs from Newfoundland (e.g., "Newfoundland Jig Melody" from *Smorgasbord,* which includes "Lots of Fish in Bonavist Harbour" and "I's the By"), through their pronunciation of "zed" instead of "zee" in renditions of the alphabet ("'A' You're Adorable" from *Smorgasbord*), and through the use of both the French and English language within a single piece (e.g., "Michaud" and "One Elephant, Deux Éléphants" from *One Elephant, Deux Éléphants*). Equally important, however, is the emphasis in many of their songs on the empowerment of children: songs reinforce the importance of practice for mastering various skills (e.g., "Is There Anybody Here?" from *One Elephant, Deux Éléphants*); they seek to develop children's self-confidence (e.g. "I'm Terrific" from *Silly and Sweet Songs*) and they also encourage creative thinking and imagination (e.g. "Dressing Up" from *Silly and Sweet Songs*). Through their inclusion of songs that are representative of various cultures, particularly on their 1979 album *Smorgasbord*, Sharon, Lois & Bram also introduce children to cultural diversity, presenting traditional songs from other cultures (e.g., "Che che koolay" from Ghana, "Mango walk" and "Hold 'Im Joe" from Jamaica, and the Hasidic Jewish song "Chirri Bim").

What is most interesting about the output of Sharon, Lois & Bram is the ways in which they engage children's voices, both in their musical performances and as active listeners to their recordings. Children are often highlighted in performances, singing songs without adults, or often in dialogue or duet with Sharon, Lois, and/ or Bram. The frequent use of verse/chorus, strophic forms, and call-and-response in their renditions of the songs allows young listeners to join in singing as well, as they can quickly learn the responses and grow familiar with the choruses with repeated listening. However, the degree of children's voices is not consistent across the albums produced by Sharon, Lois & Bram; for example *One Elephant, Deux Éléphants* greatly showcases children as soloists, in duets with the adult singers, and in a chorus by themselves, whereas *Silly and Sweet Songs* has more emphasis on the adult trio as performers. Overall the performance style of the trio encourages active listening by and participation of the listeners, at times explicitly encouraging or directing participation.

Through their creative and engaging interpretation of a variety of styles of music from diverse sources and their active performing careers in concerts, on television, and on recordings, Sharon, Lois & Bram have had a tremendous impact on children in Canada (and the United States), particularly in the 1980s and 1990s. It is significant that parents of today are still purchasing sound recordings and videos of Sharon, Lois & Bram, passing on the rich repertoire, messages of empowerment, and lessons of life and the world to their children. Their successful blend of traditional and newly composed songs, musical performances, and, most notably, their ability to engage with children through their performances put them at the vanguard of children's entertainers in the late twentieth century.

Raffi: Breaking New Ground as a Children's Solo Artist

Raffi's emergence as a powerful force on the Canadian children's music scene is due, in no small part, to the interplay between folk song and children's music and the readiness of audiences to embrace this new repertoire. Like Sharon, Lois & Bram, he emerged from the folk music scene and made the decision to move to the world of children's music. Inspired by his desire to both please his parents and live the hippie idealism of his adolescence, Raffi struggled with his commercial success throughout his career, enjoying the financial rewards while eschewing many forms of marketing and most awards and accolades (except for those he was nominated for, such as the Order of Canada in 1983 and the Fred Rogers Integrity Award in 2006, among others) and turning down numerous opportunities to make videos (he made four) and television programs (he made none) while producing twenty-one albums in thirty years and selling 15 million copies of his books, CDs, and videos (*Raffi News*). Although his financial success brought both material benefits and personal angst, Raffi embodied the folk tradition he emerged from and consciously carried many of those ideals into his music in order to influence future generations. Raffi's music is clearly evocative of folk music of the 1960s in stylistic, lyrical, and thematic approaches, a legacy of his initial attempts at a career as a folk musician.

Perhaps it is no accident that Raffi Cavoukian, of Armenian descent and an immigrant to Canada as a child, would become a significant proponent of ethnocultural awareness and inclusion for fans of his music. Since his first album in 1976, Raffi has carefully cultivated an image of a musician that both children and their parents could be proud of. Raffi's coming of age as a children's performer came at a time when several significant social and cultural shifts occurred in Canadian society. Between the rise in popularity of folk music, the implementation of multiculturalism as a policy in Canada, and increasing environmental awareness, not only is Raffi a product of his time but he also pressed these issues to the forefront to educate children who grew up listening to his music. As he writes in his autobiography, *Raffi: The Life of a Children's Troubadour*, "For me, the appeal of what we called folk songs lay in their lyrical idealism, something that I saw not as some dreamy utopian quality, but as a potent force for good as demonstrated, for example, in the civil rights movement in the U.S." (1995: 65). That idealism is seen throughout his discography in album themes, song choices, and lyrical contents.

Raffi struggled with his selfhood throughout his childhood (and, later, adult) years, eventually leaving university studies to pursue a folk singing career as a self-proclaimed hippie. While he chiefly played music for adults in his early years and made several attempts to refocus on it during the subsequent thirty years, it is children's music that has defined his career. Raffi struggled with trying to balance a career as both a children's and an adult's musician until 1979, when—after releasing an adult album alongside his second children's album, *More Singable Songs* (1977), and seeing the latter rise to astounding heights while the former achieved moderate success—he decided to strictly play for children (Raffi 1995: 110). Over the course of his career, perhaps he made peace with this choice by eventually writing and playing for older children, where he could send a more sophisticated message to his audience and satisfy his desire for advocacy and change.

His first album, *Singable Songs for the Very Young* (1976), departed from dry or syrupy educational songs or Disney cartoon soundtracks—what Raffi recognized as the two mainstays for children at the time. Raffi felt that the underlying philosophy of the album, to be "singable" songs that kids would want to sing and adults would want to listen to, dictated his choices. The nineteen tracks feature an equal number of songs about animals ("Robin in the Rain"), silly songs ("Willoughby Wallaby Woo"), and gently didactic songs ("The Sharing Song"). These were songs that children could sing and make their own through the simplicity of the message, the inclusion of children's voices in both songs and cover art, and the simple, playful arrangements. He also focused on the idea of play in this album as well as his next two releases, *More Singable Songs* and *Corner Grocery Store* (1979), both of which contained a similar mix of silly, serious, teachable and playful songs, replete with children's creativity present in their voices on several tracks and their artwork adorning the album covers. Raffi writes, "Understanding this—the importance of child play—was key to my valuing this new music. I realized that play was the way young children learned, and that songs offered a wonderfully playful learning experience that could be both individual and shared" (Raffi 1995: 111). This interest in

singable songs for the very young

✓ great with a peanut-butter sandwich

Figure 33.4: Cover art, *Singable Songs for the Very Young.*

play is clearly seen throughout these three albums, even when music is used as a teaching tool (with songs such as "Brush Your Teeth") or as a means of exposing children to diversity (by including both the secular Christmas song "Must Be Santa" and the Hanukkah song "My Dreydel" on the same album). Where these two albums depart, somewhat, from *Singable Songs* is in the inclusion of songs in other languages ("Les Petites Marionettes" and "Sur Le Pont D'Avignon") and a wider, more exploratory range of songs from ethnocultural communities other than the Anglo-Canadian children who largely comprised his audience ("Anansi" and "Pick a Bale O' Cotton," for example). It is at this point that Raffi began to challenge his audience with new sounds and new ideas. These three albums made Raffi a commercial success and a household name with young children and their parents across Canada.

Raffi's environmental awareness and activism grew over the next few years, yet his music took an unexpected turn in 1993, when, after a time of introspection about his personal life, he decided that he had become too serious. He felt it was a time to return to play as an alternate means to inner peace (Raffi 1995: 233). Raffi's inspiration came from a popular onstage gag in which he picked up a banana and pretended it was a phone. From there came the *Bananaphone* CD (1994). This CD, one of his last new albums for children, retains the maturity in message of *Evergreen Everblue* (1990), a CD aimed at older children, but reminds his older audience of the joy and fun reminiscent of *Singable Songs*. There are equal numbers of silly songs (such as the title track "Bananaphone") and songs that focus on national or ethnocultural identity (including a rendition of Canadian icon Stompin' Tom Connors's "C-A-N-A-D-A.") The balance of the CD focuses on songs related to the environment, both animals and nature (such as "The World We Love"). The lyrics of the songs directly speak to the audience, both the children and their parents, and describe values of inclusion and environmentalism quite clearly. This theme follows in a number of his later collections, including *Songs of Our World* (2008), which likewise focuses thematically on the environment and cultural diversity.

Raffi's message of inclusiveness and welcoming of all ethnocultural identities is evident not only in the content of his songs but also in the musical styles he incorporates into his songs. In *Let's Play* (2002), he includes an homage to jazz guitarist Django Reinhardt, and he acknowledges both British pop culture and Canadian fiddle music with his rendition of The Beatles' "Yellow Submarine," featuring Canadian fiddler Natalie MacMaster. Other songs feature polka, jug band, reggae, and many other musical styles from around the world. Raffi also references public figures in his song lyrics; in one of his most famous songs, "Peanut Butter Sandwich" on *Singable Songs*, he includes the line "one for me and one for David Amram," a wink to the American musician whose name he used in part to rhyme with the word "jam." His environmental message is also reflected in some of the guest artists who have graced his albums, including Canadian musician and environmentalist Bruce Cockburn, who played on the *Baby Beluga* (1980) album, and British anthropologist and chimpanzee expert Jane Goodall, who added chimpanzee calls to the song "Jane, Jane" on *Let's Play!*—although these nuances may not be immediately apparent to the children in his audience. Raffi also introduces varying musical styles integrated with his guitar playing that increases the variety of aesthetic and stylistic practices that children are exposed to at a young age. The lyrical references to important personalities and their related causes also give parents a springboard to explore these ideas and personalities further with their children.

Raffi eventually abandoned his children's music career and began to record again for an adult audience. Although this shift has led to what some might call a less "successful" career as a musician for adults, he still focuses much of his energy on what he calls "child honouring," a philosophy that encompasses diversity and inclusion, environmental awareness, and the need to show love for all children, everywhere, in as many ways as possible. Raffi has called upon those children who grew up with his early songs who are now adults, who he dubs "beluga grads," to come to action in terms of leaving a social and environmental legacy for the generations to come. As a self-described hippie and solo artist who emerged from the legacy of the 1960s coffeehouse scene, Raffi was conscious at all times of the messages he was sending children and the responsibility of what he was bringing into their homes. Although Raffi often struggled with the commercialization of his persona and his music throughout his career, he undoubtedly benefited from his iconic status among his young fans and their parents both materially and personally. He was unable to avoid the trappings of fame and fortune, but his musical journey reflected his personal life choices. He chose and wrote songs that were important to him and that reflected his values and philosophy, seeking to influence children and how they interacted with the world around them. And, along with his contemporaries, he revolutionized how both adults and children listened to music, valuing the messages that children receive through mediated sources on a daily basis.

The Legacy of Children's Performers in Canada

It is clear that in the 1970s the music industry welcomed children's entertainers to create and produce music for mass audiences. The timing of the creation of this new niche largely influenced the style and message of the music that was to be made and performed. At this time, Canadian musicians, politicians, and the general public were struggling to develop and foster a sense of national identity, in part as a reaction to the long-standing influence of American media and also due to various initiatives in Canada that promoted nationalist sentiments and ideals. The combination of the 1960s folk festival and singer-songwriter movement, the creation of an official federal policy of multiculturalism, and events such as the Olympics and the World Exposition hosted in Canada had clear and distinct effects on how Canadians felt about themselves as a country and the culture they wanted to produce as Canadians. This lay the groundwork for the specific kinds of music and musicians that were to come out of the folk movement and move into the world of children's music, enriching the musical experiences of children and their parents and providing educators with new tools to help children develop musical, language, physical, and social skills through music. Moreover, the artists from this generation confirmed in the minds of Canadian adults and children alike that a strong Canadian musical canon could be created and maintained, and many of the songs recorded and performed by these artists are now firmly embedded in the musical world of several generations.

Raffi and Sharon, Lois & Bram are two significant musical acts for children in Canada, with similar yet distinct musical styles, performance goals, and artistic agendas. While Sharon, Lois & Bram immersed themselves in everything the world of children's entertainment had to offer, prolifically producing albums, videos, and television, Raffi enthusiastically produced music while dabbling in visual media such as television and videos. Although their outputs differed, the arrangements and instrumentation on the vast majority of songs by these two performing groups are reminiscent of the singer-songwriter trend that emerged from the folk music scene of the 1960s. Although Raffi utilized guest musicians and accompanists and, indeed, sometimes featured more complex arrangements, his low-key solo act often focused on his voice, often accompanied only by his guitar, while Sharon, Lois & Bram often included multipart singing and full bands that highlighted different musical instruments and musicians. An important distinction between the two acts might be in the content of their respective repertoires. The messages Raffi conveyed through his song choice reflected his personal politics and philosophies of the environment, children's welfare, and kindness. While Sharon, Lois & Bram might be considered "flashier" performers, they likewise chose songs that they knew would entertain and engage young audiences as listeners and singers, songs that also included an educational message.

Despite their varied approaches to music, both acts share some critical commonalities. Each enjoyed—and continues to enjoy—significant commercial success through sales of their musical products. Each drew upon folk and popular musical traditions and created new songs in forming their repertoires. The two acts, along with their contemporaries such as Fred Penner and Eric Nagler, made visible and accessible the kind of musicking that adults and children were already engaged in: silly songs, rhyming, clapping games, didactic songs, folk tunes. As significant as their influence was in the 1970s, it is critical to place them not only as products of their own social and cultural contexts but also as influential for a now-healthy and vibrant children's music industry in Canada, featuring both musicians dedicating their careers to children's music (Bobs and Lolo, Judy and David) and folk/pop musicians who have turned their hands to producing children's music (Barenaked Ladies, Colleen Power). Finally, each appealed to a broad audience of children and their parents, often promoting a sense of Canadian identity and the empowerment of children in their song selection and lyrics. Indeed, the personas and products of both musical acts are directly influenced by the sociopolitical and cultural movements in Canada at that time, including Canada's official languages policy, multicultural policy, and large-scale national and international events. The inclusion of French language songs, nods to aboriginal and immigrant communities, and "Canadian" images are found throughout their albums. And perhaps the most significant commonality between them is their child-centered focus. From the inclusion of children's artwork, to children's voices, to attempts to teach children how to take care of themselves and the world around them, Raffi and Sharon, Lois & Bram, each in their own way, took children and children's music seriously and created music to empower children as the keepers of the future. And this is why many parents have made the choice to expose their children, the next generation, to the music that they grew up with, thus ensuring the longevity of Sharon, Lois & Bram, Raffi, their contemporaries, and their successors for many years to come.

NOTES

1 While there are various Franco-Canadian performers for children, this chapter will focus on performers who primarily target an Anglo-Canadian demographic. It is important to note the unique history, context, and support for Franco-Canadian artists and audiences of children's music, which are largely concentrated in the province of Quebec, with Franco-Canadian communities in other parts of the country. Due to the linguistic

and cultural differences between French and English Canada, and the ongoing relationship between Quebec and France, there is often a closer connection of Canadian Francophone arts and culture with France than with English Canada. As a result, it is important to consider the history and development of French Canadian children's music and its performers in its unique context, which is beyond the scope of this chapter.

2 See McKay (1994) for a discussion of various collecting criteria, philosophies toward the folk and their repertoire, and the use of folk song for cultural identity and tourism purposes.

REFERENCES

Anonymous. 1966. "The National Bibliography of Folk Music." *Canadian Folk Music Bulletin/Bulletin de musique folklorique canadienne* 1 (3–4): 2–11.

Carpenter, Carole H. 2002–2003. "In Our Own Image: The Child, Canadian Culture, and Our Future." *Children's Folklore Review* 25: 1–2, 47–73.

Cass-Beggs, Barbara. 1969. *Folk Lullabies: 77 Traditional Folk Lullabies from Every Corner of the World.* With Michael Cass-Beggs. Oak Publications.

Cass-Beggs, Barbara. 1974. *To Listen, to Like, to Learn.* Toronto: Peter Martin Associates.

Cass-Beggs, Barbara. 1975. *Canadian Folk Songs for the Young.* Vancouver: Douglas & MacIntyre.

Cass-Beggs, Barbara. [1978] 1990. *Your Baby Needs Music.* Vancouver: Douglas & MacIntyre.

Cass-Beggs, Barbara. 1980. *Folk Carols for Young Children.* London: Ward Lock.

Cass-Beggs, Barbara. 1986a. *Baby's Day: Musical Moments for Mother and Baby in Song and Verse.* Kingston.

Cass-Beggs, Barbara. 1986b. *Your Child Needs Music.* Oakville: F. Harris Music.

Cass-Beggs, Barbara. 1987. "A Unified Approach to Music, as Related to Children Aged Two to Six." *Canadian Music Educator* 28 (3) (March): 22–24.

Cass-Beggs, Barbara. 1991. "How Music Is First Introduced." *Ostinato* 17 (January): 15–17.

Cass-Beggs, Michael. 1973. "Bibliography of Canadian Folkmusic," *Canadian Folk Music Bulletin/Bulletin de musique folklorique canadienne* 8: 3–5

Fowke, Edith. 1969. *Sally Go round the Sun: 300 Songs, Rhymes and Games of Canadian Children.* Toronto: McClelland and Stewart.

Fowke, Edith. 1970. "Canadian Folk Songs for Children." *In Review* (Winter).

Fowke, Edith. 1972. "Anglo-Canadian Folksong: A Survey," *Ethnomusicology* 16 (3): 335–350.

Fowke, Edith. [1973, 1978] 1983. "A Reference List on Canadian Folk Music." *Canadian Folk Music Journal* 1: 45–56; rev. vol. 6: 41–56; rev. vol. 11: 43–60.

Fowke, Edith. [1977] 1987. *Ring around the Moon.* Toronto: McLelland and Stewart.

Fowke, Edith. 1990. "Collecting and Studying Canadian Folk Songs." In *CanMus Documents, 5: Ethnomusicology in Canada*, edited by Robert Witmer, 295–299. Toronto: Institute for Canadian Music.

Karpeles, Maud. 1970. *Folk Songs from Newfoundland.* Hamden, CT: Archon Books.

McKay, Ian. 1994. *The Quest of the Folk: Antimodernism and Cultural Selection in Twentieth-Century Nova Scotia.* Montreal: McGill-Queen's University Press.

Mechling, Jay. 1986. "Children's Folklore." In *Folk Groups and Folklore Genres: An Introduction*, edited by Elliott Oring, 91–120. Logan: Utah State Press.

Miller, Mark. 1992. "Sharon, Lois & Bram." In *Encyclopedia of Music in Canada*. 2nd ed. Toronto: University of Toronto Press.

Peacock, Kenneth. 1965. *Songs of the Newfoundland Outports*. Ottawa: National Museum of Canada.

Posen, I. Sheldon. 1993. "The Beginnings of the Children's (Folk) Music Industry in Canada: An Overview." *Canadian Folk Music Journal/Revue de musique folklorique canadienne* 21: 19–30.

Raffi. 1976. *Singable Songs for the Very Young*. Shoreline/Troubadour. TR 002, LP record.

Raffi. 1977. *More Singable Songs*. Shoreline/Troubadour. TR 004. LP record.

Raffi. 1979. *Corner Grocery Store*. Shoreline/Troubadour. TR 007. LP record.

Raffi. 1980. *Baby Beluga*. Shoreline/Troubadour. TR 0010. LP record.

Raffi. 1990. *Evergreen Everblue*. Rounder. 618060. Cassette.

Raffi. 1994. *Bananaphone*. Rounder. 618875, cassette; 618062, CD.

Raffi. 1999. *Raffi, The Life of a Children's Troubadour: An Autobiography*. Vancouver: Homeland Press.

Raffi. 2002. *Let's Play*. Shoreline/Rounder. 61808, cassette; 618109, CD.

Raffi. 2008. *Songs of Our World*. Rounder. CD.

Raffi. 2011. "Raffi News: Turn This World around—for the Children!" Accessed June 5, 2011. www.raffinews.com.

Sharon, Lois & Bram. 1978. *One Elephant, Deux Éléphants*. Elephant Records. LFN-78-01, LP record; reissued 2002 Casablanca Kids, Inc. 42015, LP record.

Sharon, Lois & Bram. 1979. *Smorgasbord*. Elephant Records. LFN-79-02, LP record, cassette; Casablanca Kids, Inc. 42122, CD.

Sharon, Lois & Bram. 1980. *Singing 'n' Swinging*. Elephant Records. LFN-80-04, LP record; reissued 1998, Drive Entertainment. 43246, LP record.

Sharon, Lois & Bram. 1984. *Mainly Mother Goose*. Elephant Records. LFN 8409, LP record; Casablanca Kids Inc. 42014, LP record, CD.

Sharon, Lois & Bram. 1985. *Sharon, Lois & Bram's Mother Goose*. Vancouver: Douglas & McIntyre.

Sharon, Lois & Bram. 1987. *Stay Tuned*. Elephant Records. LFN 4-8714, LP record.

Sharon, Lois & Bram. 1989a. *Car Tunes for Summertime*. Elephant Records. CAR 48901. cassette.

Sharon, Lois & Bram. 1989b. *Elephant Jam*. Toronto: Knopf Books.

Sharon, Lois & Bram. 1991a. *Sharon, Lois & Bram Sing A to Z*. Vancouver: Douglas & McIntyre.

Sharon, Lois & Bram. 1991b. *Sing A to Z*. Elephant Records. LFN4-9016. A & M 25651 0310-2; Casablanca Kids, Inc. 42101; reissued 1998 Casablanca Kids, Inc. 43214, CD, LP record, and cassette.

Sharon, Lois & Bram. 1992. *Great Big Hits*. Elephant Records. CAS-CD 42100, CD; Casablanca Kids, Inc., 42100, CD.

Sharon, Lois & Bram. 1993. *Candles, Snow & Mistletoe*. Casablanca Kids, Inc. 42103, CD.

Sharon, Lois & Bram. 1998a. *Silly & Sweet Songs*. Skinnamarink Enterprises. 02565-19836-2. CD.

Sharon, Lois & Bram. 1998b. *Skinnamarink TV*. CD; Casablanca Kids, Inc. 42102, CD.

Sharon, Lois & Bram. 2004. *School Days*. Casablanca Kids Inc. 1022, CD.

Tucker, Elizabeth. 2008. *Children's Folklore: A Handbook*. Westport, CT: Greenwood Press.

34

A HISTORICAL LOOK AT THREE RECORDINGS OF CHILDREN'S MUSICKING IN NEW YORK CITY

CHRISTOPHER ROBERTS

OVER the past thirty years, educators and ethnomusicologists have focused increasing attention on childhood musical cultures. Their works have most often explored children's songs, singing games, and musical improvisations, examining them for musical characteristics as well as the role that they have played in child culture. Researchers have probed these musical experiences, which can be referred to as musicking (Small 1998), of children in the United States (e.g., Campbell 1998, 2010; Harwood 1993) as well as Europe (e.g., Opie and Opie 1985), Asia (Lum 2009), Africa (Addo 1996), and Australia (Marsh 1995). In this chapter, I will wind the clock backward, focusing the lens on children's musical cultures in New York City as viewed through three recordings released by the Folkways record label in the middle of the twentieth century: *1, 2, 3 and a Zing Zing Zing* (FW 7003) released in 1953 (Web Figure 34.1 ⊙); *Songs for Children from New York City* (FW 7858) released in 1978 (Web Figure 34.2 ⊙); and *Street and Gangland Rhythms: Beats and Improvisations of Six Boys in Trouble* (FW 5589) released in 1959 (Web Figure 34.3 ⊙). The first two albums chronicle the songs and singing games of children a generation apart from one another. The third album, documenting the musical material of African American boys who had been involved with the juvenile justice system, brings to light the musical experiences of a group of typically underrepresented youth in the late 1950s. Together, these recordings are powerful testimony to children's creative impulses to be musically expressive alone and together, in an urban American setting in the mid-twentieth century. While the recordings have stood on their own merits for many years, this chapter provides an occasion for examining children's own music of a historical nature in light of the findings of more recent research concerning children's culture.

Both children's musical cultures (Mans 2002; Minks 2008) and children's cultures at large (James, Jenks, and Prout 1998) have been found to reflect the various communities that surround them, such as their families, neighborhoods, and cultural and ethnic groups. But children's musical cultures also comprise a culture all their own, with their own sets of traditions and meanings (Campbell 1998, 2010; Opie and Opie 1985). Historically, childhood was often viewed as an underdeveloped version of adult culture, important only in that it eventually led to more fully formed adults (Schwartzman 2001). More recent scholarship has valued childhood as important in its own right, with recognition that childhood occurs in "a culturally and historically situated place and time, a specific here and now" (Graue and Walsh 1998: 9). Studying children from a historical perspective has proven challenging, since any potential informants have long ago grown up, leaving childhood as mediated memories (Cahan et al. 1993). Historically, collections of children's music have often come in the form of books of children's songs and games or scholarly analyses of their content and meaning. Few commercially available publications or scholarly inquiries include field recordings and virtually no recordings showcase the musicking of children of the 1950s. As such, the current inquiry into music from the past century addresses a gap in the understanding of children's musical cultures.

The study of the musical experiences of urban children in the United States extends back to at least the late 1800s (Newell [1883] 1963), continuing with fits and starts through the twentieth century (e.g., Yoffie 1947) to the modern day (e.g., Campbell 2010). The current study explores three recordings from the middle of the past century, attempting to illuminate the musical experiences of children in a specific time and place. The recordings were examined for musical characteristics (rhythm, meter, melody, tessitura, and dynamics), textual patterns, and indications of cultural values that they might highlight. Liner notes from each of the albums were probed, and the archives at the Smithsonian Folkways office in Washington, DC were reviewed for supplemental information on file concerning each of the recordings. Interviews of the children were not provided on any of the recordings or supplemental material. Thus, the opinions and perspectives of participants, now viewed as a crucial part of studying children's cultures (Cahan et al. 1993; Graue and Walsh 1998), is unknown. Nonetheless, an examination of the texts, musical aspects, and performance style sheds light on the types and purposes of musicking of three groups of New York City children from the twentieth century.

1, 2, 3 AND A ZING ZING ZING

In the summer and fall of 1952, collector Tony Schwartz recorded songs and games of elementary-aged children in an area of west midtown Manhattan that was two blocks wide and twenty blocks long. *1, 2, 3 and a Zing Zing Zing* portrays groups of children that are decidedly multiracial: "Negro and white children of Puerto Rican, Irish, Italian, Jewish and other national backgrounds, who play together in the streets, back yards and supervised play centers" (Schwartz 1953: 4). Schwartz organized the tracks on the recording by game type. The track of "Bounce Ball Songs" contains three different tunes, and different musical material comprises "Jump Rope Songs," "Ring Games," and "Rhythm," for example. Listening to these field recordings provides one with a strong sense of place, as the songs and games are accompanied by the sounds of the city—cars and taxis honking, cats meowing, trumpets bugling, and children's voices eagerly singing and talking with an accent that bespeaks "New Yawk City." This type of chronicling of children's culture in a natural setting was rare in the early 1950s (Graue and Walsh 1998), placing Schwartz at the forefront of a movement to explore children's musical traditions in a context significantly different from the laboratory-based studies typical at that time in the scientific study of children's behaviors.

Released in a time before multiculturalism was a buzzword, Schwartz chose to record and select songs that, for the most part, recorded children in multiethnic contexts. This differs from many more recent studies, which have focused on children of specific ethnic or racial groups (e.g., Corso 2003; Gaunt 2006). Even the track of church hymns portrays African American and European American children singing together, which is unusual given the racial and ethnic uniformity typically found in US churches. The one recording on the album of children in a same-ethnic context is "Juan Charrascado," sung in Spanish. The song, which tells the story of a Robin Hood–type character, was sung by a group of children newly arrived from Puerto Rico. The students did not know each other, but Schwartz noted, "Singing their own Puerto Rican songs broke down the feeling of being strangers and made them feel at home" (Schwartz 1953: 6). Creating community, both interethnically and intraethnically, appears to be a focus of the album.

Children's songs and improvisations often incorporate humorous elements (e.g., Campbell and Lum 2007; Kartomi 1991; Marsh and Young 2006), and playful wordplay and fanciful stories are found in the song texts of *1, 2, 3 and a Zing Zing Zing*. For example, the rhyme "Birdie Birdie in the Sky" (Web Figure 34.4, track 1 🔊) tells the story of a bird "dropping something" in the eye of a child, who then gives thanks that cows are unable to fly. On "Camp Songs," a girl spins a tale in which sharing a straw while sipping cider with a boy leads, inexorably, to marriage and forty-nine children (Web Figure 34.4, track 2 🔊). There are numerous textual references to authority figures as well, as children tell each other to "salute to the captain, bow to the queen" and later act out being a police officer, "Policeman, policeman, do your duty." The home culture of children often affects the texts used in children's singing

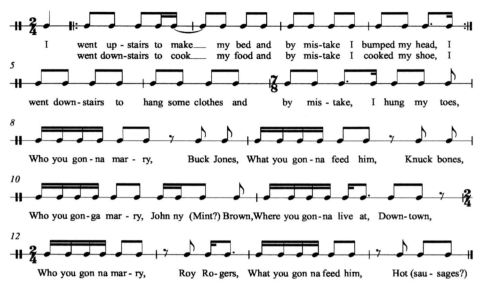

Figure 34.5: Transcription of "Who You Gonna Marry?"

games (Marsh 1995; Watts 2009), so it may be that this valuing of and respect for authority, part of the traditional mores of the 1950s (Thomson 1992) made its way into the songs of the time.

Metrically, the children's performances consist primarily of songs in duple meter (either 2/4 or 6/8). However, more complex metrical and tempo changes can be heard upon occasion, posing no apparent challenge to the children. The hand-clapping game "Who You Gonna Marry" (Web Figure 34.4, track 3 ●), for example, begins in steady duple meter, with three consecutive phrases eight beats long. It appears that the metrical pattern has been set (and that it will be continued), but at the end of the third phrase the children shift into a seemingly challenging set of rhythms in 7/8 time (see Figure 34.5). This metrical complexity is incorporated into the game with no negative impact on their vocal performance or, based on the sound of the claps in the background, the hand-clapping pattern. Children's games are typically in duple meter (Campbell 1991, 2010; Marsh 2009; Riddell 1990), although Merrill-Mirsky (1986), in her collection of songs from Los Angeles, also found occasional unproblematic forays into more "challenging" meters, and Campbell (1998) noted that children's improvisations incorporated asymmetric meters as well. While adults may view these meters as complex, children incorporate them into their play with ease (Blacking 1967; Merrill-Mirsky 1986).

Tempo changes are also occasionally incorporated into the play seamlessly. In "Head and Shoulder, Baby" (Web Figure 34.4, track 4 ●), two girls sing while performing a hand-clapping game (Figure 34.6). At measure four, when the words "head and shoulder" repeat three times in a row, the tempo increases significantly, with no detrimental impact on unison singing or the sound of the clapping pattern. The two children seem to be creating their own variant of the game, making

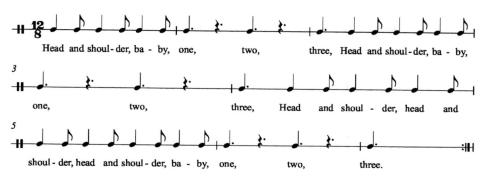

Figure 34.6: Transcription of "Head and Shoulder, Baby."

slight alterations to provide an extra challenge, a modification common in children's musical culture (Harwood 1998; Marsh 1995). Other in-song tempo modifications occur when individual children perform a rhyme, occasionally pausing in
the middle as they stumble over a word or catch their breath. These delays cause the
song to lose its steady beat, but the children continue on, unfazed. Similarly, in the
"Ball Bounce" track, one can hear the sound of a ball bouncing to the beat as different children sing or chant various songs and rhymes. Occasionally, the ball seems
to take a particularly high or low bounce, causing some words to come early or late
in the performance as the children attempt to match the beat of their word chanting
with the sound of the bounce. The children readily incorporate these tempo fluctuations without any apparent difficulty.

The majority of the musical material on the album consists of spoken chants
rather than sung material. Melodically, the songs that are included in the album generally have ranges between a seventh and a ninth. Most research of children's musical repertoire in the United States since the mid-1980s has found that playground
songs and games hold ranges of a sixth or less (Campbell 1991; Merrill-Mirsky
1986; Riddell 1990). Campbell (1991) performed a comparative analysis of songs
by children (i.e., songs created by children themselves) with songs for children
(i.e., songs taught by adults, often in pedagogical settings) and found that songs
for children generally had larger ranges. Most of the songs on *1, 2, 3 and a Zing
Zing Zing* are called "Camp Songs." As such, they could have been taught to the
children by adults, which would account for the wider range. The songs and chants
on the album unvaryingly maintain a steady dynamic level throughout each track.
Between tracks, the loudness level may fluctuate somewhat, but each individual
performance remains consistent.

Often on the recording there appears to be one child who is in charge of the
play. Harwood (1998) found a hierarchical status of performance when studying
girls' singing games in Los Angeles, in which more competent children (who were
often older) directed the activities. Marsh (2009) further noted that some children
hold more social power and may not "get out" of an elimination game when they
should. This dynamic can clearly be heard in the album's title track (Web Figure
34.4, track 5 🌐). One child begins as the lead player, "Jacqueline," while the others

attempt to topple him from this lofty status by causing him to trip up over his words in a bout of verbal dexterity. The child who begins the game as the leader has the lowest voice, a characteristic that Marsh (2009) found often indicates the oldest player. After two rounds through the game, one younger child consistently declares his or her desire to lead the game by plaintively claiming, "I'm Jacqueline!" Initially, the leader declares in a dominant voice, "No, I'm Jacqueline," moving directly into the game. Later, she or he simply ignores the other youngster when she or he tries to take charge. Eventually, this oldest child is the final winner of the game. A similar power dynamic occurs when a twelve-year-old girl shares a song learned at camp. She only wants to sing the song if the other children, aged seven to twelve, will sing with her. "Getting the children to join her was accomplished by a single sentence: 'You have to do what I say'" (Schwartz 1953: 5). Hierarchy clearly comes into play.

In play, children often make do with whatever they have at hand, and this sense of resourcefulness arises in numerous ways on *1, 2, 3 and a Zing Zing Zing*. For example, other than ball bounce and jump rope games, none of the musickings requires equipment. For a section titled "Rhythm" (Web Figure 34.4, track 6 🔊) in which teenagers were recorded in the basement of a housing project apartment building, the children used what they could find to make various rhythmic patterns, including a wooden bench, chairs, and a soda bottle. Children were resourceful with their song material as well, occasionally repurposing musical material; Schwartz notes, "Many of these selections are often used by the children for several games" (1953: 4), a phenomenon often found in musical play (Marsh 1995; Yoffie 1947). Textually, too, there are examples of enterprising behavior ("trying to make a dollar out of 99 cents"), perhaps alluding to the financial challenges faced by the families of children trying to eke out a living in a large urban environment.

Songs for Children from New York City

Songs for Children from New York City, released in 1978, also recorded the sounds of New York City children at play. Like *1, 2, 3 and a Zing Zing Zing*, this album aimed to represent the diversity of New York City children. Edna Edet, the producer of the album, observed, "The children of New York do sing 'Ring around the Rosie' and 'London Bridge Is Falling Down.' They also sing many other songs which are not part of the standard American repertoire because the children of New York are of many nations, races and cultures" (1978: 1). The songs were recorded throughout the city by informants of African, Asian, and European heritage. Of the twenty-three different songs, six tracks contained adult voices clearly leading the children. Because the purpose here is to probe the musical experiences with which children choose to engage, these six adult-directed songs were eliminated from review.

Melodically, all songs have a range of a major sixth or less. Marsh (2009) studied children's singing games in a variety of locations in the world and found that song ranges in the United States and Australia were rarely more than a major sixth, while in England, Norway, and Korea, ranges were likely to be as wide as a ninth. Despite the variety of ethnic groups represented on this album, the current findings suggest that there may be a certain "Americanization" process at work in terms of children's song range. Further, the more limited range was predominant in recent findings of child musical cultures within the United States (Harwood 1998; Merrill-Mirsky 1986; Riddell 1990). However, the range on *Songs of Children from New York City* is smaller than that of *1, 2, 3 and a Zing Zing Zing*, the latter of which was recorded twenty-five years earlier. Why the difference in song ranges between the earlier and later albums? Working in Portugal, Prim (1995) compared children's game song repertoire of the 1980s and 1990s to the recollected repertoire of adults who had been children in the 1940s and 1950s, finding that the singing range was smaller in the 1980s than earlier. It may be that in the United States, this shrinking range occurred at some point in the intervening years as well. Alternatively, it is conceivable that the songs from *1, 2, 3 and a Zing Zing Zing* were taught to the children by adults, in which case the range is more likely to be larger (Campbell 1991). Also, they may have been influenced by African American popular music of the period, which tended to have ranges larger than a tenth (Fitzgerald 2007).

Tessituras for the songs on the recording range from an A below middle C to a G above middle C, a finding similar to other researchers (Campbell 2010; Marsh 2009; Riddell 1990). The tessitura is lower than ranges suggested for singing in schools (e.g., Phillips 1996), but the lower sung vocal tessitura facilitates an easy shift between the sung and spoken parts of the same song (Marsh and Young 2006). Many of the children's songs contain a combination of sung and spoken words, with children moving easily between the two, a common pattern in children's singing games (Campbell 1998, 2010; Merrill-Mirsky 1986; Prim 1995). For example, "Miss Sue" (Web Figure 34.4, track 7 ●) begins with a spoken chant, then shifts to more clearly discernible pitches. Moreover, the spoken portion is spoken with tonal inflections similar between performers. The first time the song title's words are chanted, the pitch rises, while the second time the pitch falls, creating a type of melodic pattern. In other recordings in which the chanted text repeats consistently, the performers occasionally fall into almost perfect unison with their tonal inflections (see, e.g., "Chitty Chitty Bang Bang" [Web Figure 34.4, track 8 ●]. Marsh and Young (2006) noted that song tunes can develop from exaggerated speech inflections, which may be the case here. The phenomenon of near-perfect unison in rhymes can also be heard, perhaps, as "in-tune chanting."

Metrically, the music on *Songs for Children from New York City* falls mostly in duple meter, with the additive and mixed meters found in *1, 2, 3 and a Zing Zing Zing* not present on this recording. Rhythmically, however, syncopation is widespread. Consistently, the children anticipate the downbeat, singing and chanting syncopated patterns, even while they sometimes perform clapping patterns on the beats (e.g., "Head and Shoulder, Baby"). This further supports the contention (Campbell 2010; Harwood 1998; Marsh 2008) that music that children perform on their own holds significantly more rhythmic complexity than music that is commonly used in school classrooms. Dynamically, the recording is similar to *1, 2, 3 and a Zing Zing Zing*, in that the loudness level remains consistent throughout each individual track.

Children's singing games often incorporate musical and textual stimuli found in contemporary mediated experiences such as commercials, movies, and popular music (Gaunt 2006; Lum 2009; Watts 2009). In *Songs for Children from New York City*, children use the words "Chitty Chitty Bang Bang," a popular movie for children released in 1968. On the track "Uno dos y tres" (Web Figure 34.4, track 9 🔊), the children also sample an excerpt of the pop song "Land of 1000 Dances," originally released in 1962 by Chris Kenner as an American pop song (and performed by Cannibal and the Headhunters) and often played at sporting events today.

Individual singing games often have many different variations (Marsh 2009; Merrill-Mirsky 1986; Newell [1883] 1963; Riddell 1990). In the album's liner notes, collector Edna Edet commented that eight versions of "Here We Go, Willowbe" were found in a ten-block area of New York City (Edet 1978: 3). *Songs for Children from New York City* includes two versions of the pieces "Chitty Chitty Bang Bang," "Miss Sue," and "Miss Lucy." Intrachild variation can be found, as well. For example, on one variant of "Chitty Chitty Bang Bang," the older-sounding child leader consistently anticipates the downbeat, while the younger-sounding children speak the word on the beat. It may be that the older child is creating his or her own variant or that the younger children are not able to maintain the hand-clapping game while chanting on the offbeat. In different versions, borrowing text from other songs often occurs (Opie and Opie 1985; Riddell 1990). In *Songs for Children from New York City*, the track "Chitty Chitty Bang Bang" incorporates the text "sitting on a fence, trying to make a dollar out of fifteen cents," words that can also be found in "Miss Mary Mack" on the same album. Also, in "Hambone," one finds the text "If that mocking bird don't sing, Pops gonna buy me a mocking ring," words similar to those found in the European American lullaby "Hush, Little Baby."

Singing games often remain in existence for decades or centuries but are rarely preserved intact (Opie and Opie 1985). "Head and Shoulders, Baby," a hand-clapping game known throughout much of the United States, can be found on both *1, 2, 3 and a Zing Zing Zing* and *Songs for Children from New York City*, and a comparison of the two versions highlights some of the changes that occurred over twenty-five years (See Figure 34.7). Both games are chanted, but the later recording has more syncopation, perhaps due to the influence of popular music (Campbell 1991; Marsh and Young 2006). Metrically, children's singing games often straddle the line between simple duple and compound duple meter. The earlier recording of "Head and Shoulder, Baby" (Web Figure 34.4, track 10 🔊) is closer to 12/8, while the later rendition (Web Figure 34.4, track 11 🔊) leans toward 4/4. The texts of the opening lines are identical, but in the verses that follow, the versions diverge. The words on the earlier recording speak of various body parts to touch during the game ("knee and ankle," "eyes and nose"). On the later recording, the children begin the song with the same text but then act out movements, some of which seem likely to be far from their experience as urban youth ("cut the grass," "milk the cow"),

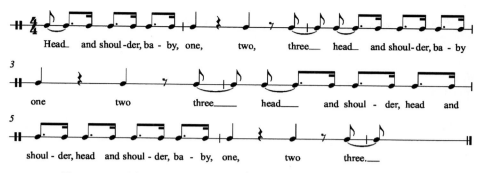

Figure 34.7: Transcription of "Head and Shoulder, Baby" (SFCNYC).

and others of which appear more urban ("soul music") or ubiquitous to childhood ("drink your milk," "comb your hair"). At the end of the song, the two players on the recording sing straight through all movements, without singing "*1, 2, 3*," stepping up the challenge in terms of the memory required to complete the task. While there is often considered a "right way" to play a game (Newell [1883] 1963), children often strive for novelty, creating their own variants to challenge themselves (Marsh 1995). Further, "master players," children who are more skilled and typically older, are often permitted to alter parts of it to provide a more challenging or musically satisfying experience (Harwood 1998). Whether the newer version on the *Songs for Children from New York City* is the variant of these two players or part of an ongoing evolution is unclear, but the skill required to successfully perform the game increased by the later recording.

STREET AND GANGLAND RHYTHMS: BEATS AND IMPROVISATIONS OF SIX BOYS IN TROUBLE

In 1959, Richard Sorensen recorded six eleven- and twelve-year-old African American boys in New York City. The children had various run-ins with the law and therefore were living in a residential training school within the city. Sorenson reports that most of the boys were members of street gangs in New York. On the recording, one hears a variety of musical styles. Percussion ensembles, using bongo drums, sticks, maracas, bottles, and even two coins struck together, send out music pulsing with energy and rhythmic dynamism. The boys also sing songs, some of which come from pop culture, others of which are children's songs, all of which are accompanied by a variety of percussion. Finally, there are a series of tracks that Sorenson calls "rhythmic and vocal improvisations reflecting personal experiences." These free-form improvisations contain spoken-word stories, typically with one boy as the main storyteller and one or two others providing occasional sound effects (sirens, etc.) and percussion accompaniment. The children had no formal musical instruction, and the performances were unwritten and unrehearsed. An album recording a group of preteen boys "in trouble" with the law seems highly unlikely to ever see release today. The Folkways label, with its bare-bones budget, kept limited supplemental information about its records, so minimal information on the genesis of this album is available.

Perhaps most notable to first-time listeners is the extent of violent activity that is revealed in the boys' improvisations. An improvised track called "Gang Fight" (Web Figure 34.4, track 12 ⬤) tells the story of a fight between rival street gangs, with specific details about the types of weapons the gang members chose to bring to the fight ("five homemade guns," "Mau Mau machete") and a final scene in which a gang member, a police officer, and a bystander all get shot. This portion of the story is told in the voice of a television or radio reporter:

> Ladies and gentlemen, there's just been a gang fight on Franklin Avenue. The Senate and Alligator Lords fighting the Vikings. The cop got shot in the back. But he say he ain't giving up. He's shooting. He done shot a lady. The lady walked by with the food. But Calvin [one of the boys] shot a man and he did got shot... [yelling] Ahhhhhhh!

On another improvised track called "Shoe Shine" (Web Figure 34.4, track 13 ⬤), the boys try to earn money by shining shoes. When they offer a shoeshine to a passer-by, the man replies, "Listen, kid, I don't need no shoe shine from a hoodlum" and proceeds to hit the child. At this, the boy rallies his gang, they surprise the prospective shoeshine client, and shoot him.

The violence often occurs as a part of everyday life. In the "Shoe Shine" example above, the boys state that they are trying to make money to go swimming on a hot summer day. In "Dumb Boy" (Web Figure 34.4, track 14 ⬤), one child copies off another child during the school day, is hit in the lip, then threatened: "Next time I catch you copying off somebody in there... I'll strangle you to death." Also, in "I Want Some Food," the principal of the residential training school hits a boy when he complains about the food that he is served. Even some of the traditional songs that are sung on the recording have texts dealing with death. In "The Fox" (Web Figure 34.4, track 15 ⬤), for example, the title character kills a goose. At times, it seems as if the boys are trying to resist inflicting violence. In "Shoe Shine," after the hopeful shoe shiner is smacked by the adult, his friend tells him, "Let's, let's get up our gang fight, man. We gotta get that man." The shoe shiner replies, "No, no, no! I don't want to hurt nobody. Remember last time?" Nonetheless, he goes along with the gang, shoots the man, and is pursued by the police.

The excessive focus on violence in the texts is an interesting commentary of New York City in the 1950s, a period that saw a spike in delinquency and rates of violence in juveniles (Fagan and Wilkinson 1998). A disproportionate number of youth in the juvenile justice system in New York City in the 1950s were African American (Baronsky 2006), so it is likely that these tales reflect the culture that surrounded the boys. However, guns, which feature consistently in the stories, were not widely available or used by gang members before the 1970s (Vigil 2003). Although

Sorenson (1953) maintains in the liner notes that most of the boys on the recording were involved in gangs, most youths involved in perpetrating gang-related violence in the 1950s were between the ages of fourteen and eighteen (Vigil 2003). As the boys on the recording were eleven and twelve, it is conceivable that the extreme violence found in the improvised texts of the songs reflects the creation by the boys of a comic book–like fantasy world. Alternatively, Corso (2003) found that musical play prepares children for their future lives through activities such as role playing, so this may be a means by which to give a dry run to the experiences of their slightly older teenage relatives and neighbors.

The song and improvisatory texts reveal other combinations of child-like and adult-like issues for the preteen boys. One hears traditional children's song repertoire sung all the way through (e.g., "The Fox"), but there are also times when known song material is elaborated upon with more mature themes. "Money Honey," a song recorded a number of times in the 1950s and 1960s by popular artists including The Drifters and Elvis Presley, recounts the tale of a person hiding from a landlord who has come to collect the rent. The tale ends with the landlord telling the tenant to pay the rent "if you want to get along with me." In the version on *Street and Gangland Rhythms* (Web Figure 34.4, track 16 ◖), an improvised section in which the tenants search for a gun and then discuss the best time to rob a nearby bank immediately follows the traditional song.

Adults in the tales are either absent or appear as persons who negatively affect the boys' lives. The police logically play a role in the gang-related tracks, but they also come up in seemingly random places. In the song "Bo Diddlie," for example, a boy is "Up on the hill now beatin' his drum," when the police come and arrest him for ostensibly playing too loud. Parents are nonexistent. Even the fox's children in "The Fox" chew on the bones of the goose, while their parents "never had such a supper in their life." Urban youth of the 1950s who had run-ins with the legal system often had parents who were neglectful at best and harmful at worst (Baronsky 2006), and the repertoire choices and textual improvisations may reflect the world around them (Campbell 2007; Mans 2002; Marsh and Young 2006). Gang violence typically occurs in low-income neighborhoods of cities (Vigil 2003), and the musical texts often reflect this lack of financial resources. In "Money Honey," when the characters in the improvisatory portion of the song are asked why they robbed the bank to pay the rent, one boy states, "I couldn't help it . . . I haven't got no money [at] home." This lack of funds often brings the disdain of others: In "Shoe Shine," a man says to the boys, "You tryin' to earn a living? You can't even wear decent clothes."

Although the grim life portrayed through the improvisations is filled with violence and unfair treatment, the musickings show ways in which the boys come together to create community. One major reason young people join gangs is to provide themselves with a sense of belonging to a cohesive group, particularly when there is a lack of traditional support structures such as the family (Thompkins 2000). In "Dumb Boy," one boy stands up for another in school, and when a man doesn't pay for his service in "Shoe Shine Shakedown" ("Look, I'm a man, you're little kids, get outta here"), a boy looks to his gang for support and, ultimately, retribution. The children demonstrate toughness and resourcefulness, as well. In "Shoe Shine," the boy stands up to the man who doesn't pay, stating, "We never run, we never cry." When they are faced with a lack of financial resources, the boys try to figure out ways to obtain money: shining shoes to pay for the trip to the swimming pool or robbing a bank to pay the rent. Even the fox in "The Fox" demonstrates resourcefulness when he figures a way to bring a goose home for his family to eat. Further, the boys still hold out hope for better things. On "I Want Some Food" (Web Figure 34.4, track 17 🔊), the speaker states, "I'm muscle-bound... want to be another Floyd Patterson," a reference to a famous champion boxer of the mid-twentieth century, and later says, "I'm gonna get outta here, if I have to break the walls down." One roots for these kids to make it but fears that they will not.

At times, the improvisations of the boys are told in story-like fashion, with no rhythmic or melodic aspect to the storytelling. The drums always accompany the tales and often reflect the intensity of the story. During periods of tension, they grow louder and faster, while when the tension eases, the drumming slows down and the volume diminishes. The voices also speed up and increase in volume when the excitement of the plot grows and slow down and soften when the plot comes to points of relaxation. The dynamic variation in the improvisations differs from the other two albums examined, in which the dynamics within songs were unfailingly consistent.

At other times, the vocal parts of the improvisations are more musical, full of rhythmic pulsing, rhyming, and assonance. Call-and-response forms, often found in children's singing games in the United States (Marsh 2009) and with African American children's games in particular (Gaunt 2006), figure prominently in the improvisations. The tale of "Gugamuga" (Web Figure 34.4, track 18 🔊) spun by one boy is punctuated by cries of "yeah" and "uh-huh," at regular intervals of four beats, slightly reminiscent of shouts of "amen" one often hears at African American churches in the United States. In "Bo Diddlie," bongo drums also serve as a response, giving structure to the improvised piece by answering the spoken tale at regular intervals, perhaps providing the storyteller the opportunity to plan his next line. Finally, on "Sister Suki," the last word or two spoken by one boy at the end of a phrase is echoed by another one of the boys, again providing a structure to that portion of the piece. For the most part, the boys' improvisations tell stories with logical plots. At times, however, the rhyming of the words appears to take precedence over its lexical meaning, a pattern often found in children's song and game repertoire (Minks 2008). For example, in "Gugamuga," one boy says,

> Sapphire... bring my food
> Put it on the table with my new shoe
> Oh no, not on the dew
> Baby, baby, baby, you got the flu

Many of the musical aspects that were found in the other two recordings in the study were also found here. Most songs, both preset and composed, are in duple meter, with syncopated rhythms. One hears vocables peppered throughout the recordings and easy shifts between sung and spoken sections of the same song. There are references to contemporary life (the cha cha cha, e.g., was a popular dance in mid-century), and the tunes and texts of popular songs, sometimes altered by the boys, are incorporated into their musickings. Further, the boys shift between spoken and sung vocalizations within the same song. Also, the voice of one boy is heard more consistently than the other two, seeming to direct the musical activities, which suggests that he may be the leader of the group, socially as well as musically. Melodically, both the songs and improvisations fall within a range of a sixth.

"Shake It to the One That You Love the Best": Children at Musical Play, Historically

The study of history helps us to understand people and societies, to deepen our sense of cultural identities, and to further understand change and how our societies function by gaining access to "the laboratory of human experience" (Stearns 1998). Children's musical histories can be studied by revisiting the recordings of children at musical play from an earlier time. The current study probed three recordings of children's natural musicking behaviors released by the Folkways record label in the mid-twentieth century, offering an occasion for exploring textual, musical, and per-formance aspects. Textually, patterns of humor, "trying on" adult ideas, and specific references to the children's social situations were found. Textual and musical varia-tion of song material was common, with variants found both within and between recordings. Musically, the songs were generally in duple meter, although additive and complex meters were occasionally incorporated into singing games with no apparent difficulty. Rhythmic syncopation was widespread. The vocal range of the children's singing was wider on the earlier recordings than the later one, and the tessituras held notes that mostly fell between an A below middle C to a G above it. Singing games were performed at a consistent dynamic level, but improvisatory tales employed dynamic contrast to heighten and lesson tension in the stories. Performance prac-tice suggested a hierarchy of performers, with stronger players directing the play. Future research could compare the findings of the current study with other recorded sources of a historical nature, both from the United States and around the world.

One of the ways children throughout the world create community with each other is through their musicking. The children in New York City in the recordings explored were surrounded by change, as the country moved from a post-World War II era of traditional mores into the time of Sputnik and Civil Rights. Throughout it all, the recordings under study highlight children working and playing together to make musical experiences that pleased them, from the giggling girls with their hand-clapping games to the tough-sounding boys with their improvisations. The recordings provide one a glimpse into the lives of these children. Some of the styles of their musicking remain consistent between recordings, while others change. Throughout, the children made music with evident joy; one can hear the light behind their eyes as they play these games and make up these stories, involved with all their beings to fill this natural human need to live out their musical impulses. In this way, they are much the same as children everywhere, both in the present day and in the past.

REFERENCES

Addo, A. O. 1996. "A Multimedia Analysis of Selected Ghanaian Children's Play Songs." *Bulletin of the Council of Research in Music Education* 129: 1–23.

Barnosky, J. 2006. "The Violent Years: Responses to Juvenile Crime in the 1950s." *Polity* 38 (3): 314–344.

Blacking, J. 1967. *Venda Children's Songs.* Johannesburg, South Africa: Witwatersrand University Press.

Cahan, E., J. Mechling, B. Sutton-Smith, and S. H, White. 1993. "The Elusive Historical Child: Ways of Knowing the Child of History and Psychology." In *Children in Time and Place: Developmental and Historical Insights,* edited by G. Elder, J. Modell, and R. Parke, 192–223. Cambridge, UK: Cambridge University Press.

Campbell, P. S. 1991. "The Child-Song Genre: A Comparison of Songs by and for Children." *International Journal of Music Education* 17: 14–23.

Campbell, P. S. [1998] 2010. *Songs in Their Heads.* New York: Oxford University Press.

Campbell, P. S. 2007. "Musical Meaning in Children's Cultures." In *International Handbook of Research in Arts Education,* edited by L. Bresler, 881–894. Dordrecht, Netherlands: Springer.

Campbell, P. S., and C. H. Lum. 2007. "Sonic Surrounds in an Elementary School." *Journal of Research in Music Education* 55: 31–47.

Corso, D. 2003. "'Smooth as Butter': Practices of Music Learning amongst African-American Children." PhD diss., University of Illinois at Urbana-Champaign.

Edet, E., collector. 1978. *Songs for Children from New York City.* Washington, DC: Smithsonian Folkways FW 7858. CD.

Fagan, J., and D. L. Wilkinson. 1998. "Guns, Youth Violence, and Social Identity in Inner Cities." *Crime and Justice* 24: 105–188.

Fitzgerald, J. 2007. "Black Pop Songwriting, 1963–1966: An Analysis of U.S. Top Forty Hits by Cooke, Mayfield, Stevenson, Holland, and Holland-Dozier-Holland." *Black Music Research Journal* 27: 97–140.

Gaunt, K. 2006. *The Games Black Girls Play: Learning the Ropes from Double-Dutch to Hip-Hop.* New York: New York University Press.

Graue, M. E., and D. J. Walsh. 1998. *Studying Children in Context.* Thousand Oaks, CA: Sage.

Harwood, E. 1993. "Content and Context in Children's Playground Songs." *Update: Applications of Research in Music Education* 12 (1): 4–8.

Harwood, E. 1998. "Go On Girl! Improvisation in African-American Girls' Singing Games." In *In the Course of Performance: Studies in the World of Musical Improvisation,* edited by B. Nettl and M. Russell, 113–125. Chicago: University of Chicago Press.

James, A., C. Jenks, and A. Prout. 1998. *Theorizing Childhood*. New York: Teachers College Press.

Kartomi, M. 1991. "Musical Improvisations by Children at Play." *World of Music* 33 (3): 2–11.

Lum, C. H. 2009. "Musical Behaviours of Primary School Children in Singapore." *British Journal of Music Education* 26 (1): 27–42.

Mans, M. 2002. "Playing the Music—Comparing Performance of Children's Song and Dance in Traditional and Contemporary Namibian Education." In *The Arts in Children's Lives*, edited by L. Brestler and C. M. Thompson, 71–86. Dordrecht, Netherlands: Kluwer Academic Publishers.

Marsh, K. 1995. "Children's Singing Games: Composition in the Playground?" *Research Studies in Music Education* 4: 2–11.

Marsh, K. 2009. *The Musical Playground*. New York: Oxford University Press.

Marsh, K., and S. Young. 2006. "Musical Play." In *The Child as Musician: A Handbook of Musical Development*, edited by G. E. McPherson, 289–310. New York: Oxford University Press.

Merrill-Mirsky, C. 1986. "Girls' Handclapping Games in Three Los Angeles Schools." *Yearbook for Traditional Music* 18: 47–59.

Minks, A. 2008. "Performing Gender in Song Games among Nicaraguan Miskitu Children." *Language & Communication* 28 (1): 26–56.

Newell, W. W. [1883] 1963. *Games and Songs of American Children*. New York: Dover.

Opie, I., and P. Opie. 1965. *The Singing Game*. New York: Oxford University Press.

Phillips, K. 1996. *Teaching Kids to Sing*. New York: Schirmer Books.

Prim, F. M. 1995. "Tradition and Change in Children's Games: Its Implication in Music Education." *Bulletin of the Council for Research in Music Education* 127: 149–154.

Riddell, C. 1990. "Traditional Singing Games of Elementary School Children in Los Angeles." PhD diss., University of California, Los Angeles.

Schwartz, T., collector. 1953. *1, 2, 3 and a Zing Zing Zing*. Washington, DC: Smithsonian Folkways FW 7003. CD.

Schwartzman, H. B. 2001. *Children and Anthropology: Perspectives for the 21st Century*. Westport, CT: Bergin & Garvey.

Small, C. 1998. *Musicking*. Middletown, CT: Wesleyan University Press.

Sorenson, R., collector. 1959. *Street and Gangland Rhythms: Beats and Improvisations of Six Boys in Trouble*. Washington, DC: Smithsonian Folkways FW 5589. CD.

Stearns, P. N. 1998. "Why Study History?" *American Historical Association*. Accessed June 10, 2010. http://www.historians.org/pubs/Free/WhyStudyHistory.htm.

Thompkins, D. E. 2000. "School Violence: Gangs and a Culture of Fear." *Annals of the American Academy of Political and Social Science* 567: 54–71.

Thomson, I. T. 1992. "Individualism and Conformity in the 1950s vs. the 1980s." *Sociological Forum* 7 (3): 497–516.

Vigil, J. D. 2003. "Urban Violence and Street Gangs." *Annual Review of Anthropology* 32: 225–242.

Watts. S. H. 2009. "Transgenerational Musical Play: Oral History Accounts of Girls' Musical Engagement." PhD diss., University of Washington.

Yoffie, L. R. 1947. "Three Generations of Children's Singing Games in St. Louis." *The Journal of American Folklore* 60: 1–51.

35

WHOSE SONGS IN
THEIR HEADS?

TREVOR WIGGINS

LYING in my bed at around 5:00 am at the beginning of another field trip to Nandom, northern Ghana, I wonder what changes I will find since my last visit seven years ago in 1999. Since then, electricity and cell phones have both arrived, together with a radio station based in the town. In 1999 there was a nascent cassette culture, as people were able to afford portable cassette recorders and a local shop sold a selection of commercial recordings from the south of Ghana and some recordings of local music. Cassettes were copied on domestic machines and were of variable quality but provided insights into the tastes and interests of local people. I expect that the arrival of the radio station will have provided a stimulus for this, widening the range of music available and offering greater opportunities for local people to make recordings and get them heard. Sure enough, soon after the call to prayer from the local mosque, the radio station came on the air with announcements in English, Dagara, and Sisaala, before moving on to music, which is the staple diet of the station. Responding to local preference for music uninterrupted by speech, tracks are played back-to-back with no announcement of the title or performer, so tracking down the identity of anything can be a challenge, but sections are often identified by the language of the lyrics. This morning we start off with songs with words in English, beginning with some Highlife (popular music from the south of Ghana). I am somewhat surprised by the second track, "Fuck you, you ho, I don't want you back."[1] Local people attach great importance to the advice offered by the words of songs and will come out during a performance to offer a small amount of money to a performer that they feel is offering good advice. I wonder what the reaction to the advice offered by Eamon will be? I know that many local children listen to the radio at home and often know much of the limited repertoire of the station by heart. I wonder what their parents might make of children singing this song?

My interest in the reaction to this song was because one of my aims on this visit to Nandom—a place I have visited for more than fifteen years—was to spend more time researching the music made and heard by local children as the town rapidly joins the twenty-first century. I was interested to inquire into the extent to which some of Campbell's conclusions in *Songs in Their Heads* might be culture specific and what might be more generally applicable, particularly in light of her summary comment that "the relationships that children individually have with their music comes as a result of the type and extent of music that has entered their ears and minds, and the manner in which they rework and reconfigure this music within their cognitive structures" (Campbell 1998: 225). All children move in a highly complex and interdisciplinary world (a maneuver that may challenge adult scholars but that is so natural and necessary for children) in which they can be subject to an intense social peer pressure to conform that draws legitimacy from cultural sources or media information and advertising. At the same time the adult world, through the medium of parents, teachers, and the nation, wishes to inculcate trained citizens who have the ability to make a contribution to society and continue the identity of that group.

LOCATION AND CONTEXT OF RESEARCH

Nandom is in the upper west region of Ghana near the border with Burkina Faso, some 900 km from the capital, Accra. The town has around 4,000 inhabitants, with a number of satellite villages bringing the total number of people for whom Nandom is the regional center up to around 10,000 spread across an area of roughly 100 square miles. Most people in this area are engaged in subsistence farming and would identify themselves as ethnic Dagara. Even the relatively small proportion of people with paid employment, such as teachers, will have their own small farm and often use the children in their class to help with the harvest at appropriate times of the year. Generally there is enough food most of the time, but the whole economy has been held at subsistence level—for example, crops yields could be increased if people were able to apply more fertilizer to the land, but this requires either more cattle or more money to buy chemical fertilizer. There is one farming season leading to harvest from September until November when almost every available able-bodied person is needed to gather, process, and store crops for the next year. Toward the end of the harvest season is the traditional time for recreational music and dance. Particularly when there is a full moon and the nights become cool, people gather in the evening to sing and dance. Some of these dances are for men and women (*Bɛwaa*) and some for women (*Kari, Nuru, Too too too*), which the men know although they will not join in. Children also have their own music and dance games, such as *Gago* (local) or *Ampe* (from southern Ghana).

After the rains stop (usually by November), the climate becomes increasingly dry then hot, with daytime temperatures typically rising to around 45°C (113°F) in April and nighttime temperatures only a little lower. During this time, there is little work farming and little energy for music and dance. It is typical that in many families, able-bodied young people who have completed education as far as they are able or can afford will travel south to stay with a relative during the dry season for roughly six months to try to find paid employment before returning to help with the farming in Nandom. People who have traveled have also experienced the wider media resources of the south, which has a far greater variety of radio and TV stations. They will have heard a greater variety of music and may view themselves as more sophisticated than their relatives back home, perhaps being reluctant to join in traditional recreational music and dance that they view as old-fashioned or "colo" (colonial). This creates a certain tension with their elders, who are concerned about the preservation of their traditions and would say, as it was expressed to me, "If you don't know Bɛwaa, you are not from Nandom."

Education and Schooling

The Ghanaian education system has three main phases after kindergarten: primary school—at least six years, usually for ages six through twelve; junior secondary school [JSS]—three years, for ages thirteen through fifteen; and senior secondary school [SSS]—three years, for ages sixteen through eighteen. This is a grade system, so students must pass the final exam in order to move onto the next level. Until 2004/2005, all children attending school had to pay school fees, which, although quite low, were beyond the resources of some parents in a subsistence economy. These fees have now been abolished for kindergarten, primary, and JSS, so the change in funding has meant that some children who had previously dropped out of school are now trying to complete their education—the eldest pupil I met in a primary school was eighteen, and in JSS was twenty-four, so there is a wide spectrum of ages in many classrooms. There is concern for the standard of education in local schools across much of northern Ghana. Teachers are conscientious and committed but local standards of education are not as high as in other parts of the country.[2] Resources are constrained and none of the schools I visited was connected to the electricity supply even though power lines often ran within 100 meters of the building. The basic government grant to provide resources to educate each pupil is just over US$3 annually. A majority of people in Nandom speak Dagara as their first language although a number of residents will speak other local languages. As the national language is English, children often learn basic English greetings by rote at an early age and are taught English as a second language during primary school. When children move on to JSS, English becomes the language of instruction although written Dagara is still taught. There is a wide variety of ability in the speaking and understanding of English among children—those whose parents also speak English to them at home are much more fluent and understand much better so that they are able to hold a conversation.

Research Schools and Students

Whereas Campbell based her research on children aged five through twelve, I used an older age group, with the youngest child aged ten and the oldest a "child" of twenty-four because I wanted to be able to talk to the interviewees directly in English and for them to understand to some extent the variety of music on offer to them. Also, as the words of songs are very important and traditionally carry a great deal of local information, advice, news, scandal, and jokes, I wanted my respondents to understand both Dagara and English words. Although some younger pupils may understand English well, it is in JSS that English becomes the medium of instruction and greater competence develops. I interviewed thirty pupils, plus either the head teacher or the teacher responsible for cultural activities and teaching, based in one primary and four JSS schools in rural and urban locations around the Nandom Traditional area.

The schools are very alike in many respects. Pupils are notably tidy and take pride in their appearance, even if their school uniform shows signs of wear. There is great social pressure to conform, to be a good citizen, to do what you are told, and to "comport" yourself appropriately. Although the relationship between pupils and teachers is quite friendly, in all schools there is a stronger hierarchical structure with teachers invariably addressed as "sir" or "madam" and a direct attitude to discipline, including corporal punishment when this is felt necessary. Both within schools and in society, children are expected to give the "right" answer to questions, and this is supported by frequent school tests to check that pupils have learned what they are taught.

None of the schools in which I worked has a member of staff with significant musical experience or knowledge. Most of the staff come from this area of the country, can speak Dagara, and have knowledge of local culture—something that was not always the case. The national curriculum for JSS was revised a few years ago to include music and dance in cultural studies under the general heading of religious and moral education (RME). There is an ongoing national debate about the maintenance of traditional culture and the ways in which this should be passed on to each new generation. Coe (2005) published results of research based in schools in the south of Ghana. She proposed that the state has attempted to produce, control, and use national culture for its own purposes and that schools are the intersection between secular, traditional, and religious concerns for the moral and cultural education of young people:

> Teachers see the cultural studies syllabus, in particular, as a top-down reform, imposed from above by government bureaucrats. Ghanaians seem more interested in learning English and French, useful for making connections in an economic system that is increasingly dependent on global flows, than in learning more about

their own languages and culture. Many teachers tend to dismiss culture in schools as only "fun," noting that children become excited and "interested" during cultural activities (their words). (Coe 2005: 55–56)

Coe's view is supported by the fact that cultural studies is only a small part of the RME curriculum. RME is required for all JSS in Ghana and seems generally to have at least two lessons allocated per week for the first two years of JSS. In the third year, the pressure to prepare for the final exams that offer entry to SSS means that RME is squeezed and often receives less attention, as it will not be part of the curriculum at SSS level. The textbooks (in three volumes, one for each year of the syllabus) that are available for use in JSS to teach RME were prepared in the department of religions at the University of Ghana (Gibed [2002] 2005). Book One is mostly concerned with a detailed description of religious practices for Christianity, Islam, and traditional Ghanaian religions. In the whole book, other than within the description of traditional religion (always third after Christianity and Islam), there is little evidence of Ghana's rich cultural heritage of music and dance and no mention of the moral and social significance often attached to such activities. In Book Two the main sections are Work, Money, Leisure and Time, Responsibility, Human Rights and Privileges, Religious Personalities, Religious Festivals, Rites of Passage, and Chastity and Immorality. Music and Dance appear mostly in the section on religious festivals, which briefly describes some of the main celebrations from around Ghana and also asks pupils to find out about any traditionalist festival in their community and why and how it is celebrated. "Playing musical instruments" is mentioned as a hobby under the "Proper Use of Leisure Time" and among the "Reasons for Leisure" (p.16) is stated, "Through leisure we can relax and refresh ourselves after work." Versions of this phrase came up several times in the interviews with students, and it is clear that music is placed in this category—an appropriate activity for relaxation and refreshment. Book Three is much slimmer and its sections are Moral Teachings and Commitment, Reward and Punishment, Religious Youth Organizations, and Decency and Substance Abuse. There is little mention of traditional culture, let alone cultural activities of any sort. Of course, these volumes are only a written source and are prepared to contain the information that students will need in order to pass the exams in RME, so they may not represent the actual curriculum experienced by students. They do provide a very full syllabus to be delivered in the time available, leaving little room for teachers to bring in local cultural activities drawing on musicians, dancers, and artists in the local communities.

In other parts of Ghana, teachers felt that "the content of the cultural studies subject posed real problems," claiming that, according to the syllabus, "teachers were supposed to teach about customs and festivals that devout Christians avoided"[3] (Coe 2005: 121). In the Nandom region, no teacher, nor the local Roman Catholic priest, saw a problem with teaching and demonstrating traditional cultural activities in the classroom. When I asked the priest about his opinion of the teaching of traditional religion as part of cultural studies in school, his response was, "It's a good thing. People need to know the culture of their people so that they can be integrated, so for me, it's a good thing" (Patrick Segkpeb [parish priest of Nandom Catholic church], personal interview, November 3, 2006). The Nandom Catholic church has organized two choirs in recent years: one that sings predominantly in Dagara and is accompanied by two local xylophones plus hand drums and rattles; and one that has more young members singing mostly in English accompanied by an electric keyboard and conga drums. The English repertoire is mostly contemporary songs that would be recognized by many people around the world who attend a Christian church.

ASKING QUESTIONS

Within this cultural and educational context for my inquiry, what did I learn from my respondents? I spoke with a random mixed group of boys and girls, ranging in age from ten through twenty-four (although most were between fifteen and eighteen).

Farming is the principal occupation of the parents of 80 percent of students questioned. All the students understood the local Dagara language and also spoke English. A few students spoke other Ghanaian languages such as Waale, Moshi, or Twi, learned either from their parents or from visits to other parts of Ghana. In school, they spoke English and with their friends, and although many of them claimed to use the opportunity to practice their English, I mostly heard the local language with some English words added, creating a personal peer group language common in many groups of young people.

I asked all the students what they liked most and least about school. Many of them cited learning and socialization generally as key benefits, mostly with a view to future earnings and success in life. Others identified particular subjects or areas of study that they most enjoyed. On the negative side, various forms of misbehavior by other students were much disliked, and caning (corporal punishment) was also a concern. Some students, mostly in the town, did not like cultural studies because they did not know how to do some of the activities (e.g., dances) and they could not see much future use for it, but this was more than balanced by the number of students who felt it was important to "know your culture." Several students also disliked feeling very tired in school, usually as a result of getting up very early, typically 4:30–5:00 am, in order to complete domestic chores before setting off for school. When I asked students about their preferred activities outside school time, around half of them talked of helping their parents with chores around the house or farming, including growing their own crops. Reading was also a preferred activity, with a majority reading the lesson notes they had made in school that day. Of course, a good number also mentioned playing football or local games such as *Ampe* and *Gago*, sewing, cooking, and listening to the radio.

I also asked about the future career aspirations of the students. Unsurprisingly, most of them aimed for professions (medicine, law, accountancy) that generally combined a good salary and prospects with the perception of a positive contribution to the community. No student wanted to follow the career of their parents—this may be typical of a generation gap, but it seemed quite extreme and also mostly unrealistic given the proportion of these students who will not pass exams to enter secondary education. Teachers, parents, and the government have succeeded in raising the aspirations of this generation, and this aspiration carries into the cultural and musical world they occupy.

My initial questions about music to all students were "Do you like music? Why?" There was an interesting range of properties ascribed to music:

- I like to listen to music because music reflects our mind and helps people to know so many things. Music also gives people more ideas.
- Music refreshes our mind. When you listen to music, you forget all the bad things that happen to you.
- I like it because we learn moral lessons from it.
- Because music gives us knowledge and teaches lessons about the world. It also gives us moral lessons to show us how to behave well in society and how to be committed to God.
- I like music because it lets you be comfortable in times of sorrow. If you listen to some music you become comfortable.
- Because it makes me happy all the time.

There is a clear expectation of a moral, spiritual, and/or religious dimension to music. The students are also clearly aware of and use music as a means to influence and change mood. For these students, as DeNora observed of people in the United States and United Kingdom,

> Music is an accomplice in attaining, enhancing and maintaining desired states of feeling and bodily energy (such as relaxation); it is a vehicle they use to move out of dispreferred states (such as stress or fatigue). It is a resource for modulating and structuring the parameters of aesthetic agency—feeling, motivation, desire, comportment, action, style, energy. (DeNora 2000: 53)

The expectation that music itself, complimenting any words associated with it, will instruct you in good moral behavior as well as putting you in an appropriate frame of mind came through in many of my conversations. There was some convergence in the responses from students in each school, possibly both because of their instruction in music within the RME curriculum and because of the widespread experience of religious and Gospel music. A focus on the words of songs is common throughout Ghana. When a Ghanaian talks of "composing" a new song, they are often referring to changing the words of a song they have heard and/or adding some new lyrics to it. However, this interest in the lyrics for their moral content seemed to operate more strongly in Dagara than in English—the words of the Eamon song quoted earlier did not seem to register powerfully although some students mentioned another song in English, "I Want to See You My Father" by King Ayisoba as their favorite because of the good advice it gave to fathers to spend more time with their families and less with their girlfriends!

A majority (57 percent) of students cited Gospel songs (in English) as some-thing they sang most frequently although none of the students at the primary school gave this response, probably because of their, usually, only basic knowledge of English at this point. Gospel songs had mostly been learned from the church and included several that have wide recognition globally, such as, "When We Walk with the Lord," "I Will Lift up Your Name on High," and "What a Friend We Have in Jesus," but there were also a number of songs that had been learned from the radio, including some in the Twi language from the south that local students could not fully understand. The next most common category was traditional Dagara songs, either recreational or used in the observance of the *Bagre* traditional religion. Some students also mentioned reggae or Highlife styles and songs in French (mostly from a school where they are taught the language by one teacher).

The sources for the songs were quite predictable: mostly the church, the radio, and their peers, with a few from cassettes, parents, grandparents, teachers, and the Kakube local cultural festival. Many of the students were confident singers and, particularly those who had learned songs from the radio, could imitate stylistic ele-ments in addition to the words and tune. A few were less confident and pitched the start of a chosen song too low so were unable to maintain the melodic con-tour. Issues of pitch and tuning are interesting in this region. The main traditional pitched instrument is a large pentatonic xylophone having sixteen to eighteen bars with the highest note around C_5 and the lowest C_2 (where C_3 is middle C on the piano). The tuning of the bars of these instruments is not standardized, and makers copy the pitches from another instrument in their possession. Most instruments are tuned so they have few intervals as small as a tone (200 cents) but also do not have intervals as large as a minor third (300 cents) to give the distinctive gapped pattern of a Western pentatonic scale (if the instrument was tuned equipentatonically, each interval would be 240 cents). This is perhaps best illustrated by a graph (Figure 35.1) showing the intervals tuned on a typical instrument made by a local xylophone maker, Bedohir.

Recordings I made in the 1990s showed that local people were completely immersed in the traditional tuning and sang everything using it. So, even on a few occasions when they were accompanied by a Western-tuned electronic keyboard, they continued to sing the pentatonic xylophone tuning, obviously (consciously or not) viewing the keyboard as a poorly tuned xylophone. The only occasion I heard anything different was in the Catholic Church, when the choir performed a few sections of the Mass in the Latin tones and had clearly learned to sing music with semitones. Language usage is also significant in communicating local adaptations. The Dagara word for xylophone is *gyil* and for a white person is *nasaala,* so when the early missionaries brought a harmonium to accompany this singing in church, this was *nasaalgyil.*

A brief case study of the children's game song *Gago* may highlight some of the issues.

Figure 35.2 is a transcription of *Gago* as sung and danced by the children at the Nandom chief's palace in November 2006 (See Figure 35.4 and Web Figure 35.3 ⊙.)

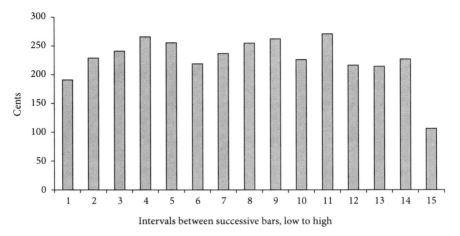

Figure 35.1: Comparison of interval sizes between successive notes on a xylophone.

A translation of the words is "Gago eh, Girls' leader for Gago has gone to Kumasi. If you enter the dance, can you dance Gago?" (Si-li-la-lo are vocables for the start of the faster dance step, in time with the clapping.) This has a typical "call-and-response" structure to the first section with everyone joining the refrain of "Eh Gago eh" every second bar although the lead sections also had more than one singer. In the first section, the dancers jump in the air while whirling one arm around. In the second section where the pulse is doubled, the dancers bend their back and knees and stamp each foot twice in alternation.

I had previously recorded this song in the village of Biligang (about a mile northeast from Nandom) in 1994 (Web Figure 35.6). There are a few differences: some words are different, and there are also some rhythmic and tuning changes.

Figure 35.2: Transcription of *Gago*.

Figure 35.4: Children playing *Gago*. Photo: Trevor Wiggins.

The rhythm changes show up in the transcription where the tuning changes do not. Figure 35.5 is a transcription of the 1994 performance.

In this version the call-and-response is much more marked (bold text shows the chorus sections interspersed with solo leads). The length of each section is more dependent on the invention of the leader in the first section (with words between the chorus responses throughout although not decipherable in some places), and the stamina of the dancers in the second (the dance section might be repeated up to ten times before stopping at *fine*). Most of the differences are what could be expected within an aural tradition, but the rhythmic and tuning changes are indicative of particular trends. The older songs in this region tend to have a complex rhythmic structure that overlays units of two, three, four, and six, as this brief extract of the song "Vielu daa" shows (Figure 35.7).

Recent songs as well as those from villages to the south often use a tune that has a four-beat unit aligning with the dance step rather than overlapping it as above. The later version of Gago shows this tendency, going to a simple rhythm in the dance step rather than maintaining the "3 & 2" feel (represented by quaver and dotted quaver pulses) of the earlier recording.[4] The aspect the notation cannot show is the tuning. In the earlier recording, the notes shown as C, D, and E are consistently very wide tones (so that E is sung almost as F, and the note shown as A is sung

Figure 35.5: Transcription of *Gago* at Biligang.

as close to B♭). This is in line with the typical xylophone tuning noted earlier. In the later recording, the notes are sung much closer to Western pentatonic tuning, particularly noticeable on the repeated first three degrees of the scale in the dance section. This indicates a general trend toward more "Western" rhythms and tuning in particular that I also observed in my interviews.

The students I interviewed who sang Western songs heard on the radio generally followed the Western tuning (within the limits of their vocal ability), but when they were singing a local song, they reverted more to the traditional tuning. It will be interesting to see how long it is before children in this region absorb Western tuning and have to be specifically taught the traditional tuning if they are to learn it. The main attributes for a good traditional singer in Nandom are a powerful voice, usually with a nasal quality that can be heard above the xylophones and drums often used for accompaniment. Students singing Western songs were also well able to imitate the stylistic features of these, including vocal delivery—very different

Figure 35.7: Transcription of *Viɛlu daa na Nandomme minyu* (Nandom people drink very good beer).

from the traditional style. In most of Ghana, there is more emphasis on learning than teaching in study outside the school curriculum and this presents a curious dichotomy: in school, the expectation is that a student will be able to repeat with great accuracy the information imparted by teachers and the focus is on preparing students to pass exams. In traditional culture, a person may sometimes be shown something, but it is expected that she or he will learn from observation and then try to develop her or his own version of the model. Direct imitation is not valued as much as making one's own version of something, such that it still fulfills the function and stylistic norms of the original. This links much more with the modes of learning identified in popular music, usually outside the formal curriculum, found in the United Kingdom (Green 2002).

When I asked Nandom students if they played a musical instrument, there was a highly positive response, with only 20 percent saying they did not play anything. While this high level of engagement is striking, it also masks a level of detail that is interesting. Of the students who claimed to play, fourteen played the local xylophone, six the drum (either a local gourd drum or a conga), two played the rattle (used to accompany songs particularly in church), and one each the bass drum (in the brass band attached to the Catholic church), the electric organ (keyboard), and guitar, plus one student who said he played the radio (not a joke but the way he understood the verb). The student who plays the organ has one at home and has parents who are professional and able to afford this, but the student who plays the guitar does not have her own and is only able to play this at the house of a friend. Local xylophones are quite expensive (around a month's wages) but there are quite a few of these available and the schools try to maintain an instrument if possible. Twelve of the students who played the xylophone had one at home, usually played by a parent or elder brother, who was the main source of their learning. For a majority of students, there was clearly quite a musical environment in their home, and more than 60 percent had either a father or a sibling (usually an elder brother) who played the xylophone, and many of the students mentioned that their father or elder brother had learned from their grandfather. Clearly a number of the students understood the question "Do you play a musical instrument?" as "Have you played a musical instrument?" since when I asked what they could play they were not able to name anything. My best estimate was that five students (17 percent of the group, all boys) could play with some level of expertise, and two of these were evidently expert and played for a local dance group that would compete at the Kakube festival.

As a result of the availability of instruments, it is not surprising that the repertoire of music for the students engaged in playing an instrument is mostly Dagara and all material is learned aurally. Although a large number of students expressed an interest in more international musical styles such as reggae, Gospel, and modern Ghanaian popular music, there are few resources for them to play this music for themselves. Thus these young people are moving very rapidly from a situation in which music was mostly live, local, and participatory to one in which it is mostly recorded, international, and receptive. The extent to which this is a contested ground, exhibiting tensions between issues of tradition and modernity, between local and international cultural locations, and between generations of local people with a particular focus on their level of education, is something I explored in the other questions I asked.

Campbell (1998: 161) notes, "Few children directly defined music, and I did not probe for an exact definition of it." It is an oft-repeated fact that there is not a word for "music" in most African languages and this is true for Dagara; the words used are those for a specific event or activity such as *Kari*, *Bεwaa,* or *Gago*, and this word then encompasses all activities involved in that event, including music and dance. The students I interviewed seem to have taken on the Western concept of "music" as implied by the English term—everyone was positive that they "listened to music" and understood that to be either live performance or the radio/cassette. There were clear preferences about the music they liked to hear, usually on the radio, and some evidence of the diversity of opinion with their parents.

Do you listen to music? (Some responses have been conflated)

- In the evening time, after the news [on Radio Freed] they will play Dagara cassettes or Highlife. Sometimes they play reggae all evening. I don't like reggae but Highlife they often play, you can dance to.
- I like Gospel songs.
- I like the Dagara songs.
- On the radio. [I like] the English mixes. They play the Dagara ones too but I don't feel it.
- [I listen] to the radio. I like "My Father." The words are "I want to see you my father. The way you do, it is not fine, your girly friend …" It is telling us about what some fathers do. They are not there for their children and would rather have a girlfriend. [This is the track by King Ayisoba referred to earlier.]

The source of music for most students was the local FM radio station with 90 percent having a radio in their home. There was a cassette player in 34 percent of students' homes, while only 3 percent had a TV. When I asked what they would buy if they had some money to spend on music, 50 percent would buy a radio as first choice, and 23 percent a TV with the remainder wanting either a cassette player or a xylophone first.

What kind of music do your parents listen to/like?

- They like to dance *Bine* [funeral dance/music]. I don't like to dance *Bine* because I can't dance it.
- If we are playing English songs they say we should put that off, it is not our culture. If I sing English songs they don't like it but I don't like Dagara songs. Why should I leave the English songs? I know the Dagara songs but I don't want to sing them.
- They listen to Gospel songs. [*Is there anything that you play that your parents don't like?*] No—music is music.

- My father likes only Dagara music because he hasn't been to school so cannot understand the words of the other songs.

Another interesting way of coming at the students' musical preferences is to ask what music they like to dance to. Virtually all traditional music has dance movements associated with it, sometimes illustrating the words but more often providing another message or effectively contributing to the sonic aspects through the rhythmic movement.

Do you like to dance to music?

- I don't like reggae but Highlife they often play, you can dance to. I also like to dance to Dagara songs like *Bɛwaa*.
- Yes, reggae, Highlife.
- Yes, my favorite song [*Gago*].
- Yes, I dance the Hiplife because it's fast. I saw it on the television in Accra.
- Yes, I dance in church [to Gospel music].
- Yes. Dancing makes you exercise your body. Any music is good to dance.

Dancing is probably the main participatory cultural activity in northern Ghana, and only one student said he didn't dance for enjoyment but then admitted to dancing "to exercise my body" because he has been told it is good for him. There is a complete mix of styles here, with most people knowing both the local dances and Ghanaian popular styles and reggae (although there is no set style of dancing for these of course). Learning of local dance styles is entirely informal at present, but there is some evidence that fewer students now know the more difficult traditional dance (*Bine*) for funerals and are not motivated to learn it if they are approaching their midteens and have not learned it already because they feel self-conscious and know they will be criticized for not knowing their culture.

Music teaching and activities in school are patchy and dependent on the interest and ability of the teacher responsible for RME—it is rare for a school at any level to employ a specialist music teacher. Students were not sure whether music should be in the curriculum or not. They are told that traditional culture is an important part of their identity as Dagara and they should know it well, but this is not reflected in the time and apparent importance allocated to it in the curriculum. There is also a sense from the students (and teachers) that, unless one is planning to be a musician, knowledge of music is of little use to the student in a future career, given the stated career aspirations of the majority of students. I asked the teachers and the students about music in school. A typical response was as follows:

> [RME] covers the lifestyle of the people and their religious background. It contains a lot about music. Theoretically we teach them in the classrooms and we also practice it outside, so through cultural dance and other things the community comes here to witness the students and they also go into schools to perform. I can remember that this school even came first in the last cultural competition held at Nandom. We are really lacking the musical instruments. We are always trying [to get them]—the school is really lacking them, but when the need demands, we

beg from the community. We don't have electricity in the school, so we can't use recording easily. Mostly we use the xylophones and other instruments. If we want to use a recording at all, sometimes we try to get batteries and a small [cassette] recorder. We write some things on the board and the students copy it, also there is information in their textbooks concerning music. Yes, we bring [in local people] as resource persons. Sometimes we also send them [the students] to the community when they are doing this. They really enjoy it [music]. When you do it practically, they participate a lot.

The perception of students was a little different, typically as follows:

- We used to play the xylophone and sing as we marched into our classrooms but the xylophone got burned so now we only sing.
- No, we sing music to march into our classrooms.
- Yes, [we sing] when we have a [Catholic] Mass in school.

In Ghana, only a small number of institutions, mostly at a more advanced level such as training colleges for religious orders or teachers, have set out systematically to teach music. The music curriculum in such institutions is an area of potential cultural conflict (see Flolu 2004). In the past, the music taught was usually based on the Western tradition of church music and staff notation. Ghanaians have now reclaimed this territory to a fair extent, and traditional music is used and taught alongside the Western classical tradition, but this is not universally accepted, as some churches view traditional music as associated with the worship of idols and devils. So the appearance of traditional music and dance within the curriculum of RME is an innovation, moving to the school something that children would previously have been expected to absorb from their environment. Given the variety of music within Ghana, no musician/teacher could offer instruction in the whole range, so this would seem to be an ideal opportunity to involve the local community and musicians in schools. But, of course, it's not that simple. There is little money to pay local musicians for this teaching, and the traditional music takes on a different character when taught in a necessarily brief way within a crowded curriculum. As one of the students observed, "[The teachers] say that we are not going to write [an exam] for music therefore they only teach us those nine subjects [that will be examined]."

Summary and Analysis of Research Findings

What is the cultural framework within which we should consider this inquiry? Of course, comparison is a basic tool, but comparators are always difficult—whose view of Ghanaian music/society am I comparing with its American equivalent? In a recent survey of children's musical learning cultures around the world, Campbell characterizes West Africa as "Musical grooves from infancy onward." She describes the traditional environment where,

> In the arms of their mothers, or strapped to their mother's backs, children learn from infancy the rhythms and tunes of their culture. In rural societies, they continue as infants and toddlers in a cultural practice of listening and feeling the rhythmic movement and sound vibrations of their mothers at work, walking, talking, chopping, stirring, stamping, singing. (Campbell 2006: 426)

The situation in West Africa is changing rapidly. In the highly rural community around Nandom, babies are still carried on their mother's backs for the first few months and will never be far away while being breastfed. Their mother will doubtless be carrying out much of her work in a traditional way, chopping and pounding food for example, but her direct musical activities will be much reduced because the constant source of music in most homes has become the radio. Children often start to attend nursery school from around the age of four and, from that point on, are far more part of a formal educational system of a sort familiar in more industrialized countries. The changes in cultural knowledge and experience can already be seen in the students I interviewed, with particularly those based in the town being less familiar with traditional culture. For the students from the outlying villages, their cultural induction may have been more traditional, but they are mostly in their midteens and are not part of the "radio" generation being born in the past few years. The traditional methods of learning music, through listening and imitation, are still the main mode of transmission and likely to stay so, as they are an integral part of the musical style, and only the Western-trained musician would even consider any other method. There is general awareness on the part of local people that their traditional culture is being eroded/compromised/integrated[5] with more national and international elements. When I interviewed the paramount chief for the Nandom area in 1996, he was very certain of resisting external influences:

> Custom and tradition is something that you can never change. Once you are a Dagara you can, for instance, put on a suit but when you die they won't put a suit on you. This [indicating his traditional batakari dress] is how you will go into the grave. (Naa [Chief] Puoure Puobe Chiir VII, personal interview, December 1996)

This same interview showed that the chief recognized that music learned in a school setting was not the same as immersion in traditional culture, and students in Ghana are increasingly being taught *about* their culture in school. While this is preferable to their traditional culture not being represented in school, without the resources to spend more on educational facilities to support culture, there is a significant loss. The situation in urban centers is even further removed from the tradition, but there is still a strong sense of Ghanaian cultural identity and young people are clearly aware and proud of their own culture and, if they value it, they will remake it for their generation. As Agawu[6] points out, there is a danger that focusing too much on small areas of difference between cultural artifacts, specifically music, obscures the far larger areas of similarity (Agawu 2003: 151–171).

In surveying global practices, commentators have a tendency to identify and be struck by those areas that are not familiar and may represent places like Ghana as very different from their previous experience. As media availability and communication improves, these differences may become smaller and focused more on smaller areas of difference that become significant in maintaining individual identity.

There are also other conundrums that are not yet sufficiently explored. Campbell observes,

> Children are a product of social organization, and they do not move through increasingly advanced stages of their biological and neurological growth without being shaped by a constellation of forces within their environments, not the least of which are the musical genres which their societies value and thus preserve. (Campbell 2006: 434)

In the society of northern Ghana, what are the drivers for preservation—the feeling that the society and culture is under threat? How is preservation to be effected—by the continued usage within the society or by recordings made by researchers? The majority of parents believe that their Dagara culture is important and they value and use it, but this does not mean that they don't listen to, for example, the radio, which has probably only around 25 percent of Dagara music in its output. Children make cultural and individual decisions every day, influencing their peers as they themselves are influenced. One of the factors evident in Dagara society, as in many others, is the generation gap: children do not want to be like their parents, do not want to listen to "their" music. This is not necessarily an indication of adolescent "storm and stress" (Walker 2006: 455) or even, given the limited sources in Nandom, of the media hype that is sometimes blamed for this, but an awareness on the part of the young people that there is another world out there that they want to be part of. The main reason Nandom students gave for wanting to buy a TV was "because from television we can hear and see what other countries do." They neither want to be excluded from the world of their parents nor that of their global peers.

What thoughts and conclusions are prompted by my inquiries? I learned that the students in Nandom have plenty of songs in their heads—some learned, some created—and they use music to structure and order their world, sometimes not understood by the adult world—a head teacher observing a group of students returning again to their game said, "These songs [*Ampe* and *Gago*], they like them too much!" The differences are around the extramusical meanings that are loaded onto the music; the significance of one music over another (and particularly the language of the words) that indicates allegiance to traditional Dagara culture, to Ghanaian culture, to the Christian church, or to membership of a global popular music audience with a particular focus on the perceived wealth of the United States. Nandom students are well aware of the implications of these and they are constantly being given good advice from the older generation about valuing their traditional culture. At the same time, the Ghanaian government, through the schools, wants a highly trained and educated workforce, and musical skills are not perceived as an essential part of this, so traditional arts get little time within a curriculum focusing on producing good citizens. The economic context means that there is not a great range of music available locally. What is significant at the moment is the role that the radio station and the church play as the providers of alternative cultural materials. The Nandom radio station is highly concerned to promote Dagara culture, but it also has to meet economic targets for survival, and these depend on the extent to which it meets the needs of its listeners. The Catholic Church also wants to support local culture and uses traditional music, but of course, the music's function is changed with the new context and it thus acquires a different meaning. Each of these agencies carries a great responsibility for Dagara culture, but each of them would also point to other main imperatives for their existence. In the middle of this, as in any society, are the people enjoying and using music. For all our concerns about tradition versus innovation, commercial exploitation, global culture, and cultural imperialism, most of the time, they are simply listening to music. As one student said, "Music is music," but underlying that simple statement are many questions about the ownership and origins of the songs in their heads.

Notes

1   From the album, *I Don't Want You Back* by Eamon (Jive 2004). The lyrics include the lines "Fuck what I said it don't mean shit now, Fuck the presents might as well throw 'em out, Fuck all those kisses, it didn't mean jack, Fuck you, you ho, I don't want you back." (Accessed February 26, 2007. http://www.lyricsandsongs.com/song/19574.html.)

2   Referring to the north of Ghana as a whole, the following is from http://www.isodec. org.gh/Alerts/salvatingeducation.htm (accessed December 3, 2007): "The standards of primary and secondary education has fallen abysmally within the last three years in the Northern Region. On the average, some 82.1 percent of all students who attempted the Senior Secondary School Certificate Examination (SSCE) from 2003 to 2005 could not secure the minimum entry requirements of tertiary institutions across the country. For the Basic Education Certificate Examination (BECE), an average of 44.1 percent males and 56 percent females who sat for the examination in the Northern Region over the same period failed to qualify for SSS."

3   Traditional Ghanaian religious practices are centered on "animism," the belief that plants, animals, and all material objects (including the earth) have souls or a spiritual dimension. These spirits must then be consulted, placated, and offered tribute as appropriate or indicated.

4   My decision to use a change of time signature for the dance section in the first transcription makes the difference look more dramatic—always a problem with staff notation—but I have not found a better solution to show the rhythm accurately.

5   Choose your preferred term according to your view of "world culture" and the "global village."

6   One of Campbell's sources of information about musical practices in West Africa (Campbell 2006: 426, referring to Agawu 1995).

REFERENCES

Agawu, V. K. 1995. *African Rhythm: A Northern Ewe Perspective*. Cambridge: Cambridge University Press.

Agawu, V. K. 2003. *Representing African Music: Postcolonial Notes, Queries, Positions*. New York: Routledge.

Campbell, P. S. [1998] 2010. *Songs in Their Heads: Music and Its Meaning in Children's Lives*. Oxford: Oxford University Press.

Campbell, P. S. 2006. "Global Perspectives." In *The Child as Musician: A Handbook of Musical Development*, edited by G. E. McPherson, 415–438. Oxford: Oxford University Press.

Coe, C. 2005. *Dilemmas of Culture in African Schools*. Chicago: University of Chicago Press.

DeNora, T. 2000. *Music in Everyday Life*. Cambridge: Cambridge University Press.

Flolu, J. 2004. "Music Teacher Education in Ghana: Training for the Churches or for the Schools?" In *Sounds of Change: Social and Political Features of Music in Africa*, edited by S. Thorsén, 164–179. Sida Studies No. 12. Stockholm: Swedish International Development Cooperation Agency.

Gibed, D. [2002] 2005. *Religious and Moral Education for Junior Secondary Schools*. 3 vols. Accra, Ghana: Masterman Publications.

Green, Lucy. 2002. *How Popular Musicians Learn: A Way ahead for Music Education*. Aldershot, UK: Ashgate.

Walker, R. 2006. "Cultural Traditions." In *The Child as Musician: A Handbook of Musical Development*, edited by G. E. McPherson, 439–460. Oxford: Oxford University Press.

INDEX

....